Handbook on Quality and Standardisation in E-Learning

Ulf-Daniel Ehlers
Jan Martin Pawlowski

Handbook on Quality and Standardisation in E-Learning

With 91 Figures and 51 Tables

 Springer

Dr. Ulf-Daniel Ehlers
Universität Duisburg-Essen
Wirtschaftsinformatik der Produktionsunternehmen
Universitätsstr. 9
45141 Essen, Germany
ulf.ehlers@icb.uni-essen.de

Dr. Jan Martin Pawlowski
Universität Duisburg-Essen
Wirtschaftsinformatik der Produktionsunternehmen
Universitätsstr. 9
45141 Essen, Germany
jan.pawlowski@icb.uni-essen.de

ISBN-10   3-540-32787-8 Springer Berlin Heidelberg New York
ISBN-13   978-3-540-32787-5 Springer Berlin Heidelberg New York

Cataloging-in-Publication Data
Library of Congress Control Number: 2006929200

Springer is a part of Springer Science+Business Media

springeronline.com

© Springer Berlin · Heidelberg 2006
Printed in Germany

SPIN 11683001   Printed on acid-free paper – 42/3100 – 5 4 3 2 1 0

Note from editors

The motivation to publish the Handbook for Quality and Standardisation in E-Learning has its origin in numerous discussions during the last few years with colleagues from all over the world, in research projects, from universities or on policy level. They gave us the chance to learn that quality for e-learning on the one hand is of utmost importance and on the other hand is a field of great uncertainty. How to achieve high quality e-learning experiences is still subject to investigations and highly dependent on the context considered. During several voyages through the quality landscape we had the opportunity to look at successful models and learn from sophisticated strategies. The handbook is intended to be a travel diary in the best sense of the term. It covers the state-of-the-art of current burning questions and discussions around the field of quality in e-learning in order to help stakeholders in the e-learning scene in their every day quest for quality.

It is intended to provide guidance for learners, professionals, and educational practitioners, to facilitate researchers' investigations and help policy makers in their decision making towards a 21 centuries' learning society. It is also our intention to provide a concise overview on the knowledge field of quality research which can be used for teaching purposes.

We chose the format of a handbook because it is a possibility to bridge the gap between theory and practice. All contributions therefore contain theoretical foundations and research questions as well as methodologies for quality development on the one hand, and state practical examples and factors of success as well as experiences on the other hand.

We have been able to synthesize work in this publication which partly was carried out under the E-Learning Action Plan of the European Commission which supported research into the quality of e-learning at various levels. A project cluster led to intensive debate about instruments and concepts, but it has also been concerned with basic aspects of the definition of quality and has given rise to over 100 events in 20 months (2003 and 2004), has initiated workshops and discussions, and has contributed publications to a variety of conferences in the field. We believe that our synthesis will have a positive impact on the community of all those involved in e-learning.

However, publishing a handbook is a collaborative exercise because it brings together researchers and experts to form a discussion community. A work of this extent would not have been possible without the immense effort of all the authors who contributed their work to this handbook, agreed to take part in reviews and provided input for great discussion and debates. We have been able to build on a network of supporting organisations, whose commitment and willingness to help have constantly carried us forward, making the impossible possible and finally enabling us to present this handbook. Due to this support it is a handbook comprising over 30 articles from authors coming from over ten countries. We would like to express our sincere gratitude to all authors for their great support.

Apart from the authors we also would like to thank all persons and organisations without whom this handbook would not have been realised. Brian Holmes and Maruja Guttierez-Diaz from the European Commission have supported our work to a great extent and always been contributed constructive advisers throughout our project. Prof. Dr. Heimo H. Adelsberger deserves a special thanks for promoting our work in a very encouraging manner on personal and professional level. In the same way a big thanks goes to all our colleagues who contributed with their ideas and reviews and without whom this handbook would have not been possible.

Essen, May 2006

Ulf-Daniel Ehlers & Jan M. Pawlowski

What can you expect?

When you really get down to analysing it, the promises of e-learning often have yet to materialise. The question how e-learning can be successful becomes more urgent as we move from an 'early adopter' stage to a more general offering. In a global educational market, for e-learning it is critically important to gain understanding of quality in e-learning. Many different concepts and approaches have been developed so far for many different contexts and purposes. The *Handbook on Quality and Standardisation in E-Learning* provides a European and global perspective on these issues. It involves all important actors and draws a picture of the situation in quality development. The Handbook is directed to learners, professionals, researchers and policy makers in e-learning. It covers topics of a rather foundational nature in quality research, the description of quality approaches and instruments as well as experiences and best practises. It is structured into three main parts dealing with methods, standards and practical experiences.

Part A: Quality development: Methods and approaches

Part A of the handbook focuses on introductory background topics of quality development in education and especially e-learning. It gives an overview on the topic of educational quality research, describes developments and the relevance of quality development and introduces the cultural dimension. Methods, models, concepts and approaches for the development, management and assurance of quality in e-learning are introduced. The chapters are all structured alike: First the theoretical model is described in detail and then a practical implementation and the challenges and experiences connected to it are accounted for.

Part B: E-learning standards

Part B focuses on standards for e-learning. The controversial discussion on standards of the last decade is reflected: On the one hand, cost-reduction, secure investments, and new market potentials are expected. On the other hand, there is the fear of limitations for creative solutions. Standards are often misunderstood, and perceived as restricting flexibility or creativity or huge additional effort, especially in the education community. Therefore, we draw a clear picture what can and what cannot be achieved by the use of standards. The main goal of e-learning standards is to provide solutions to enable and ensure interoperability and reusability of systems, components, and objects. The handbook gives an overview on a variety of standards and discusses their practical use and benefit for e-learning.

Part C: Fields of practice and case studies

Part C focuses on quality development in practice and case studies. Transversal themes which set quality development in relation to the cultural dimension, business models and elaborate on quality development in different educational sectors are presented. Also a number of articles of foundational nature, introducing future challenges in the field of quality for innovation of e-learning in the 21st century are included in this part.

Contents

1 Quality in European e-learning: An introduction

Ulf-Daniel Ehlers, Jan M. Pawlowski

University of Duisburg-Essen, Germany

1.1 Introduction: Quality in e-learning as emerging leitmotif

There is no doubt that quality is the most decisive factor determining the future of e-learning. This is the reason for the great variety of concepts, suggestions and debates which now encompass a large section of society and effect many social sub segments. It shows that the question of quality touches the heart of the learning debate. We can regard quality more and more as a subjectively individual and collectively influential category. How should learning opportunities look like and learning environments be structured, now and in the future? How do we meet the demand for building high quality learning capacities which are needed to transform our societies into learning societies? Quality in e-learning brings together the field of education, technology and economy in comprehensive concepts in order to contribute to societal development, to innovate formal, non-formal and informal learning opportunities, and empower learners as citizens to take part in the building of a shared European knowledge and learning space. It becomes clear that the debate on quality is a debate about how learning and education should look like in the future. It is a debate about values and cultures and it takes place on basis of diverse experiences and convictions.

The concept of quality in the public perception and debate today has gained the significance of a leitmotiv for the educational field in all European countries, having the same importance like "equality" or "scientific orientation" in the educational debates of the 1970s in some European countries. Such concepts do not appear as empirical accurately defined and operationalised notions but are rather constituted by a dense bundle of a broad range of arguments, objectives, convictions and procedures (Terhart, 2000, p. 809). Quality in e-learning in this sense has become a leitmotiv for educational policies, a slogan for practitioners and a huge demand for learners. Achieving high quality is a hotly debated and much-sought-after goal in all segments of society and education. It is less characterised by its precise definition but rather by its positive connotation. The very impact of the word "quality" on behavior demonstrates its meaning. The word merely signifies "composition" (Latin: qualis) but in everyday language it is used to distinguish a characteristic of an object as being of a higher calibre than that of another object.

The task to develop or to provide a high quality educational experience is, however, especially in the field of e-learning an extremely difficult challenge. First, it is necessary to find a valid perspective and definition of quality. This requires an answer to the question for which processes of the educational scenario quality development has to be carried out, which quality and from which perspective it is defined – a learners' view may differ considerably from the view of a teacher, developer or the government.

1.2   E-learning quality: A field of great diversity

E-learning quality – or educational quality in a wider context – is a diverse concept. It is not an absolute and fixed category but rather depends on the situation in which it is employed. No country has reached a social, political or academic consensus on what educational quality actually is. Different methods are used to assure quality, ranging from market-oriented instruments, government-driven consumer protection mechanisms and accreditation concepts to institutional strategies and individual instruments. Approaches can have an explicit intentional character or can be rather implicit – when quality development is left to individuals' professional competences.

The definition of quality always takes place as a normative act, referring to a specific context. Consequently, situations and interests always influence its definition. This applies specially to the sector of social and educational services, since here we can not follow patterns which are virtual laws of nature and always turn that which we deem suitable in its composition to fulfil a certain requirement – i.e. quality – into a negotiable issue between various propounded academic theories and subjective, political and social interests.

To critically analyse quality it is helpful to identify the basic points of the debate. We can distinguish between three fundamentally different aspects in the discussion (Ehlers, 2003):

- different interpretations of quality
- different stakeholders with different perspectives on quality
- different forms of quality (input-, process-, output-quality)

Together these three aspects provide a general frame of reference for the described debate.

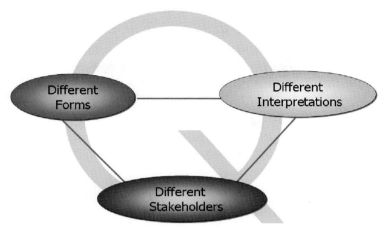

Source: Ehlers, 2003

Fig. 1-1: Dimensions in the quality debate

One dimension is the different *interpretation* of the meaning of quality. Numerous definitions from various fields are available. For example, economics adopt the product based definition which views quality as a physical characteristic of an object. The quality of a piece of jewellery then depends on its gold fraction and the quality of a whisky on the length of its storage. There is also a user based approach which relates to individual customer preferences. Under this interpretation optimal fulfilment of demand signifies the best possible quality: An often borrowed book therefore attains a higher quality than a seldom borrowed volume. We also have the production based approach which sets standards, compliance with which equals quality. Here, the main focus is on functionality. All books which do not fall apart then have the same quality.

Of course these attempts of definition can not easily be transferred to the educational sector. Unlike businesses education does not involve classic supplier-customer relationships. It is an association of co-producers. An e-learning program supplies technology and content but it is down to learners themselves to actively use it, i.e. learn. This interaction between the learning environment and the learner is known as a co-production process. In education, we can currently identify about five different meanings of quality (Harvey, Green, 2000):

- quality as an exception, describing the surpassing of standards,
- quality as perfection, describing the state of flawlessness,
- quality a functionality, referring to the degree of utility,
- quality as an adequate return, measured by the price-performance or cost-benefit ratio,
- quality as transformation, describing the above mentioned co-producer relationship between the learner and the learning environment and referring to the learners progress in terms of a learning process.

However, there are not only different interpretations of quality but also different stakeholders' perspectives: the enterprise as a user of a training measure, the tutors supervising an e-learning-program, the human resource managers who establish a framework for continuing education in their sector, and the learners. Each of these players generally has divergent interests and differing quality requirements and interpretations. It is therefore important to regard quality not as a static element but as a negotiation process between different stakeholders involved in the social process.

Last but not least, quality can also refer to different educational processes or levels. We can cite the different levels of the famous quality triad by Donabedian (Donabedian, 1980a):

- e-learning prerequisites (input or structure quality): availability or capability of the technological infrastructure, qualification of tutors, etc.,
- the learning process (process quality): the interaction of learners, learning formats, corporate learning culture, learning content and desired training goals,
- the result (output/ outcome quality): the increase in learners professional competence.

Quality can not be generalised. There is no direct relation between action and impact. Quality development – as much as education – is rooted in cultural and learning contextual conditions. Defining quality therefore means navigating this multidimensional space. There is no easy answer or standard quality assurance solution. We have to abandon the hope of only having to define quality criteria once to be able to appraise e-learning-services and formats properly in the future. A key factor for e-learning thus will be a concise *quality orientation* which spans all processes and puts learners first. They must take the pole positions in the quality debate since their (professional) development is on stake – regardless of formal or informal environments.

Even more dimensions of diversity which influence the quality debate can be identified. There is, for example, the notion of quality in different subjects and topics. From a European perspective the cultural diversity places enormous challenges on the quality debate. Nagel (2004) reports that students are viewed from different angles in Anglo-Saxon, Scandinavian and southern European countries. In Anglo-Saxon countries, he reports, students are seen as investors in their own carrier, in Scandinavian countries they are viewed as young citizens and in southern European countries as family members. It becomes manifest that the structure of educational systems determines the answer to the quality question to a high degree, and cultural diversity has t be taken into account.

1.3   Quality & standards for e-learning

In the quality debate, we can distinguish between the idea of developing quality *for* e-learning – using methods and instruments – and the concept of improving quality *through* e-learning – using e-learning as a means to improve educational opportunities, access and learning. This chapter focuses on the first meaning of quality development – describing quality methodologies and instruments to improve quality for e-learning. Different approaches and methodologies have been developed to meet the goal of high quality for e-learning throughout all European countries. Today, the question which arises when developing quality is not any longer, where to find a suitable approach, but how to find out which of the available approaches could fit the individual purposes.

1.3.1   Classification of standards

Standards for Quality and for e-learning have been discussed controversially in the last decade: On the one hand, cost-reduction, secure investments, and new market potentials are expected. On the other hand, there is the fear of limitations for creative solutions. Standards are often misunderstood, especially in the education community. They are perceived as restricting flexibility or creativity or huge additional effort. However, new generations of quality standards provide only a basic framework and help organisations to develop quality systems according to their own requirements. In the same way, learning technology standards provide descriptive specifications to develop interoperable solutions. A variety of standards has been developed and adopted for different contexts and have improved the flexibility and effectiveness of e-learning. Fig. 1-2 shows a classification for standards in the field of learning, education, and training.

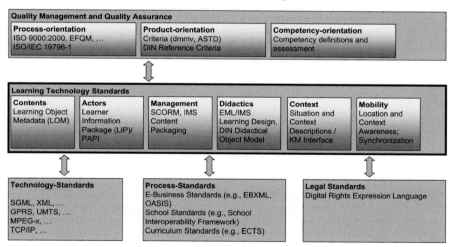

Fig. 1-2: Classification of standards

- *Quality Standards* support quality development in organizations according to their specific needs and requirements. The standard should improve flexibility, reusability, transparency, and comparability and is widely accepted in the community. Usually they are classified into standards for processes, products, and competencies.

- *Learning Technology Standards* deal with the interoperability of components of learning environments, such as authoring systems, learning management systems (LMS), and learning resources and services. The variety of these standards contains standards for content, management, actors, and didactics. Recently, new areas such as context description or mobility aspects gain more importance. They contribute to fulfilling the quality objective of interoperability.
- *Related standards* are used within quality or learning technology standards, such as technology, process, or legal standards. They are usually developed in other domains.

This book deals mainly with the first two classes of standards. Related standards are mentioned within the articles and specifically in chapter 19.

1.3.2   Methodology and instruments to develop quality for e-learning

In the following, we provide a brief survey of methods and instruments in the field of quality, based on (Ehlers, Pawlowski, 2004).

Quality management approaches

Quality management approaches can be used to ensure or optimize the quality of an educational process. They generally do not follow a product-related quality understanding; they are directed at creation, implementation, and performance processes. According to this understanding, QM approaches focus on customer and, specifically, learner requirements for planning, implementing and providing a product (such as an educational product like an e-learning course). Due to their generic scope, these approaches can be applied in different branches and contexts. For e-learning, there are currently no generally recognized quality management approaches. However, concepts are increasingly being developed that are based on the generic process orientation of quality management approaches and are then especially adapted for the educational field or e-learning.

Quality assessment on the basis of criteria lists and checklists

Quality criteria are mostly normative-static tools for the assessment, development and selection of learning platforms, learning software or learning environments. Assessment tools based on quality criteria lists are relevant and popular because they seem to make it relatively easy to evaluate learning effectiveness, although this is usually only possible with time-consuming empirical methods. As a result, these tools enable people to assess the quality of a learning arrangement or learning software without prior empirical studies.

Quality criteria are defined as a characteristic attribute of a learning program whose learning effectiveness has been proven in a validity study. Many quality criteria lists, however, contain criteria for which no explicit validity prove exist, but which are simply assumed to be effective for learning. Meier (1995) points out that many quality criteria lists mainly contain criteria from the area of "screen interface design" or "technical usability"; however, pedagogical/ didactic criteria are often underrepresented. Metastudies on the learning effectiveness of multimedia learning environments, though, show that in particular the didactic concepts implemented in e-learning-modules and learning arrangements have a greater effect on the learning process than the so-called "delivery technology" that is used (cf. Weidenmann, 1997), (Kulik, 1991), (Kulik, Kulik, 1994).

Evaluation as a quality approach

Evaluation approaches can be used for assessing learning situations in which e-learning is used. These methods do not focus on a product itself, but a learning process and thus puts the learners in the focus of attention.[1] Specialised evaluation approaches for assessing e-learning require a learning-theoretical basis to determine which processes in media-supported learning affect each other and how. Only by this means it is possible to investigate assumptions about how or whether someone learns effectively or not, using evaluation methods. Possible theoretical foundations are described in chapter 11.

Further quality approaches for e-learning

In addition to the previously described quality approaches, there are other methods for assessing or assuring quality. These include above all approaches such as

- Benchmarking (for example, "Quality On The Line" of the Institute of Higher Education Policy, USA, 2001), which attempts to compare different offers – for example, from e-learning-providers – on the basis of specified criteria,
- Accreditation and certification approaches (for example, from the ZFU, being the State Office for Distance Learning in Germany), in which providers of e-learning must submit to one-time or regular audits and are then awarded a certificate, or
- Quality mark organizations (e.g. British Learning Association, eQCheck, Weiterbildung Hamburg e.V. in Germany etc.) are usually associations of several organizations in the educational field and award a self-developed mark of quality to their member organizations when these meet previously defined criteria.

---

[1] Strictly speaking, the assessment of e-learning offers using quality criteria lists is also a form of quality evaluation, a so-called expert assessment or product evaluation. However, since it clearly differs from more process-related evaluation approaches in its conceptual approach and implementation, both types – quality criteria assessment and evaluation – are considered separately (Tergan, 2000).

1.3.3   Learning technology standards

Another development is the introduction of standards for e-learning arrangements, -platforms and -content. These standards mainly serve the goal to achieve interoperability and reusability. They focus on various aspects from a technological as well as pedagogical/didactical perspective. However, the intention of standardization is not, as often assumed, to reduce and unify the didactic or technological options, but to standardize their description. The goal is to attain a greater transparency for all users of learning technologies (learners, teachers, etc.) and a greater interoperability and reusability. This is more and more important in e-learning, particularly in global education markets. A progressive understanding of standardization in this sense means to provide structured information about learning resources to enable learners, teachers, and systems to adjust to the respective teaching/learning context. Learning technology standardization as quality approach is therefore related to a quality in the sense of a pedagogical, process-related quality. As a basic requirement for multi-system, interoperable e-learning, standardization is becoming a critical success factor as Europeanization and globalization progress. In general, standards should follow these guiding principles:

- Transparency: Standards should improve transparency of processes and systems. This means that all stakeholders should have access to clearly structured, accurate information.
- Openness: Standards should be developed in a consensus process. In this process, all stakeholders should be involved, such as developers, teachers, designer, and, most important, learners.
- Adaptability: Standards should be adaptable to national, regional, local, or organizational requirements. This means that harmonization can be done on an abstract level, whereas profiles are built based on specific requirements and needs.
- Extensibility: Standards should be open for extensions when new requirements or developments occur. This means that the basis can be stable for a longer period of time, only extensions need to be integrated.

Using these principles, the adoption and acceptance of new standards will be improved and accelerated.

1.4   Preview on the book chapters

The handbook is structured into three main parts. After a general introduction on challenges of European quality development in a Europe of shared visions and divers goals (Brian Holmes), part A gives an overview on methods and approaches which can be used for the development of quality in different educational contexts. Part B focuses on e-learning standards, as there are quality and learning technology standards. The third part of the handbook, part C, brings together articles centring around practical experiences and case studies. All articles are bridging the gap between theory and practice. They lay out basic concepts and theoretical foundations, describe methodologies and finally give practical examples and suggestions for realisation.

Part A on *Methods and approaches for quality development in e-learning* starts with chapter 3 on "Quality of e-learning: Negotiating a strategy, implementing a policy" by Claudio Dondi, Michela Moretti and Fabio Nascimbeni. They state in their article about that dialogue among individuals, organisations, policy makers and other involved stake-holders is a pre-condition to create clarity and trust without which a quality strategy for e-learning may not progress. A phased approach on how to build public policies and institutional strategies for e-learning quality is suggested.

Chapter 4, by Julia Flasdick, Amaury Legait and Lutz P. Michel, focuses on accreditation ("The maze of accreditation in European higher education"). They describe the accreditation process, give an overview of the tools and methods and thus help to select appropriate accreditation for particular circumstances. Additionally they sketch out the future evolution of accreditation in the European Higher Education Area.

In chapter 5, "Adopting quality standards for education and e-learning", Jan M. Pawlowski shows how to implement and adapt the quality standard for e-learning ISO/ IEC 19796-1. The Quality Adaptation Model shows the steps to develop and implement quality in organisations: the main steps (Context Setting, Model Adaptation, Model Implementation and Adoption, and Quality Development) are explained in detail to show how an organisation can develop its individual quality system.

Christian Stracke explains in chapter 6 about "Process-oriented quality management" the importance and relevance of process orientation in quality management for educational organisations. First, the relevance of process orientation for a holistic quality management concept is described and then an overview on several quality management concepts is given.

In chapter 7, Markus A. Wirth approaches quality management approaches from a different perspective: "An analysis of international quality management approaches in e-learning: Different paths, similar pursuits". The contribution intends to break with some commonly accepted statements that solely emphasise the heterogeneity of nowadays quality approaches. A systematic overview of four generically different fields of quality management approaches points out some basic differences in the underlying objectives and the ways in which these goals are prosecuted. However, a deeper look below the surface reveals some striking similarities between various quality management approaches.

Thomas Lodzinski and Jan M. Pawlowski describe a new quality mark in chapter 8, "The quality mark e-learning: Developing process- and product-oriented quality". The presented Quality Mark e-learning (Qualitätssiegel e-learning, QSEL) is an example of a holistic quality mark. It analyses the quality of organisations and its products and services.

In Chapter 9, John Erpenbeck, Lutz P. Michel focus on "Competency-based quality securing of e-learning (CQ-E)". The article deals with crucial questions of measuring and making up a balance of professional competencies – in contrast to skills and qualifications. The article sketches a proposal for a special model of securing the quality of formal as well as informal learning, based on the concept of competencies.

Thomas Berger and Ulrike Rockmann describe the use of product oriented quality criteria in chapter 10 "Quality of e-learning products". The contribution provides background information about the concept and the development of the Reference Quality Criteria Catalogue. The catalogue contains quality criteria for e-learning products and processes and is part of the Public Available Specification (PAS) 1032-1 of the German Institute of Standardisation, and also annexed to the standard ISO/ IEC 19796-1.

Evaluation is on stake in chapter 10, about "Quality Evaluation for e-learning", by Ulf-Daniel Ehlers and Lutz Goertz. They give an overview on evaluation concepts for e-learning and describe evaluation as a means to find out whether e-learning is effective, in which contexts and for what groups of learners.

The last chapter of part A focuses the question how to find the best quality model. Barbara U. Hildebrandt and Sinje J. Teschler describe in chapter 12 about "Towards a model for structuring diversity: The EQO approach for better quality in e-learning" a possibility to structure the diversity of quality approaches and strategies in European e-learning. The EQO Analysis Model enables a consistent description and thus comparison of quality approaches based on a harmonised metadata scheme.

Part B on *E-Learning-Standards* starts with a journey into the sometimes confusing standards jungle. Kai Heddergott shows how better transparency can be achieved using standards. His journey leads us to the parts of architectures and frameworks, management standards, standards for contents, didactical standards, learner model standards and inter-face standards. The orientation serves as a guideline for the complex field of standards.

In chapter 14, Rolf Lindner gives a survey of architectures and frameworks as the conceptual umbrella for standards. He shows how architectures and frameworks for e-learning relate to quality aspects. He outlines the major approaches and explains their features, strengths and weaknesses. He concludes with identifying the major differences between educationally-oriented approaches favoured in Europe or technology-oriented approaches found in the USA.

In chapter 15, Christian Prpitsch and Patrick Veith describe the most adopted standards so far: For the description of Content, Learning Object Metadata (LOM) and in the field of management standards, SCORM and IMS Content Packaging. They focus on the procedure to adapt these standards using application profiles for a context specific.

In chapter 16, Michael Klebl introduces didactical standards or, as he names them, educational interoperability standards. He shows two alternatives: IMS Learning Design (IMS-LD) and DIN Didactical Object Model (DIN-DOM). A description of examples and issues in practical use concludes this article.

In chapter 17, Cleo Sgouropoulou describes learner profiles and their contribution to the development of the European education area. Her article presents an overview of the new European educational setting, discussing issues and initiatives.

Michel Arnaud describes in chapter 18, how e-portfolios contribute to creating employment opportunities. He shows the need to have common references for competency definitions with the learner competency model: IMS LIP as well as an e-portfolio format in agreement with IMS Reusable Definition of Competency or Educational Objective (RDCEO), Europass Diploma Supplement, Data Protection and Privacy procedures. He concludes how the e-portfolio can provide an opportunity for the European Union to have a stronger implication in improving European employability through its promotion.

In chapter 19, Markus Bick describes the integration of business information systems and learning systems. The goal is to integrate learning and business tasks and other enterprise applications. He shows corresponding standardisation activities for integrated information systems, especially emphasizing how learning and business systems can be integrated into a common framework. He describes selected data exchange standards, especially the Extensible Markup Language (XML) and infrastructure standards, like the Open Management Architecture (OMA) and Web services.

Chapter 20 focuses on accessibility aspects of standards. Pythagoras Karampiperis, and Demetrios Sampson present in their work on "Facilitating learning objects reusability in different accessibility settings" a methodology for defining an accessibility application profile that captures the accessibility properties of learning objects in a commonly identified format. This in-formation is critical in order to be able to match learning content with learner accessibility preferences, as well as, to allow the use of generic hypermedia and multimedia based educational content which is not originally developed for a particular group.

With chapter 21, Wayne Hodgins concludes this part of the book with an outlook into the future of standardization. He describes the first steps and initiatives. A main conclusion is that supporting tools and technologies are readily available today. He shows how we enter a new era for standards to develop new tools, specs, and standards. Finally, he provides a look ahead at the next deacades and the future of standards for technology enabled learning.

Part C of the book puts forth practical experiences in form of case study accounts or reports about implementation, chances, benefits and pitfalls of quality development in e-learning.

Based on 5 national studies, from Finland, France, Poland, Spain, and Switzerland, Bernard Dumont and Albert Sangra present and analyse in chapter 22 organisational and cultural factors that can facilitate or block the implementation of Quality in Higher educational institutions in general and for e-learning in particular: "Organisational and cultural similarities and differences in implementing quality in e-learning in Europe´s higher education". They make a comparison between these factors, some of them being common to the 5 countries, the other being relevant for only one or more countries.

Chapter 23 gives a visionary account on "Rethinking quality for building a learning society" by Maureen Layte and Serge Ravet. The article explores how the issue of quality in the knowledge economy and learning society of the 21st century might dramatically differ from that we have known in the industrial age.

Ulf-Daniel Ehlers focuses in chapter 24 on the learner perspective of quality development: "Myths and realities in learner oriented e-learning-quality". The article describes the concept of learner oriented quality development for e-learning in various educational sectors. Learner orientation is viewed as a necessity rather than an option for quality development in e-learning. Four questions are answered in particular: What is learner orientation? Why is it important? What do learners think about quality? How can learner orientation in quality development be achieved in a participative way?

Chapter 25 also focuses on the learner. Anne-Marie Husson presents "The e-learning path model: A specific quality approach to satisfy the needs of customers in e-learning". Focusing on the satisfaction on the various customers all along the offering, the quality approach presented has been elaborated by a team of "quality" and "e-learning" experts under the leadership of Le Préau.

In the contribution "Pedagogic quality - supporting the next UK generation of e-learning", chapter 26, John Anderson and Robert McCormick show how to enable educational practitioners (teachers and learners) in order to make more informed decisions about the value of resources and tools to support effective pedagogical practice in their context.

Chapter 27 "Quality in cross national business models for technology based educational services" by Stefan Fischer, Martin Gutbrod and Helmut W. Jung describes that technology based educational services (former e-learning) are built on a complex partner network with most different service sectors.

Thomas Reglin, in chapter 28, focuses on "e-learning quality and standards from a business perspective". The article discusses quality requirements for e-learning from the perspective of vocational education and training. It points out that the complexity of e-learning projects demands a specific process model that describes the manifold feedback loops between producers and customers as well as within interdisciplinary teams of experts, didacts, technicians.

"A framework for quality of learning resources" is put forth in chapter 29 by Frans van Assche and Riina Vuorikari. They argue that in order to better understand the complex question of quality of web-based learning resources it is beneficial to look at the different processes during the life of a learning resource: what are the aspects of quality that are related to the creation of material, its discovery and eventually its use and re-use for learning purposes? This chapter therefore looks at the different processes related to learning resources and the roles involved in these processes with the aim to understand the quality aspects of the processes as well as the roles, which have responsibilities regarding the quality for these processes.

Erik Duval presents a concept for measuring the "real quality": "LearnRank: Towards a real quality measure for learning" in chapter 30. The chapter starts from the notion that quality is context dependent and proposes "LearnRank", a context-dependent ranking algorithm focused on learning applications, as a vision for how to really measure quality.

Miho Taguma, in chapter 31, reports on current initiatives regarding 'quality' in tertiary education e-learning drawing upon the results of the OECD/ CERI international case studies: "Quality of e-learning in tertiary education: Managing a balance between divergence and convergence". The case studies examined the tertiary e-learning practices in 19 postsecondary education institutions from 13 countries (Australia, Brazil, Canada, France, Germany, Japan, Mexico, New Zealand, Spain, Switzerland, Thailand, UK, and US). Six institutions are from Europe.

Chapter 32, by Rob Edmonds on "Best practices for e-learning" lists more than 40 best practices in e-learning (and provides full details of 17). The results are particularly useful for organisations looking to improve their e-learning and learning implementations but are also useful for learning developers and vendors that need to improve the efficiency and effectiveness of their customers' learning operations.

2 Quality in a Europe of diverse systems and shared goals

Brian Holmes

European Commission, Europe

Quality is at the heart of Europe's vision to become a worldwide reference for education and training by 2010. And information and communication technologies (ICT) are seen as a vital tool for achieving this – opening up our systems to the world, improving access for all and increasing learning effectiveness. But more than this, ICT is seen as a catalyst for change in our efforts to reform and modernise education and training for the knowledge society.

So how does e-learning contribute to improving the quality of Europe's education and training, and how is its implementation influenced by the political vision of Europe as an Area of Lifelong Learning with diverse systems and shared goals?

Quality can be simply defined as "fitness for purpose". This article will explore some of the policy drivers for quality in e-learning (the purpose) whilst exploring the extent to which these are currently being met (the fitness).

2.1 Europe: A worldwide quality reference

Quality in education and training has always been an important issue in Europe. Ask any teacher or trainer and they will explain the considerable lengths they go to in order to ensure their pupils and students learn. It is this commitment and dedication that has helped Europe to develop a worldwide reputation for excellence in learning.

At a time when European politicians are focusing on achieving the goals of Lisbon and trying to catch up with the USA and Asia in terms of competitiveness and productivity, it is interesting to reflect on our position in the world regarding education. Take the results of the PISA study conducted in 2000, for example (OECD 2002). The American social critic Jeremy Rifkin noted in his recent book that whereas the USA spends about the same proportion of GDP on education as do countries in the European Union, for reading literacy you will see eight European Union countries ranked ahead of the USA, lying in fifteenth place. For mathematics literacy there are twelve European countries ranked higher and for science literacy there are eight. He concludes that

> "When we think about criteria for determining good quality of life – what an economy should be all about – what comes immediately to mind is access to a decent education, assuring our good health, providing adequate care for our children, and living in safe neighbourhoods and communities. In most of these particulars, the European Union has already surpassed the United States of America" (Rifkin, 2004).

So if Europe is doing so well in relative terms, why are we focusing so much on improving quality? The answer lies partly in the detail; if we compare the Pisa results for the various European countries, we see that some are doing very well whilst others are not. There is a considerable variation in the quality of education across Europe. At the same time our society is changing radically and our education and training systems need to reform to meet the new challenges. It is for these reasons that the Members States – normally strict upholders of their right to develop education and training policy independently – decided to work together more closely, to share good practice and to learn from one other. Education and training have become key policies issues at a European level and this is where the discussion on quality becomes really interesting.

This article looks at the issue of quality from the perspective of policymakers. It examines the implications for the use of ICT in education and training (e-learning) and presents some key issues, based upon lessons learnt.

2.2   Diverse systems, shared goals

Some countries believe strongly that it is the duty of the state to educate children, in a way which is equal and consistent, regardless of family situation, religion or other factors. For them quality implies access for all, shared values and a strong social responsibility. Other countries, however, believe that education is a responsibility to be shared with parents, whom they encourage to take an active part in their children's education. They encourage children to excel and may even encourage competition.

Who is to say that one system is better in terms of quality than the other? To try to do so would miss the point. Rather we should recognise that Europe's systems are diverse and have different approaches which reflect our deep rooted cultures and values. It is better for us to focus on identifying shared goals, opportunities for collaboration, co-operation and peer-learning; to build upon the strengths in Europe and develop towards our shared aspirations.

The Lisbon Objectives and Education & Training

Europe should become, by 2010, ...

*"the most competitive and dynamic knowledge-based
economy in the world, capable of sustainable economic growth with more
and better jobs and greater social cohesion"*

European Council
Lisbon March 2000

The future objectives for education & training ....

• Increasing the quality and effectiveness of education and training
  systems in the European Union
• Facilitating the access of all to the education and training systems
• Opening up education and training systems to the wider world

Education Council
Brussels February 2001

Source: European Commission 2005d, e

Fig. 2-1: The lisbon objectives and education & training

In response to the challenges identified in Lisbon, the European Council adopted in 2001 three strategic goals (and 13 associated concrete objectives) to be attained by 2010: education and training systems should be organised around *quality, access* and *openness to the world*. A year later it approved a detailed work programme for the attainment of these goals, called *Education and Training 2010*, and supported the ambition of the Ministries of Education to make Europe '*a worldwide quality reference by 2010*'. Quality was placed firmly at the top of the political agenda and Members States committed themselves to work together, through an approach called the 'Open Method of Co-ordination'.

2.2.1   Education – a global market

The desire for Member States to work together is set against the backdrop of education becoming global. Students are prepared to travel more to get the best in education. They are also more demanding in terms of what they expect. So in many respects a worldwide market is developing in which European universities need to compete with the best on offer in the USA, Asia and elsewhere. At the same time, information and communications technologies (ICT) and the Internet are allowing institutions to offer their courses on line, so that 'virtual mobility' is also on the increase. Indeed in 2002, the Massachusetts Institute of Technology (MIT) decided to post on the Internet, free of charge, the contents of many of its courses. UNESCO hailed this decision as '*a huge opportunity for universities in poor countries*', however European academics were alarmed at the prospect of losing valuable fee-paying students (UNESCO, 2002). But as the furore over this decision passed, people realised that it wasn't such a challenge to Europe after all. Learning is a social process and the context of learning, with fellow students and experienced teaching staff, is as important – if not more important – than the content. From the point of view of quality, free online content is only a small part of the learning equation.

2.2.2   'Massification'

The demand for higher education is also growing significantly, as countries try to increase the number of young people passing through university – 'massification' as it is often termed. In the UK, for example, the number of students attending a higher education institute increased from 125 000 in 1962 to over 1 million in 1996 (Lomas, 2001). This has led some to claim that quality is decreasing. They take the view that quality derives from excellence and that 'more means less'. The alternative view of quality as 'fitness for purpose' presupposes that as long as systems are put in place to address the learners needs and assure quality, then greater numbers does not necessarily mean lower quality. However, there is general agreement that massification increases the challenge for quality. In this respect, ICT and e-learning are again seen as important tools for increasing effectiveness and efficiency, and thereby increasing quality.

2.2.3   Lifelong learning

The developing global market for education and massification were not the only things driving change when the work programme for Education and Training 2010 was agreed (European Commission, 2003a, c, e). There was also the desire to make learning more relevant to the needs of society; not only during one's youth, but continuously throughout life. Lifelong learning was emerging as major political objective, to improve the skills of the workforce but also to improve people's quality of life and aid social inclusion through better understanding and tolerance for cultural differences.

Lifelong learning is not a second-class form of education or something one does only later in life. Rather it is a concept covering the whole of one's existence: from cradle to grave. It emphasises the need and desire to learn continuously, as part of our work, our relaxation, our life.

In reality we have a long way to go to achieve good participation in lifelong learning in all countries. Statistics published in the Commission's report on progress towards the Lisbon objectives for Education and Training 2010 (European Commission, 2004a) show a wide disparity in the participation of adults in lifelong learning across Europe (figure 2-2), from 35.8% in Sweden down to only 3.7% in Greece.

Percentage of population aged 25-64 participating in education and training in 4 weeks prior to the survey (2004)

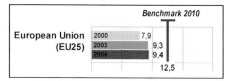

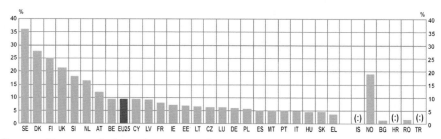

Source: Eurostat, Labour force survey[2]

Fig. 2-2: Participation in lifelong learning

Traditionally our education and training systems have focused on young people, supporting them as they pass from one discrete stage of their education to another. The transition from school to college, from college to university, is often dramatic and little attention has been paid to supporting connections between these stages of learning. But under a philosophy of life long learning this must change. Schools must co-operate more closely with universities, to guide pupils towards choosing what is best for them and equipping them with the key competencies they will need in later life; such as learning to learn, communication skills, maths, science and digital literacy, to name just a few. But more than this, universities must co-operate with industry and with local communities to extend learning beyond youth. Governments must also invest in continuous vocational education and training (VET) and lifelong learning centres – museums, libraries, community centres, etc. Learning must not stop when we leave school or graduate from college and our education and training systems need to adapt to this widening window of learning opportunities.

Quality in education was easier to handle when we had more predictable intakes of students, with similar ages, experience and background. But now – with increased mobility, more mature learners, etc. – things are radically different and our model of quality needs to adapt to these changes. Also education and training has traditionally been the remit of the school, university or training college. But now new stakeholders are involved: parents, industry, local communities, governments and let's not forget, the ever more demanding and discerning learner. Quality needs to embrace a multi-stakeholder, multi-modal approach involving a wide variety of learning contexts, experiences and learner maturities.

---

[2] http://www.europa.eu.int/comm/education/policies/2010/doc/progressreport05.pdf.

2.2.4   The changing learning paradigm

The discussion on quality is also set against a backdrop of a fundamental change that is taking place in the way we teach and support learning. We are moving from a paradigm based on the *transfer* of knowledge (or rather information) from the all wise teacher to the pupil (or trainer to the student), to one based on learner *acquisition* and *construction* of knowledge through active dialogue with other learners, content and the teacher. In the latter scenario, the teacher takes on the role of facilitator, guiding the learner, inspiring and motivating them as they follow their own path of learning. This learner centred approach is more dynamic, more flexible to the needs of the learner, but also a greater challenge to our traditional educational institutions. Indeed it is the loss of control and the shift in power that poses a problem for some teachers.

Our notion of quality changes substantially when we adopt this learner centred approach. Instead of focusing on parameters which affect the delivery of learning – such as the ability to pass a clear and consistent message to many students, the quality of the teaching material, etc. – we are more likely to be focusing on such things as the possibility for the students to communicate effectively, to collaborate, to interact and modify the learning content, and for the teacher to be able to follow the different learning paths and offer tailored guidance where necessary.

The learner centred paradigm is not new, many would argue, rather it is becoming more widely recognised for its advantages. Some teachers, trainers and tutors have been operating this way for a long time. But now it is becoming more institutionalised as 'the way we do things here'. As such, this way of learning is starting to impact the quality of the institution as a whole, instead of the work of just a few pioneering teachers. There is growing recognition that *innovation* is important for education and training institutions, and that in order to improve quality they need to make better use of the knowledge, experience and ideas of their most important asset – the teaching staff.

The implications of this paradigm shift are that we need to focus not only on the quality of the content (such as books), but also on the quality of the learning process and the key actors involved, such as teachers, tutors and trainers.

2.2.5   The introduction of new technologies

The advent of new technologies and the Internet has opened-up a whole new range of opportunities for enhancing learning. Not only in terms of facilitating distance learning, through online forums, virtual classrooms, etc, but also in ways in which face-to-face learning is enhanced, through Internet connected electronic whiteboards, the use of digital cameras in the classroom, etc.

The integration of ICT into education and training (e-learning) has been recognised as a powerful tool for improving learning at the highest political level. It can help us in our endeavours to achieve the three strategic European goals mentioned earlier, namely quality, access and openness to the world. It can help improve quality by facilitating more learner-centred, flexible and contextualised learning. It can improve access to learning for people in remote places or with special needs. And it can help Europe to open up its systems to the world, through better communication and interaction.

This is precisely why the Commission proposed the *e-learning* Action Plan in 2001 and the European Parliament helped to launch the *e-learning* Initiative to fund pilot projects (figure 2-3). The initiative developed into a programme in 2004 and will take the work on e-learning forward until the *Integrated action programme in the field of Lifelong Learning* starts in 2007.

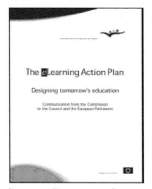

eLearning Action Plan helps co-ordinate community actions concerned with e-learning, mobilising the educational and cultural communities, as well as the economic and social players in Europe

eLearning Initiative 2000-2003
Funded 65 projects, 27.2 million €

eLearning Programme 2004-2006
44 million €

Source: European Commission 2005d

Fig. 2-3: ICT for education and training: E-learning

Results from the *e-learning* Initiative and other programmes supporting the use of ICT in education and training – such as the Minerva action line of the Socrates programme, the Leonardo da Vinci programme and the Information Society Technologies (IST) programme – have shown the added value of e-learning. However, they have also shown that integrating ICT doesn't automatically lead to better learning. On the contrary, it is very easy to reduce quality by applying technology inappropriately and forgetting to address the all important pedagogical and organisational issues.

2.3   Quality and the impact of ICT

Much of this article has focused on quality in education and training in general and we have only now turned our attention to the subject of e-learning. There is a clear, deliberate reason for this – quality for e-learning primarily concerns quality for learning. Indeed, results from the various e-learning projects support this assertion; when attention is placed on the technology rather than the impact on learning, then the overall quality reduces.

That is not to say that e-learning is simply learning with an 'e', but rather to emphasise that we mustn't forget where our centre of attention should lie: with the learning.

2.3.1   The scope is wide

E-learning is helping to improve access to learning, to improve its availability, its effectiveness and, in some cases, its efficiency. Yet this only part of the story. E-learning is also providing us with a unique opportunity to transform the way we learn; to open-up our education and training systems, breaking down the barriers to lifelong learning; to forge new partnerships with the local community, with industry and commerce; and most importantly to put the learner in control of his or her own learning. Many schools, universities and training colleges are rising to this challenge, integrating ICT, transforming their processes and implementing organisational change. Within this context of radical change, the scope of quality is wide and potentially very complex.

As a starting point, we need to know what we mean by e-learning. The e-learning Action Plan defines it as "the use of new multimedia technologies and the Internet to improve the quality of learning by facilitating access to resources and services as well as remote exchanges and collaboration''. Central to this definition is the idea of improving learning through increased collaboration, better access to resources and improved services. It builds upon the tenet that learning is a social process and that e-learning is only a tool, albeit a valuable one, to be used in context with appropriate pedagogical practices.

In its report presenting a possible model for quality for training, Le Préau sees e-learning as a service, involving collaboration over networks, supported by a third-party training provider and involving validation (Le Préau, 2002). It lambastes attempts to treat the e-learner as a consumer at the end of a *'linear, industrial process'*. Instead it advocates co-production, with a *'wide range of diverse competencies, a multiplicity of actors who are positioned at the crossroads of numerous and varied professions and within different technological and pedagogical fields'*. The learner his/herself has to have *'skills in the field of cognitive, organisational and social autonomy as well as the ability to take on responsibility for their learning process'*. Le Préau sees these as important factors in a quality approach which *"must encourage motivation, guard against possible failure, reduce the drop-out rates, and help the learners develop responsibility for learning, free them from temporal and spatial constraints, and provide them with evaluation tools"*. What we see here are many of the points raised earlier in this article, about multi-stakeholder involvement, about taking a holistic view to learning that develops essential competencies at an early stage in life and about the need for innovation.

2.3.2   The dimensions are many

In its report on the use of ICT in Schools, the OECD highlights eight dimensions which it considers important for the quality of educational software (OECD, 2001).

- *Educational purpose:* much educational content is produced not for schools, but for businesses and commerce. Functions which are most interesting for the classroom, such as a straightforward x/ y plot in a spreadsheet, may only appear after some time.
- *Mode of use:* the designer of an e-learning system has made many decisions about the selection of content, how it is presented, the speed of progression and the nature of feedback that in total represent 'an implicit pedagogy' which may not be appropriate for the context in which it is being used.
- *Needs of individual learners:* it is important that the complexity of the content and the language used be appropriate to the different types of learner. The challenge is to avoid 'edutainment' where the need of the market for standardised products outweighs those of the learner.
- *Robustness and user friendliness:* it is important that software meant for schools is robust and low-maintenance.
- *Added value:* e-learning must add value for the learner. It is doubtful whether simply transferring information available in books to web pages achieves this. What is needed is additional interactivity and possibilities to edit, manipulate and create content.
- *Cultural relevance:* European is rich in cultural and linguistic diversity and e-learning content must reflect this. It is not simply a question of translating content made for the largest market; the content must be designed from the outset with the specific needs of the various learners in mind.
- *Avoidance of stereotypes:* images can carry powerful messages and it is important that stereotypes are not reinforced by inappropriate content. In this respect media literacy becomes very important – several projects were launched under the *e-learning* Initiative to look into this important topic.
- *Affordability and mode of delivery:* the added value of e-learning needs to be carefully balanced against the costs involved, some of which are not always immediately obvious such as maintenance of equipment and royalty payments.

What is interesting about the OECD's criteria is their emphasis on the users' perspective and their sensitivity to culture. They also highlight that what may be appropriate for the business world is not necessarily appropriate for the classroom – on the contrary.

2.3.3   Islands of quality initiatives – the need to build bridges

In his work on the SEEL project (see below) Kennet Lindquist argued that early attempts at quality in e-learning were '*overly technology-centric, atomistic and pedagogically 'foreign'*', adding that most approaches are procedural and focus on delivery. He does, however, see a trend towards approaches which are increasingly '*user-centred, contextual and with societal perspectives*' (Lindquist, 2003). He calls for these '*islands of quality initiatives*' in Europe to be better coordinated and for us to focus more on the users' perspective.

In order to help build bridges between the various quality initiatives and coordinate work in Europe on quality in e-learning, the European Commission launched a call for proposals in 2002 under the *e-learning* Initiative. This resulted in the launch of four strategic projects: EQO, QUAL-E-LEARNING, SEEL and SEEQUEL[3]. Such has been the success of these actions, that several are continuing their work jointly under a new project called TRIANGLE, launched in March 2005, and have the aim of establishing a European Foundation for Quality in E-learning (EFQUEL).

2.3.4   Standards

Nowhere is the debate on quality in e-learning more heated and more sensitive than in the area of standards.

Standards have been around in education and training for decades. They are used by institutions and governments to ensure that learning is predictable, fair, consistent, and economic and achieves at least a minimum level of quality acceptable to society. These are laudable goals for any organisation; however in the world of education, standards are some times interpreted by the teaching staff as an attempt to limit their creativity, freedom and ability. After all, we cannot treat the education of children in a school the same we as we treat the production of cars in a factory.

The debate on standards has become event more fraught with the introduction of ICT, which has added a technical dimension to learning. So it is best for us to separate right from the beginning the discussion on *educational standards* from the one on *technical standards*. Discussion on the former, as already mentioned, has been continuing for decades and is becoming even more difficult as we aim to compare and contrast the different educational policies at a European level. But it remains a fundamental question associated with education and training in general, and in this context e-learning and the use of ICT is just a side issue. With the latter (technical standards) the situation is quite different. Here there is a clear appreciation that if the technology is to work and to become transparent in the learning process, then we must have standards. Not local ones or European ones, but global

---

[3] EQO: European Quality Observatory; QUAL-E-LEARNING: Quality in E-learning; SEEL: Supporting Excellence in E-learning; SEEQUEL: Sustainable Environment for the Evaluation of Quality in E-Learning.

standards.

The European Commission has been supporting Europe's involvement in the development of global technical standards for e-learning for many years. Through the Information Society Technologies (IST) Programme, for example, with the ARIADNE project. Through the *e-learning* Initiative and the EQO project, for example. And most importantly, through support for the CEN's working group on learning technologies.

The emphasis is on developing technical standards which free the user from being locked in to one particular technical system or provider (Open Standards). That allows the user to freely communicate between learning environments, transferring content and other essential data for learning (interoperability). This work is essential for ensuring that good quality is possible. However, it only presents the user with a level playing field; with the prerequisites for e-learning to be successful. It helps ensure consistent quality but does not guarantee high quality. For the latter, we need to look at the dimensions of quality in learning already described in this article, such as appropriate teacher/ trainer training, relevant pedagogy, organisational change, etc.

2.3.5   Quality is improving

Early attempts at e-learning solutions were often unsuccessful: they isolated the learner, they were inflexible and dictated how we must learn, and they tried to replace the teacher or trainer with automated checklists, pop-up menus and help-pages. In those early days technology was king and we were so concerned with trying to connect schools to the internet and putting PCs in classrooms that we often forgot to think about the process of learning.

At work too, there was so much emphasis on reducing cost and increasing efficiency that we often neglected the effectiveness of the learning itself. In-house company training was replaced by do-it-yourself, CD-ROM based learning. But as a result, the drop-out rate from training courses increased significantly. Learners just didn't like this new way of learning and many companies started to question their investment in technology.

But thankfully we have learnt from those early days. Pedagogical approaches have been adapted, technology has advanced significantly and quality has improved. Modern e-learning solutions now recognise the importance of learning as a social process and offer possibilities for collaboration with other learners, for interaction with the learning content and for guidance from teachers, trainers and tutors. These learner-centred approaches have put the learners back in command, with a wealth of learning resources at their finger tips.

Teachers and trainers once more play a central role, using virtual interactions together with traditional face-to-face meetings to obtain a 'blended' approach. An approach in which they and the learners are no longer seen simply as consumers of pre-determined e-learning content, but as editors, authors and contributors to a contextualised learning scenario.

2.3.6   Much has still to be done

With more than 93% of European schools now connected to the Internet, with the average number of pupils per PC now down to 13 and with the rapid uptake in broadband (36% of PCs now connected), we see that e-learning is starting to become mainstream in education. Does this imply that a work on e-learning is nearing completion? No; but it does show that our work is bearing fruit. However a lot more still needs to be done to increase the overall quality of e-learning.

As an example, a recent study on the use of e-learning in SMEs funded by the European Commission, showed that respondents found that the quality of e-learning was lower than traditional training for many aspects, including availability of content, different language versions, availability of topics, etc (see figure 2-4) (Unisys, 2005).

Table 2-1: The satisfaction of SMEs is less with e-learning than traditional training for many aspects

	Traditional Score	E-learning Score
Training is available in a language understandable to all staff	3,3	4
Trainings are an opportunity to develop a network of new acquaintances	2,4	3,8
Topics developed are well covered, from basic to expert level (Completeness)	2,9	3,6
The training infrastructure is available	3,5	3,6
Topics available do cover the training needs of my company	2,7	3,5
Training certificates are available at the end of the course	3,1	3,5
Guidance is available to help me find my way in the training offer	2,8	3,4
Training courses react to the input of the learner (interactivity)	3,1	3,4
Effective user/learner support is available when needed	3,1	3,4
The quality of the learning process is continuously improving	3,4	3,4

1 denotes Excellent, 5 denotes Poor

For some aspects, however, they found that e-learning offered advantages, particularly in terms of flexibility, efficiency and cost (see figure 2-5).

Table 2-2: The satisfaction of SMEs is higher with e-learning than traditional training for some aspects

	Traditional Score	E-learning Score
Training is available when needed (Timeliness)	3,9	2,6
Training is tailored to the needs of the learner (own rhythm, no judgment)	3,7	2,8
Training courses are efficient (shorter time needed to learn)	3,4	3,1
Training/training materials is/are available on the job (Support function)	3,4	3,1
Training costs are reasonable (affordable)	3,4	3,1

1 denotes Excellent, 5 denotes Poor

In conclusion, the study states that:

- There is a lack of awareness as to how e-learning can benefit enterprises
- The e-learning materials are generally not well adapted to practical and specific needs of SMEs
- Success in the use of e-learning is often accompanied by local support
- Learning in SMEs is mostly informal and that e-learning is still predominantly formal
- There is a need to combine e-learning with other forms of business support, such as knowledge management, change management, peer collaboration, etc.

Each of these points relate to the quality of learning being offered to SMEs through e-learning and they clearly show that many fundamental changes still need to be made before it can be considered to be a useful alternative to traditional training.

2.3.7   Strategic and long-term objectives

In its progress report for 2003, the working group on ICT for the *Education and Training 2010* work programme, provided four recommendations for the use of ICT in education and training institutions:

- Embed ICT policies and strategies into long term educational objectives;
- Ensure new support services for education;
- Empower educational actors and train for the management of change;
- Develop research, establish new indicators and provide access to results.

These recommendations were derived from an analysis of what is taking place in the Member States and an exchange of good practice. They echo similar conclusions emerging from other studies and projects. In particular that we should not expect e-learning to deliver quick wins. Rather investment in ICT should be seen as a strategic decision, requiring important organisational change and continuous professional development for teaching staff on the pedagogical implications. Only when this approach is adopted will the quality of e-learning improve.

2.4   Conclusion

Quality in education and training is at the top of the political agenda in Europe. Politicians have realised that continuous education and training throughout life (lifelong learning) is an essential prerequisite for Europe to achieve its aspirations for improving competitiveness, innovation and growth. Commissioner Figel' – responsible for education, training and multilingualism – in his speech on the priorities for education and training for the next five years, referred to the *triangle of knowledge* comprised of research, education and innovation (European Commission, 2005c).

The use of ICT in education and training (e-learning) has been shown to be an effective tool for helping to make learning more accessible, effective and efficient. But only when important factors are taken in to account, such as the need for teachers, trainers and tutors to receive appropriate training on the pedagogical implications of using ICT; for the use of ICT to be accompanied by appropriate organisational changes; for the process of learning itself to be redesigned to take full advantage of the possibilities offered by technology; for content to be interactive, multilingual and highly contextualised. These are just a few of the key lessons learnt from our now quite extensive experience of using e-learning in practice. Put these altogether and you start to get a valuable picture of how we can assure and raise the level of quality in e-learning.

Part A: European quality development: Methods and approaches

Part A of the handbook focuses on introductory background topics of quality development in education and especially e-learning. It gives an overview on the topic of educational quality research, describes developments and the relevance of quality development and introduces the European dimension. Methods, models, concepts and approaches for the development, management and assurance of quality in e-learning are introduced. The chapters are all structured alike: First the theoretical model is described in detail and then a practical implementation and the challenges and experiences connected to it are accounted for.

3 Quality of e-learning: Negotiating a strategy, implementing a policy

Claudio Dondi, Michela Moretti, Fabio Nascimbeni

SCIENTER, Italy

Although everybody recognises that lack of confidence in e-learning and lack of perceived quality in early e-learning, a major mobility factor to adoption of and investment in e-learning. The approaches to quality, governmental and institutional policies that can be observed are as many as the cases that can be studied.

The article explores the issue of quality concepts as one deeply rooted in people's visions of the world and values, that naturally and culturally diverge. Any policy that "imposes" one particular concept of quality is therefore likely to fail – at least partially – in its objectives.

It argues that dialogue among individuals, organisations, policy makers and other involved stakeholders is a pre-condition to create clarity and trust conditions without which a quality strategy for e-learning may not progress and suggests a phased approach on how to build public policies and institutional strategies for e-learning quality.

3.1   Is quality in e-learning a "clear" concept?

The analysis of state of the art of the debate on Quality in e-learning shows different recurrent factors/ elements:

- Quality seems to be in the eye of the beholder. The way in which stakeholders approach and see quality in e-learning is different. The difference emerges not only between education and industry sectors, but among the stakeholders belonging to the same sector[4].

---

[4] Boonem, A.; van Petegem, W. (Eds). Mapping of approaches to quality, Desk research Interim report, SEEQUEL project, 2005. This paper can be download from European eLearning Quality forum http://communities.trainingvillage.gr/elearning_forum.

- Quality is a concern for all the stakeholders. The development of quality in e-learning is a long-term strategy/ objective for stakeholders, especially those involved within education and training institutions if they are going to be able to offer added value to learners and citizens. For best effect, quality needs to be inherent and designed into a process rather than applied after the process has been developed.
- There is a diffuse perception about lack of quality of e-learning provision[5]. Despite ever increasing focus on the assurance of suitable quality input there exists a great variance in the observed quality levels of available courses and resources. Indeed the ever increasing volume of available material is not readily matched by available quality levels.
- The focus of existing quality initiatives/ approaches/ strategies/ frameworks diverge. It ranges from e-learning materials to services, from the user perspective to that of institutions with some specific actions addressing both regional and societal dimensions[6]. The different approaches rely on quality concepts which vary in their scope and goals: excellence, fitness for purpose, conformance, performance, re-usability, user satisfaction, personalisation, standardisation, innovation, human-interaction, etc.

Currently, there is a significant number of initiatives driving discussions and aiming at consensus building as regards quality in the new learning technology systems and the emerging learning processes, required to support the developments in the Information Society. These initiatives have originated from the need to establish a comprehensive framework for making judgments about the inflows and outflows of the recent, and sometimes innovative, ICT-supported learning processes (what we call e-learning), and have established working groups and discussion fora, which are trying to consolidate the various approaches and provide a common framework of understanding about quality in e-learning, mainly addressing – either in an explicit or in an implicit way – the needs of intermediaries of learning, namely the teachers and trainers as well as the policy makers.

Despite the effort, the different visions and perspectives on quality and the variety of existing approaches have shown the complexity of the quality concept and the multiplicity of "heterogeneous voices" in the e-learning arena.

The reality shows that quality is linked to individuals' visions, perspectives values, roles, contexts, and that a "one size fits all" model for quality does not exist.

There is no simple definition of quality in e-learning and any definition we might wish to consider runs the risk of constraining people vision of what quality means and it significance in their particular context.

---

[5] Massy, J. Quality and eLearning. Summary Report 2002, Biz Media.

[6] In this respect, it is worth mentioning the four European Quality projects (Seequel, SEEL, EQO, and QUAL-e-Learning) supported by the European Commission (DG Education and Culture) within the eLearning Action Plan that focused on the quality of eLearning from different perspectives.

3.2   Why quality in e-learning is not a unified concept?

It is important to introduce the approach, the reflection and the outputs achieved in the *SEEQUEL project*[7]. The driving objective of SEEQUEL was to reach consensus on a comprehensive analysis framework, encompassing the different "quality cultures", that are representative of the interests and long-standing priorities of the various user groups such as industry, academia, professionals, students[8].

The first phase of the SEEQUEL project consisted of a mapping of the different approaches adopted with respect to quality in e-learning by different stakeholders; this was done through an in-depth desk research and documentation activity (collection of experiences, practices, models) that covered the following eight sectors:

1. industry providing e-learning,
2. industry seen as content provider,
3. government at EU, national and local level;
4. school education,
5. higher education,
6. initial vocational education and training,
7. informal learning,
8. continuous professional development.

The desk research was articulated keeping in mind the following questions: Who is the group? How is it articulated? Which points of view are inside? Which criteria do they adopt for defining quality in e-learning? Which is their approach?

---

[7] SEEQUEL project was supported by the European Commission (DG Education and Culture) and coordinated by the MENON Network, which aimed at building dialogue around the issue of e-learning quality among all the stakeholders involved in the e-learning discourse.

[8] The partnership represented in itself the dialogic principle of the project: if one of the main problems of e-learning quality is the difficulty of different approaches and visions to talk to each other, having in the same project some key players of the industry world and some highly representative bodies from different E&T settings is, by itself, a necessary as well as an unusual starting point. The eLearning industry side is represented, in the project consortium, by the European eLearning Industry Group – Elig and on the education and training side, SEEQUEL has gathered some key players of the eLearning fields, Cedefop - the European Centre for the Development of Vocational Training, is the EU's reference centre for vocational education and training. EIfEL (European Institute for E-Learning) is a European professional association dedicated to the support of the continuing professional development of individuals and the transformation of organisations who wish to enter into the knowledge economy and society.The European Distance and E-Learning Network (EDEN) is the most comprehensive European association in open, flexible, distance and e-learning, aiming to foster developments in this constantly evolving field through offering services in a non-hierarchical manner. EuroPACE is a trans-European network of universities and their partners in education and training, i.e. private enterprises, regional and professional organisations and public authorities. ESIB - the European Federation of National Unions of Students is the umbrella organisation gathering 50 national unions of students from 37 countries and representing over 10 million students.Two UK universities: the University of Edinburgh and the University of Reading.

SEEQUEL coordination was carried on by MENON, a European research and innovation network8 which is running a number of observation and stakeholders' analysis activities, concerning the developments in e-learning across the board, with particular attention on the issues of quality, and their long-term perspectives. MENON comprises five expert organisations in the fields of e-learning as well as innovation in education and lifelong learning, namely: FIM NewLearning, HUT Lifelong Learning Institute Dipoli, Lambrakis Research Foundation, Scienter, Tavistock Institute of Human Relations.

Which are the components of the e-learning system at the core of their quality approach? Do they focus on conformance or performance? How?

The results of the desk research were finalised in individual sector report and in "starting a positioning document" which served the purpose to start the discussion within the *European e-learning Quality Forum.*

The European e-learning Quality Forum was designed in order to support an exchange of opinions and approaches and to store all the project discussion results and outcomes. The Forum, hosted by CEDEFOP (which is still running outside the project life-span at the following web address
http://communities.trainingvillage.gr) is structured both by sector and by theme, in order to provide to each user an easy entry point.

The Forum is still populated by more than 800 users and it is testifying the interest of the European Education and Training community on the issues of quality and their implications on e-learning.

From the desk research and forum debate, its emerge that:

- Each sector in entering in the debate on quality of e-learning stressed different elements/ criteria/ positions, among the possible ones:

  - *industry providing e-learning*: conformance, interoperability, standardisation, provision of scalable integrated learning services, product oriented process[9];
  - *industry seen as content provider*: competence and expertise of the producer of the educational material, content-oriented and production quality process;
  - *government at EU, national and local level*: control on content & curriculum, control on 'equal opportunities',' equal access', protecting learners as customers, improving efficiency and effectiveness of learning processes;
  - *school education*: customer satisfaction , curricula integration, educational value and use of learning services, user-friendliness and usability of resources;
  - *higher education*: Material/ content is scientifically state-of-the-art and maintained up-to-date, prestige and recognition of the authors, accreditation;
  - *initial vocational education and training*: support to contextualisation, quality of the product, clearly explicit pedagogical design principles appropriate to learner type, needs and context, high level of interactivity;
  - *informal learning*: Accessibility by different target groups in particular the ones have been excluded before, low-cost, support to individual path, avail-

---

[9] Conformance: the process to verify that a given product or a process complies with general and accepted set of rules.

Interoperability: the ability of two or more systems or components to exchange information and to use the information that has been exchanged (Institute of Electrical and Electronics Engineers - IEEE).

Product oriented process: In regard to quality for e-Learning there are basically two different fundamental approaches. The Process-oriented approach is guided by the observation that there can hardly be quality without clear and concise process definitions and quality measures for each process, sub process (like e-learning management, content development, content management, etc) and activities. The other way around the introducion of a process-oriented quality apporach can singificantly ehance quality.

ability of support mechanism that help people overcome any obstacle that might have prevent them from engaging in formal learning;

- *continuous professional development*: content of the programme and the quality of resources, accreditation system for centres to deliver their qualification programmes, relevance to work processes and working contexts.

• In order to make different stakeholders and sectors to dialogue and work together, there was a need to design *a core quality framework* as "universal lens" (see next paragraph).

• The importance of the *e-learning Quality Laboratory*, which was foreseen in the project as a priority-setting environment able to transform the needs and the problems raised in the Forum into priorities for action and to design new tools. The working groups within the quality Laboratory must be formed by more than a category of stakeholders in order to assure that different perspectives are taken in account.

During the project it became possible to understand the main needs related to e-learning quality and the approaches and positions of the different groups of stakeholders, and to "filter" these needs through the Quality Lab working group and through the Core Quality framework criteria, and resulting from this a set of tools has been developed[10].

A quality conceptual framework

The creation of a conceptual framework trying to integrate in a single structure the very different values and criteria that lie behind the different approaches to e-learning quality was undertaken in order to identify and, collate all the quality concerns coming from the different stakeholders in relation to the elements of an e-learning system/ experience. To this end, the resulting framework can be used as a "universal lens" that empowers any user from any education and training setting to look at e-learning quality with his/ her own eyes and at the same time to be aware of how other people view the concept of quality.

The SEEQUEL Quality conceptual framework focuses on the user (the subject) and on his/ her perception of quality, attributes this perception to three dimensions that are proper of every user:

---

[10] Four "tools" have been produced:

• The (e)Learner's Bill of Rights: a chart of fundamental rights of the (e)learner that, in prospective, every e-learning material/service should comply with to be considered of quality.

• The eLearner's Quality Guide: an usable collection of guidelines and hints able to guide the novice as well as the expert eLearner in any decision process about e-learning.

• The Quality Guide for informal learning: a guide conceived to encourage the adoption of quality approaches within less structured and more informal learning environments.

• A Quality tool able to help industry decision makers: a step-by-step iterative tool that can help industry and SMEs decision makers facing an e-learning related problem to look at the issue from a multiple perspective, taking into account a comprehensive set of criteria.

- the Sector to which he/she belongs (school education, university, VET, industry, etc.),
- his/her Role into the sector (e.g. inside school: school teacher, school pupil, school parent, school administrator),
- and the users' Vision of the world.

This third element is the most innovative aspect of the SEEQUEL framework, and allows justifying the fact that not all teachers have the same understanding of e-learning quality, as not all university managers do, and so on.

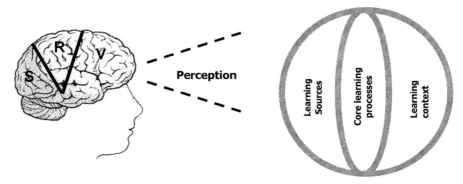

Fig. 3-1: Individual quality perception

Six visions of the world[11] are introduced, each one linked to a set of values and to a specific view on e-learning:

Table 3-1: Six visions of the world

Vision of the world	Reference Values (on which also the concept of Quality is based)	e-learning is perceived as...
World of Inspiration	Singularity, difference, innovation, originality, irrationality, imaginary, spirituality, unconscious, chance.	A huge opportunity to open up curriculum boundaries and to generate new knowledge and content through grass-roots energy mobilisation.
Domestic World	Confidence, responsibility, merit, respectability, convention, dignity, tradition, hierarchy, rank; parents, children, generation; rules and confidence, principles; harmony; the "natural"; the duty.	A potentially dangerous development that needs appropriate legislation, quality control, protection of young learners and a high level of structuring of learning paths and activities before being considered as a serious complement to traditional teaching methods.

---

[11] These visions have been borrowed from the work of two French sociologists, Boltanski and Thevenot (Luc Boltanski, Laurent Thévenot, De la justification, Les économies de la grandeur, NRF Essais, Gallimard, 1991).

World of Opinion and Image	Image, reputation, fame, success, honour, acknowledgement, visibility, audience, credibility, identification.	A recent development in the education and training area, that should be trusted only when proposed by a well-established organisation which could provide prestigious titles.
Civic World	The general will, the common interest, generosity, self-abnegation, sacrifice, pride, the group, collective action, collective entities (ideas, values, symbols and institutions).	An interesting opportunity to develop community-based learning, to give access to learning opportunities to people who would be excluded. BUT ALSO A risk of de-contextualising the learning experiences through the dominance of global providers.
Merchant World	Wealth, money; variety of choice, business, fair deals, good deals, bargain; interest, attentions to others; contract; competition, freedom.	The way to maximize the access to learning opportunities and to minimize the costs of both producing and purchasing learning. An opportunity to challenge conservative education and training systems. A new opportunity to develop new services and contents for a potentially huge market.
Industrial World	Progress, future, functionality, efficiency, optimality, performance, productivity, professionalism, reliability, far-sightedness, system	A modern and efficient way to rationalize provision of education and training, guaranteeing standard quality and seamless access. A way of facing huge training needs in a short time and without depending on variable quality teachers/ trainers and organisational constraints

Every view of e-learning quality, as well as every approach, is legitimate because it is grounded on individual visions and values. No one single vision can be judged as the best one through which to describe the concept and people can subscribe to more than one vision at the same time.

Quality depends on the vision of the world: in other words quality depends upon the viewpoint of the observer. If you are a user of e-learning materials you will have a view on what is perceived as quality. It will probably have a lot to do with the fitness for purpose and the actual experience encountered in using the materials. A teacher will have one view of quality and the student may have another. The designer of the e-learning experience will perceive quality as a complicated function of the visual experience and the degree to which the learning objectives are achieved by the type of learner for which the experience was designed. The materials may contain graphics and video sequences, animations and simulations all of which will have associated issues of quality in their preparation and use. In general there will be many people involved in the development and delivery of learning. Each will have a defined role and each will contribute to the overall quality of the experience. In other words the perception of quality in e-learning will be dependent on the viewpoint and role of multiple stakeholders (Baker, Johns, Williams, 2004).

This approach implies the need for every institutions/ organisation/ company working in e-learning to:

- have a clear and shared "own vision" of the quality of learning. This means self-analysis and positioning each organisation within the quality discourse.
- become aware that its own vision of quality is not the exclusive one and the various stakeholders can have a different and rightful visions. This means understanding that in approaching "quality" a subject as well as an objective components coexist and have to be taken into account.
- make an effort and start a process for understanding the different view points that the players/ actors involved at different levels may have. This means that only an open minded dialogue and a receptive position can be suitable to support the process.
- realise that the different views points on quality are key factors for choosing and defining a quality strategy and policy. This means that any quality strategy should take into consideration the multiperspectives and multistakeholders dimensions by understanding what the involved parties consider relevant in defining quality.
- understand that there are objective criteria for defining quality (can someone disagree that: accessibility, cost-effectiveness, coherence of the experience with the purpose, scientific correctness of the contents are not valid criteria?) but not everybody will attribute the same importance to the same criteria.
- assure that the quality strategy which will be adopted is the results of a negotiated processes which has taken into consideration the different perspectives and has clarified on which components of the learning experience is focused.
- avoid reinventing the wheel but benefit of, if possible, the existing Quality approaches and tools. This means that after one has define the own vision of quality and the approach to adopt, the organisation must verify that the are available tools and procedures allowing to implement the approach chosen.

3.3   The components of the learning experience and related quality criteria

The key focus of quality in e-learning is the learning experience. Many factors affect the learning experience, including some that don't seem to be directly relevant. The investigation of e-learning quality undertaken at European level identifies three key areas of an e-learning experience as: Learning Sources, Learning Context, and Core Learning Processes.

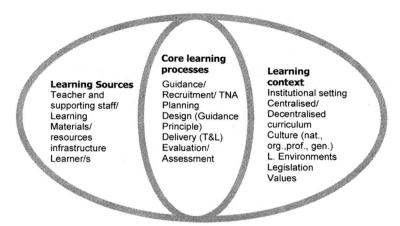

Fig. 3-2: E-learning experiences

- *The Learning sources* encompass all the sources from which the learning takes place. It comprises not only the technical infrastructure and the learning materials but also the human resources in their functions of teaching and supporting learning. Supporting sources also include peer groups and single learners.

- *The Learning processes:* Any learning experience consists of a series of processes. There are two main types of processes. Firstly there are those that occur during the actual learning experience – learning processes. Secondly, there are a series of processes set up around a given learning experience. These support processes underpin any learning experience, but are separate from the learning experience itself – for example recruitment of teachers, which does not take place as part of the learning experience, but still has a definite impact on the learning experience itself. The processes identified are typical of any training action such as: training needs analysis, guidance, recruitment, design (macro and micro), delivery and assessment/ evaluation.

- *The Learning context* is the environment in which learning takes place. It is viewed in its double perspectives: intrinsic and relative. The quality of a learning experience depends both on the quality of the context itself and on the relationship of the designed and implemented experience to the context in which it occurs.

- *The learning context* is very important in terms of quality, as all learning takes place within a specific setting and the details of this setting strongly influence the suitability and quality of the learning.

- *The quality of a learning experience* as a whole is related to the quality of the individual learning processes that compose the particular learning experience. In turn, the quality of each learning process is related to the environment in which the process takes place, and the sources used in the process.

In particular the approach took into account aspects presented in existing and well-known quality approaches such as ISO 9000:2000 or EFQM to mention but a few.

In other words,

- The customers/ users are at the centre of the system. It is particularly true in the SEEQUEL approach, which is based on the subjectivity and legitimacy of different view points and on the common dialogue used to define the vision of the different stakeholders.
- The institutional dimension is guaranteed by the criteria which relate to the organisation that is designing/ delivering the learning experience, and recognises its value and priorities.
- Attention to the quality of resources is given in the learning source area.
- The context dimension (one of the three components/ areas) is of particular relevance for vocational training, non-formal and informal learning.
- The quality concept conceives e-learning as a system in which the three areas are interdependent.

The SEEQUEL approach processes a set of objective criteria for defining quality in e-learning, and to this aim a Core Quality Framework has been design (as one of the key out of the project).

SEEQUEL believes that there are objective criteria for defining quality in e-learning, but also believe that the weight/ importance given to each criterion is based on a user's particular sector, together with their individual role and personal vision of the world.

For example if a user's vision of the world reflects that of the "world of opinion", s/ he will consider very important that the e-learning experience is provided by a well-established organisation (values: acknowledgement, visibility). This criterion would not be considered so relevant for defining the quality of an e-learning experience by a user whose values mirror closely those of "world of inspiration". Such user would probably place a stronger importance to criteria such as innovative didactic methods, individualisation of the learning paths and diversification of learning resources (value: originality, innovation…).

The Core Quality Framework is based on a matrix where a list of common quality criteria applicable to the whole e-learning experience can be weighted by the various user (people or organisation), enabling any category of stakeholders to position their perception of quality with respect to the perceptions of another stakeholders' category. SEEQUEL *allows each one to enter the debate on quality with his/ her own vision* and in this way recognises that different visions co-exist and that only by understanding multi-perspective factors and the complexity of the concept of "quality", can consensus amongst the involved actors be achieved. This issue is dealt with in greater detail in the subsequent chapter.

The core quality framework is an entry point for designing other tools which will take into account the specificity of the contexts and the learning scenarios.

The SEEQUEL Core Quality Framework is much more than a matrix, and synthesizes a subjective (weight) and an objective (criteria) dimension of quality systems.

Weight can be attributed to each criteria following the below scale:
2 = key/ core criteria for defining quality of the object
1 = important criteria for defining quality of the object
0 = non relevant for defining quality of the object

Table 3-2: The SEEQUEL core quality framework

Object	criteria	weight
1. Learning sources		
1.1A Supporting staff		
	Ability to support learning (based on past experience)	
	Ability to support the motivation to learn	
	Adaptability to change/ flexibility	
	Capacity to manage complexity	
	Communication skills (e.g. establish relationship with learners, communicate appropriately)	
	Specific educational background in e-learning	
	Intuitive and lateral thinking (e.g. thinking outside the box")	
	Open mindedness	
	Organisational skills	
	Practical skills	
	Problem finding and solving	
	Ability to initiate and manage activities that will facilitate learning	
	Relevant experience in e-learning	
	Respect for diversity including multi-culturalism	
	Ability to give encouragement	
	Team player skills	
	Technology orientation (ability to work with ICT and e-learning tools)	
	Ability to monitor learning progress	
	Ability to assess learning progress	
1.1B Teaching staff		
	Ability to support learning (based on past experience)	
	Ability to support the motivation to learn	
	Adaptability to change/ flexibility	
	Communication skills (e.g. establish relationship with learners, communicate appropriately with new means)	
	Ability to initiate and manage activities that will facilitate learning	
	Relevant experience in teaching	
	Relevant experience in the subject to be learnt	
	Respect for diversity and multi-culturalism	
	Ability to work with ICT and e-learning tools	
	Ability to work with online technology (e.g. usage of virtual classroom tools)	
	Ability to monitor learning progress	
	Ability to assess learning progress	
1.2 Learning materials		
	Content reliability and updated	
	Integration property (it can be used in different contexts/ org)	
	Technical quality	
	Aesthetic quality	
	Conformance to standards	
	Interoperability with other systems	
	Portability with other system	
	Reusability	
	Security	

Object	criteria	weight
	Metadata attribution	
	Relevant background of the authors of materials	
	Brand recognition	
	Suitability of the language and contents to the targets	
	Clear objectives	
	pre-requisites identification	
	Clear organisation of the content and structure	
	Content which stimulates controversial debate	
	Non controversial content	
	Coherency with the purpose	
	Ease of use	
	Interactivity	
	Multiple ways of accessing in term of background knowledge and skills	
	Materials are learner driven	
	Low cost	
	Modularity/ granularity	
	Motivating	
	Multiculturalism including language	
	Cultural specific	
	Multiplayer (e.g. role-play game)	
	Standardized layout	
	Personalized layout	
1.3 Learning infrastructure		
	Accessibility (e.g. people with disabilities, organisational difficulties)	
	Adaptability to users' need	
	Interoperability with other systems	
	Database for management of information	
	Plan for the information security of the database is operational	
	Ease of use	
	Learning platforms support a range of pedagogic methods (including 'home alone' and self-paced learning)	
	Reliability of the Technical infrastructure	
	Availability of different communication tools	
	The course authoring and production tools are able to cover a variety of actual and future delivery formats (paper based, web based, wap, etc.)	
	The technological platform used to deliver learning is consistent with the pedagogic approach of the Institution	
	Tolerance to users' mistakes	
	Tools to enhance the pedagogic effectiveness of technologies are provided: help on line, map of the environment, tracking of the learner's path, structure of the page, usage of icons etc	
	Uniform interface	
	Personalized interface	
2. Core learning processes		
2.1 A Guidance/ Training Needs Analysis		
	The Institutional objectives/ mission and the needs of the public/ market in which the institution operates are periodically checked by a governing body for alignment	
	Standard procedures/ tools for new and existing customers' Training Needs Analysis are operational	
	Specialist in Training Needs Analysis/ guidance is available	
	Recognition of previous achievements/ prerequisites/ informal and non formal learning is guarantee	
	Standard guidance services/ tools are in place	

Object	criteria	weight
	Individual learners guidance services are in place	
	The delivery structure of the course will be sensitive and coherent with the learners' needs identified by the guidance results	
2.1 B Recruitment		
	Different payment facilities for the course fee are operational	
	Means and strategies for reaching (promoting/ marketing/ informing) different categories of potential users are in place	
	Materials and procedures for informing the potential learners (prior to enrolment) about the course characteristics, aims and methodology are provided	
2.2 Learning design		
	The learning course is aimed at developing knowledge	
	The learning course is aimed at developing competences	
	Ex-ante, in itinere and ex-post course evaluation procedures and tools are in place	
	Clear definition of the target groups	
	Coherence of the didactic strategy with course objectives	
	Community building and social nature based	
	Content structure and organisation coherent with the didactic model	
	Appropriate use/ mix of different media	
	Effective design of the communication strategy	
	Granularity of the content	
	Tools for detecting emerging needs of the learners during the course are in place	
	Flexibility of the learning path is assured in the module or course	
	Identification of the learning objectives is assured – wasn't this already done in the learning materials?	
	The course design is based on a competence model	
	The course design is based on a knowledge model	
	Learner controlled	
	Teacher controlled	
	Learning accreditation system is available and linked to the national/ European accreditation system context (e.g. ECTS)	
	Activation of Learners' Motivation	
	Problem-solving procedures are in placed	
	Supporting learners' diverse needs is assured	
	Technical assistance in course development is assured	
	Peer and tutor support processes are in place	
	Supporting Progression in learning (e.g. the learning experience allow to reach different level/ steps of learning outcomes)?	
2.3 Learning Delivery		
	Accessibility	
	Adaptability to User's requirements (context/ individual)	
	Reliability and robustness of the online services	
	Throughout the course students are provided with technical support for using the services available (individual and group level)	
	Throughout the course students are provided with pedagogical support for using the services available (individual and group level)	
	Availability of systems and services to support communication among students and staff	
	Measures are adopted to avoid drop out during the course	
	Open endedness	
	Software to collect statistical data on student and staff utilisation of services	
	Support staff regularly informed on the most frequent questions and problems encountered by students	

Object	criteria	weight
	Measures to monitor and rectify common technical problems	
	Traceability of the learners use of the online system	
2.4 A Evaluation of the course		
	Availability of evaluation experts	
	Alignment of the evaluation tools, actions and timing with the objectives	
	Effectiveness (Technical)	
	Effectiveness (pedagogical)	
	Efficiency in the use of the organisation's resources (Economic)	
	Efficiency in the use of the organisation's resources (Technical)	
	Identification of the evaluation objectives, objects and sources	
	Procedures and tools for monitoring and reviewing the systems are implemented	
	Quality standards for evaluating course and learning services are adopted	
	Student's feedback on the services and on the course is requested and regularly collected.	
	Use of the evaluation results in the overall improvement process	
2.4 B. Assessment of the learners		
	Availability of assessment experts	
	Identification of the assessment objectives, objects and sources	
	Both staff and student assessment procedures and methods are represented within the decision–making process	
	Alignment of the assessment tools, actions and timing with the objectives	
	A process of "reflective review" is promoted and encouraged by different means and tools	
	The mode and the tools for assessing learning is negotiated with the learners	
	Measures to avoid misuse of the online assessment are in place e.g. logins, time passworded, internet access denied	
	Tools and procedures for assessing the outcomes of the learning process are implemented	
	Use of the assessment results in the overall improvement process	
3. learning context		
3.1 Institutional setting		
	E-learning Strategy is in place	
	Policy for technology planning is in place	
	Monitoring and evaluation procedure link to the administrative and management system	
	Quality is focused on the impact of the learning process	
	Knowledge management system is in place	
	Education/ training quality policy is in place	
	All the stakeholders are involved in the design and decision process	
	An overall plan and measures for managing the technical resources is operational	
	Authoring tools and authoring support systems (such as database of images, simulation software) are available	
	Collaborative working procedures and tools are adopted in the institutional environment where learning is taking place	
	Course Design and Delivery Guidelines are available for relevant staff	
	Guidelines, instructional material, training and support services are provided to teachers in order to support them (if required) in the process of moving from conventional teaching to on-line teaching.	
	Measures are adopted in order to check, maintain and update the software, hardware and productivity tools	
	Measures are adopted in order to solve technical problems	
	Monitoring and Content Management System for collecting student's feed-	

Object	criteria	weight
	back and documenting usage of resources is operational	
	Research and monitoring results are transferred into teaching/ learning/ management practice	
	Standard criteria/ procedures for cataloguing materials are operational	
	Technical services to support staff interaction are implemented and provided on a permanent basis	
	Procedures for the management of human resources are in place	
	Educational choices are made at central level	
	Educational choices are made at department/ unit level	
	Strategy and policy are in place to foster and support social inclusion	
3.2 Cultural setting (national, organisational, professional, general)		
	Flexible pedagogic and learning delivery models are adopted to meet different users' needs and socio-cultural specificities	
	Institution adopts 'open access' policy for student and staff recruitment	
	Staff competences include training and/ or experience in working with disadvantaged learners	
	A Technology based system is implemented in order to track and collect statistical data on the behavior of the user population and in particular about excluded groups	
	Individual personality of the staff is supported	
	Equal opportunity policy is operational	
	Tools and services targeted at disadvantaged categories are implemented	
3.3 Learning Environment		
	System misuse/ corrective action is in place	
	Control of non-conformance is in place	
	Supporting collaboration	
	Supporting personalisation	
	Supporting competence representation (mapping) and recognition	
	Supporting interaction/ communication	
	Respecting different learning paces/ modes/ styles	
	Supporting individual work	
	Supporting team work	
	Supporting contextualisation rather than abstraction	
	Supporting individual behavior patterns rather than common behavior patterns	
	Supporting divergent thinking	
3.4 Legislation		
	IPR and Copyrights related to the materials' content are respected	
	The accreditation system is recognized by professional associations	
	The credits achieved are transferable between programmers	
	The accreditation system is recognized by other educational & training organisations	
3.5 Financial setting		
	The organisation invests in resources and systems to provide effective user-friendly systems for students	
	Specific financial aid measures are devoted to disadvantaged categories (e.g. grants, participation fees)	
	Procedures/ Tools for monitoring the costs related to Staff and teachers are in place	
	Procedures/ Tools for monitoring the costs of delivery of e-learning are in place	
	Procedures/ Tools for monitoring the costs of developing of e-learning resources are in place	
3.6 Values systems		
	Supportiveness (both of climate and service)	

Object	criteria	weight
	Open-mindedness	
	Valorisation of Learning results	
	Encouragement for collaboration	
	Encouragement for competition	
	Encouragement of learner's autonomy	
	Orientation to customer satisfaction	
	Orientation to staff satisfaction	
	Openness to pedagogical innovation	
	Openness to institutional change	
	Openness to technological innovation	
	Openness to socio-cultural diversity	
	Recognition of staff results/ competences	
	Decentralized curriculum is supported	
	Centralized curriculum is supported	
	Supporting learners diversity	

The above table illustrates the core quality framework and is articulated in two main columns. The first column presents a list of objectives criteria which can be used to assess quality of a learning experience (the objective dimension). The second column is placed to allow each stakeholder to weight the importance of the criteria (the subjective dimension).

The following paragraph presents the main steps for the implementation quality policy which any body/ institution/ company should follow in order to define, select, adopt a quality approach.

The steps are the following:

- Context and problem identification,
- Dialogue building,
- Choice of a strategy,
- Implementation of the quality approach adopted.

3.4   Quality policy implementation steps

A *policy* is an intention, direction, a plan or course of action, of a government, political party, business or organisation to address a given problem or interrelated set of problems and intended to influence and determine decisions, actions, and other matters.

The following scheme is an attempt to suggest, represent and simplify, the process that a body/ institution/ company which desires to implement a quality approach might follow to assure its own "position/ vision" is taken into consideration together with the view points of the actors interested in and involved with an e-learning system.

Obviously, decision making processes are not quite so linear as this, as many complicating factors may emerge during the different suggested steps. Nevertheless, the proposed scheme highlights the complex and negotiated process necessary to define a quality strategy and implementing a quality approach.

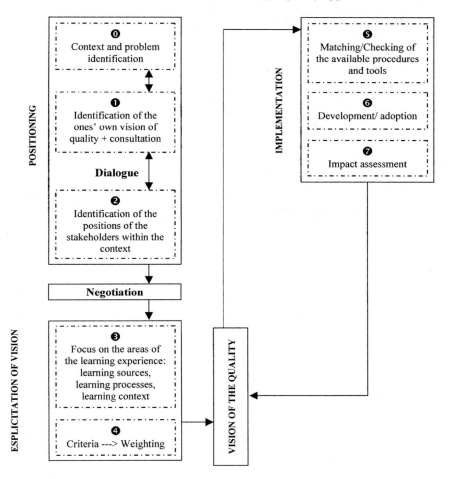

Fig. 3-3: Quality process

0. *Context and problem identification.* The policy definition starts with the process of identifying the problems which need to be addressed by the policy and the context in which the policy will come into force or will be adopted. This is true at any level from government to single organisations. Of course if one refers to a single organisation (e.g. training centre, school, company) two different levels enter into the picture: the policy and the constraints derived from the context in which the organisation is positioned - the institutional level which the organisation refers to (e.g. regional, national) - and the policy which the organisation considers coherent with its mission and objectives.

Until now research on quality in e-learning has focused principally on resources and followed by the learning processes; while attention to the context in which the learning experience takes place has remained in the background. The quality of the learning experience depends both on the quality of the internal context (if for example the internal context considers "learning" a positive value) and on the relationship between the designed e-learning system and the context in which it is delivered.

In reality, the quality of the relationship between the learning action and the context in which is realised is fundamental if you consider that one of the main aims of training and learning is to create the conditions to change, improve and innovate the competences of the learners to interact with their social, cultural and working environment.

The quality policy defined by an organisation should be based on:

- positioning itself in the general and specific contexts in which it is operating,
- identifying different elements (presented in the steps 1,2,3): the self-analysis of its quality visions, weakness and strengths; the analysis of the visions, values and viewpoints of all stakeholders which will attribute a positive or negative significance to the learning experience which will influence the results and thereby the impact of the policy;
- its ability to take into consideration and negotiate the quality approach to be adopted.

1. *Identification of the ones' own vision of quality & consultation*: the starting point is the analysis and the recognition of the ones' own point of view:

   - 1a. the point of view of the single person;
   - 1b. the point of view of the organisation toward the quality of e-learning.

What are the aspects that I consider the important for defining quality of an e-learning system? How is e-learning perceived within the organisation? What's the vision of quality within the organisation? Which elements are considered fundamental to assure quality (context/ resources/ processes)? Are there different positions among the staff/ personnel who are acting in the e-learning system?

Through consultation the process allow the expression of the different view points of quality within the organisation.

2. *Identification of the positions of the stakeholders within the context:* after the "internal" analysis the organisation should identify the visions and the points of view of all the stakeholders acting in the context in which the e-learning system will be implemented (e.g. professional bodies, trade unions, end users etc). The process of dialogue will not only allow organisation to become aware of the elements perceived as important within the external context but also to achieved a greater level of credibility among the actors/ people themselves.

3. *Focus on the areas of the learning experience: learning sources, learning processes, learning context 4. Criteria ---> Weighting:* at this point the or-

ganisation has a map of the relevant information which will allow it to decide, in respect of the learning experience and its components, on which areas it is necessary to focus when setting up and implementing a quality system. In other words, it is time to define the objectives of the quality system and the criteria through which values which are considered important can be transferred (phase 1 and 2). As mentioned before, the SEEQUEL core quality framework has defined a set of criteria, but it is up to the organisation, taking into consideration the different visions, to establish a level of priority to each criteria (e.g. some criteria could be considered relevant but not immediately applicable).

4. *Matching/ Checking of the available procedures and tools:* once the vision of quality and the approach to be adopted has been defined, the organisation should check if tools and procedures, necessary for implementation of the chosen approach, are already available. All the approaches are legitimate but the choice depends on the decisions previously taken in phase 3 and 4.

5. *Development/ Adoption:* in those cases where the tools are already available, the organisation will adopt them (e.g. *benchmarking*, guidelines etc.) by following the defined procedures. In those cases where they are not available, the organisation should develop its own tools, paying particular attention to the overall coherence of the system and keeping in mind the objectives and the visions.

6. *Impact assessment:* the process ends with the assessment of the impact of the results achieved by implementing a quality approach and the return/ benefit/ satisfaction achieved by all the parties involved.

3.5   Conclusions

The concept of quality underlines plural perspectives: there is not a unique vision on quality which can be considered the best one. This implies that quality has a "subjective", contextual and "objective" components. The latter involves defining a set of common criteria by which the quality of e-learning can be assessed, but it is undoubted that the way that different stakeholders will weight the criteria can be very different.

If the object of the quality is defined as the "learning experience" considered in its three components - sources, processes and internal/ external context - quality means complexity and systemic view.

Every organisation/ institutions/ body which is working at any levels in an e-learning system should be aware of the multiplicity and multiperspectives of the visions on quality and be ready to start a process of understanding other view points and negotiate the approach to be adopted.

The key elements for supporting European quality in e-learning are understanding, dialogue action and review of results to date, that is a typical quality assurance loop.

Furthermore, in this perspective it emerges the need to work together among the different stakeholders in order to define common needs and to start a fruitful and valuable peer learning process which represent the new frontier of the collaboration within the European scenarios.

4 The maze of accreditation in European higher education

Julia Flasdick, Lutz P. Michel

MMB Institute for Applied Media and Competence Research, Germany

Amaury Legait

Independent Consultant, France

This article is relevant to higher education institutions needing to gain better perspectives on accreditation. It describes the accreditation process, gives an overview of the tools and methods and thus helps to select appropriate accreditation for particular circumstances.

With the creation of the European Higher Education Area[12], quality and accreditation are becoming important issues. Students will be moving from the best higher education institution to equally ranking universities. International ranking is often based on research results[13]. At the level of a curriculum, accreditation gives an evaluation of quality.

But accreditation processes and criteria differ from one accreditation body to the other. Can we compare two accreditations? Unfortunately, this is not possible at the moment. In this article we present the maze of accreditation: processes, standards, criteria and bodies. We also try to sketch out the future evolution of accreditation in the European Higher Education Area.

---

[12] The European Higher Education Area is the objective of the Bologna process - to create more comparable, compatible and coherent systems of Higher Education in Europe (http://www.bologna-bergen2005.no).

[13] http://ed.sjtu.edu.cn/ranking.htm.

4.1   Introduction

Basically, accreditation is a process that gives public recognition to institutions or study programs that meet certain standards. It ensures that the institution has qualified staff, adequate facilities and equipment, operates on a sound financial basis and offers a approved study program. A successful accreditation may as well be interpreted as a promise to provide the quality of education being claimed by the institution (DETC, 2005).

Regarding the assurance and improvement of quality in Higher Education, accreditation is one of multiple methods like summative or formative evaluation, standardisation, certification, audit or benchmarking. In the past years, accreditation has become quite popular in Europe: Countries such as Germany, Norway and the Netherlands share the opinion that accreditation should be the main type of quality assurance of higher education in their country (ENQA, 2003).

Accreditation in Higher Education is a process of external quality review based on self- and peer assessment for public accountability and improvement of academic quality. Peers assess the quality of an institution or academic program and assist the faculty and staff in improvement (CHEA, 2001). An accreditation of an academic programme or an entire institution typically involves three major activities: Self-evaluation by the applicant, guided peer-review, and decision by the accreditation agency. Once an institution has been accredited, it is periodically reviewed via the reaccreditation process to ensure it continues to meet accreditation standards. As a means of quality assurance, accreditation in higher education is also important in connection with the Bologna Process.

Assuring and improving quality in Higher Education, accreditation may have various positive effects: It will give confidence to potential and current students as well as to potential employers. It will also foster academic improvement. In some regions, it helps to ease transfer of credits (European Credit Transfer System, ECTS) and sometimes, accreditation may give access to public funding. There are many accreditation systems, many national (or regional), and often they differ according to the various subjects taught in higher education (medicine, architecture, engineering, etc.).

Accreditation has been at work for many decades in higher education, and it became virulent in connection with the Bologna Process as a means of the equalisation of European Higher Education systems. In some countries, it is mandatory and implicit as only accredited diplomas are available. In some other countries, accreditation is left to the initiative of the educational institutions. For the Master of Business Administration, accreditation is required if it wants to be in the top one hundred listed in the Financial Times.

Accreditation body: Accreditation bodies review the quality of academic programms or institutions of higher education on the basis of principles and guidelines. If the review is successful, the applicant gets the accreditation which has to be refreshed after a fixed period of time. In Germany, accreditation bodies are in turn accredited by the German Accreditation Council and are not allowed to operate without its permission.

Examples for accreditation bodies:

- ANECA – Agencia Nacional de Evaluación de la Calidad y Acreditación. Spanish accreditation agency. Webaddress: http://www.aneca.es
- ASFOR - Associazione per la formazione alla direzione aziendale. Italian accreditation agency. Webaddress: http://www.asfor.it
- AQAS – Agentur für Qualitätssicherung durch Akkreditierung von Studiengängen. German accreditation agency for Bachelor and Master programs. Webaddress: http://www.aqas.de
- DETC – Distance Education and Training Council. Accreditation agency in the USA. Webaddress: http://www.detc.org
- NVAO – Nederlands-Vlaamse Akkreditatieorganisatie. Accreditation agency in the Netherlands. Webaddress: http://www.nvao.nl

4.2   Accreditation bodies

Many students and sometimes professors are not aware of the existence of accreditation bodies and their work. In the case of national diploma in France, the requirements are defined by the French ministry of education and the local universities have to comply to the national definition of the diploma. Professors are recruited at the national level and it is assumed that they have equivalent qualification and abilities.

The Masters of Business Administration (MBA) have developed both – systems of accreditation and ranking. The three international accreditation bodies (Association for MBA (AMBA), European Quality Improvement System (EQUIS) and Association to Advance Collegiate Schools of Business (AACSB) are providing a complementary view to the rankings published by, for example, the Financial Times. The accreditation bodies – which are mainly government agencies or non-profit organisations – try to look at the inside of the curriculum while the rankings focus on the achievements of the alumni (Related with the development of the European Higher Education Area, we may quote the ECTS label[14] (European Credit Transfer System) which is a very preliminary step toward accreditation).

In Germany, accreditation is made by non-profit agencies, with a federal admission by the German Akkreditierungsrat. In the USA, accreditation organisations were organised with the development of private universities after the Second World War and three regional organisations have to coordinate their activities.

For distance education, some existing accreditation bodies have evolved from

---

[14] http://europa.eu.int/comm/education/programmes/socrates/ects_en.html#7.

education by mail to education by Internet. Some new accreditation bodies are established at the national level in various European countries.

In order to demonstrate the quality assurance of accreditation procedures to the public, many accreditation bodies have set up a *"Code of good practice"* which states binding guidelines. It represents a measure to define internal quality assurance procedures and to ensure the transparency of the accreditation procedure[15].

4.3   Accreditation processes and evaluation methods

According to the various accreditation agencies in Europe, their different legal basis and objects[16], there is a huge variety of accreditation procedures which try to meet the special requirements of the agencies at each time. Albeit this specialisation, there are some general, structural characteristics which are definite for all accreditation procedures. Those similarities allow to divide the accreditation process into four main steps as shown in the figure below: Preparation, application, evaluation, decision.

Accreditation object: An accreditation object may either be an institution of Higher Education itself or a single study programme.

Similar to the variety of procedures, there is a set of methods which can be used during the accreditation process. Those principle methods range from guided peer review, assessment of student achievement with respect to the objectives of the programme and the institution to the (on-site) evaluation of staff, faculty and premises. Just like the accreditation procedures, the selection of the evaluation methods depends on the accreditation object[17].

The following sections outline a synopsis of the different accreditation procedures. It is based on a grid analysis of eight different accreditation bodies and their accreditation approaches, carried out by the Special Interest Group of Distance Learning Accreditation in Europe (SIG DLAE)[18] in spring 2004.

---

[15] ECA (European Consortium for Accreditation) developed a "Code of good practice" in order to guarantee comparability of accreditation procedures throughout Europe and to define internal quality assurance measures of accreditation organisations.

[16] A recent study about "Quality Procedures in European Higher Education" (ENQA, 2003) indicates that the accreditation's favourite object is the study program (overall 56% of all respondents in the survey) - especially by German-speaking accreditation agencies, by agencies in the associated countries, by Dutch agencies as well as by Nordic and southern agencies. In contrast, accreditation of institutions is done on a regular basis by only 22% of the interviewees. In some countries (e.g. Germany, Netherlands), also accreditation agencies themselves can be the object of accreditation.

[17] Another distinction can be made between accreditation processes which precede the launching of new programs and those which evaluate existing programs (ex-ante vs. ex-post accreditation).

[18] The main objective of the Special Interest Group for Distance Learning Accreditation in Europe (SIG DLAE) is to draw a proposal for a European accreditation system in e-learning and blended learning. The project started in January 2004 and expires in July 2005. It is partially founded by the European Union, further information can be obtained from: http://dlae.enpc.fr.

In general, the preparation phase of the accreditation process should give a clear idea of the necessary steps of the procedure and establish the needed contacts for it. It will also give the applicant insight into the accreditation process and provide information about the resources in terms of time and money which have to be allocated to the accreditation.

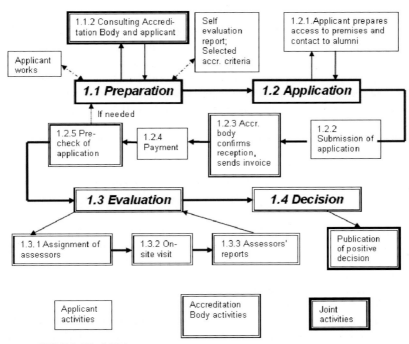

Source: SIG DLAE, 2004

Fig. 4-1: Accreditation process

4.4   Preparation phase

The first step of the preparation phase varies depending on whether or not the accreditation object does already exist or not. Usually, the accreditation procedure for new programmes is much shorter and simpler than the accreditation of existing ones, because the applicant has just to fill in a programme description or hand in an information dossier which describes the accreditation object in detail. Additional external assessments (e.g. on-site visits) which are normally part of accreditation procedures of already existing programmes are carried out quite rarely only.

The initial contacts between the applicant and the accreditation agency for a first-time accreditation should provide a global assessment of the feasibility of the accreditation. The eligibility of the applicant to the accreditation process is checked out during this phase on the basis of special criteria (eligibility criteria). In a first step, the accreditation body checks those eligibility criteria which are usually published on the agency's website.

Eligibility criteria: Preconditions stated by the accreditation body that qualify the applicant for the accreditation.

Another task during the preparation phase is to define the time scale, forms and fees for the accreditation procedure. After having agreed upon the procedure, the accreditation body delivers a draft version of the accreditation contract with pricing for the accreditation process to the applicant. If an individual set of accreditation standards was defined by the accreditation body, it has to be given to the applicant as well.

During the preparation phase, the accreditation body usually is responsible for supporting the applicant with all needed information and provide him with all necessary documents. Subsequently, the applicant starts working on the application, writes a self-evaluation report and completes the other requested documents and forms. Additionally, some accreditation agencies (e.g. Association of MBAs (AMBA) or German accreditation agency for Bachelor and Master programes (AQAS)) offer initial meetings or workshops to familiarise the applicant with the procedure and the related documents.

4.5   Application phase

The second phase of the accreditation process is the submission of the application and the payment of the fee. Along with the application, the applicant guarantees that it provides access to the (campus) facilities for the number of assessors the accreditation body will find necessary to perform the accreditation procedure. Within some accreditation procedures, the applicant will also be asked to provide contact with former students in order to conduct interviews. Afterwards, the staff of the accreditation body will consider the application documents. At this stage, the application may be rejected in very obvious cases, e.g. lack of documentation, inappropriateness of the information, etc. However, in principle, the preparation phase should prevent this situation from occurring. The application should be finished within a defined time limit, usually between one or two month.

4.6   Evaluation phase

The evaluation and assessment of the application is the most crucial part of the accreditation procedure.

Selection criteria for experts: Rules established by the accreditation body in order to ensure the competence and independence of the experts involved in the accreditation process.

To ensure high quality, it should be performed by a team of independent and competent experts

(1) on accreditations per se,
(2) in the specific academic field,
(3) in general pedagogical aspects, as well as
(4) in distance education/ e-learning (peer-group review).

It is an advantage if one assessor is able to cover several of these competencies. The assessors should be selected on the basis of special criteria (selection criteria for experts).

Peer-Group Review: Peer-group review is the general principle of accreditation. It means that the accreditation object is evaluated by a group of independent assessors who are experts in the corresponding educational field ("peers"). After the assessment, the peers write a report which forms the basis for the decision of the accreditation body.

During the assessment, the assessors check the documents provided by the applicant and evaluate the given information. Additionally, most accreditation bodies carry out on-site visits which include interviews with teachers, students and sometimes deans or members of administrative staff. Another way to conduct the on-site visit is – in case of accrediting e-learning or blended-learning courses – a test of the virtual learning arrangement.

The evaluation of the documents and the results on-site visits are stated in an assessment report (peer report) which should emphasise the positive aspects of the accreditation object and always pave the way to improve deficiencies[19]. Depending on the accreditation procedure, this report will either already include the accreditation decision made by the assessors/ peers which is checked and notified by the accreditation body.

In a more complex procedure, the peer report will be (1) handed over to an expert team, an accreditation commission, council or board who (2) discusses the findings and (3) issues the final decision on the accreditation (e.g. Institute for Accreditation, Certification and Quality Assurance (ACQUIN), Agency for Quality Assurance by the Accreditation of Study Programs (AQAS)).Traceability of the accreditation procedure can be established if any material concerning the accredi-

---

[19] In order to facilitate the assessor's work, some accreditation agencies provide special tools for the evaluation of the delivered documents and the results of the on-site visits which have taken place during the accreditation procedure. Some accreditation bodies (e.g. DETC, DLAE) have developed time-saving rating forms which allow the assessors to note very quickly if the course or institution meets an accreditation standard or not. Explanations and recommendations have to be stated in a detailed report.

tation process is made public on the website of the accreditation body. Thus, maximum transparency of the relevant accreditation standards and the main steps which led to the accreditation decision can be ensured. This may help the customer to orientate himself and to have confidence in the decisions made by the accreditation agencies. Moreover, transparency and traceability might be used as well-sounding marketing arguments for an accreditation agency.

4.7   Decision phase

The final phase of the accreditation process is the decision and the notification of the result to the applicant which is usually done by the accreditation body. In general, positive decisions are made public on the website of the accreditation agency and might additionally be announced by the applicant as well.

In order to account for the various changes which occur in higher education programmes or institutions, the accreditation decision has to be renewed after some years, usually not later than seven years after the latest accreditation. For this renewal, many accreditation bodies offer a reduced and simplified accreditation process with lower fees.

4.8   Accreditation standards and criteria in the field of education and training

Criteria and standards are the core of any kind of quality assessment – at least, they should be! Especially in the case of higher education we are convinced that accreditation without clearly defined and openly communicated criteria would be pretty much the same as sailing a ship without a compass. This is underlined by a recent study on quality procedures in European Higher Education, where it says that "not only in accreditation but also in quality assurance in general, the use of criteria and standards has become a common element of the evaluation process." (European Network for Quality Assurance in Higher Education 2003, p. 34).

What is the difference between criteria and standards? What kinds of criteria and standards can be distinguished? How are they developed? How can one make sure, that criteria and standards can be applied and measured? These are some crucial questions, which every accreditation body has to answer.

Concerning the definition of the terms criteria and standards, the above cited study on European accreditation processes comes to the conclusion, that "the distinction between the term 'criteria' and 'standard' is blurred" (Ibid). There is no clear definition of both terms, and even the leading European accreditation agencies do not share a common understanding of these two key terms.

Generally speaking, it can be stated that standards in accreditation "seem to be used as thresholds values, often formulated by government or other educational authorities" (Ibid) (an example from accreditation of new bachelor's and master's degree courses in Germany: "More than 50 per cent of academic staff must have a Ph.D. degree."). Criteria, on the other hand side, seem to be less fixed, "but function as suggestion or recommended points of reference for good quality." (European Network for Quality Assurance in Higher Education 2003, p. 34) An example from Germany again: "Online-support is provided." (Cf. WebKolleg 2003).

Although there is no unanimous definition of those terms in the scientific community so far, the authors like to propose the following distinction which is also the bases for the development of a European accreditation system for e-learning and blended learning proposed by the DLAE project:

Standard: Normative, qualitative and/ or quantitative specification with regard to the fulfilment of fixed quality demands[20]. It describes specific aspects of a programme or an institution, e.g. "The programme is relevant for the professional needs".

Criteria: Characteristic, distinct feature (cf. ibid.). Criteria are used to define and operationalise the standards, e.g. for the example mentioned above: "A learning needs analysis has been performed".

Except for a small group of official norms (set by law or defined by Government bodies), all criteria and standards are individually developed by the respective accreditation body or taken over from existing accreditation concepts. Usually the procedure follows the method of deduction – that means that all criteria and standards refer to a theory of "good teaching". Unfortunately, this theory or best practice model is never explicitly stated nor disclosed in most cases. Thus, most lists of criteria and standards resemble the Ten Commandments, Moses brought down from Mount Sinai.

To avoid the suspicion that criteria and standards are unquestioned "a priori" settings, it is advised that accreditation bodies should clearly define their model of "good teaching". As a commitment to certain principles, also the *"Code of good practice"* of an accreditation agency can be considered as a (rather implicit) foundation for accreditation standards and criteria.

The minimum requirement for an objective and professional accreditation is from our point of view:

- criteria and/ or standards have to be clearly formulated and made publicly available;
- criteria and/ or standards have to be consistent and non-contradictory[21],
- criteria and/ or standards should be operationalised; making sure that the applicant as well as the assessor have a clear understanding of the meaning of each criteria and the way the quality of courses and/ or institutions is assessed.

---

[20] http://www.go-cert.de/htm/glossar.htm.

[21] This is what universities expect from accreditation, as a recent survey by the DLAE team indicates (cf. DLAE 2004: p. 6).

Following the structure of the process oriented accreditation approach underlying this article (fig. 4-1), we distinguish the following types of criteria and standards as shown in the figure below:

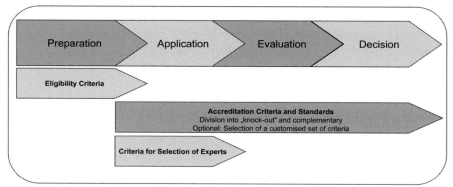

Source: SIG-DLAE, 2004

Fig. 4-2: Criteria & standards in the accreditation process

In the preparation phase, the applicant has to check its eligibility. In order to facilitate the process and assure maximum transparency, the eligibility criteria of the accreditation body are usually publicly available on its website. According to the character of the accreditation body and its accreditation objects, eligibility criteria vary from case to case: Whilst some agencies set up a multiplicity of criteria, others content themselves with a handful of it[22]. In general, eligibility criteria may concern either the programme or the institution and refer to different analytical levels.

The following examples quoted from the Distance Education and Training Council (DETC) and the Special Interest Group of Distance Learning Accreditation in Europe (SIG DLAE) give an impression of two different ways in setting up eligibility criteria:

Distance Education and Training Council (DETC 2005)

- The *institution* is in fact a "bona fide distance education institution and/ or training provider;"
- it has been in operation and enrolling students for at least 2 years;
- it is properly licensed; and
- it has completed and submitted DETC's "Application for Accreditation."

Special Interest Group of Distance Learning Accreditation in Europe (SIG DLAE); (cf. DLAE, 2005)

- Your degree is at the master level.

---

[22] Also in the field of eligibility, the term „criteria" is not used in a common way. In the sense of the authors, the "criteria" mentioned in the examples below do rather have the character of "standards".

- Your programme is distance e-learning supported (a minimum of 20% and a maximum of 80% of its modules or overall duration is delivered by teaching and learning methods within the range of e-learning; 20% is the present class minimum level; 80% is the present class maximum level).
- Your institution has an explicit quality policy.
- Your programme has at least been running during the past two years.

If the applicant has passed the eligibility check, it will start applying for accreditation. According to the characteristics of the accreditation object (programme vs. institution and further specifications), the accreditation agency may select an customised set of accreditation criteria and standards which is the basis for the following accreditation procedure. However, unsurprisingly, there is also no homogenous proceeding within European accreditation approaches in this respect: whilst some agencies customise their accreditation criteria and standards, others hand over the whole range of criteria and standards and let the applicant select the relevant ones by itself (and check its choice critically afterwards).

Moreover, the accreditation body has to make some crucial distinctions concerning the criteria and standards by defining the following types of criteria:

- *Rejection (or essential)* criteria and standards: Each single criteria and standard in this group is fundamental for a successful accreditation and therefore immediately leads to rejection of the application if the accreditation object does not comply to all of them;
- *Complementary* criteria and standards: Within this group, criteria and standards can compensate each other. In general, accreditation agencies define a minimum overall score for this group of criteria and standards which is necessary to pass accreditation successfully (mostly this score ranges from 70 to 80 percent).

The following examples for *rejection* criteria and standards have been derived from admission policy from the German e-learning provider *WebKolleg* (WebKolleg, 2003):

- The tutorial support is ensured.
- The technical premises are stated unambiguously.
- The target group is apparent from the course description.

For the evaluation of the documents delivered by the applicant and the conduction of on-site visits or interviews with alumni, a team of external experts is needed for the last two phases of the accreditation process. As the selection of those experts is "of key importance for any quality-oriented accreditation procedure"(ECA, 2005), accreditation agencies should decide upon the admission of an assessors on the basis of clearly defined criteria and standards.

In our example, the members of the European Consortium for Accreditation (ECA) agreed – amongst others – upon the following principles (ibid):

- Any decision regarding the composition of the expert team is to be based on the rules […] of the accreditation organisation or on pertinent legislation […].

- Experts must be independent and in a position to make unbiased judgements.
- […] Expert teams should bring together the relevant expertise.

Recapitulating the current situation, there are different types of criteria and standards which are important in certain phases of the accreditation process. So, if we talk about criteria and standards in accreditation, there could be quite various meanings hidden behind these terms. This maze of connotations could be lifted if scientists and accreditation experts would agree upon a common definition of the main terms used within that field.

4.9   Sketch for the future

At the time of the creation of a unified European Higher Education Area, it is doubtless that accreditation will gain importance as a method of quality assurance in Europe. It is clear that Europe will manage a change, an evolution and will not do a revolution. We will evolve from what is mainly a set of national accreditation systems to a European system. It will take five or ten years.

There are two ways to manage the accreditation in higher education and especially in distance education: by mutual recognition and by a European central agency. For many years, higher education in Europe has used mutual recognition either at the level of institutions or often at the level of professors: "I send you my best student, you send me your best student". Problems such as legal framework, country-specific regulations were solved by the mutual respect of professors and institutions.

In order to achieve the objectives of the European Higher Education Area, new methods have to be developed. In a first step, mutual recognition will be developed between institutions. In a second step, mutual recognition of accreditation agencies will take place. The third step will be the definition of a common European approach to accreditation in higher education in Europe.

As said before, mutual recognition is based on knowledge and respect for another person or institution. A common European approach will require more time to develop. It will be necessary to agree upon and respect:

- Processes;
- Standards and criteria specific to topic (architecture);
- National standards and criteria (they will not disappear);
- Standards and criteria specific to distance learning;
- Assessors (a database of recognised assessors with their qualification).

Currently there are three projects in Europe which are concerned with the establishment of European accreditation approaches:

- The European Consortium for Accreditation in Higher Education (ECA);
- The Accreditation of European Engineering Programmes and Graduates (EUR-ACE) in engineering

- and the Special Interest Group for Distance Learning Accreditation in Europe.

Those three projects exchange information and try to converge their developments to a united European accreditation approach. At a time where many valuable professors are going to retire, the question of the database of qualified assessors is also gaining importance.

4.10   How to find a suitable accreditation body, process and criteria?

To find a suitable accreditation body is task for a thorough market analysis. What is the demand? Do you work with national students or with students from abroad? Who are your competitors? What is the offer on the same market segment? What are the costs of an accreditation in comparison with the benefits (number of students, price of the education)?

Accreditation is required twice, once to get access to the market and second to get access to the most profitable share of the market. In the case of distance learning, accreditation is especially important to support students as well as companies judging the quality of distance pedagogies compared to the face to face teaching.

Having an idea of your market, you should consider the various accreditation bodies available (reputation, etc.), the accreditation process and criteria. You should be able to evaluate the amount of work to be done and your return on investment.

The following questions can be read as a checklist that might help you to choose a suitable accreditation body:

- What is your accreditation object: Your institution or one (or more) study programme(s)?
- What are the markets' demands?
- Who are your competitors? What do they offer?
- What kind of students do you work with: National or from abroad?
- How many students do you have?
- How big will be the workload for the accreditation in your institution (time and human resources)?
- What will be the benefit of the accreditation? Will it overweigh the arising expenses?
- Which accreditation bodies offer the kind of accreditation you need (institutional/ programme-based)?
- Do they have a good reputation?
- Do they provide measures to ensure their internal quality (e.g. Code of good practice; ISO certification; cyclical, external evaluation)?
- Which eligibility criteria have to be fulfilled by the applicant?

- Which accreditation criteria are basic? Which of them are compulsory, which voluntary? Are there "knock-out" criteria?
- Is there a focus on a certain category of criteria? If so, does this focus meet your requirements?
- What are the conditions (time, costs) for the re-accreditation?

5 Adopting quality standards for education and e-learning

Jan M. Pawlowski

University of Duisburg-Essen, Germany

This article shows how to implement and adapt the quality standard for e-learning ISO/IEC 19796-1. This standard is a general framework to describe and develop quality management and quality assurance for educational organisations. It provides a framework to develop quality based on the organisations requirements and needs. The Quality Adaptation Model shows the steps to develop and implement quality in organisations: the main steps (Context Setting, Model Adaptation, Model Implementation and Adoption, and Quality Development) are explained in detail to show how an organisation can develop its individual quality system.

5.1 Introduction

This article shows how the new quality standard for learning, education, and training, ISO/IEC 19796-1 (ISO/IEC, 2005a), is used, implemented, and adapted. It shows how to use and adapt the abstract standard to meet the needs of an educational organisation. It shows step by step how to develop a quality system in an educational organisation.

Quality in the field of e-learning has become an issue of increasing importance in both researchers' and practitioners' communities. A variety of approaches has been developed and implemented successfully. However, the high number of approaches and their different scopes and objectives lead to confusion in the users' and decision makers' communities (see chapter 12). Therefore, a harmonised quality standard has been discussed and consensually approved in the standardisation committee ISO/IEC JTC1 SC36 (International Organisation for Standardisation/ International Electrotechnical Commission, Joint Technical Committee 1, Subcommittee 36: Information Technology for Learning, Education, and Training).

The article first discusses the concept of quality standards and shows a classification framework for quality standards. After a description of ISO/IEC 19796-1, the Quality Adaptation Model (QAM) is presented. QAM is a concept for the adaptation, implementation, and use of this standard in educational organisations. The model explains step-by-step how a quality system can be implemented in educational organisations.

> *Harmonisation* of quality approaches means to provide a common framework to make them transparent and comparable. Harmonisation does not mean to unify approaches but to create a common description and understanding of concepts while maintaining flexibility.

5.2   Quality standards

Quality Standards are often misunderstood, especially in the educational community. They are perceived as restricting flexibility or creativity or huge additional effort. However, new generations of quality standards provide only a basic framework and help organisations to develop quality systems according to their own requirements.

5.2.1   Classification of quality standards

Quality Standards provide harmonised, consensual concepts to manage, assure, or assess quality. In the field of learning, education, and training, a variety of standards, quasi-standards, and related standards are available.

Generally, three classes of standards can be distinguished:

- *Generic Quality Standards* provide concepts for quality management or quality assurance, independent of the domain of usage. As an example, ISO 9000:2000 (see Chapter 6.4.2) is used in different sectors and branches. As a generic quasi-standard, the Excellence Award by the European Foundation for Quality Management (EFQM, see Chapter 6.4.4) is widely used but not agreed on by a formal standardisation body.
- *Specific Quality Standards* provide quality management or quality assurance concepts for the field of learning, education, and training. This means that specific requirements concerning processes or products are incorporated.
- *Related Standards* are used to manage or assure specific aspects of quality. As an example, learning technology standards (see Section B: E-learning standards) are used to assure interoperability as a specific quality objective. As another example, ISO 9241 assures the usability of systems by providing specific requirements and guidelines for user interface design.

However, this is only a very rough classification. To describe quality standards in depth, the following aspects help to distinguish quality concepts:

- *Context and Scope:* For which context is an approach intended (e.g., schools, Higher Education, Vocational Training), which are the processes covered (e.g., design, development, realisation)?
- *Objectives:* Which are the quality objectives which can be achieved by an approach (e.g., cost reduction, process consistency, learner satisfaction, product reliability)?
- *Focus:* Does the quality approach focus on 1) organisations/ processes, 2) products/ services, or 3) competencies?
- *Perspective:* For which stakeholders and from which perspective was a quality approach designed (e.g., developers, administrators, learners)?
- *Methodology:* Which methods and instruments are used (e.g., benchmarking, criteria catalogue, guidelines, information provision)?
- *Metrics:* Which indicators and criteria are used to measure the success (e.g., drop-out rate, return on investment, learner satisfaction)?

> *Quality Standard:* A quality standard supports quality development in organisations according to their specific needs and requirements. The standard should improve flexibility, reusability, transparency, and comparability and is widely accepted in the community.

This classification shows the variety of possibilities to design a quality approach.

5.2.2   Quality systems

The survey of the European Quality Observatory (Ehlers, Hildebrandt, Goertz, Pawlowski, 2005) showed that different user groups have different requirements towards a quality standard. From the results of this survey, a framework for quality systems was developed, defining the levels and components to cover all aspects of quality. It suggests that an organisation planning to implement a Quality System[23] (see figure 5-1) should discuss and consider the following aspects:

- *Quality Culture:* Quality should be anchored in the culture of an organisation. Aspects of this are a quality vision, reflecting the meaning of quality for all areas of an organisation. A quality policy and strategy show the long-term objectives of an organisation's quality system.
- *Quality Awareness* covers the attitude of the organisation's staff towards quality. Every staff member should be aware of its individual contribution towards the overall quality of an organisation.
- *Quality Management* covers all activities the planning, steering, and improving quality in organisations. This term is usually used for process-oriented quality instruments.

---

[23] The term quality system is used for all quality related concepts, methods, and activities of an organisation.

- *Quality Assurance* covers all activities to evaluate, control, and measure quality in organisations. This is usually related to products and services.
- *Quality Components* cover several aspects of quality, e.g., the quality of processes, products/ services, or competencies of staff members.

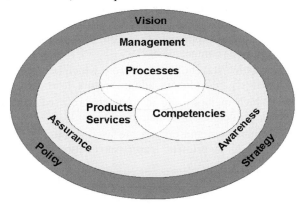

Fig. 5-1: Levels of quality systems

To implement a quality system, various alternatives for all parts of the system can be considered. A quality standard should cover all aspects of a quality system.

5.3   The quality standard for learning, education, and training: ISO/IEC 19796-1

The Quality Standard ISO/IEC 19796-1 is the basic framework for a harmonised quality standard developed by experts in the international standardisation group ISO/IEC JTC1 SC36. It serves as a framework for quality development and the description of quality approaches. In the following, the use of this standard will be explained.

5.3.1   Description of ISO/IEC 19796-1

Specific Quality Management and Quality Assurance Standards for e-learning provide the framework for the use of standards in organisations. Whereas many organisations have adapted general standards like ISO 9000:2000 or the EFMQ Excellence Model, currently specific standards for e-learning are being developed: The new standard ISO/IEC 19796-1 provides a "reference framework for the description of quality approaches" (RFDQ) (ISO/IEC, 2005b). A reference framework gives an orientation which aspects should be covered and how solutions for these aspects can found. The standard is an instrument to develop quality in the field of e-learning. It consists of three parts:

- A description scheme for quality approaches
- A process model as a reference classification
- Reference Criteria for evaluation

It supports the development of quality profiles for organisations (such as objectives, methods, relations, people involved). "Quality profiles" mean that the generic standard is adapted to the needs and requirements of an organisation. It does not provide specific requirements or rules – it is a framework to guide actors through the process of quality development in the field of e-learning.

The *Description Model* is a scheme to describe quality approaches (such as guidelines, design guides, requirements). It documents all quality concepts in a transparent way. It bases on the CEN/ ISSS CWA 14644 (CEN/ ISSS, 2003a, b). Each process can be described by this scheme:

Table 5-1: Description model for quality approaches of ISO/IEC 19796-1

Attribute	Description	Example
ID	Unique Identifier	ID1234
Category	Main Process	Course Development
Process Name	Process name	Method selection
Description	Description of the process	"Within this process the didactic concept and methods are evaluated and selected"
Relations	Relation to other processes	"Before the method selection a target group analysis must be performed"; [Process 1.6]
Sub-processes/ sub-aspects	Sub-processes/ sub-aspects/ tasks	Method identification Method alternatives Method priorisation
Objective	Objective of a Process	Adequate selection of one or more didactic concepts according to learner preferences and learning styles
Method	Methodology for this process	Method selection shall be based on the target group taking into account their competencies and learning styles. Methods are selected based on the teachers' experience.
Result	Expected result of a process	Method specification Documents
Actors	Responsible/ participating actors	Team didactical design, Project leader
Metrics/ Criteria	Evaluation and Metrics for this process	Criteria catalogue 3.2.2-3.2.6
Standards	Standards used	DIN EN ISO 9241, LOM See Method Guidelines Handbook
Annotation/ Example	Further Information, Examples of usage	

This model serves only as a base to provide a harmonised scheme to describe quality approaches.

The *Process Model* is a guide through the different processes when developing learning scenarios. The process model includes the relevant processes within the life-cycle of information and communication systems for learning, education, and training. The process model is divided in seven parts. Sub-processes are included referencing to a classification of processes.

Table 5-2: Process model of ISO/IEC 19796-1

ID	Category	Description/ Sub-Processes
1	Needs Analysis	Identification and description of requirements, demands, and constraints of an educational project
		1.1 Initiation 1.2 Stakeholder Identification 1.3 Definition of objectives 1.4 Demand analysis
2	Framework Analysis	Identification of the framework and the context of an educational process
		2.1 Analysis of the external context 2.2 Analysis of staff resources 2.3 Analysis of target groups 2.4 Analysis of the institutional and organisational context 2.5 Time and budget planning 2.6 Environment analysis
3	Conception/ Design	Conception and Design of an educational process
		3.1 Learning objectives 3.2 Concept for contents 3.3 Didactical concept / methods 3.4 Roles and activities 3.5 Organisational concept 3.6 Technical concept 3.7 Concept for media and interaction design 3.8 Media concept 3.9 Communication concept 3.10 Concept for tests and evaluation 3.11 Concept for maintenance
4	Development/ Production	Realisation of concepts
		4.1 Content realisation 4.2 Design realisation 4.3 Media realisation 4.4 Technical realisation 4.5 Maintenance
5	Implementation	Description of the implementation of technological components
		5.1 Testing of learning resources 5.2 Adaptation of learning resources 5.3 Activation of learning resources 5.4 Organisation of use 5.5 Technical infrastructure
6	Learning Process	Realisation and use of the learning process
		6.1 Administration 6.2 Activities 6.3 Review of competency levels

7	Evaluation/ Optimisation	Description of the evaluation methods, principles, and procedures
		7.1 Planning 7.2 Realisation 7.3 Analysis 7.4 Optimisation/ Improvement

Finally, ISO/IEC 19796-1 contains a comprehensive list of *reference criteria* for the assurance of quality of learning products which is provided in the criteria catalogue. The catalogue contains as well functional as media and learning psychology related reference criteria. Furthermore, it includes criteria related to data security and (special marked) criteria related to national laws in the area of distance learning.

These criteria can be used for assessment and evaluation of learning processes and environments within the process model, described in the last section. Only criteria which are suitable for a certain context should be used. Hence, the criteria just provide a comprehensive list – when implementing a quality management or quality assurance system, adequate criteria can be chosen from this list.

The reference catalogue shall provide a common basis to build country and domain specific catalogue profiles. These profiles contain a relevant selection of criteria and can specify priorities e.g. by marking criteria as "must-criteria". Such a criteria profile based on the reference catalogue is deployed in the evaluation of processes based on the process reference model. For this purpose each process specification in the process reference model contains a reference to the relevant section of the reference criteria catalogue. The list can be amended and changes according to the contexts.

Furthermore the reference catalogue can be applied to create criteria profiles which allow comparisons of learning products or support certification of learning products (according to quality standards).

The list of reference criteria is structured into catalogue sections, to allow easier access to certain criteria. Each criterion appears only once in the catalogue. A criteria profile however may use another structure.

Table 5-3: Quality criteria of ISO/IEC 19796-1

Section No.	Section/ Category	No of criteria	No of descriptive criteria
1	ISO 9241		
2	General Conditions	101	32
3	Technical Aspects	103	23
4	Data storage and Data processing	37	14
5	Functionalities	69	29
6	Theoretical Aspects	80	17
7	Encoding of Information	59	3
8	Special modes of presentation	31	0
	Total	480	118

5.3.2   Usage scenarios

The standard itself is a reference model which can be applied in different scenarios:

Developing quality systems

The main objective of ISO/IEC 19796-1 is to provide a transparent description model to clearly describe and document quality management and quality assurance approaches. The description model describes processes to develop e-learning scenarios by specifying:

- Quality objectives
- Methods to ensure the quality
- Actors involved in this process
- Relations to other processes
- Evaluation methods to assess the success of a process
- Standards and references

Using this model, individual quality approaches can be developed including parts of approaches which apply to the context of usage. The adaptation process will be described in detail in the next chapter.

Combining quality approaches

The model provides a clear terminology and description formats to assemble individual quality concepts from existing approaches.

Process model as a guideline

The second part is a reference model containing all processes of the e-learning lifecycle. It can be used as a guideline to develop quality concepts from the first idea ("I would like improve my seminars´ flexibility") to the optimisation and improvement. Therefore, ISO/IEC 19796-1 can be used to support quality development for all actors.

Reference source for evaluation criteria

Many organisations need to develop evaluation criteria for their education and training programs. ISO/IEC 19796-1 provides a collection of criteria to be used in evaluations for different purposes.

However, the most important purpose is to develop quality in organisations. The next chapter shows how to implement quality development using ISO 19796-1.

5.3.3   The Quality Adaptation Model (QAM): Adapting ISO/IEC 1976-1

The reference framework needs to be adapted to requirements of an organisation. Adaptation in this context means that the reference model can only serve as a guideline which aspects should be considered.

The *Quality Adaptation Model (QAM)* follows a process in four steps. These steps are not performed iteratively but should be individually scheduled.

- *Context Setting* covers all preparatory activities for the adaptation process.
- *Model Adaptation* contains activities to implement the reference model based on the needs and requirements of an organisation.
- *Model Implementation and Adoption* means the realisation and the broad use of the quality system.
- *Quality Development* means that quality systems should be continuously improved and further developed.

These steps contain several activities explained in the following paragraphs.

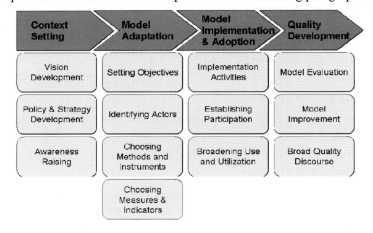

Fig. 5-2: The quality adaptation model

Context setting: Providing the basis for quality development

This phase sets the context for quality development. It should ensure that quality development is anchored and present in all parts of the organisation.

The organisation's long term objectives, externally and internally, are contained in its vision, strategy, and policy. If an organisation is committed to quality development, this should be contained in these statements. However, in most organisations quality, and specifically quality of e-learning, is not adequately represented. Therefore, the process to improve the vision, strategies, and policies needs to be established.

The redefinition should not be only the management's responsibility. The process should be at least transparent to all staff members. It can be recommended to include participants from all staff groups into this process which actively sets new directions for organisation. As an example, the strategy/ policy should explain what "Quality of e-learning" means related to the organisations' core competencies and how it influences the main operations.

Directly related is the process of awareness raising. Quality development will not be successful if it is a top-down regulation. Quality development should be part of everyday operations and related to all activities. Therefore, all members of an organisation should be aware of quality and its meaning for their personal actions.

The outcome of this phase should be revised vision, strategy, and policy documents showing the organisations long-term view of quality and the consequences for all parts of an organisation. All staff groups should be aware of and involved in this process.

Model adaptation: Individualising ISO 19796-1

To establish the details of quality development in an educational organisation, the reference model ISO/IEC 19796-1 can be used as a guideline.

First of all, the *relevant actors* for quality development should be identified. It is useful to involve actors of all departments and all staff groups in this process. Actors, acting as multipliers for their groups should be involved. They should be fully committed to supporting the quality development process. The outcome of this phase is a list of actors responsible for quality. Usually, this also leads to changed job descriptions and agreements with these actors.

Secondly, the *processes* relevant for an organisation should be identified. E.g., for producers of learning media, only some sub-categories (such as design and production) might be relevant. As another example, for tutors only the learning processes would be relevant. Additionally, processes specific for an organisation should be added. The outcome of this phase is a comprehensive list of processes for the organisation.

The main step of adaptation is the *setting quality objectives* for each process. Quality objective means that for each process it should be defined how quality results can be achieved (e.g., process "technical concept": "the objective is to develop a clear, unambiguous specification of technologies used which meet the users' needs and preferences."). The quality objectives for each process cannot be defined by just one individual – they are subject to a negotiation process and should be agreed on in consensus with the relevant actors.

Based on the objectives, *instruments and methods* should be identified and selected. In this context these are concrete activities to achieve, assure, or assess quality for the given objectives. Instruments to achieve the quality objective "24 hour availability of the support hotline" could be an assessment of the call centre's staff, test calls, or technical monitoring. The selection of adequate instruments is crucial for the success of a quality system: these instruments need to be adequate for the quality objective, the effort should be small, and they should be well accepted by the participants. Therefore, it is useful to inform and train staff members in the use and interpretation of these instruments.

Finally, usually connected to the choice of instruments and methods, *metrics and indicators* are chosen to assess and measure the success. Metrics should reflect the success of achieving a quality objective. Typical metrics are for example drop-out rates, return on investment/ education. However, these metrics need to be developed for each quality objective and have to be evaluated continuously. In any case, there should also be a procedure how to interpret metrics and which actions are taken based on the interpretation.

The outcome of this phase is an organisation's process model including quality objectives, responsible actors, methods/ instruments, and metrics/ indicators. By this description, the organisation's actions to achieve their quality are transparent, explicit, understandable, and repeatable. An example of a full process description is given below.

Table 5-4: Model implementation and adoption: Making the concepts work

ID	Category	Process	Description	Relation
2.2	Framework Analysis	Analysis of staff resources	Identification and description of actors, their qualifications and competencies, and availability	
Sub-processes/ Sub-aspects		Roles/ functions Competencies/ formal qualifications Availability of actors		
Objective		To clearly identify and correctly assess the roles/ functions, competencies/ qualifications, gaps, and availability of actors and users who will be involved in top management courses.		
Method		Methods of empirical social-/ educational research (e.g. document analysis); consultation of specialists; staff profile analysis		
Result		Description of roles/ functions of staff Description of competencies/ formal qualifications of staff Description of availability of staff		
Actors		Project manager; HR experts, learners		
Metrics/ Criteria		Categories 2, 3, 4 of Reference Quality Criteria		
Standards		Project management and documentation guidelines; standards for social researches		

In the initial adaptation process, usually only small groups of actors are involved. Therefore, an *implementation strategy* should be developed. This strategy should describe actions and activities that the quality system is used. Furthermore, it is of vital importance that all actors are aware and involved. This does not mean that every staff member should know the entire quality system, but they should be aware of quality objectives for core and related processes they are involved in. To establish participation, there should be opportunities for actors to influence, change, and improve quality objectives and methods. Usually, the first implementation is done in representative test groups. Therefore, further users need to be involved and become familiar with the quality concepts to systematically broaden the use of the quality system.

Quality development: Improving the organisation's performance

A Quality System must be continuously evaluated, updated, and improved to be aligned to new developments in an educational organisation. Therefore the following steps are necessary. The Quality System should be evaluated at least on a bi-annual base. Specifically, it should be evaluated if the quality system has led to overall improvements in the organisations performance. Furthermore, the adequacy of methods, instruments, and metrics needs to be evaluated. Based on this evaluation, improvement actions should be taken, such as the change and refinement of the system's components. Again, for this phase a broad commitment and participation is necessary to reflect the staff's opinions and attitudes toward the system. This should lead to a broad awareness and discussion on quality.

The outcome of this phase is an evaluation strategy, improvement concepts, and, most important, a broad discourse on quality. Specifically in the field of education, this will lead to a participatory process designing and developing learning scenarios.

5.4   Summary

To implement a Quality System in an educational organisation, four main steps are necessary: Context Setting, Model Adaptation, Model Implementation/ Adoption and Quality Development. Each step should be performed including a broad range of actors to raise awareness and consensus. To facilitate this process, the use of the ISO/IEC Reference Model for the Description of Quality Approaches was recommended. It was shown how to adapt this model to develop a Quality System for an organisation.

Currently, a variety of tools is developed to support this process, such as the initial choice of a quality approach (see chapter 12.3) or the choice of quality instruments (Hildebrandt, Stracke, Pawlowski, 2005), (Pawlowski, 2005). For the future, it can be expected that a variety of tools are available to support this process and to integrate quality into a broad range of educational organisations.

6 Process-oriented quality management

Christian Stracke

University of Duisburg-Essen, Germany

In this contribution process-oriented quality management, its importance and its relevance for educational organisations will be examined. Process-oriented quality management is a generic term for a lot of approaches with a variety of meanings and range. Therefore, first the relevance of process orientation for a holistic quality management concept will be described. According to the requirements of a holistic quality management the four main quality management concepts (KAIZEN, BPR, Six Sigma, TQM) are analysed. Total Quality Management (TQM) as the most comprehensive holistic approach will be explained in detail. The general philosophy and the multitude of facets of TQM will be described. In introducing and realising the TQM ideas, quality standards and reference models can offer a decisive support. The standards family ISO 9000:2000ff. and the EFQM Excellence Model will be explained as the two most important instruments of introducing a comprehensive quality management system and the TQM idea. Finally, the introduction and use of the quality management systems in educational organisations will be outlined.

6.1 Introduction

The objective of this contribution is the description of the need for holistic and process-oriented quality management due to the changes of economies, and the analysis how the four main quality management concepts fulfil these requirements. Specifically, the importance of these approaches for educational organisations will be demonstrated. With the enterprises and in the political economies a fundamental change has taken place, which has been intensified since several decades: The new organisation of labour and enterprises, the industrial and technological progress, the globalisation tendencies and the emerging IT economy, which is also called the new fourth sector, have led to a loss of significance of the primary and, in the end, of the secondary sector, too (cf. Bruhn, 2004), (Zink, 2004). The tendency towards the tertiary sector and the development of the service branch to the decisive economic power has massively changed the structural challenges to enterprises and organisations as well as their orientations (cf. Bruhn, 2004; service is used here in the Anglo-American meaning as a comprehensive term which relates to both the product and its development process). With the service offers, customer and quality orientation have more and more come to the fore at the same time. Three central long-term paradigms for successful organisations can be recognised (cf. Bruhn, 2004), (Ebel, 2003), (Seghezzi, 2003):

1. *Customer orientation:* Instead of the provider/ prducer view and the fixation on products, the customers more and more come to the fore.
2. *Process orientation:* Instead of the functions and rigid hierarchies in organisations, overlapping processes become more important.
3. *Quality orientation:* Instead of quantity and the mere sales volume, quality becomes more decisive for the customer relationship and the business success.

This requires a comprehensive holistic and integrated management that takes all three paradigms into consideration. For that process-oriented quality management offers a disposition that aims at the long-term sustainable and continuous improvement and optimisation of the complete organisation.

At first, a general survey of the beginning of the quality idea is given and the concept of the Integrative Management is introduced (chapter 6.2). Influential quality management concepts are shortly outlined and, with reference to this concept, are examined concerning their range. Total Quality Management (TQM) is more intensely dealt with as the most comprehensive approach for process-oriented quality management (chapter 6.3). The standards family ISO 9000:2000ff. and the EFQM Excellence Model as the main quality standards and reference models for the introduction and realisation of TQM are explained in the following. Finally, some remarks are given how to implement quality management in educational organisations (chapter 6.4).

6.2   Quality management and quality development

Quality is of fundamental importance, this is true over all the borderlines of organisations, branches and political economies. Their manifold dimensions lead to different views and definitions of the quality term and to different approaches to quality management. In this chapter, the basis of process orientation for a holistic quality management system will be discussed first. Then, by means of a four-dimensional classification of the management, the demands on Integrated Management concepts are identified. The analysis model of the Integrative Management concept will be presented. This will be the basis for the analysis of the quality management approaches in chapter 12.

6.2.1   Process orientation and holistic quality management

When the economy was still based on solid seller markets, quality was often re-garded product-oriented as a given or desired characteristic. Organisations made use of methods of quality assurance in order to guarantee the constant product quality. Through the pressure of stronger competition and with the rise of cus-tomer orientation, new management concepts and faster (re)action times became necessary. The quality of the processes came into the focus of interest. Quality management became a task of the complete organisation and involves all employ-ees and processes. After World War II the quality movement gained numerous supporters and chiefly started from Japan (cf. Ebel, 2003). Especially with the KAIZEN philosophy the optimisation of products through a comprehensive qual-ity management and customer orientation was pushed ahead. Moreover William Edwards Deming and Joseph M. Juran, who successfully introduced and pleaded their convictions, were influential there (cf. Deming, 1982), (Juran, 1951), (Bruhn, 2004). Already before that, there had been statistic procedures and methods of su-pervising and directing processes and of statistical process control (SPC, cf. Seghezzi, 2003). Influenced by Deming and Juran a new idea of a comprehensive quality management was developed, which, with the help of the KAIZEN phi-losophy, also includes a continuous improvement and a systematic model for im-plementation and realisation in general. In the western countries the philosophy of the Total Quality Management (TQM) was more generally accepted (cf. Zollondz, 2002).

After the oil crisis in 1973, a second wave of the Total Quality Management began in Japan (cf. Frehr, 1993). This made them more intensely deal with quality management and its introduction. With the development of the standards family ISO 9000ff., in the middle of the eighties, the international discussion and consen-sus development on the direction and aims of a comprehensive process-oriented quality management began.

Process orientation has stood up to other possible perspectives in quality man-agement as one among some possible views in the meantime. In principle the di-verse dimensions of quality can be divided in different ways. A distinction into three basic quality dimensions has become widely accepted. According to Dona-bedian (1980b) and Bruhn (2004) the following three quality dimensions can be distinguished:

1. Potential dimension
2. Process dimension
3. Result dimension

This distinction applies to quality management, too. Next to process-oriented qual-ity management, product-oriented and potential-oriented quality management ap-proaches have been developed. To achieve a comprehensive and holistic concept for organisational management all these three aspects must be considered. The process orientation has gained a crucial role within integrative management meanwhile due to the changes of economies towards customer markets and to-wards the growing importance of the service sector. Process orientation has frequently replaced strict organisation structures based on functions. Horizontal business processes crossing all functional units were defined and so allowed for a radical change in management. Process reengineering and process optimisation became the impulsive forces of economic growth (cf. Ebel 2003), (Schmelzer, Sesselmann, 2003).

The four classic management processes of analysis, planning, realisation and controlling can be recovered in process-oriented quality management. Quality management serves to achieve the organisational objectives and to support the management (cf. Bruhn, 2004), (for another distinction of the management functions in planning, realisation and controlling cf. Juran, 1992). Thus a process-oriented standard cycle was introduced analogous to the four management processes. The four phases of the standard cycle of quality management picked up in many variations are:

*P*lan, *D*o, *C*heck, *A*ct (PDCA, cf. Deming, 1982, 1986)

This standard cycle was originally developed by Walter Shewhart, what Deming himself has pointed out (cf. Deming, 1986). It has become well known by publications by Williams Edwards Deming and therefore it is often called *Deming Cycle*. The cycle has especially influenced many Total Quality Management approaches where it can be retrieved in several modified versions.

6.2.2   Integrative management

Management in its functional dimension is sub-divided into different layers which are supplied with different structures, aims and functions. To this topic there have already been a lot of different attempts to classification in categories and to structuring (cf. Ulrich, 1992), (Zink, 2004). Integrated management concepts have been developed with quite different aims, emphasis and ranges, and they are subject to changing fashions. Above all they can be characterised by the following qualities (cf. Ebel, 2003), (Seghezzi, 2003):

- Comprehensive and holistic approach
- Expanded management philosophy
- Inclusion of the complete organisation
- Customer, process and quality orientation
- Cycle of continuous improvement

With the four dimensions of the Integrative Management a combination of the concept of the integrated management of Switzerland´s St. Gallen school (cf. Bleicher, 1999), (Seghezzi, 2003) and classical management levels (cf. Bruhn, 2004), (Ebel, 2003) is introduced here.

The basis of all management activities is the general management philosophy. In order to achieve comprehensive quality in the sense of business excellence, it has to realise especially a holistic view in regard of its systemic approach, of its orientation on all relevant target groups within the organisation, of its sustainability and of its future orientation (cf. Zink, 2004). Out of the management philosophy, the vision of the organisation and its organisational culture are developed which, as paradigmatic principles determine the management (cf. Bleicher, 1999), (Zink, 2004). For the analysis model of the Integrative Management the following four dimensions of the management are distinguished:

Normative management

The normative management determines the structure of the organisation, the fundamental missions and aims of the organisation and the predominant organisational culture. It results in missions that substantiate the sense and the object of the organisation.

Strategic management

The strategic management is decisive for the organisational structures, changes the aims into programs and deals with problems respectively with their avoidance in advance. It results in strategic programs that realise the missions.

Tactical management

The tactical management creates the preconditions for the strategic programs and their direct realisation in the organisational units and thus serves as the connection between customer requirements and organisational aims. It results in organisation projects supporting the strategic programs.

Operative management

The operative management is responsible for the organisational processes, the customer orders and aims at achieving performance and cooperation. It results in concrete orders.

It becomes clear that all the four dimensions are interdependent and influence each other. The rising international competition pressure and the stronger customer power or, system-theoretically respectively economically expressed, the growing environment complexity and dynamics demand (new) management concepts (cf. Luhmann, 1998). These concepts need to be based on a management philosophy and a long-term vision. They have to focus and comprise in a holistic way all the four dimensions at the same time. In the following the four main quality management approaches are introduced and it is analysed whether they can serve as a comprehensive and holistic quality management concept.

6.3   Influential quality management approaches

In the following part, influential management approaches are shortly outlined and examined with regard to the question whether they are a comprehensive management concept in the sense of the above described Integrative Management used as analysis model. In addition each concept is shortly examined by its support for educational organisations.

6.3.1   KAIZEN and CIP

The KAIZEN philosophy aims at optimising processes and products by a comprehensive quality management and customer orientation. Imai who invented KAIZEN unites process-oriented management with his Japanese concept of innovation in small steps and three levels of KAIZEN (management, groups and persons) (cf. Imai, 1986, 1997). In KAIZEN every process is standardised after its improvement before it is released. Insofar his Imai cycle SDCA (Standard, Do, Check, Act) named according to its inventor Masaaki Imai, is different from the Deming cycle PDCA (Plan, Do, Check, Act; cf. chapter 6.2.1). In the SDCA cycle a continuous optimisation in small steps is realised. The standardisation protects the enterprises from surprising setbacks and direct strong falls because standardised processes are less subject to mistakes. This, however, prevents sudden innovations that are possible in the PDCA cycle and it strongly clings to the status quo. KAIZEN thus consequently realises the idea of the continuous improvement process (CIP) which Deming introduced to Japan. The western concept of the continuous improvement process (KVP = Kontinuierlicher Verbesserungsprozess) in Europe and the U.S.A. is not only closely connected with KAIZEN concerning its terms and in many aspects leans on it (cf. Womack et al. 1990) but often both concepts are identified (cf. Schmelzer, Sesselmann, Zink, 2004). It remains to ask whether CIP in its western adoption always implies the comprehensive change of consciousness and attitude as Imai postulates it.

KAIZEN cannot be considered as an integrative management concept because a closed holistic system-oriented approach is not given (cf. Zink, 2004): A lot of interesting management approaches are sub-summarised under the umbrella of KAIZEN but a comprehensive and stringent elaboration which would include all forms of control alternatives (process reengineering) is not given. KAIZEN is an influential management philosophy which focuses the innovation of processes in small steps and the standardisation of processes and which can be an essential part of a comprising integrative management (cf. Imai, 1986, 1997), (Westerbusch, 1998).

Therefore KAIZEN is a good source for review and improvement especially for enterprises like educational organisations dealing with process-oriented services. But it cannot serve as an integrative management concept for the development and realisation of learning offers.

6.3.2   Business process reengineering (BPR)

Business Process Reengineering (BPR) intends the radical restructuring and re-definition of business processes. Thus innovative and enormous development and quality leaps can be gained. In their BPM-*Manifesto* which earned great resonance both in Europe and in the U.S.A., Hammer and Champy even promise a business revolution in their sub-title (cf. Hammer, Champy, 1994). By delimitating from continuous improvement processes in small steps as in KAIZEN they, however, do not meet the holistic demands of an integrative management (cf. Hammer, Champy, 1994), (for its criticism cf. Deming, 1986), (Feigenbaum, 1986), (Juran, 1992) and (Zink 2004), (for a broadening of the concepts to a Business Process Management cf. Schmelzer, Sesselmann, 2003). In a certain way BPR can be called the complementary opposite to KAIZEN. So BPR remains a method to radically innovate processes which does not offer a holistic concept for integrative management but which is often a condition for its introduction (cf. Hammer, Champy 1994), (Champy, 1995), (Zink, 2004).

Educational organisations have often the opportunity and the need to a radical change management of their business models due to the uncertain learning market. Therefore BPR can support well the quality management of educational organisations. But BPR is not the compensation for a quality management but helps to improve the adaptation of the learning processes to the customer's needs.

6.3.3   Six sigma

In 1996 Six Sigma was introduced by Motorola as an instrument of quality planning, at first for the production field (cf. Harry, Schroeder, 2000), (Zink, 2004). The name of Six Sigma is derived from the stochastics: The Sigma factor designates the variation (deflection from the nominal value) in a Gauß-distribution in which two of one million parts are outside the range of Six Sigma (cf. Seghezzi, 2003). "Motorola as the pioneer of Six Sigma, for understandable reasons, has allocated 3.4 parts outside Six Sigma. According to that his model is constructed, too." (Seghezzi, 2003, p. 266). Six Sigma, according to the definition by Motorola, then means that only 3.4 mistakes occur in one million possibilities and that thus a faultless output of 99.99966 % is achieved. With this result the underlying zero defect philosophy is already near (cf. Crosby, 1980). In Six Sigma critical customer related measuring values are defined and the accompanying key processes are determined. Strong improvement aims are set, which are measured and evaluated electronically with the help of a lot of statistic methods. In order to enlarge the customer satisfaction the processes are optimised and the defects eliminated. Insofar Six Sigma is fundamentally a method of performance measurement and performance improvement which can be applied in every quality management (cf. Schmelzer, Sesselmann, 2003), (Zink, 2004).

In the meantime Six Sigma has extensively been developed further (cf. Harry, Schroeder, 2000), (Seghezzi, 2003), (Zink, 2004). By including systematic project management and permanent participation in improvement projects Six Sigma, together with its strong computer use, is even partly regarded as modern KAIZEN (cf. Seghezzi, 2003). By introducing a qualification system with certifications Six Sigma remains a continuous organisation process. In accordance with far-eastern competitive sports the interested supporters of Six Sigma get different belts after passing the examination successfully, beginning with green belts beyond black belts for examined project manager to the black Master Belts for the organisation-internal Six Sigma program manager. In addition to that Six Sigma was extended by further TQM instruments, e. g. by the leadership idea realised by introducing the declaration of champions. Six Sigma cannot be called an integrative management (yet?), but it is justified to speak of a comprehensive management strategy which meanwhile far exceeds the statistic registration of defects (cf. Seghezzi, 2003), (Zink, 2004).

With Six Sigma educational organisations find an interesting approach which development is still in progress. Actually it is not an appropriate quality management system but the enrichments and development of Six Sigma is going in that direction. Educational organisations can use Six Sigma as an instrument for reviewing and redefining their processes obtaining a comprehensive quality management concept. It has the potential to become a holistic approach in future.

6.3.4   TQM and TQC

Total Quality Management (TQM) reached Japan especially through the two Americans William Edwards Deming and Joseph M. Juran where their philosophy was widely spread and used under the term Total Quality Control (TQC). TQM is a holistic management philosophy that can be characterised as the most comprehensive quality management approach (cf. Seghezzi, 2003), (Bruhn, 2004) and that therefore will be described more extensively in the following.

Both the Americans Deming and Juran represented the idea of TQM first and imported it to Japan. There TQM was absorbed strongly and reached, under the name Total Quality Control (TQC), wide dissemination and realisation (cf. Feigenbaum, 1986). The Deming Price awarded already in 1951 for the first time contributed to this development to a great extent. In Japan TQM was regarded as a comprehensive organisation wide management philosophy and task almost from the beginning (cf. Zollondz, 2002). The situation in the U.S.A. and in Europe was quite different first: There process-oriented quality management was regarded predominantly as a task of single organisational business units. Here, too, the establishment of quality prices caused a broader view. The American Malcolm Baldrige National Quality Award (MBNQA) was adopted by the US-American Congress by law in 1987 and was awarded in 1988 for the first time. Its model delivered practical measurement categories and led to a strong TQM movement in the United States (cf. Seghezzi, 2003). In Europe the European Quality Award (EQA) was developed by the European Foundation for Quality Management (EFQM) in cooperation with the European Commission and the European Organisation for Quality (EOQ) and awarded in 1992 for first time (cf. Zink, 2004). Both prices, like the Deming Price, aim at the dissemination of the TQM idea and its realisation.

The main objective of Total Quality Management (TQM) is a continuous improvement process (CIP) that is called KAIZEN in Japan: KAIZEN improves the processes by many little single steps and reduces existing performance failures (cf. chapter 6.3.1). Beyond that TQM is the organisational management concept dealing with quality as the core focus of all activities and used by all the employees (for comments cf. Schmelzer, Sesselmann, 2003). TQM is an ambitious and holistic organisation philosophy characterised by these five aspects (cf. Seghezzi, 2003), (Soin, 1992):

1. Customer orientation in consideration of all stakeholders
2. Use of all knowledge resources and link to individual and organisational learning
3. Continuous improvement by little as well as by radical steps
4. Quality responsibility by each single person and by all the teams
5. Working in processes

Total Quality Management is not a consistent and coherent quality management approach, but is a combination of a lot of different concepts. The most important impulses and thinkers and their influence will be described shortly in the following part.

Deming has emphasised the quality development in processes and its subjective assessment within his "14 Points for Management"-Programme (cf. Deming, 1982, 1986), (Bruhn, 2004). For him quality is not measurable in an objective way, but always the individual result of the customers' measurement concerning value and performance given for the money. In parallel he has introduced the Continuous Improvement Process (CIP) principle which is contained as the fifth point of his "14 Points for Management"-Programme (cf. Deming, 1982, 1986), (Bruhn, 2004), (Zollondz, 2002).

Juran argues similarly with his customer-oriented quality definition called "Fitness for use" for products and services (cf. Juran, 1951, 1992), (Bruhn, 2004). He has transferred the Pareto-principle to the quality assurance by his concept "vital few, useful many". His quality definition can be used for all kinds of products, for all hierarchical levels, for all organisational functions and for all branches (cf. Juran, 1992). Juran has expanded the customer definition by introducing the "internal customer" and also takes into account the internal quality processes within an organisation. His "Quality Triology" consisting of the three processes quality planning, quality control and quality improvement represents a holistic management approach for continuous quality improvement. Statistical methods and measurement are used mainly, whereas the importance of the colleagues seems to be minor (cf. Bruhn, 2004), (Oess, 1993).

Feigenbaum has decisively formed the Japanese vocabulary with his Total Quality Control (TQC) approach. Feigenbaum calls for the integration of all internal organisational interdependencies and for the responsibility of all the employees. He especially focuses on technical quality assurance and introduces the consideration of quality costs. His main objective is the fulfilment of customer expectations and the adaptation of the quality to the customers' requirements and standards (cf. Feigenbaum, 1986), (Zollondz, 2002), (Soin, 1992).

Crosby has formulated his "Four Absolutes of Quality Management" for a comprehensive quality-oriented organisation culture while he, in the sense of the performance standard of zero defects, postulates "Do it right the first time." Analogue to Deming he has composed a "14-step Quality Improvement Process" for its realisation (cf. Crosby, 1980), (Bruhn, 2004), (Zollondz, 2002).

Ishikawa has developed the Company Wide Quality Control (CWQC) concept (and also the well-known fishbone diagram). This approach is based upon the concepts of Deming and Juran (cf. Bruhn, 2004). He considerably extends the meaning of internal customers (cf. Ishikawa, 1985). Ishikawa recommends the integration of all the employees into a participative management concept and proposes the establishment of Quality Circles for the first time (cf. Bruhn, 2004), (Zink, Schick, 1998).

Within all these developments and different approaches in parallel, a movement can be observed from pure quality assurance to process-oriented quality management in the sense of a comprehensive Total Quality Management. Worldwide acceptance and realisation of Total Quality Management was reached and supported strongly by the development of international quality standards and reference models and especially by the development of the standards family ISO 9000ff.

Finally, it can be summarised that TQM is the most holistic quality management concept of the four discussed quality management approaches (KAIZEN, BPR, Six Sigma and TQM). TQM fits best the defined sense of an integrative management concept. Among the other three concepts Six Sigma has shown the best potential for its development. But actually TQM is the most complete integrative management concept fulfilling all requirements. Especially TQM is suitable for educational organisations due to its accentuation of process orientation. Therefore, the main quality standards and reference models of TQM and their relevance for educational organisations are described in the following chapter 6.4.

6.4   Quality standards and reference models

Process-oriented quality management has won recognition against statistical failure control and product-oriented quality assurance. The holistic focus on quality management processes has made possible an avoidance of mistakes in advance and a strong customer orientation. In this combination Total Quality Management is the most comprehensive approach among many concepts the most influential of which have been outlined in chapter 6.3 above. In this chapter the relevance of process-oriented quality management for educational organisations will shortly be dealt with. Quality standards and reference models are gaining more and more in importance. Therefore the standards family ISO 9000ff., the reference models of ISO/IEC 19796-1 and PAS 1032-1 (cf. DIN, 2004a) and the EFQM Excellence Model (cf. EFQM, 2003b) will be presented in the following as the most relevant quality standards and reference models for the implementation and realisation of the Total Quality Management philosophy.

6.4.1   Process orientation and educational organisations

Process-oriented quality management and especially Total Quality Management can raise the service quality just in education and vocational training. The reason for this is that the products and services, i. e. the learning offers, can be examined, assessed and evaluated hardly before their usage. The consumers of learning offers, i. e. the potential learners must trust the information given about the learning offers by the providers. They can try and check a learning offer only very seldom. Especially face-to-face training parts cannot be tested in advance, but also electronic learning resources can be tested only partly as demo versions, otherwise these learning products would lose their monetary value. On the other hand the examination and certification of every learning offer by external evaluation would be very expensive and not economic. And there is the general problem that the quality of materials and products cannot give a hint about the overall quality of learning offers: The quality of the learning services like individual coaching and tutoring as well as the competencies of the learning provider, the teachers and the tutors cannot be evaluated in advance. Therefore, quality standards can be a valuable aid, especially in organisational education and vocational training. Quality standards do not only offer indications for the quality management of one's own, but also for the comparability of learning offers and for the transparency during their planning, development, realisation and evaluation. They are not a guarantee for excellent quality of products and services but a useful instrument to ensure the organisational process quality on provider's side and an indicator for efficient learning offers on customer's and user's side. In the following part, the standards family ISO 9000:2000ff. and existing reference models (PAS 1032-1/ ISO/IEC 19796-1 and EFQM) will shortly be dealt with because they are most important for the process-oriented quality management. Every chapter will be concluded by some hints how educational organisation could use the specific approach.

6.4.2   The standards family ISO 9000:2000ff.

The standards family ISO 9000:2000ff. is supporting the development, implementation and improvement of quality management systems. The following model of a process-based quality management system serves as the basis of the standards family ISO 9000:2000ff.:

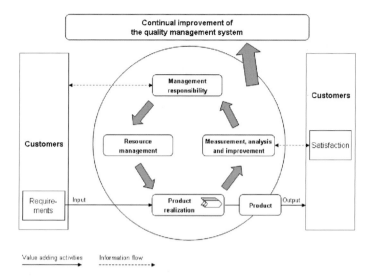

Fig. 6-1: Model of a process-based quality management system from ISO 9001:2000

The analogy to the PDCA-Cycle is evident and intended. In conjunction with the clear customer orientation and the emphasis of the need for continuous improvement, this model requires a comprehensive quality management system in the sense of a Total Quality Management. The necessary principles are included in ISO 9000:2000 as well as in ISO 9004:2004 (cf. ISO 9000:2000; ISO 9004:2000; DIN 2001). The following eight quality management principles form the basis for the quality management system standards within the standards family ISO 9000:2000ff.:

Customer focus

Organisations depend on their customers and therefore should understand current and future customer needs, should meet customer requirements and strive to exceed customer expectations.

Leadership

Leaders establish unity of purpose and direction of the organisation. They should create and maintain the internal environment in which people can become fully involved in achieving the organisation's objectives.

Involvement of people

People at all levels are the essence of an organisation and their full involvement enables their abilities to be used for the organisation's benefit.

Process approach

A desired result is achieved more efficiently when activities and related resources are managed as a process.

System approach to management

Identifying, understanding and managing interrelated processes as a system contributes to the organisation's effectiveness and efficiency in achieving its objectives.

Continual improvement

Continual improvement of the organisation's overall performance should be a permanent objective of the organisation.

Factual approach to decision making

Effective decisions are based on the analysis of data and information.

Mutually beneficial supplier relationships

An organisation and its suppliers are interdependent and a mutually beneficial relationship enhances the ability of both to create value." (ISO 9000:2000-12, p. 7).

The standards family ISO 9000 has been developed and edited and will be revised and developed further by the ISO Technical Committee 176 "Quality Management and Quality Assurance" (ISO/TC 176). The first edition of the standards series ISO 9000ff. took place in 1987, and already in 1990 it was decided to further develop it in two steps. To assure its consistence and continuity in practical implementation, a first revision with slight changes only was published in 1994. The long-term further development with radical changes was (provisionally) ended in 2000, with the publication of the new series ISO 9000:2000ff. The most important innovations were *formally* the consolidation of the formerly more than twenty standards into four main standards with a similar structure and *in substance* the general process orientation.

The standards family ISO 9000:2000ff. consists of these four standards:

- *ISO 9000:2000-12:* Quality management systems. Fundamentals and vocabulary
- *ISO 9001:2000-12:* Quality management systems. Requirements

- *ISO 9004:2000-12:* Quality management systems. Guidelines for perfomance improvements
- *ISO 19011:2002-12:* Guidelines for quality and/ or environmental management systems auditing

ISO 9000:2000 defines the fundamentals and the vocabulary of quality management and quality management systems. It contains the eight quality management principles that can also be found in ISO 9004:2000, as well as the model of a process-based quality management system (also contained in ISO 9001:2000 und ISO 9004:2000). ISO 9001:2000 determines the requirements for quality management systems. Core meaning has been given to the overall performance, efficiency and effectiveness of a quality management system to meet and fulfil the customers' needs. ISO 9004:2000 offers a guideline for organisations whose top management aims at a continuous performance improvement. The standard ISO 9004:2000 broadens the objectives of ISO 9001:2000, especially to support the measurement and the improvement of the overall performance, efficiency and effectiveness of an organisation. ISO 19011:2002 has been developed to uniformly supersede the former standards for quality auditing (ISO 10011) and for environmental auditing (ISO 14010ff.) and has been prepared jointly by Technical Committees ISO/TC 176 "Quality management and quality assurance" and ISO/TC 207 "Environmental management". ISO 19011:2002 contains guidance on managing audit programmes and on conducting internal and external audits of quality and environmental management systems as well as the description of the competencies needed by an auditor. It also defines the principles of auditing, with the help of which auditors should gain equal evaluation results (cf. ISO 19011:2002).

Both ISO 9001:2000 and ISO 9004:2000 were formed as a consistent pair with similar structures during the great revision of the standards family ISO 9000:2000ff. ISO 9001:2000 is almost completely included in ISO 9004:2000. "ISO 9001 specifies requirements for a quality management system that can be used for internal application by organisations, or for certification, or for contractual purposes. It focuses on the effectiveness of the quality management system in meeting customer requirements. ISO 9004 gives guidance on a wider range of objectives of a quality management system than does ISO 9001, particularly for the continual improvement of an organisation's overall performance and efficiency, as well as its effectiveness. ISO 9004 is recommended as a guide for organisations whose top management wishes to move beyond the requirements of ISO 9001, in pursuit of continual improvement of performance." (ISO 9001:2000-12, p. 14) Thus ISO 9004:2000 as well as ISO 9000:2000 are not intended for certification or for contractual purposes. A certification is therefore possible on ISO 9001:2000 only. ISO 9001:2000 can be used also for contractual purposes as well as for internal application by organisations. It is important to note that ISO 9001:2000 does not standardise a quality management system and it does not contain concrete specifications. The standard describes 'only' the requirements on a quality management system and offers support for organisations to develop and establish their own quality management system that is to fit to the special needs of the organisation (cf. ISO 9001:2000).

The standards family ISO 9000:2000ff. has achieved, together with their eight quality management principles, a great dissemination and over 400.000 enterprises worldwide have been certified until their radical revision in year 2000 (cf. Seghezzi, 2003). Process-oriented quality management has considerably won consideration and reputation by the revision and new formulation of the standards family ISO 9000:2000ff. Their implementation and realisation have considerably grown. Just within the service sector, the new standards with their process orientation have contributed to give more place to the ideas of quality management and to establish the philosophy of Total Quality Management.

The standards family ISO 9000:2000ff. can be used efficiently by educational organisations especially after its revision and new given process orientation. The standards support educational organisations by the development and implementation of a holistic quality management system. To implement such a quality management system in educational organisations, the commitment of the top management is necessary for defining the organisational vision and the derived missions. Another crucial factor is the identification of the processes and involved stakeholders and the participation of all employees. The success of the implementation depends on the consciousness, on the attitude and on the support of all people developed and improved by internal communication, workshops and processes.

6.4.3   Reference models (ISO/IEC 19796-1 and PAS 1032-1)

Reference process models are well fitting for implementation, analysis, evaluation and reengineering of organisational processes. The new standard ISO/IEC 19796-1 and the specification PAS 1032-1 are the first two reference process models especially developed for the education and vocational training sector with special focus on e-learning. It is important that the DIN-Reference Process Model included in PAS 1032-1 is a comprehensive process model that covers all aspects and requirements of the providers as well as of the users of learning offers in the same way (cf. DIN 2004a). The new standard ISO/IEC 19796-1 based on this model is in addition an internationally accepted quality standard that has acquired its worldwide acceptance by a long-term consensus process. The new standard ISO/IEC 19796-1 and the specification PAS 1032-1 will be described and explained in detail on a different place of this book. That is why here it may be sufficient to mention them and to refer to them (cf. DIN 2004a, 2005).

6.4.4   The EFQM excellence model

The organisation European Foundation for Quality Management (EFQM) was founded in 1989 by leading European major enterprises with the support of the European Union. The main objective of EFQM is the dissemination and implementation of the TQM philosophy in Europe (cf. Zink, 2004). Therefore the European Quality Award (EQA) was established following the Japanese Deming Price and the American Malcom Baldrige National Quality Award. The EQA was awarded in 1992 for the first time. The base of it is the *EFQM Excellence Model* (EFQM, 2003b) launched in 1991 for the application of the *Fundamental Concepts of Excellence* (EFQM, 2003a). These eight Fundamental Concepts of Excellence of the EFQM are:

Results orientation

Excellence is achieving results that delight all the organisation's stakeholders.

Customer focus

Excellence is creating sustainable customer value.

Leadership and constancy of purpose

Excellence is visionary and inspirational leadership, coupled with constancy of purpose.

Management by processes and facts

Excellence is managing the organisation through a set of interdependent and inter-related systems, processes and facts.

People development and involvement

Excellence is maximising the contribution of employees through their development and involvement.

Continuous learning, innovation and improvement

Excellence is challenging the status quo and effecting change by utilising learning to create innovation and improvement opportunities.

Partnership development

Excellence is developing and maintaining value-adding partnerships.

Corporate social responsibility

Excellence is exceeding the minimum regulatory framework in which the organisation operates and to strive to understand and respond to the expectations of their stakeholders in society." (EFQM, 2003a)

The EFQM Excellence Model (EFQM, 2003b) is based on nine criteria (five 'enablers' criteria and four 'results' criteria). The following figure shows the relationship between the nine criteria and their weighting at the EQA:

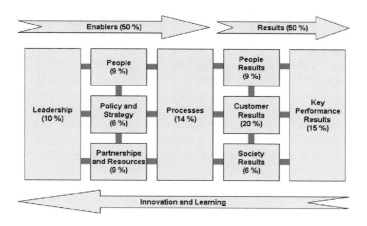

Fig. 6-2: The EFQM excellence model

In 2000 the criteria of the EFQM Excellence Model were revised while for the first time three sub-criteria for customer orientation and the RADAR approach of continuous improvement processes were integrated (cf. Zollondz, 2002), (Zink, 2004). RADAR stands for:

*R*esults, *A*pproach, *D*eployment, *A*ssessment and *R*eview.

The RADAR approach emphasises the importance of continuous improvement in the sense of the PDCA-Cycle as well as of the focus on achieved results. In addition that underlines that the EFQM Excellence Model is a comprehensive TQM approach. The EFQM Excellence Model especially recommends the self-assessment (in difference to the standard ISO 9001:2000). The EFQM proposes different methods for the self-evaluation (cf. EFQM, 2003c), (Zink, 2004):

1. Self-Assessment by workshop
2. Self-Assessment by matrix diagram
3. Self-Assessment by check list
4. Self-Assessment by standard form
5. Self-Assessment by the simulation of a proposal of a national or international price
6. Self-Assessment by involvement of colleagues

The EFQM Excellence Model is suitable for educational organisations especially due to its emphasis of the processes' relevance. To introduce the EFQM Excellence Model, first the commitment and support by the top management has to be fetched and a careful planning of the assessment units, of the methods, of the resources and of the task distribution has to be realised. In addition to that especially the information and qualification of all the stakeholders according to their functions and roles within the self-assessment has to be taken notice of in the forefield. During the self-assessment the data will be collected, documented, prepared and finally assessed. Different methods can be mixed up at the stage of documentation and assessment. It is important to obtain a common consensus at the assessment eventually by external support. The results of such a consensus process must influence the whole organisation and the strategic management. And this influence should not be the ending point of self-assessment but the starting point for the next self-assessment (cf. Zink, 2004). In the sense of the RADAR model every result of a self-assessment is only the base for the permanent process cycle to continuous improvement.

6.5   Summary

Quality management is a concept that has permanently grown up and been improved, and it integrates customer orientation, process orientation and quality orientation. Total Quality Management covers all the requirements of an Integrative Management concept. The revision and further development of the standard family ISO 9000:2000ff. have led to internationally accepted quality standards for the development and implementation of a quality management system and for its certification. Process-oriented quality management can look back on a long-term development that, in the sense of a continuous improvement process cannot be finished, but has always to be evaluated and further developed. For that reason quality will be remaining the complex crucial success factor for the entire management in the future.

7 An analysis of international quality management approaches in e-learning: Different paths, similar pursuits

Markus A. Wirth

University of St. Gallen, Switzerland

An analysis of quality approaches in the field of e-learning reveals different ways to tackle the quality challenge but similar aspirations and implicit agreements on what quality is about. By stating this, the following contribution intends to break with some commonly accepted statements that solely emphasise the heterogeneity of nowadays quality approaches. First of all, it's true - there are considerable differences between the various existing quality approaches. A systematic overview of four generically different fields of quality management approaches points out some basic differences in the underlying objectives and the ways in which these goals are prosecuted. However, a deeper look below the surface reveals some striking similarities between various quality management approaches. Thus, much of the complexity we experience in today's quality management landscape is due to a lack of information and knowledge of what is inside a certain quality management conception. Hence, users should not accept anymore 'black box' quality management approaches but must demand explicit and comprehensible documentation of quality criteria, indicators and standards, underlying quality understandings and conceptions as well as relevant evaluation methods.

7.1 Introduction: How to differentiate quality management approaches?

It cannot be overlooked that during the most recent couple of years, many efforts have been taken to design and implement instruments for quality assurance in many different economic sectors and to bring them finally forward to educational challenges - and to e-learning in particular. In the meantime, there exist several publications that systematically describe and explain these approaches and their respective backgrounds (see Gonon, 1998), (Riddy et al., 2002), (also Srikanthan,

Dalrymple, 2002, p. 216)[24]. Impressively, the various existing publications on quality approaches reveal a large and hard to count number of different offerings for quality management in the educational sector. Already a smaller study by the Danish Institute for Evaluation identifies and analyses up to 34 quality assurance agencies in 24 countries (Danish Evaluation Institute, 2003, p. 17). A Cedefop study by Bertzeletou (2003) even comes up with 90 national and international quality approaches for quality certification and accreditation. Woodhouse (2003) counts more than 140 quality approaches that are associated with the International Network of Quality Assurance Agencies in Higher Education (INQAAHE). Most of these certification and accreditation bodies follow their own quality approaches and have their own evaluation, certification and accreditation offerings. To make things even more complex, above mentioned studies and papers mostly address traditional certification and accreditation frameworks for higher education and only rarely include newer quality approaches that specifically focus on recent educational innovation and e-learning.

> *Quality Management Approaches*: Explicitly stated structures, activities and processes that were designed to plan, assure, improve, and/ or evaluate the quality of an institution, a product or a service.

In respect to an overview of and complexity among nowadays quality frameworks, three aspects are pointed out by above stated brief overview: first, a useful categorisation and systematisation of existing approaches should help to better and more validly compare the unmanageable wealth of coexisting quality approaches. Second, it has to be acknowledged that a fully comprehensive discussion of all existing quality approaches is not feasible and that a useful selection of approaches must be made that should be as representative as possible. Third, different quality approaches come from and base on different contexts. Leaving out this contextual information would mean to leave out some of the most essential information that is necessary to understand the goals, methods and concepts of a specific quality approach[25]. Thus, it becomes obvious that validly comparing different quality approaches one by one is possible to a limited extent only. Existing systematic views (similar Faulstich, Gnahs, Sauter, 2003, p. 9), (see Kiedrowski, 2001, p. 137ff.) that differentiate input-, process- and output-oriented approaches seem to be far too simplistic for the complex offerings of today. This is mainly because in most of nowadays' approaches you will most likely find a certain mix of input, process and output oriented quality criteria. Other proposals for a systematic view (like the one in Bertzeletou, 2002, p. 5) also have some difficulties to holistically describe quality approaches, because the dimensions they use (i. e. generic vs. specific, process oriented vs. product oriented) do not exclude each other but make both part of a well balanced quality approach. Despite of the important differences be-

---

[24] See also the European Initiative ‚European Quality Observatory' (EQO, www.eqo.info, 01.01.2005).

[25] See for example the importance that is given to contextual information within the ‚European Quality Observatory' (EQO, www.eqo.info, 01.01.2005).

tween the various quality approaches, some of the well renowned publications in this field do not use any systematisation at all (i. e. Gonon, 1998), (also Seghezzi, 2003), (Srikanthan, Dalrymple, 2002) - as a consequence of this, different approaches on different levels with different focuses stand next to each other without an explicit differentiation and explanation (also compare Francés et al., 2003, p. 9), (see the discussion in Gonon, 1998).

Thus, as a first step, it seems to be appropriate to start with a generic systematisation of existing quality management approaches that should allow for a better understanding of different purposes and underlying goals of specific quality management approaches. In search of an appropriate systematisation framework, this paper builds on the well known Deming-Circle terminology (see for example Seghezzi, 2003, p. 13) which supports a comprehensible and useful typing:

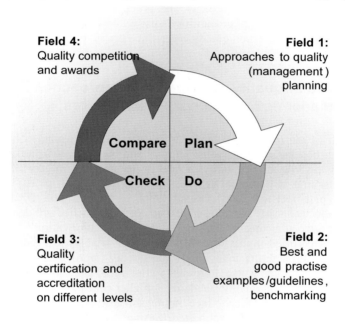

Fig. 7-1: Different starting points of quality management approaches

In field 1, focus on process and quality management documentation prevails. As such, to systematically plan and implement quality in educational institutions becomes a central concern of quality management. As a result of such quality management approaches, generic and holistic quality models are targeted that are intended to serve as reference points for the design of an institution- or programme-specific quality management conception. In contrast to this, approaches in field 2 much more focus on the realisation of learning and e-learning solutions and try to accompany the relevant implementation processes with tangible instructions. This finally results in a continuous self assessment against best or good practise examples which is known as benchmarking. Differently to this, it's not self evaluation but an assessment of an institution's or a programme's quality executed by an external accreditation or certification body that characterises quality management approaches in field 3. Whereas quality approaches in field 2 rarely operationalise their benchmarks, elaborating on evaluation methods and indicators of quality criteria is a crucial element of valid quality evaluation. Finally, in field 4 it's not the evaluation of a specific institution or programme against preset criteria that is of interest but the competitive comparison of specific learning or e-learning solutions. In contrast to best or good practise examples in field 2 that focus on a certain space in time (like implementation of e-learning), approaches for quality awards are much more point-in-time oriented. Different to quality accreditation or quality certification, there are not preset standards and criteria (minimum criteria, 'pre-Olympic model') but on a competitive ranking ('Olympic model') that is intended to effect high quality services and products. Thus, it is basically about competitively best meeting a certain jury's expectations at a certain point in time and less about meeting certain quality criteria at a pre set minimum level.

7.2   Use of quality management approaches in the academic and the corporate sectors

Independent of the implementation of a specific quality management approach, various contributions in international journals and books show some considerable reservations towards the feasibility of quality management in general and in the field of e-learning in particular (Eaton, 2003), (Franz, 2004, p. 107), (Fröhlich, Jütte, 2004, p. 12), (Leef, 2003), (Ravet, 2002, p. 272), (Simon, 2001, p. 155)[26]. As such, Tulloch, Sneeds' warning in respect to 'best practice' guidelines is valid as a major criticism against quality accreditation and certification too: There is a big danger of certified input, process and output variables to become inflexible rules that may stifle future innovations and quality improvements (see Tulloch, Sneed, 2000, p. 9). Even worse: in respect to the use of e-learning, Tulloch, Sneed conclude that traditional quality standards in higher education mislead many institutions to imitate classical face to face trainings instead of fostering and leveraging strategic advantages of media supported learning scenarios (see Tulloch, Sneed, 2000, p. 9). In this context, it must be assumed that quality assurance measurements that purely focus on traditional quality goals (e. g. physical infrastructure like library, public working space) negatively affect the overall quality because they result in an inefficient use of funds and capacities in new and change educational environments. Meyer in particular draws a negative picture of accreditation: „Accreditation has become a battlefield between those who would use traditional accrediting standards to forestall the changes wrought by distance education and those who would change accreditation" (Meyer, 2002, p. 9). Friend-Pereira et al.

---

[26] See also Merchel's criticism against quality certifications of institutions and services in the social sector which in its main features can be brought forward to the educational sector as well, Merchel, 2001.

(2002, p. 22) agree to this by concluding that quality accreditation may become dangerous if it ends in itself and only serves for legitimation. Recently, an empirical study by Lagrosen et al. (2004, p. 65) clearly indicated that internal quality evaluation gains more and more in importance compared to external quality assessments. In contrast to these results, Pellert & Welan (1995) observe an evanescent trust in internal quality controls - especially with universities and public schools. As such, an increased pressure for justifications and a growing demand for discussing the quality of universities seriously express the loss of confidence in their self regulatory quality assurance schemes (Pellert, Welan, 1995, p. 88). Beyond the academic sector, an own study confirmed the diminishing confidence in internal evaluation and revealed a growing need for external quality evaluation with both learners as well as teachers (Wirth, in print, p. 420). Thus, more and more quality evaluation and certification by an external and independent evaluation body is reasoned by a broader acceptance (learners, employers, politicians, investors, and others more) (see van Damme, 2000, p. 3) and credibility of measurements towards quality improvement (Danish Evaluation Institute, 2003, p. 14). It is striking that despite the fact that quality accreditation and certification is able to evaluate minimal standards only, the public generally expects the assurance of highest possible standards through quality certification and accreditation (Wirth, in print). As this makes it clear, aspects and trade-offs between practicability and acceptance are relevant for academic and corporate quality assurance (similar Franz, 2004, p. 107): Quality assurance has to meet high expectations, process complex relationships and at the same time must allow for an efficient evaluation and economic justification (Fröhlich, Jütte, 2004, p. 13). In this respect, it is very interesting to have a closer look at the dissemination of existing quality management approaches in the academic as well as the corporate sector. An empirical study among European universities (N = 241) that was conducted on behalf of the EU commission reveals that more than half of the institutions at least partly apply a quality model for e-learning (53 %) (PLS Ramboll Management, 2004, p. 70). Quality evaluation comprises in most of the times learner satisfaction or evaluation by external peers (17 universities), creation of an internal quality position (5 Universities), external quality assessment (3 universities), and guidelines as well as standards for course development (8 universities). In addition to this, 24 universities confirm that they apply the same quality assurance methods for e-learning and for traditional educational settings (PLS Ramboll Management, 2004, p. 70). Other research very much confirms these findings (see for example Fraunhofer IPSI, 2003, p. 32). In the corporate sector, user feedbacks (orally or by means of so called 'happy-sheets') are still very much in the spotlight of quality management, whereas only few institutions decided yet to go for quality certificates (only 7 - 8 % Unicmind, 2002, p. 20, 26). Fraunhofer's Integrated Publication and Information Systems Institute states that standardised quality assurance approaches are hardly ever applied (Fraunhofer IPSI, 2003, p. 33) which, in respect to the number and diversity of quality certification and accreditation frameworks, is quite astonishing. However, even if the currently observed use of quality management approaches is not overwhelming at all, in the last couple of years, a distinctive increase of quality related activities took place (see the results in Balli,

Krekel, Sauter, 2002, p. 17). In particular, the increasing number of country-, region- and even world-wide rankings and benchmarkings are dedicated indicators for this development (see Danish Evaluation Institute, 2003, p. 21), (Federkeil, 2004, p. 63). Surveys among providers of further education in Germany clearly show that market conditions for free riders and so called 'rotten apples' got worse (Gnahs, Kuwan, 2004, p. 50f.). Hence in respect to quality, reasons for the tremendous increase in the use of quality management approaches can be tracked down to increasing competition, the improvement of quality of the quality approaches (see Falk, 2000, p. 557), a growing understanding of quality as a major differentiator on the market and changing legal limiting factors (see Bötel, Krekel, 2004, p. 25), (Bötel, Seusing, Behrensdorf, 2002, p. 36). In this context, Fröhlich & Jütte emphasise that even if nowadays' quality management approaches may not be completely satisfying yet, they at least must be seen as a chance to become more sensitive towards current challenges and innovative ways to solve quality issues (Fröhlich, Jütte, 2004, p. 13). Finally however, the use of quality management approaches in e-learning has to be evaluated under economical and not just under ideological conditions.

7.3   Selection of a representative set of quality management approaches

It must be clear, that this paper does not allow for an indefinite number of approaches to be discussed but asks for a rigorous selection of a representative set. In the following short paragraph, the necessary selection follows the four fields introduced above and lists the quality management approaches that will be included in the subsequent analytic discussion. The selection of certain approaches mainly bases on the respective relevancy in the quality management community and the availability of background information that allows to understand a specific conception (for more detailed information, see Wirth, in print, p. 159ff.).

- In field 1, mainly three large organisations can be identified that drive developments in respect to quality management approaches (Bötel et al., 2002), (Dembski, Lorenz, 1995), (Gonon, 1998), (Schroeter et al., 2003). For a long time already, the European Foundation for Quality Management (EFQM), the International Organisation for Standardisation (ISO) as well as the Deutsche Institut für Normung e. V. (DIN) have been offering approaches for the corporate context. All times, the transferability of these approaches to the educational sector was discussed very controversially. As a reaction to these discussions, there were mainly three specific developments initiated (ISO 10015, DIN PAS 1032, DIN PAS 1037) in recent years that dedicatedly focus on educational matters and e-learning issues in particular.

- European Foundation for Quality Management: EFQM Excellence Model (TQM, www.efqm.org)
- International Organisation for Standardisation (ISO): ISO 9001:2000, ISO 10015:1999 (www.iso.org)
- Deutsches Institut für Normung e. V. (DIN): DIN PAS 1032-1:2004, DIN PAS 1037:2004 (www.din.de, www.beuth.de)

- In field 2, there is a huge variety of recommendations (i. e. American Federation of Teachers, 2000), (Hollands, 2000), guidelines (i. e. Open and Distance Learning Quality Council (ODLQC), 2001) or criteria catalogues (i. e. Gottfried, Hager, Scharl, 2002), (SODIS, without date; Wright, without date) and checklists (i. e. American Council on Education, 2001), (Bellinger, 2004), (also Scalan, 2003, p. 1). A discussion on the value of all these approaches is very difficult because most of them only provide criteria and do not furnish them with relevant context information and underlying quality conceptions. Most recently, a few guidelines seem to prevail. As such, the Institute for Higher Education Policy described the development of their criteria in a very detailed way in the well known 'quality on the line'-publication (Phipps, Merisotis, 2000). A more recent initiative in France also targeted towards a comprehensive set of best practise recommendation and finally led to a French code of practise (AFNOR, 2004). In England finally, the Institute for IT training at the University of Warwick developed several best practise documents by which the quality of e-learning services should be assured and strengthened.

  - Association française de normalisation (AFNOR)/ Forum français pour la formation ouverte et à distance (FFFOD): French Code of Practice in e-learning (http://www.afnor.fr, AFNOR, 2004)
  - Institute for Higher Education Policy (IHEP): Quality on the Line-Benchmarks (www.ihep.org, Phipps, Merisotis, 2000)
  - Institute of IT Training, University of Warwick (IITT): Code of practice for e-learning providers, Web site usability standards, Competence framework for e-learning designers and developers, Competence framework for e-tutors, Charters for learners (www.iitt.org.uk)

- In field 3 - similar to field 2 - there is a hard to count number of quality approaches including accreditation and certification offerings that mainly focus on different educational aspects and levels. Thus, to make the analysis more comprehensible, three subgroups are built, of which the first is focusing mainly on educational institutions, the second one focuses on business education, and the third subgroup focuses on e-learning products and services.

  - Accreditation and certification of higher and further education institutions

    - Distance Education and Training Council (DETC): Distance Learning Accreditation (www.detc.org)
    - Schweizerisches Qualitätszertifikat für Weiterbildungsinstitutionen (e-duQua, ww.eduQua.ch)
    - Quality Assurance Agency (QAA) – Accreditation of educational insti-

tutions following the ‚Guidelines on the quality assurance of distance learning' (www.qaa.ac.uk)

- Accreditation and certification of management oriented education (institutions and programmes)

  - Association of MBA's/ Ambassadors for MBA Quality (A-MBA, www.mbaworld.com)
  - Association to Advance Collegiate Schools of Business (AACSB, www.aacsb.edu)
  - European Foundation for Management Development (EFMD): European Quality Improvement System (EQUIS, www.efmd.be/equis)

- Accreditation and certification of e-learning (products and services)

  - Gesellschaft für Pädagogik und Information e. V. (GPI): Comenius-Siegel and -Medals for learning software (www.gpi-online.de)
  - QualitE-Learning Assurance Inc.: eQCheck (basing on the Canadian Recommended e-learning Guidelines/ CanREGs, www.eqcheck.com)
  - American Society for Training & Development (ASTD): E-learning Courseware Certification (ECC, www.astd.org/astd)

- There is hardly any international e-learning organisation that does not award a price for outstanding e-learning solutions. As such, there is a wide range of tutor awards, software awards, and other Oscar-like jury awards. Again, three approaches are selected within this field that will be included in the subsequent reflections:

  - European e-learning Award (EureleA, www.eurelea.org)
  - Deutscher Bildungssoftware-Preis (Digita, www.digita.de)
  - Mediendidaktischer Hochschulpreis (Medida-Prix, www.medidaprix.de)

The above mentioned selection of quality management approaches will be analysed in the next section and hence will serve as a reference basis for the following conclusions.

7.4   Breaking down complexity: From niche-qualities to generally agreed on concepts

Fröhlich & Jütte clearly set out that the heterogeneity and complexity of today's quality approaches distract from the core quality issues that must be addressed (Fröhlich, Jütte, 2004, p. 13). Thus not only models and concepts but also dedicated explicit quality goals and an adequate and comprehensible operationalisation are needed. At the first glance, an analysis of above listed selection of 18 major quality management approaches supports the heterogeneity and polymorphy stated and anticipated by Fröhlich & Jütte. In fact, most of the approaches have their specific peculiarities. Quality concepts in the planning sector very much base on a central design and controlling instrument called quality handbook that incorporates a comprehensive and detailed process description. In the second field ('Do'), project oriented quality concepts (French Code of Practice) and quality charters for elearners (Institute for IT-Training, University of Warwick) seem to be very specific. In Field 3, some of the quality accreditation approaches evaluate conformity with local fire police and healthcare requirements (Distance Education and Training Council) and put much weight on a fully developed library infrastructure (i. e. Quality Assurance Agency). Others use a construct called 'internationality'[27] (i. e. EFMD's European Quality Improvement System) to judge the quality of an educational institution which is not very much supported by literature (see Knight, 2001, p. 233). Other approaches in field 3 that focus on checking the quality of e-learning software focus on (de-)installation issues, interface design and handbook comprehensibility. In contrast to this, approaches within field 4 (like Digita and Medida-Prix) do focus on unique selling propositions - or in other words they do award scenarios that are in some ways unique and innovative. At the same time and in contrast to this, EureleA - another quality competition - evaluates how well a specific scenario can be transferred to another enterprise and whether or not (just to give an example) Scientology exclusion clauses have been incorporated into a specific project (part of the BVDW quality criteria that were integrated into the EureleA evaluation scheme). As this short excursion has shown, the context dependence of the quality criteria mentioned does not allow for the identification of a general-abstract conception of 'good' e-learning (see also European Commission, 2003d, IV) - but however, the differences between the various approaches are smaller than expected. Thus, beside some considerable 'at a first glance'-differences, a more in depth view reveals a broad consensus on crucial quality dimensions and criteria (Lockee, Moore, Burton, 2002), (Parker, 2004, p. 386), (Ravet, 2002), (also Scalan, 2003, p. 1), (similar Twigg, 2001).

By means of a qualitative content analysis (for further research methodological information see Mayring, 2002, p. 114ff.), quality criteria of above mentioned quality management approaches were analysed. Seufert & Euler identified five dimensions (pedagogical, economical, technical, organisational, cultural Dimensions) that their study revealed to be relevant for sustainable e-learning innovations (Seufert, Euler, 2003; Seufert, Euler, 2004, 2005). As an orientation framework, these dimensions are subsequently used to gain a holistic view on quality issues addressed by the various approaches these dimensions. Guided by these dimensions, the quality dimensions and criteria observed were systematically evaluated and interpreted and finally brought together to generic groups of quality issues. It is obvious that this was a cyclical process that by continuously summarising and reviewing existing classifications finally led to 18 stable quality areas that are covered by most of the quality management frameworks. However, it has to be stated that due to the openness of some quality management frameworks, interpretations of the quality criteria some time was quite hard and sometimes needed normative decision making.

---

[27] Internationality is measured by the ratio of English speaking students and faculty to native students and faculty coming from the specific institutions' home country.

Table 7-1: Overview of central quality areas that were identified to be implicitly agreed among different quality management approaches

Dimensions	Commonly agreed quality dimensions that are addressed by the indicated quality management approaches	Field 1 — EFQM / ISO[28] / DIN[29]	Field 2 — FCoP / IHEP / IITT	Field 3 — DETC / eduQua / QAA	Field 3 — EQUIS / AACSB / A-MBA	Field 3 — Comenius / eQcheck / ASTD	Field 4 — EureleA / Digita / Medida
Strategic Goals	**1** Analysis of the targeted market, strategic goals.	2 / 2 (2) / 2 (2)	2 / 0 / 1	2 / 2 / 1	2 / 2 / 2	0 / 0 / 0	2 / 0 / 1
	2 Management and documentation of the specific educational measurement.	2 / 2 (2) / 2 (2)	2 / 2 / 2	2 / 2 / 2	1 / 1 / 0	0 / 2 / 2	2 / 1 / 0
	3 Description of the target group.	2 / 1 (2) / 2 (2)	2 / 2 / 1	0 / 2 / 0	2 / 2 / 2	2 / 2 / 1	2 / 2 / 2
Pedagogic Dimension	**4** Pedagogic concepts and learning goals.	0 / 0 (2) / 2 (2)	2 / 1 / 2	2 / 2 / 2	1 / 2 / 2	2 / 2 / 2	2 / 2 / 2
	5 Added value and integration of e-learning and other teaching and learning methods.	1 / 0 (1) / 1 (1)	2 / 0 / 2	1 / 0 / 0	0 / 0 / 2	2 / 1 / 0	2 / 2 / 2
	6 Interaction (among learners, between learners and teachers and interaction with learning contents).	0 / 0 (1) / 2 (2)	2 / 2 / 2	1 / 0 / 2	1 / 2 / 2	2 / 2 / 2	2 / 2 / 2
	7 Development and delivery of learning contents.	1 / 0 (2) / 2 (0)	2 / 2 / 2	2 / 1 / 2	0 / 0 / 2	2 / 2 / 2	2 / 2 / 2
	8 Assessment of the learning success/ progress.	0 / 2 (2) / 2 (2)	2 / 2 / 2	2 / 2 / 2	2 / 2 / 2	0 / 2 / 2	2 / 0 / 1
Economic Dimension	**9** Sustainable financial planning.	0 / 0 (2) / 1 (2)	1 / 0 / 0	2 / 0 / 2	2 / 2 / 0	0 / 2 / 0	0 / 0 / 2
	10 Cost structures and budgeting.	0 / 1 (2) / 1 (2)	2 / 0 / 0	2 / 1 / 1	2 / 2 / 0	0 / 2 / 0	0 / 0 / 2

---

[28] ISO 9000:2000, details of ISO 10017 are indicated in brackets.
[29] DIN-PAS 1032:1, details of DIN-PAS 1037 are indicated in brackets.

Dimensions	Commonly agreed quality dimensions that are addressed by the indicated quality management approaches	Field 1 EFQM ISO[28] DIN[29]	Field 2 FCoP IHEP IITT	Field 3 DETC eduQua QAA	Field 3 EQUIS AACSB A-MBA	Field 3 Comenius eQcheck ASTD	Field 4 EureleA Digita Medida
Technological Dimension	⑪ Planning and implementation of the technological infrastructure	0 0 (0) 2 (1)	2 2 0	2 0 2	0 0 2	0 2 0	0 0 2
Technological Dimension	⑫ Reliability, usability and accessibility of the e-learning software used.	0 0 (0) 2 (0)	1 2 2	0 0 0	0 0 2	2 2 2	2 2 2
Technological Dimension	⑬ Reusability of the technological environment and learning contents.	0 0 (0) 2 (0)	0 0 2	0 0 1	0 0 0	0 2 2	0 1 0
Organisational Dimension	⑭ Organisation and support services for teachers and/ or learners	1 2 (2) 2 (2)	2 2 2	1 2 2	1 2 2	0 2 2	0 0 2
Organisational Dimension	⑮ Qualification and competency development for teachers and staff.	2 2 (2) 1 (2)	0 2 2	2 2 0	2 2 2	0 2 0	2 0 1
Organisational Dimension	⑯ Continuous quality improvement and responsiveness towards students' and teachers' complaints.	2 2 (2) 2 (2)	1 2 2	1 2 2	2 2 2	0 1 0	2 0 2
Cultural Dimension	⑰ Implementation and keeping momentum for the innovation process.	2 0 (0) 1 (0)	0 2 0	2 1 1	1 2 0	0 0 0	1 0 2
Cultural Dimension	⑱ Engagement of employees, teachers, and incentives.	2 1 (1) 0 (2)	0 2 0	0 2 0	0 0 1	0 0 0	0 0 2

Caption: 0 = no such nomination, 1 = partial nomination, 2 = explicit nomination

7.5   Conclusion

As Gonon correctly concludes in his overview on quality management approaches in the Swiss educational sector, there is no single best quality management system that can be used all the time and in any context (Gonon, 1998, p. 88). Hence, a systematic view on existing quality approaches revealed some basic insights in respect to strengths and limitations of approaches that support the planning of a quality management system ('Plan'), guide the implementation of e-learning ('Do'), provide for an evaluation framework for solutions ('Check'), and competitively compare different solutions ('Compare').

So different the forms of quality management frameworks and approaches may be, their core quality concepts and understandings come closer and closer to each other. Almost all observed quality management approaches do believe that interactive learning is important for the quality of e-learning. None of the education oriented quality approaches denied learning goals and pedagogic concepts to be important for a high quality e-learning offering, just to give two examples. Thus, can we conclude that it does not matter which quality management approach to use because they all are the same anyway? Of course not, once the fog of mystery has lifted from the 'black box' quality management approaches, we get aware of much difference in the professionalism by which the commonly targeted quality goals are implemented and operationalised. And that's exactly where we have to start working with existing approaches!

8 The quality mark e-learning: Developing process- and product-oriented quality

Thomas Lodzinski, Jan M. Pawlowski

University of Duisburg-Essen, Germany

Quality Marks intend to improve the quality of organisations and/ or products and services by certification. However, the scope, objectives, and outcomes vary. Therefore, it is necessary to match the objectives of a quality mark with the requirements of an educational organisation. Sometimes, the only outcome of a quality mark is the marketing effect. However, quality marks can start and maintain a quality development process in organisations. As an example, we present the Quality Mark e-learning (Qualitätssiegel e-learning, QSEL) as an example of a holistic quality mark. This quality mark analyses the quality of organisations and its products and services. In this article, we show the requirements of the quality mark and how this process can lead to a change process. The objective is to establish a learning, quality-aware organisation.

8.1 Introduction

Quality marks are a popular method to assure the quality of products and services. However, they vary in their scope, applicability, and their usefulness. This means that quality marks do not always meet the quality requirements of organisations and their customers. Therefore it is necessary to analyse the scope of quality marks and the benefits and added value for organisations using them.

In this article, we will describe the Quality Mark e-learning (Qualitätssiegel e-learning, QSEL) as an example of a holistic quality mark. After a review and analysis of existing quality marks for learning, education, and training, in particular e-learning, we identify the main requirements for a harmonised, adaptable approach which can be used in various contexts. QSEL follows a descriptive, adaptable approach increasing transparency of processes, products, and services in the field of learning, education, and training. Even though QSEL contains specific components for e-learning it can be applied to face-to-face settings as well.

We will describe the main principles, concepts, and categories of the quality mark and show first experiences. We conclude with an outlook on future activities, specifically in the field of quality standards.

8.2   Quality marks for e-learning

A quality mark is an instrument to assure quality by a certification by a well accepted certification body. In general, quality marks also cover a variety of approaches: some quality marks certify the quality of organisations, some are limited to the certification of products, such as courses.

A quality mark therefore only covers certain aspects of quality. This means, it is necessary to prove if the scope of a quality mark meets the demand on an organisation and its customers. In this article, we demonstrate the scope of different quality marks. As an example of a holistic quality mark we present the Quality Mark e-learning (QSEL), covering a wide range of quality aspects.

8.3   Requirements for a quality mark

In the last years, quality has gained more and more attention in the field of learning, education, and training (Ehlers, Hildebrandt, Goertz, Pawlowski, 2005). Providers, intermediaries, and customers request flexible and practical solutions to manage, assure, and measure quality. Quality marks are a popular approach in the field of quality. On the one hand, quality marks provide guidelines and recommendations for processes as well as products. On the other hand, quality marks are used for marketing and trust-building purposes.

> *Quality Mark:* A quality mark is an instrument to assure quality by a certification by a well accepted certification body. Quality marks also cover a variety of approaches, ranging from the quality of organisations to the quality of products, such as courses.

An analysis has shown that a variety of quality approaches are either used or considered for use. A survey was done by the European Quality Observatory (Ehlers, Hildebrandt, Goertz, Pawlowski, 2005) to determine which quality approaches are used in Europe and what the different requirements are on the European level. This survey showed that various quality strategies and concepts (N=650) are used in European e-learning:

Table 8-1: Quality approaches in organisations

Quality Concept	Approach used or considered for use (N=650)
ISO 9000	127
EFQM Excellence Model	51
SCORM	38
TQM	25
Public Available Specification 1032-1 of DIN	23
AFNOR, Code of Practice	19
AICC	19
BAOL Quality Mark	12
Learning Object Metadata	12
EQO-Analysis Model	11
IMS-Learning Design	9

Source: Ehlers, Hildebrandt, Goertz, Pawlowski, 2005

This result also shows a huge variety of choices and alternatives for organisations who consider using a quality approach or quality mark. Even learning technology standards are considered as quality approaches even though they only focus on assuring quality in regard to interoperability. This variety of approaches illustrates the need to have an instrument specifically designed for e-learning which can be adapted to the needs of an organisation. Such an instrument should cover a wide range of quality aspects and the possibility for organisations to use the aspects in which they want to develop quality. As an example, one organisation might only want to improve its course design while a different organisation might want to include e-learning quality on a strategical level. Therefore, when choosing a quality mark an organisation should clearly state what their quality requirements are. As a next step they should choose a quality mark meeting those needs.

To illustrate this decision problem, we present selected quality marks and their different focuses:

- The efmd Certification for e-learning (CEL) (European Foundation for Management Development 2004a, 2004b, Euler, Seufert, Wirth, 2004) is a quality mark focusing on managing and ensuring quality for management programs in Higher Education. It provides criteria, recommendations, and indicators for processes as well as products of e-learning. It is limited to the domain of business schools (MBAs) and programs using more than 20% of e-learning.
- The Gütesiegel e-learning (Bruder, Offenbartl, Osswald, Sauer, 2004) focuses on products, such as courses and modules. It provides a comprehensive list of criteria for assessing quality.
- The Quality Mark of ArtSet LQW (Zech, 2003) provides a framework for institutions mainly based on self-assessment and one external audit. It covers a variety of components, from strategies to products, aiming at training institutions.

- The criteria of WebKollegNRW (WebKolleg NRW, 2003) define criteria which have to be fulfilled to submit (Blended Learning) materials to a repository/ educational portal. These criteria are minimum requirements for courses and modules.
- Several quality standards (DIN, 2004a; ISO/IEC 2005; CEN/ISSS, 2003a, b) provide frameworks for quality which have to be adapted, e.g., concerning quality objectives, methods, or criteria. They can serve as a guideline to develop individual approaches but do not contain recommendations or procedures.

Based on an analysis of existing approaches we have defined the following principles for a quality mark:

- *Transparency:* The quality mark shall provide means to inform all stakeholders about the quality of processes, products and services. It will not prescribe concepts, but describe the way organisations act to achieve high quality solutions.
- *Learning orientation:* the quality mark should contribute to a better learning experience
- *Holistic approach:* The quality mark shall include concepts to ensure quality for processes (e.g., design, development, evaluation), products (e.g., modules, platforms), and services (e.g., support, administration). It shall cover all levels of quality development, from quality awareness and strategies to quality of learning materials.
- *Adaptability:* The quality mark shall provide methods to adapt the concept to the needs of an organisation.
- *Extensibility:* The quality mark should be extensible taking into account new concepts, technologies, or innovations.
- *Quality development:* The quality mark should lead to a continuous quality development in organisations. It shall not focus on maintaining the current state but aims at continuously improving quality.
- *Participation:* Quality is seen as a negotiation process between all stakeholders. It shall ensure participation on all levels.
- *Harmonisation:* The quality mark does not aim at developing new solutions. It should take existing practices and quality marks into account.
- *Standardisation:* The quality mark should be based on recent standards, such as ISO/IEC 19796-1 or DIN PAS 1032-1.

Following these principles, a quality mark needs to be generic enough to serve a variety of scenarios, but is flexible to fulfill the individual requirements of organisations.

8.4   Quality mark e-learning

The Quality Mark e-learning (Qualitätssiegel e-learning, QSEL) combines both, process- and product orientation and takes existing quality marks into account. Products and services should not be analysed separately without taking production, realisation and the organisational context into consideration. Therefore, the QSEL quality mark comprises two main: *Quality of educational organisations* and *Quality of components*.

8.4.1   Quality of educational organisations

The quality of educational organisations contains quality development concepts for an organisation, including its vision, strategy, processes, and results. One of the main focuses is the analysis of processes related to the conception, development, use, and optimisation of learning environments. To reach consistency with other process-oriented quality marks, this part takes the several important approaches into account: the EFQM model and it's application in the quality mark of the British Association for Open Learning (2001), ArtSet LQW2 (Zech, 2003), and CEL (European Foundation for Management Development 2004a, 2004b). Accordingly, the following categories have been identified:

1. Policy and Strategy
2. Management
3. Resources
4. Processes
5. Learner-orientation
6. Staff management and -contentment
7. Outward appearance/ Innovation
8. Results

The following table shows the main organisational components of the quality mark.

Table 8-2: Main components of QSEL

Category	Components	Sample Instruments
Policy and Strategy	Strategy Mission statement Definition of successful Learning and e-learning External Transparency Internal Transparency	Existence of a Strategy concept Defined and published mission statement Definition of successful learning and e-learning Proof of publication for strategy concept and mission statement Defined procedure for mission statement development

Category	Components	Sample Instruments
Management	Leadership Fields of Leadership Development planning Communication Quality Reporting and Controlling	Management concept includes: - Concept for target agreements and result control - Organisational concept - Concept for quality management - Participative development planning - Communication concept
Resources	Finances Infrastructure Materials Staff	Financial program and control instruments for budget monitoring Program of infrastructure and -development Index of Materials Staff list Staff development program
Processes	Processes Sub-processes Program information Requirement inquiry General framework Concept Production Rollout Realisation Evaluation Optimisation	Documentation of Processes and sub-processes Model for workplace and procedure descriptions Standardised descriptions of educational program and courses Concept for requirement inquiry Concept for general framework determination Documentation of conceptual design for educational offerings Production concept Rollout concept Concept for realisation and use Evaluation concept Optimisation concept
Learner-orientation	Learning processes Learners' Participation Information Service	Concepts for: - evaluation and optimisation of learning processes - learners' participation - internal and external communication - service- and customer management
Staff management and -contentment	Staff-contentment Staff skills Professional training Staff participation	Concepts and systems for measuring Staff-contentment Consistent company-wide documentation and taxonomy for staff skills Staff consulting and list of relevant training actions Proof and documentation of rights and actions for staff participation

Category	Components	Sample Instruments
Outward representation/ Innovation	Outward representation Marketing Innovation	Concepts for: - public relation - marketing - monitoring and implementation of innovation
Results	Performance Net operating profit Objectives Courses	Proof of: - balance between product portfolio and strategy/ mission statement - output agreements and according control instruments - objective agreements and according control instruments - documentation and reflection of course outcomes

In the following, we outline these components and the quality development process in details.

8.4.2   Policy and strategy

The main objective is to assure the awareness and strategic embedding of education and training within an organisation's strategic planning. Quality awareness is a main success factor of quality management (Ehlers, Hildebrandt, Goertz, Pawlowski, 2005). Without the support on the strategic level, operational issues will not be successful.

Table 8-3: Example for the component policy and strategy

Component	Requirement	Instruments	Certification
Strategy	Learning is anchored within the organisation's culture	Participatory strategy development	Self assessment (self-audit); Review of the organisation's strategy (external audit)
Definition of successful Learning and e-learning	A consensual definition of „Successful Learning and e-learning" exists which was negotiated with representatives of all stakeholder groups.	Document/ Documentation about „successful Learning and e-learning"	Self assessment (self-audit); Review of the concept (external audit)

8.4.3   Management

The main objective of this category is to ensure successful action of the management. Organisational quality mainly depends on successful management. Diverse organisational concepts should be consistent, related to each other, and should be continuously updated. Therefore, all management processes should be clearly defined and ratable.

Table 8-4: Example for the component management

Component	Requirement	Instruments	Certification
Leadership	A concept for declaration of objectives and for monitoring of results exists	Management concept	Self assessment (self-audit); Review of the management concept (external audit)
Quality	A concept for quality management exists, which integrates all stakeholders and contains concerns of politics, planning, control, protection and optimisation	Quality management concept	Self assessment (self-audit); Methodological Review of the quality management concept (external audit)

8.4.4   Resources

The main objective of this category is to draw attention on the adequate allocation of material and human resources to ensure financial and personal sustainability for educational products and services. In a separate process, the material and human resources programs are reviewed.

Table 8-5: Example for the component resources

Component	Requirement	Instruments	Certification
Finances	Proof of an existing financial program which ensures financial sustainability for running educational offerings	Financial program and control instruments for budget monitoring	Self assessment (self-audit); Review of the financial program and control instruments for budget monitoring (external audit)
Staff	A Staff list and a Staff development plan exist	Staff list Staff development program	Self assessment (self-audit); Review of the staff list and the staff development program (external audit)

8.4.5   Processes

The main objective of this category is a precise description of all processes of the e-learning-Lifecycle in the organisation. From the identification of educational demand, the conceptual design and rollout to the final optimisation, all processes should be transparently described.

Table 8-6: Example for the component processes

Component	Requirement	Instruments	Certification
Realisation	A concept for realisation and use of an educational offer exists	Concept for realisation and use	Self assessment (self-audit); Review of the concept for realisation and use (external audit)
Evaluation	A concept for methodical analysis of the use and excellence of educational offerings exists	Evaluation concept	Self assessment (self-audit); Review of the evaluation concept (external audit)

8.4.6   Learner-orientation

The main objective of this category is to draw focus on learners' needs and participation in educational processes: The results of learning processes, services, information and participative action are included as an integral part into the optimisation process of the whole organisation. Beyond this, concepts for quality improvement of learner related information- and service activities are elaborated and verified.

Table 8-7: Example for the component learner-orientation

Component	Requirement	Instruments	Certification
Service	A concept for customer service- consulting- and management-activities exists	Service concept	Self assessment (self-audit); Review of the concept for customer service- consulting- and management-activities (external audit)
Learners´ participation	Learners actively take part in the design of educational processes (regarding objectives, matters, methods, materials, competences and the definition of learning success)	Concept for learners´ participation	Self assessment (self-audit); Review of the documentation of conjoint development for objectives, aimed competence, contents, materials, methods in terms of conformance with strategy and mission statement of the organisation (external audit)

8.4.7   Staff management

The main objective of this category is to reveal the skills and potentials of the working staff and to ensure their participation. To reach organisational success, professionally trained staff is needed. Therefore, guidelines for standardised competence classification, measurement of staff-contentment and individual professional training are examined.

Table 8-8: Example for the component staff management

Component	Requirement	Instruments	Certification
Professional training	Staff members are counseled and informed about professional training offerings and continuously take part in professional training activities	Staff consulting concept and list of relevant training actions	Self assessment (self-audit); Review of the staff consulting concept and the list of relevant training actions (external audit)
Staff skills	Textual, methodical and social staff skills are documented, continuously updated and enhance the competence field of the organisation. Proof of analysed skill overviews which form a starting point for human resources development	Consistent company-wide documentation and taxonomy for staff skills	Self assessment (self-audit); Review of the consistent company-wide documentation and taxonomy for staff skills (external audit)

8.4.8   External appearance/innovation

The main objective of this category is to define processes for innovation monitoring and meaningful integration of organisational, technological and didactical advances. Secondly, a consistent concept for cooperation, marketing and adequate representation of the organisation should exist.

Table 8-9: Example for the component innovation

Component	Requirement	Instruments	Certification
Public Relations	A concept for public relation and outward representation exists	Concept for public relation and outward representation	Self assessment (self-audit); Review of the concept for public relation and outward representation (external audit)
Innovation	Development of organisational, technological and didactical aspects is monitored. A development concept exists for implementation of organisational, technological and didactical innovation.	Concepts for monitoring and implementation of innovation	Self assessment (self-audit); Review of market monitoring provisions and the strength of innovation implementation (external audit).

8.4.9   Results

The main objective of this category is to create awareness for the need of continuous development of the organisation considering both, financial and educational outcomes. Defined and measurable outcomes directly lead to follow-up actions and improvement procedures.

Table 8-10: Example for the component results

Component	Requirement	Instruments	Certification
Performance	The products and services offered are concurrent to the strategy and the mission statement of the organisation	Proof of balance between product portfolio and strategy/ mission statement	Self assessment (self-audit); Review of the balance between product portfolio and strategy/ mission statement (external audit)
Net operating profit	The net operating profit relates to the objectives and was achieved concurrent to the strategy and the mission statement of the organisation	Proof of output agreements and according control instruments	Self assessment (self-audit); Review of output agreements and according control instruments (external audit)

The presented categories help to ensure quality in all parts of an organisation covering a variety of aspects. It is also possible to only certify selected areas (such as processes or components). However, the main goal of the quality mark is to start and maintain an awareness-building process within an educational organisation. This process can be started using a quality mark. However, the process is a continuous ongoing process which can even change the culture of organisations towards a learning organisation. As a result, quality should not be seen as additional work, but be an integral part of everybody's daily operations.

8.4.10   Quality of components

This section of the QSEL quality mark inspects the components of services and products of an educational organisation (such as e-learning courses or learning management systems). QSEL is based on criteria of different approaches, such as WebKollegNRW (WebKollegNRW, 2003) and Gütesiegel e-learning (Bruder, Offenbartl, Osswald, Sauer, 2004), as well as the reference criteria of DIN PAS 1032-1 (DIN, 2004a).

The components are analysed based on the criteria. However, when analyzing a component the processes to produce a component should always be analysed as well. As an example, when analyzing an e-learning module, the design and development processes should be analysed as well.

The criteria cover products as well as services of e-learning (e.g., modules, platforms, support services) and include the following items:

1. Learning objectives
2. Textual design
3. Didactical design
4. Roles and activities
5. Organisational design
6. Technical design
7. Use of media
8. Communication alternatives and modes
9. Testing and Examination
10. Maintenance and care

To provide elaborated quality assurance for the above mentioned items, the component criteria are divided in three sections:

- Common Criteria
- Learning management systems (LMS)
- Courses/ Modules

The following table (table 8-11) shows the main component-related units of the quality mark. In total, 86 are examined. Table contains only examples of components and examples of adequate sample instruments which are checked in the certification process by the audit-team.

Table 8-11: Sample criteria for components

Category	Components	Sample Instruments
Common Criteria	Didactical design Use of media	Existence of a didactical concept Proof of conformity with software ergonomic standards
	Tracking	Existence of tools for tracking action and user efforts
	Communication alternatives and modes	Existence of different communication alternatives to communicate with the learner
	Maintenance and care	Continuous and closing evaluation Existence of textual and technical support
Learning management systems (LMS)	General	Existence of interfaces for system expansion action
	Function	Proof of ability to integrate external tools
	Modularisation	Proof of ability to integrate additional modules and media objects
	Information	Existence of documentation and manuals

Category	Components	Sample Instruments
Courses	Learning targets	Existence of defined learning targets which were developed in participation of the learners
	Textual design	Proof of up-to-dateness of the course topics
	Didactical design	Use of different didactical methods if reasonable
	Roles and activities	Support for active and proactive learning Specified roles for each group of stakeholders
	Organisational design	Advice and support prior to course-start
	Technical design	Use of technical standards (e.g., SCORM, LOM, Learning Design) Course is designed modularly
	Communication alternatives and modes	Coaching and support through different communication channels (e-mail, voice, fax, forum)
	Testing and Examination	Flexible examination disposition and defined periods for publication of examination results
	Information	Existence of published information concerning main facts of the education program
	Billing	Existence of e-payment options and information about payment modalities
	Certification	Existence of certification options

The component-related categories presented above ease the process of component certification by providing general as well as specific criteria. Through the persistent use of an elaborated vocabulary, the component-certification process becomes transparent. Together with the organisational components, the described criteria contribute to a multifaceted view on both, the organisations operative and strategic e-learning alignment and contribute to assist the organisations' continuous learning development.

8.4.11   Certification workflow

The certification procedure consists of well defined workflows to achieve the QSEL quality mark. It is presented in the proximate chart and described briefly in the following sections. The certification focuses on facilitating quality development, rather than a strict and inflexible auditing.

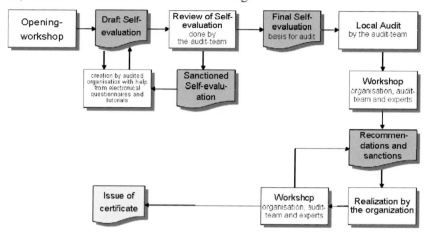

Fig. 8-1: Certification of QSEL

The following main steps show the principles of the certification:

- Opening workshop: When the initial criteria are met, the applying organisation enters the certification procedure which starts with an opening workshop. The certification process is explained and a common view on quality is build. Additionally, the individual review process is prepared.
- Self-evaluation: During the step of self-evaluation, the organisation is analysed internally, creating a "self-report" which contains both organisational and component-related statements. This step is supported by a set of electronic questionnaires and tutorials which cover aspects of existence, accessibility, storage and deployment of the information needed.
- Review of Self-evaluation: The results of the self-evaluation are handed over to the experts of the audit-team and reviewed. Improvement suggestions are made by the audit team.
- Local Audit: The Local Audit session is realised as a meeting of the audit-team experts with the organisation's staff where the organisation is examined to meet the requirements of the QSEL quality mark. This procedure helps to identify the strengths and to reveal potential optimisation fields of the organisation and the audited educational components.

- Workshops: The existing and future potentials identified in the Local Audit session are discussed in workshops with particular experts from the certification agency, the audit-team and the persons in charge within the educational organisation to be certified. This commission discusses future concepts, visions and improvement actions for the organisation. Concrete tasks are agreed on to improve the organisation.
- Issue of certificate: Finally, the certificate is issued and awarded to the audited organisation which is then authorised to call itself "QSEL-certified".
- Evaluation and quality assurance of the certification process.
- From the opening workshop to the certification, the process is monitored permanently by experts from the certification.

8.5   First experiences

A prototype of QSEL has been evaluated in expert workshops and two prototype certification processes. The main results are:

- QSEL is a starting point for organisational change. Changes towards a quality culture and increased quality awareness have been reached in all organisation levels involved.
- Long term changes might be reached but cannot yet be validated.
- The efforts to fulfill the requirements of QSEL are reasonable compared to expected benefits.
- The flexible structure (such as allowing different instruments and methods) leads to various solutions to improve quality.
- Organisations not involved in quality development need intense support by experts. The workshops clarified open questions and led to organisational changes.
- Workshops led to more organisational changes than the audit when the organisation was already involved in quality development.
- Sometimes, huge organisational changes are needed (e.g. innovation, or staff participation) which cannot be fulfilled within the short time period of certification.

The results show that QSEL can lead to organisational changes and improvements if the organisation is willing to adopt new concepts and change towards a learning, quality-oriented organisation. However, long-term improvements need to be evaluated in the future.

8.6   Summary and future developments

In this article, we have shown quality marks for e-learning, in particular the holistic, harmonised approach of the Quality Mark e-learning, QSEL. QSEL is directed to improve the quality of an organisation, as well as its products and services. The quality mark will be submitted to standardisation organisations in order to further harmonise quality marks and to ease the orientation for e-learning providers and customers.

9 Competency-based quality securing of e-learning (CQ-E)

John Erpenbeck

Humboldt-University Berlin, Germany

Lutz P. Michel

MMB Institute for Applied Media and Competence Research, Germany

Throughout the 20th century professional education and training concentrated on teaching occupational qualifications and skills. Only in the „post-fordistic" era competencies of employees – e.g. their personal capacities, their ability to learn self-guided, etc. – came into focus.

The article deals with crucial questions of measuring and making up a balance of professional competencies – in contrast to skills and qualifications.

First, the fundamental difference between skills and qualifications on the one hand side and competencies on the other hand is discussed in short. With this theoretical understanding in mind, the different forms of learning in small and mid-sized companies are analysed on a profound empirical basis.

The following part of the contribution deals with most common methods and procedures of measuring professional competencies and outlines an actual, theoretically and methodologically sophisticated approach to make up balances of competencies.

Finally, the article sketches a proposal for a special model of securing the quality of formal as well as informal learning, based on the concept of competencies.

9.1 Introduction

The role of evaluation, security and development of competencies within occupational and operational activities is increasingly important. Adequate quality of required and procured competencies can only be secured:

- If competencies can clearly be distinguished from necessary expertise, as well as from the likely indispensable abilities and qualifications, and when this can be put into reference with e-learning.
- If it can clearly be analysed, which type of learning enables which quality security based on the concept of competencies, and which function e-learning will have in this process.
- If it is clearly outlined, how competencies are characterised and evaluated. It should then be demonstrated with the help of examples, how elaborated methods of competence evaluation can be connected with e-learning.
- If from the previously mentioned analysis a concept for, based on competencies can be deduced.

This program will be analysed in more depth within the following disquisition.

9.2   E-learning and the consignment of know-how, abilities, qualifications and competencies

Know-how, e.g. knowledge in a detailed sense, abilities, qualifications are not to be equated with competencies, they are not sufficient for competent acting. Competencies require skills, abilities and qualifications, while being much more than that. This is shown in figure 9-1.

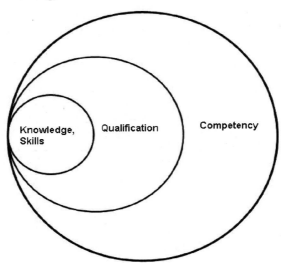

Fig. 9-1: Showing the relation between know-how (knowledge in a detailed sense), abilities, qualifications and competencies

Especially important is the relation between qualifications and competencies. Development of competencies requires a high level of qualification. Highly competent persons are always qualified at the same time.

Nevertheless, highly qualified persons might be fully incompetent. Competencies are founded on qualifications, they take them for granted – and still are more than that and different. We can, with Arnold (2000), compare qualifications and competencies as follows:

Table 9-1: Regarding the relation between quality an competency

Qualification	Competency
Qualification always intends to serve a given purpose. Therefore it is *externally organised*.	Competency includes the ability of *self-organisation*.
Qualification is limited to the compliance of concrete requests and/ or requirements. Therefore it is *object-related*.	Competency is *subject-related*.
Qualification is restricted to immediate activity-related knowledge, abilities and skills.	Competency refers to the entire person. Therefore competency pursues a holistic demand.
Qualification relates to elements of individual abilities, which can be certified within a judgement context	Learning competencies open the possibility to issue-focussed learning opposite to the necessities to arrange for the interposition of qualities. Competency includes the variety of all individual acting dispositions.
Qualification is disorienting from the classical ideal of education (Humboldt's „proportional education of all resources") by focussing on utilisable abilities and skills	Competency is orienting towards the classical ideal of education using a new, contemporary way.

Source: Arnold, 2000

Controlling concepts for education, with the intention of quality assurance for learning in general, are obliged to not lose sight of the interposition of know-how, skills, qualifications and competencies. Valuation of the individual learning propositions (curricular aspect), of the learning process (procedural aspect) and of the learning results, which are manifested within mental and physical acting (performance aspect) are to be considered.

The emphasis can be put on the aspect of available propositions when looking at the know-how, and the controlling actually verifies the difference between proposal and memory contents, while the main focus of skills rests with the procedural aspect, and the difference between the standardised and the real process of acting is valuated.

Qualification deals with the ability to reach a given aim; therefore with the difference between intended acting result/ reached acting result.

Competencies also stand in context with acting results, but these are self-directed, and reached by self-organisation.

They therefore are subject to the valuation of the difference between various acting results, which can be reached by creative means, and which are not pre-defined in detail. Competency manifests within the performance.

Figure 9-2 symbolises the connections.

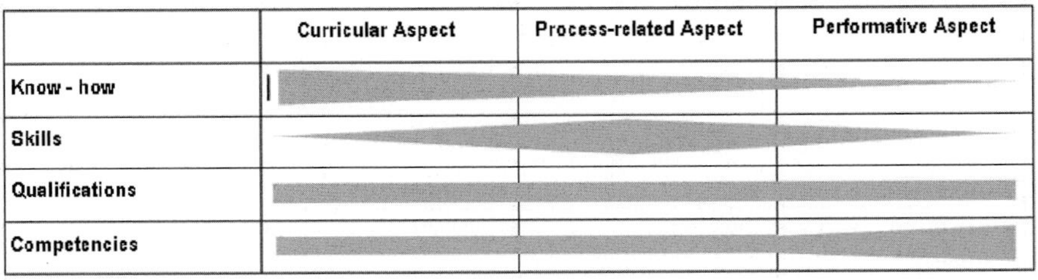

	Curricular Aspect	Process-related Aspect	Performative Aspect
Know - how			
Skills			
Qualifications			
Competencies			

Fig. 9-2: Emphasised aspects within the controlling of education regarding know-how, skills, qualifications and competencies

> "We understand competencies as evolutionary grown, generalised self-organisation dispositions of complex, adaptive systems – such as human individuals, or corporative actors – for reflexive, creative acting with the intention of problem solving focussed on general classes of complex, selectively important situations (paths)" (Kappelhoff, 2004).

Competencies therefore can be described as self-organisation dispositions. An example shall illustrate the term's meaning within that sense:

"You want to get to know Brazil together with some friends and fellows on your own account. You rent a car and start driving at random. Without aim (contrary to *self-directed* with a predefined aim) – but with the intention to get some understanding of the country and its people.

You want to discover something new for humanity: Indian relicts, people who never came into touch with our civilisation, unknown animals or plants. You organise your route from beginning to its end on your own and manage many situations of chaotic decisions, whereas, only by a fraction of an inch, the decisions could have been passed completely different. By this process, you write your very own and not repeatable story. You cannot rely at all on your qualities – in the wilderness you have no usage of acquired educational degrees or certifications. Your know-how and knowledge of methods only serves for the background, so that you will not need to give up when your engine fails working, when illnesses are approaching, when you lose your direction; all this must be embedded within a big treasure of experiences, motives and hopes – therefore it needs to represent *professional-methodical competencies.*

Additionally, you need a pertinent portion of self-confidence, courage, creativity – namely *personal competencies.* You and the people you meet need to be able to stick together no matter what situation you will be in, or at least you need to be able to tolerate them. You need persuasiveness, cooperativeness and candidness –

therefore social-communicative competencies.

Last but not least, all professional, personal and social competencies are not of any use, if you are not able to accomplish your imaginations and plans with strong will. Therefore you need *activity and accomplishment competencies.*

All this is not only valid for acting and learning in the Brazilian wilderness. It applies to all learning and acting under the conditions of a risk community – a community possessing numerous political, economical and social processes, which are complex and dynamical.

We are not only in need of capabilities, which enable us to navigate from a clearly defined start situation – a task, a problem – to a clearly defined end situation – the fulfilment of the task, the solution to the problem. These are rather part of much broader abilities, namely to develop novelties creatively and innovatively – solutions, which will not only surprise the user, but also the developer.

Generally, we deal with abilities of self-organised thinking and acting: With reference to oneself, (P: personal competencies), with more or less impulsion to transfer plans into acting (A: activity related competencies), based on professional and methodical knowledge, experience and know-how (F: professional-methodical competencies) and usage of ones own communicative and cooperative possibilities (S: social-communicative competencies)."

By this, a central problem of e-learning becomes apparent: *Know-how* can be easily and effectively transported via this new medium. *Skills* can be transmitted via e-learning, in case they deal with information processing, since then the subject and the medium become identical. Development of other skills, precision mechanical for example, requires a highly developed and with the learning media coupled measurement body in order to be successful.

The pure description of skills, for example as "tips and tricks", supported by multimedia displays, can be helpful, but is no substitute for own experiences, which the skills are based on.

For qualification, e-learning becomes more and more important, because the entire target-oriented thinking and activity process can be mapped and therefore its compliance can be evaluated. Professional and methodical competencies are more than know-how and methodical knowledge. They include experience, creativity and an open mind for novelties. Subjects belonging to the areas experience and expertise, can only be acquainted by ones own acting, within autonomous problem solving processes. This can be combined with activities on and with the computer, of course, but there it does not exhaust itself in any way. More problematic even is the question, whether personal or social-communicative competencies can be distributed via e-learning. Those competencies always include elements of valuation elements which are gained by learning processes depending on cultural differences (Schmidt, 2005).

Values are not learned in the sense of knowledge, but are gained through mental processes of dissonance and *labilisation* (Erpenbeck, Weinberg, 1993). It is difficult to transfer those via the media of e-learning (Erpenbeck, 2004).

It becomes more and more important to arrange for a transfer of competencies, combined with the quality security within learning processes occurring in the modern risk community, especially since economical and political developments change faster and faster, and chaotically.

This is reason for two questions: Where, within a modern enterprise, does one need the presence and/ or the transfer of competencies at all? And: How can one analyse available competencies, and how can one discover deficits of competencies, as well as how can one eliminate them with the help of e-learning?

It is not intended to declare any necessary professional training, any important qualification as development of competencies, as it might be fashionable at present[30]. Quite the contrary: Taking illustration 9-1 seriously, the requirement of up to date development of competencies goes hand in hand with the requirement of solid training of know how and skills, as well as of founded qualification.

We can reveal this well by viewing the various forms of learning which are applied in modern enterprises.

9.3   E-learning within the context of job-related operational learning forms

Within different branches of economy and different job groups, we find different ways of learning. Besides a range of comprehensively valid forms of job-related learning, particularly innovative branches of economy and jobs which are affected by them show important differences within the learning culture. A widely arranged study of this matter which was performed for the BMBF was firstly published in 2002 (Heyse et al., 2002).

Within this study, an extensive census among the senior management of three particularly innovative branches (IT/ Software, multimedia- and biotechnological businesses) was raised. Also, for comparison, a traditional branch (Electrical engineering business) was given the same questions. Altogether, 511 telephone interviews were held.

Job-related requirements of learning and competencies were firstly examined in the frame of this investigation, e.g. how they differ from one another, relating to tasks, jobs and branches.

That profession-related quality requirements - for example for a programmer or a marketing executive - will show differences is no surprise. But how about the competencies in a broad sense, which professionals of various activity groups should dispose of? Furthermore, the study also examined, how the employees of various job groups gain the required knowledge, and what type of knowledge – rather explicitly documented knowledge or rather implicit and person-related knowledge – is gained by the employers.

The branch- and job related cultures of learning determine the selection of the appropriate sets of learning forms. This should be illustrated with the help of the following example of the future branch IT/ Software. The following eight job

---

[30] As in former times, when qualifying was en vogue, all competency development was declared to be a development of "key-qualifications".

groups have solidified within the last three decades (index by frequency[31]):

System Programming, Marketing/ Distribution, IT-Consulting, Data Base Development, Net Administration, System Administration, Software-/ Application Development and System Analysis

Which connections can be observed between the requirements, that need to be fulfilled by the employees working in the IT-/ Software branch and their specific job- and activity groups?

To give a first empirically founded answer to this question, the referring executive managers were asked to evaluate the meaning of the *four competency* dimensions which were introduced by the interview prior to the census. How important are the following individual competencies from the view of the interviewed executive manager:

- *Person-related* competencies, as for example authenticity, personal responsibility, creativity;
- *Activity-related* competencies, as for example energy, mobility;
- *Professional-methodical* competencies, as for example know-how, conceptual strength;
- *Social-communicative* competencies, as for example communication ability, cooperative ability.

The evaluation was supported by a 4-level scale (level 1: very important; level 4: completely irrelevant; the values 2 and 3 represent different shades in between). First analysis of the answers already showed the importance of all four competencies were rated very high to high. The average rating value lies in between 1.2 and 2.0 (the theoretical maximal value was at 1.0, the minimal value at 4.0). Therefore, none of the competencies can be unnecessary. But, as a result of this first evaluation, the different shades between the values needed to be analysed.

Table 9-2: Requirements of competencies within the IT/ Software branch (this competency is „very important")

	Personal-related	Activity- related	Professional-methodical	Social-communicative
System Programming	55	40	62	36
Marketing/ Distribution	78	63	36	78
IT-Consulting	77	45	62	60
Data Base Development	43	25	73	32
Net Administration	53	44	53	37
System Administration	36	40	84	28
Software-/ Application development	21	35	79	22
System Analysis	53	42	74	53

Source: Heyse, Erpenbeck, Michel, 2002

---

[31] Only vocations and professional activities which can be found in at least 3 percent of the companies have been added to this list.

As expected, the *importance of each individual competency* for the eight most important IT professions was *stated very differently*. Within the following, we focus on the results for the strongest characteristic ("very important"), because here we find a wider spectrum of differences than within average values. The question to be raised is: For which activity groups is the percentage of employees in personal management, which rated one of the four competencies as "very important", very high? The following table shows all four competencies in an overview.

If one looks closely at the strongest peculiarities it becomes clear that six activity profiles at each one competency reach a value bigger than 70 percent. This means that an obvious majority of the personnel administrative employees – namely about 3 of 4 queried persons – sees an indispensable prerequisite for a qualified professional performance in this.

This is valid for the professional-methodical competency of *system administrators* (84% "very important"), *software/ application developers* (79%), *system analysts* (74%) and *data base developers* (73%), as well as for personal-related competencies of *IT consultants* (77%) or *marketing/ distribution professionals* (78%). For the last group, social-communicative skills also play an equally important role (78%). Within the group of *system programmers* and *net administrators* no such peculiar values exist.

If one focusses on the individual activity groups and the values which were placed here, one can differ between "one-way competent", "double-competent" and "multiple-competent" profiles.

The activity groups *system administration, software-/ application development, data base development* manifest as "one-way competent". Their qualifying foundation lies mainly in professional-methodical competencies.

System programmers and *net administrators* count as "double-competent" activity groups. For those jobs personal and professional-methodical competencies are stated as particular important to (about) the same extent.

The remaining three IT activity groups can be rated as "multiple-competent".

Respectively three of four competencies are rated as very important within those professions by a majority of the interviewed persons. Two professions receive a similar rating: activity-related competencies play a rather subordinated role for *IT consultants* and *system analysts*, while those competencies are an essential module within the set of occupational competencies for the *marketing professionals*.

In a further step, the occupation-specific meaning of formal learning (for example a conventional classroom training) and/ or of informal learning (for example a discussion with an experienced colleague) was examined. Evaluation of the answers show that the interviewed companies prefer informal learning for all IT professions. At the same time, however, it becomes obvious, that not only the competency requirements, but also the learning forms within the IT branch, clearly differ from one profession to the other (see figure 9-3).

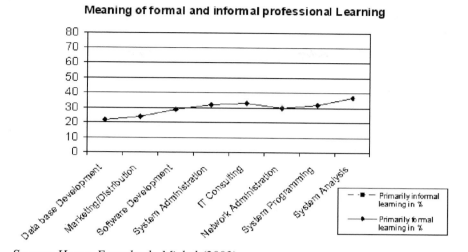

Source: Heyse, Erpenbeck, Michel (2002)

Fig. 9-3: Meaning of formal and informal professional learning within the IT-/ Software branch

The support of informal learning within the activity groups *data base development and marketing/ distribution* receive particularly high values. Traditional training measures are only rated as the most important method of competency instrumentality for a small minority of personnel administrative employees.

Less strong is the dominance of informal learning within the other six activity groups. Here, after all a third of the interviewed persons (between 29 and 37%) assign the biggest importance to formal learning.

Which role does initiative of ones own and motivation as well as self-organisation within the occupational learning of IT professionals actually play? To find the meaning of these two basic types of learning processes (externally organised vs. self-organised) for each activity group, the average values of each type were ascertained. For this, the values of respectively five learning forms of one type of learning[32] were collected and the arithmetic mean was calculated (see figure 9-4).

---

[32] Primarily externally organised learning: 1) directives (fundamentals, regulations); 2) informational events, cross company training events; 3) cross-company workshops, target-group specific workshops 4) individual information seminars; 5) training of behaviour, activity-concomitant training.

Primarily self-organised learning: 1) taking over of special tasks, participation in projects, task forces, quality circles; 2) usage of training media in one's free time; 3) individual private studies, self-chosen correspondence course, evening classes, study travels; 4) voluntary exchange of exprreriences among the colleagues in- and outside of the company; 5) non-intentional, therefore virtually incidental learning in every day's life, outside the job.

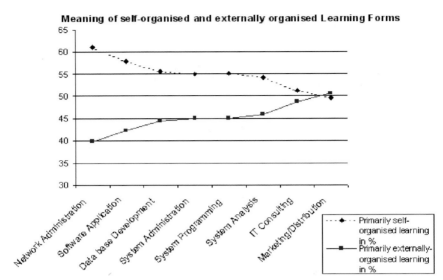

Source: Heyse, Erpenbeck, Michel, 2002

Fig. 9-4: Meaning of self-organised and externally organzied learning forms within the IT-/ Software branch

There is no IT profession which learns the same way as another one. This can be stated as a first result of the analysis of the comparison of learning types. While the primarily technical oriented activity groups (net administration; development etc.) show a definite preference of self-organised learning forms, the activity groups IT consulting, marketing/ distribution, which dealing closely customers make use of both types of learning forms. Externally organised learning, for example in seminars and workshops, possesses the same importance as self-organised learning within the process of work or in one's free time.

Product of each learning process, therefore also of the professional learning, is knowledge. We need to distinguish between two forms of professional knowledge: explicit knowledge, which means clearly defined and documented knowledge which can be transferred as such, and implicit knowledge, which is a knowledge tied to a person, in the shape of competencies, values, motivations, expertise etc. The interviewed administrative employees were asked to point out, for each activity area apparent in their company, whether rather explicit or rather implicit knowledge is needed for the profession. Analysis of the answers results in clearly different competency profiles (see figure 9-5).

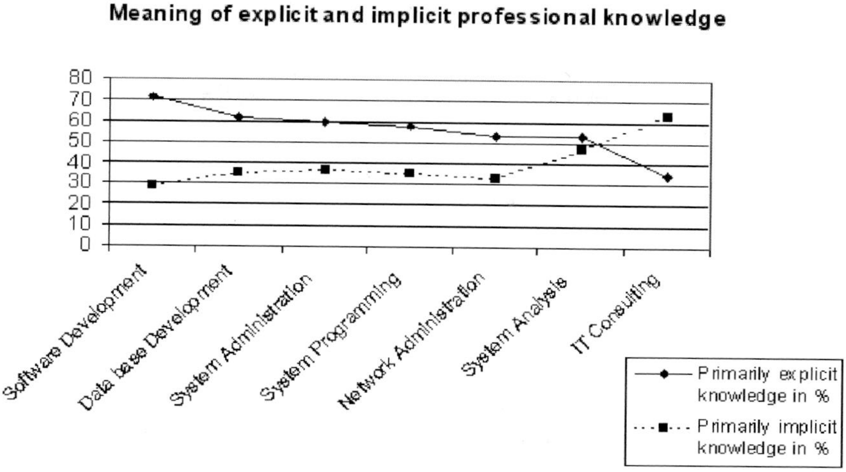

Meaning of explicit and implicit professional knowledge

Source: Heyse, Erpenbeck, Michel (2002)

Fig. 9-5: Meaning of explicit and implicit professional knowledge within the IT-/ Software branch

The illustration exemplifies clearly: For most IT-professions, the majority of the interviewed personnel experts employed within six out of eight most important activity groups back on explicit knowledge. This is valid for the primary creative activity groups *software-/ application development* (71%), *data base development* (62%), *system programming* (58%), as also for the rather operative activity groups *system administration* and *net administration* (60 and 53%). Within these activities implicit knowledge only plays a subordinated role according to the majority of the interviewed persons.

Less definite are the requirements for *system analysts*. Here as well, codified, explicit knowledge plays the most important role, however, the difference to implicit knowledge results in only 6 percent and represents therefore the smallest gap comparing all activity groups. Viewed from the knowledge perspective, the profession of a system analyst is therefore a "hybrid job". For the activity groups, dealing closely with customers, *marketing/ distribution* and *IT consulting*, implicit knowledge plays definitely the essential role (65 and 63%). Explicit knowledge is only for a third of the interviewed persons on rank one.

9.4   E-learning, competency measurement and competency training

Modern learning processes can and must at least assure the preservation, but normally also lead to extension of competencies of the learning person. Also, the on-passing of know-how, of skills and qualifications remains ineffective, if it does not result in the profit of competencies. This also holds without any restrictions for the processes of e-learning. Insofar it is possible to describe competence measurement as verification of efficiency and a touchstone of e-learning (Erpenbeck, 2004). Knowledge tests, skill checks, qualification certifications are not sufficient for the evaluation of learning results, especially results from e-learning. The learning person as well as the employer are both after all interested in the learned subject matter effecting the acting of the learning person, and that the flexibility, employability and entrepreneurship of the employee does increase. Not before the effectiveness in acting (performance) is proofed, it can be concluded, that the learning person gained abilities, dispositions, within a new, open situation, facing unclear or missing objective, to act self-organised and creatively.

Only when this can be proofed, we can state a raise of the person's competencies.

Modern methods of competency measurement must enable competency evaluations independent from whether the competencies were gained either by traditional learning processes and formally or outside such processes, therefore informally.

To measure competencies or proof them, one has – within the otherwise common variety of terminology (Haase, 2001), (Bjornavold, 2001), (Rychen, Salganik 2001) – to agree on an operational definition of the competency term. A simplifying nomination of the formerly mentioned definition summarises competencies as dispositions of self-organised acting, as self-organisation-dispositions (Erpenbeck, Rosenstiel, 2003). Within this definition, dispositions are understood as, at a definite time of acting, inner prerequisites for regulation of activities. Therefore, dispositions comprise not only individual equipment but also results of individual development (Clauss et al., 1995).

Systematics, worked out on this basis, distinguishes between *competency types* (referring to self-control strategies/ gradient strategies vs. self-organisation strategies within a closer sense/ evolution strategies); *competency classes* (referring to subject – object or object – subject relations, / (P) personal, (A) activity and accomplishment related, (F) professional-methodical and (S) social-communicative competencies); *competency groups* (methodologically referring to motivation- and personality psychology, activity- and occupational psychology, cognitive psychology and education, as well as social- and communication psychology); *competency developments* (differentiating between an *instantaneous status* and *timed development)*; *competency observation* (differentiating between *objective* and *subjective methods*); *competency research* (differentiating between *quantitative* and *qualitative methods*).

Competency measurement therefore is understood as result of the basic comprehension of *competency type, competency classes, competency groups, competency development, competency observation and competency research*. Finally, the *specific* set of competency measurement methods, which goes into action at a concrete competency measurement procedure, results only from the totality of understandings, perspectives, views, inclinations and preferences. Competency measurement therefore must be understood, in a broad sense, as a generalised transmission of competencies. Where measurements of competencies cannot be measured, we are often compelled to measure competencies assigned to activities and acting persons. Therefore very different procedures of competency measurements have to be examined, namely the

- quantitative measurement (Competency test)
- qualitative characterisation (competency passport)
- comparative description (competency biography)
- simulative analysis (flight simulator)
- evaluating observation (work samples)

Not the exactest, but the most appropriate competency measurement procedures, supplying decision supporting tools best possible in shortest time, have established within operational and educational practise. In Germany, for assessments, qualification- and recruitment tests, career consulting, personnel studies etc. a variety of competency measurement procedures of international origin (mainly from USA) as well as developed within German-speaking countries are used. The lately published "Handbuch Kompetenzmessung" (Handbook of Competency Measurement) lists the original German procedures extensively and describes them in-depth (Erpenbeck, Rosentiel, 2003). To enumerate or characterise them here would go beyond the scope of this essay.

In Germany, procedures of competency balancing, which integrate a range or all of the mentioned forms of competency transmission, which, besides tests, work samples and perhaps simulations also include qualitative and particularly biographical aspects, are still standing at their begining. While the French Bilan de Compétences and the Swiss handbook of qualification CH-Q already present established and frequently applied procedures, in Germany a first, cross-border and governmental supported balancing initiative has been started with the so called profile pass. More advanced are the profit oriented working centres for competency balancing (CeKom), which summarise quantitative procedures as KODE® (Erpenbeck, 2000) and KODE®X (Erpenbeck et al., 2001) as well as, based on the European Biography (European Comission, 2002) qualitative, biographical analysis methods.

On basis of such measurements, competencies cannot only be determined, but also developed further systematically. In this connection, hardly instructional methods, but in truth training methods are required. From competence measurement procedures, systematically procedures of *competency training* can be derived (Heyse, Erpenbeck, 1994).

The result is definite: competencies can be scientifically declared, as well as practically, they can be measured and certified successfully. Competency developments can be comprehended and illustrated. They can increasingly also be measured with the help of online-procedures (Ritter et al., 2004).

Modern competency measurements are methodically on a par with the traditional qualification certifications, but concerning the contents, always then outclassing, when dealing with abilities, which help performing in activity- and decision open situations; and additionally "more democratic" within the sense, that they do not enquire into social origin, but into social effectiveness, the real employability of individual acting capability.

As far as e-learning is not directed towards pure on-passing of fact- or methodical knowledge or focussing on calculating- or programming skills, measurement of learning effects in the sense of *competency measurement becomes essential* as well withal. This at first refers to all *professional-methodical* competencies, which in shape of probational acting without given goal, requiring experience, expertise - within a net or outside – can be evaluated. The imparted competencies can be *acquired* with appropriate above mentioned competency measurement forms either offline or online. But, *personal, social-communicative* and *activity-related* competencies can be *acquired* via e-learning only in a difficult way. This states a basic contradiction, which pervades the entire history of e-learning so far:

- On one side, the increasingly extensive usage of education- and information technologies of e-learning is an irrevocable process.
- On the other side, the development from – traditional – professional further education to professional competency development is also an irrevocable process.
- The efficiency of present education- and information technologies of e-learning does definitely not cover the performance requirements of modern professional competency development:
  - Their strength lies in the support of information gathering, calculating- and programming skills, professional- and methodical knowledge and qualifications.
  - Modern professional competency development is mainly directed towards personal, activity related and social communicative competencies. These are hardly or not at all transmittable via e-learning.

This represents a fundamental problem within times of a quickly escalating knowledge- and competency management. How far can competence development be achieved with the help of e-learning *itself*? When and where does one have to purely accept other education forms within the sense of a "blended learning"? Where are the borders of e-learning in competency transmission? Answers to such questions must be given by a modern controlling of e-learning and by endeavours for quality and standardisation of e-learning.

Initially we had determined that, when dealing with competency transmission, one has to assume a broad, rule and norms including term of knowledge. Knowledge management and competency management become factual identical, meta competencies, basis competencies (key competencies), and competencies derived from those as well as comprehensive competencies represent therefore particular knowledge in form of dispositions for self-organised acting, which kernels are constituted by values. This way, all difficulties and paradoxes of value internalisation, the acquirement of values, come into play. Since for formation of competencies value internalisation is compulsory, all quality security of learning, based on competencies, has to check up the appropriate procedures on powers of labilisation, irritation, generation of dissonances etc. (Draschoff, 2000).

This is of essential importance when personal, activity-related and social communicative competencies are distributed, and less important for transmission of professional and methodical competencies. Therefore, the question should always be, how, and to which extend can education- and information technological methods as e-learning support the internalisation of values, and with that, particularly the development of competencies in general? From the manifold of net- and multimedia based education technologies especially those are of interest, which can contribute to the internalisation of values and therefore to the development of competencies within the professional further education, within the work process as well as during free time, in the social surrounding. This leads to the following basic questions:

1. Can professional competency development and its kernel area, the self-organised learning including the internalisation of values, be supported by e-learning, and where are the borders of competency transmission supported by that media?
2. Which potential do already successfully applied e-learning approaches possess to transfer activity-related and social communicative competencies?
3. Which already successfully applied methods of competency development (particularly coaching and training procedures) can be supported or substituted by e-learning?

Thereby one has to consider that e-learning, when imparting competencies, can be applied in two ways. This is shown in the following analysis:

(A) Either e-learning programmes carry the *learning contents themselves*.

(A0) Usually this is the case when professional-methodical contents becomes transferred. This will lead to only little emotional labilisation of the user, or none at all, and therefore hardly any transfer of competency can be expected.

(A1) Or they indeed make the effort for a problem- and conflict inducing and therefore labilising design[33], which is, however, only little emotionally and motivationally accessible for the user. As a consequence, labilisation- and competency learning effects remain rather little as well.

(A2) Or, the e-learning programs offered are designed in such way, that they inspire the user with problem situations and conflicts, resulting in cognitive dissonances, so that the user becomes emotional labilised and therefore is enabled to internalise new value attitudes and thus to learn new competencies. The experiments of Lohausen-type of Dietrich Dörner have shown this very illustrative.

(B) The other form of e-learning programs examined here is the one which only serves the purpose as *medium of transport*.

(B1) Distance learning or – classes via the internet, transfer of lectures, distance consulting by experts will normally hardly produce any emotional- motivational labilisations. Though the transferred information might be highly important and represent a basis for professional-methodical competencies later, but they do hardly impart competencies on a direct way.

(B2) It is different when looking at all other arrangements where teams are competing, where the participants struggle for achievement of best results refer-

---

[33] Ibid.

ring to financial operations or to project designing tasks, but also, when looking at medially transmitted consulting activities, which bring out individual abilities and defaults. In the first case, social-communicative competencies can be learned and developed very well; in the second one, personal competencies.

The appropriate learning processes can be characterised consistently as training processes. Consequently, *competencies can only be imparted as training forms.*

A new „Handbuch Kompetenztraining"(Heyse, Erpenpeck, 2004) (Handbook of Competency Training) which has been developed for each of the 64 derived competencies of Modular Information- and Training programs (MIT), which include, as *objective* modules, definitions, training units, techniques, exercises, as *subjective* modules self-evaluation, possibilities of changing, braking, personal aims, and personal consequences.

Some of the training units also include hints on e-learning variants, but actually there are other medias of available, relating to a much stronger concentration of value- and experience of competencies, which are clearly more effective. Probably they will be mostly available within the area of blended learning (Sauter, Sauert, 2002).

Competency measurement within the sense of *certification of efficiency* of e-learning can, as a result, only be understood and practised as a form of *difference measurement*: Methods of competency transfer, where e-learning is involved in any way, but which are actually independent from e-learning, have to be placed vis-à-vis, with reference to contents, and only the additional profit of competencies can then be interpreted as such, when it has been gained by usage of the modern media.

9.5   E-learning and quality security of learning based on the concept of competencies (CQ-E)

From the results which have been developed formerly, we now find a rather clear way of procedures of quality security, of learning based on competencies within the e-learning area (CQ-E). We will finally illustrate our conclusion as a tree of decision making. Its elements are explained explicitly within the text.

Table 9-3: Competence-based quality securing of e-learning (CQ-E), schematic plan of procedures

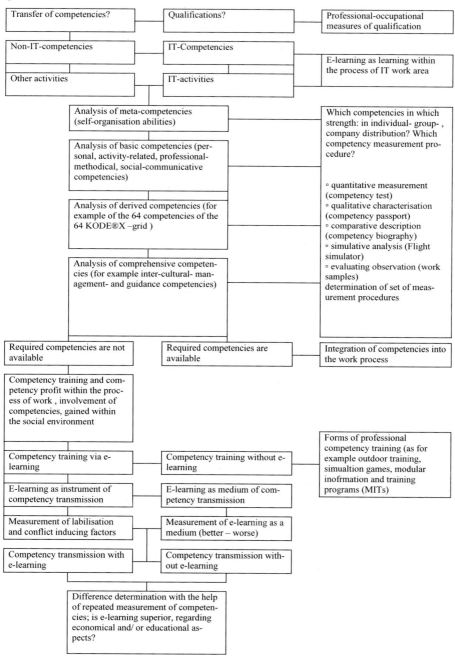

10 Quality of e-learning products

Thomas Berger

Institute of interdisciplinary Research inter.research e.V., Germany

Ulrike Rockmann

Carl von Ossietzky University Oldenburg, Germany

This contribution provides background information about the concept and the development of the Reference Quality Criteria Catalogue. The catalogue contains quality criteria for e-learning products and processes and is part of the Public Available Specification (PAS) 1032-1 of the German Institute of Standardisation, and also annexed to the ISO Standard ISO/IEC 19796-1. The criteria of the catalogue are based on relevant ISO-standards for software and multimedia user interfaces, relevant laws and regulations, and consolidated empirical findings from relevant scientific areas.

Furthermore, we provide examples how the catalogue has been used as a tool for quality assurance of e-learning products. The relationship between the process model (PAS 1032-1 and ISO/IEC 19796-1) and the reference criteria catalogue will be illustrated.

10.1 Introduction

A lot of work has been done in the field of product quality for e-learning so far. The concept presented here focuses primarily on product quality[34]. Within the framework of the development-concurrent standardisation of the DIN e.V. and in the internationally operating Information Technology Standards Committee (sub-workgroup NI-36 Learning Technology), a quality criteria catalogue for e-learning

---

[34] For recommendations on the high-quality design of the production process itself please refer to PAS 1032-1 (DIN e.V.).

products (QCC-eL; PAS 1032) has been developed.

An e-learning-product is software that is developed for learning purposes taking pedagogical, didactical and psychological aspects into account. They differ in size and extent. An e-learning product could be a small simulation, static html-pages, or online courses.

QCC-eL can be integrated into the production process as a guideline for product planning and the assessment of e-learning-products at different development stages. Furthermore, it can be used to control the quality of final e-learning-products. Therefore, QCC-eL is of interest for product developers, decision makers, and purchasers.

QCC-eL was evaluated by experts who carried out independent analyses, including extensive assessments of a total of 30 e-learning products (Rockmann, 2004).

The catalogue QCC-eL is used to describe and/ or to verify the pedagogic and didactic product characteristics, the features having an effect on learning and motivation as well as the functional product characteristics. The criteria are based on:

1. relevant ISO-standards for usability of software and multimedia user interfaces (ISO/EN/DIN 9241, 14915; see 10.2.1),
2. relevant EU and German laws and regulations (see 10.2.2), and
3. consolidated empirical findings taken from the relevant scientific areas (see 10.2.3).

The borders between these areas are fuzzy since consolidated scientific findings have now been incorporated into laws and standards. The criteria are not directed at quality assurance of the contents as this can only be provided by experts in the relevant domain/ scientific fields.

10.2   Quality criteria

10.2.1   Criteria derived from international standards

The relevant standards must be adhered to, even though they are a form of voluntary agreements and have no legal standard quality. However, since they are incorporated in laws, they have gained indirect importance. In accordance with the EU interpretation of the law, the international standard ISO 9241 thus acts as a basis for the definition of the ergonomic principles for software.

ISO 9241 deals with general principles that have to be taken into account in designing dialogues between humans and information systems. The suitability of the software for fulfilling the desired task through humans is focussed. Components of suitability are the support of learning, individualisation, conformity with user expectations, self descriptiveness, controllability, and error tolerance.

ISO 14915 establishes design principles for multimedia user interfaces, provides recommendations and requirements for the design of multimedia user interfaces and the organisation of the content. It addresses applications for professional activities such as learning and working not applications for entertainment.

ISO/EN/DIN 9241 consists of a total of 17 parts, where sections 3, 8, 10 – 17 describe the ergonomic criteria for software products (Rockmann, 2002). Whilst ISO 9241 covers the general ergonomic requirements for software, ISO/EN/DIN 14915 (parts 1-3) focuses more specifically on multimedia, although the specific topic of learning is not dealt with.

These ISO-standards are not regulated standards. In other words: the standards themselves do not specify which methods are to be used to determine whether or not standards are being met. Such an analysis therefore requires the operationalisation of the standards.

The product criteria catalogue (QCC-eL) provides this operationalisation. From the product criteria defined in this catalogue, a total of 216 are an adoption of ISO 9241 and detailed under the category *Software Ergonomics*. The operationalisation of ISO 14915 with 100 criteria, however, covers several categories (see 10.3).

It is worth noting that because of the standardisation processes, formulations sometimes are quite difficult to reconcile with this claim for universality and which will indicate, for instance, that ISO 14915, placed very little emphasis on learning.

Table 10-1: Demand taken from ISO 14915-3[35]

5.6	Supporting user preferences	As long as it is appropriate for the task, alternative forms of media[1] should be made available to users, from which they can select a preferred medium or deactivate specific media.

Table 10-1 shows an example which learning psychologists immediately associate with an infinite number of research results reporting subjective preferences for TV as a medium, yet with only a very small retention capacity, or with research results showing that in many instances familiarity rather than effectiveness is a decisive factor for the media selection. It is this kind of problems which were taken into consideration for the operationalisation of the standard (see table 10-2).

---

[35] In accordance with definition ISO 14915-2: Media = various specific forms of presenting information to the user (text, video, graphics, animation, audio).

Table 10-2: Extract of the operationalisation

The objective of using e-learning products is that you learn whilst using them. Are different forms of media available?	
If yes:	**If no:**
Are the media contents justified conclusively within the framework of the overall concept (e.g. redundant presentation of information so that the students can experiment to see how they learn with the different media)?	Is the availability of only one medium a shortcoming within the framework of the overall concept?
Have these media been selected appropriately with regards to the information to be conveyed? (Can the media selected basically be used to convey the information?)	Has this medium been selected properly?
Are the media designed appropriately with regards to the information to be conveyed (see 2, table 3, category 7)?	Has this medium been designed properly?
Are students encouraged to think about why they use a certain medium (e.g. by having the system record the selections made and by issuing appropriate messages)?	

Source: Rockmann, Olivier, 2005

10.2.2   Criteria derived from laws

Depending on the type and area of application of e-learning products, other regulations and laws may also become relevant. In Germany, these regulations include, for instance, federal and/ or national data protection laws, the distance learning protection act, or the ordinance on barrier-free information technology. These laws and ordinances are also incorporated into the criteria, whilst taking into account that they may vary from state to state.

As far as consumer protection is concerned, it is essential to specifically check over-the-counter products to see whether potential purchasers have the opportunity to inform themselves thoroughly about the objectives and quality of the product, its technical and contextual prerequisites, about objectives that may be achieved by using a product and the resulting costs before buying a product.

10.2.3   Criteria derived from scientific findings

The core objective of e-learning products is to ensure that users learn something by applying these products. This is why findings from the areas of learning and motivational psychology, media psychology, pedagogic and didactic findings from the scientific sector are of great importance for the design.

Meta analyses from studies carried out in the relevant areas show that there is not one correct theory, but that there are several theories, theoretical trends and settings, which are potential candidates for building a theoretical foundation for e-learning products.

Table 10-3: Example

Instructional design, situated or problem-based learning approaches can form the theoretical basis of the development, depending on the topic and target group.

    ♪   Depending on the theoretical learning context that has been chosen, different learning styles or learning strategies may be postulated so that manufacturing of the products can be aligned with it.

           ♪   Depending on the definition of the learning strategies (e.g. surface and deep strategies) the most suitable working methods are implemented, which can then be recommended by the system if necessary, and selected by the user or predefined by the system.

It becomes obvious that the quality criteria must be comprehensive in order to adequately cover the different theoretical approaches. It is only possible to assess whether the theoretical foundation is in keeping with the learning objectives, the framework conditions and the target group and whether an appropriate adoption was implemented (see 10.2.).

10.3   Different categories of criteria

With its 682 criteria the QCC-eL is so extensive that it has to be divided into categories (Rockmann, Olivier, 2005, see table 10-3). The selection of categories is based on the fact that specific areas – if not required – can be easily omitted from the quality assessment, and either evaluated or replaced by other procedures. This depends, for example, on whether the product

- is used privately, at work or for educational purposes,
- is used in Germany or in other countries,
- is used online on a server by the operator or offline by users themselves,
- incorporates specific functions (e.g. automatic indexing; logging of user data) or whether encoding (e.g. moving pictures) is used or not.

Table 10-4: Categories of QCC-eL

No.	Category	Subcategory	No.	Category	Subcategory
1	Software ergonomics (ISO 9241)	Symbol design (Part 3) Colour design (Part 8) Dialog design (Part 11) Ergonomic requirements (Part 12) User guidance/ error management/ help functions (Part 13) Dialogue navigation: direct manipulation (Part 16) Dialogue navigation: screen forms (Part 17)	4	Data storage and analysis	Specification of data saved Data display tools Data analysis
			5	Programme features	Control system Control support Support features Communication
			6	Theoretical aspects	General psychological aspects Aspects related to the psychology of learning Didactical aspects User concept
2	Organisational aspects	Organisational aspects Target Target group Quality assurance Conditions for participation	7	Information encoding	Content-equivalent information transport Picture Moving pictures Text
3	Technical aspects	User Operating company Product	8	Format and Design	Animation Simulation Questions and exercises Speech recognition Overall design

Source: Rockmann, Olivier, 2005

In the following the category *Theoretical Aspects (category 6)* should serve as an example for detailed discussion. The category includes criteria which verify if the product is based on a didactic, pedagogic or psychological learning concept. Tests are carried out to see whether the specified concept has been suitably adopted. In particular the following aspects must be verified, if a product is supposed to

- propose learning paths based on previous knowledge: it must include features capturing the previously acquired knowledge in the preparatory phase and/ or during the learning process;
- follow the drill and practice approach: the product must include tasks and exercises in order to check the level of achievement;
- support different learning preferences with regards to a selection of the learning medium: it must provide redundant information using different media;

- allow explorative learning: it must include fundamental characteristics which support exploration (availability of navigation, research and localisation features), anchor points, etc. Other characteristics should not be available (for example: program control which the user cannot manipulate).

A few questions to be verified by the tests are given here as examples:

   - Are the technical requirements, e.g. for navigation purposes, implemented in such as way that they support search operations?
   - Is it possible to quickly return to significant points or states or is it possible for users to set significant points by themselves?
   - Are users always able to find out where exactly they are within the multimedia application at a given moment in time, where they started from and where they can navigate to from this point? (see also ISO 14915-3)

- allow asynchronous communication among learners: it must provide the respective tools (such as annotation, forums, and publication tools); for each of the tools, provided quality criteria can be applied to describe and evaluate the tool. For the example of the annotation tool questions such as

   - "It is possible to switch on and off annotations or their representation on the screen?"
   - "Is it possible to share annotations (with other learners or tutors)?"
   - "Is it possible to label annotations (make different type of annotations such as comments, references etc. visible)?"

would be used to verify the tool.

10.4   Using the QCC-eL - An example from category 6

The catalogue developed has been implemented for quality assurance purposes for the sport science online academy *ILIS* (http://www.sportwissenschaft-akademie.de). One of the main requirements of QCC-eL is that e-learning products must be based on an overall concept which also has to be documented (see table 10-3, category 6).

In the case of ILIS, a blended learning approach is followed throughout the overall concept, where "blended" refers to the use of books in combination with online courses (Rockmann, Reiter, Olivier, 2005). The books produced to form the suite of books for the basic study of sport science are not only interlinked amongst themselves but are also connected with the corresponding online courses. The same applies to online courses that are offered at an online academy.

One central feature is the autonomy of both media, i.e. all books as well as all online courses are suitable for learning purposes even if used individually. The media are designed in such a way that both the book and the corresponding course offer a comprehensive and structural redundancy as far as the key statements are concerned. On the one hand, this is essential since these statements have to be available even if only one of the media is used. On the other hand, this kind of approach offers a quicker orientation when it comes to changing a medium.

In accordance with the verification that is based on the criteria, it is interesting to determine whether the concept described is actually available, and the links from the book to the Internet and vice versa, can actually be found by the users.

In this example, we are only looking at the verification of the latter item. It shows that the search for the book-links in the online course is supported by three different functions, which are presented to the user on the main page under the heading *Hints*.

- The chapter number in the book – e.g. 2.1.3 corresponds with the chapter number of the online course.

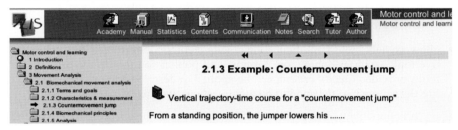

Fig. 10-1: Interrelation between text book and online course

- The online course includes a site that can be used to directly call up all links from the books.

	Link	Topic	Page in book
5 Motor Learning / Animations / Videos / Questions / Links / Downloads / Last Page	2.1	**Biomechanical Analysis**	
	www213	"counter movement jump" (CMJ)	43
	www2142	"squatjump" (SJ)	47

Fig. 10-2: Finding links mentioned in the book

- The search function can be used to find the relevant page when the link reference is entered.

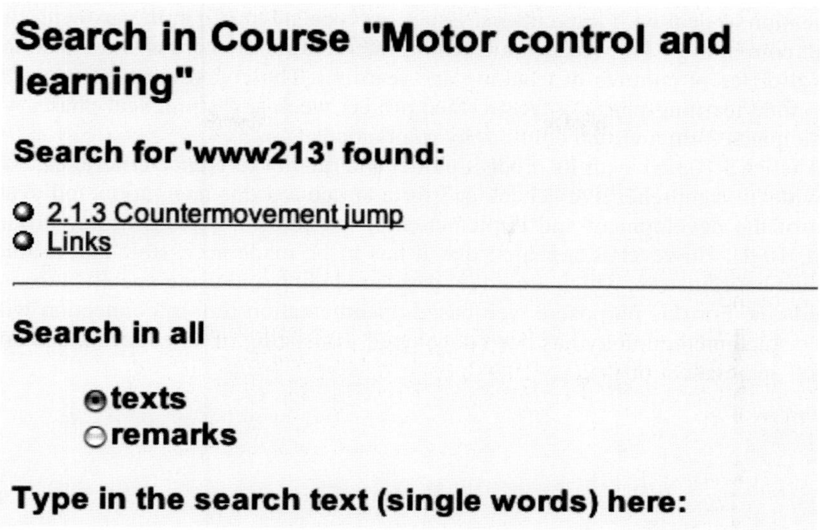

Search in Course "Motor control and learning"

Search for 'www213' found:

- 2.1.3 Countermovement jump
- Links

Search in all

- **texts**
- **remarks**

Type in the search text (single words) here:

Fig. 10-3: Searching in the online course

Conclusions:

The brief examples from above should show that the quality assurance of e-learning products is a complex problem, which is also indicated by the verification of the catalogue QCC-eL with its 682 criteria. When examining the products on the market it becomes obvious, however, that quality assurance is of utmost importance (see also "Stiftung Weiterbildungstests" (foundation for testing consumers' goods), http://www.stiftung-warentest.de, e.g. documents 8/2003, 11/2003, 5/2004).

Analysing the deficits it shows that especially criteria concerning learning concepts are disregarded. In the case, the product development is finished when deficits occur it is difficult, to eliminate them. Therefore it is better to integrate the criteria in the development process.

10.5   Methods and tools of combining a product and a process oriented approach

The following example describes experiences in the use of the quality reference criteria catalogue and the process model of the PAS 1032-1. Methods and tools described below have been tested in the framework of the e-learning project "Teaching Culture!" (www.teaching-culture.de; funded by the European Union).

The Teaching Culture! (TC) Project is a cooperation project of thirteen adult education institutions, universities and research institutes from nine European countries. Its aims at developing a training course which enables teachers in adult education to deal with intercultural issues appropriate to life in the growing European community. TC focuses on teaching intercultural awareness while also looking at different cultures of teaching and learning. The course concept consists of an online learning phase, a face-to-face project week and a practical phase, when participants form a virtual community of practice.

The PAS 1032-1 with its process model and quality reference criteria catalogue provides a comprehensive "checklist" for a structured documentation and evaluation of the development and implementation process for the TC online products (Fig. 10-4). However it appeared that it has to be made accessible and usable to project coordinators, which are not experts in reading and using specifications and standards. For this purpose a web-based documentation tool in connection with a three stage methodology has been developed, consisting of an editorial, documentation and evaluation stage.

CHOOSE STAGE

THE PROCESS MODEL

Needs Analysis	Framework Analysis	Conception/ Design	Development/ Production	Implementation	Learning Process/ Realisation	Evaluation/ Optimization
Initiation	Analysis of the external context	Learning objectives	Content realization	Testing of learning resources	Administration	Planning
Stakeholders Identification	Analysis of Staff Resources	Concept for contents	Design realization	Adaption of learning resources	Activities	Realization
Definition of objectives	Analysis of target groups	Didactic concept/ methods	Media realization	Activation of learning resources	Review of Competency Levels	Analysis
Demand analysis	Analysis of the institutional and organizational context	Roles and activities	Technical realization	Technical Environment		Optimization / Improvement
	Time and budget planning	Organisational concept	Maintenance	Organization of use		
	Environment analysis	Technical concept		Technical Infrastructure		
		Concept for media- and interaction design				
		Media concept				
		Communication concept				
		Concept for test and evaluation				
		Concept for maintenance				

Fig. 10-4: The process model

In the editorial, stage the relevant criteria from the reference catalogue are assigned to processes of the process model. The process model provides a more user friendly "interface" to the process specifications and to respective evaluation criteria as the format of the standard documents PAS 1032-1 can provide.

In the documentation phase the project work is documented, based on the process specifications. The criteria are used as a kind of checklist to cover all relevant aspects in the documentation. Results of the documentation stage provide the basis for the evaluation stage, when results are evaluated based on the quality criteria and evaluation results are documented. Those stages have a cyclic nature, i.e. all results of the three stages are revised periodically during a project life cycle.

The Web browser is the interface for the user of the documentation tool. The so called "view concept" allows that in the editorial stage different language versions can be added to the standard process model or additional explanations can be made by the editor. The user can e.g. in the documentation stage switch between the standard text from the PAS 1032-1 and the additional versions (views). Fig. 10-5 shows the use of the web based documentation tool of the TC project. The example focuses on sub process CD.9 ("Communication Concept" in the Category "Concept and Design").

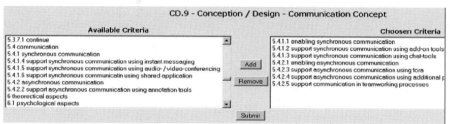

Fig. 10-5: Usage of the documentation tool in the editorial phase

In the editorial stage all quality criteria from subcategory 5.4 of the reference criteria catalogue ("Communication" is the fourth subcategory of category 5 "Programme features"; see tab. 10-3) are selected to be assigned to sub-process CD.9.

In the documentation stage the communication concept chosen for the first pilot run is documented (fig. 10-6).

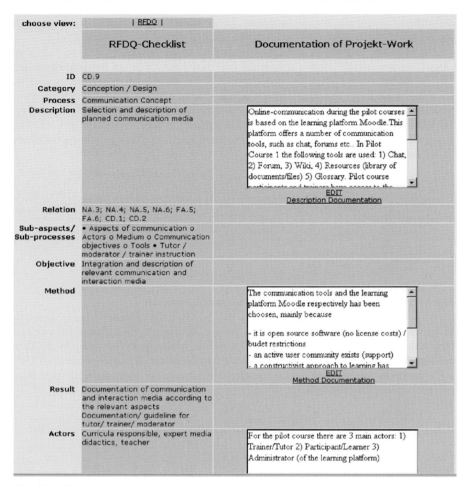

Fig. 10-6: Documentation stage

At the time of writing this article the first results from a questionnaire targeted to participants of the pilot course were available and documented as part of the evaluation stage. Based on the documented evaluation results design, technical or concept changes will be done for pilot run two and documented as part of a cyclic documentation stage (fig. 10-7).

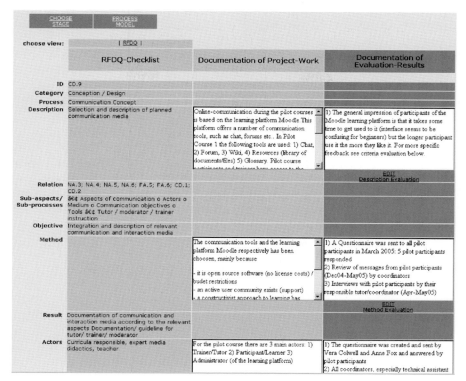

Fig. 10-7: Usage of the documentation tool in the evaluation phase

10.6   Outlook

Since the development of an e-learning product is a complex project with many people involved, only guidelines can assure that the resulting products derive great benefit from the potentials of computers in a way that is useful for the learning process. For structuring the process of planning, implementing and evaluating the PAS 1032-1 can be used. Since documentation is on the one hand necessary but on the other hand unpopular a documentation tool can support the continuous documentation.

The e-learning sector is a very dynamically developing caused by the technical development and the increase of scientific findings in the learning media area. Therefore every guideline needs a continuous evaluation and expansion. Working groups e.g. of the German Institute of Standardisation provide a platform for practitioners, experts and users to contribute to the further development of the PAS 1032-1 and its application in practice.

11 Quality evaluation for e-learning in Europe

Ulf-Daniel Ehlers

University of Duisburg-Essen, Germany

Lutz Goertz

MMB Institute for Applied Media and Competence Research, Germany

The development and provision of e-learning is a rapidly expanding area of education and training. Whether this is through an intranet, the internet, multimedia or computer based training, e-learning is seen as a key corner stone for building the future knowledge society. However, what is known about these innovative approaches to training has been limited by the shortage of scientifically credible evaluation. Is e-learning effective? In what contexts? For what groups of learners? How do different learners respond? Are there marked differences between different ICT platforms? Does the socio-cultural environment make a difference? What problems has it created for the teachers? E-learning is also one of the areas that attracts the most research and development funding. If this investment is to be maximised, it is imperative to evaluate e-learning processes and produce tools which are flexible in use but consistent in results.

11.1 Introduction: Evaluation for e-learning

The article gives an overview over basic concepts and methods of evaluation and then elaborates specifically on the subject of models and methods for the evaluation of e-learning. In addition to that, problems which have relevance in the context of evaluation will be elaborated.

Evaluation looks back at a long tradition reaching far back into history up to the Antique: Aristotle, for example, suggested an empirical benefit analysis of political activities which were directed to improve social situations. Especially for the analysis of political programs evaluation meanwhile has gained importance.

Looking at pure terminology, evaluation means to assess the value of something. Depending on the area in which evaluation is used, different concepts are used to determine the different dimensions of the object to be evaluated, the so-called process of operationalisation. The actual process of evaluation can then be carried out in different forms (e.g. at the end of a development in form of a summative evaluation or parallel to a development process, as a formative evaluation) using the whole canon of empirical research methods.

Through extended funding of projects and initiatives by the European Commission a culture of evaluation has grown throughout Europe. The research and project proposals contain usually – apart from the description of objectives and goals – also a plan how the achievement of these goals and objectives can be assessed. How these assessments are carried out methodologically is not standardised and opens a broad field of methods which, however, has to be understood intersubjectively. It remains a question if the evaluation instruments and procedures which are described in this article form a European culture of evaluation or if they are rather a collection of independent tools and instruments.

11.2   Evaluation: What is it about?

Evaluation meanwhile is an everyday term. Almost everyone can give a description of what it means or relates to. Still – or maybe because of that - it is difficult to give a general definition which isvalid for all disciplins and areas. This section is introducing elemtns of a definition for evaluation and then gives an overview on insitustions and expert networks in the field of evaluation, which are concerned with evaluation in Europe.

11.2.1   An overview on terminology, concepts and methods

The term evaluation is - as previously already mentioned - multifacetted and differently defined. This diversity of defitions also shows in literature. Fricke (Fricke, 2002) gives a large list of literatur references: (Stufflebeam, 1969, 1972, 1994), (Wulf, 1972), (Stiefel, 1974), (Lange, 1983), (Prell, 1981, 1986), (Gerl, Pehl, 1983), (Wittmann, 1987), (Fricke, 1986), (Wottawa, 1986), (Lösel, Nowack, 1987), (Will et al., 1987), (Rossi et al.,1988), (Wottawa, Thierau, 1990), (Berendt, Stary, 1993), (Götz, 1993), (Seidel, Park, 1994).

The term of the evaluation cannot be defined generally, since it is used in very different contexts and theoretical connections. Evaluation, however, extends over the mere measurement of single variables and items, like for example in the tradition of empirical pedagogical teaching and learning research, an uses a comprehensive variety of generated data and analysis methods.

Four elements for the definition of evaluation are especially emphasised by Will et al. (1987):

1. Evaluation is goal and usage oriented. It is primarily intended to improve practical measures, to legitimise them or to decide over them.
2. Basis for every evaluation is a sound data basis about the conditions, the processes and the impacts of the evaluation object.
3. Evaluation includes a value statement, i.e., the data will be interpreted on basis of values and according to certain rules.
4. Evaluation is not so much focussing on assessing the performance of individuals but is rather concerned with evaluating the development, design and control of educational processes as a whole.

In contrast to the assessment of e-learning with quality criterion catalogues or check lists, evaluation places not so much emphasis on product-related characteristics but rather on the evaluation of learning processes and judgements concerning quality, effect (acceptance, success in learning) and perceived benefit.

In evaluation research, usually the differentiation between formative and summative evaluation is made. Formative evaluations mainly serves purposes of quality assurance. Its goal is the uncovering of weak points in a process. The research is conducted accompanying the process and are used to optimise the ongoing process. Summative evaluation on the other hand, are used to control the quality, the impact or the benefit of an educational offer. The evaluation is therefore usually timed to the end of a process. Different process for evaluation are also elaborated by Stufflebeam (1972) in his evaluation model.[36]

Another differentiation is done by Tergan (2000) who differentiates between process and product evaluation. He differentiates between those evaluations in which the object of evaluation is the development process and those evaluations which relate to the final product at the end of a development process. For evaluation concepts for e-learning this means that they demand for a theoretical foundation on which processes in media supported learning are influenced in which way. In section 12 specific evaluation concepts for these purposes are described.

11.2.2   European initiatives and actors in the field of evaluation

If someone needs help in the fields of evaluation, it is useful to draw on a professional agency or institution. The following list gives an overview on Evaluation associations, initiatives and networks specifically in the field of evaluation:

- Danish Evaluation Society (Dansk Evaluerings Selskab DES, in Danish only)
  http://www.danskevalueringsselskab.dk
- European Evaluation Society (EES)
  http://www.europeanevaluation.org
- Finnish Evaluation Society (Suomen arviointiyhdistyksen, FES)
  http://www.finnishevaluationsociety.net

---

[36] Götz (1993, p. 105ff.) describes further evaluation models, amongst them input vs. output evaluation, external vs. internal, part vs. holistic evaluation, subjective vs. objective evaluation, direct vs. indirect evaluation, intrinsic vs. extrinsic evaluation, an more.

- French Evaluation Society (Société Française d'Évaluation, SFE, in French only)
  http://www.sfe.asso.fr
- German Evaluation Society (Deutsche Gesellschaft für Evaluation, DeGEval, in German only)
  http://www.degeval.de
- International Program Evaluation Network (IPEN, Newly Independent States)
  http://ipen21.org/ipen/en/default.html
- Irish Evaluation Network (IEN)
  http://www.policyinstitute.tcd.ie/Irish_Evaluation_Network.html
- Italian Evaluation Association (Associazione Italiana di Valutazione, AIV, in Italian only)
  http://www.valutazioneitaliana.it
- Polish Evaluation Society (Polskie Towarzystwo Ewaluacyjne, PTE)
  http://www.pte.org.pl
- Spanish Public Policy Evaluation Society (Sociedad Española de Evaluación, SEE)
  http://www.sociedadevaluacion.org
- Swedish Evaluation Society (Svenska utvärderingsföreningen, SVUF)
  http://www.svuf.nu
- Swiss Evaluation Society (Schweizerische Evaluationsgesellschaft, Société suisse d'évaluation, SEVAL)
  http://www.seval.ch
- UK Evaluation Society (UKES)
  http://www.evaluation.org.uk
- Walloon Evaluation Society (Société Wallonne de l'Evaluation et de la prospective, SWEP, in French only)
  http://www.prospeval.org

(This list is comprised by the European Evaluation Association which can be found at http://www.europeanevaluation.org).

An overview on European projects and activities in the field of evaluation, as well as articles and good resources, e.g. a guideline for evaluation specifically for project managers, can be found at: http://www.evaluate-europe.net.

A very important topic in the context of evaluation are emerging evaluation standards which are made to secure a minimum quality in evaluation processes. They become more and more accepted in evaluation projects. The US American standards have been published in the "Handbook of Evaluation Standards" (Joint Committee on Standards for Educational Evaluation 2000), the German Society for Evaluation (www.DeGEval.de) has published own standards which are related to the American version and which can be accessed at http://www.degeval.de/standards/standards.htm. In addition to that there are also standards for the evaluation of learners (Student Evaluation Standards) (ibid. 2003) as well as standards for the evaluation of personnel (Personnel Evaluation Standards) (ibid. 1998).

11.3 Evaluation concepts for e-learning

Kirkpatrick (1994) has formulated an evaluation approach which is differentiating between four levels of evaluation, and which meanwhile has become widely accepted: *Reaction level, Learning level, Transfer level, results level.* According to this model, evaluation should always begin with level one, and then, as time and budget allows, should move sequentially through levels two, three, and four. Information from each prior level serves as a base for the next level's evaluation. Thus, each successive level represents a more precise measure of the effectiveness of the training program, but at the same time requires a more rigorous and time-consuming analysis.

Apart from this, a number of evaluation concepts, especially for media supported learning exist. Reigeluths' (1983, p. 77ff.) instructional design concepts can be taken as a basis for evaluation of computer supported learning environments. For the construction of such learning environments he differentiates between five steps:

1. *Instructional Design:* Selection of suitable goals and related instructional and teaching methods for achieving a defined goal for a defined target group.
2. *Instructional Development:* Development and construction of teaching methods.
3. *Instructional Implementation:* Precise adaptation of the teaching methods to the specific context.
4. *Instructional Management:* Specific planning for the application of a qualification activity, e.g. in a company.
5. *Instructional Evaluation:* This aspect relates to „[…] understanding, improving, and applying methods for assessing the effectiveness and efficiency of all […] activities" (Reigeluth, 1983, p. 9).

The evaluation model of Ross and Morrison also elaborates on some of the described aspects (Fricke, 2002, p. 451). Formative and summative, quantitative and qualitative methods, from the area of instructional design s well as from constructivist learning theory are combine to a common approach here. Their evaluation model describes five steps which build on each other.

1. *Needs analysis:* Defining the goals and questions of the evaluation study.
2. *Methodology*: Selecting appropriate evaluation methods and implementation of the methods in five steps
   a. *Program Analysis:* Analysis of the teaching goals
   b. *Participant Analysis:* Definition of the target group/ sample
   c. *Evaluation Design:* Definition of the evaluation plan and the methods of measurement (formative as well as summative; qualitative as well as quantitative methods)
   d. *Instrumentation:* Assembling of the evaluation instruments to a coherent evaluation concept and plan under consideration of the given restrictions

and conditions.
   e. *Implementation:* Definition of a timeline for the evaluation

3. *Data analysis and Interpretation:* Analysis of data and interpretation of results.
4. *Disseminating Results:* Documentation of final conclusions and dissemination of the report.

Ross und Morrison emphasise that evaluation has to be seen as an iterative process, which leads to a permanent improvement of the program.

Another evaluation approach which also builds on an instructional theory, the so-called "Universal Constructive Instructional Theory" (UCIT, see Dijkstra et al. 1997, Tennyson et al. 1997), has been developed by Schott et al. (2000). It starts with a construction process: Needs analysis, formulation of a overall objective, conception of the learning environment by defining the learning activities, the learning environment, the learner group and the external frame. Finally, a specific and situated learning solution is developed. The evaluation process is now going the other way round. From the end it assesses if with the used software the desired goal has been achieved and the problem for which the software was developed has been solved. The claimed theoretical foundation of the evaluation is guaranteed by being interwoven with UCIT, however, only few practical experiences with the described model exist so far (Schott et al., 2000).

Zimmer and Psaralidis (2000) also develop an evaluation model for learning software. They argue that the learning success defines the quality of a learning software – and that this success is defined through the gain of competencies of a learner. So far a lot of evaluations based on the assumption that the quality of the learning software determines the success of the learning process – and not the other way round. The authors criticise these evaluation models as too close to "machine-like" models of impact research (ibid.). Their evaluation approach defines the learning situation as a holistic situation which can only reveal a conclusion on the quality of learning software if assessed in a holistic way. To answer the primary evaluation question – which learning processes and successes was directly caused by learning with the learning software – the evaluation object first has to be defined. The evaluation object in this case is not the software itself but rather the learning success and the gained competencies. Methodological they suggest the method of logical reconstruction. They suggest to analyse the connection between the learning success and the activities which led to this learning success a detailed way for a given fixed point of time and a specifically defined learning goal.

Such a holistic understanding as in the above described approaches which does not only relate to the measurement of achieved effects but which also relates to accompanying optimization of construction processes can also be found in Tergan (2000), Schenkel (2000), and Mandl/ Reinmann-Rothmeier (2000). It becomes clear that evaluation can be used as a method of quality assurance. However, evaluation approaches do not deliver a sound theoretical basis on which learning processes can be analysed but rather defines a methodological framework for the analysis of quality.

11.4   Evaluation of e-learning

11.4.1   Special characteristics of the evaluation of e-learning

Baumgartner (1997) mentions that the evaluation of e-learning has to take special characteristics into account. He states that e-learning challenges learning scenarios though new learning constellations and opportunities. This has necessarily also be taken into account when evaluating e-learning (Baumgartner 1997, p. 10). Baumgartner elaborates especially on five aspects of e-learning which especially have to be taken into account in the evaluation process:

1. *Access:* Through the possibility of individualised access to learning resources (anytime – anywhere) there is no common time, no common and public accessible spaces for learning processes.
2. *Situation and Needs:* E-learning allows for a potentially heterogeneous groups of learners and learning situations (at home, at work, on travel but all in the same course). This is also true regarding demographic variables (position in job, educational status etc.), regarding the content components (pre-knowledge, skills etc.) and the learners' learning experiences. Above that: What when and how long learners learn is in their own control.
3. Regarding the learners need e-learning allows a similarly heterogeneous situation amongst the groups of learners. Potentially learners' goals and motivation structures can vary in media supported learning. These varying motivations and goals do not only influence learners success but are also constituting tits definition.
4. *Optional offerings:* E-learning allows seemingly – through the used media – to separate content from learning process. This separation is, however, an illusion (Baumgartner, 1997). In reality it is the objective to evaluate not a static quality of material but rather the ability of this material to stimulate lively and interactive learning processes. Therefore the checklist-type evaluations can only be used with great caution to evaluate the quality of learning software.
5. *Learning situation*: The special learning situation of e-learning should be taken into account. Especially a differentiated evaluation of the effects of the delivery technology and of the didactical potentials of learning software – instruction technology – should be envisaged.
6. *Costs:* An analysis of costs and usage shows that two aspects have to be considered that are not yet in the common focus of interest. On the one hand, he argues with Levin not only to consider economical and financial costs but also social costs:

   „In economic terms, a cost is a sacrifice of an option. If a resource is applied to one use, it is not available for another use. In a purely economic sense, the cost of any decision is the value of what is sac-

rificed with respect to the best alternative use of that resource."
(Levin, 1981:30)

On the other hand one has to make a difference between a cost-and-usage-analysis
and a cost-effect-analysis. Whereas in the first case several different content related areas are compared with each other (e.g. educational vs. transport system)
this does not apply for the analysis of costs and effects.

Another underestimated effect tops off the thoughts of Baumgartner. He
stresses the aspect that not only the individualisation of the web-based learning
causes special demands during the evaluation, but also the possibility of social interaction forces require a new way of thinking about the evaluation of group-
assisted learning processes. Learning is therefore an interactive social process that
is negotiated between subjects (situated learning) (see Brown et al. 1988), (Chaiklin, Lave 1993), (Collins et al., 1989), (Lave 1988), (Lave, Wenger 1990), (Suchman 1988). A success of learning is not only caused in the cognitive achievement
of an individual person but of the whole learning system.

11.4.2   Methods of evaluation: A guideline

In the paragraphs above several approaches of evaluations, models and special
characteristics in the evaluation of e-learning have been described. In this paragraph, concrete methods and tools for e-learning users to prove the quality of e-
learning are shown. With these tools one can check during any stage of the e-
learning production if the results match with one´s own targets.

Reigeluth (1983) and Reinmann-Rothmeier et al. (1996) emphasise the importance of formal evaluation during the construction and usage of e-learning applications: „For the educational technology field, evaluation was now being viewed as
an integral and ongoing part of the instructional development process." (see also
in Fricke 2002: 450) For this purpose we suggest approaches of formative evaluation and focus on the question: How will a formative evaluation dealing with the
production and implementation be managed?

As in every scientific project the research on e-learning applications start with a
"research question" derived from a problem. An example: The first conception
phase of an e-learning curriculum shall be evaluated. So the question could be:
Does the intended content fit to the predispositions and needs of the learners?

In this way, one can express concrete questions for each phase of the e-learning
production process. In the following list, we present some example questions that
can emerge during the production and implementation of e-learning content –
from the perspective of an e-learning-provider:

The phase of e-learning production

1. Identification of needs/ conditions

   - For which demographical groups, sectors, positions in companies with which needs is the e-learning environment intended?
   - Is there a need on the side of potential users and decision makers for that e-learning environment? What is the budget?
   - Which competitors can we find in the market? Are there similar products in the market? How are the sales rates?
   - How many potential users can be expected?
   - How large is the interest to use and to buy the learning environment?
   - Which research results dealing with didactics, technology and usage are useful for the development of the learning environment?
   - Is there already an e-learning environment that fits the needs of the user organisation (small need for customisation) or shall the application be a completely new product („make or buy")?

2. Design of pedagogical concept

   - Does the didactical and creative design fit to the learning content and learning goals?

3. Production

   - How can the quality of the production process or of the final product be guaranteed?
   - Which tools (e.g. learning management systems, authoring systems or virtual classrooms) are available on the market? Can they be useful for the development of the own product?

The phase of e-learning implementation (e.g. in user-companies or in higher education institutions)

4. Introduction

   - How about the usability of the e-learning application for a future user (in the pilot phase as well as in the implementation phase in the company of the customer)?
   - Are there suggestions for improvement by authors, designers and developers who work on the implementation?
   - Is there really a need for the application by potential users and decision makers in the user company? How about the usability for users in the customer company?

5. Realisation

- How can one assure the quality of the implementation process and the quality of the final product?

6. Evaluation (as a summative evaluation)[37]

- how high is the rate of learning success after the training?
- are the users satisfied with the conditions, the learner's support and the application in general?

These different questions need different empirical methods of data generation and data analysis. The following table shows various methods for the measurement of quality – including advantages and disadvantages.

Table 11-1: Empirical research methods for evaluation in the social sciences (related to the learning process)

Method	Explanation	Advantages	Disadvantages
Survey			
Narrative Interview/ Guided Interview	elaborate interview with guiding questions. All answers are docu-mented basically	getting a lot of (also unexpected) de-tailed information, comfortable dia-logue situation	it takes a lot of time, great amount of work to take the minutes, weak comparability be-tween interviews
orally-standardised interview	interview guided by a systematic question-naire with pre-determined answers	good comparability of answers, high probability to real-ise the interview, because of face-to-face contact with the interviewer	at least 30 inter-views necessary to get valid results, risk that inter-viewee is not "hon-est" ("reactivity")
Written Interview	Interviewees receive a printed self-administering question-naire with pre-determined categories	great number of re-alised interviews by with low personal [or personnel] ef-fort „honest" answers, because of a lack of social control dur-ing the interview, local independence	no feedback possi-ble, high effort to gain interviews – often contact by telephone neces-sary, costs for mail postal charges
Telephone Interview	like orally standardised interview but via tele-phone	great probability to realise interview because of direct contact, local inde-pendence	great personnel ef-fort, telephone costs

---

[37] Normally the evaluation is a continuing process parallely to the e-learning production and im-plementation. It is no isolated step in the whole process.

Method	Explanation	Advantages	Disadvantages
Written interview (online)	survey with a standardised questionnaire via World Wide Web	can be used during online learning, immediate storage of (digital) data, no postal charges, local independence	no feedback possible, high effort to gain interviews – often contact by telephone necessary
Further methods			
Focus-groups/ discussion groups (qualitative research)	discussion with a group of learners supported by a guideline	participants are motivating each other to answer	single participants try to play a dominant role
Online-forum (synchronous und asynchronous)	discussion held in a newsgroup or a virtual classroom	embedded into a natural learning situation	great effort to motivate participants, great Amount of work to document and to evaluate the discussion
Tracking/log files	with the support of a special tracking software the different actions of a user will be traced and evaluated	"passive" method, in which a user can not be distracted by the instrument, low costs	only actions will be traced, not attitudes
"Desktop-research"	search in the internet or in archives for sources dealing with the same subject	low costs, no own survey or inquiry necessary	certain information is not available or not accessible
Observation	a well-trained observer documents actions, gestures and spontaneous statements utterances of an observed person guided by determined categories	documentation of actions which the observed person would not mention orally	changing of behaviour during an open observation (reactivity)
content analysis	evaluation of documents written by learners, e.g. diaries guided by a system of categories	written documents are manifest and always present, no limitation of the period of inquiry	great effort for diary writers, material is often incomplete

These methods can be used by everyone – detailed explanations about each method can be found in Diekmann (1995) and other publications about methods in social sciences. Nevertheless is it recommended to ask an expert during the conception of a questionnaire or for the implementation of tracking software – another advice: By combining two or more research methods you are likely to receive a deeper insight into your evaluation object (e.g. interviews plus tracking). This method mix is called triangulation and represents an own methodological approach.

To get elaborated answers to the above named questions it is necessary to approach different target groups. The following list shows which groups play a role in the production and implementation of e-learning and which methods are suitable.

- *Competitors/ market/ producers:* Information about the market – as an overview or good-practice-examples – are provided by brochures about companies and by websites of enterprises in the internet. E-learning associations and sector orientated newsletters and online magazines publish detailed overall views of the market. This way of "desktop research" is also a 'secret' way to get relevant information.

- *Experts:* They help with their knowledge to see ideas in a greater context and to estimate their relevance. Experts are listed in congress programmes and as authors of books and articles about e-learning. They can also be board members in councils and associations. Often they are representatives of e-learning companies and training academies. As experts have a wide knowledge and can explain things in a differentiated manner the „narrative interview" is an adequate interviewing method.

- *HR managers/ CEOs (potential customers):* For the distribution it is important if the decision makers in customer companies can be convinced by the product. They can have various positions in the enterprise – mainly they are HR managers, sometimes pedagogical managers or in-house trainers. In some cases they are the head of the IT department. In smaller companies, the e-learning decision maker is often the CEO himself. In this group, it is important to get a lot of details of expert's opinions. Therefore, it is recommended to ask a small number of that target group in narrative interviews.

- *Teachers/ Docents/ Tutors:* Another target group consists of people who use e-learning in their lectures (e.g. in a blended-learning training) and who care for the learners. This group has lots of experiences in the production and/or the implementation of e-learning that should be documented extensively. Again the narrative interview is recommended.

- *Learners/ potential learners:* Most important for the quality of e-learning is the learning success. The approaches in chapter 12 show how this success can be operationalised. For the exploration of the learners one can generally use the whole spectre of research methods. It depends on the learning situation which instrument is suitable e.g. if a user is online most of the time or if he learns in presence lectures. For online learners, telephone interviews or online questionnaires are adequate means for research. More and more we find recorded collaborative sessions that can be used for evaluation. In case of written interviews the feedback is only small. Additionally one can use log file-tracking usability-tests with a group of test users who represent a certain target group. This usability test can help to find out the future acceptance of an e-learning application as well as questions of software ergonomy.

- *Authors:* Also the authors of learning content can contribute useful facts for an evaluation of an e-learning application. They make experiences that can be relevant for the optimisation of the product. We can distinguish between authors working for an e-learning producer and authors on the side of the customer but also e-learners themselves. The suitable method for this group is the narrative interview and for a larger number of authors a self-administrated questionnaire.

These lists show the great variety of interesting questions and research methods. Although many methods can be used by e-learning producers or by e-learning users it is always a good idea to ask professional consultants and research institutes who have specialised on the support of research projects.

11.5   Conclusion: Evaluation of quality on every level

So far, the evaluation of further education training is often limited to surveys with participants regarding satisfaction with the course program. At the most can we find an evaluation of learning results at the end of the course (e.g. tests, see also Bliesener, 1997). But as it was shown, there are several evaluation models regarding e-learning. In these models quality assurance is more than just the control of learning effects. It is necessary to regard all factors of influence – the learner, the subject, the intended results, the technological and social surrounding (work place, learning culture in the company, private learning situation etc.). An effective quality assurance has to cover the whole process from the first plan up to the development and implementation until the assurance of transfer.

The position of the learner and the factors that influence him have to be considered in actions for quality assurance more than before. The aim of learning is an increase of competence. That means that the primary yardstick of quality is the increase of competencies and skills and not – to pronounce it in an exaggerated way – the quality according to criteria which can be measured well but do not influence the learning process. Quality assurance is not only limited to a good planning or preparation but it has to cover all phases in the qualification process and has to include the learner. Most important is therefore a "tailor made" concept of evaluation in order to assure quality. The concept of evaluation has to fit to the situation.

It is an error to believe that e-learning just has to be planned and prepared to achieve an intended success. A detailed concept of quality assurance covers all phases of the qualification process and goes beyond the standard evaluation methods for training programs. Those concepts will integrate the planning and development phase and additionally the evaluation of the implementation phase as well as the effects of the training (e.g. the return on investment of further education trainings in companies) and administration and management processes.

12 Towards a model for structuring diversity: Classifying & finding quality approaches with the EQO model

Barbara U. Hildebrandt, Sinje J. Teschler

University of Duisburg-Essen, Germany

There exists a great variety of quality approaches in Europe which are applicable to the field of e-learning. To structure that diversity, a systematic procedure is needed that supports the user first in evaluating those approaches and second in finding a suitable quality approach for a specific situation: The EQO Analysis Model enables a consistent description and thus comparison of quality approaches based on a harmonised metadata scheme. The appliance of this model is embedded in the EQO Decision Cycle that supports the quality management in four steps: analysing quality needs, analysing and comparing quality approaches, making decisions and practically implementing quality strategies. Based on the theoretical background, this article also gives a practical example to illustrate how the appliance of the EQO Decision Cycle and the EQO Analysis Model can support and improve the quality management in e-learning.

12.1 Introduction

The general e-hype is over and reality has shown that the "e" in e-learning doesn't necessarily make learning easier, better or cheaper than traditional pedagogical methods. Especially the field of continuing education has been strongly influenced by new e-learning solutions, but e-learning didn't keep its promises. The ongoing discussion about quality in e-learning demonstrates the hype has now led to a search for adequate concepts and instruments to assure and improve the quality of continuing education especially regarding the use of e-learning. But, screening the discussion about quality in the numerous publications, it gets obvious that there is no common understanding of what this term "quality" actually means – not to mention what has to be done to enhance this quality. There are numerous different dimensions, criteria, perspectives and corresponding vocabularies used when discussing about this topic and the need for a common understanding comes clear quite obviously.

Pushed by the ongoing discussion about quality management in general and about quality in education specifically, a variety of quality approaches has been developed in the past to enhance the quality of the different educational scenarios. But these quality approaches are as diverse as the general discussion about quality so that it is a real challenge to find the right quality approach for each context of usage. The experiences from the past have shown that even the usage of these quality approaches does not necessarily lead to a real improvement of the quality. In each context of usage, the term quality has to be specified by appropriate criteria and concerning the different needs and perspectives of all stakeholders involved in the educational process(es). And then, based on these criteria, the next step is the search for the right quality strategy fitting to these needs. After this, the next challenge consists in applying the selected quality strategy to the user's organisation or educational processes, because the general model is often very different from actually applying it to a specific context. So in most of the cases, there is adaptation necessary in many ways. And in the end, the usage of a quality strategy will only influence the business and educational processes in a positive way if all stakeholders understand how to integrate the quality procedures into their everyday business.

So far, quality management activities in continuing education can be characterised as a rather provider- and decision maker-steered process (Ehlers et al., 2005). On the one hand, there is a lack of integrating the user's/ learner's demand and the people on operational level, and on the other hand, there's also a lack in understanding how to integrate the activities of quality management into the proper business processes.

Based on these understandings, the European Quality Observatory (EQO) has developed a reference model for analysing and describing quality approaches for the field of European e-learning. It is a framework, based on a metadata model describing many different criteria to characterise educational scenarios/ contexts and to define the meaning of quality in these different cases. So the EQO Model provides a classification scheme for the discussion about quality in e-learning and thus enables the analysis and comparison of the different quality approaches. But the process of selecting the right quality approach is not the only challenge in this field; EQO also provides a decision (support) cycle to guide the user through the process of how to find and to adapt the right quality approach to his or her context of usage.

Reference Model: A reference model is a framework which defines concrete steps and criteria as an exemplary template.

In this article, we show how this support by EQO looks like in practice. Therefore in the next chapter, a basic overview on the process of decision-making in general and possible support by computer-based systems throughout this process will be introduced. Then, based on this general insight it will be illustrated how EQO can provide support in the specific field of deciding about a quality approach for European e-learning.

12.2   Decision support

The variety of existing quality approaches leads to the decision-making problem of selecting the best fitting one(s) for a specific e-learning situation. For a better understanding, first the general process of decision-making will be explained and different types of corresponding computer-based systems will be introduced. Then, based on these insights in the following chapter the specific problem and its support by the EQO approach and system will be discussed in detail.

Today's decision makers generally face a lot of information they have to consider when making their business decisions. To break down all these information into a feasible way and thus to enable founded decisions a lot of different support systems have emerged during the last decades. The (interdisciplinary) scientific field which is dealing in a systemic way with the behaviour of individuals and groups when taking decisions is called *decision theory* (e. g. Laux, 2003, p. 1). A *decision* in this context means to choose one out of several alternative options where this selection must be taken consciously (Laux, 2003, p. 1; Mag, 1977, p. 3). The process of decision making can be subdivided into several steps. Especially regarding the support of computer-based systems Curtis and Cobham for example describe the process of decision making using the following four-step model (Curtis et al., 2005, p. 6):

1. *Intelligence:* The decision maker first needs to be made aware that there is a problem requiring a certain decision. This means that corresponding information needs to be presented in a manner conductive to this recognition.
2. *Design:* The possible alternatives to choose from have to be identified (Davis, 1988, p. 30) which involves the recognition of the range of acceptable solutions to the problem as well as the implication of each of them. Therefore it is also necessary to examine "all the factors that influence the value, risk or acceptability of each candidate proposal" (Davis, 1988, p. 30). For the support by a computer-based system this means, that at this stage "information needs to be supplied to aid the decision maker in predicting and evaluating these implications" (Curtis et al., 2005, p. 6).
3. *Choice:* After formulating all possible alternatives in the previous stage, the decision maker now has to choose the most suitable solution for his/ her problem. Davis subdivides this stage into three more steps: first "evaluate and analyse each alternative in terms of some set of objectives or requirements" then "compare and rank the possible outcomes", and in the end, "select the alternative that provides the best, or most acceptable, course of action" (Davis, 1988, p. 30). The more information is available to the decision maker at this stage, the more straightforward or certain is the possible analysis of the situation. If a full analysis of the options is not possible, "the deci-

sion maker may have to choose between incomplete and perhaps incomparable alternatives" (Curtis et al., 2005, p. 6).

4. *Implementation:* In the last stage, the chosen decision has to be carried out. The proper implementation of a solution usually exceeds the scope of the computer-based information or decision support system, but still the system could support the user in providing information on how to implement the selected solution into practice or by stating experiences other users made when implementing a comparable solution in a comparable case.

It is obvious that the quality of the decision-making process is extremely influenced by the extent and quality of available information at each stage. To give particularly managers the best possible support a lot of different kinds of computer-based support systems have been developed in the past. To fully classify and describe all the types of support systems would by far exceed the scope of this article as the range covers (management) information systems, management support systems, decision support systems and expert systems, to enumerate only some examples. Although a lot of definitions exist, it is not possible to distinctly classify the different types of these systems since they differ in scope and objectives but also have some characteristics in common. Laudon & Laudon for example use the term *information system* and define such systems "technically as a set of interrelated components that collect (or retrieve), process, store, and distribute information to support decision making and control in an organisation. In addition to supporting decision making, coordination, and control, information systems may also help managers and workers analyse problems, visualise complex subjects, and create new products" (Laudon et al., 2006, p. 13). Elsewhere they describe "primarily standalone systems [which were] isolated from major corporate information systems that used some type of model to perform "what-if" and other kinds of analyses" and call such systems *model-driven Decision Support Systems* (DSS). DSS provide "analysis capabilities based on a strong theory or model combined with a good user interface that made the model easy to use" (Laudon et al., 2006, p. 466). Curtis and Cobham also identify different types of DSS characterised by the kind of support provided by them. In the scope of this article the following definition states applicable functionalities: *Computational support for structured decisions* " [...] involve[s] using existing general data held on a database and computation together with details of individual cases to arrive at information for a decision" (Curtis et al., 2005, p. 245f). But also the following definition of another type of support system is interesting within the scope of this article: an *expert system* is "[...] a computerised system that performs the role of an expert or carries out a task that requires expertise" (Curtis et al., 2005, p. 605). *Experts systems* "are computer systems that mimic the expert in being effective consultants in a particular knowledge area or domain. In common with experts they can provide explanation for their advice and conclusions. They are distinguished from other decision support systems by possessing general knowledge in a specific domain of expertise" (Curtis et al., 2005, p. 255). In the scope of this article, we use the general term "*support system*" and the domain of expertise is the field of quality in e-learning.

In this article a *Support System* is a computer-based system which supports its users in solving a problem (in a specific domain) by guiding the user through the different steps of a decision-making problem by providing information and additional explanatory material.

As stated before, there is a great variety of quality approaches which are very different regarding scope, objectives, methods, instruments, quality goals, target group, etc. It is obvious that the procedure to select an appropriate quality approach for a specific context of usage has to be planned and considered in detail and that there is a lot of systematically prepared information necessary to enable and support a competent decision.

Such a structured procedure for selecting quality approaches for European e-learning and a corresponding computer-based support system have been established by the European Quality Observatory. In the following, it is shown in detail how this can look like.

12.3   How to find a suitable quality approach?

Dealing with the field of quality in e-learning is a very complex topic since many different aspects have to be considered and information is often available only on a very abstract level. Quality approaches are very different regarding their characteristics and it is not possible to compare them against each other offhand. So it is necessary to provide more structured information on the different quality approaches.

In the following, we show how the EQO Analysis Model enables a consistent description and thus comparison of quality approaches based on a harmonised metadata scheme. Then it will be explained how the EQO Decision Cycle using the metadata scheme supports the quality management in different steps in practically implementing quality strategies.

12.3.1   EQO metadata model

Quality approaches for e-learning are abstract conceptualisations of "good e-learning" – so far no consistent descriptions of them have been available. Therefore in the European Quality Observatory there has been developed a metadata scheme for the analysis, description and thus comparison of quality approaches applicable for European e-learning. The EQO Model (EQO, 2004) is a standardised description model and takes a theoretical analysis as well as a description of practical experiences of quality approaches into account. Therefore it is divided into two main parts. On the one hand, quality approaches are analysed on a theoretical basis by quality experts using the official documentation and publications about the different approaches. On the other hand, experiences users made in practically implementing quality approaches are categorised and analysed as well. The model is conformant to existing metadata schemes like the results of the CEN/ ISSS Workshop Learning Technologies (CEN Workshop Agreement 14644) (CEN/ ISSS, 2003a, b) and common metadata schemes as e.g. Learning Object Metadata (LOM) (IEEE, 2002).

The description of the quality approaches is done using a hierarchy of many single criteria (data elements) grouped in categories and subcategories. For a better comparison the value spaces for the data elements are defined by involving predetermined vocabularies and classification schemes wherever possible. The theoretical analysis of approaches covers the following three main categories (figure 12-1):

1. *General:* In this category general information on the quality approach are analysed. It deals with information such as title (name of the approach), version, the language in which this approach is expressed, the location where it can be accessed as well as copyright and other restrictions for using this approach (such as costs and charging schemes). This category is considered to contain all information needed to clearly identify the quality approach.

2. *Context:* This category analyses the intended area of usage and the educational context the quality approach is applied to. Information about the educational context, such as the educational level (e.g. "university") and/ or the industry sector or educational institution the approach is related to (e. g. "manufacturing industry") is summarised. Also the target group this quality approach aims at is defined (e. g. "author" of learning materials) as well as the cultural or regional coverage of the approach (e.g. "not restricted to a country"). Furthermore, the EQO model expresses if the quality approach was developed for a specific topic within a classification scheme and for which educational processes it can be applied. In a last subcategory the quality goals that the approach addresses and in particular the sense in which quality is defined in that approach are expressed. Additionally, the user is given the possibility to rate the importance of certain criteria here.

3. *Method:* This category summarises information about the scope of the quality approach. It defines whether the quality approach focuses on the results of a process or the process itself (e. g. "product-oriented") and the methods the quality approach uses (like "benchmarking", "evaluation", "standards", etc.).

The so far described categories and elements of the EQO Model describe the generic approach and cover details about what this quality approach is intended to be and to effect. But often, the general intention of the model is very different from its instantiation when actually applying this model to a concrete context of usage. In addition to the theoretical analysis there is also a category "experiences" dealing with the experiences people made in concretely applying these generic approaches to specific implementations. The EQO project expects the experiences part to provide valuable information to quality practitioners since especially this category enables to explore the demand and point up requirements for adaptation of an quality approach. People can profit from other people's experiences and directly see which aspects of a certain quality approach needed to be adapted and how they were adapted when applying a quality approach for a concrete use case. Also information about indicated factors for success or failure in adapting quality approaches can be derived.

title,
description,
actual version,
language,
copyright,
...

General Information

Context of Usage

educational level,
target group,
cultural/regional coverage,
specific topic,
...

Quality Approach

scope,
product-/process-oriented,
methods (evaluation/bench-marking/...),
...

Method of Quality Approach

Experiences

experiences users made,
specific Implementations,
other valuable information,
...

Fig. 12-1: The EQO metadata model

The EQO Model provides standardised information about quality approaches on a level and granularity which makes this abstract topic manageable. To support the decision maker in the best possible way, there is also a process model available which guides the user through the process of selecting a quality approach which is suitable for his/ her situation. The EQO Model has been implemented as a corresponding computer-based support system providing the descriptions and analysis of quality approaches. The following paragraph will illustrate how the EQO Model is used during the process of deciding on a quality approach.

12.3.2   EQO decision cycle

Based on the previously illustrated EQO Metadata Model a process model has been developed to support any actors involved in quality in e-learning in finding the appropriate quality strategy for any e-learning scenario: the EQO Decision Cycle (figure 12-2).

Walking alongside the EQO decision cycle all four stages of the general process model of decision making (described in chapter 12.2) are covered in four different steps: analysis of quality needs, analysis and comparison of quality approaches, decision support and adaptation and implementation of recommendations.

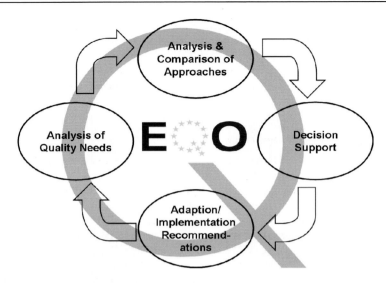

Fig. 12-2: The EQO decision cycle

Analysis of quality needs

A good point to start is the analysis of the quality needs of the current situation – no matter if somebody just started to deal with the field of quality in e-learning or if this person is already well experienced in this area. This corresponds to the stage called "intelligence" of the general model of the decision-making process (cp. chapter 12.2). Either the user already is aware that there is a need to create a new or better quality strategy or the user will be made aware of the potential of quality activities at this stage. Therefore a set of criteria defining the different aspects of quality is needed which is provided by the EQO Model and which consists of many different criteria to describe these different aspects. They can help to define what is understood by "quality" and thus supports them in defining their quality needs and requirements. This description model contains many aspects which might not be applicable to a specific situation, because there are really many different aspects to be taken into consideration to cover the whole field of quality in e-learning and to most situations only a more or less substantial subset of these different aspects will be applicable. However, people will find criteria which otherwise they didn't even think about or realise that they might be important for the quality in their organisation.

In this first step, the user is supported in getting a clear idea of the precise aspects of quality of his or her current situation. The definitions of aspects for a specific context – this may be for example a special course in an organisation that focuses on customer support – determine the characteristics a quality approach needs to fulfil to be an appropriate one for the specific situation. Therefore a standardised description framework like EQO can deliver helpful support. The EQO model is the basis for the EQO repository which is a web-based support system to analyse and compare quality approaches. According to the categories and criteria of the EQO Model the user can browse through the different descriptions of quality approaches and thus get a clearer idea of what quality approaches there are available at all and what aspects of quality could be considered in general and especially regarding his/ her concrete context of usage.

Analysis and comparison of approaches

After the relevant criteria have been defined, in a second step different quality strategies, or quality approaches, how they are denoted in EQO, need to be analysed and compared according to their appliance to these previously defined criteria. This corresponds to the "design"-stage of the general model of decision-making. Regarding the great variety and bandwidth of different quality approaches it is not easy to profoundly compare them against each other. The scale covers small checklists containing few criteria for very specific contexts of usage up to holistic approaches like total quality management approaches. It is obvious that because of the huge number and great variety it is hard to get an overview of all these different approaches and to compare them against each other. Again EQO offers support by providing a standardised description framework of predefined criteria to describe the whole bandwidth of different quality approaches no matter if they have been specifically developed for the quality assurance of e-learning materials or if they originally have been developed for quality assurance in general, but now also are applicable for e-learning courses.

According to this standardised description framework, the user has different possibilities to access analysed quality approaches in the EQO repository. The first option is the browse-interface where the quality approaches can be accessed by selecting different categories. For example if an author of e-learning materials wants to search for quality approaches which provide quality criteria to be considered during the process of creating e-learning courses one possible search strategy would be to go to the browse-interface of the EQO repository and select in the category "target group" the criterion "author". Another option is a full text search on many fields in the database. For users who are already more experienced with quality approaches there are advanced search functionalities which provide a search according to (previously defined) user's ratings and preferences (in detail in: Manouselis et a., 2004).

No matter if starting with the browse-interface or with either of the search interfaces after executing the search the user will be presented a list of results containing all quality approaches which are currently in the repository fitting to the search criteria. All the descriptions of analysed quality approaches in the repository follow the categories and criteria of the EQO Model. According to the four categories of the EQO Model the analysis is spread over four tabs: general, context, method and experience (cp. figure 12-3).

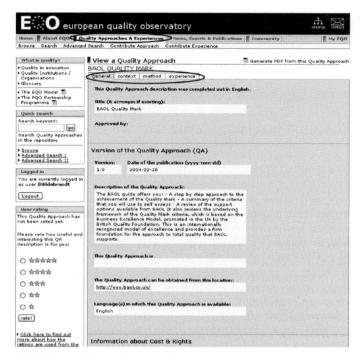

Fig. 12-3: The EQO-repository: View a quality approach

This structured description enables the user to analyse and compare the different quality approaches against each other[38].

Decision support

After the different quality approaches have been analysed according to their appliance to the previously specified quality criteria and after the user has found out which ones of them can be applied or adapted to the considered e-learning scenario in the next step the best fitting quality approach is selected. Corresponding to the stages of the general decision-making process model the user in this step of the cycle has to make a "choice" (cp. chapter 12.2). But still in most of the cases there won't be a quality approach perfectly fitting to all of the criteria and some adaptation will be necessary. With the help of EQO people are able to have a look at all existing criteria of the listed results that are stored in the database to get detailed information about further characterising criteria of the approaches. In addition to the complete list of criteria of an approach the category of experiences gives useful information from other users. These descriptions of experiences contain detailed information about the process of adaptation other users passed

---

[38] A helpful feature in this context is the function of creating a PDF either of a single description of a quality approach or of all quality approach currently analysed in the repository.

through when applying this quality approach to their concrete use cases. Moreover they contain recommendations these users make according to their experiences for future appliance and adaptation processes.

Adaptation and implementation recommendations

Based on the collected information, the user will be able to examine which quality approach is the best fitting one to fulfil her or his needs. In the following next step this quality strategy or quality model has to be applied to the considered e-learning scenario, corresponding to the "implementation"-stage of the general process model of decision-making (cp. chapter 12.2). In some cases, the user will face the fact that the chosen quality approach does not perfectly fit to all of the specified criteria. In this case, it is possible to search for these special criteria in a further search process to find quality approaches which are excellent only in these special aspects. Based on the result list, the user can decide which quality approaches from this second search delivers the most suitable solution for the specified aspects and if and in how far they can be integrated into the previously selected approach. In a further step single parts of different quality approaches fitting to the concrete scenario and fulfilling the requirements can be integrated. In that way, a combined quality approach especially satisfying the user's needs is determined.

The last step which might be the most challenging one is the application of the selected quality strategy into practice. For this step further support exceeding the information of the experiences category would be very helpful, but so far could not be covered by the EQO support system (but will now be developed in another project called Q.E.D. (Quality initiative e-learning in Germany). For strategies to adopt and implement quality standards, see chapter 5 of this book.

In the end, after the appliance of the personal quality strategy to the specific e-learning scenario the whole decision process will start again, because the definition and assurance of quality is an always ongoing procedure and subject to change.

12.4   Conclusion

The ongoing discussion about quality management in general and about quality in education specifically shows that there are numerous different dimensions, criteria, perspectives and corresponding vocabularies that have to be taken into account when applying a quality strategy. There has been developed a variety of quality approaches in the past to enhance the quality of the different educational scenarios.

As there is existing a great variety of quality approaches in the field of e-learning a support system is needed to support the user systematically to make the right decision in choosing an approach that fits to the special needs in each situation. Generally, the process of decision-making can be characterised using a four-step model. The European Quality Observatory has developed the EQO

Decision Cycle, based on the EQO Metadata Model, that supports users in finding the right quality approach and in making decisions. Focus of the metadata scheme is to give criteria and elements to describe, compare and handle different approaches – even to give structured information and thus to provide decision support. With the Decision Cycle there has been developed a process model to support any actors involved in quality in e-learning in finding the appropriate quality strategy for any e-learning scenario.

With the results of the EQO project first important steps have been made to provide the urgently needed support for dealing with the complex field of quality approaches in e-learning. However, it is obvious that this was only a starting point and that there is great demand for further research in this field to provide better support for the process of implementing quality approaches.

Part B: E-learning standards

Part B focuses on standards for e-learning. The controversial discussion on standards of the last decade is reflected: On the one hand, cost-reduction, secure investments, and new market potentials are expected. On the other hand, there is the fear of limitations for creative solutions. Standards are often misunderstood and perceived as restricting flexibility or creativity or huge additional effort, especially in the education community. Therefore, we draw a clear picture what can and what cannot be achieved by the use of standards. The main goal of e-learning standards is to provide solutions to enable and ensure interoperability and reusability of systems, components, and objects. The handbook gives an overview on the variety of standards and discusses their practical use and benefits for e-learning.

13   The standards jungle: Which standard for which purpose?

Kai Heddergott

MMB Institute for Applied Media and Competence Research, Germany

The developing e-learning market needs some standards in order to offer the producers of e-learning applications a guideline for the production process and to provide the customers with instruments for a better transparency in the evaluation of e-learning products. In this overview, the currently discussed approaches of e-learning standardisation, their goals and their limits are systematically described in a brief typology, which provides an introduction to further contributions on the approaches. The standards can be distinguished in Architectures and frameworks, Management standards, standards for contents, Didactical standards, Learner Models standards and Interface standards.

13.1   Introduction

To provide the e-learning-market with interoperable products that can be used in different companies, different learning environments and by different types of learners, there has to be a common sense about the description of learning content and course design. In this context, instruments aiming at the standardisation of e-learning play a decisive role. They offer producers of e-learning-applications certainty in the production process and provide customers with the possibility to evaluate the functionality and applicability of products who are claiming to be made accordingly to the standardisation requirements. Moreover, standards in e-learning allow to transfer learning content from one learning environment to another, e.g. in companies with widespread subsidiaries with different learning-platforms.

Discussing standards in e-learning means talking about a matter, that mostly cannot be recognised at first sight – from a learner or customer view, one is talking about an "invisible subject". Generally, most standards are for developers only. From a technical view this is because most benefits of standards indeed are created underneath in the thicket of markup languages.

Today neither any e-learning producer nor any company using e-learning can afford to ignore current and future e-learning standards. But besides this accordance about the meaning of standardisation in general, there is a lack of understanding how the actual needs and demands concern Learning Technology standards like SCORM or AICC in detail.

When it comes to present the relevance of e-learning standards to the users of e-learning, one has to be a well-prepared and experienced guide for a rough walk through a jungle of buzz words, explanations, references and different instruments. Moreover there are two perspectives on the meaning and use of e-learning standards: the view of the producers and the view of the users and customers of e-learning products and concepts.

Therefore it is necessary to create an aisle in this jungle for a better understanding of the standards themselves, their relevance in the context of quality development and improvement. The goal is to give a common understanding for all actors in the field of e-learning – at least to provide the knowledge "of the other side". The following text will give you an overview and leads to further contributions on Learning Technology e-learning Standards in this handbook.

13.2   Standards and standardisation – what are we talking about?

To achieve the aims mentioned above and to work with the oncoming contributions in this handbook, we have to give an explanation what Learning Technology Standards are in general and how they are generated. First of all, the process of standardisation has to be described:

- Standards are the result of a standardisation-process. The International Organisation for Standardisation (ISO) describes the formation of standards as follows: "There are three main phases in the ISO standards development process. The need for a standard is usually expressed by an industry sector, which communicates this need to a national member body. The latter proposes the new work item to ISO as a whole. Once the need for an International Standard has been recognised and formally agreed, the first phase involves definition of the technical scope of the future standard. This phase is usually carried out in working groups which comprise technical experts from countries interested in the subject matter. Once agreement has been reached on which technical aspects are to be covered in the standard, a second phase is entered during which countries negotiate the detailed specifications within the standard. This is the consensus-building phase. The final phase comprises the formal approval of the resulting draft International Standard (the acceptance criteria stipulate approval by two-thirds of the ISO members that have participated actively in the standards development process, and approval by 75 % of all members that vote), following which the agreed text is published as an ISO International Standard"[39].

- *To put it briefly, Standardisation is the process* of establishing a (technical) standard with the inclusion of related national and international bodies, who are willing and assigned to attend this process[40].

- The (technical) *standard is the result* of the standardisation, which describes the consensual specifications of a given subject, service or product after discussing it with qualified experts. For those, who complete in the related market, it is highly recommended to consider or follow this standard or to take part in its further development. Regarding the impact and the national or international relevance, one can distinguish different kinds of standards:

- There are several pre-standards, which represent an agreement of a selected community: The highest level of consensus is gained by formal standards by ISO, CEN or DIN, also called norms.

- On a national level there is the "Publicly Available Specification (PAS)", on an European level there are "Workshop Agreements (CEN/CENELEC-CWA)". The international level is covered by the "Publicly Available Specification (ISO/IEC-PAS)" and "International Workshop Agreements (ISO-IWA).

Standardisation means being the first in an undiscovered jungle to explore a subject, to arrange a safe way through the thicket and to prepare the trail for the rearguard – which in our context are the producers and customers of e-learning. To erase the "white spots" on the map of e-learning it is necessary to do these first steps – and, at the same time, it is needful to keep the process going and gain momentum in the further development of the e-learning-market. Basis is the participation of several stakeholders, who create standards conjointly by building a consensus: producers and manufactures, users and vendors, governmental institutions, engineers, researchers and consumer groups, which are all involved voluntarily.

These stakeholders meet in working groups, which are initiated by themselves or by the standardisation bodies. Such bodies are e.g.:

- the IEEE LTSC (Learning Technology Standards Committee of the Institute for Electrical and Electronic Engineers),
- the ISO/IEC JTC1 SC 36 (Subcommittee 36 of the Joint Technical Committee 1, formed by national bodies from ISO and IEC)
- the CEN/ ISSS WS LT (CEN/ ISSS Workshop on Learning Technologies)
- the ADL Collaboration (Advanced Distributed Learning, established by the Department of Defense of the United States of America with partners industry and in the academic sector)

---

[39] http://www.iso.org/iso/en/stdsdevelopment/whowhenhow/how.html (last modified 2003-09-30).

[40] Refer to www.ieee.org, www.iso.org, www.cenorm.be, www.din.de. See also ISO/IEC (2005). On the work of a standardisation body, see the contribution by Jan Pawlowski about Quality Management Standards in Section 3.Methods. Furthermore, the Learning Technology Standards Committee (LTSC) of the IEEE and the Advanced-Distributed-Learning-Network (ADL) have to be mentioned: http://ltsc.ieee.org, www.adlnet.org.

- IMS Global Learning Consortium (Academic sector and IT- and e-learning-industry)

Moreover, correspondent standards are given by other bodies, such as W3C (World Wide Web Consortium), which defines standards and frameworks for the use and production of websites. These specifications have an important impact on the conceptual design of web based e-learning-solutions.

13.3   A hot spot on the map – what are the purposes of learning technology standards?

Once one has understood how standards are generated, it comes to the question, what kind of purposes are served by these specifications. In the context of e-learning, there are several purposes[41]:

- the unification of relevant terms
- the application of defined procedures
- the description of an ideal type of the production process of e-learning products[42]
- the management of quality assurance in the production and the use of e-learning
- the description of quality criteria of e-learning-products
- the provision with instruments and methods for reusability and interoperability of e-learning elements/ contents in other than the primary contexts
- the promotion of a greater transparency on the market of e-learning products

At this point, the guide has to remember the travelling group on its way through the jungle, that learning Technology standards do not have the capability to evaluate the quality of the e-learning content itself – actually, they are very helpful to clarify and review specific items and parameter in a given context. For example, by using standards it is possible to exchange e-learning-content between different learning-platforms or learning-management-systems (technical interoperability) or between different courses and didactical concepts (semantic interoperability).

It becomes apparent, that there are superordinated goals of Learning Technology standards – but they can also be distinguished by their theoretical background[43]. These approaches can be described as follows:

- *Architectures and frameworks:* This type is a generic type; further specifications are derived from a basic description of cornerstones. Rather standardisa-

---

[41] An overview in German is given by Heddergott/Pawlowski (2002).

[42] The DIN-PAS 1032-1 is a good example for a reference model for quality management and quality assucrance. Refer to DIN (2004).

[43] Lindner distinguishes in his contribution in this handbook from another starting point of view "Formal Standards" and "De-facto Standards", regarding the bindingness of standards.

tions bodies or developers than costumers or users deal with this level of standardisation in an early stage in the definition of future standards (see also chapter 14).

- *Management standards:* They handle the process of transferring e-learning content into other environments like learning management platforms or toolsets for the production of e-learning. They tell the e-learning-producer how to handle the elements and let them "arrive safely". The keyword here is "interoperability" (see also chapter 15).

- *Standards for contents:* The description of the content metadata is the main topic of this type of learning technology standards. These metadata contain information about the used language, the learning subject, used media and a wide range of other descriptors of e-learning-content. It always provides the interoperability of e-learning content, but on a smaller scale on the level of the content elements themselves. Producers of e-learning, who are aiming to offer their content and learning-modules for different learning-platforms, should have a closer look on this type of standard (see also chapter 20).

- *Didactical standards:* The main topic of this type is the description of learning targets. E-learning-applications which focus on the didactical concept and structure of the learning-solution should be developed by reflecting and using this type of standard (see also chapter 16).

- *Learner Models standards:* The indication of learner-related previous knowledge as well as the definition, mapping and tracking of individual competencies are main targets of Learner Models standards. They have to assure, that the learning progress and the consideration of learning paths could be tracked and that the data is secured from illegal access. These standards have relevance for vendors of e-learning-courses with greater numbers of learners, which are interested in getting information about their learning process, their progress and their learning behaviour.

- *Interface standards:* These standards have to ensure that e-learning-applications do fit in existing standards concerning the design and the use of business information systems and their corresponding standards like XML, EDI and so on. The integration of learning and information is the main topic and mainly e-learning-producers should be interested in getting information about this type of standard (see chapter19).

13.4   After passing the jungle: What lies ahead?

The success of e-learning depends on the success of Learning Technology Standards – this assumption is widespread among e-learning-experts and vendors of applications. The viability of the products is in fact a key factor for the further development of the market and it is for sure that the standardisation has great importance for the diffusion of computer-based learning solutions. The more learners can use a certain e-learning product equally in different learning environments the more the market will grow – without the necessity of providing different groups with different products. The future lies in the interoperability and reusability of e-learning content.

But besides this point of view it seems to be clear that the way to a common acceptance of e-learning standards is not untinged of certain obstacles. Mainly, we have to work out which expectations e-learning producers do have in mind when they talk about standards. We also should know what the actual needs of the customers in this respect are.

13.5   Good reasons for the use and support of learning technology standards

For the *vendors* of e-learning, the advantages of the use of standards could clearly be described:

- The development costs can be reduced by keeping in mind the possibilities of reusing learning contents ("Economies of scale")
- International markets can be addressed by using customisable learning elements which are compliant to foreign learning concepts[44]
- The usage of e-learning standards approved by the „official" bodies can be part of the marketing activities of a vendor („approved quality")[45]

On the other hand, the producers have to monitor the development of e-learning standards by taking part in the ongoing professional discussion; this means the attendance in standardisation bodies and committees followed by special costs.

More often, *customers* do ask whether an e-learning product follows current standards or is approved by a responsible body. Moreover, setting the focus on standards in e-learning have other effects for customers:

- The consideration of e-learning standards do concern the advanced training and the human resources development; worldwide companies have to think about the reusability of e-learning-content between the subsidiaries in different countries.
- By using e-learning-products which are following current e-learning standards customers maintain and enlarge their competitiveness (e.g. because of cost-reduction and the increase of efficiency).
- Finally, being independent of proprietary standards means a greater flexibility when it comes to choose products or suppliers without having the necessity to

---

[44] The example of the vendor WBTsystems may show, how the producers focus on the advantages of e-learning-standards by showing success-stories from their customers. See some of these casestudies online on: http://www.wbtsystems.com/customers/casestudies

[45] Vendors, who have been certified by AICC (Aviation Industry CBT Committee), are listed with detailed certification-reports on the AICC-Website. See the reports online on: http://www.aicc.org/pages/cert.htm

change previously used e-learning components. Furthermore the customers can decrease the investment risks by using standards.

13.6   Lessons learned for future trips through the jungle

The are several key findings having a closer look on Learning Technology Standards:

- Actually we are talking about instruments to specify e-learning-products rather than evaluating learning quality[46]. Evaluating e-learning-applications and -solutions in the respect of considering standards means to proof whether the product is capable to improve interoperability by fitting several standards. A learning-platform aiming to the connection of the learning environments of an academic institution with a greater company is a good example for the need and use of interoperability.
- A certain common ground is prepared for vendors as for users of e-learning although the diffusion of Learning Technology Standards has still to become greater.
- The further development and diffusion depends on the active participation of all actors on the e-learning-market: without the feedback of the customers the vendors could not realise the needs; there has to be a professional dialogue.

---

[46] On quality issues, see the article by Ehlers/Pawlowski/Goertz (2003).

14 Architectures and frameworks

Rolf Lindner

University of Darmstadt, Germany

This article shows how architectures and frameworks for e-learning relate to quality aspects in this domain. It explains which levels of standards are found and what are the characteristical properties of standards for e-learning architectures and frameworks. It outlines the major approaches and explains their features, strengths and weaknesses. In doing this, it also reveals the major differences between educationally-oriented approaches favoured in Europe or technology-oriented approaches found in the USA.

E-learning is a term that currently has many ambiguous meanings. In this article, *e-learning* denotes all kinds of learning, teaching, training, education, knowledge creation, etc. where a substantial amount of support based on information and communication technology is found. It is evident that *e-learning* is a "soft" term.

14.1 Introduction

In this chapter information will be provided which contributes to answering the question:

What can be expected from standards for architectures and frameworks in the context of employing Information and Communication Technology (ICT or, shorter, IT) for supporting Learning, Education, and Training (LET)?

Following, we will use the acronym ITLET for addressing both this support and this field of application.

ITLET is an acronym for "Information Technology for Learning, Education, and Training". This composite term addresses the employment of information (and communication) technology (i.e. machinery, networks, software, and data) for supporting the dissemination, harmonisation, and progression of knowledge, skills, education, literacy, culture, etc. in environments made up of humans and technology. This implies that *ITLET* is inherently related to diverse and varying disciplines and phenomena and cannot be clearly assigned to one of those.

Well-designed ITLET architectures and frameworks ease and particularly foster common agreement on the conception of the phenomena which are related to ITLET. They do this necessarily at a high abstraction level as they have to be suitable for a wide range of possible implementations and use cases. The outcome of making use of widely agreed ITLET architectures and frameworks are well-focussed and well-designed, mutually interoperable implementations of ITLET components, tools, services, and environments and further ease their description, specification, evaluation, selection and use.

E-learning is a term that currently has many ambiguous meanings. In this article, *e-learning* denotes all kinds of learning, teaching, training, education, knowledge creation, etc. where a substantial amount of support based on information and communication technology is found. It is evident that *e-learning* is a "soft" term.

14.2   Quality and e-learning architectures or frameworks

Architectures and frameworks for ITLET aim at supporting the human understanding of the effects and the mutual interaction of the diverse processes in LET environments. A good comprehension of the effects and the interaction of the processes is a precondition for

- prudential design of components and interfaces for such environments
- appropriate configuration of such environments for particular purposes
- optimal use of such environments

Quality of learning results from optimised use of appropriately configured environments which are built from prudentially designed components and interfaces. It needs not mentioning that education and knowledge building go closely together with learning and are always implicated here where for simplicity reasons just "learning" is mentioned.

While in LET scenarios the "quality of learning support" will be in the centre of interest, further kinds of quality exist, reflect the interests of the other stakeholders, and need to be considered.

In general, the "level of quality" is an attribute that is associated with a product or a service and that may be given a value. This value expresses to which degree the expectations of the evaluator are matched. Frequently, the evaluation is performed by a representative group of users. It may be guided, analysed, and summarised by evaluation experts.

A value for a "quality of learning support" may depend on many factors which may each have different importance for different users. In a very crude model, the value could be seen as a normalised ratio of effect and effort.

In theory, the effect of learning could be measured by comparing the performance of the learner in the field, the learning is done for, before starting and after finishing the learning. In practice, the situation is much more complicated like in cases where the learning takes place preparatorily, e.g. for an examination (no reference exists for the comparison, any pre-examination is already an act of learning).

The same degree of difficulties as for judging on the effect of learning is found for estimating the effort of learning. In addition to the cost for, e.g., a course, the learner's time spent on attending the course and on doing accompanying preparations and repetitions counts. It makes a difference for the learner's effort whether the course is entertaining or sober, challenging or relaxed. Some learners like it the one way, some the other way.

Finally, the quality of learning support will be measured by the observed satisfaction of the learners and the observed gain in performance. Both judgements are subjective. The first one reflects the subjective, summarising estimation of the learner, the second one reflects the specific view of those who decide what to observe and how to interpret the observed hints relative to a particular set of claims.

14.3   Standardisation: Architectures and frameworks

The following subsections explain major criteria which can be used to categorise "standards" focussing on diverse aspects, and the general approach for building standards in the field of architectures and frameworks. They exemplify architectures and frameworks for e-learning by outlining four different approaches. The different level of detail of these descriptions reflects the personal estimation of the author regarding the impact and suitability and of the different approaches.

Architecture and *framework* are two related terms that are commonly used with ambiguous meanings. In this article, both terms are used in the context of the conception and the design of systems. When we use the term *architecture*, we have a stronger focus on the particularity of aggregating components and are more unspecific concerning the typology of the components. When we use the term *framework*, we have a stronger focus on the typology of the components and are more unspecific concerning their particular aggregation.

14.3.1   A simple standards typology

There are several definitions for what "Standard" means (see also chapter 13).

In the context of which kind of information standards specify, standards may be (possibly combinations of):

- "Interoperability Standards", specifying a certain, revisable way of implementing or combining systems or products in order to assure (technical or semantical) interoperability among the systems or products which abide by the standard.
- "Conceptual Standards", specifying a certain, revisable way of conceiving services or practices in order to assure conceptual comparability among the services or practices which correspond to the standard.
- "Level Standards", specifying a certain, revisable level of "quality" for systems, products, services or practices. These standards are frequently the basis for certifications that aim on providing orientation for users regarding their selection processes.

In the context of which body builds and adopts standards, different levels can be distinguished (including cross-level efforts of liaising and co-operating):

- "Formal Standards", adopted by formal Standards Bodies. The formally appointed National Standards Bodies, like ANSI (ANSI) in the USA, DIN (DIN) in Germany, or JISC (JISC) in Japan, and their worldwide federations: ISO (ISO), IEC (IEC), and ITU (ITU) are unanimously accepted to be "Formal Standards Bodies". Another example for a body which adopts "Formal Standards" in Europe is CEN (CEN).
- "Community Standards", adopted by certain, representative communities. These communities conduct bodies which clearly do standardising work resulting in "Standards", "Specifications", "Recommendations", "Guidelines" etc. which may be very broadly accepted and obeyed to. Typical "Community Standards" in the field of technical support for LET are produced by IEEE (IEEE) and its IEEE SA (IEEE SA), the W3C (W3C), or by MPEG (MPEG).
- "De-facto Standards", sometimes also named "Industry Standards" typically start with proprietary regulations and specifications which are accepted by large user communities and, following, by further supporting industries and communities. In many cases, these standards lack publicly available or purchasable specifications and are not based on consensus building in representative communities. Nevertheless, they may have large influence on the market of systems, products, or services, and may effectively influence common practices.

In the context of the state of standards, we may distinguish between:

- "Final Standards" which are stable and undergo well-defined processes for revisions, advancements or withdrawal.
- "Proposed Standards" which may be in different stages of development and consensus achievement.

Making use of this simple "standards typology", we can state that, regarding the field of architectures and frameworks for ITLET, no final formal standard, a single final community standard: IEEE LTSA (IEEE LTSA, 2002)(IEEE Draft LTSA, 2001), and no final de-facto standard exist. Plans for a less technology-driven standard have been discussed to some extent in ISO/IEC JTC1 SC36 (ERILE,

2001), however have been renounced in 2005 without reaching any formal state. Some further, more technology-driven proposals exist which may contribute to future standards and for which it is not yet clear which body might adopt them. Two of them, the IMS Abstract Framework (IMS Abstract Framework, 2003a) and the approach Service-oriented Frameworks (Wilson et al, 2004) are outlined below.

14.3.2   Typical properties of ITLET architectures and frameworks

It can be expected that standards for ITLET Architectures and Frameworks represent combinations of "Conceptual Standards" (these might typically be named Architectures) and "Interoperability Standards" (these might typically be named Frameworks), where the stress might be on the one or the other type.

ITLET Architectures and Frameworks standards must embrace a large percentage of implementations, as a high demand for interoperability exists (for many reasons that cannot be discussed here in detail). Therefore, these standards clearly need to abstract from the implementations. The large variety of already practised, expected and requested ITLET implementations complicates this abstraction considerably. The experience with these kinds of implementations is limited and experience exchange is handicapped as a widely accepted conceptual model for ITLET implementations is still missing.

This relationship between adjacent abstraction/ implementation layers of an architectures respectively a frameworks is excellently described throughout the latest publicly available draft of the IEEE LTSA (IEEE Draft LTSA, Annex G – Methodology, sections 15.8 to 15.10). In the final standard, a large amount of this methodology description has regrettably been omitted.

One of the central concepts in the methodology used for specifying the IEEE LTSA is the "abstraction/ implementation boundary" in a multilayer model. Crossing this boundary means to go from one layer to an adjacent one, either "upward" or "downward", where "upward" means moving to a description at a higher level of abstraction, and "downward" means moving to a description at a higher level of detail.

On the first glance and wrongly, this approach seems to build a taxonomy for learning environments, where all possible kinds of very specific environments would be the leaves of a taxonomy tree and the nodes on the different levels of the tree would represent all environments below this node in a higher level of abstraction.

Looking at the above approach more closely, a specific environment needs a description on every abstraction/ implementation layer to be completely specified, and all elements on every abstraction layer may play a role in this description.

The task of abstraction is particularly awkward as a large diversity of disciplines and their communities is inseparably involved. Each discipline has its own way of abstraction, and agreement on a common one is hardly found.

14.3.3   Strategy of abstraction in the IEEE LTSA

The IEEE LTSA focuses on the normative third abstraction/ implementation layer in a five-layer model. The informative layers above (layers 1 and 2) and below (layers 4 and 5) are described annexes. The five layers represent:

- Layer 1: Learner-environment interactions (informative)
  This layer places the learners into the centre of the model. The concept of a "learner entity" is presented that represents a group of collaborating learners. The concept of an "environment" is presented that represents further humans acting and interacting in roles and all the involved technical items and data.
  Throughout the standard, information and control flows between components are described and depicted in Yourdon notation (Coad et al, 1990). Readers have to take into consideration that the figures just show the dominant directions of the flows and restrict to the major components and flows. This, however, leaves much room for interpretations that have not been intended.
  The decision of distinguishing in this layer of the model between the (groups of) learners on the one side and the remaining humans, technical components and data on the other side has unfavourable implications for the layers below as it hides the conceptual symmetry between human and artificial properties and functions. The (at that time) "politically" advantageous learner centric view implies a asymmetry of the interests of the diverse stakeholders and at the same time excludes important processes like knowledge building, capturing, and coding for reuse purposes.

- Layer 2: Learner-related design features (informative)
  In the final standard, the learner-related design features have been nearly completely removed (three lines of text in Annex C.3 "Learner design features" compared to LTSA draft 6 containing 10 pages of text and figures in the informative clause 5.3 "human-centred and pervasive features" and the equally titled informative annex D). Only some of the aspects are also found in the examples of the informative annex D "Illustrations of stakeholder mappings".
  It is recommended to make supplementary use of the previous LTSA drafts (IEEE LTSA History, 2001) of the standard.
  As a consequence of the strictly learner-centred orientation of layer 1, the design features of the other stakeholders are also missing in layer 2.

- Layer 3: System Components (normative)
  This layer is the centre of the final standard and makes extensive use of a graphical representation of the normative concept of this layer.
  In this representation (following the IEEE LTSA), ellipses represent processes, rectangles represent stores, solid arrows represent information flows, and dashed arrows represent control flows.
  What is easily seen is an overall loop of four processes, supported by two stores.

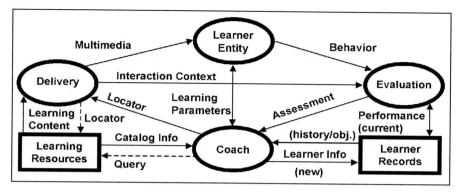

Fig. 14-1: The LTSA system components

- On top of the diagram, the learning process of a single or a group of learners (inside the process "Learner Entity") is represented.
- Observable information ("Behaviour") concerning this learning process, the context of the current learning activity ("Interaction Context"), and stored "Performance" information regarding the "Learner Entity" are provided to the process "Evaluation".
- The process "Evaluation" judges on the assumable learning progress and provides as well "(current) Performance" information for the "Learner Records" store as "Assessment" information for the process "Coach".
- The process "Coach" provides guidance and information for the Learner Entity. It makes use of what is stored in the "Learner Records" about the performance and the learning objectives of the "Learner Entity" and issues new entries in this store reflecting findings and decisions ("Learner Info (new)"). It sends out "Queries" to the store "Learning Resources" and selects the most appropriate resource. It sends the "Locator" of this resource to the "Delivery" process.
- The process "Delivery" uses this "Locator" to acquire the "Learning Content" (the Resource) and to transform it into a appropriate form ("Multimedia") for the purpose of interaction with the "Learner Entity". At the same time, the "Delivery" process provides the "Interaction Context" (which may be derived from Learning Object Metadata and the status of the delivery) for the "Evaluation" Process.
- The vertical, double-tipped arrow in the middle of the diagram represents the information exchange between the "Learner Entity" and the Coach for the purpose of negotiating the requested and the recommended kind of guidance.
  An obvious limitation of this model is again resulting from the restriction to the support of acquiring expertise from existing resources. The opposite way of creating new resources from creative aspects of the learning process is closed in this diagram. It could be opened by a few additional flows between the "Coach" Process and the "Learning Resources" store.

An important aspect of using this diagram is the regulation that, as far as the processes represent human activities, they represent just these activities and not the humans themselves. This allows to model simultaneous activities of one human in several processes (like in self-directed learning where the same human might simultaneously play the roles "Learner Entity", "Evaluation" and "Coach").

- Layer 4: Stakeholder Perspectives and Priorities (informative)
  The information in this layer consists of a large variety of learning environment categories (in annex D of the standard respectively annex C of LTSA draft 9) and examples (in annex F of the standard respectively annex E in LTSA draft 9) that are described by making use of the system components of layer 3.
  Effectively, these two annexes seem to have the main purpose of proving that the model in layer 3 reflects the wide field of use cases for learning environments. At the same time, layer 4 provides many examples that ease the understanding of the System Components model in the layer above.
  From the examples F.3 in annex F of the standard (annex E, 13.3 in LTSA draft 9) it becomes evident how difficult it is to represent stakeholders like, e.g., learning material producers or user and material administrators.
- Layer 5: Codings, APIs and Protocols (informative)
  Like done for layer 2 [learner-related design features] of the overall model, the information on this layer 5 has been nearly completely removed either. While in LTSA draft 5 some pages of information about bindings, encodings, APIs and calling conventions, codings and data formats, protocols and communication layers were included, these have already been dropped in LTSA draft 6. Apparently, this has been done because this level of description came out to be quite general and not sufficiently specific to ITLET. This shortcoming seems to be typical for many of the technology-driven approaches and is a clear consequence of the design decisions for layer 4 [stakeholder perspectives and priorities] that is rather presenting arguments for layer 3 [system components] than providing guidance for presenting ITLET environments at a technical level.
  The version history of the LTSA is very helpful for understanding the controverse discussions across the educational and the technical communities. Trying to satisfy both by masking out all information that provokes either the one or the other community, the remainder is not satisfying. It seems that a terminology is needed which is new for both communities and allows to build common agreement.
  The LTSA approach represents an architecture and, in its approach, is neither technology- nor educationally-oriented. From its wording, however, it seems to be technology-oriented, however is not. This technical wording is also responsible for many of the misunderstandings, the approach is suffering from. During the consensus building process, the approach has been stripped down to a version that does no longer comprise some of the important concepts contained in earlier versions. One of the weaknesses of the LTSA approach is its

restriction to a subsection of e-learning only: the delivery scenarios (in contrast to the phenomena resulting from cross-role knowledge building scenarios). The major strengths of the LTSA approach are its neutrality regarding technology or educational orientation and its high level of abstraction.

14.3.4   Strategy of abstraction in the ERILE proposal

The ERILE proposal is an attempt to learn from the shortcomings of the LTSA approach. The work on this proposal started in the end of the nineties and tried to harvest the experience acquired from designing, implementing, using, and evaluating an ITLET platform (the IDEALS MTS (IDEALS MTS, 1996), see example F.3 in annex F of the IEEE LTSA (or example 13.3 in LTSA draft 9).

In contrast to the IEEE LTSA, that aims at explaining the support of learning in a process model, the ERILE approach focuses on the representation and exchange of expertise in ITLET.

Expertise as used in this article denotes a generalisation for phenomena like knowledge, skills, aptitude, qualification, competency, etc. These phenomena are associated with actors (represented by humans or also computing machinery). In the case of computing machinery, these phenomena are usually represented by carriers and, separately, associated specification of semantics. Regarding humans, the explicit separation of carriers and semantics is not usual as it is not easily observable. *Expertise* may be available or practiced, and, also may be observed, specified, mediated, stored, and reused. Provision of *expertise* in computing machinery requires adequate representation (i.e. coding for building carriers) and description (for specifying the semantics). It requires also appropriate runtime systems that bring the carriers into action and take care of the application context. Employment of *expertise* is related to any practicing and, in ITLET environments, to didactic and pedagogic strategies, learning, teaching, and inherent knowledge progression.

- The model aims at a strict symmetry of human and computer-based activities.
- It is specified for the purpose of characterising instances of learning environments by declaring, to which percentages activities were performed by humans, by computing machinery, or by a flexible allocation.
- The general concept of expertise allows for integrating diverse levels of expertise, such as topical, didactical, educational, technical, administrational expertise with an unlimited possibility of extensions.
- The definite separation of (human or computer-based) actors and roles that can be associated with actors is the attempt to overcome the conceptional difficulties observed in the IEEE LTSA System Component Model. As for the list of expertise categories, the list of possible roles is an open list.
- Specific importance is given to the concept of capturing, coding, replicating and reusing expertise by using a scale that covers the expertise representation

spectrum from usable instances over templates and wizards up to highly automated tools.

A proposal of a graphical representation of this model is suggested as shown below:

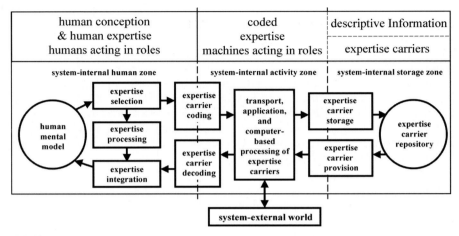

Fig. 14-2: The ERILE model

Different from the modelling in the IEEE LTSA, no particular roles and no particular processes are separated in this general diagram. Instead, the "hidden" phenomena inside and the "observable" phenomena outside the involved humans are
contrasted.

Only for the purpose of pointing out that the ITLET systems under observation
here may have an interface to a system-external world, whose details remain hidden in our observations, a system-internal zone is separated from a system-
external one.

It should be assumed that the "human mental model" will typically be associated to more than one human being.

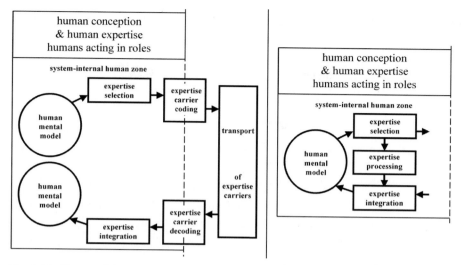

Fig. 14-3: Human dialogue and contemplation

Figure 14-3 shows how a dialogue between two humans (where there is no number restriction) or how the contemplation of a single human are modelled. Of course, in a dialogue a continuous switching of the talker role and the listener role occurs; even the simultaneous association of both roles with both humans is possible when both humans talk at the same time (and hopefully listen as well...). This abstraction in this model allows also more complicated dialogues among several humans acting in different (and possibly continuously changing) roles, such as learner and teacher, learning material author and content manager, or learner and user interface designer.

An important and disputed concept in this model is that of "expertise carriers". These carriers are the observable signals or data exchanged among actors in the system. These signals (like speech or gesture) or data (like coded video, audio or text) do in fact not simply carry expertise. They even do not simply carry meaning, however they finally do this in combination with the context in which they are generated or brought by the receiving actor (allowing all the obvious phenomena of understanding and misunderstanding that are around).

Several categories of "expertise carriers" represent those entities which are commonly named "digital resources". The awareness of these resource categories is growing and clearly exceeds the classical resources like media files or Web pages. The steps from descriptive data towards meaning and finally "expertise" or "competency" are continuously developed in research and practice.

When using the term "actor", both humans and software agents (computing machinery enabled by software and data) are addressed: one of the most important features of ITLET environment in comparison to traditional LET environments is the employment of computers as acting and responsive actors.

At first glance, the appearance of humans (left side) and software agents (middle and right side) in figure 14-2 does not look symmetrical, however, in fact is. On the one hand, the processes of expertise selection, processing, and integration being not directly observable in connection with humans, are observable in connection with software agents. The same applies to the coding and decoding of expertise carriers. In connection with the software agents these five processes are contained inside the central block. On the other hand, expertise carrier storage and provision are observable activities in connection with computing machinery, however not with humans.

In ITLET environments, the context of the signals and data required for the reconstruction of meaning may to some extent be represented by descriptive data (frequently named "metadata") associated with the expertise carriers. Substantial context information is represented, however, by the "understanding of the communication status". In human-to-human dialogue, one of the main activities observed is the continuous verification of context correspondence. Where computing machinery is engaged in dialogue, descriptive data is indispensable for using expertise carriers. In dialogues between humans and computing machinery, the lack of appropriate descriptive data results in continuous "misunderstanding".

Naming these carriers (signals and data, associated with descriptive data) "expertise carriers" reflects the basic intention of ICT support for LET, which is the reuse of expertise. The purpose for reusing expertise is the enhancement of its availability (in terms of multiplicity, time and location) and the attempt of consolidating widespread expertise in a way which is suitable for local and individual needs. The precondition for reusing expertise is the possibility of extracting, coding, transporting, storing, replicating, and activating it by responsive and acting computing machinery.

On the basis of this abstraction strategy, it is quite obvious how the counterparts for human expertise and activities can be built by engaging data and computing machinery. Subject to the diverse categories of expertise and the role-specific activities already well-known from traditional, human-based LET, the corresponding representations for "expertise carriers" can be developed, experienced, and advanced. This can be done stepwise, reflecting the growing insight into such systems and the most urgent needs.

This development process, which is a learning process of its own, would start with the definition of roles and categories of expertise. In contrast to the limitations of the IEEE LTSA, no limitations exist here in connection with the activities found in environments applicable for the management, the advancement and the dissemination of human knowledge.

The ERILE approach represents a framework and is neither technology- nor educationally-oriented, as it attempts to mediate between both orientations. It focuses on the human expertise which is related to the effect of humans and technical means and on the artefacts the technical means are accepting, communicating, and bringing into action. The major weaknesses of the ERILE approach are its high abstraction level and, surprisingly, one of its main strength: the introduction and use of a terminology that is positioned between the technical and educational communities. It will take some time for these communities to conceive the advantage of such a neutral terminology and to harmonise it. The major strengths of the

ERILE approach are its community-neutral approach, its symmetry in the context of humans and computing machinery, and its "expertise carrier" concept.

14.3.5   Strategy of abstraction in the IMS abstract framework

The IMS (IMS Global Learning Consortium) Abstract Framework undertakes to analyse a wide range of use cases, a rich set of IMS specifications, and a variety of existing or developing reference models and architectures (mainly selected from US-dominated initiatives) in order to integrate these in a single, abstract framework.

Several aspects are considered, such as

- a "logical architecture", reflecting the OSI (OSI, 1996) view,
- a "physical architecture", reflecting a 3-tier "User-System-Interface - Process-Management – Database-Management" view (Sadoski et al, 2004),
- a "functional model", reflecting the processes and communicated artefacts, and
- the "functional person model", reflecting the integration of "human resources" into an e-learning framework.

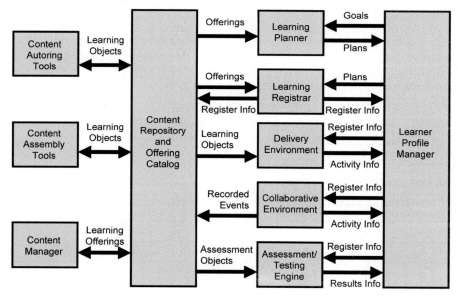

Fig. 14-4: A functional model for using learning material

Figure 14-4, following the IMS Abstract Framework White Paper, shows the functional view of an e-learning framework as a typical example.

The IMS Abstract Framework, though doing this in a really abstract manner, points out implementation layers, while the ERILE approach focuses on the effects and does not refer to any implementation strategies.

The functional model of the IMS Abstract Framework (see figure 14-4) identifies a variety of activities and communicated artefacts. In doing this, it corresponds to the approach taken in ERILE, however, in contrast to the ERILE approach, is very unspecific regarding the expertise carried by different categories of learning objects.

The IMS Abstract Framework focuses on dedicated technical categories of tools and, thus, is clearly technology-oriented. One of its weaknesses is the insufficient association of educational phenomena with different kinds of "Objects", "Offerings", "Plans", "Events", and "Infos". Its major strength, and at the same time a major weakness, is its orientation towards existing technical modules, by this easing its adoption by at least the technical community (at the same time scaring away the educational community).

14.3.6   Strategy of abstraction in a service oriented framework

There are several attempts of abstracting ITLET environments by addressing their components in a very general sense. This approach is the combination of general system design and a repository of all the concepts, phenomena, functionalities, and tools which are of relevance in the context of ITLET.

By ordering these concepts in a way which represents activity-related coherence (in figure 14-5: horizontally) and manifoldness (in figure 14-5: vertically), the components can be associated with services that can be combined for providing all functions required for an ITLET environment, at the same time avoiding duplications and assuring consistency.

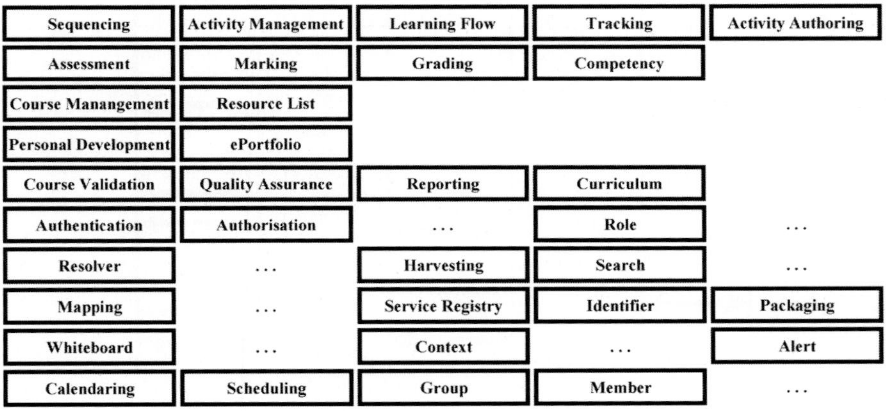

Sequencing	Activity Management	Learning Flow	Tracking	Activity Authoring
Assessment	Marking	Grading	Competency	
Course Manangement	Resource List			
Personal Development	ePortfolio			
Course Validation	Quality Assurance	Reporting	Curriculum	
Authentication	Authorisation	. . .	Role	. . .
Resolver	. . .	Harvesting	Search	. . .
Mapping	. . .	Service Registry	Identifier	Packaging
Whiteboard	. . .	Context	. . .	Alert
Calendaring	Scheduling	Group	Member	. . .

Fig. 14-5: E-learning framework

Figure 14-5, following a publication on service-oriented frameworks (Wilson et al, 2004), gives an impression of an example of an e-learning framework in this kind of abstraction.

The Service Oriented Framework in fact represents a typical framework and focuses on a mix of dedicated functional categories of services, processes and actors. By doing this, it is clearly technology-oriented. One of its weaknesses is the insufficient separation between processes, actors, and artefacts. Like already found for the IMS Abstract Framework approach, the major strength, and at the same time a major weakness, of the Service Oriented Framework approach is its orientation towards existing technical objects, by this easing its adoption by at least the technical community (at the same time scaring away the educational community).

14.4   Practical use of e-learning architectures or frameworks

There are many different ways of making practical use of specifications and standards for ITLET architectures and frameworks. What might have become evident from the short presentation and explanation of examples is the fact that a single standard will not match all needs. Different strategies for abstracting the manifoldness of imaginable ITLET environments will provide orientation and help for different categories of users with different interests.

The IEEE LTSA is well suited for understanding the orientation of an ITLET environment as soon as its mapping to the LTSA System Components model is provided. Such an abstracted representation does not allow to deduct any quality assertions easily. The graphical coding of the involvement (colour coding) and the significance (line width) of the processes and flows provide, however, clear hints regarding the forming of particular processes and potential support from them. This allows from the System Component model and its accompanying textual description some judgements on the suitability of a system for different LET applications.

This possibility is illustrated in the annexes of the IEEE LTSA by a very rich set of examples that show how different categories and examples of ITLET environments appear differently in this mapping. The mapping provides a good overview of the main characteristics of an ITLET environment.

Regrettably, for real ITLET environments it is not at all easy to map them to the LTSA System Components model, particularly if the environments go beyond course delivery towards knowledge management. Overcoming this shortcoming has been a major design goal for the second example of abstracting ITLET environments.

The ERILE approach has qualities that suggest to use this kind of abstraction for unambiguous mappings of ITLET environments or demand specifications to a representation that can be used for automated comparison of provisions and demands (i.e. automated suitability evaluation). At the same time, this approach provides a good conceptual model for understanding the mechanisms of ICT support for LET.

Carrying on this approach will result in extracting the major concepts for ICT support for LET. These concepts are associated with well-known educational, psychological or physiological information, processes, and activities, represented as well traditionally as by employing ICT. Using these concepts allows sufficiently precise specification of demanded quality for ITLET settings and description of their quality potentialities.

An additional advantage of the ERILE approach is bringing the technical and the educational communities into a substantial discussion and have them link together their differently focussed expertise.

Both framework approaches, the IEEE LTSA and ERILE, aim rather at providing design orientation for technical implementers than representing a conceptual help for educational experts. It must be kept in mind, however, that the components of these frameworks need to be derived from abstract approaches like those of the IEEE LTSA or ERILE. All four approaches outlined here are specific conceptual projections of the same phenomena and should not be seen as alternative, exchangeable approaches. They are closely interrelated and support each other while providing differrent information and orientation.

We can expect an ongoing learning process inside the involved, different communities, and hopefully also across those. Obviously, ITLET focuses on learning and at the same time undergoes a learning process. The amount of interdisciplinary awareness in the diverse communities confines the consensus on really useful architectures and frameworks for e-learning. The same awareness is required for making progress on e-learning quality. Work on terminology is a third stage where awareness can be advanced and harmonised. Experience from practice is one of the most important fields for supporting conceptual progress. Taking this into account, it is of secondary importance, where in these fields progress is made – as long as progress is made at all.

15 Content and management standards: LOM, SCORM and Content Packaging

Christian Prpitsch, Patrick Veith

University of Duisburg-Essen, Germany

Interoperability of learning scenarios is a critical factor. A variety of initiatives have developed specifications and standards for e-learning. For the description of Content, Learning Object Metadata (LOM) have been widely adopted. In the field of management standards, especially SCORM and IMS Content Packaging have grown in importance. They enable users to package contents and share, distribute and reuse them between different learning management systems. However, several steps are necessary to implement these standards in an efficient way. This article introduces LOM, the Sharable Content Object Reference Model (SCORM) and IMS Content Packaging and explains the use of application profiles for a context specific reuse of e-learning resources.

15.1 Introduction

E-learning contents in general consist of interlinked resources, which are a multimedia representation of the content, normally stored and run within a Learning Management Systems (LMS). The Hyper Text Markup Language (HTML) is most commonly used and as such each HTML document can only be used to its full extend together with all referenced files (e.g., graphic or audio files referenced within the HTML document). All files for a specific e-learning offer bundled in one compressed file, is what we call an e-learning content package. This includes all HTML documents, all media files, all style sheets and all scripting components used within the content. This definition of e-learning content packages excludes a measure how much content such a package includes. Thus, a content package could just consist of a short text about one topic, while another package could consist of a full fledged university course with simulation programs, questionnaires, and text documents. The design process to build consistent content and to modularise the content is not within the scope of this article, which will focus on the technical interoperability of such packages.

Content packages are used within different applications. First of all, most content packages are created using authoring tools. Learning Management Systems (LMS) use these packages to provide the included content for their learners. LMS commonly add services they can provide to the package to enable their learners to better use these packages. For example, a forum could be used to enable learners and teachers to communicate within their learning context. Applications which specialise in storing and indexing content packages are called repositories. While these do not provide support for the learners' learning processes, repositories aim to enable learners to retrieve content packages, which are best suited for them and their situational context.

This article is about reusing e-learning content packages. Reuse is not a trivial process: it must take several constraints into account, such as the organisational or personal context of a learning situation. Reusing e-learning packages can include any combination of the following activities:

- Retrieving packages from repositories based on learner preferences.
- Exchanging packages within a learning scenario.
- Searching through repositories to find packages with suitable learning objectives.
- Retrieving a description of the didactic concept of an e-learning package.
- Extracting competencies, which either are needed for or are achieved with the package.
- Retrieving cooperation information on the package. For instance if the package was designed for teams of learners or individual learners.
- Repackaging e-learning content to individualise content.

The activities to be supported to build an efficient, reusable package depend on the context for the reuse. As such, it is impossible to provide support for every possible form of reuse, but if the need for reuse can be specified prior to the reuse, the packages can be tailored to comply to these needs. The most promising way to do this is to provide an individualised set of metadata for each e-learning package. These sets of metadata are called application profiles. Later in this article, we provide an example to build specific application profiles.

This article focuses on standards in e-learning which were designed to provide a better technical interoperability between the different tools involved in the learning processes. SCORM for instance provides a technical standard for interoperability of e-learning content packages between LMS and e-learning content authoring systems.

This article starts of with an overview of the IEEE Learning Object Metadata, IMS Content Packaging and SCORM standards which help to make e-learning packages interoperable. In a second step, we introduce the concept of profiles for metadata to achieve a better reusability/ retrieveability of e-learning packages. Additionally, we describe recent work within standardisation bodies, which provide specific application profiles to address problems within their scope. To illustrate the practical use, we present one scenario with specific needs and show how we designed an application profile to cope with them at our university. The article closes with a short summery and a short glimpse on the future of standardisation activities in the field of management standards.

15.2   IEEE learning object metadata (IEEE LOM)

The standard IEEE Learning Object Metadata (IEEE LOM) was designed to facilitate search, retrieval, acquisition and use of learning objects by, for instance, learners, instructors or software processes. To achieve this IEEE LOM specifies a conceptual data scheme and the corresponding XML-binding (IEEE, 2002).

The idea of IEEE LOM was that metadata about learning resources was needed much like a library catalogue record. The catalogue had to provide structured descriptions for learning objects and thus enable repositories to make the described learning objects searchable by selected attributes like title, author or subject. By defining a set of metadata, the description can be stored separately from the learning objects or packaged with the resource.

15.2.1   The basic structure of IEEE LOM

IEEE LOM consists of nine categories, which group the included Data elements respectively. Cancore (CANCORE, 2005) was used as a base for the description given here.

General

The General Category groups general information describing a learning object as a whole. This includes identification criteria, language of the learning object, the title, a short description and keywords as well as its coverage, structure and aggregation level.

Lifecycle

This category describes the current state of the learning object and provides the entities that have affected this learning object during its most current evolution. To give a more complete overview of the evolution of the learning object from version to version, each predecessor can be referred to in the Relation category.

Meta-Metadata

Here the metadata of the learning object are described. The data elements here can be used to identify which schema the metadata adheres to. Usually in IEEE LOM, this refers to the version of LOM used.

Technical

Information about technical features of the learning object are grouped in the Technical Category. Here the physical size, the location, technical requirements to use the learning object and the duration to complete the learning object are given. IEEE LOM currently assumes a one-to-one correspondence between metadata and the resource it describes, which is commonly not the case. To accommodate this, the Relation Category can be used to refer to included elements.

Educational

The educational dimension of the learning object is described within this category. Data elements include a description of the interactivity and context of the learning object, as well as the role of its intended end user and his typical age range.

Rights

This category describes the intellectual property rights and conditions of use for the learning object. This category is limited to a very minimum of data elements, as the ongoing work on Digital Rights Management (DRM) in the internet community is expected to provide a standardised description in the future. Right now opinions about DRM range from the U.S. government, who has already passed a "Digital Millennium Copyright Act" (U.S. Copyright Office, 1998) to enforce DRM, to the open-source community, which is discussing DRM controversial (see Stallman, 2002).

Relation

The relationship between the described learning object and other learning objects is described here. It is possible to define multiple relationships by adding multiple instances of this category to a learning object. Each relation to a learning object is described in a new relationship instance.

Annotation

Comments to the educational use of the learning object can be entered here.

Classification

The Classification category is used to describe the learning object from different perspectives or for different purposes using named classification systems.

15.2.2   Integration of IEEE LOM in other standards

IEEE LOM was the first of the learning standards to become an officially en-dorsed standard. It also was widely accepted from the very beginning and thus it was integrated into almost all further e-learning standards, which in turn also helped to further establish IEEE LOM as the backbone of the e-learning standardi-sation.

15.3   IMS content packaging (IMS CP)

"The objective of the IMS CP Information Model is to define a standardised set of structures that can be used to exchange content" (IMS, 2004a).

The IMS Content Packaging (IMS CP) standard consists of two components: the Information Model (IMS, 2004a) and its corresponding binding (IMS, 2004c). The CP Information model describes the data structure of IMS CP, which ensures the interoperability between LMS and authoring tools. The IMS CP XML Binding Specification describes the representation of the data structure using XML (W3C, 2005). Additionally a best practice guide is also available from IMS (IMS, 2004b).

While the information model describes the data used to make IMS Content Packages interoperable, the XML Binding offers a technical solution to extract the data from each package. This is realised by adding one metadata file to each IMS Content Package which includes the metadata. This file is called manifest and added to the top level of the package which also includes all content files of the package.

The manifest file is structured in four categories: Metadata, Organisation, Re-sources and Sub-Manifest, which will be described in the following paragraphs.

General

This section specifies an identification key, the version and the relative offset for included content files of the package.

Metadata

The metadata section can contain the metadata describing the package as a whole. IMS suggests the IEEE Learning Object Metadata (LOM) (IEEE, 2002) to de-scribe the package.

Organisation

The organisation section is the key part for the interoperability within IMS Con-tent Packaging. It describes the structure of learning resources. A learning re-source specifies either a structure of other learning resources or refers to a set of resources in the resource section (see below). Each learning resource can be used on its own and thus represents reusable content. The hierarchical structure of the organisation section is used to rebuild the default structure within applications using these packages. As an example, LMS are enabled to access the structure of IMS Content Packages and include the structure in the navigation. Each learning resource can include either inline metadata or refer to a file within the package which includes its metadata. IMS CP suggests IEEE LOM as metadata, but other metadata standards (such as Dublin Core) can also be included.

Resources

Resources in IMS CP refer to files or groups of files within the package which are needed for learning resources specified in the organisation section.

Sub-Manifest(s)

In this category, different organisations can be specified. An application using the package can provide learners with a variety of alternative navigations for the content.

Figure 15-1 shows how IMS CPs are expected to integrate into the content management processes within a learning platform. The aim was to design a standardised way to specify LMS independent e-learning content. IMS CP focuses on import and export functionalities for compliant LMSs and thus does not need to provide a full-fledged view on the content. It is tailored to help authors to produce e-learning content which can be imported in and extracted from LMS easily. Other than that the LMS has to cope with the content of the package on its own, as IMS CP does not support learning activities directly.

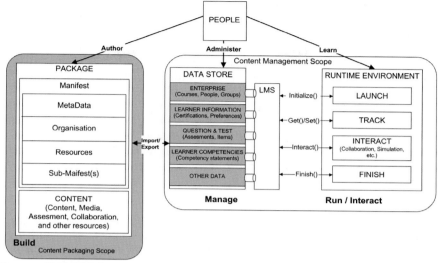

Source: IMS, 2004b

Fig. 15-1: IMS content framework

15.4   Shareable Content Object Reference Model (SCORM)

The Sharable Content Object Reference Model (SCORM) is designed to make electronic learning objects interchangeable between Learning Management Systems (LMS) and to reuse them. These goals are achieved by creating so called SCORM-packages and by specifying a runtime-environment for these packages. SCORM uses and integrates standards from various organisations. SCORM supports the learning process by enabling the LMS to present some kind of learning resources to the learners and to let them do tests after that. SCORM is developed by the Advanced Distributed Learning Initiative (ADL) (ADL, 2004a).

Most of the standards used by the SCORM are adapted from IMS Global Learning Consortium (IMS, 2005a). The recommended standard for metadata is Learning Object Metadata (LOM) as defined by IMS (see section 15 of this book). SCORM packages are created according to IMS Content Packaging. To describe the sequencing of learning objects in the SCORM package IMS Simple Sequencing (IMS SS) (IMS, 2003a) could be used. IMS SS defines a method for representing the intended behaviour of authored learning content for LMS to represent the content as intended by the author. Within a SCORM package, this is mainly achieved by sequencing the included objects as described in the IMS SS metadata included in the package.

A SCORM package is an archive in a common format (e.g., zip as defined by RFC1951 (Deutsch, 1996)) built with a predefined structure of its content. The most important part of the content is an XML-file called manifest-file containing all information about what is in the package, what it is for and how it is used (see section 15.4.1). The package also contains the resource-files itself. It may contain metadata-information about everything in it which is strongly recommended by the SCORM.

To achieve reusability, the content of a complete package is divided into smaller parts called *Sharable Content Objects (SCO)*. A SCO is the smallest reusable unit in the context of the SCORM. It includes all necessary files to use its content and additionally software to communicate with a SCORM compatible LMS. This software is the *SCORM API-adapter client* component. Each SCORM conform LMS has to include the *SCORM API-adapter server* component. A SCO may contain web-content or any other content. Each SCO has to communicate with the LMS using its SCORM API-adapter. The lowest requirement is to notify the corresponding LMS that the SCO is loaded or unloaded using the API-adapter. The API-adapter is recommended to be implemented as a JAVA-applet which has to handle the specified data-fields. These are described in (ADL, 2004b) and cover data for tracking the learners' performance and other information provided by the LMS. The API-adapter is also responsible to control the access to the fields, to check the data-type and to make the data persistent. Web content can access the JAVA-applet via ECMA-Script (also known as JAVA-Script), which enables the LMS to grant access to learning content based on the performance of learner on a test. Some examples for both, the API-adapter and the usage via ECMA-Script, are available at ADL (www.adlnet.org).

15.4.1   The SCORM manifest file

Every SCORM package has to include a manifest file (as described in the section 15.3 above) named "imsmanifest.xml" which has to be located on the top level. This file is used to describe and structure the content of the whole package. It consists of metadata, one or more organisations, resources and sub-manifests.

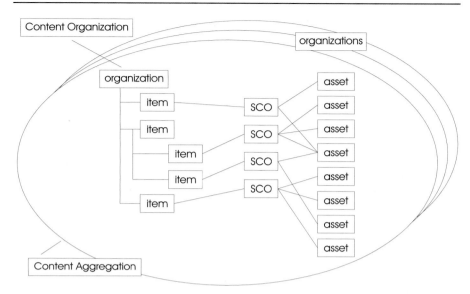

Fig. 15-2: Structuring elements in a manifest file

The metadata for each SCO and the package itself are optional but recommended. Every XML-format of metadata is allowed, but SCORM suggests the use of IEEE LOM (IEEE, 2002). There are two ways of connecting metadata to the manifest. The first one is to simply include it in the structure. The second way is to reference to it by a link to a file within the package so that the metadata are available in separate XML-files. Metadata can be specified for every kind of resource, every organisation item, and for the whole manifest.

Resources define the groups of media files and links in this package. They can be ordered hierarchically. There are two kinds of them: SCO and asset. In the vocabulary of the manifest-file, all files are *Assets* and groups of them are called *SCOs,* if they match the requirements mentioned above. Otherwise they are called *grouped Assets*. The major difference between SCOs and Assets is that SCOs are required to be useable within an LMS on their own, while this is not the case with assets. Additionally, an SCO must be able to communicate with a LMS. Every resource gets a unique identifier.

In (IMS, 2004b), the use of Assets is recommended for grouping files belonging together and/ or used together. As an example, usually one asset is defined including files for the SCORM-API adapter which all SCOs refer to. Additionally each SCO in the SCORM package refers to assets which include all media files representing its content.

The organisation section of the manifest file structures the resources. There may be more than one organisation, but there has to be at least one specified. In an organisation definition, the main element is the *item*. Items can be ordered hierarchically. They refer to a SCO in the resources section. Every item has a unique identifier and a title. Items can contain other items. They can include information for the SCORM-runtime of a LMS, like information about the data the SCO will send to the LMS. This is mainly specified in the item section. By declaring more organisations it is possible to vary the information each SCO sends. A SCO can thus be used in different contexts by reacting to the data the actual LMS is able provide.

It is possible to add metadata to an organisation and to every item. Every organisation and item is required to have a title and a unique identifier. Each item is assigned a title. If metadata is used this field becomes redundant as the title is also included in the relevant metadata, but the field must still be filled.

A manifest may include multiple sub-manifests. They are specified the same way as the manifest described above and represent different learning sequences for the same set of SCOs, for example to provide additional learning sequences for different learning preferences.

The structure of a manifest is shown in figure 15-2. Every manifest contains one or more Content Aggregations, represented by sub-manifests within the main manifest. The Content Aggregation contains any number of content organisations, called "organisations". Every organisation structures the content of the package by ordering the included SCOs. The definition of SCOs and Assets is given in the section "resources". The reusability of the content is put into effect by the definition of organisations or manifests for every intended target group. This is common practice for creating packages containing learning objects used in different contexts.

As an example, a learning object named "theoretical definition of a system" for a university course can be used in many different courses with very different contexts, for instance engineering and political science. The first target group needs the theory to understand how to build a concept for operating systems of computers. The second group is not interested in operating systems but needs the abstract definition of a system to understand models used to simulate activities in politics and society. A teacher can create one learning object covering the abstract definition for both contexts. This learning object can then be included in both contexts and even in one SCORM package. This would result in two organisations for the same package. The metadata of the organisations can be used to describe how to use the learning object within each context.

15.4.2   LOM and SCORM

The usage of IMS-LOM is recommended by the SCORM specification. As already mentioned above, the usage of other metadata formats is possible. In the specification of SCORM (ADL, 2004c), there are sets of metadata-fields declared, depending on the kind of described object. Because every declared object in a manifest can have assigned metadata there is a great variety of different objects to describe, e.g. a complete manifest or just a single asset. The suggested profiles all include the required fields from the specification by IMS. As LOM is specifically tailored to e-learning, its usage in SCORM is widely accepted, for example both the Canadian (CanCore, 2005) and the English (cetis, 2005) initiatives for learning resource metadata use LOM. Other standards as for example the Dublin Core (DCMI, 2005) standard usually do not cover the special needs of learning objects because they are not designed for this purpose.

15.5   A short note on learning design and other didactic standards

In contrast to SCORM, the IMS Learning Design (LD) specification can depict a wide range of pedagogies in online learning (IMS, 2003b). This is achieved by providing a generic and flexible language to represent the didactic conception, such as learning activities, of learning scenarios. IMS specifies activities to be performed with each content object and thus adds the didactic concept as metadata to its packages. As in SCORM, IMS LD specifies a package and a runtime environment for it and uses IMS CP to structure its content. Thus IMS LD inherits much of the merits of SCORM and adds a new level of reusability: The didactic concept of an e-learning package. IMS LD can provide all functionalities SCORM provides and additionally provides a representation of the used didactic conception. Chapter 16 in this book elaborates more on this topic, so it suffice here that standards like learning design can be used to describe e-learning much more detailed and make e-learning more transparent. For example, this is done by specifying (software-) services needed for use the e-learning package. It is likely that SCORM will include Learning Design in one of its next versions.

15.6   Profiling metadata to enhance reusability

Application profiles are a collection of metadata that are tailored to the needs of a specific community of users. To efficiently use metadata in e-learning, it is not necessary to provide all entries for each used metadata standard. This would be too much to cope with. The IEEE LOM standard for instance has over 60 entries. Therefore, application profiles define a subset of mandatory entries typically based on a metadata standard to reduce the complexity of the standard. Additional elements can also be defined. In general, a very specific profile for a community requires less data to be collected. An example for such a profile could be one country government, which creates an application profile to describe educational learning resources targeted for the country's schools use. The application profile could be tailored to help people to find digital learning resources that they need from this sector and thus exchange content between schools. Another example is shown in the 13.7 below, which tailors a profile to one specific organisation.

Application profiles usually aim to reduce the mandatory entries to a minimum, which supports the aims of the profile to its full extent. Most of the work involved in building such a profile is to evaluate which entries are needed and how they should be used to improve interoperability between partners. As such, global and local application profiles are developed in different standardisation bodies. Below some example of developed profiles are given.

Standardisation project with global scope

International Standardised Profiles (ISP) are developed in ISO JTC1 SC36/ WG6 and can be found on http://isp.jtc1sc36.org/index.html. Aim of this workgroup is to define profiles for established e-learning standards to foster the use of these.

To achieve an accepted profile and foster the use of standards the work group decides on a theme to work on and then get together a body of experts from all over the world to work on the theme. They will then try coordinating the different activities world wide and recommend a profile with global scope. Activities right now include for example defining a participant information profile. Information about these activities can be found on the work groups website mentioned above.

European standardisation project

The UK LOM Core initiative adapts IEEE LOM for use in the UK educational context and a description of the project is hosted on http://www.cetis.ac.uk/content/20030731165743. This is done twofold: The UK LOM Core initiative defines a minimum set of elements of IEEE LOM metadata for the UK educational community and writes an implementation guide for all IEEE LOM elements including the additional requirements for the UK educational community.

National projects outside Europe

The Treasury Board of Canada also issued a project to harmonise Canadian application profiles. The project can be found on http://www.tbs-sct.gc.ca/im-gi/mwg-gtm/ems-sml/intro_e.asp. The main tasks of the e-learning subgroup are:

- To investigate several Canadian and international metadata initiatives in the field of e-learning.
- To seek to reach consensus on the means by which to create educational metadata.
- To gather and disseminate best practices and guidance.

To achieve these goals the actions are coordinated by a work-plan published on the homepage of the project. Activities this year include define a vocabulary for the educational community of Canada.

The Ministry of Education Taiwan started a project to create a metadata application profiles and suggest a system for educational resources for use in Taiwan schools. A description of the project can be found on http://www.sinica.edu.tw/~metadata/project/project-homepage/m1-3-e-learning_eng.htm.

The aim of the project is to improve the curriculum of the Grade 1-9 by using information technology and by promoting instructional design and experience sharing. This is done by integrating educational resources from internet communities managed by counties, cities and educational organisations and encourages communication between these internet communities.

15.7   Example of use

In the following, we describe a short example how to use SCORM with LOM metadata for representing the structure of a complete course of studies. The prerequisite to implement this example in a university was the acceptance from the teaching staff. To support this, a predefined set of standardised metadata was used to reduce redundant information entries in the workflow concerning the courses held by each staff member.

The environment of this example is one course of study at a university. The requirements are made by four stakeholders: The administration of the course of study requiring a handbook to describe all modules and courses including prerequisites and dependencies. Every single teacher is required to provide metadata for courses. These were used to detect overlapping parts with other courses. The students needed more information about what courses they could take and which courses depended on one another. The administration of the university needs reports about which courses were held.

Aim of the implementation was to avoid redundancy in the stored data and to provide a user-friendly application. The idea of implementation is the usage of a metadata-profile and SCORM-packages to provide possible e-learning-content. Other documents should be automatically generated by specific style sheets. There are different possibilities of creating printable documents (transform to HTML and print via browser or transform to any text-format). The decision was to use an XML-based format for a text-application. The OpenOffice.org-format (Brauer, 2005) is completely written in XML. This made it easy to create a style sheet and transform the metadata to OpenOffice.org-documents. The main benefit is to produce documents being editable in a cross-platform word processor (OpenOffice.org Writer).

The goal to detect overlapping course content could easily be achieved by indexing the created metadata for every course and search them for redundancies. To choose one metadata profile we did the following. First all requirements were translated into metadata-fields. With this translation one could go through relevant metadata-sets –like LOM for instance- and see if it could be used in this case. Another prerequisite was the availability of a common XML-representation. This was needed to integrate the metadata into SCORM-packages and to be able to add additional information to the defined profile; the data set had to be extensible.

LOM was selected because of its wide acceptance and its integration in SCORM. Additionally, the XML-representation is extensible and widely used. The required fields had to be translated to either existing fields in LOM or added as extension-fields to LOM. The new profile was ready for use and the courses could be described using the developed set of metadata.

The next step is to create the output-files from the metadata files. As already mentioned above, the use of the OpenOffice.org document-format enabled us to transform the XML-based metadata files with XSLT to the specified format. This technique was used for creation of the module-handbook and all other reports for the universities administration. The web-based output for the students was also done with XSLT and a customised style sheets. The creation of SCORM-packages was also very easy to handle because the LOM metadata-set is the recommended one in the SCORM and the used applications already provided support for SCORM. The redundancy of course metadata was avoided by using the same metadata files for all four kinds of output. The created model is extensible to future requirements by just adding some more required metadata-fields or customising the style sheets to create new kinds of output.

We used our own application called Essen Learning Model application (ELM application) (Pawlowski, 2001) as user-interface. This application is able to edit extended LOM metadata and the e-learning content can also be edited within this application. The ELM application provided the tools for the implementation of the solution, for example it includes a XSL-transformation facility. So the generation of all needed output was be implemented by providing the corresponding style sheets. Additionally, the teaching staff could be assigned different access rights to the courses and the ELM application helped to detect redundancies by providing a search facility based on the metadata of the included learning objects. The application is designed as a client-server program so that the data is accessible to all the staff and stored in one central server. This solves the problem of holding inconsistent data on many computers. Some users were assigned special rights to do the administration of the whole course of studies and were also enabled to edit the output-locations for the transformation results.

15.8   Future trends

E-learning resources can be described in an interoperable format by LOM. IMS CP added a framework for packaging learning resources. SCORM added interoperability function to these e-learning packages. LD adds another level of description to the package to depict the activities in learning processes. While SCORM is widely used, LD has just started to gain influence in e-learning. In the near future, standards LD will probably improve reusability and transparency of e-learning.

Another aspect already in the standardisation work is the development of learner and teacher profiles to enable users of learning content to select the learning resources best for their preferred style of learning.

Finally, it seems possible to reach a state, in which learners can learn anywhere the way they prefer, by using the developed profiles to their full extend. For example, by providing functionalities to build individual tailored e-learning packages from repositories based on the skills, the learning preferences and the situational context of an individual learner. Thus in the near future learners should get tools to select and adapt learning content to their context, by providing their e-learning profiles to LMSs and repositories. Musa (Musa et al., 2004) already elaborated on a possible ontology for web services and how it can influence e-learning. It seems feasible to design adaptive e-learning resources to provide learners with a maximum of flexibility for their life long learning. For the long term trends, please see chapter 20.

16 Educational interoperability standards: IMS learning design and DIN didactical object model

Michael Klebl

University of Eichstätt-Ingolstadt, Germany

In emerging educational markets, fostered by developments in learning technology and educational media, not only resources for learning are subject to exchange and trade. Educational services providers design, operate and evaluate complex learning scenarios as a service. Hence, technical interoperability as well as quality issues focus the teaching-learning-process itself. In order to meet this objective, Educational Interoperability Standards propose a framework for a comprehensive description of the teaching-learning-process. This article gives an overview on two alternative Educational Interoperability Standards: IMS Learning Design (IMS-LD) and DIN Didactical Object Model (DIN-DOM). The introduction focuses on the paradigmatic shift from description of content to description of process. How educational interoperability standards add quality is discussed in the second part of this article. The third part presents common core concepts of IMS-LD and DIN-DOM and gives a comparison of these standards. A description of examples and issues in practical use concludes this article.

16.1 Introduction on educational interoperability standards

16.1.1 From content to process

The notion of a single learner in self-study activities within a long distance learning scenario in interaction with digital learning content is often related closely to the term "e-learning" – it is related so closely that it might not be reflected any more. Nearly all recent approaches to learning with educational media and information systems have dismissed this notion: When we create blended learning scenarios, we emphasise the integration of web-based self-study and traditional classroom teaching. When we talk about Computer Supported Collaborative Learning (CSCL), we examine how computer- und web-based tools can be used for learning in groups. On a theoretical level we discuss learner-centred approaches like situated learning and social-constructivist learning.

Roughly speaking, a paradigmatic shift away from a content-based knowledge delivery to a social and learner-centred paradigm can be stated for most parts of the current e-learning discussion. In academic discussion as well as in designing learning scenarios we take care of learner activities, interaction within a group of learners and different supporting roles of teaching staff like tutoring, coaching and informing.

For quite a long time the development of interoperability standards in e-learning focussed on learning content. Especially metadata standards and content packaging principles (see part 15) are designed for the management of digital media for education. In these standards only few potential is given to describe how learning (and teaching) in a certain learning scenario may take place. While metadata offer some descriptive information on some educational aspects for a single digital learning resource, content packaging is used to arrange these resources in a certain order. Resources for learning can be various: we consider texts, figures, exercises, lectures, simulations, experiments or problem statements as resources for learning.

However, learning scenarios are based upon *interaction* with resources for learning, upon *communication* within a group of learners and upon *supporting* and *teaching* activities by teaching staff. Generally speaking, a whole learning scenario is more than perception of learning content – it is a process of interaction between people in learning situations using resources for learning within a designed environment. Activities of persons in learning scenarios build up to a sequence in time, a fact that is best expressed by different meanings of the term "course".

Learning scenario: A learning scenario is a social setting dedicated to learning, education or training. It is a process of interaction between people in a specific learning situation using resources for learning within a designed environment. People in role of learners perform activities directed towards learning objectives using resources for learning. Learners may work on their own or in a group of learners. They may be supported by teaching staff.

When we consider a learning scenario as interaction between people in a group of learners or interaction of a single learner with educational media directed towards learning objectives, it becomes quite obvious that this process of teaching and learning can be described as a workflow or, more appropriate, as a learning flow. For workflow management, complex tasks are broken into single process elements. Actors (for workflow management human or machine) in role perform single tasks using resources in order to fulfil sub-goals of the whole process. By organising single learning activities (together with supporting activities), the process of teaching and learning can be described as a learning flow. Figure 16-1 gives an impression what a learning flow can look like:

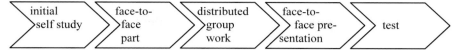

Fig. 16-1: Exemplary learning flow

This could be a typical learning flow within a blended learning scenario. Learners prepare in self-study with educational media for a first face-to-face part. This part is lead by a tutor. Apart from teaching, hands-on experience and discussion, groups of learners are formed during this part. These groups then work collaboratively and with web-based tools. In a second face-to-face part the groups present the outcome of their collaborative work. This is part of assessment by a tutor as well as an individual test which follows some time later.

> *Learning flow*: A learning flow is a formal description of a teaching-learning-process within a learning scenario that is based on concepts of workflow management. These concepts are actors, roles, tasks, goals, process elements, interaction, resources and outcome.

Only a few interoperability standards try to capture the learning scenario within a framework, which enables instructional designers to propose a comprehensive plan of such a learning flow as a teaching-learning-process. In this article the term "Educational Interoperability Standards" is used for those standards (respective specifications). Sometimes they are referred to as "Educational Modelling Languages" – in short EML.

16.1.2   History

The term "Educational Modelling Language (EML)" was coined at the Open University of the Netherlands. A research project was started there in 1998 in order to build a semantic notation for complete courses (Koper, 2001, p. 3). One outcome of this project was a comprehensive information model for "units of study" called "Educational Modelling Language (EML)". Based on a binding in XML, EML provides elements to describe both content and outline for a unit of learning to be run (this is: to be taught) in an institution like an open university. The version 1.0 of the information model and the XML binding was released in December 2000.

An instance of this information model is the result of the instructional design process and can be used to run a unit of learning within a learning scenario. On the one hand, resources for learning are aggregated within this instance. On the other hand, this aggregation of resources for learning is completed by a description of learning objectives, prerequisites, learning activities, teaching activities and services used in the learning situation.

Providing the possibilities to describe these educational elements beside content within an outline for a unit of learning, EML enables to integrate one or more instructional designs in a learning scenario, e.g. problem-oriented-learning, group discussion with presentation, collaborative learning, self study, project method, case-study. An instructional design itself is an instance of a pedagogical model. In his widely acknowledged paper Koper (Koper, 2001) describes a pedagogical meta-model underlying the information model of EML, which is meant to be pedagogically neutral. Single pedagogical models – like a behaviouristic model of learning, a cognitivistic approach towards understanding teaching and learning or a social-constructivist paradigm for creating learning scenarios – can be described within the pedagogical meta-model (Koper, 2001, p. 8ff). In order to be versatile and to be accepted in different educational contexts, the pedagogical meta-model must not force instructional designers to use a certain approach to teaching and learning. Instead, a pedagogical meta-model should allow instructional designers to create and describe their own models of teaching and learning.

The Educational Modelling Language of Open University of the Netherlands has been leading in the development of "Educational Interoperability Standards". Given EML as a conceptual prototype, the term "Educational Modelling Language" was adopted as a generic term for information models (and their binding in XML), which enable instructional designers to describe a comprehensive plan of a teaching-learning-process. From 2001 to 2002 a project of the CEN/ ISSS Workshop on Learning Technologies started a survey and analysis of "Educational Modelling Languages" in order to achieve a CEN/ ISSS Workshop Agreement (CWA) as part of further standardisation work. Within this project a working definition of an "Educational Modelling Language" was given. This definition is here proposed as a definition for "Educational Interoperability Standard", hence the term "Educational Interoperability Standard" is used instead of the term "Educational Modelling Language" in this article:

> "An EML [respectively an Educational Interoperability Standard] is a semantic information model and binding, describing the content and process within a 'unit of learning' from a pedagogical perspective in order to support reuse and interoperability." (Rawlings, Rosmalen, Koper, Rodríguez-Artacho, Lefrere, 2002, p. 8).

Given this definition an Educational Interoperability Standard provides a semantic notation for units of learning. In order to support reuse, exchange and interoperability, this notation has to be a standard. The notation has to be both pedagogically rich and pedagogically neutral, in order to enclose pedagogical information and not to restrict instructional designer on specific pedagogical models.

Educational interoperability standard: An Educational Interoperability Standard is a semantic information model and binding, describing the content and process within a unit of learning from a pedagogical perspective in order to support reuse and interoperability. It is a form of standardised notation for units of learning used by instructional designers to lay down their comprehensive plan for a learning scenario.

While the CEN/ ISSS Workshop on Learning Technologies was carrying out their survey and analysis of Educational Modelling Languages, a workgroup at IMS Global had already chosen the specification EML from Open University of the Netherlands as a starting point for a specification of an Educational Interoperability Standard called IMS Learning Design. The specification IMS Learning Design was published by the Learning Design Workgroup at IMS Global in February 2003 (Koper, Olivier, Anderson, 2003a; b; c). Basic concepts of EML from Open University of the Netherlands were taken over while EML was being integrated with other specifications at IMS Global, especially IMS Content Packaging und IMS Simple Sequencing.

Parallel to this process at IMS Global a working group at the Deutsches Institut für Normung DIN e.V. focused on a standardised process model for planning, developing, realising and evaluating processes in learning, education and training. Within this reference model for instructional design processes another Educational Interoperability Standard was specified: The Didactical Object Model (DIN-DOM) provides a notation for units of learning that can be handed from one step in this process to another. As a Public Accessible Specification (PAS 1032-2, Deutsches Institut für Normung e.V., 2004b) the DIN-DOM was published in summer 2004. Both EML from Open University of the Netherlands and the specification IMS Learning Design in development were considered while developing the DIN-DOM.

At present, IMS Learning Design and DIN-DOM are prominent and alternative approaches in Educational Interoperability Standards, especially in Europe. Though they build on common basic concepts, there are some differences in notion and usage. But when we look at the shortly abridged historical development above, we may consider them as mainly influenced by European approaches towards teaching and learning with digital educational media.

The common basic concepts of IMS-LD and DIN-DOM are summed up by the following aspects:

- Educational Interoperability Standards describe rather the process of teaching and learning than learning content.
- They are a form of standardised notation for units of learning used by instructional designers to lay down their comprehensive plan for a learning scenario.
- This plan might be run by a learning management system, but it also can be used in a traditional way as a lesson plan for both learners and teaching people.
- A learning scenario is described not only by resources for learning, but also by a description of learning objectives, prerequisites, learning activities, teaching activities and services used in learning situations.
- In order to be a comprehensive framework, Educational Interoperability Standards have to be applicable not only for a single learner in self-study activities

(within a long distance learning scenario in interaction with digital learning content), but also for teaching and learning in classroom, for vocational training and for learning in groups.

• To be versatile and widely accepted, an Educational Interoperability Standard has to be both pedagogically neutral and pedagogically rich to incorporate pedagogical information within the outline for a unit of learning without forcing the use of a certain pedagogical approach.

Pedagogical flexibility: Pedagogical flexibility is a fundamental requirement for an Educational Interoperability Standard. In order to be versatile and widely accepted, an Educational Interoperability Standard has to be both pedagogically neutral and pedagogically rich to incorporate pedagogical information within the outline for a unit of learning without forcing the use of a certain pedagogical approach.

16.1.3   Documents and scope

This article gives an account of the core concepts of IMS-LD and DIN-DOM starting from objectives and scope of both specifications in this section. The specifications themselves consist of documents which describe context, conceptual model, information model as well as examples and description of best-practice. For further reading some summarising articles can be recommended. The "Designer's Guide" gives a good introduction to IMS Learning Design (Koper et al., 2003a, pp. 20-47). An overview can also be found at (out Olivier, Tattersall, 2005). A good introduction to the DIN Didactical Object Model is given in (out Deutsches Institut für Normung e.V., 2005). For both specifications the information model itself is provided as a binding in XML. This binding (in both cases implemented as XML-schema) can be used to create plans for units of study which are compatible to the respective specification. Both documents and XML-schema-files are available on the web.

Objectives and scope of IMS learning design

The specification IMS Learning Design starts with a very comprehensive objective:

> "The objective of the Learning Design Specification is to provide a containment framework of elements that can describe any design of a teaching-learning process in a formal way" (Koper et al., 2003b part 2.1).

Given this rather extensive objective for the specification IMS Learning Design, eight more specific goals derive from this global objective (ibid):

- The first of these, "Completeness", identifies aspects of learning scenarios that are to be described: Activities of both learners and teachers as well as resources and services used during learning, in order to support a wide variety of approaches to learning for both single and multiple user models of learning together with support for mixed mode (blended learning) as well as pure online learning.

- A second goal, "Pedagogical Flexibility", explains the notion of support for a wide variety of approaches to learning. The pedagogical meaning and functionality of elements in a learning scenario has to be expressed. This expression has to be flexible in the description of all different kinds of pedagogies thus not prescribing any specific pedagogical approach.

- The third goal, "Personalisation", emphasises adaptability within learning scenarios for individual learner. Hence, IMS Learning Design has to facilitate the adaptation of learning content and learning activities based on the preferences, portfolio, pre-knowledge, educational needs and situational circumstances. The flexible control over the adaptation has to be laid either in the hands of the learners, the teachers, the learning management system or the designer, as appropriate.

- Another five derived goals ("Formalisation", "Reproducibility", "Interoperability", "Compatibility" and "Reusability") denote essential organisational and technical requirements for reuse, exchange and trade of plans for learning scenarios.

Furthermore, the specification IMS Learning Design states some aspects that are not within the scope of IMS Learning Design. Requirements for authoring tools and runtime environments (delivery of learning scenarios) are not part of the specification. In order to support a wide range of pedagogical approaches less abstract pedagogical principles, which would refer particularly to preconditions, educational needs and situational circumstances, are also not part of the specification. The relation of learner preferences to instructional design, the interpretation of content from one educational context to another and issues of quality are not directly within the scope of IMS Learning Design. (Koper et al., 2003a part 1.1)

Objectives and scope of DIN didactical object model

The DIN Didactical Object Model refers with a comprehensive objective primarily to the intended use: Exchange, comparability and transparency for instructional concepts, learning scenarios and teaching-learning methods in different areas of education are denoted as the global objective. (Deutsches Institut für Normung e.V., 2004b, p. 4)

In order to achieve this, elements of a learning scenario have to be described within unifying and understandable categories for different actors in both the instructional design process and the learning scenario itself. Two aspects of the intended use are differentiated (Deutsches Institut für Normung e.V., 2004b, p. 4):

- Instructional designers as well as teaching persons may use the DIN-DOM for designing, operating and evaluating learning scenarios.
- Teaching persons as well as persons responsible for educational and training matters may use the transparent description conformant to the DIN-DOM for decisions of use and choice according to educational intentions and situational needs.

As stated above, the specification DIN-DOM relates explicitly to IMS Learning Design. Therefore objectives and goals of IMS Learning Design are not repeated. Instead, the relations to instructional design processes and decisions are accentuated.

16.1.4   Intended use

In traditional classroom teaching one single person is responsible for planning, developing, realising and evaluating processes of teaching and learning – let this person be a teacher, a lecturer or a trainer. Only the definition of learning objectives and attainment targets is usually not within the scope of a single teaching person. Apart from situations in teacher training and apart from evaluating the performance of a teaching person there is no need for them to explain any step in the process of planning, developing, realising and evaluating units of learning.

On the contrary, the production of digital educational media and the realisation of computer supported learning scenarios are only possible with systematic workflows that integrate skills of different experts like subject matter experts, instructional designers, graphic designers and software developers. While traditional classroom teaching can be considered as craftsmanship, the development and operation of media-based learning scenarios can be identified as industrial (Moonen, 2001, p. 154f).

The increasing use of digital educational media leads to the disintegration of the traditionally close linkage between a single teaching person and the responsibility for a teaching-learning-process. Different people take care and work cooperatively on creating and running a learning scenario. Different tasks like developing a general concept, producing learning content, designing learning scenarios, teaching in class, moderating groups of learners, mentoring single learners, assessing or testing students and evaluating or administrating courses are assigned to different actors in specific roles.

Research and studies in instructional design pay great attention on systematic workflows for planning, developing, realising and evaluating educational media and computer-supported learning scenarios. To organise different roles and tasks for collaboration in a team producing educational media and services, an instructional design process has to be managed. Systematic approaches to instructional design develop reference process models, described und used to coordinate the workflow in an instructional design team (see part 12). In figure 16-2 an example for instructional design process is given (again, just to have an example, see Deutsches Institut für Normung e.V., 2004a):

Fig. 16-2: Exemplary instructional design process

Systematic approaches and Educational Interoperability Standards are closely interrelated. In a team producing educational media and services, different actors have to share plans for learning scenarios. These plans must be designed to incorporate pedagogical information in order to foster communication between different actors in the instructional design workflow, flexible adaptation on context or individual needs and reflection on pedagogical aspects of the teaching-learning-process. A semantic information model and binding, describing both content and process for a "unit of learning" from a pedagogical perspective is basal for this purpose. In a standardised form this information model is an Educational Interoperability Standard.

The connection between the process of instructional design and the teaching-learning-process itself is shown in figure 16-3 below. The teaching-learning-process itself is embedded within the instructional design process. The interrelation between Educational Interoperability Standards and the instructional design process is obvious: Descriptions of the learning scenario are handed from one step in process to another – regardless whether they are first drafts, elaborate plans or a formal description that can be run by a learning management system. Hence, Educational Interoperability Standards are used to create blueprints for the teaching-learning-process.

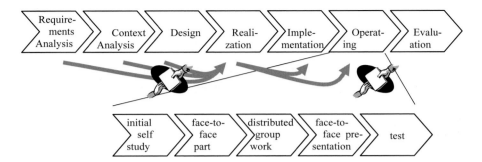

Fig. 16-3: Interrelation of instructional design process and teaching-learning-process (exemplary)

Within the instructional design process intended use and a notion of benefit of Educational Interoperability Standards like IMS-LD or DIN-DOM are at hand. Instances of both are standardised descriptions of learning scenarios. Their usage aims at a seamless data flow within the instructional design process. This can lead to faster development cycles as well as to a reduction of failures and costs. Furthermore, this provides the basis for communication between actors in the instructional design process.

Let me now come to the main points for the intended use of Educational Interoperability Standards:

- Educational Interoperability Standards act as a blueprint for teaching-learning-processes within the instructional design process.
- They enhance communication between actors and thus provide the basis for transparency and quality in instructional design.
- Their use within information systems for instructional design (i.e. authoring environments) and within learning management system (as a runtime environment) can enhance efficiency in both designing and operating computer supported learning scenarios.

At this point a statement about designing units of learning is to be made: Instructional designers create plans for teaching-learning-processes. For this purpose they may use an Educational Interoperability Standard or not. But in any case: The plan for a teaching-learning process must not be mistaken for the teaching-learning process itself. During the run of a unit of learning learners and teaching staff may follow a plan laid out in a special notation, represented as a lesson plan simply on a chalk board or within a learning management system. But following a plan in reality always means dealing with uncertainties, acting individually and reacting spontaneously on contextual influences. Instructional designer do well not to reduce a teaching-learning-process to an arrangement of rigorous steps. According to learner centred approaches like situated learning and social-constructivist learning the learners (as well as teaching people) are to be encouraged to take care of their teaching-learning-process actively. But on the other hand: Plans are extremely useful in areas to be discovered. No-one would go on a hiking tour without having a map and a notion of paths and goals. While exploring new areas of knowledge and skills, guidance is surely appreciated by learners.

16.2   Educational interoperability standards in relation to quality

As stated above, through communication and transparency Educational Interoperability Standards provide a basis for quality in planning, developing, realising and evaluating learning scenarios. Considering their relation to quality, other meanings of the term "educational standard" may interfere. The term "educational standards" (Ravitch, 1995) may refer to a certain level in achieving learning objectives (performance standards), to learning content covered by a curriculum (content standards) or to a guaranteed level in quality of schooling and teaching (opportunity-to-learn standards). Educational Interoperability Standards must not be mistaken with educational standards themselves. While the later are a normative construct, an Educational Interoperability Standard is a technical construct which can enhance quality in teaching-learning-process, but never guarantees it. In other words: You can do bad schooling, teaching or training while using an Educational Interoperability Standard, but you are more likely to notice it.

Nevertheless Educational Interoperability Standards relate to educational quality in different ways, indirectly. Some aspects of this indirect relationship can be stated as follows:

- *Integrated learning scenarios:* An Educational Interoperability Standard provides a differentiated and comprehensive framework for designing and operating integrated learning scenarios. Learner activities, interaction within a group of learners and different supporting roles of teaching staff like tutoring, coaching and informing are taken into account within the description of a learning scenario. Following the premise that the named aspects enhance learning, as the contemporary discussion on learner-centred approaches like situated learning and social-constructivist learning suggest, one can hardly deny that Educational Interoperability Standards contribute to quality in computer supported learning scenarios. Especially the possibility of paying attention to classroom-like learning situations including the use of non-digital media or real objects as resources or tools for learning to reveal new aspects of educational quality.
- *Broader range of methods for teaching and learning:* An Educational Interoperability Standard enables the integration of one or more instructional designs in a learning scenario, e.g. problem-oriented-learning, collaborative learning, project method. Within a pedagogical meta-model, a formal description of a teaching-learning-process is largely open to different approaches towards teaching and learning. Hence, an increase in the variety of methods for teaching and learning can be expected. This leads to a variety of methods for the learner,

in elaborated cases up to adaptive selection of learning methods according to individual learning preferences.

- *Learner's competence in learning:* If learning methods in a learning scenario as an outcome of instruction design are described formally in a unit of learning, it can be useful to represent the learning methods to the learner in the graphical user interface. A learner, informed about the process of teaching and learning, will probably acquire knowledge about his or her own learning process. This knowledge can be thought of as meta-cognition which leads to the development of learning skills.
- *Free market economy for educational services and products:* Since Educational Interoperability Standards promote the transparency for teaching-learning-processes within the instructional design process, they support the comparison of services and products in an educational market. In an idealised free market the possibility to compare educational services and products will lead to innovation and quality.
- *Quality management:* An Educational Interoperability Standard serves as a standardised instrument within instructional design processes to document educational concepts, pedagogical models and lesson plans. Hence, an Educational Interoperability Standard is indispensable device for quality management. Instructional design processes are managed according to reference processes in order to create continuously high quality outcomes.
- *Best practice sharing:* The ability to describe learning scenario formalised and standardised allows reuse and sharing of successful approaches to teaching and training. Regardless whether reuse, exchange and sharing is done cooperatively, e.g. between colleagues in an educational institution or commercially, e.g. from educational content providers to educational institutions, approved concepts or single learning scenarios can spread more easily (Liber, 2002, p. 197f).

The indirect relationship between Educational Interoperability Standards and educational quality can be summarised as enhancement of communication and transparency within the instructional design process. The term "instructional design process" may suggest a restriction for the use of Educational Interoperability Standards to e-learning in higher education or to distance learning scenarios. But processes of planning, developing, realising and evaluating learning scenarios are carried out in every educational field regardless of the learner's age and regardless of how formalised these processes are. Educational Interoperability Standards allow reflection on what is going to happen in teaching-learning-situation and they allow communication amongst people responsible for education. Hence, they are a valuable instrument in teacher training as well where they can be used as a notation to transfer pedagogical knowledge. The specification IMS Learning Design states this relation to quality especially for e-learning scenarios – but this statement can be transferred to any educational scenario:

"The absence of agreed and compatible ways to describe teaching strategies (pedagogical approaches) and educational goals is a constraint that will hold back the development of the industry. As best practice evolves in systems that support e-learning, it follows that some of these pedagogical approaches will be codified, leading to the presentation of opportunities that facilitate successful learning experiences" (Koper et al., 2003a part 1.).

16.3   IMS learning design and DIN didactical object model: Elaboration and comparison

In order to give a short introduction to both IMS Learning Design and DIN Didactical Object Model common core concepts are described and discussed in the following part. While both specifications share "units of learning" as a common starting point and have activities as a core concept, for resources for learning, adaptability and life-cycle some differences can be stated.

16.3.1   "Units of learning" as a starting point

Both IMS Learning Design and DIN Didactical Object Model start from a common concept: The outcome of an instructional design process refers to a "unit of learning" (Koper et al., 2003b part 2.3). What is handed from one step in this process to another gives an outline for a single learning scenario limited in time and space related to specified learning objectives and learning content. Common terms of this concept are "course", "module", "lesson" or "learning experience" in relation to Educational Interoperability Standards they are sometimes called "unit of study" or "unit of instruction". The DIN-DOM introduces another term for this unit: "didactical object" (Deutsches Institut für Normung e.V., 2004b, p. 7f).

> *Unit of learning:* A unit of learning is a part of education or training that is designed towards one or more learning objectives. Hence, a unit of learning is a self-contained period in a teaching-learning process, limited in time and dedicated to a certain issue of a subject that is studied.

A unit of learning consists of a description of learning objectives, prerequisites, learning activities, teaching activities and services along with an outline of the teaching-learning-process and along with resources for learning used in this process (or at least references to these resources). Complexity and granularity of a unit of learning cannot be determined in general. A specific extend of a unit of learning is defined by semantic and pragmatic aspects: Resources and services are coherently interrelated within a teaching-learning-process directed towards learning objectives – this unit cannot be broken into parts without loosing meaning. This inner meaning for a unit of learning is accomplished by a distinctive separation from other units of learning. Units of learning have a limited extend in time and they are self-contained in process, in learning objectives and in learning content. A connection between units of learning can only refer to prerequisites – completion of one unit of study can be a prerequisite to start another on both individual's and learner's group level. Both IMS-LD and DIN-DOM allow recursive nesting of units of learning within other units of learning. This is a slight contradiction to considering a unit of learning as an entity which is meant to be singular, coherent and self-contained.

In a pragmatic view anyone responsible for learning scenarios in any educational context will know how to determine extend, complexity and granularity of units of learning. Obviously planning, developing, realising and evaluation learning scenarios focus on meaningful units, regardless whether they are twenty minutes pieces of web-based training or several weeks training units. Causes that influence determination of units of learning can be various: coherent learning objectives or attainment targets, a thematic area of knowledge or simply a given phrasing in time.

16.3.2   Conceptual core: Activities

According to the paradigmatic shift from description of content to description of process in learning scenarios, a teaching-learning-process can only take place when there are meaningful learning activities performed by the learner. To be meaningful, activities have to be directed towards learning objectives.

Consequently, activities are the core concept of an information model that can be used as a notation for learning scenarios. Both IMS Learning Design and DIN Didactical Object Model base their information model on activities (Deutsches Institut für Normung e.V., 2004b, p. 9), (Koper et al., 2003b part 2.3). In general, an activity is something to be done by someone in order to achieve a purpose. In a learning context, activities are directed towards learning objectives. Learners perform learning activities while teaching staff perform supporting activities. Both use resources for learning, e.g. educational media or tools, and both interact and communicate directly or via special devices, i.e. both use web-based services. These elements form a conceptual core of any learning scenario: *People in roles of either learner or staff perform structured learning activities (respective support activities) within an environment of resources and services for learning in order to achieve learning objectives.* Thus, activities as the core concept for a comprehensive description of a teaching-learning-process imply related concepts like roles, learning objectives and environments with resources and services. All these concepts form together a process element as a smallest unit to describe a teaching learning process shown in figure 16-4 below:

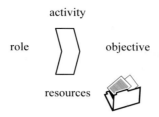

Fig. 16-4: Learning activity as process element

Learning activity: A learning activity is intentional action performed by learners within a teaching-learning-process. It is often, but not always prompted by an instruction. Learners perform learning activities within an environment of resources and services for learning in order to achieve learning objectives.

From an educational as well as from a psychological point of view you can say a lot about learning activities. Different theories of learning emphasise different connotations of learning activities. A behaviouristic model of learning comprises learner's activities as a way of perceiving knowledge. For a cognitivistic approach learners' activities are related to mental operations. Thus, an outer and an inner part of an operation can be described. Within a social-constructivist paradigm learning activities can only be described as an interaction between subject and (social) environment (Koper, 2001, p. 11).

16.3.3   Aggregation of activities

Given learners' and teaching staff's activities as smallest process elements, the teaching-learning-process is basically assembled through aggregation of activities (not as aggregation of content). In both IMS-LD and DIN-DOM activities ("Handlung" in DIN-DOM) can be nested within activity structures ("Handlungsstruktur" in DIN-DOM). A composition of activity structures assembles to a specific learning flow which is a method of teaching and learning in both specifications. Here a difference between IMS-LD and DIN-DOM has to be stated. While IMS-LD introduces a special taxonomy the aggregation of activities, in DIN-DOM levels of aggregation are described as an attribute of the method itself.

The levels of aggregation in IMS-LD can be examined at a graphical representation of the information model (as an UML diagram see figure 16-5 below):

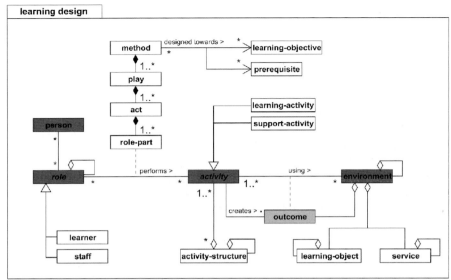

Source: Koper et al., 2003b part 2.2.2

Fig. 16-5: Information model IMS learning design level A

In IMS-LD, activities are aggregated to activity-structures which can be recursively nested and which are either a sequence or a selection of subordinate activities or activity-structures. With role-parts activity-structures or single activities are assigned to different roles within an act. Multiple acts follow sequentially within a play, which is a synonym for a certain teaching-learning-method (Koper et al., 2003b part 2.3). Since activities or activity-structures can only be assigned to roles within an act using multiple role-parts elements, acts serve as a synchronisation element and mark phases within a unit of learning. Only within an act can different roles do parallel tasks, while the transition from one act to another applies to all roles, i.e. to all people in the teaching-learning-process (Koper et al., 2003b part 4.4).

Figure 16-6 shows a graphical representation of the information model for DIN-DOM (as an UML diagram):

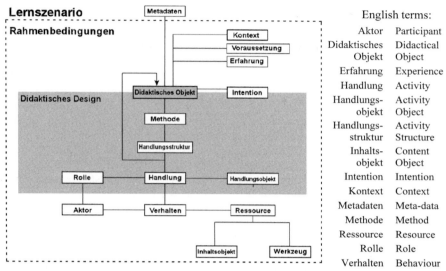

Source: *Deutsches Institut für Normung e.V., 2004b, p. 7*

Fig. 16-6: Information model DIN didactical object model

In contrast to IMS-LD there is no special taxonomy for the aggregation of activities ("Handlung") in DIN-DOM. Subordinate activities, subordinate activity structures or whole units of learning ("Didaktisches Objekt") can be aggregated as a sequence, parallel, complementary or unordered within an activity structure ("Handlungsstruktur"). Only activities themselves (as leaf elements) can be assigned to roles. Hence, in DIN-DOM the recursive nesting of activities is very flexible and not determined by aggregation levels (like role-part, act and play in IMS-LD). The specification DIN-DOM uses an attribute to the method element to describe levels of aggregation. Methods used in a unit of learning are classified as micro-, macro-, or meta-methods:

- A micro-method is the smallest unit of teaching-learning-methods. It is to be considered as a mental operation (like reading, structuring, observing, interpreting, generalising or explaining).
- A macro-method consists of micro-methods and contains phases in the teaching-learning-process (like role-play, discussion, self study, text study, coaching, brainstorming or feedback).
- A meta-method is the dominating form of organising a teaching-learning-process (like project method, web based training, simulation, case-study or learning by doing) (Deutsches Institut für Normung e.V., 2004b, p. 9).

With aggregation of activities IMS-LD and DIN-DOM share a common concept. This concept separates them clearly from specifications for learning content. Aggregation of activities is done with different accentuation: While the IMS-LD implies a special taxonomy for the aggregation of activities within the information model, in DIN-DOM levels of aggregation are described semantically.

16.3.4   Resources and services within a learning environment

In order to attain learning objectives people in learning situations (learners as well as teaching staff) use resources and services for learning. The term "learning object" was introduced for resources for learning. Along with developing implementing learning content repositories and standards for metadata or content packaging the concept of learning objects was discussed largely. To describe resources of learning, they have to be qualified in terms of their pedagogical function and use. The specification Learning Object Metadata (LOM) for instance proposes a classification of different types of learning objects (in element 5.2 Learning Resource Type, Learning Technology Standards Committee of the IEEE, 2002, p. 25): exercise, simulation, questionnaire, diagram, figure, graph, index, slide, table, narrative text, exam, experiment, problem statement, self assessment and lecture.

Both IMS-LD and DIN-DOM only refer to a descriptive classification of resources given by specifications like LOM. In their own information model they only offer a basic, but important classification:

- IMS-LD separates learning objects from services. While learning objects are defined as resources for learning that are instantiated during developing and realising a unit of learning (during "design time"), services are instantiated during operating a unit of learning (during "runtime"). Hence, learning objects can be used, addressed and referred to whether a unit of learning is running or not. They are contained or referred to in a plan for a teaching-learning-process. A service however has to be created for each single run of a unit of learning. Common web-based services for communication like chat or newsgroups are formally described in a plan for a teaching-learning-process, but not contained. A runtime environment for IMS-LD has to create them and assign users to them, when they are needed during the run of a teaching-learning-process. (Koper et al., 2003bpart 2.3)
- DIN-DOM separates content objects ("Inhaltsobjekt") from tools ("Werkzeuge"). A content object is defined as a representation of a learning content. Tools are defined as devices used during a teaching-learning-process. While content objects are bound to content, tools are content independent. Tools serve as a device to transport or transform content. Given this abstract definition, communication services as well as applications used for learning can be subsumed under tools. (Deutsches Institut für Normung e.V., 2004b, p. 10)

This basic classification of resources for learning differs slightly between IMS-LD and DIN-DOM. Furthermore, the connection of resources for learning to learning activities follows different concepts:

- The information model of IMS-LD introduces an element named "environment". Environments are the linking elements between activities and resources. Resources cannot be assigned to activities directly. Environments are container elements that serve as packages in which an instructional designer puts anything a learner needs at a certain step in a teaching-learning-process. Through reference these packages can be reused during a teaching-learning-process more easily than a set of resources, which would be referred to directly from a learning activity. (Koper et al., 2003b, part 2.3)
- The information model of DIN-DOM makes a distinction between a resource for learning (it may be a content object or a tool) and its use within the teaching-learning-process. The use of a resource for an activity is described in a wrapper element named activity object ("Handlungsobjekt"), which describes the function of a resource for an activity. Content objects or tools are regarded to exist independently from a unit of learning, their use within a teaching-learning-process turns them into a learning object. (Deutsches Institut für Normung e.V., 2004b, p. 10)

With the element of environment the specification IMS-LD not only offers a useful tool for instructional designers to organise resources used in a teaching-learning-process, it also reflects a notion of creating learning scenarios as a specially designed arrangement of resources in which learning can take place. The specification DIN-DOM however emphasises another notion: any digital media, non-digital media, real object or communication device can be used for learning, whether it is especially designed for learning or not. The use of an object (digital or real) as a resource or tool for a learning activity converts this object into a learning object.

16.3.5   Adaptability: Level B, C in IMS-LD

The specification of IMS Learning Design supports three levels of implementation and compliance. All concepts described so far – activities, roles, learning objectives, environment, resources and services – are enclosed in a basic Level A. Using Level A, a teaching-learning-process can be planned and operated in a rather unambiguous way. At Level A, there can be alternative paths within the learning flow based on selection of single activities or activity structures. Level B of IMS-LD adds three concepts which allow the creation of more elaborate learning flows within a unit of learning: properties, conditions and monitor. Properties (like services) have to be instantiated at runtime and record outcomes of activities during operating a unit of learning. The outcomes of an activity can be various: They can be learner related and thus record results of assessment, information on choices or on learner's preferences or documents submitted by a learner that form a learner's portfolio. Furthermore, properties that store information can refer not only to a learner as a single person, but also to information about roles and about the whole group of learners, therefore store information about the actual situation during the run of a unit of learning. Given logical and arithmetic expressions in combination with if-then-statements in the condition element, modification in the learning flow can be planned and executed during runtime on the basis of properties. Although the modification of the learning flow applies mainly to hiding and showing elements of the learning flow, adaptive learning scenarios can be designed with Level B reacting on single learners (for personalisation) or situated on a group of learners. Predefined parts of the teaching-learning-processes like different activity structures that represent different learning methods can be chosen and presented (i.e. shown) according to information evaluated and stored in properties during the run of a unit of learning (Koper et al., 2003b, p. 4f).

Level B of IMS-LD also introduces a special service called "monitor", which can be used to enhance interaction between learner and teaching staff or within a group of learners on the basis of properties, too. For example, a student's working result like an essay can be submitted as a property. In order to allow a person in a teaching role to review this work a monitor service can be used – monitor services connect roles to properties and thus allow structured ways of interaction on results and outcomes of learning.

With Level C IMS-LD extends adaptability further more. A single added element called "notification" adds the possibility to send messages from the runtime environment to learners in roles triggered by events in the teaching-learning-process. Given this opportunity especially collaborative activities in the teaching-learning-process can be planned to react on activities of learners rather than on a predefined learning flow. Hence, IMS-LD can be used to design learning scenarios based on role plays or simulations. (Koper et al., 2003b, p. 7f)

The elements of Level B and C in IMS-LD – e.g. properties, conditions, monitor and notifications, here just briefly mentioned – are very abstract concepts. They are generalised from real learning scenarios in order to be functional instruments for creating flexible and adaptive learning flows. The specification DIN-DOM does not include similar concepts.

16.3.6   Lifecycle: Context and annotation in DIN-DOM

The specification DIN-DOM is closely related to a reference process model for planning, developing, realising and evaluating processes in learning, education and training (Deutsches Institut für Normung e.V., 2004a). The reference process model identifies and describes process categories and process elements. Process elements are described by e.g. sub-processes, actors, targets and outcomes. The specification DIN-DOM is considered to serve as a notation for outcomes of process elements in the instructional design process. Instances of the DIN-DIN information model are to be used as documentation for units of learning that can be handed from one step in this process to another.

The reference process model of the PAS 1032-1 refers not only to the processes of planning, developing and realising a learning scenario, but also to evaluating and, in addition, to revising learning scenarios. For example, units of learning are often designed to be operated as regularly repeating courses – e.g. year to year. In order to support the lifecycle of a plan for a unit of learning, the specification

DIN-DOM adds some elements to the notation of this plan: context, experience and conditions (in a sense of prerequisites) (Deutsches Institut für Normung e.V., 2004b, p. 8).

The concept of context captures the relation between the development of a plan for a unit of learning and the intended application of this plan. A single context element represents information about intended settings in political, social and economic aspects or about institutional, personal and organisational resources. The experience element is used to annotate information that is derived from previous runs of a unit of learning. A record of an experience can refer to a context element to note the application context of this single experience. Records of experience can thus be characteristic case examples for the operation of a unit of learning in a sense of good practice or lessons learned.

The category condition covers all conditions and resources necessary for the operation of a unit of learning, which can be personal, institutional, technical or organisational. For example, the use of a teaching-learning-method can be made dependent on the learning preferences or on the level of achievement of a learner. In contrast to the specification IMS-LD that captures conditions with logical and arithmetic expressions, the conditions are described only in natural language using text in the specification DIN-DOM. Thus, the category condition in DIN-DOM is rather to be compared with the concept of prerequisites in IMS-LD.

The distinctive elements context and experience in DIN-DOM are basic concepts to support a lifecycle of unit of learning. They are not considered as metadata (where they could also be included), but as an essential annotation feature. The specification IMS-LD does not include similar concepts.

16.3.7   Practical use: Examples and issues

Educational Interoperability Standards imply complex requirements for implementation in information systems used for teaching and learning as well as for integrated authoring environments. A wide range of implementations in information systems for learning are to be expected, thus examples for runtime environments are presented in the following part only briefly. For authoring environments central issues are described shortly as well. Instead of listing particular development tools an overview of principles for representation of a plan for a learning scenario in a graphical user interface is given.

16.3.8   Runtime environments

A runtime environment is used for representing a unit of learning, which is conformant with an Educational Interoperability Standard, to both learners and teaching staff. Both are relieved from routine tasks during operating the learning scenario, like providing resources for learning at the right time or submitting assignments, if a unit of learning can be operated by processing a plan for the teaching-learning-process.

Trends for runtime environments

Use and impact of an Educational Interoperability Standard will depend on whether soon runtime environments are being developed. For implementation of Educational Interoperability Standards in information systems for learning (like learning management systems) different trends are to be expected:

- Some new developments of learning management systems will build directly on the concepts and principles of an Educational Interoperability Standard. Especially the separation of content and activities as the conceptual core of IMS-LD and DIN-DOM offers a good basis for the separation of structures for unit of learning along with their operation from learning content, which leads to Learning Content Management Systems.
- However, the most important trend will be the integration of functions for an Educational Interoperability Standard into existing web-based learning management systems. Some learning management systems (not all) already offer functions to structure a unit of learning in a sense of a plan with phases, activities and resources. These systems can adapt their course structure management to the structure of an Educational Interoperability Standard. In addition to this, they will offer possibilities for import and export of units of learning compliant to those specifications.
- Another approach will be the use of Educational Interoperability Standards with non-compliant learning management system or without learning management system at all. As shown above Education Interoperability Standard addresses aspects of the instructional design process at least equally to aspects of operating teaching-learning-processes themselves. Hence, an Education Interoperability Standard may support the instructional design process, while developed plans for a learning scenario are transformed to simpler format for the run of a learning scenario. This simpler format can be a typical content aggregation format (like SCORM™) with descriptions of learning objectives, learning activities and so on converted to static content objects. A simpler format can also be a printed lesson plan for teaching staff as well as for learners. This way, automated functions within a learning flow are not available. Nevertheless, a unit of learning planned with an Education Interoperability Standard can be operated without a fully compliant learning management system. This approach opens up opportunities for the development of integrated authoring environments as well as for units of learning, where the latter can serve as best practice examples.

Examples of runtime environments

Starting from publication of the specification IMS Learning Design in February 2003 several developments of information systems for learning were inspired by the notion of describing rather the process of teaching and learning than learning content. Far from being complete, only three developments ought to be listed here:

- *Open-Source Engine for IMS-LD – CopperCore:* (Eaton, 2003), (Franz, 2004, p. 107), (Fröhlich, Jütte, 2004, p. 12), (Leef, 2003), (Ravet, 2002, p. 272), (Simon, 2001, p. 155) In order to support wide and accelerated implementation of IMS Learning Design in different learning management systems, the Educational Technology Expertise Centre of the Open University of the Netherlands started the development of an engine for IMS-LD called CopperCore. Copper-Core was initiated as an open source software project. In information systems for learning CopperCore can be used as a module to process plans for learning scenarios conformant to IMS-LD, thus providing developers an elaborated starting point. Platform independence results from implementation in Java and J2EE (Martens, Vogten, 2005, p. 91ff). CopperCore is intended to be an engine within the application layer for the use of IMS Learning Design in different learning management systems. Hence, it is not intended to be a single full run-time environment for IMS-LD-conformant units of learning. Nevertheless, a graphical user interface for users is provided within the current distribution of CopperCore. This IMS-LD-player may offer an impression of the use of IMS Learning Design (any Educational Interoperability Standard respectively). It clearly reflects the three basic concepts of delivery and representation of a unit of learning within CopperCore. The graphical user interface of that player is divided in three major areas. While the activity tree is situated top left, the environment tree is situated bottom left – both like navigation trees. Elements like activities and resources for learning are presented in a main area right.
- *Learning Activity Management System (LAMS):* Developed by WebMCQ Pty Ltd. in cooperation the Macquarie E-learning Centre of Excellence (MELCOE) at Macquarie University, Australia, the Learning Activity Management System (LAMS) emphasises the aggregation of learning activities as the core concept for designing and operation learning scenarios. LAMS is not fully compatible to IMS-LD, but dedicated to the notion of describing rather the process of teaching and learning than learning content. Learning activities can be sequenced in a flow chart and are represented to users (learners and teaching staff) in the same way (Dalziel, 2003).
- *lab005 – Lern- und Arbeitsbereich:* As a graphical user interface to be used in classroom teaching as well as for self study, a web-based learning environment called "lab005" was developed in a research project at the Catholic University Eichstätt-Ingolstadt, Germany. This prototypical runtime environment for IMS Learning Design was build on Moodle (Dougiamas, Taylor, 2002), an open source course management system. Development and use of the runtime environment lab005 were intensely evaluated from the perspective of users in mixed mode learning scenarios, both staff and learners. A formative approach was chosen for usability evaluation of the web-based learning environment, in order to understand strengths and challenges of both IMS Learning Design and its tentative implementation in lab005. Though limited in scope, the successful implementation of IMS Learning Design in higher education proves the possibility to support mixed mode learning scenarios (blended learning) (Klebl, 2005).

Several more implementations of Educational Interoperability Standards, both commercial and open source (respectively developed in research projects), are currently being developed or already in use. More runtime environments are to be expected. Particular implementations may be close or distant to the specification and further on, they can be classified weather they are dedicated to specific or general purposes (Griffiths, Blat, Garcia, Vogten, Kwong, 2005, p. 117). Interested readers might retrieve information about recent implementations through the web. The EU founded project UNFOLD is establishing a network for people working on IMS Learning Design (http://www.unfold-project.net). Information on IMS Learning Design is also collected by the Educational Technology Expertise Centre (OTEC) at the Open University of the Netherlands (http://learningnetworks.org).

16.3.9   Authoring environments

The use of an Educational Interoperability Standard for designing and operating media enhanced learning scenarios shortly leads to an increase in expenses and costs. Considering the relation of expenses and benefits, integrated authoring environments are essential in order to support instructional designers.

Instructional designers are challenged by difficult tasks creating learning scenarios compliant to an Educational Interoperability Standard like IMS-LD or DIN-DOM. Authoring Environments provide functions for editing plans for learning scenarios. The following directions of development for authoring environments can be expected:

- *Course Structure Management Tools in Learning Management Systems:* Some learning management systems already implement functions to design courses in a sense of planning a unit of learning. The organisation of learning content or communication services, the planning of learner's tasks (in a sense of learning activities), of conditions for transition from one phase in the learning flow to another in addition to assessments can be done with course structure management tools in a specific way. Often this is possible within the web-based interface ("edit-in-place"). If these course structure management tools in learning management systems are adapted to an Educational Interoperability Standard and functions for export and import are implemented, the learning management system itself is used as an authoring environment. In this case the opportunity is given to develop learning scenarios during the first run of a course (a quite normal approach) and, after a critical revision if necessary, then reusing the course plan for repeated runs.

- *Independent Integrated Authoring Environments:* Regardless the availability of compliant learning management systems, independent integrated authoring environments for Educational Interoperability Standards can serve as important tools for planning, developing, realising and evaluating teaching-learning-processes. Like tools for computer aided engineering they facilitate effective, efficient and pedagogical proficient creation of learning scenarios, which can be operated by teaching staff, e.g. in blended learning scenarios enhanced by digital educational media. A meaningful representation of elements in the information model for a unit of study, an ease of use and collaborative functions are essential to the acceptance of these tools.

- *Use of Standard Applications:* Since Educational Interoperability Standards are implemented in XML (eXtensible Markup Language) as a key technology for interoperability, standard XML editors may be used for implementing units of learning compliant to Educational Interoperability Standards. A skilful content developer can efficiently perform tasks in realising units of learning with an arrangement of standard applications for word processing, image manipulation and editors for XML and HTML. For each individual case it is to be weighed whether the development of integrated authoring environments is preferred against a cooperative thus specialised working scenario that leaves the coding to experts.

Tools for creating learning scenarios treat content objects as given – either within a repository for learning objects or created with external content editing tools. Hence, authoring environments for learning scenarios focus on creating, editing, storing, retrieving and selecting plans for teaching-learning-processes (Wilson, 2005, p. 41). Especially independent integrated authoring environments offer great potential for supporting instructional designers and subject matter experts through educational and pedagogical knowledge. For example, methods for teaching and learning like problem-oriented-learning, case study or project method can be given as predefined "learning design patterns" that allow instructional designers to use different pedagogical approaches in created units of learning.

Furthermore, procedures for the test of consistency for units of learning are to be developed (extending the validating against the XML-schema). Functions like the graphic representation of a plan for a teaching-learning-process, reports e.g. regarding the prospective duration in time or the proportion of learner's activities in relation to teacher's activities or simulated trial runs support decision on design and quality.

16.4   Conclusion

In order to support modularity, reuse, exchange and interoperability of digital educational media a pedagogically rich and meaningful notation for learning scenarios is crucial. Within this notation an aggregation of resources for learning, i.e. learning content, has to be completed by a description of learning objectives, prerequisites, learning activities, teaching activities and services used in the learning situation. Learning and teaching activities form the conceptual core to lay out a teaching-learning-process in a plan for a learning scenario as a learning flow; concepts of roles, environment, properties and context complete the notation. Educational Interoperability Standards provide elaborate information models for a standardised notation, which are abstracted from single learning scenarios as well as from single pedagogical approaches. Hence, Educational Interoperability Standards entail rather abstracted concepts, which, however, are versatile in use.

A notation that is proposed by an Educational Interoperability Standard has to be both machine-readable and human-readable. A formal description of elements that can describe any plan for a teaching-learning process within a containment framework can be processed by different learning management systems, as long as they are compliant to an Educational Interoperability Standard. Obviously, interoperability for learning scenarios (not only for learning content) that are to be exchanged between learning management systems depends on a machine-readable notation in a standardised format. But a formal description for a learning flow is of value beside interoperability. If learning scenarios can be operated by processing formal notations of a plan for a learning flow, human actors are relieved from routine tasks like providing resources for learning at the right time, setting up communication services or assigning users to courses, content, tools and services. Hence, teaching and supporting staff in learning scenarios can concentrate on educational tasks like teaching in class, moderating groups of learners and mentoring single learners. Still, as stated above, the plan must not be mistaken for the realisation. But acting upon a plan provides a stable basis for dealing with uncertainties and reacting spontaneously.

Readability for human actors has to be supported by authoring environments, of course. Integrated authoring environment for Educational Interoperability Standards with graphic representations of plans for a teaching-learning-process, reporting and simulating feature serve as tools for planning, developing, realising and evaluating teaching-learning-processes. They foster communication between different actors in the instructional design workflow, flexible adaptation on context or individual needs and reflection on pedagogical aspects. They thus provide an important basis for evaluating and managing quality in learning, education and training.

17 Developing and handling learner profiles for European learner information systems

Cleo Sgouropoulou

National Technical University of Athens, Greece

Learner profiling has become a high priority action item within the European education area. Indeed, the recently developed Europass framework aspires to provide the common basis for the well-structured recording of European learners' private and institution-owned information. The need for related support services at a European level, ranging from secure management and exchange of learning-related history, goals and accomplishments, to new learning and employment opportunities discovery, will soon begin to emerge. It is most obvious that such services should rely upon open and interoperable information systems. This article presents an overview of this new European educational setting, discusses issues and presents initiatives for the production of mappings and application profiles of Learning Technology interoperability specifications that can drive the design and development of European Learner Information Systems for the fomentation of European learning and employment mobility.

17.1 Introduction

In our dynamically changing world learners are given opportunities for enhancing their knowledge capital with a diversity of resources. The competitiveness of learners, as well as their partners in the learning process, depends heavily on the ability to deal with the great diversity of natural and technological resources currently available.

The imperious need for future actors of learning to become competent in *"knowledge economics"* undoubtedly assumes the use of technology for the provision of tools and services capable of resolving the main knowledge resource management issues within the learning process context: awareness on the availability of resources, rapid location of available resources, validation of resources in accordance with the learner's educational needs (Sgouropoulou et al, 2005).

Inline with this constantly evolving setting, Learning Management Systems

(LMS) aspire to provide learners with advanced, adaptive support based on their needs, preferences, background and other characteristics. However, the initial, ad hoc development of heterogeneous systems, lacking any provision of interoperability mechanisms, turned out hindering for the achievement of successful e-learning and delayed the longed for transition from the 'early adopter' to a more general offering stage, leaving many of the promises of e-learning yet immaterialised.

The development and utilisation of e-learning technology standards in the LMS design and implementation processes is now offering a new perspective towards the resolution of former limitations. Standards-based, open, interoperable systems will be key to the formation of a common marketplace and the broadening of borderless learning pathways.

The Learner, constituting a core entity within the learning process, has been the subject of standardisation efforts aiming at the production of information models capable of expressing learner profiles and records. The most highlighted use of leaner profiles is that of aiding in the personalisation of learning resources acquisition (Rousseau et al., 2004). However, a longer-term strategic aim of learner-centred information systems points to the need for facilitating the lifelong learner mobility within and between higher education, vocational education and training sectors and for supporting the communication of competencies and qualifications for employment purposes or for admission to learning schemes.

Responding to this need, the enhancement of lifelong learners' mobility and the establishment of a framework for the transparency of qualifications and competences by means of open, interoperable systems with focus on learner needs, have already been identified as mainstream issues across the European Education Area (EEA).

In its first part, this article provides a brief overview of the European initiatives and actions for the realisation of the EEA, as part of the mandate for European education systems to become 'a world quality reference'. Emphasis is put on the recently adopted Europass framework for the transparency of qualifications and competences, a standardised instrument which sets up some initial requirements towards the development of a European Learner Profile standard, capable of driving the design and implementation of European-scale Learner Information systems. The article continues with an analysis, on a two-stage process basis, of the actions involved in moving from requirements to actual implementations. It discusses the current European policy making procedures, presents the learning technology standardisation efforts and introduces the activities related to the expression of the European requirements and concerns for the development of emerging Learner Information systems.

17.2   Requirements for a European Education Area: The europass framework

At its Lisbon meeting in March 2000, the European Council set a goal for the Union to "become the most competitive and dynamic knowledge-based economy in the world capable of sustainable economic growth with more and better jobs and greater social cohesion" (Report from the Education Council, 2001).

Making this happen will mean a fundamental transformation of education and training throughout Europe. Actions in these fields involve the development of the European Higher Education Area (the "Bologna process") and the enhanced European co-operation in Vocational Education and Training (the "Copenhagen process"). As part of the Lisbon mandate, the Commission has taken initiatives to establish synergies between both processes for the design of national frameworks of qualifications and an overarching European Qualifications Framework (EQF) for Lifelong Learning, taking into account the work done in the Bologna and Copenhagen context.

Qualifications frameworks can be defined as "a systematic description of an education system's qualifications where all learning achievements are measured and related to each other" (Realising the European Higher Education Area, 2003).

The aims and purposes of qualifications frameworks are manifold. In particular, they intend to:

- Facilitate the comparability and compatibility of degrees and qualifications through the use of common reference points for competences.
- Facilitate the recognition of degrees, as well as the recognition of experimental, informal and non-formal learning.
- Ease mobility, mostly through the easier recognition within and between the university sector and other types of post-secondary education.
- Build the link between higher education and lifelong learning.
- Contribute in the improvement of the European cooperation with regards to quality assurance.
- Foster the social dimension, mainly through providing more flexible learning paths, thus promoting social inclusion.
- Provide good guidance for curricula changes e.g. in terms of shifting from teaching-based to learner-centred systems.

- Provide more transparency for the labour market and for learners, as it will become more visible and understandable what skills and competences are achieved at a given level or in a given degree.

Qualifications frameworks can achieve their full benefit in combination with instruments and devices, two of the most essential being the "European Credit Transfer System" (ECTS) and the "single Community framework for the transparency of qualifications and competences" (Europass).

With the decision 2241/2004/EC the European Parliament and the Council of Europe have established Europass by means of the creation of a personal, coordinated portfolio of documents, which citizens can use on a voluntary basis to better communicate and present their qualifications and competences throughout Europe (Decision on Europass, 2004). Each of the Europass documents defines information structures for the presentation in a clear and comprehensive way of several types of learner information. In particular, Europass consists of the:

- Europass-CV, a curriculum vitae structure for the presentation of an individual's qualifications and competences.
- Europass-Mobility, which records periods of learning attended by its holders in countries other than their own.
- Europass-Diploma Supplement, providing information on its holder's educational achievements at higher education level.
- Europass-Language Portfolio, providing individuals with the opportunity to present their language skills.
- Europass-Certificate Supplement, describing the competences and qualifications corresponding to a vocational training certificate.

Apart from providing these standardised information structures, the "Europass decision" sets the way ahead for the creation of an open, interoperable Europass Internet-based information system, parts of which will be managed at national level in the different stakeholder countries, while others administered at Community level. The Europass information system is expected to facilitate submission and exchange of information among the interoperating parts, and shall be developed taking into account the opportunity of future developments, with particular reference to the integration of information services on job and learning opportunities (Decision on Europass, 2004).

17.3   Implementing European requirements through learning technology standards

Despite of the possible resistance to change, it is inevitable that certain information about European citizens will be captured, stored, processed and transferred between emerging information systems.

The requirement for open, distributed information systems to support the exchange of learner information throughout Europe, in a transparent manner, is a highly demanding task. In order to provide viable support for the emerging European Learner Information systems and dissuade European service providers from developing proprietary services and platforms, it is essential that interoperability standards for the representation of learner profiles are agreed upon. By mapping profiles to a common interoperability specification, the exchange of operational data between systems will be enhanced and it will also become easier to move reference data into new systems as software is upgraded or replaced. In addition, issues about privacy and data protection need to be investigated and dealt with.

The process of moving from requirements to actual implementation involves two stages (JISC-CETIS, 2001):

- *A Policy Development Stage*, to agree the human, organisational and educational questions as to what information needs to be gathered and exchanged, for what purposes, in what contexts, and how this information should be organised.
- *A Technical Stage*, to evaluate currently available interoperability specifications and standards, in order to provide technical formatting (mappings) of profiles information, thus enabling its accommodation and exchange between systems.

The following paragraphs introduce actions and issues involved in each of the above stages for the implementation of European requirements through Learning Technology standards.

17.3.1   Policy issues regarding the attributes of learner profiles

The establishment of the Europass information structures constitutes one of the initial steps towards the formation of a European Learner Profile and the achievement of the European Qualifications Framework objectives. Europass is a significant standardisation tool, setting a common basis for the representation of a major part of the learner information that is typically required in a number of learning, training or employment business processes. However, as the need for more services grows, additional profile structures will need to be determined and integrated in the overall learner information scheme.

The following scenario of a learner seeking admission in a technical school, college or university within the EEA, is an example providing a good basis for pinpointing additional attributes of the Learner Profile domain (CEN/ ISSS WS LT, 2004). In particular, the learner presents an application which might comprise:

- A letter of application (or application form) in which the learner explains her motivation, makes claims and provides evidence of achievement.
- A Europass-CV
- A set of diplomas or more detailed 'transcripts' setting out formal qualifications, such as the Europass-Certificate Supplement or the Europass-Diploma Supplement.

In addition, the learner may provide:

- A testimonial from a teacher (or ask a teacher to provide a reference letter, directly).
- A testimonial from a workplace supervisor, offering an opinion on how well the learner can exercise the competency which he or she claims to have develop at work and which qualifies her for a particular programme of study.
- A report including a presentation of what she has learnt through experience, for example in employment.
- A testimonial from a person who has supported the learner's personal and educational development and which the learner can read without special permission.

The scenario illustrated above highlights a number of issues, apart from the information structuring, subject to consideration throughout the policy development stage (CEN/ ISSS WS LT, 2004), (Grant et al., 2003). For example:

- The Learner Profile should comprise both academic, vocational or professional related information owned by the corresponding educational, training or employing bodies, and information owned by the learner, in which the learner provides a profile of him or herself. The Europass-Diploma Supplement is an example of documents falling into the first category, whereas Europass-CV represents learner owned information.
- Detailed descriptions of eligible business processes among individuals and organisations should be elaborated.
- A specification of regulations concerning the processing of personal data and the protection of privacy should be compiled.
- Scaleable contextual information should be provided e.g. of the nature and status of the organisations a profile refers to, in order to enhance understanding in uses of the same profile across Europe.
- Suitable packaging of different profile information for presentation to different audiences should be supported. For example, in some cases the different documents making up the profile a learner wishes to present to an audience may best be packaged together, which implies certain technical requirements for security. In other cases the different documents may best be communicated as separate packages, for example where an e-portfolio accompanies an application like the one outlined above.

17.3.2   Learner Information interoperability specifications

Standardisation efforts in the Learner Information field are oriented to the production of information models capable of adequately describing learner characteristics, and the provision of mechanisms for the exchange of information among diverse learning systems. Currently the most dominant specifications related to the Learner Profile domain, are the IMS Learner Information Package (LIP) from the

IMS Global Consortium and the IEEE Public And Private Information (PAPI), the further elaboration of which has been undertaken by the ISO/IEC JTC1 SC 36 Participant Information Working Group.

IMS learner information package

Learner information in the IMS LIP specification offers a data model that describes characteristics needed for the general purpose of recording and managing learning related history, goals and accomplishments; engaging the user in a learning experience; discovering learning opportunities (IMS Global Learning Consortium Inc., 2001). The typical sorts of learner information supported by LIP are:

- Education record, the record of educational achievement from school through to college/ university
- Training log, the record of training activities undertaken, e.g., courses carrying formal certification
- Professional development record, the record of professional development activities undertaken including membership in the appropriate professional bodies
- Resume/ CV, a record of personal achievement that includes relevant work experience, qualifications and education history
- Lifelong learning record, a cradle-to-grave record of the learning activities and achievements of an individual.

The specification supports the exchange of learner information among a variety of information systems used in the learning process, which are referenced as learner information systems regardless of any other functionality they possess or roles they fulfil. IMS LIP is a structured information model which defines fields that hold the learner data and the type of data that may be accommodated by these fields.

Typical data might be the name of a learner, a course or training completed, a learning objective, a preference for a particular type of technology, and so on. Metadata about each field can include: time-related information, identification and indexing information and privacy and data protection information. This metadata is available for each and every field in the information model, either directly or via inheritance. The primary learner information as specified in IMS LIP is presented in figure 17-1.

IEEE public and private information

IEEE PAPI was created to represent learner records, specifying the semantics and syntax of associated information. It specifies data interchange formats, facilitating communication between cooperating systems (IEEE LTSC, 2002). User records are divided into personal information and performance information and these are maintained separately. A key feature of the standard is the logical division, separate security, and separate administration of several types of learner information. The current specification splits the learner information into the following areas:

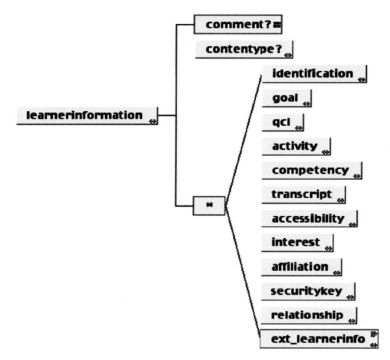

Fig. 17-1: Primary learner information as specified in IMS LIP

- Learner personal information: name, address, and telephone number (private to learner).
- Learner relations information: learner's relationship to other users of learning technology systems, such as teachers, instructors, and other learners.
- Learner security information: learner's security credentials, such as: passwords, challenge/ responses, private keys and public keys. This is private to the learner (with the exception of public information).
- Learner preference information: describes information that may improve human-computer interactions. This type of information is similar to personal information except that it may be public.
- Learner performance information: relates to the learner's history that is created and used by learning technology components to provide optimum learning experiences. Generally, learner performance information is created and used by automated learning technology systems.
- Learner portfolio information: is a collection of a learner's accomplishments and works that is intended for illustration and justification of his/ her abilities and achievements.

The high level architecture of the PAPI Learner Information is depicted in figure 17-2.

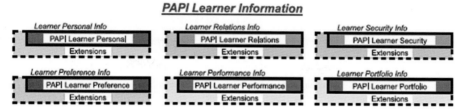

Fig. 17-2: IEEE PAPI learner information

17.3.3   European learner profile interoperability specifications

The first information structures for building European learner profiles in the form of the Europass documents are now a fact. Furthermore, the learning technologies standardisation community has produced enabling technical specifications for the accommodation and exchange of learner information.

The European standardisation body for learning technologies, CEN/ ISSS Workshop on Learning Technologies (WS LT), as part of its headline objective to encourage the development and use of relevant and appropriate specifications and standards for learning technologies in Europe, has undertaken a set of actions dealing with the development of data models, protocols and bindings capable of effectively meeting the specific European requirements and concerns for learner information that allow secure handling of this information in open and distributed learner information systems (van Assche et al., 2003).

In particular, CEN/ ISSS WS LT, in terms of its work item "Handling of Learner Profiles in IT-supported learning environments from a European perspective" has carried out the following actions, presented in detail in CEN/ ISSS WS LT, 2004:

1. *Evaluation of the currently available interoperability learner information specifications and standards.* After investigation of the IMS Learner Information Package and the IEEE PAPI Learner Information (including its successors), the workshop agreed on the endorsement of IMS LIP as a normative basis for emerging European Learner Information Standards.
2. *Integration of enhanced language capability to IMS LIP.* This action was concerned with information regarding the languages learners read, understand and write. Elaborating on prior work (CEN/ ISSS WS LT, 2002b), the workshop compiled and proposed a structure for enhancing the IMS LIP "3.3 Language" data element. The enhanced data model contributes to the creation of fine descriptions of learner language capabilities, usable in a large range of communication situations, with varying levels of proficiency.
3. *Mapping of the Europass-CV to IMS LIP.* This action item produced a first mapping of the Europass-CV information structure to the IMS LIP data model (association of each piece of the CV information with an IMS LIP element) (figure 17-3).

European CV Category	IMS LIP 1.0 Element	Value for typename
Personal Information		
Name	`<identification><name>`	
Address	`<identification><demographics><date>`	
Telephone	`<identification><contactinfo><telephone>`	
Fax	`<identification><contactinfo><facsimile>`	
E-mail	`<identification><contactinfo><email>`	
Nationality	`<identification><ext_identification>`	Nationality
Date of Birth	`<identification><demographics><date>`	

Fig. 17-3: Excerpt from the europass-CV mapping to IMS LIP

The suggested technical specification constitutes an initial implementation proposal for the development of information systems to exchange European learner CV data. Experimentation with and several revisions of the proposed mapping are of course necessary, before a fully interoperable Europass-CV schema evolves.

4. *Mapping of the Europass-Diploma Supplement (EDS) to IMS LIP.* Within this action item a first mapping of the EDS information structure to the IMS LIP data model was introduced (figure 17-4). Member states can use the suggested mapping as a basis for the production of national mappings. This process is necessary in order for European countries to gain experience on the appropriate representation of information required by EDS and contribute in the subsequent elaboration of an overarching, interoperable EDS, usable by all European educational institutions. As a mapping example of a national transcript (main source of EDS information) to IMS LIP, the case of the UK transcript was presented.

DS Data Element	IMS LIP 1.0 Element	Comment
2 **Information Identifying the Qualification**		
2.1 Name of qualification and title conferred	`<qcl><title>` `<activity><definition><description>` `<activity><learningactivityref>`	An electronic DS name of the qualit the programme le institution's datab:
2.2 Main field(s) of study for the qualification	`<qcl><ext_qcl >`	In some member statistical returns vocabulary of sub
2.3 Name and status of Awarding Institution	`<qcl><organization>`	There is currently of organisations represent organis perhaps following require a second institution, perhap
2.4 Name and status of institution administering studies	`<affiliation><organization>`	Same comment a

Fig. 17-4: Excerpt from the europass-DS mapping to IMS LIP

5. *Definition of the European need for privacy with regard to Learner Profile information.* This action was intended as a starting point for discussion concerning issues such as the appropriate use, ownership and privacy of data within any learner information package. In particular, a variety of documents in current use in UK were discussed (e.g. the use, privacy and ownership definition for the UK Transcript/ Diploma Supplement) and the need for investigation and elaboration of privacy definitions for the exchange of the European learner information was highlighted.

In addition, and in order to further enhance the learner information domain, CEN/ ISSS WS LT has initiated a work item for the production of a European information model for expressing learner competences (CEN/ ISSS WS LT, 2005b). Competences are typically referenced by learner profile structures, e.g. the Europass-CV and the Europass-Certificate Supplement, and constitute the basis for a number of services regarding skill gap analysis and learning/ employment opportunities tracking.

17.4   Conclusion

The European Union has already set up the processes for transforming European education in a '*world quality reference*'. The fulfilment of this ambitious goal involves the development and adoption of a European Learner Profile for the expression of European citizens' learning, training and employment related information across the entire European Education Area. Europass constitutes an important step towards this direction. Learning technology standardisation initiatives both at a European level and within several member states (UK, France, etc.) have contributed in the production of the corresponding technical interoperability specifications, setting the grounds for the implementation of European Learner Information Systems.

18 Improving European employability with the e-portfolio

Michel Arnaud

University Paris X, France

The e-portfolio is a web-based information management system that uses electronic media and services to provide a lifelong learning device for users, a monitoring tool for training institutions and an improved access to employment opportunities.

To reach that goal, there is a need to have common references for competency definitions with the learner competency model: IMS LIP as well as an e-portfolio format in agreement with IMS Reusable Definition of Competency or Educational Objective (RDCEO), Europass Diploma Supplement, Data Protection and Privacy procedures.

The e-portfolio can provide an opportunity for the European Union to have a stronger implication in improving European employability through its promotion, provided there is a coordinated action regarding competencies certification and validation across Europe, using the same format, protecting personal data and finally ensuring system interoperability. Standardised interfaces will facilitate the use of customised and efficient e-portfolio services.

18.1 Introduction

The goal of this paper is to present e-portfolio's potentials in terms of improving European workforce's employability. An e-portfolio allows a customised follow-up on a person's education and career development if correctly used. European citisens may gain from adopting it, for self-monitoring and evaluation, to get better counselling for training as well as for job placement. Quality criteria apply to e-portfolio in order to optimise its usages as a learner's knowledge and professional skills tracking tool. Obstacles have to be overcome to that effect, related to a European common framework for competencies certification and validation, for personal data protection procedures and for across-the-board system interoperability. These aspects have to be part of the quality insurance process to be monitored by specific indicators.

18.1.1   Definition

A general e-portfolio contains information about digital and non-digital works created by the subject, activities in which the subject has participated, is participating, or plans to participate, competencies (skills, etc.) of the subject, achievements of the subject, whether or not certificated, results of any test or examination of the subject, contextual information to help the interpretation of any results, any notes, reflections, or relevant assessments. It is also possible to find information on the subject's preferences, goals and plans, interests and values as well as about creation and ownership of parts of the e-portfolio.

The EDUCAUSE NLII defines an e-portfolio as "a collection of authentic and diverse evidence, drawn from a larger archive, that represents what a person or organisation has learned over time, on which the person or organisation has reflected, designed for presentation to one or more audiences for a particular rhetorical purpose." The "larger archive" may contain multiple views of its contents directed towards multiple audiences. This collection usually takes the form of a set of pieces of evidence of learning and performance, reflections, or interpretations on that evidence, and representations of relationships between and among the evidence, interpretations, and evaluation criteria. Broadening out from just learning, an e-portfolio could also evidence personal qualities and attributes, or any "competencies" that are relevant to the particular audience, who could be potential employees or colleagues interested in performance at work, as well as academics interested in the outcomes of learning.

The subject of the e-portfolio may also be the same person as the audience, and the purpose may be reflection. In this case, there are no particular bounds to what is relevant, and the whole of the archive can be considered to be the e-portfolio. While the subject of an e-portfolio is always the overall owner of the portfolio, some evidence, reflections, relationships, and criteria may have been created and may be owned by another individual or group. The authenticity and integrity of these parts may need to be verifiable with some third-party authority.

This expanded version of the NLII definition describes the most complicated and sophisticated structure of e-portfolios found in practice. In many concrete applications, certain elements may be unnecessary. Many e-portfolios contain only a single view. Some e-portfolios contain only parts owned and authored by their subject. Some e-portfolios contain no reflections, while others contain no assessment information. Some contain information about how to render their contents, while some do not. This specification provides the means to represent both complex and simple e-portfolio types.

Major types of e-portfolios include:

- personal development e-portfolios (a process undertaken by an individual to reflect upon his/ her own learning, performance and/ or achievement and to plan for his/ her personal, educational and career development),
- learning e-portfolios (used to document, guide, and advance learning over time),

- presentation and assessment e-portfolios: they tend to demonstrate achievement to some authority by relating evidence within the e-portfolio to performance standards defined by that authority.

18.1.2   Relevance for target groups

The benefits of e-portfolios can be summarised under three areas: a learning tool for the user, a monitoring tool for institutions and a mechanism for employment opportunities. This interaction between institutions, instructors, advisors, employers and peers creates a varied learning community and improved job market conditions.

The European citizen should be able to take an e-portfolio offered at one stage of learning into the next stage of learning, whether in education or employment. In this way a European citizen will use a Lifelong e-portfolio. To that effect, active services and tools that enhance learners' development should be included in the European definition of e-portfolio. Teachers and learning institution administrators have to be trained to know how to use e-portfolios of learners they have in charge. Developers have to receive clear and agreed instructions on e-portfolio system interoperability.

Policy makers may be interested in promoting the widest use of e-portfolio as it can help increase job opportunities for European citizens and meet the needs of the European economy for a highly skilled and flexible workforce.

Pilot exchanges of learner information are being undertaken within Member States, but not yet between States. Scenarios of use suggest that a common European instrument such as the Europass Diploma Supplement would provide a useful starting point for pilots between States and leads on directly to richer information that a wider e-portfolio should provide. National governments and the Commission have an important role to play in promoting the use of e-portfolio throughout society.

18.1.3   Challenges

In order to develop advanced systems and services that help improve European citizen employability, through the promotion of e-portfolio, there is a need to have common references for:

- e-portfolio format: the scenario online template has to include general information (language, description, creator, audience, source, other contributors;), scenario flow diagram from different perspectives, a list of stakeholders and other actors, information about resource's format and contribution's rights management, information about the person who enters the object/ resource (role of the creator/ publisher of the scenario).
- competency definitions through the model of learner competency (IMS LIP), based on RDCEO and to be applied all over Europe,

- personal data protection : the IPSE approach seems adequate,
- interoperability of e-portfolio on different platforms and environments.

A strong case is emerging for the development of a European standard to support these technical initiatives and pilot their implementation to exchange learner information between member states. Standardised interfaces will facilitate the way towards customised and efficient e-portfolio services from a training and work-related perspective.

18.2   Related research and experiences

The Learner Information Packaging Group based in the UK is coordinating the development of a set of scenarios to illustrate some typical uses of e-portfolios across Europe. Each scenario provides an illustration of how a learner may typically use an e-portfolio. Workshops are being arranged to develop further scenarios. Scenario's main elements are:

1. Metadata about who has provided this specific scenario.
2. A short statement providing context for a scenario, explaining briefly how it relates to other practices and policies within a particular education or employment sector and within a particular region or state.
3. A scenario's simple flow diagram. Typically this will show how different kinds of people make use of e-portfolio and of systems which support it.
4. The 'story' or narrative about using an e-portfolio told from the perspective of an external narrator. This can cover paper-based practice, face to face meetings and use of other technology in addition to e-portfolio. Comments are invited on how a user may move from present practice toward using an e-portfolio.
5. The narrative told from the perspective of one or more persons involved, always including learner's perspective.
6. A list of stakeholders involved in the scenario and of what they want the system to provide.
7. A list of other persons and systems, supporting the process.
8. Definitions of terms.
9. References and bibliography.

Scenarios contribute to the development of European e-portfolio White Papers, outcomes of the INSIGHT European Schoolnet knowledge base for new technology and education. This is equivalent to the White Paper for North America published in November 2003 by ePortConsortium. Scenarios are also intended to inform the development of formal technical standards by European standard and specification bodies.

5 European projects are funded either by the DG Education and Culture under the Socrates - Grundtvig programme or by the 6th Framework Research Program, developing e-portfolios formats and systems.

- EPICC (from 01/03 to 06/05) presents an e-portfolio state of the art and develops specifications of e-portfolio systems. Among key findings of this project, the conceptual framework for e-portfolios describes conditions to enhance a greater interoperability. E-portfolio plugfests are organised to demonstrate e-portfolio technologies and enhance interoperability between e-portfolio platforms and other information systems.
- Key-PAL (from 09/04 to 08/06) develops e-portfolio for essential skills as a benchmark of national approaches towards the definition and supports to the development and accreditations of essential skills.
- TELCERT (from 01/04 to 06/06) develops conformance testing of technology enhanced learning as well as the European Diploma supplement (EDS) Application Profile (technical specifications) with CEDEFOP, the European vocational training agency, for e-portfolio public specifications and standards.
- OSMOSYS (from 10/04 to 09/06) promotes small and medium organisation learning with the e-portfolio as a support for learning and accreditation.
- INFLOW (from 10/04 to 09/06) promotes informal learning at the workplace with the e-portfolio.

While e-portfolios previously took the form of static web pages, the growth over the last few years has been fuelled by the availability of commercial and open source e-portfolio tools in the form of database-driven, web applications. E-portfolios are beginning to be used as tools for personal development planning, lifelong learning, and learning in the workplace. E-portfolios are also beginning to be used for high-stakes assessment and credentialing. But, to be portable e-portfolios need to ensure educational continuity between programs within an educational institution that use e-portfolios, integration of evidence about learning over time, and smooth transfer of verifiable information about learning and evaluation between institutions, levels of education, and employers. From an individual perspective, information about and artefacts of a person's performance and achievement, as recorded in an e-portfolio, need to operate across institutions and countries throughout their lifetime.

18.3   E-portfolio: The concepts

The following aspects are essential for a more efficient and wider use of e-portfolios in Europe. Common definitions of terms are needed to provide coherence and stability for European competency grids. Technical specifications as well as certification procedures have to be implemented in a coherent approach in order to enhance greater interoperability. Personal data protection has to be guaranteed across all e-portfolio management systems so that European citizens feel secure about aspects they want to keep private and not being revealed to potential employers.

18.3.1   Common definitions

Common definitions need to be used to guarantee coherence among e-portfolios. A technical report presented in JTC1SC36-WG3 about proposed standards concerning Participant Information data models, features various templates for describing competencies, capabilities, impairments, performance, educational objectives and other related issues. It intends to provide a map of the described concepts which are used in Information Technologies for Learning, Education and Training, and in particular in Participant Information data models. Based on these definitions and the relationships between terms, this technical report proposes a coherent conceptual model, referring to current research work in the domains involved, in which each term listed fits.

Knowledge: Knowledge means a set of facts, information, skills, understanding that one has gained on a given topic. Specialists distinguish the following categories of *knowledge:* factual knowledge, or declarative knowledge, i.e. knowledge of facts (knowing what…), procedural knowledge, i.e. knowledge of procedures (knowing how to do…), and practical knowledge or know-how. This latter is also considered as tacit knowledge, which means that it cannot be explained by words, or formalised.

Skill: A *skill* is the effective use of knowledge, understanding and know-how to perform an activity. *Skills* develop through practice.

Educational objective: An *educational objective* describes precisely the aim of an educational or training sequence in terms of evolution of knowledge, know-how and skills of the participants. An *educational objective* can be expressed according to different viewpoints: the customer will express it in terms of targeted competences, whereas a training or educational services provider will express it in terms of abilities to acquire. This form is sometimes called "pedagogical objective", and is used both to design and implement the educational or training sequence, and to evaluate the abilities acquired by the participants. Pedagogical objectives define and structure learning activities.

Task: A *task* is a set of operations which must be achieved in order to reach a goal and get a given result. Description of *tasks* aims at facilitating the achievement of a given production according to a given process. A *task* correspond to an external vision of an activity: the term "activity" often describes the actual work which is performed, whereas the term "task" is used to describe work assigned by an authority, in other terms work "prescribed" as stated in work analysis

Ability: An *ability* is a set of natural or acquired dispositions in which a person is proficient. Ability is expressed by a sentence like: he/ she is able to…*Ability* can be demonstrated in a professional or vocational context, or indirectly measured by tests. *Abilities* are very often expressed in terms of sets of various knowledge, know-how and skills.

Aptitude: An *aptitude* is a supposed ability to perform a given activity. An *aptitude* is therefore the vision that someone has of somebody else's ability. At the end of training, a certificate may guarantee that the trainee has the *aptitudes* required by the qualification, but not that he/ she has the abilities to perform any given task! This term is mainly used in Education and Training.

An impairment: An *impairment* is a loss of substance or an alteration resulting from a pathological state and which affects body structure or appearance, or a physical or mental function. The Directive 95/46/EC of the European Parliament and of the Council of 24 October 1995 on the protection of individuals with regard to the processing of personal data and on the free movement of such data prohibits storage and processing of certain categories of data (Art. 8), to which pertain *"impairments"*.

Competence: Competence is, generally speaking, the ability to solve a problem in a given context. It corresponds to the implementation of knowledge, know-how, skills, behaviours, procedures, ways of reasoning to perform an activity. *Competence* is therefore considered as the reactive conjunction of a person's actual and potential abilities and the situation in which they are put into action. By extension, "professional *competence*" means the ability to perform adequately a given activity. Therefore, the result of somebody else's *competence* appears as the performance he/ she achieves.

Qualification: Qualification is a set of aptitudes or abilities, acquired through training or experience, which fits a person for a given job. *Qualification* is often testified by a diploma or a certificate. Performance is the result obtained at the end of a test or of an activity performed in a given situation which reveals the competences in use. Performance is the proof of somebody's *competence* for somebody else. It is measured in terms of operations or activities successfully achieved.

Based on agreed definitions of key terms as presented above, a common conceptual model can be used to assess the relevance of Participant Information data models which are proposed for various e-portfolios, in a quality-based approach.

18.4   Related specifications

Currently available systems, known to the IMS e-portfolios Development Committee, store e-portfolios in formats that have no facilities for importing and exporting e-portfolio information conformant with accepted standards. This makes it difficult or impossible to move e-portfolios data between systems, and leads to inefficiency and redundancy when integrating e-portfolio tools with other enterprise systems. Technical specifications have been issued for software developers designing e-portfolio tools, integrating them with other systems and with e-learning tools that incorporate e-portfolio-related functions to increase their interoperability.

IMs learner information package (LIP) and IMS reusable definition of competency or educational objective (RDCEO)

IMS Learner Information Package (LIP) provides a very flexible way of representing information about the activities, achievements, etc. of a learner. IMS Learning Information Package Accessibility for LIP (ACCLIP) can be embedded in LIP to provide the accessibility component of learner information. IMS Digital Repositories Interoperability (DRI) Portfolios share characteristics with repositories. Recent versions of the DRI and e-portfolio specifications are aligned accordingly.

IMS Reusable Definition of Competency or Educational Objective (RDCEO) provides a way to represent a definition of what it means to be able to do something. This is particularly useful for e-portfolio definition of assessed ability which may include a pointer to some RDCEO data. Where vocabulary data types are defined in IMS specifications, the community of use may choose to define its own vocabulary. The RDCEO definition construct includes the idea of a definition model: a template for defining competencies, educational objectives, etc. The great variety of models in use means that communities using e-portfolios will generally have to define how their model is expressed in RDCEO.

To perform a multi-dimensional assessment needs to define a complex set of interrelated criteria and would usually be visually represented as a table. This sort of rubric generally has three elements: dimensions of quality, levels of mastery, commentaries. A dimension of quality is identified, for example to present a piece of evidence as an item for assessment. The intersection of a dimension of quality and level of mastery is identified, for example to interpret a score. An individual criterion is identified, for example when expressing how a level of mastery is shown.

Europass diploma supplement

The e-portfolio can be complemented by other instruments aimed at strengthening overall recognition of qualifications in Europe. The Europass Diploma Supplement is an annex, an explanatory note attached to a diploma awarded by a higher education institution. It helps to explain the diploma which may often be understood only within the country concerned. When fully completed this document provides all the information necessary to make a valid assessment of any degree or qualification. The Supplement should be issued to every student, upon graduation, together with their official diploma, free of charge, in a widely spoken European language.

Institutions should disseminate information regarding the purpose and content of the Diploma Supplement among their own students as well as to local organisations, employers and other interested persons. In this connection, the EUROPASS initiative of the Commission should be noted. The European Commission proposes to integrate the different transparency instruments developed for vocational training (like the Europass CV, Europass Mobility, Europass Diploma Supplement, Europass Certificate Supplement, Europass Language Portfolio) and bring them together in a single European Framework for Transparency of Qualifications and Competences.

The task to be fulfilled by the network of national ENIC/ NARIC centres is to provide adequate, reliable and authenticated information, within reasonable time as prescribed by the Lisbon Recognition Convention, national and EU legislation, on qualifications, education systems, and recognition procedures to individual holders of qualifications, higher education institutions, employers, professional organisations, public authorities, ENIC/ NARIC partners and other interested parties.

Data protection and privacy (DPP)

E-portfolio systems should be protected since they hold personal and private information. W3C XML Digital Signature Syntax and Processing (Dsig) provides a vehicle whereby information can be proven to have originated from an entity and not been changed. Digital signatures are important because they avoid the need to go back to the origin of information for verification and so reduce the need for large repositories of persistent information.

The CEN ISSS Workshop on Data Protection and Privacy (CEN/ ISSS WS/ DPP) is extended beyond 2005 as a project team whose aim is to help organisations to comply with the Data Protection Directive and relevant national legislation by facilitating harmonisation of practice, developing the understanding and predictability of detailed or sector practices, contributing to resolving ICT technical compliance issues, and encouraging consistency of assessment and oversight. The Workshop took due regard of the provisions of the relevant EU legislation on data protection and privacy, including Directives 95/46/EC, and 2002/58/EC.

The Workshop prepares a legal opinion and model clause concerning anonymisation of personal data and the demarcation line between identifiable and non-identifiable data. Article 2 of the Data Protection Directive (DPD) gives a definition about 'personal' data by which a natural person can be identified 'directly or indirectly'. According to alinea 26 of the DPD, non identification is assumed if the amount and the nature of the indirectly identifying data are such that identification of the individual is only possible with the application of disproportionate effort, or if assistance by a third party outside the power and authority of the person responsible is necessary. The results will be published in the form of a CEN Workshop Agreement and report. The baseline data protection audit framework will include a set of norms from a compliance perspective and a privacy governance perspective, guidance sections for organisations considering an audit, preparing for an audit and for organisations executing the audit and explanatory notes on how to tailor the standard to the local legislation.

18.5   Practical examples which illustrate the quality approach/concept in practice

Among various software to handle e-portfolios on an electronic medium, some are private such as iWebFolio, produced by Nuventive, some are open source such as the Open Source Portfolio Initiative (OSPI). Many experiments are ongoing at different stages of magnitude in terms of the number of actors involved.

The e-portfolio framework is used to match users' needs and e-portfolio services which contribute to assessment, personal development, pathway, guidance. These services have reference models which identify common requirements and show how one or more services can be used to meet users' needs. These reference models lead to reference implementation where quality procedures are implemented as guidelines (Rees Jones, 2005).

For example of a reference model, the employer identifies the gaps in learning required for the job. The teacher identifies the gaps required to bring the learner up to the minimum standard. The learner identifies the gaps required for his/ her long term ambitions. The actors negotiate a learning flow customised to the needs of the employer meeting the minimum standard and personalised by the learner. The plan is executed.

A pattern book containing reference implementations can be used by any of the actors to find a particular type of plan for a particular type of learner, job, learning problem or goal. An agent can help any actor to navigate the pattern book, customise the learning and the learning flow. Each actor can specify conditions when the plan will alert them, for example by poor diagnostic assessment results or attendance. The plan is therefore a learning flow and an active resource. Quality process can be applied to measure how the reference implementation has been taken into account for building a specific learner's plan.

To submit an e-portfolio to an external review system is a crucial step in the assessment process. For example, a student is enrolled in a program of study in preparation to enter a profession. The curriculum maps with certification and accreditation requirements for that profession and requires each student to submit an e-portfolio demonstrating their completion of these requirements to an institutional assessment system prior to graduation. In order to reach that result, the student has to collect evidence of his performance and map the evidence to the standards in a personal e-portfolio tool. To that effect, the help of instructors and counsellors is needed to provide feedback as the quality of the review correlates to improved student performance. Critiquing an e-portfolio requires instructors to be explicit and consistent in applying assessment criteria. E-portfolio must provide tools to assist instructors in providing improved commentary on student work. In turn, faculty can create a teaching e-portfolio to demonstrate how they help students learn and revise their pedagogy based on the same representation, reflection, and revision cycle. At the institutional level, e-portfolio offers an ideal tool for providing evidence of improved student learning, which is meaningful to accreditation agencies and funding sources.

Three obstacles to institutional uptake of e-portfolio have been noted at the

University of Minnesota where e-portfolios are used extensively by 34.000 students: lack of easy ways to protect intellectual property rights of students, concerns about increased workload for faculty, 'inverted value' of e-portfolio to students (Acker, 2005). The first aspect needs to add digital right management to data protection procedures. In case of collaborative learning, the question of who has written what in a group document can become divisive. There is a need to protect students' ownership on produced texts. The second problem rises from the increased interaction allowed by using e-portfolios between faculty and students. As a prerequisite, faculty needs to develop new skills for handling e-portfolio procedures. Assessment workload is increased because of more explicit feedback than in a regular classroom, prone to more contentions and discussions. Finally, 'most students are outcome, rather than process, oriented. They want to graduate, rather than track their academic growth between early and late educational experiences. This explains why e-portfolio often is presented as a career showcase, rather than a process for documenting learning.' This third aspect should be addressed in the e-portfolio framework where reference models and implementations for learning plans may be defined along the lines of a quality process where outputs are outlined as a guarantee for learning contracts to be passed between learners and all other actors involved in using e-portfolios.

18.6   Conclusion

With a particular focus on competency grids, format harmonisation, system interoperability and protection of personal data and security issues, quality insurance process regarding e-portfolio concentrates on recommendations for further work on specifications and standards as well as building reference models and implementations to better match users' needs.

The e-portfolio will provide an opportunity for the European Union to have a stronger implication in improving European employability through its promotion, provided there is a coordinated action regarding validation of competencies across Europe according to the Learner competency model developed by CEN, respecting personal data protection in the format used for e-portfolios and finally implementing system interoperability. A direct effect expected from developing appropriate European standards in this domain will be an increase of ease of use and efficiency of e-portfolios. The wider use of e-portfolio depends also on the human factor, namely the reactions of users and other stakeholders which have to be tackled by appropriate methods to be measured by quality procedures.

19 Interface standards: Integration of learning and business information systems

Markus Bick

ESCP-EAP European School of Management, Germany

Jan M. Pawlowski

University of Duisburg-Essen, Germany

The integration of business information systems is actually not a new challenge. To facilitate business tasks, enterprise applications must communicate with one another and share data (Deitel et al., 2003). Therefore, corresponding standardisation activities have been conducted to obtain integrated information systems. The main goal of this paper is to give a general review of relevant standards in the area of business information systems integration, which can be applied in learning systems as well. At first, selected data exchange standards, especially the Extensible Markup Language (*XML*) are being described. After that, corresponding infrastructure standards, like the Open Management Architecture (*OMA*) and *Web services* are reviewed. Recommendations for future works are being suggested as part of the conclusion.

19.1   Introduction

The integration of computer-based business information systems – in the following shortened as information systems – is actually not a new challenge. Integration of corresponding applications is as old as applying information technology to business processes. Data exchange between certain applications as well as between supply chain partners is the main emphasis on this aspect. Moreover, various approaches suggest the integration of additional information systems classes, e.g., knowledge management systems (KMS) or learning management systems (LMS) to an integrated knowledge-based workplace-environment (Adelsberger,

Bick, Lodzinski, Pawlowski, 2005). Typically, a learning management system and a human resource management system require the same personal records, e.g., name, gender, role, competencies, etc. This maintained data is passed from the human resource management system to the learning management system (figure 19-1). After course/ training completion corresponding information is returned to the human resource management system, e.g., result information, etc. (IMS-E, 2000).

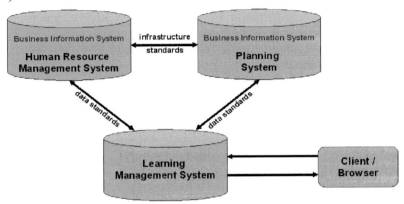

Fig. 19-1: Systems integration potentials

Österle (Österle, 1996) identifies three major reasons for information systems' distribution and integration. At first he asserts *corporate reasons*, especially the transformation from an industrial society to an information society. In principle, there are no (longer) stable structures in organisations. We currently experience numerous divisions, mergers, and alliances. Thus, information systems, which have been never designed and implemented to work together respectively to exchange data, must be integrated. Consequently, he annotates *implementation specific reasons*, like individual software solutions as well as standard software suites developed in autonomous teams. These software solutions are applying various data and function models, diverging architectures and diverse hardware and software platforms. Besides this, numerous *technical reasons* for multi-tier applications could be named, e.g., a steadily increasing number of transactions and data transfer, or security reasons.

In addition, information systems, like production facilities, are rated as long term investments. Thus, the complete replacement of critical parts is quite impractical regarding time efforts and costs. Consequently, a whole enterprise rather an entire business/ industry sector should employ only one information system without redundant data and functionality (Österle, 1996).

Following Chen and Vernadat (Chen, Vernadat, 2004) the development of standards in the area of Enterprise Integration and Engineering can be assigned to the end of the 1970s, with the adoption of the ISO 7498 – standard for Open System Integration also know as the OSI model or the ISO/OSI reference model. Considering section 3.3.1, standardisation activities with regard to enterprise integration and engineering are carried out as well at various levels. Thus, numerous standardisation organisations respectively bodies are active in this area, whereas most of the work is performed by institutional organisations such as the ISO (International Standardisation Organisation), the IEC (International Electrotechnical Committee), or the CEN (European Committee of Standardisation); the latter especially within the CEN TC310 WG1 (System architecture). Furthermore, various not-for-profit organisations, e.g., the OMG (Object Management Group) or the OAGi (Open Application Group, Inc.) also accomplish relevant pieces of standardisation work (Chen, Vernadat, 2004).

The CEN TC310 WG1 distinguishes between three levels of integration (Vernadat, 1996):

- *physical integration:* Interconnection of devices, NC machines etc. via computer networks,
- *application integration:* Dealing with interoperability of software applications and database systems in heterogeneous computing environments, and
- *business integration:* Coordination of functions that manage, control and monitor business processes.

In principle, this distinction is quite similar to current three-tier – respectively multi-tier – information systems' architectures; dividing applications' functionality into separate, logical levels: *presentation, application logic,* and *data* (Weitz, 2002).

As already mentioned earlier by Lindner (chapter 14), different levels of standards can be distinguished, e.g., "Formal Standards", or "De-facto Standards". Certainly, these various levels of standardisation can also be found within the area of business information systems respectively enterprise integration. Thereby, major activities have been conducted on *data* and *infrastructure* standards to obtain integrated information systems.

Within the field of system integration, we can identify a differentiation of the terms integration and interoperability in many cases; although often used synonymously. Whereas integration mainly focuses applications and processes, interoperability describes the ability of a system to use functionalities of another (remote) system. Interoperability-based approaches focus on the exchange of more meaningful, context-driven data between autonomous information systems (Pollock, 2001). This differentiation actually mirrors the historical development with regard to corresponding standards.

In the remainder of this chapter, I will present a survey of relevant standardisation activities in the area of business information systems integration, which can be also applied in ICT-based learning systems. In consideration to the limited space available in this paper, I only present selected standardisation activities. Due to the fact that data is the basis of every information system as well as application and consequently system integration, I look at data exchange formats and data standards provided by various standardisation bodies at first. After that, I review certain infrastructure standards providing application integration and – in addition – interoperability. Finally, a concluding summary and some recommendations for further work are given. Thus, we trace the evolution from typical business data

278 Markus Bick, Jan M. Pawlowski

exchange formats, like EDI (Electronic Data Interchange), up to complex interoperability approaches, like emerging Web services technologies.

19.2   Data standards

The exchange and sharing of specific data within or between enterprises demand compatible data formats. Data exchange formats can generally be divided into four groups: CSV, EDI, XML, and miscellaneous (Leukel, 2004). The first and the last group of exchange formats will be excluded from further discussion. Particularly the miscellaneous formats support just data exchange between proprietary application systems, e.g., Microsoft Excel (.xls). Of course we will not negate data import and export potentials applying proprietary formats, especially applying the comma separate value (CSV) format. But with regard to targeted application integration and interoperability these cannot contribute in an adequate way. For further discussion cf. (Leukel, 2004).

Despite these formats, data standards for the exchange of product data as well as production data have been developed. The ISO Technical Committee 184, technical industrial automation systems and integration, Sub-Committee industrial data (ISO TC184/ SC4) published the ISO 10303 (*STEP*) and ISO 15531 (*MANDATE*).

The *Standard for the Exchange of Product model data* (STEP) covers the computer-interpretable representation of product data, and its exchange. The objective of ISO 10303 is to provide a mechanism, that is capable of describing product data throughout the whole life cycle of a product; independent of any particular computer system. The nature of this description makes it suitable not only for a neutral file exchange, but also as a basis for implementing product databases and for archiving data (ISO TC184/ SC4, 2004). Besides, the ISO 15531, Industrial automation systems and integration- manufacturing management data exchange (MANDATE), includes the representation of data relating to the management of the production processes and the exchange and sharing of management data within or between companies (ISO TC184/ SC4, 2004). Comparing MANDATE with STEP, MANDATE deals with the data defining the processes used to manufacture the products that are described by STEP (Chen, Vernadat, 2004).

19.2.1   EDI

As computers became essential to business, organisations wanted to use electronic capabilities to reach their markets faster and more efficiently. Many organisations have invested in EDI technology to link business partners and help mange supply chains (Deitel et al., 2003). Electronic Data Interchange (EDI) is the computer-to-computer exchange of structured business information by agreed message standards from one computer application to another by electronic means and with a minimum of human intervention (Wiki, 2005b). Every supplier, manufacturer and distributor in a supply chain is linked to the EDI system through a value added network (VAN) – a closed network that includes all members of a production process (Deitel et al., 2003). EDI documents contain the same data that would normally be found in a paper document used for the same organisational function (Wiki, 2005b).

In common usage, EDI is understood to stand for specific interchange methods agreed upon by national or international standards bodies for the transfer of business transaction data. The EDI standards were designed from the beginning to be independent of lower-level technologies and can be transmitted using Internet protocols as well as private networks (Wiki, 2005b). Appropriate EDI standards arose at the end of the 1970s. An important/ significant role plays the UN/ EDIFACT Standard (EDI for Administration, Commerce and Transportation) (Leukel, 2004). UN/ EDIFACT is the only international standard; in fact, a United Nations recommendation (Wiki, 2005b). With regard to UN/ EDIFACT various EDI subsets have been derived, e.g., EAN (European Article Number) respectively EANCOM (EAN Communications) in the commerce sector (Leukel, 2004).

Although EDI systems improve efficiency, they can be expensive to operate. Installation costs can easily reach 50.000 Euro, not including additional online fees. Many suppliers and distributors are small machine shops and shipping companies that do not have the technology to link into a traditional EDI system. Furthermore, the systems that send and receive EDI messages are not standardised, so a supplier or distributor that conducts business with multiple customers or partners might require separate EDI connections for each relationship. Also, EDI systems can be difficult to maintain, because they are tightly coupled. If a developer changes one component of a tightly coupled system, the developer must re-program all components in the systems that rely on the altered component (Deitel et al., 2003).

Applying Internet technologies like Hypertext Transfer Protocol (HTTP) and Extensible Markup Language (XML), EDI traffic can now be carried over the Internet; providing an opportunity to proper costs reduction and accessible data exchange to more organisations. Furthermore, XML (section19.2.2) additionally supports the exchange of multimedia data, in contrast to EDI. Corresponding XML-based standards facilitate the reference to specific multimedia data supplemented by corresponding metadata, especially in learning systems. For further discussion preferably cf. chapter 15.

19.2.2   XML

Derived from ISO 8879 (Standard Generalised Markup Language – SGML), XML is a very flexible text format. Originally designed to meet the challenges of large-scale electronic publishing, XML is also playing an increasingly important role in the exchange of a wide variety of data on the Web and elsewhere (W3C, 2005).

Following SGML, the separation of content from its presentation is the essential characteristic of XML. Because XML documents describe only data, any application that understands XML has the ability to apply and format XML data in different ways. All applications employing XML are able to communicate, provided that they can understand each other's XML markup, or vocabulary (Deitel et al., 2003).

XML is a widely accepted standard for describing data and especially creating markup languages. Accordingly, numerous XML-based markup languages have been designed so far, focussing various domains, e.g., education, commerce, or human resource management. With regard to its degree of familiarity, even in the area of learning systems, we will briefly review selected exponents, i.e., catalogue standards (commerce) and standardisation activities on human resources data[47]. For further discussion on learning technologies standards preferably cf. the previous chapters in this part of the book or (Pawlowski, 2004). Moreover, we will describe a short example of integrating knowledge management principles and methodologies and e-learning requirements.

XML-based catalogue standards

Contrary to most data stored in information systems, catalogue data is exchanged between enterprises by definition. The transmission of electronic product catalogues using e-business standards refers to the first and most common applications of XML in e-commerce (Leukel, Schmitz, Kelkar, 2004). While the exchange of product model data is standardised by the STEP standard (section 19.2), corresponding web-based approaches show a different picture. The rise of XML has led to a variety of different, often from-the-scratch catalogue standards, e.g., BMEcat 1.2 (BME, 2005), cXML (cXML, 2005), or xCBL (xCBL, 2005).

Current standardisation activities in this domain focus the prevailing limitations regarding configuration requirements. The capabilities of corresponding XML-based standards often do not match the requirements on the representation of parameterisable or configurable products. Thus, configurable products can not be handled in a standardised way (Leukel, Schmitz, Kelkar, 2004). Also the afore mentioned catalogue standards only provide some concepts towards these issues. With its new version of BMEcat – BMEcat 2005/ BMEcat 2.0 – the German Federal Association of Procurement Managers (BME) bridges the predominant gaps in this area (BME, 2005).

XML-based human resources standards

Human resources management encompasses a diverse range of business processes, e.g., advertising open positions or recording changes in employee status appropriately in internal information systems as well as in systems of external partners and service providers. In principle, these processes are bound together by the need to synchronise human resources (HR) data across internal and external systems (Allen, Pilot, 2001).

Compared to business data exchange (section 19.2), great diversity in corre-

---

[47] With regard to the objectives of this paper as well as chapter 9, we especially decided to describe current standardisation activities in the field for human resource-related data.

sponding data formats predominated. CSV, variants of EDI transaction sets, or vendor-specific XML, are common ways of how data are formatted (Allen, Pilot, 2001).

The HR-XML Consortium is one of the leading organisations concerning human resources-related data exchange standardisation. The mission of the HR-XML Consortium is the development and promotion of a standard suite of XML specifications to enable the automation of human resources-related data exchanges (HR-XML, 2005). The consortium's working groups develop various Document Type Definitions (DTDs) and XML schemas defining messages for key HR transactions, i.e., recruiting and staffing, enrolment, payroll, cross-process objects, time reporting, staffing industry data exchange standards (SIDES), competencies, and stock (HR-XML, 2005)[48]. By developing and publishing those open standards, HR-XML provides the means for companies to transact with one other without having to implement numerous separate exchange mechanisms (Allen, Pilot, 2001).

IMS enterprise

The IMS Enterprise specification (IMS-E, 2000) is a concrete XML-instance, to support the integration between business information systems and learning management systems. In contrast to the more business-oriented XML standardisation approaches presented in this section, the IMS Enterprise specification specifically supports the exchange of information about people and groups of people engaged in learning. Thereby, the specification is focused on defining integration between systems within the same enterprise or organisation (IMS-E, 2000).

The IMS Enterprise specification, like other IMS specifications[49] and many other XML-based vertical sector specifications (section XML-based catalogue standards), is based on a domain information model. The information model is designed to achieve integration between various business process components which typically require interaction between such systems: e.g., personal profile data maintenance, group management, enrolment management, and final processing (IMS-E, 2000). Therefore, the IMS Enterprise specification comprises three core data objects: *person, group*, and *group membership* (IMS-E, 2000). These core data objects are assigned to an XML binding as underlying structure which is designed to contain any number of person, group and membership structures, to exchange data between integrated systems applying an IMS Enterprise XML instance file (IMS-E, 2000).

---

[48] Furthermore, HR-XML is cited reference of the IMS Reusable Definition of Competency or Educational Objective – Information Model.

[49] The IMS Enterprise Specification is related to other IMS specifications, e.g. IMS Learner Information Package (LIP) (IMS-LIP, 2005), etc. as well as to various standardisation approaches, e.g. HR-XML (section 0), etc. For further discussion see (IMS-E, 2000).

Matching MASK/IMS-LD

In this section, we will briefly introduce an integrated approach to design e-learning activities by matching the MASK[50] knowledge management methodology and the concepts proposed by the IMS-Learning Design (IMS-LD) modelling language.

This work was carried out by Benmahamed, Ermine, and Tchounikine cf. (2005) suggesting the construction of learning scenarios from knowledge management systems applying MASK and IMS-LD. When the knowledge, that is to be acquired, is part of the company's knowledge management system, for them it is obvious to build the learning activities scenarios from the corresponding data stored in the knowledge management system.

MASK proposes seven different models to help experts and knowledge engineers structure knowledge under systemic, ergo-cognitive, psycho-cognitive, historical and evolution aspects. Accordingly, this allows various points of view to study in depth the expert's knowledge and their systems of value at different levels of granularity. MASK facilitates its use for dividing, decentralising, learning and adapting this knowledge and describing the company's activities.

The IMS Learning Design specification supports the use of a wide range of pedagogies in online learning, providing a generic and flexible language. This language is designed to enable many different pedagogies to be expressed. The approach has the advantage that only one set of learning design and runtime tools then need to be implemented in order to support the desired wide range of pedagogies. For further discussion cf. chapter 16 or (IMS-LD, 2005).

Matching MASK and IMS-LD demands three stages which have to be followed: identifying general scenarios from MASK Domain Model, identifying the scenarios from MASK Main Activities Model, and then generating the IMS-LD description.

---

[50] Méthode d'Analyse et de Structuration des Connaissances (MASK) – approximately: Method to Analyse and Structure the state of Knowledge.

Learning activity general structure for "project management"				
Course title: Learning how to manage a project.				Timing: xxx
Global teaching objectives: developing high level competences in the project scenario definition, dashboard construction, men management, ...				
Global prerequisites: fundamental knowledge on the project devices & knowledge of the project ecology...				
Didactic principles & synopses: How does the course archieve its objectives? - alternate individual and collective learning steps, - alternate synchronous and asynchronous learning steps, ...				
Learning steps (Learning steps references and execution conditions)				
Ref.	Starting with?	Waiting the end of learning step	Learning step title	Next step
1	Yes	/	Preparation of the upstream project	2
2	No	1	Project beginning	3,4,6
Learning steps scheduling: developer choice ☒ actors choice ☒ cf. previous table ☑				

Source: Benmahamed, Ermine and Tchounikine, 2005, p. 133

Fig. 19-2: A sample learning scenario

Figure 19-2 presents an example of a general learning scenario, in this case for project management, derived from the above mentioned process. The general scenario, described as a structured document, can be transferred into an IMS-LD description, respectively a corresponding XML document. Thereby, the obtained scenarios cover the key knowledge that is proposed in the MASK models.

Besides, the suggested approach is currently performed semi-automated, because some e-learning specific issues are not part of the MASK models and must be added additionally, e.g., environment materials, etc. (Benmahamed, Ermine, and Tchounikine, 2005). Nevertheless, the presented integrating approach is a promising suggestion for the integration of learning systems and knowledge management systems. Particularly, model-based approaches to knowledge management and e-learning show major convergences which can be used to study the transfer from knowledge engineering models to e-learning scenarios.

19.3   Infrastructure standards

Chen/ Vernadat (Chen, Vernadat, 2004) define an Integrating Infrastructure as a set of software agents providing services that will allow software components, technical as well as human operators, to be managed and to be interoperated in distributed, heterogeneous, and multiple source environments. As already mentioned, standardisation activities within the area of Enterprise Integration began with the adoption of ISO 7498; the ISO/OSI reference model (section 19.1). Consequently, this standard is the basis for information systems' integration as well as interoperability[51].

Information technology infrastructure standards focus services built upon various layers covered by the OSI model. For example CEN introduced the experimental standard Enterprise Model Execution and Integration Services (ENV 13550), which focuses on services to allow execution of an enterprise model to control industrial processes. Besides, ISO 15414, named Information Technology – Open distributed Processing – Reference Model, supports the integration of computer system distribution, inter-working and portability (Chen, Vernadat, 2004).

Additionally, various not-for-profit organisations, e.g., the Open Management Group (OMG) or the Open Applications Group, Inc. (OAGi), established and maintained corresponding standards. The Open Management Architecture (OMA), respectively its corresponding middleware platform CORBA, is probably the most common exponent of infrastructure standards. Accordingly, middleware is one of the enabling technologies of Enterprise Application Integration (EAI). Newer EAI technologies involve using Web services as part of a service-oriented architecture as a means of integration (Wiki, 2005a). Companies are already implementing Web services to facilitate a wide variety of business processes, such as application integration and business-to-business transactions (Deitel et al., 2003).

19.3.1 Middleware

Following the above mentioned definition of an Integrating Infrastructure, middleware technologies provide various services. Within heterogeneous environments middleware services enable heterogeneous applications written in various languages running on various platforms to interoperate (Wiki, 2005c). The interoperation for specific procedure calls applies standardised interfaces, e.g., Application Programming Interfaces (APIs). Thus, middleware is an additional layer within a multi-tier information system's architecture (section 19.1), based on standardised interfaces and protocols, providing services for a transparent communication within distributed systems. The middleware layer is integrated between the application layer and the system software layer. Following this, current thinking is that the best (metaphoric) approach to middleware is to use a message bus to connect numerous separate systems together (Riehm, Vogler, 1996).

Naturally, there are various approaches to middleware technology, e.g., Remote Procedure Call (RPC), Microsoft's Distributed Component Object Model (DCOM), or CORBA. Due to limited space, we will focus on OMA/ CORBA in the following.

---

[51] However, the main driver of enterprise integration is the TCP/IP stack, standing up to the more theoretical ISO/OSI reference model. In contrast, TCP/IP actually only covers data transport across networks; leaving application interaction to specific services/protocols, e.g., World Wide Web (WWW) / Hypertext Transfer Protocol (HTTP), electronic mail / Simple Mail Transfer Protocol (SMTP), etc. It is named after the two most important protocols in it: the Transmission Control Protocol (TCP) and the Internet Protocol (IP). The Internet Engineering Task Force (IETF) governs the evolution of corresponding standards.

The OMG's Open Management Architecture supports application integration, which focuses exclusively on issues affecting object-oriented systems. With regard to the above mentioned layer classification, it depends on the presence of an adequate system software, e.g., operating system and communications (Chen, Vernadat, 2004). The OMA reference model contains five components cf. (figure 19-3).

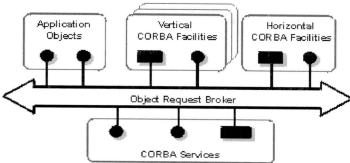

Source: OMG, 2005

Fig. 19-3: Open management architecture

- *Object Request Broker* is the integral part which – following the bus metaphor – allows applications respectively objects to communicate transparently via specific messages. The Object Request Broker is also known as CORBA: Common Object Request Broker Architecture.
- *CORBA Services* provide necessary basic functionalities, including Naming service, Object Trader service, and Persistent State service.
- *Horizontal CORBA Facilities* include higher level services shared by many or most systems, regardless of application or content area. Four major sets are identified: User Interface, Information Management, Systems Management and Task Management.
- *Vertical CORBA Facilities* represent standardised application areas. They support the domain-specific tasks associated with vertical markets.
- *Application Objects* are created by software developers. They are components specific to end-user applications representing an enterprise model.

These allow CORBA-based applications to interoperate with one another, on almost any other computer, operating system, programming language, and network

19.3.2   Web services

Web services provide a standard method to enable the integration and interoperability between information systems over a network. Actually, Microsoft coined the term web services in 2000, when the company introduced web services as a key component of its .NET initiative. Web services encompass a set of related standards respectively specifications that can enable any two computer applications to communicate and exchange data via the Internet. Because web services facilitate communication among disparate applications and platforms, standardisation is crucial. Thus, the most important advantage of web services over previous distributed-computing technologies is the employment of open standards. The World Wide Web Consortium (W3C) and other standard bodies are committed to ensure that web service protocols and specifications remain open and interoperable across vendor implementations. Even major software vendors, especially the members of the Web Services Interoperability Organisation (WS-I), are also promoting interoperability among web services implementations.

Web services are modular applications that are self-describing and that can be published, located, and invoked from anywhere on the web or within any local area network (LAN) based on open internet standards. Web services are packaged in the form of modules that can be reused, without worrying about how the service is implemented, or even what language, operating system, or component model was used to create it. When packaged as a web service or set of web services, an application provides a reusable interface that can communicate with other properly configured applications. This means that applications can share processes, rather than only content, without the need for customised, one-to-one solutions.

As already mentioned, web services use XML-based standards, predominantly[52]:

- *SOAP* provides a communication mechanism between services and applications.
- *WSDL* offers a uniform method of describing services to other programs.
- *UDDI* enables the creation of searchable Web services registries.

Figure 19-4 depicts the role of various standards in common Web services architectures.

---

[52] Rather than competing with the W3C to develop basic standards such as the above mentioned specifications the not-for-profit organisation OASIS (Organisation for the Advancement of Structured Information Standards) has made contributions to various Web service-related initiatives. Most relevant is the creation of electronic business XML (ebXML). Also ebXML is a framework through which companies could communicate and exchange data via the Internet, encompassing aspects of core Web services technologies to enable e-business (Deitel et al., 2003).

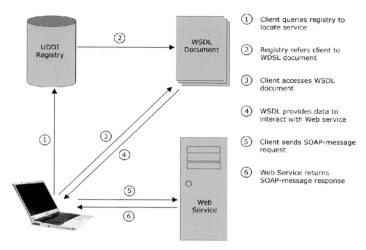

1	Client queries registry to locate service
2	Registry refers client to WDSL document
3	Client accesses WSDL document
4	WSDL provides data to interact with Web service
5	Client sends SOAP-message request
6	Web Service returns SOAP-message response

Source: Deitel et al., 2003, p. 3

Fig. 19-4: SOAP, WSDL, and UDDI in a web service interaction

SOAP

SOAP originally was an acronym for Simple Object Access Protocol, but the acronym was dropped in Version 1.2 of the SOAP specification (Wiki, 2005d). The purpose of SOAP is to enable the data transfer between systems distributed over a network. When an application communicates with a web service, SOAP messages are the most common means for two systems' data exchange. A SOAP message sent to a web service invokes a method provided by the service, meaning that the message requests a particular task executed by the service. The service then uses information contained in the SOAP message to perform its function; if necessary, the web service returns the result via another SOAP message.

SOAP is layered over an Internet protocol, such as HTTP or SMTP, and can be used to transfer data across the web and other networks. The use of HTTP allows web services to communicate across firewalls, because most firewalls are designed to accept HTTP service requests[53].

WSDL

The Web Services Description Language (WSDL) describes the public interface to web services (Wiki, 2005f). It provides a grammar for describing services as a set of endpoints that exchange messages (Cauldwell et al., 2001). These WSDL descriptions convey to other applications the methods that the service provides and

---

[53] Several protocols could be used instead of SOAP to enable Web services, e.g., the RPC pattern – up to now the most common technology that provides similar functionality (section 19.3.1).

how those methods can be accessed (Deitel et al., 2003); namely the protocol bindings and message formats required to interact with the web services listed in its directory (Wiki, 2005f).

A WSDL document defines the kinds of messages a web service can send and receive, as well as specifying the data that a calling application must provide for the web service to perform its tasks. WSDL documents also provide specific technical information that inform applications about how to connect to and communicate with web services over HTTP or other communications protocol.

Most web service development tools generate WSDL documents automatically. This means that, if a programmer develops a web service, the software used to build it, creates an appropriate WSDL document for that service.

UDDI

With the Universal Description, Discovery, and Integration (UDDI), developers and businesses are enabled to publish and locate web services on a network (Wiki, 2005e). As its name implies, the specification allows companies to describe their own services and electronic processes, discover those of other companies and integrate other's services into their systems. UDDI began as a means for users of e-business exchanges to share information about their businesses and business processes with potential partners and affiliates (Deitel et al., 2003).

UDDI defines an XML-based format in which companies can describe their electronic-capabilities and business processes; the specification also provides a standardised method of registering and locating the descriptions on a network, such as the internet. Companies can store their information either in a private UDDI registries, which are accessible only to approved business partners, or public UDDI registries, which any interested party can use (Deitel et al., 2003).

A UDDI registry's structure is conceptually similar to that of a phone book. Registries contain:

- *White pages* list contact information in textual description of themselves.
- *Yellow pages* provide classification information about companies and details on companies' electronic capabilities.
- *Green pages* describe technical data relating to services and business Processes.

Provided information regarding businesses and services is highly categorised, enabling companies to search for desired partners or services. Appling the technical information in the registries, UDDI simplifies the process of creating e-business relationships and connecting electronic systems to exchange data and services (Deitel et al., 2003).

19.4   Conclusion

The main objective of this paper was to review various standardisation activities in the area of business information systems integration, which can be also applied in learning systems. Therefore, we classified the standards by two categories: data exchange and infrastructure.

At first, selected data exchange standards (section 19.2), especially the Electronic Data Interchange (EDI) and the Extensible Markup Language (XML) were presented. With regard to interoperating information systems and learning systems, we focused on the human resources XML (HR-XML) as one promising approach to transfer corresponding data between such systems. Furthermore, we gave an example of an integrated approach to design e-learning scenarios applying a specific knowledge management methodology (MASK) and the IMS Learning Design (IMS-LD).

After that, due to the fact that standardised data exchange demands an integrated information system infrastructure, corresponding standards were introduced. Thereby, we focused on the Open Management Group's OMA/ CORBA specification which is probably one of the most common exponents according to Enterprise Application Integration (EAI), applying middleware technologies. Since newer EAI approaches apply Web services as a means of integration, corresponding specifications were presented.

However, all reviewed standards and specifications provide advantages as well as disadvantages. For instance EDI systems improve efficiency, but they are expensive to operate. In contrast, XML solutions are less expensive and also support the exchange of multimedia data; unfortunately corresponding data exchange traffic is increasingly high. Middleware platforms specifications, e.g., CORBA, had been submitted to standards organisations with the expectation that companies would choose it as a universal distributed-computing standard. However, this did not occur, because organisations had already made significant investments (Deitel et al., 2003). The most important advantage of web services over previous distributed-computing technologies is their employment of open standards. Nonetheless, SOAP and WSDL are under development by the W3C, and UDDI has not yet been submitted to a standards organisation. This means, that the protocols and specifications are likely to change near-term. Furthermore, Microsoft and IBM are currently refusing to release their intellectual property rights to certain web services standards, suggesting that vendors might attempt to charge royalties on web services technologies. Another impediment to web services adoption is the lack of standard security procedures. Thus, many businesses wait until the underlying technologies are stable before adopting web services (Deitel et al., 2003). Consequently, the detailed and necessary standards for information system integration and interoperability are not yet available.

Nevertheless, we suggest web services as a promising approach to information systems' and leaning systems' integration. We identified various projects, e.g., (CMU, 2005) or (IMS-GWS, 2005) analysing and applying web services within the area of e-learning, strengthening our suggestion. Thereby, some approaches already focus on so called semantic web services adopting technologies developed in the semantic web context, e.g., a Web Services Tool Suite (KAON, 2005).

20 Facilitating learning objects reusability in different accessibility settings

Pythagoras Karampiperis

Advanced e-Services for the Knowledge Society Research Unit, I.T.I, C.E.R.T.H., Greece

Demetrios G. Sampson

Department of Technology Education and Digital Systems, University of Piraeus, Greece

During the last years, accessibility has been recognised as a key design consideration for web-based educational systems. However, in real life, each e-learning services provider uses its own training approach (either driven by theory or driven by the years of practical experience) to design e-learning programmes and uses its own e-learning environment (typically, commercial or open-source Learning Management Systems) to deliver e-learning courses. As a result, the end users (both learners and their tutors) of this particular e-learning services provider cannot easily access other resources available on the web and, moreover, they are entirely dependent from the specific e-learning environment in use. This is a recognised drawback to the wide spread take-up of e-learning in several contexts of use, including lifelong learning and vocational training. It becomes an even more significant problem for the application of e-training in Learners with Special Abilities. The reason for this is that quality e-learning resources and courses are particularly expensive to develop. Therefore, it is important to be able to built generic e-learning systems that would allow the reuse of existing learning resources in different accessibility settings. Towards this end, in this book chapter we present a methodology for defining an accessibility application profile that captures the accessibility properties of learning objects in a commonly identified format. This information is critical in order to be able to match learning content with learner accessibility preferences, as well as, to allow the use of generic hypermedia and multimedia based educational content which is not originally developed for a particular group.

20.1   Introduction[54]

During the last years, accessibility has been recognised as a key design consideration for web-based educational systems (Mirabella et. al, 2004) (Schmetzke, 2001). As a result, a number of systems have been proposed aiming to meet the educational needs of people with special abilities. Such systems include among others HOPE (García, 2002), VisiCAST (Bangham, 2000) and SMILE (Kronreif et. al, 2000). However, these web based educational environments suffer by the fact that most available tools and content are only developed to meet the "local" needs of specific user groups with limited potential for reuse and take-up by other e-learning organisations.

In real life, each e-learning services provider uses its own training approach (either driven by theory or driven by the years of practical experience) to design e-learning Programmes and uses its own e-learning Environment (typically, commercial or open-source Learning Management Systems) to deliver e-learning courses. As a result, the end users (both learners and their tutors) of this particular e-learning services provider cannot easily access other resources available on the web and, moreover, they are entirely dependent from the specific e-learning Environment in use. This is a recognised drawback to the wide spread take-up of e-learning in several contexts of use, including lifelong learning and vocational training. It becomes an even more significant problem for the application of e-training in learners with special abilities. The reason for this is that quality e-learning resources and courses are particularly expensive to develop (see also Part A: European quality development: Methods and approaches). Therefore, it is important to be able to built generic e-learning systems that would allow the reuse of existing learning resources in different accessibility settings (Karampiperis, Sampson, 2005 a, b).

Accessibility is a central issue when considering the quality of web-based education. Since the Lisbon European Council in March 2000, achieving an Information Society for All, has become a political priority for the European Union (European Commission, 2000). A key objective of the eEurope 2002 Action Plan was to achieve the participation for all in the knowledge-based economy (European Commission, 2002b). This plan stresses the need for a renewed approach focusing upon the identification and removal of the various barriers preventing disabled people from obtaining equal opportunities and achieving full participation in all aspects of social-economical life. This has been reinforced with the eEurope 2005 Action Plan (European Commission, 2005a). To this end, on March 2002, the European Union adopted the W3C Web Accessibility Initiative Guidelines (W3C WCAG, 1999) on accessibility of public web sites and their content (European Commission, 2003b). Thus, the need for providing European Learners with web-

---

[54] Acknowledgements: The work presented in this paper is partially supported by European Community under the FP6 Information Society Technologies (IST) programme ICLASS contract IST-507922, the Leonardo da Vinci programme eAccess contract EL/2003/B/F/148233 and the the CEN/ISSS Learning Technologies Workshop, Project Team "Accessibility properties for Learning Resources", contract CEN/EXPERT/2004/09.

based learning content that matches their accessibility needs and preferences has been identified as an important issue in web-based education.

Although, the W3C Web Content Accessibility Guidelines (W3C WCAG, 1999) provide design techniques and requirements that should be followed in order to design accessible web-based content, the identification of learning content accessibility properties and the definition of a metadata model for describing accessibility information for learning resources remains an open issue. Several initiatives already exist trying to deal with this issue, including the CEN/ ISSS Learning Technologies Workshop Accessibility Working Group (CEN/ ISSS WLT), the Dublin Core Metadata Initiative Accessibility Working Group (DCMI AWG) and the IMS Accessibility Working Group (IMS AWG).

Towards this end, in this book chapter we present a methodology for defining an accessibility application profile that captures the accessibility properties of learning objects in a commonly identified format. This information is critical in order to be able to match learning content with learner accessibility preferences, as well as, to allow the use of generic hypermedia and multimedia based educational content which is not originally developed for a particular group. Furthermore, we present a full application profile of the IEEE LOM standard based on the accessibility metadata requirements defined in IMS Accessibility for LIP specification.

20.2   Methodology for defining an accessibility application profile

As discussed in section A, the definition of accessibility properties of learning resources is an important issue towards the design of web-based educational systems that bare the potential to serve different accessibility settings. Those properties, once properly defined, can be used for matching web-based educational content to learners' accessibility preferences. The development of a set of commonly agreed accessibility metadata is expected to facilitate the description of learning resources using the same metadata sets and, therefore, support sharing of accessible resources (Nevile, 2002), (Hofman, 2002). This is particularly important in web-based education of learners with special needs, since, on one hand, the development of quality educational courses is already expensive, and, on the other hand, these groups of learners do not constitute a monetarily interesting target group for commercial content providers.

Although a generally accepted standard for the description of learning objects already exists, namely, the IEEE Learning Object Metadata (LOM) standard (IEEE, 2002), this metadata model lacks information on accessibility properties of learning objects. As a result, in order to describe the accessibility characteristics of learning objects, the definition of accessibility metadata is needed, leading to an accessibility application profile (see info box on Application Profiles for Learning Objects). In our previous work (Karampiperis and Sampson, 2004 a, b), we have presented the main principles for defining such an accessibility application profile, as well as, initial results of this process. In this book chapter, we present a full proposal of an accessibility application profile for learning objects based on the IEEE LOM standard.

Application profiles for learning objects: As more and more applications are developed exploiting educational metadata, it became obvious that it would be difficult for a single metadata model to accommodate the functional requirements of all applications. This becomes more evident, in the case of applications that need to combine metadata specifications from different models, such as simple resource discovery (Dublin Core), digital rights management (INDECS), multimedia content (MPEG-7), educational content (IEEE LOM) and/or museum content (CIDOC CRM), to satisfy their specific requirements. As a result, application profiles aim to facilitate the application-oriented implementation of metadata specifications by allowing the designers to 'mix and match' metadata models as appropriate. Thus, an application profile is an assemblage of metadata elements selected from one or more metadata models. The purpose of an application profile is to adapt or combine existing metadata models into a new one which is tailored to the functional requirements of a particular application, while retaining interoperability with the original base metadata models. Some examples of application profiles already published are the Le@rning Federation Application Profile (www.thelearningfederation.edu.au), the Cancore Application Profile (www.cancore.ca), the Celebrate Application Profile (www.eun.org/eun.org2/eun/en/index_celebrate.cfm), the European Treasury Browser (ETB) Metadata Application Profile (www.en.eun.org/etb), the SCORM Metadata Application Profile (www.adlnet.org), the UKLOMCore (www.cetis.ac.uk/profiles/uklomcore), the RDN/LTSN LOM application profile (www.rdn.ac.uk), the SingCore Application Profile (www.itsc.org.sg) and the Curriculum Online Application Profile (www.curriculumonline.gov.uk)[55].

Based on the three main accessibility dimensions in web-based education, (namely, the *Learner,* the *Content* and the *System* dimension), we can identify the key drivers that influence the definition of an Accessibility Application Profile for Learning Resources. Figure 20-1 presents a schematic representation of this process by identifying the main anticipated Guidelines (namely, Learner Specific Guidelines, Content Specific Guidelines and Application Specific Guidelines) and their corresponding available specifications (namely, the IMS Accessibility for Learner Information Package specification, the W3C Web Content Accessibility Guidelines and the IMS Guidelines for Developing Accessible Learning Applications).

---

[55] Duval E., Hodgins W., Stuart S., Stuart L. W. *Metadata Principles and Practicalities.* D-Lib Magazine, vol. 8(4), 2002 [online]. Available from Internet:
http://www.dlib.org/dlib/april02/weibel/04weibel.html [cited 24.09.2005].
    Duval E., Hodgins W. *A LOM research agenda.* In Proc of the 12th International World Wide Web Conference (WWW2003), Budapest, Hungary, 2003, pp. 659-673.

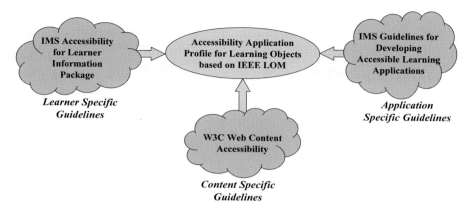

Fig. 20-1: Guidelines and Specifications that influence the definition of an Accessibility Application Profile for Learning Resources

Then, for the definition of an Accessibility Application Profile, we propose the following methodology. First, all three Guidelines are scanned and the main checkpoints which are important for the application in hand are identified. Then, for each checkpoint the following steps are repeated:

- *Step1: Identify the related IEEE LOM Element.* During this step an analysis of the specific checkpoint is conducted in order to identify the most related with this checkpoint IEEE LOM element. The identification of the related element is based on the match between the requirements introduced by the particular checkpoint in hand and the functional description of the element.
- *Step2: Extend the Value Space of the IEEE LOM Element.* During this step, possible extensions required in the value space or the vocabulary of the related IEEE LOM element are identified, so as to satisfy requirements of the particular checkpoint in hand. The appropriate extensions are then developed.
- *Step3: Add new sub-elements to the related LOM element.* During this step new elements are added (if necessary) to the information model with special attention in avoiding overlaps with other already existing elements.

Alternatively, instead of directly extending the metadata model of the IEEE LOM standard in order to meet the functional requirements of an application in hand, a separate accessibility category could be defined. This approach has been proposed by the Accessibility properties for Learning Resources Working Team of the CEN/ ISSS Learning Technologies Workshop (CEN/ ISSS WLT). Although we have no evidence on which of the two approaches is more preferable, it is obvious that defining a separate accessibility category bares the potential to ensure interoperability with existing systems, whereas, the proposed approach is expected to overcome possible overlaps with other existing elements of the IEEE LOM information model.

Other similar works have also been reported in the literature (Nevile et. al., 2005), aiming to define a metadata model that describes the modalities used in educational resources. This approach focuses more on the separation of the constituent parts of a learning object, in order to enable disaggregation and reaggregation of a learning object to meet the individual learner needs, rather than describing the accessibility properties of learning resources to enable direct match with learners' accessibility preferences. These efforts have lead to the definition of the IMS Access For All (IMS AccMD, 2004) specification. This specification focuses on describing modality information used in a learning object, as well as, information on equivalent alternatives for that resource.

20.3   An accessibility application profile based on IEEE LOM

In this section, we examine the design of an accessibility application profile based on learner specific guidelines and, more precisely, the IMS Accessibility for LIP Information Model specification (IMS AccLIP, 2003a) (see info box on the IMS Learner Information Package and its accessibility related extensions). More specifically, we present an Accessibility Application Profile based on the IEEE LOM standard and the IMS Accessibility for LIP recommendations, that has been created following the methodology presented in previous section.

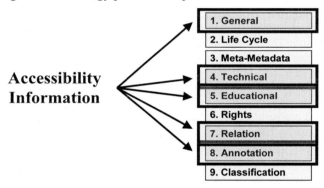

Fig. 20-2: IEEE LOM Accessibility related Metadata Categories

The IMS Accessibility for LIP Information Model provides a list of checkpoints identified as metadata requirements for enabling the match between learner's accessibility preferences with educational content. For each checkpoint we have identified the related IEEE elements and have defined the possible extensions required to satisfy the requirements of the checkpoint on hand. Figure 20-2 presents a generalised view of the IEEE LOM categories that we identified to be related with accessibility properties of learning resources during the design of the accessibility application profile.

Next, the introduced elements of the Accessibility Application Profile are presented for each related IEEE LOM category identified in figure 20-2. More specifically:

IMS learner information package and accessibility related extensions: The IMS Learner Information Package (IMS LIP, 2003a) specification provides a way of packaging learner information (for example, individual learner information such as a learner submitting his/ her resume to an e-learning system or, organisational exchange information such as the certification of a learner's achievements to a third-party institution). The IMS LIP specification is an Open Model, that is, nearly all metadata elements are optional and they can be defined depending on the requirements of the application in use.

Regarding accessibility, the IMS LIP information model includes the "accessibility" element aiming to describe learner accessibility *information* regarding learner's language capabilities, disabilities, eligibilities, as well as, learner's accessibility *preferences*, including learning preferences (e.g. issues of learning style), physical preferences (e.g. a preference for large print) and technological preferences (e.g. a preference for a particular computer platform). An extension to the IMS LIP information model is the IMS Accessibility for LIP Information Model (IMS AccLIP, 2003a) specification, published on July 2003. This specification defines accessibility preferences that go beyond supporting learners with special needs, to include other types of accessibility requirements such as mobile computing, noisy environments, etc. The IMS AccLIP specifications refine the metadata model used in IMS LIP for describing accessibility preferences through the definition of display, control and content preferences (IMS 2001, 2003d).

20.3.1   Extension of the IEEE LOM general category

The IEEE LOM General/ Language element describes the human languages used within a learning object to communicate to the intended user. Since sign languages can also be a case in the communication with the intended user, an extension of this element is needed. In this case, only an extension of the value space is required to include also sign languages as shown in table 20-1.

Table 20-1: Extension of IEEE LOM general/ language element

IEEE LOM Element	Original Value Space	Proposed Value Space
1.3 Language	LanguageID =Langcode ("-"Subcode) * with Langcode a language code as defined by the code set ISO 639 or ISO 639-2, and Subcode a country code from the code set ISO 3166-1:1997.	SignLanguageID=SignLangcode - Langcode("-" Subcode) with SignLangcode a single 3-letter code, sgn, Langcode, a language code as defined by the code set ISO 639:or ISO 639-2, and Subcode, a 2 letter country code from the ISO 3166

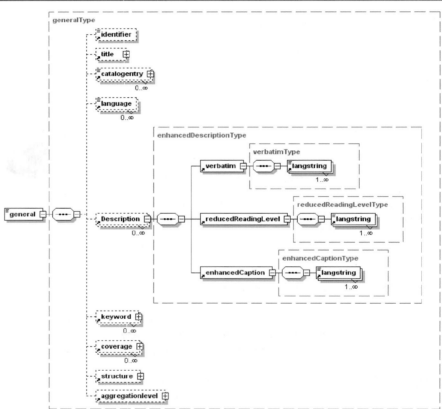

Fig. 20-3: Extending the IEEE LOM general/ description element

The IEEE LOM General/ Description element provides a textual description of the content of a specific learning object. The language and the terms that are to be used in this element are intended for those who make decisions on whether a specific learning object is appropriate and relevant for those that will use it.

Table 20-2: IMS AccLIP metadata requirements for textual description

AccLIP Elements	Definition	Meta-Data Required
1.3.1 captionType	What form of text caption is preferred.	(container)
1.3.1.2 verbatim	Enable verbatim captions which may include descriptions of sound effects.	Meta-data on caption that includes pointer to primary video, synchronisation file if necessary and a label verbatim.
1.3.1.3 reducedReadingLevel	Reduce the reading level	Meta-data on caption that includes pointer to primary video, synchronisation file if necessary and a label of reduced reading level.
1.3.1.5 enhancedCaption	Enhance the captions to include more information. This includes the use of video layers to provide information about the paralinguistic content of speech, music, and other non-speech sounds.	Meta-data on caption that includes pointer to primary video, synchronisation file if necessary and a label of enhanced

Thus, analytic textual descriptions, even in the case of multimedia-based learning objects, are needed in order to enable access through screen readers or other text-to-speech engines. Table 20-2 presents the IMS AccLIP metadata requirements concerning the content description of a learning object.

As shown in figure 20-3, the required extension includes the addition of three new sub-elements, namely, the "verbatim", the "reducedReadingLevel" and the "enhancedCaption" elements, which are defined as follows:

- *Verbatim:* A single instance element containing verbatim descriptions which may include descriptions of sound effects. This element is mutually exclusive with the reducedReadingLevel element. The data type of this element is language string with smallest permitted maximum equal to 1000 characters.
- *reducedReadingLevel:* A single instance element containing textual descriptions that refer to reduced reading level (e.g. to learners that require low reading speed of a text-to-speech engine). This element is mutually exclusive with the Verbatim element. The data type of this element is language string with smallest permitted maximum equal to 1000 characters.
- *enhancedCaption:* A single instance element containing textual descriptions that aim to enhance the existing captions by providing more information. The data type of this element is language string with smallest permitted maximum equal to 1000 characters.

20.3.2   Extension of the IEEE LOM technical category

The IEEE LOM Technical category describes the technology (hardware, network, software) that is required for using a learning object. It also provides characteristics, such as the size or the location of a learning object. In the case of multimedia-based learning objects (image, video etc.) specific technical properties concerning the use of colours in learning objects should be specified, otherwise people with colour blindness could not access the learning objects. Table 20-3 presents the IMS AccLIP metadata requirements concerning the colour avoidance schema for a learning object.

Table 20-3: IMS AccLIP metadata requirements for colour avoidance

AccLIP Elements	Definition	Meta-Data Required
1.1.4 colourAvoidance	Preferences regarding the use of colour in display of information	(container)
1.1.4.1 avoidRed	Avoid the use of red to display Information	Meta-data on content specifying that red is avoided or is used.
1.1.4.2 avoidRedGreen	Avoid the use of red and green to display information	Meta-data on content specifying that red and green in combination are avoided or are used.
1.1.4.3 avoidBlueYellow	Avoid the use of blue and yellow to display information.	Meta-data on content specifying that blue and yellow in combination are avoided or are used.
1.1.4.4 avoidGreenYellow	Avoid the use of green and yellow to display information	Meta-data on content specifying that green and yellow in combination are avoided or are used.
1.1.4.5 avoidOrange	Avoid the use of orange to display information	Meta-data on content specifying that orange is avoided or is used.
1.1.4.6 avoidRedBlack	Avoid the use of red and black to display information	Meta-data on content specifying that red and black in combination are avoided or are used.
1.1.4.7 avoidPurpleGray	Avoid the use of purple and gray to display information	Meta-data on content specifying that purple and gray in combination are avoided or are used.
1.1.4.8 useMaximumContrast Monochrome	Use monochromatic displays at maximum contrast.	Meta-data on content specifying maximum contrast monochrome

In this case, the extension required is the addition of an extra container element, namely, the "VisualProperties" element, that contains information about the visual properties of a learning object. More precisely this element contains information about the colour avoidance schema, as well as, the maximum contrast and the colour brightness used within a multimedia based learning object. This element has meaning only if element "4.1 Technical.Format" has the value of "image/xxx" or "video/xxx". The "VisualProperties" element consists of three sub-elements, namely, the "ColourAvoidance", the "ColourDifference" and the "ColourBrightness", as shown in figure 20-4, which are defined as follows:

- *ColourAvoidance:* A single instance element containing preferences regarding the use of colour in display of information. This element contains 7 sub-elements, each one corresponding to a different colour combination schema, namely, the "avoidRed", the "avoidRedGreen", the "avoidBlueYellow", the "avoidGreenYellow", the "avoidOrange", the "avoidRedBlack" and the "avoidPurpleGray" elements. All these sub-elemets are single instance elements with a "yes", "no" value space which indicates if the corresponding colour combinations are avoided or used for the display of information in the learning object.

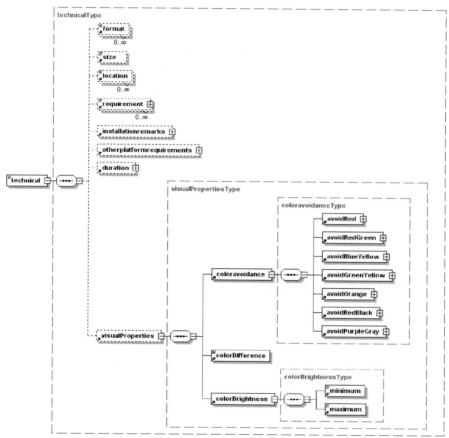

Fig. 20-4: Extending the IEEE LOM Technical category

- *ColourDifference:* A single instance element containing information about the maximum contrast used within a learning object. This element has a numbered value space between 0 and 100. The value of the ColourDifference element is defined using the following formula from W3C Techniques For Accessibility Evaluation And Repair Tools (W3C, 2000):

$$Color\ Difference = \frac{1}{7.65}\left[\left[\max(R)-\min(R)\right]+\left[\max(G)-\min(G)\right]+\left[\max(B)-\min(B)\right]\right]$$

where R, G, B are the corresponding values of the Red, Green and the Blue colour respectively. *ColourBrightness:* A single instance element containing information about the minimum and maximum colour brightness of the colours used in a learning object. This element consists of two single instance subelements, namely, the "minimum" and "maximum" sub-elements, which contain the minimum and maximum colour brightness respectively. These subelements have numbered value spaces taking values between 0 and 100. The value of the ColourBrightness/Minimum and ColourBrightness/Maximum elements is defined using the following formula from W3C Techniques For Accessibility Evaluation And Repair Tools:

$$Color\ Brightness = \frac{1}{2550}\left[(299 \times R)+(587 \times G)+(114 \times B)\right]$$

where R, G, B are the corresponding values of the Red, Green and the Blue colour respectively.

20.3.3   Extension of the IEEE LOM educational category

The IEEE LOM Educational category describes the educational or pedagogical characteristics of a learning object. These characteristics include the interactivity type, the semantic density and the level of difficulty of a learning object, the time that a typical user takes to work with it, etc. In the IEEE LOM information model there exist an element describing the technical requirements for a learning object (e.g. the operating system, required plug-ins etc), that is, the technical/ requirements element. However, from the educational aspect in many cases in order for a learner to concentrate on the focus of the learning activity, the existence of specific tools is required. Examples of such tools include a dictionary, a calculator etc. To this end, extension to this category is required in order to include links with learner scaffold tools. Table 20-4 presents the IMS AccLIP metadata requirements concerning the support of learner scaffold tools.

Table 20-4: IMS AccLIP metadata requirements for learner scaffold tools

AccLIP Elements	Definition	Meta-Data Required
1.4 learnerScaffold	Analogous to a book bag, a scaffold is a place to carry common tools.	Meta-data on learner scaffold specifying: dictionary, calculator noteTaking, peerInteraction, abacus thesaurus, spellchecker, homophoneChecker, mindMappingSoftware outlineTool.

As shown in figure 20-5, the required extension includes the addition of one new element, namely, the "learnerScaffold" element, defined as follows:

- *LearnerScaffold:* A multiple occurrence element with smallest permitted maximum equal to 10 items, containing information on the required peripheral tools to allow the learner concentrate on the focus of the learning activity. The value space of the LearnerScaffold element is a vocabulary containing the following values: "Dictionary", "Calculator", "noteTaking", "Peer Interaction Abacus", "Thesaurus", "Spell Checker", "Homophone Checker", "Mind Mapping Software" and "Outline Tool". Of course, depending on the application, this value space can be expanded to include also other learner scaffold tools.

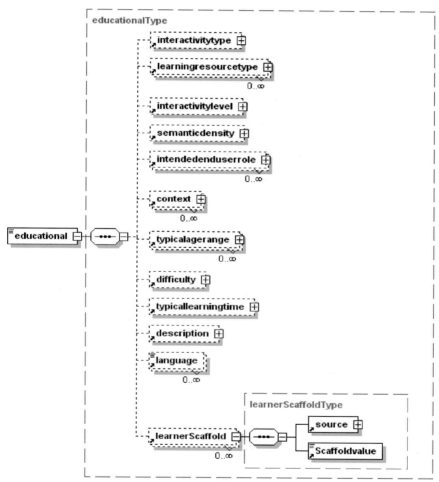

Fig. 20-5: Extending the IEEE LOM educational category

20.3.4   Extension of the IEEE LOM relation category

The IEEE LOM Relation category defines the relationships between learning objects. In order to locate and retrieve an alternative learning object, relationships with the primary learning object should be defined. This process requires the extension of the IEEE LOM Relation category to include the link to and from visual, text or auditory alternatives of the primary learning object. In this case, only an extension of the value space is required to include also alternative modality relations as shown in table 20-5.

Table 20-5: Extension of IEEE LOM relation/ kind element

IEEE LOM Element	Original Value Space	Proposed Extensions
7.1 Relation/ Kind	ispartof/ haspart, isversionof/ hasversion, isformatof/ hasformat, references/ isreferencedby, isbasedon/ isbasisfor, requires/ isrequiredby	isVisualAlternativ / hasVisualAlternative, isTextAlternative/ hasTextAlternative, isAuditoryAlternative/ hasAuditoryAlternative

20.3.5   Extension of the IEEE LOM annotation category

A critical factor in using a learning object in an accessible way is to provide information on the real experience of its application use, good practices or even guidelines for best use. To facilitate this, the extension of an existing element of the IEEE LOM information model is required, namely, the "Annotation/ Description" element. This element provides comments on the educational use of the learning object and information on when and by whom the comments were created. The extension includes the addition of a new single instance sub-element, namely, the "category" sub-element, which categorises the provided annotation comments into three categories: the "General Comment", the "Educational Usage Comment" and the "Accessibility Comment", as presented in figure 20-6.

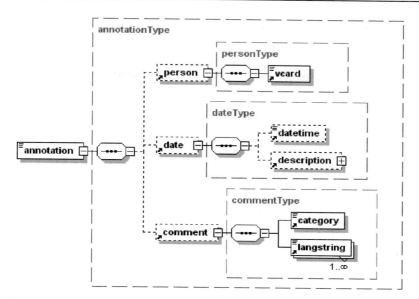

Fig. 20-6: Extending the IEEE LOM annotation category

20.4   Case study: The eAccess project

The eAccess project (www.ask.iti.gr/e-Access) intends to promote access to the European Vocational Training by facilitating searching, sharing and reuse of accessible e-Training Resources and/ or accessible e-Training Courses. To this end, a web-based repository containing accessible learning objects for learner communities with special needs (in particular, communities of visually impaired people and motor disabled people) has been built. The Accessibility Application Profile of the IEEE LOM standard presented in this book chapter, has been used for describing the accessibility properties of the learning resources contained in the eAccess repository. To enable access to the contents of the eAccess repository, a web portal has been created, namely the eAccess Portal, which offers an easy-to-use searching facility for accessible learning objects, as shown in figure 20-7.

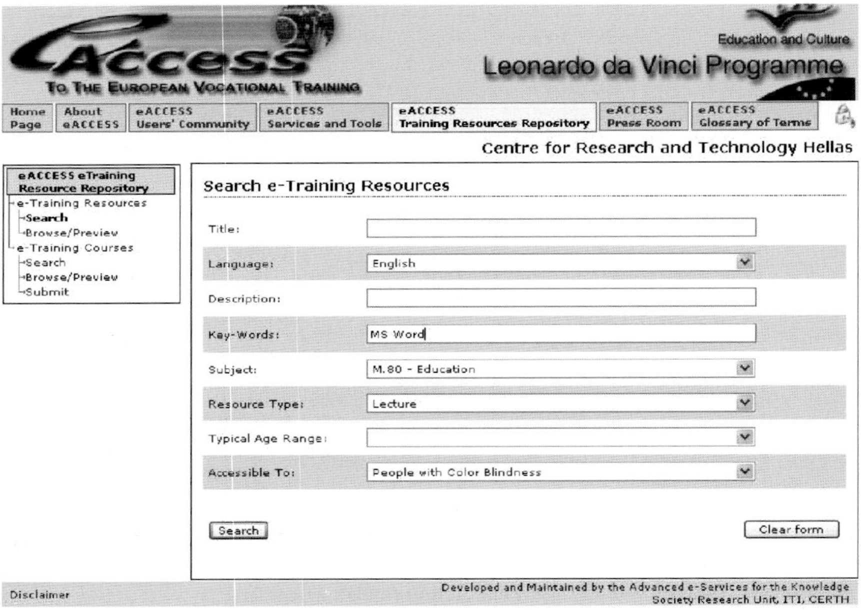

Fig. 20-7: The eAccess resource searching facility

When users of the eAccess searching facility request appropriate accessible learning resources for a particular target group, their request (that is, the search criteria) is transformed to a record of metadata requirements that is compared with the metadata descriptions of the learning resources contained in the repository. This comparison filters the contents of the web-based repository and retrieves the desired set of accessible learning objects. For example, when searching for accessible learning resources suitable for people with colour blindness, this means that the corresponding metadata requirement is the avoidance of all problematic colour combinations. For convenience of the search results, the user, except from obtaining the resulting learning objects, has the ability to inspect the entire metadata record of the retrieved learning objects (see figure 20-8).

Furthermore, the eAccess Portal supports not only those users that need to find and use accessible learning objects, but also those who create them and intent to describe them with accessibility metadata. To this end, a specialised tool has been developed, namely, the Accessibility Metadata Authoring and Repository Management Tool (ASK-AccLOM-RM), for the authoring and management of accessibility metadata in Learning Objects.

Educational	
Interactivity Type	mixed
Learning Resource Type	Narrative Text
Intended End User Role	Learner
Educational Context	Vocational Training
Typical Age Range	Initial Vocational Training
Difficulty	medium
Typical Learning Time	0.25 didactic hour
Description	

Classification	
Source	NACE
Subject	M.80 - Education

Accessibility		
Description	Has Visual	no
	Has Auditory	no
	Has Text	yes
	Has Tactile	no
	Uses Stylesheets	no
Color Avoidance	Avoid Red	yes
	Avoid Red-Green	yes
	Avoid Blue-Yellow	yes
	Avoid Green-Yellow	yes
	Avoid Orange	yes
	Avoid Red-Black	yes
	Avoid Purple-Gray	yes
Visual Properties	Maximum Contrast	100
	Minimum Brightness	90
	Maximum Brightness	100

Fig. 20-8: Partial view of a metadata record

This tool provides an easy-to-use environment capable of authoring, storing and managing the metadata produced for describing the accessibility properties of learning resources. The ASK-AccLOM-RM (figure 20-9) offers a number of features to support the above processes, including the creation of learning object metadata repository, the authoring of accessibility metadata, importing existing metadata descriptions conforming with the IEEE LOM standard, overview of learning object metadata repository contents, searching the learning object metadata repository and exporting the metadata repository contents in XML format.

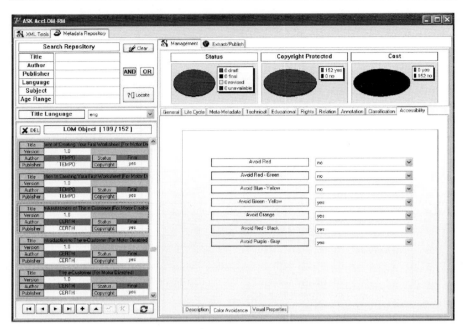

Fig. 20-9: The ASK-AccLOM-RM tool

20.5   Conclusions

In this paper we established the need to define an accessibility application profile for learning resources and presented a methodology for defining such an application profile based on the three main accessibility dimensions. We presented the first step towards the definition of such an application profile. The proposed Accessibility Application Profile of the IEEE LOM has been developed in the context of CEN/ ISSS Learning Technologies Workshop as an initial proposal produced by our research group for consideration in the project team entitled "Accessibility properties for Learning Resources". Future work includes the creation of an integrated accessibility application profile based on W3C and IMS ACCLIP guidelines utilising mappings of W3C WCAG with IEEE LOM, as well as, the identification of other content specific accessibility guidelines and application specific accessibility guidelines as influence factors to the accessibility application profile.

21 Out of the past and into the future: Standards for technology enhanced learning

Wayne Hodgins

www.learnativity.org, United States

Even before the term „e-learning" came into existence in about 1999, the need for common standards has been recognised as a requirement for the realisation of the promise of technology enabled learning(TEL) and the vision dramatically improved learning. Intriguingly most of the current work on standards for learning began in 1997 including such groups as CEN/ ISSS Workshop for Learning Technology, IEEE Learning Technology Standards Committee (LTSC), Advanced Distributed Learning initiative (ADL), SCORM, and IMS Global. Today (2005) after 7+ years; most of the initial objectives have been met, the specifications and standards have been released, supporting tools and technology are readily available, thousands of organisations around the world are hard at work implementing these daily, and millions of people worldwide, cutting across all industries and the domains of academia, government, defence and business are beginning to reap the benefits. We are therefore now entering a new era for standards for TEL; one of implementation and maintenance of the results of the first era, discovery of new requirements for the next and the development of new tools, specs, standards and the groups to create all these. This chapter will briefly review the past and present situation and then provide a look ahead at the next new era and the future of standards for technology enabled learning.

21.1 Introduction

No examination, planning and focus on quality would be complete without an examination of the role of standards. History has shown rather conclusively that the takeoff point for any new era or innovation includes the adoption of common standards. Examples would include railway track gauge, telephone dial tones, video tape formats, email protocols, and the Internet and World Wide Web themselves. Without such common adoption of standards, the development and adoption of technology, products, services and whole new practices simply stalls. Consider the historic battle between VHS and Beta that withheld the explosion of the video industry. Or, look to current examples such as the lack of common standards for DVD recorders or Instant Messaging. These stories often start out with proprietary specifications from an individual company or source. Unfortunately, this often means that emerging technologies are built using proprietary specifications and will not work well with other similar or competing products. Since these technologies often do not meet the needs of end-users, the market typically drives the various leaders from business, academia, and government to work together to develop common "standards." This allows a variety of products to co-exist. This convergence of technologies is very important for the consumers of these technologies. Products that adhere to standards will provide consumers with wider product choices, more competition and a better chance that the products in which they invest will avoid quick obsolescence.

In the world of learning, common standards for such things as learning object metadata, content packaging, sequencing, discovery, learner profiles, and run-time interaction are requisite for the success of the knowledge economy and the future of learning. Breaking from the tradition of conflict as noted in some of the examples above, in the case of learning technology standards there has been a delightful lack of competing standards. Even with this significant advantage, it has taken many years of extremely hard and thankless voluntary work by many individuals and groups from the world learning community such as[56] AICC, ARIADNE, Dublin Core, IMS and countless other acronyms. They have designed and developed these specifications and are now being ratified, generalised, and globalised through standards bodies such as IEEE and ISO to create fully accredited standards.

As a result, and with a nod of thanks and appreciation to these efforts, robust accredited standards and working reference models such as the Advanced Distributed Learning (ADL) SCORM or Shareable Content Object Reference Model are now available and are being implemented everyday around the globe in real world situations with scalability. The attention therefore now shifts to the many issues and questions of how we will integrate these standards into our current projects and the need to start further planning for the future[57].

It would appear to be particularly appropriate and apropos that we take advantage of this point in the evolution of TEL and their standards to look at the long and short term future. Whether you feel it is a long time or short, we have been working on developing standards for TEL for about 8 years as intriguingly most of the current standards we have today and their respective groups all began in about 1997.

In this sense, the current state of learning technologies is not unlike the state of the Web around 1994 when the basic web standards (HTML, HTTP, and URL) were stable and focus shifted to the development of browsers and authoring tools. Even though additional development of XML, web services and other technolo-

---

[56] See Reference section at end of this article for URL links to each of these organisations.

[57] For a MUCH more in depth coverage of standards in learning, please see the recent Industry Report produced by The MASIE Centre and available at www.masie.com/standards.

gies is not without merit, the breakthrough of the Web is more directly caused by the development of tools and the experimentation which lead to such things as the broad use of Email, instant messaging, Amazon, Google and eBay. We now need to devote time and energy to the development of equivalents for learning.

All this makes it both ideal and necessary to start planning for the future of standards and keep the road ahead well planned and paved for the increasing progress forward. For context and clarity we will take a quick look at the past and at the present so we know where we are today and how we arrived. However, the focus of this paper will be on the future of standards. We will be looking ahead for the purposes of longer range planning, enabling and augmenting smart choices and decisions we need to make TODAY and in the near term future in order to best steer the course for the future of standards for TEL.

21.2   Overall assumptions and perspectives

The overall perspective[58] taken in this paper is that we are currently in a state of great transition. The initial development of the specifications and standards, and the creation of the organisations to develop these are winding down. We have a rich collection of enablers in the form of completed and stable standards and technology for learning. Now begins the necessary and challenging mass adoption of the resultant standards and reference models. There is thus a need to put more focus on how to successfully implement what we have now, how to maximise the potential benefits, and to assess what is needed next to best achieve the goals of improved learning and performance.

Success of standards = adoption

The direct success of standards is best defined by the degree to which they are voluntarily adopted and how transparent they become to those who are actually using them. Using current and past success of standards, we can see how effective transparency has been and how it evolves over time as the standards take hold at an exponential rate of adoption. Recent examples include web standards like HTML, HTTP, TCP/ IP that have enabled the Internet and World Wide Web's dramatic rise and success, or telephone standards that give us the ubiquity of global telecommunications.

---

[58] With the limits of the space available in this paper, this is NOT intended to be a complete or comprehensive coverage of all areas within TEL that would benefit from or require standards. Rather, this is intended to provide a good cross section of some of the more prominent areas for standards development in the future. If you have further questions or input, please contact the author via Email at wayne.hodgins@autodesk.com.

STANDARDS have an integral role as one of the key enablers for the realisation of the vision of personalisation of learning at a planetary scale. Therefore the ultimate success of standards will be determined by how well they assist in meeting these grand challenges and advance us towards this grand vision for the future of learning.

21.3   Out of the past

Depending on your point of view it has either been a very short or very long time since work began on the development of standards for TEL. In either case it is interesting to note that in spite of an extremely diverse range of original sources and purposes, most of the work on standards and the formation of the respective standards bodies and organisations doing this work, all began about the same time; 1997.

Just to put this into perspective, in 1997 the term "e-learning" did not yet exist (~1999) and all of the following began in 1997:

- Advanced Distributed Learning (ADL) developers of SCORM
- IEEE Learning Technology Standards Committee (LTSC) forms first Study and Working Groups
- Creation of IMS
- Creation of the European CEN/ ISSS Workshop for Learning Technology

21.4   Up to the present

Today, standards are in transition as they move from a state of mass confusion to one of mass adoption and implementations. Most would likely agree that the world of standards has been rife with confusion, uncertainty and doubt. One has only to look at the number of acronyms for the standards and standard bodies involved to see this situation[59]. AICC, IMS, IEEE, LTSC, ISO, CEN/ ISSS, AICC, SCORM, ADL, LOM, CMI, DREL, and too many more. None of this should be that surprising as everything from TEL itself, the subsequent specifications and standards, and most of the individuals involved were completely new. It is easy to forget that the standards and groups we now take for granted, did not yet exist prior to 1997. However, it would appear that we have emerged from this fog and that there is much greater clarity and understanding.

In any case, there are certainly many indications of massive rates and degrees of implementation of standards in TEL worldwide and across literally every spectrum from commercial to education and government, and being applied to most domains of learning and performance within these.

---

[59] See References section on Standards Related Organisations for all URL links to these organisations.

Bringing us up to the present day: of 2005. There truly has been a great deal of progress in "only" 8 years! In spite of all odds and only after a truly unbelievable amount of work, collaboration and effort, major promises and commitments have been met including such notable ones as:

- The completion of SCORM 2004. Having met all the original technical requirements and a point of reasonable stability, the latest release of SCORM 2005
- Successful completion of fully accredited standards from IEEE such as:
  - LOM data model
  - LOM XML binding
  - ECMA script
  - CMI
- Specifications from: IMS, AICC, ARIADNE, CEN/ ISSS, AICC, MPEG including such specs as:
  - Learning Design
  - Assessment
  - Learner Profiles
  - Reusable Competency Definitions
- Ongoing work on the international scene with ISO/IEC JTC1 SC36
- MASSIVE adoption and use at scale and globally
- Tools incorporating standards are widely available

But have we made any significant progress at improving learning through standards? Do we have any results to show for this? And of course most importantly in the context of this paper; what do we need to start planning for and working on next to ensure that we continue our progress to date and the development of enabling standards into the future?

21.5   Into the future

21.5.1   The near term future (2005 to 2007)

Looking out 18 months takes us to the end of the first decade of standards for TEL. (as was noted previously, almost all of the work on current standards began in 1997 In this near term (18 months) it is perhaps most critical that we collectively work to deliver on the promise and potential of both TEL and their supporting standards, that remains largely unrealised. Most of the initial expectations and predictions from the 1997 beginnings have been met or exceeded as they delivered an excellent foundation of the base standards and specs as was outlined in the previous section. The oft cited "abilities" list of such things as interoperability; manageability, affordability, accessibility, etc. have been provided for in the currently published standards and first versions of the technology tools to implement them. As we noted earlier, success of standards is best measured by their voluntary adoption, so in order to fully achieve success of the initial phase, the most important things for standards is their implementation and use.

During this stage of implementation the priority wants to be more on technique that on technology. It has always been the ideal that standards are lead by practice and not the other way around. While not always possible with the rapid rate of change and advancement in the world of technology enabled learning, as much as possible this is what to strive for. In this time of transition, we now have an excellent opportunity to put the existing standards and specifications into practice. By so doing, we are actually laying the important foundations for the longer range, and largely unknown, future of standards. As usual "learning by doing" is often the best, and the learning that is derived from the experiences of our collective implementations will prove to be invaluable for the next wave of standards and for the evolution and advancement of TEL.

21.5.2   Gain from pain

Looking at standards development in the near term future, the most progress will most likely be made by focusing on a relatively small number of specific „pain points" (there are so many to choose from!) In particular and to be expected, there are some new challenges that have been produced as we implement the current standards and new models of TEL. For example standards have enabled the exponential growth of content and the corresponding metadata that is beginning to accumulate in large collections and repositories. Just as is the case with the Internet and the web, the problem of greater accessibility, interoperability and choice is how to get what you want, when you want it?! Simply put, having everything available is great, but of little use unless it can be readily *discovered, located and delivered*.

21.5.3   GUIDs

As in life, some of the most important and difficult things are the smallest and simplest. Such is the case with figuring out how to uniquely identify each and every "noun" or "object" in the world: every person, place and thing. Content, metadata, technology, person etc.

The need for so called Globally Unique Identifiers or GUIDs has been known for some time. For example, there is a metadata element reserved just for GUID's in the IEEE Learning Object Metadata (LOM) standard, which is also what is used in SCORM and many other implementations. While simple in concept and obvious in need, their implementation is anything but simple. However, there appears to be a well developed solution in the near term and being addressed by a well established system called "Handle" and a new initiative called CORDRA that we will get to next.

21.5.4   Finding & discovery vs. searching & directing

Rather than searching what we most often want is finding. Rather than having access to what we already know is out there, we want to be able to discover what others have made available and what is related and relevant to our needs but not directly what we thought we were looking for. Most of us experience that great AHA! moment of finding something extremely valuable in the least likely place or from an unusual source or within a very foreign context. Just as using a thesaurus in addition to a dictionary, finding things "like this" or being made aware of things that are related to and similar to what we were directly looking for often proves to be the most valuable.

21.5.5   CORDRA: Already working on the future

Not surprisingly then, this set of related new challenges that are emerging from the implementation of the first set of standards and reference models such as the ADL SCORM 2004, have been collected together and are being vigorously worked on under the latest new acronym: CORDRA. Content Object Repository Discovery and Resolution/ Registration Architecture.

As defined by the CORDRA organisers, CORDRA is aimed at providing a model for a global infrastructure for learning and content by being *"an open, standards-based model for how to design and implement software systems for the purposes of discovery, sharing and reuse of learning content through the establishment of interoperable federations of learning content repositories"*. For more details and some excellent resources, please refer to the CORDRA web site at www.cordra.org.

CORDRA is a logical follow on from SCORM and will also be developed in the style of a "reference model" rather than a standard in and of itself. In fact CORDRA represents a great example of focusing for the near term on implementation and maximum leverage of the current standards. The overview of CORDRA clearly states that it will not be a completely new specification or a standard itself and will rather be

"As part of the notion of economy of re-use, CORDRA will be based on existing standards for learning content, repositories and digital libraries. The CORDRA project's proponents believe that sufficient standards and technologies exist; what is needed is to utilise them in combination to achieve interoperability. Thus, while the "blueprint" for the CORDRA model will combine and refine other standards documents as necessary, the CORDRA model should NOT be regarded as a completely new specification".

21.5.6   Wanted: Implementation of SS&N

To site but one example, though perhaps the most compelling and underdeveloped, there is a particular need for the implementation of one of the newest aspects of the standards, the so called "Simple Sequencing and Navigation (SS&N) that is detailed in SCORM 2004. Unlike most of the other components of SCORM and the other current standards such as LOM, Content Packaging, and CMI, SS&N has not been worked on for several years nor has the amount of practical implementation, tools or technology.

Though relatively new, there are already some excellent resources to assist with the implementation of SS&N. The CMU Learning Systems Architecture Lab (LSAL) web site at http://www.lsal.cmu.edu has some very well done and useful guides for overall content development and particularly good coverage of how to use SS&N such as the document on "Simple Sequencing Services" at http://www.lsal.cmu.edu/lsal/resources/standards/ssservices/services-v02.pdf.

The ADL web site at www.adlnet.org also has some excellent resources for implementing SS&N including.

21.5.7   Assessment

Given the fundamental role that assessment and evaluation plays in learning, it is a surprise that this whole area has such limited related standards. While there is the IMS Question and Test Interoperability (QTI) specification, it is about the only instance of any work on specs or standards for assessment and for many reasons even this does not seem to have much acceptance or adoption. More commonly the need for assessment is dealt with individually and with proprietary tools, many of which work very well but they suffer the common limitation of any non standard approach: they don't scale or provide for mass adoption, interoperability, and all the other limitations which standards address.

Some have suggested that the basic functional requirements for handling assessments could be sufficiently handled by the existing standards from IEEE and in SCORM 2004 of CMI, SS&N and LOM. If true, then perhaps in the short term it would be best to look at how we can use the current CMI data model to support assessments and then look longer term at providing the needed additional functionality for the broader issues of assessment and evaluation.

21.6   Medium term future: 2005 to 2010

2010 may sound like a truly futuristic date, yet as of this writing (May 2005) it is less than 5 years away. Back in 1997 when most of the work on today's standards for TEL began, few would have imagined it would take 5-8 years to complete the first versions! Therefore looking out to 2010 (and beyond in the next section) is not as far fetched as it might seem. Indeed, we would only be good students of history to take such a long view and be that much better prepared for the typical "premature arrival of the future".

As noted previously we will want to use what we learn from the current implementations and near term future to shape and guide these future standards and efforts. However, given the long development times involved, and using what has been learned to date, the current transition time provides us with an opportune time to start the early stages and planning. Looking out to 2010 and within the limited space we have available in this paper, the following categories can already be discerned.

21.6.1   C'ing the Future of Standards

More than a simple play on the words and their common first letter, the future for standards can largely be summarised as involving the three C's of Content, Context and Competencies. Indeed much of the future of overall learning and human performance improvement can be synthesised within these three C's. Below is a brief overview of the specific areas that would benefit from or require development of specifications and standards in each category.

21.6.2   Content: (All)

While not learning in itself, there is a clear relationship and dependency between learning and content. Much work has been done in the first decade of standards and TEL to address the foundation requirements, however much remains to be done by building upon these foundations with work on standards for some of the following areas:

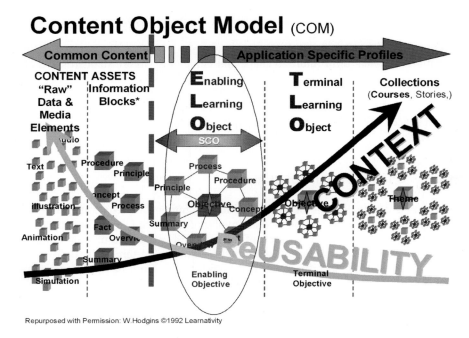

Repurposed with Permission: W.Hodgins ©1992 Learnativity

Fig. 21-1: Content object model

A content object model (COM)

Arguably the most critical concept that remains unaddressed by standards or even common understanding is a structural model for content (see figure 21-1 for one example). SCORM for example, is silent on this and defines a SCO or Shareable Content Object as simply the smallest unit which can be tracked by a Learning Management System. This makes good sense from the perspective of the LMS and managing learner's use of content. However it leaves unanswered the question of how content is to be structured which has led many to develop their own definitions and to also use these to address the disaggregation and aggregation of content. Many of these are working increasingly well and are finding that they all have much more in common than ever originally imagined.

It is worth noting that this is not limited to or unique to content for learning as such a modular or object based model appears to work equally well for almost any type of content and any application. For example these content models seem to apply equally well and be largely the same for content for technical publications and manuals, content for performance support, and most others. So the stage is set with this combination of demand and some existing practice to hopefully lead to the relatively rapid and successful work on creating standards for a common Content Object Model.

Getting beyond text?

Almost all of the content and standards to date are focused on only one type of content: text. While understandable and probably smart to start with, this has produced a critical need to address all the other forms and types of content: video, music, speech, photos, illustrations, 3D models, simulations, games, to name but a few! No where is this omission more glaring and critical than for learning. This is all the more surprising and critical in this time of massive access to and ease of production of multimedia.

This area is also a good example of where we as the learning community will be best served by joining forces with other domains and experts in these respective content domains and applications such as video, music, illustrations, etc. Equally important and helpful to accelerating this work on standards is the opportunity to embrace and extend the work of other standards organisations in these respective areas such as MPEG.

Metadata

Metadata has received a lot of attention and successful standards development in the first phase with Dublin Core and the IEEE Learning Object Metadata standard being the two most prominent examples. These have provided very good foundations and sources of great learning and experience which leads us into the needs for additional attention to metadata issues.

The field of metadata is rather fragmented at the moment, with initiatives such as Dublin Core (DC), Learning Object Metadata (LOM), the Moving Picture Experts Group (MPEG-7), the Resource Description Framework (RDF) and others.· Such fragmentation can be intimidating to prospective developers and thus hinders adoption and uptake of the very notion of metadata.· More importantly, this situation leads to " balkanisation" of metadata, where tools typically work with one kind of metadata only, so that end users either need to work with parallel sets of tools, or will have only a portion of the global set of metadata available to them. This situation is all the more regrettable as the world of "learning content" is not clearly separated from content in general (targeted by DC) or audio-visual content (the focus of MPEG-7). As an intermediate solution, we should develop a better understanding of the ways in which application profiles can allow us to "mix and match" metadata elements from diverse origins. Especially when the architectural assumptions are not evidently compatible, such mixing of elements does not seem to be straightforward to implement.

Longer term there is both a growing need and amount of work and research on the automation of metadata generation and metadata management. This includes what could be referenced as "subjective" metadata such as preferences, usage data and contextual information. This is in addition to but often more valuable than the more "objective" metadata (title, author, revision date, etc.) which has been the focus of metadata work and standards to date.

21.6.3   Context

Context is the collection of relevant conditions and surrounding influences that make a situation unique and comprehensible. The human cognitive and perceptual systems are designed to identify and use context automatically as we go about our daily lives (Anderson, 1995), (Hasher, Zacks, 1984).

Context is also largely the vision of the Semantic web or at least one of its largest characteristics. In the case of learning it is hard to imagine anything more relevant and critical than context, yet it has so far escaped much attention and certainly much work on standards for context.

Capturing context

However I am seeing more and more examples that this is increasingly being recognised and dealt with. In several meetings and conferences with different groups around the world in the last year, "capturing context" has emerged as their conclusion of the single most important and critical missing component for personalised learning and content. Capturing content can be understood to mean the ability to capture such attributes (metadata) as (Degler, Battle, 2000):

- Who the users is
- What the users is doing now
- Location
- Time
- Who else is available now
- Resources available now

Attention please! Do we all have ADD?

With no disrespect intended for those (including the author) who suffer from the real form of Attention Deficit Disorder (ADD) it would appear that this could be an all too accurate description of what is afflicting everyone living in the information age. Not so much the lack of attention but the challenge of figuring out WHAT to pay attention to and when and how? We are all bombarded daily with a growing volume and variety of "information" all vying for our attention. Equally we are often searching, and all too rarely finding, the "right" thing to pay attention to. What document or part of, to read? Who best to call? Who to ask the question? What session to attend? The list goes on, the choices grow exponentially.

This is part of context as it is the context that largely determines the value or what makes something or some one "right" relevant and real. We need help; assistance making smart decisions, being aware of what is "best" for us at any given time and situation. We have begun to see a glimmer of hope and some excellent examples (and flaming failures) in such diverse areas as retail sales, dating services and entertainment. For example there are increasingly effective recommender systems which can do an almost frighteningly accurate and highly valuable job of recommending a song to listen to, a movie to watch, an interesting (to you) person to meet, the right shirt to go with your outfit etc.

However two issues are already apparent: how to apply this to learning and how to manage your preferences and other "attention" information. In addition to obvious concerns for privacy and disclosure of this information consider the following for the latter issue of managing this data:

- How do you differentiate between items you buy for yourself from those you buy as gifts for others?
- How to you track the TV, movies and music preferences (likes and dislikes) in a house with more than one person?
- How do you aggregate all this preference data so you can take it with you and use it on whatever site, merchant or purpose that YOU want?

Not so simple is it? And not much use if you can't do this right?

Attention.xml

And now for the best part and the link back to standards. With the advanced warning that this is extremely new and a long way from being any standard, one of the most exciting new developments I've become aware of this year is that of *Attention.xml*[60]. It is gaining a good deal of attention itself (pun intended) and is attracting a growing number of groups and individuals who are assisting with its development and application.

Attention.XML is an open standard, built on open source that helps you keep track of what you've read, what you're spending time on, and what you should be paying attention to. As Steve Gillmor, the originator puts it

> "We hear every day about the problem with too much information splintering our attention. More news, more feeds, more pressures to keep informed. But the connected world is progressing toward a more sophisticated way to stay in touch. A world where attention is shared across the network, between machines, that distribute and share it or don't share it, based upon your preferences, likes or dislikes"[61].

As for applying this to learning, I'm even more optimistic about our ability to make rapid progress with this aspect. Just start to think how valuable it would be to have every learner receive recommendations on the 5 best things for them to read today that are the most relevant to them personally, the tasks they are working on, the others they are working with, etc. Imagine a project manager being able to would learners, students, teachers and managers.

For now, I would recommend that most in the learning community simply be

---

[60] See Attention.xml Dev Wiki: http://developers.technorati.com/wiki/attentionxml.
[61] http://endeca.com/resources/pdf/Endeca_ProFind_Overview.pdf.

aware that this is happening and put their focus on the issue of how and where to apply this to learning. Whether it is Attention.xml itself or some other future derivative that emerges as the de facto standard there is no question that we will see such a standard emerge in the next few years. Let's make sure that we have a hand in shaping this new standard and taking maximum advantage of it for learning and performance.

21.6.4   Competencies: Connecting content, learning and performance

Straddling the near and long term future timelines and connecting content with human performance and learning, an extremely important area for learning and standards development is that of overall human competencies. In this context competencies are to be understood in the most general sense and relative to learning.

IEEE LTSC WG20: Reusable competency definitions

The definition of *'competencies'* provided by the relatively new IEEE LTSC Working Group 20 for Reusable Competency Definitions provides a good base line by defining competencies as being:

> "... any form of knowledge, skill, attitude, ability or educational objective that can be described in a context of learning, education or training. Note—The word competency here is to be interpreted in the broadest sense to include educational objectives (those things that are sought) and competency or competencies (those things that are achieved). The word 'competency' is also used to include all classes of things that someone, or potentially something, can be competent in...."[62]

Originating with the work done at IMS on the specification for Reusable Definition of Competency or Educational Objectives (RDCEO), the IEEE standard for Reusable Competency Definitions (RCD) defines an information model for describing, referencing, and exchanging definitions of competencies, primarily in the context of online and distributed learning. The RCD standard provides a means to create common understandings of competencies that appear as part of a learning or career plan, as learning prerequisites, or as learning outcomes. RCD provides unique references to descriptions of competencies or objectives for inclusion in other information models.

---

[62] For full text see http://ltsc.ieee.org/wg20.

Learning objectives

In addition to the work on competencies themselves, there is also a need for and the beginnings of work being done on the special case of objectives (see figure 21-2). The omission of objectives in previous work on standards is rather surprising given the strong and historic consensus about the central role that objectives play in learning and especially in the development of content for learning. Furthermore, objectives are the nucleus of the author's original conceptual model for Learning Object and the overall Content Object Model (see figure 21-1).

For example, the author has initiated and is involved with several large organisations that are developing what could be described as a specification for *performance passed objective statements*. The purpose of this work is to provide objectives with all the common attributes of standards; consistency, interoperability, scalability, reusability, etc. While objectives are certainly nothing new and they tend to be very commonly understood and constructed, they remain sufficiently informal and different from one developer or community to the other to prevent any amount of reuse, access or sharing. So the need is to have a way to capture and express objectives in a consistent and interoperable way. Equally, it is clear and important that this must NOT be about instructions or procedures on how to write objectives, nor any specific pedagogical or andragogical approach, nor any one type of content nor any specific technical "binding" of the objective statements. These are elements which are best left up to the decisions of each individual community of practice, culture, discipline and domain.

Following common nomenclature and learning design, the initial work on objective statements has suggested following a simple and traditional two part structure of terminal objectives which are composed of one or more enabling objectives. These objectives will be performance based (NOT restricted to any one learning model or venue) and have the common components of an observable action (verb); at least one measurable criterion (standard of performance) and the conditions of performance (environment).

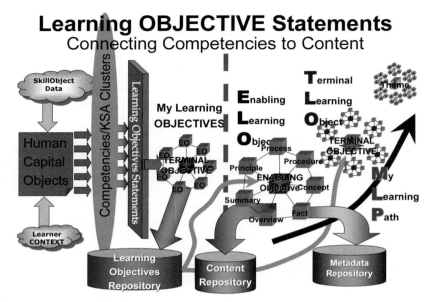

Fig. 21-2: Learning objective statements

As noted in the figures, these objectives will also serve as the trigger or catalyst for the assembly and aggregation of content assets to form Terminal and Enabling Learning Objects. Having a standard way of capturing objectives will lead to the creation of stand alone objective statement "objects" which can be stored in repositories, federated, reused, discovered, etc. Perhaps most promising of all, these objective statements will logically connect competencies with content and are likely to also finally enable the dramatic increase in the content available for learning by embracing the full range content and learning styles or types including Performance Support, Games & simulations, Embedded learning, e-learning, Classroom, and instructor led training, Technical publications, manuals and content of all types. When you get down to it, what content does NOT have any potential as a resource for learning? What content for learning would we not want to make available for other purposes?

21.7   The long term future: Into the next decade, 2010 and beyond

In my role as so called "Strategic Futurist at Autodesk Inc. my time frames are extremely long range relative to most. Typically in the 10 to 50 year range. So to finish this look at the future of standards, here are some observations from peering into the future through such a long range telescope:

21.7.1   The magic of metadata and beyond

Unlike current experiences many have had with metadata, in the future most will be derived automatically and will adequately describe every piece of data, every object, every event, and every person in the world. Objective metadata, almost all of which can be generated automatically, describes physical attributes, date, author, operational requirements, costs, identification numbers, and ownership and so on. Subjective metadata are the more varied and valuable attributes of a learning object, and are determined by the person or group who creates the metadata. The label on a can of tomato sauce provides objective metadata; your opinion of whether that tomato sauce worked well as an ingredient in your favourite recipe is an instance of subjective metadata. It is especially the subjective attributes of metadata that create the ability to capture what is otherwise tacit knowledge, context, perspectives, and opinions. Leveraging and extending beyond metadata we are seeing tremendous work and advances in developing the vocabularies, taxonomies and ontologies that bring the true power and ability to get it all "just right."

21.7.2   The next big thing? Getting small!

Standards are following what I've referred to as a "meta trend" for the past 10 years or so and that is the trend of getting small. In this context, "small" refers to breaking things down into very small but stand alone standard component which can then in turn be assembled into larger and infinite numbers of custom collections. Doing this with standards rectifies their history of being too monolithic and inflexible. Thus the meta trend of "getting small" applies to standards as well by creating standards that are modular, designed to be reused, taken down to the smallest possible unit sise and made to be interoperable. This has already started to happen to some extent within existing standards bodies such as IEEE Learning Technology Standards Committee (LTSC) and the Advanced Distributed Learning Initiative (ADL) and SCORM. They have developed specifications, standards and reference models which are made up of smaller, interoperable modules which can be individually selected on an as needed basis and assembled into a custom solution. Be prepared to see this trend continue every downward on the smallness scale as today's standards are themselves broken down into smaller individual components.

21.7.3   Getting to all the letters in ADL?

When are we going to start making the BIG improvements in learning? When are we going to get to all the letters and vision of ADL? This group name; Advanced Distributed Learning seems to be very enduring and prescient. While certainly only one of many important organisations, the vision of ADL (not just SCORM) is as well articulated as any and the names in the acronym are intriguing. We seem to have started in the middle and done a good job of addressing the "D" for Distributed with the existing standards and SCORM. But when are we going to get to the 'A' for Advanced in ADL? We need to address the need for specifications and standards for such things as Games, Simulations, Adaptive learning, Intelligent tutors and automated dynamic content assembly to name but a few.

And what about the "L" for Learning? When will we see a dramatic improvement in learning itself? What of advancing on the vision for learning that is truly "just the right" person, content, time, context, location and way? When will we get better at the skill of learning? How about learning what is out of date, proved to be wrong or ineffective? What about informal learning? I hope that by providing the prior review of the near and mid term future of standards, you will be able to assist with and contribute to answering these questions as we progress towards the future.

21.8   Conclusion

21.8.1   Back from the future

While my long standing involvement with standards certainly makes me biased, all our recent history seems to have shown rather conclusively that there simply is no future without standards. We just need to make them "right" and make them work and keep them in perspective as a means to an end; the realisation of the vision for personalised learning for all. As we approach the completion of the first decade of standards for TEL, we have much to be proud of and much to be humbled by. But there is no turning back. The only alternative to standards is no standards and that is no longer an option. We've answered the initial question of "do we need standards?" with a resounding YES!

21.8.2   Underestimation experts

One thing we certainly seem to be consistently very good at is underestimating. However this is actually a good thing! Looking at how far we have come since most of our work on standards for TEL began in 1997 I think it is fair to say that almost no one expected it to take this long. But equally almost no one foresaw just how far and where it would lead us. Similar to the Internet and the web which no coincidentally also began to take off about 1997. No one would have imagined what and where this would take us.

And as with these other examples such as the web and the net, the work doesn't get any easier, just different. I want to salute all of you, most of you reading this I'm sure, for the roles you have played, knowingly or unknowingly in bring standards and TEL so far. Keep the faith, keep up the great work and keep those eyes on that price!

Hoping that we can learn from this history, let's agree that we can probably not possibly imagine just how much work likes ahead and equally we can probably not fully imagine just how bright and beautiful the future of standards based TEL will be!

Part C: Fields of practice and case studies

Part C focuses on quality development in practice and case studies. Transversal themes which set quality development in relation to the European dimension, business models and elaboration on quality development in different educational sectors are presented. Also a number of articles of foundational nature, introducing future challenges in the field of quality for innovation of e-learning in the 21st century are included in this part.

22 Organisational and cultural similarities and differences in implementing quality in e-learning in Europe's higher education

Bernard Dumont

Consultant, France

Albert Sangra

Universitat Oberta de Catalunya, Spain

Based on 5 national studies, from Finland, France, Poland, Spain, and Switzerland, the authors present and analyse organisational and cultural factors that can facilitate or block the implementation of Quality in Higher educational institutions in general and for e-learning in particular[63].

They make a comparison between these factors, some of them being common to the 5 countries, the other being relevant for only one or more countries.

This study is supported by the *e-quality* Minerva Project (Socrates Programme). It aims the production and validation of training material to train teams in charge of ODL in these 5 countries.

One encounters here one of the important issues on international norms and standards: How to find equilibrium between the need for such specifications and the specificity of each country in terms of organisation and cultural representation of "Quality concepts"?

---

[63] We thank the authors of the e-quality national reports on which important parts of this article has been based.

22.1   Introduction: Facing with quality in open and distance practices

Quality has become in the last years, a very relevant aspect for the organisational life. It should be connected directly with the strategic planning and with the improvement and it can affect any product, process, service, person, etc. In this sense, it affects even the organisational culture. Absolutely anything goes close with quality, and ODL Higher Institutions (ODL HI) are not an exception. In the model we present, the student is located as the user, the main element because of his/ her role of "client".

It is remarkable that to create a model that includes the whole universe of the ODL HI, at last three different views must be included: institutions, teachers and students. The quality treatment would have different aims depending on the selected object. Secondly, each one has different standards to attend. For instance from an institutional perspective there are different focus areas, such as: Governance and regulation, Curriculum design, Learning experience, Medium of delivery, Student support, Content of programmes, Financial viability, Qualification, Administrative support, Organisational process (Harvey, 2003).

These standards, moving into a more in depth detail would be divided in more aspects, for example roles, activities, artefacts or of course others (e.g. Governance and regulation is a standard that needs the role of the decision maker and the educational laws as instrument, etc.). Concluding, quality could face one or more elements related to specific and concrete scenarios, where the cooperation and interaction between the elements of the different levels are needed.

Going to an educator's level, the picture is quite different; Institutional Commitment, Technology, Student Services, Instructional Design and Course Development, Instruction and Instructors, Delivery, Finances, Regulatory and Legal Compliance, Evaluation. However, educators are not of course the only involved roles, there are others, such tutors, programmers, head masters, etc., with their specific standards (Frydenberg, 2002).

Our model has a student centred perspective, as it is argued in the forthcoming points of this document, and it is an organic element of the project, completely interconnected with the rest of the elements that create a system. Overall, this model should be linked to further actions in the quality field to enhance a more qualified learning, improving the academic achievements, a better knowledge and understanding, a better development of skills (professional too), a high level of satisfaction, etc.

Implementation of quality in Higher Education is nowadays a very important issue. To do it particularly with those programs regarding Open and Distance Learning (ODL) or e-learning is still a real challenge.

To face it, a group of European universities have initiated a project, partly funded by the European Commission under the Socrates/ Minerva Programme[64],

---

[64] The 3 year e-Quality project (Project number: 110231-CP-1-2003-1-MINERVA-M – 2003-2006) is supported by 7 institutions from 5 European countries:
The Pôle Universitaire Européen de Montpellier-Languedoc Roussillon (France), that is in charge

in which it is proposed to offer a ground for practical design and implementation of a quality methodology, a training package for staff in charge of its implementation, a validation field and a knowledge data base for results and best practice dissemination.

ODL: Open and Distance Learning is a general expression covering all forms of learning and teaching different from traditional face-to-face training. E-learning is only one form of ODL but ODL is more general in terms of technological means. "Open" refers to Open Universities. Used also as "Online and Distance Learning" for instance at Athabasca University.

The pedagogical approach puts the student's needs at the root of the ODL quality process. This approach is comprehensive: it encompasses all the processes needed to validate in real situation the produced methodology and documents.

22.2   Methodology and design of the case studies

The *e-quality* project starts with the comparative analysis of the partners' context that permits to be aware and detect a set of existing blocking factors in the implementation of quality.

A questionnaire has been designed and validated by partners, to describe the situation in all participating countries: Finland, France, Poland, Spain and Switzerland. This questionnaire is built from general information to more specific one:

- The educational context

  - General information (population, unemployment rate, national policy on ICT use…)
  - General information about the access to computers and Internet
  - General aspects of the Higher Education system with some questions about: evaluation process for Higher Education institutions, typology of teachers, use of ICT in teaching, quality
  - General aspects of ODL in the Higher Education system

- Representation and implementation of quality

  - Models of quality applied in the country

---

of the management of the project, on behalf of the UO-MLR (Open University - Montpellier-Languedoc Roussillon);

The University Montpellier 2, France;

The UOC (Open University of Catalunya), Spain;

The University of Tampere, Finland;

The Technical University of Szczecin, Poland;

The University of Applied Sciences (Haute Ecole Valaisanne Spécialisée), Switzerland;

The University of Lausanne, Switzerland.

The external evaluation is lead by the Belgian company ATiT.

- Efforts carried out by national agency(ies) on the implementation of quality in the public and private sectors
- Main challenges for implementation of quality in the country (problems to solve, areas to improve...)
- Global view on quality implementation in the country
- Organisational and cultural specificity of the country that can influence the representation and the implementation of quality in the public organisations
- Organisational and cultural specificity of the country that can influence the representation and the implementation of quality in the Higher Education institutions
- Cultural specificity that can influence the representation and the implementation of quality in ODL services or departments within the Higher Education institutions
- Implementation of quality in traditional universities
- Current situation of quality implementation in institutions currently offering only ODL courses (if any)
- Current situation of quality implementation in institutions currently offering both ODL courses and face-to-face courses

• Implementation of quality in the partner's institution

National studies have been conducted in the 5 countries using this common questionnaire. Reports have been written. The synthesis includes also an interesting comparison on blocking or helping factors for quality implementation in Higher Education institutions, in general and for ODL in particular. This collaborative work has been used to elaborate the objectives and to build the material of the training of national teams working for ODL development and delivery[65]. These national reports and a synthesis of them can be found on the project website[66]. This article presents the main results of this first step of the project.

22.3   Quality in higher education: 5 case studies

We present here, after some general references and the position of the European Ministers in charge of Higher Education, the situation of quality implementation in the 5 participating countries as seen form the national reports.

---

[65] The project aims to produce a training package to train, in face to face and at distance, several teams of concerned staff (both trainers, technicians and administrative, with students as observers) on quality, at least one in each participating country. Each trained team is to experiment these supports in their own ODL training programme.

[66] www.e-quality-eu.org.

22.3.1   Different models for different geographical areas

As described by Kells (Kells, 1993), there are three main models of quality assessment in education, regarding four basic variables: the assessment purpose, the evaluation framework, the wideness of the approach and the main procedures of the system. Also Kells considers, from a worldwide approach four basic models: the American, the European Continental, the British and the Scandinavian ones.

The American tries to improve the institutional programmes and give guarantee to the users. It is focused on the achievement of institutional goals. The European Continental is based on the fact of extending the guarantee not only to the users, but to the Administration and Government as well. Peer-assessment is usually adopted.

The British model emphasises on academic degrees standards and to establish quality criteria. Peer-assessment and performance indicators are the tools used the most. Finally, the Scandinavian one is a diversification of the European Continental one, introducing accountability purposes and external assessment practices.

As the five countries analysed in our project belong to the European Continental and Scandinavian models, similarities are quite evident. We will try to point out mainly on the differences.

It is also true that most of these models are attempts to adapt to the educational field the corporate sector certification standards. Quality management systems are not so commonly used in education, because they have not suited well enough for the quality of education, even if, in professional and vocational education, there are some standard and certificated systems which have been used, e.g. in the demonstration of competencies.

22.3.2   Standards and guidelines for quality assurance in the European higher education area

As mentioned in the Communiqué of the Conference of Ministers responsible for Higher Education in Berlin in 2003 (*Realising the European Higher Education Area*, 2003): "The quality of higher education has proven to be at the heart of the setting up of a European Higher Education Area". After reaffirming that each institution is responsible for its own Quality Assurance, based on the principle of institutional autonomy, the Ministers "stress the need to develop mutually shared criteria and methodologies" and they fixed 2005 as a deadline for ENQA[67]"to develop an agreed set of standards, procedures and guidelines on quality assurance, to explore ways of ensuring an adequate peer review system for quality assurance and/ or accreditation agencies or bodies".

In fact, during the Bergen conference in May 2005, the Ministers adopted "the standards and guidelines for quality assurance in the European Higher Education Area as proposed by ENQA" (Bergen, 2005), stressing that "there is still progress to be made, in particular as regards student involvement and international coopera-

---

[67] ENQA: European Association for Quality Assurance in Higher Education. http://www.enqa.net/.

tion.". From this date, these "standards and guidelines" (ENQA, 2005) must be considered as the main reference for quality assurance in Higher Education at the European level and are also relevant for ODL, even if in this case some other criteria have to be taken into account.

22.3.3   The situation in Finland

EFQM, TQM, and ISO 9000 certification standards, are common in Finland[68]. Many subjects affect the quality in the public Finnish organisations. There are well-built infrastructures, high standard of education and technological knowledge is high. There are also stable social welfare and equal circumstances. Quality management systems are very common in Finland and there are many rationales to implement a quality system, e.g. the motivation of staff, competitiveness, marketing advantages, better quality in all functions, better communication and organisational culture. University is based on Humboldian ideals of autonomy, freedom of research and teaching and the unity of research and teaching. The Ministry of Education and The Finnish Higher Education Evaluation Council (*FINHEEC*) favour decentralised quality work. The universities have been opposed to the establishing of a national quality agency. Quality assurance is considered as the universities' task. The Ministry of education recommends that universities and polytechnics develop quality assurance systems, which should a) meet the developing quality assurance criteria of the European Higher Education area, b) be part of the operational steering and management system, c) cover the entire operation of the higher education institution, d) be interrelated as part of the normal operations of the higher education institution, e) be continuous, f) be documented, and g) enable the participation of all members of the higher education community in quality work. The *FINHEEC* gathers information about the quality work in the universities; it doesn't produce formal quality models for the universities' purposes. Quality models that are created by individual institutions are not very formal models, but more guidelines on how to enhance quality. However, these quality systems are not very visible or transparent systems for the universities' personnel or the outside actors to perceive.

22.3.4   The situation in France

There are specific and formal models applied in France for quality management mainly: ISO 9000, EFQM and TQM. A few public Higher Education institutions have implemented a formal quality step. But all are involved, at least, in a self-evaluation based on the "Book of reference"[69] edited by the National Committee for Evaluation (*CNE*[70]), the agency in charge of the evaluation of Higher Educa-

---

[68] EFQM Annual Quality Award ceremony and seminar were organised in Finland in Autumn 2003.
[69] English short version: http://www.cne-evaluation.fr/WCNE_pdf/bulletin38bis.pdf.
[70] http://www.cne-evaluation.fr/.

tion institutions. It is independent from the Ministry. "The book of references and the logic of demonstration" explains the new approach to the evaluation of Higher Education institutions; it is designed as "a tool to support the setting up of quality assurance procedures and as a document that will facilitate institutions' entry into the European Higher Education area".

22.3.5   The situation in Poland

In Poland, product certification is performed by Polish Research and Certification Centre (PCBC[71]). Their main objectives are investigation and certification of products, Quality management certification and auditor's certification. About difficulties to implement Quality in Poland, one can mention:

- Society does not force the use of quality standards;
- Lack of funds;
- Lack of formal support on quality initiatives.

In Poland, *the State Accreditation Committee* (SAC[72]) is the only organisation authorised-in-law operating to control quality in education process in Higher Education institutions. *SAC* negative rating implies the decision from Ministry of Education to withdraw its authorisation on particular institution which does not respond with applicable quality indicators (restricting the fault specialisation at the higher education institution).

Poland suffers from lack of institutions supporting quality in ODL in general. The ODL process establishment and formation are considered 'fresh', challenging, not widespread. Only few higher education institutions exist offering ODL courses and these are parts of traditional institutions (universities and technical universities). The distance learning student does not represent legal student status (only as extern student status). Therefore, the quality implementation is at a very limited and restricted level.

22.3.6   The situation in Spain

The Spanish Education law (LOGSE) opted for the application of different European quality models, overall the EFQM model (but it was not the only one), quality being defined in the following phrase: "the users' satisfaction of the public education services, of the teachers and staff personnel, and the impact in the society can be achieved through a leadership which fosters the planning and strategy in the educational institution, its human resources management, resources and processes to improve the results permanently". The National Agency for Quality Assurance and Accreditation, *ANECA[73]*, is a State foundation. Its purpose is to as-

---

[71] http://www.pcbc.gov.pl/certyfikacja.html.
[72] Source: http://www.men.waw.pl/pka/index.php.
[73] http://www.aneca.es.

sure quality in the Spanish university system, assessing and publicising Higher Education performance, and reinforcing transparency and comparability in the Spanish system. Nevertheless, autonomous communities have the possibility to create specific quality agencies, and this is what the Catalan and Andalusian regions have done. At this stage, both Spanish and Catalan Agencies for Quality in Higher Education are developing quality and accreditation criteria for the new fully online courses.

In discharging its functions, the *ANECA* is likewise bound to co-ordinate and co-operate with the external assessment bodies existing for similar purposes within and under the laws of the different Autonomous Governments.

22.3.7   The situation in Switzerland

The Centre of Accreditation and Quality Assurance of the Swiss Universities (*OAQ*[74]) is an academically independent institution, trying to define its own certification model. Each Academic University defines its own model of quality, which has to be validated by the *OAQ*. Applied Universities refer to eduQua and ISO 9000 but not specifically for ODL courses.

A specific norm called eduQua[75] has been developed for continuing education institutions. It qualifies a good formation, assures and develops the quality in the continued education institution, offers more transparency for the consumers. Presently, 406 education enterprises are certified eduQua. Nevertheless, the students will preferably choose a certified institution, but it is only one of the criteria for them and not the most important one.

22.4   Organisational and cultural specificities that influence the implementation of quality in higher education institutions in 5 European countries

We present here, based on the national studies, some specificities that can explain why differences exist between these European countries in term of implementation of quality in their Higher Education institutions. We consider two main aspects, as they are explicitly mentioned in the objectives of our project: the organisational aspects (i.e. the status of the different kinds of teachers, the way institutions are evaluated or not…) and the cultural aspects (i.e. the general representation of quality in education, the interest of teachers for pedagogy, the use or not of an evaluation of courses by students and its impact on teachers…).

---

[74] http://www.oaq.ch.
[75] http://www.eduqua.ch/002alc_00_fr.htm.

22.4.1   The situation in Finland

Main challenges in Higher Education institutions have an influence on quality implementation. First of all, autonomy of universities is an important issue. Universities differ from other educational institutions due to their large size and the heterogeneous nature of the different departments. This is the reason why changes and even improvements are adopted slowly in universities. Multidisciplinary universities have difficulties in creating quality models that are general enough but yet compatible with the department's own culture.

There are in some departments much expertise on leadership, management, and quality assurance that could be used for the benefit of the whole of the University. In order to benefit from this strength, the University needs an effective mechanism for transferring its knowledge and expertise in academic quality assurance not only across departments within a faculty, but also across faculties. Another difficulty is a lack of transparency in administrative decisions.

Support by the administration is needed. The lack of support is a common challenge in quality development. It influences the teacher's work, e.g. the teacher can feel that the work s/he does for a better quality is not appreciated.

Quality work is often seen as a hard and time consuming work.

22.4.2   The situation in France

In spite of so called "university autonomy" most of university organisation is defined by a law, most of university budget comes from the state, nearly all of university staff (including researchers and professors) are paid by the state. At university level, professors are recruited on their thesis and research and on their bibliography and scientific publications; their career is done mainly on the same base, with little consideration on the involvement in pedagogy. The same is true of ODL: pedagogy being not a specific issue, if one knows a subject, one can teach it face-to-face; if one can teach face to face, one can teach at a distance... Professors' evaluation by students is very seldom done. Quality of teaching and students' success are not the priority of the majority of teachers at university level. Universities have problem with quality implementation because they can hardly address the questions: "What are the services that an university must deliver? How are they evaluated? By whom? Do the universities deal with clients? Who pays for what?». Teaching/ teacher is at the core of university organisation, not learning/ learner. Pedagogical approaches, learner centred, are not obvious in French culture.

Another blocking factor still remains: the status of ODL teaching is not fully recognised for University teachers: only on-campus teaching is recognised by French legislation to fulfil teaching obligations. Several universities have by passed the problem but with not fully legal arrangements. This situation is one of the most blocking factors for further development of ODL in Universities.

22.4.3   The situation in Poland

Three main issues are important in Poland in regard with quality: the number of High Education institutions, the lack of thorough participants' verification, because of evolving staff, and varying conditions and also the lack of clear and responsive quality normative body for Higher Education institutions.

22.4.4   The situation in Spain

Similarly to school education, in the last 10 years Spain has lived two changes of government, whose have proposed educational reforms with some differences. It is quite probable that the last law (LOU) is discussed again due to the new changes in the government.

There is a continuous debate about the university: its function, the appropriateness of the increasing use of ICT, the growth of the university participation, the new importance of 'humanism training', the relationship with the labour market and the importance of the 'professional function'.

Concerning the role of the teacher, it is moving from a mere transmitter of knowledge to an academic counsellor or facilitator and someone which may fit the students' needs. At last we have to mention the importance of the value of autonomy and the function of quality agencies in the evaluation, certification and accreditation processes.

22.4.5   The situation in Switzerland

Cooperative Federalism is one of the most important cultural aspects that influence quality evaluation process in Switzerland. With 4 official different languages[76], one has to take into account different points of views. In German part, people are more quality oriented than in French or Italian parts. Focusing on learning quality evaluation process, it is to note that in this country, one generally thinks that if every minor task is certified, the whole process will present the best quality and doesn't think about including a large creative vision of the process. Learners are generally considered like any other "product" and pedagogy is not often included in the norm. This point of view on learning process qualification will not increase quality of future qualified institutions. ODL has a very short history in this country so quality is oddly not the first preoccupation of ODL course developers and sustainers.

---

[76] French, German, Italian and Romanche.

22.5   Examples of quality strategies in institutions offering ODL courses

We present here several examples of existing quality strategies in institutions that deliver ODL courses in 3 of the participating countries, to illustrate the on-going process of quality implementation.

22.5.1   Examples in France

We can mention two examples with interesting results.

In 2001, the French National Centre for Distance Education (CNED[77]) has launched a quality step and a Director of Quality has been appointed. Within the framework of the institution programme (2005-2007), a quality policy, accompanied by objectives/ criteria and by indicators, is in final phase of elaboration around four axes:

- Quality of the services,
- Satisfaction of the customers,
- Satisfaction of the staffs,
- Look for financial balances.

This situation is to be mentioned as CNED is the oldest and largest French institution dedicated to ODL and has a reputation of being conservative, very heavy to move and kind of old-fashioned. Such quality "offensive" – learner centred – is quite surprising but illustrate a real change in the policy of the institution: they have to get more students and – above all – to keep them, in a difficult environment where CNED has many competitors.

In 2003 a study was lead for the Ministry of Education on the quality process within the "Campus numériques" (Digital Campuses)[78].

Several main points must be noticed:

- The quality improvement aims first the trainees;
- Certification is not a crucial objective for most of the respondents;
- Main objective: a good level of satisfaction for both students and staff.

In 2003, 64 ODL formations obtained a label to which four campuses concerning the electronic environments of work added[79]. This study shows that a change appeared in the representation of training in these institutions: trainees' satisfaction

---

[77] http://www.cne-evaluation.fr.

[78] Details on: http://www.educnet.education.fr/superieur/CN-demarchkal.htm.

[79] http://www.educnet.education.fr/superieur/qualintro.htm,
http://www.educnet.education.fr/chrgt/CN-demarchkal.pdf,
http://www.educnet.education.fr/superieur/campusqualite.htm,
List institutions having obtained a quality label:
http://www.educnet.education.fr/superieur/CNlabel.htm.

is an objective and is linked with quality. This evolution is in accordance with Bergen communiqué.

22.5.2   Example in Poland

The ODL department on Technical University of Warsaw (called OKNO), at the bachelor level, has implemented two quality systems, one focused on the didactic process, the second one on the computer infrastructure. All didactic materials and production procedure are standardised. The quality factor is increased by the feedback between the teachers and the students.

22.5.3   Example in Spain

UOC has its own quality model, based on the EFQM model, which is also used for institutional evaluation purposes. Concerning the organisational part, the UOC model follows the lifecycle of the learner, from the beginning of the student-institution relationship until the end of these. This vision is very pragmatic as it allows to design and evaluate processes fitting the learners' needs during all their lifecycle at UOC. The way in which we design the process map follows the EFQM model. On the second hand, the quality must also be focused in learning processes. This is the 'evaluation of the methodology', centred in three macro-indicators: learners' success, learners' satisfaction and learners' drop-out level. These indicators are measured by asking learners about them in several e-learning fields (learning materials, virtual learning environments, teachers' role and tasks, assessment, contents…). An organised system of structured questionnaires has been created, called 'Balance Scorecard for methodology', which allows to gather information about the situation in the UOC's subjects and degrees. This is a measurement process, but not an evaluation one (understanding measure as getting information and evaluation as decision making).

   The results obtained by these questionnaires are the basis to generate hypothesis, for instance: "students from technical degrees have less problems to use virtual tools than other students"; "the drop out level during the first month is very high because learners are not motivated by the institution"… The data obtained from this MCQ system allow to go in depth with the evaluation of specific aspects of the courses, which will be carried out through interviews with learners, teachers, staff… and through specific questionnaires.

22.6   Summary: Organisational and cultural factors blocking or helping quality implementation

The political commitment of the European Ministers in charge of Higher Education for Quality Assurance, as presented in the Communiqué of Berlin in 2003, and confirmed during the Bergen Meeting in 2005, is, potentially, a strong opportunity to develop quality steps in the Higher Education institutions in general and in ODL in particular. However there still exist some critical factors that will influence this initiative and overall any other implementation of quality in the ODL.

As it had been said before, five different countries with their concrete reality had been analysed under the frame of the *e-quality* Project. After the data obtained had been studied, four main categories have been built up when dealing with favourable or blocking factors for the quality implementation in ODL in Higher Institutions. The first one is dedicated to the favourable factors that are common in the whole countries. The second category is related to the favourable factors just detected in some scenarios. The third category deals with the blocking factors that appear in the five national reports, while the fourth and last group of factors is devoted to just specific blocking dimensions in four or less countries.

22.6.1   Facilitating factors for quality development

Moving to the first category of common favourable factors, some similarities exist for the university evaluation process. For instance, quality is a compulsory process in all the countries with no exception. Furthermore, quality is a process that is always defined by the state. The five states count with national agencies that are in charge of quality, even if they don't have the same status, especially in Finland. Another coincidence is the practice of an internal and an external evaluation. And lastly, quality is always an implicit or explicit objective at the university level.

Apart of the university evaluation process and going in depth with ODL Higher Institutions, there is a set of favourable factors for the whole countries such these:

- The new European degree organisation (Bachelor Master Doctorate) will lead universities to publicise their training programmes and to facilitate to their students an access to training modules from other universities;
- The ECTS system with possible equivalence of credits will promote student virtual mobility;
- With an easier and faster access to Internet, the universities begin to face concurrence with other European universities;
- ODL appears as a new reality and a means to attract national and foreign students;
- The evolution of technologies, including high-speed access to Internet, development of e-mail communication, forums, videoconferences, streaming video etc., make possible the condition for high level ODL services.

However a large effort is still needed to help teachers and technical staff to produce better training material and to offer better services (e.g. tutoring), as far as there are blocking factors dedication to overcome the situation is needed.

The second category, non common favourable factors in all the countries, represent almost all the countries trends but with just one or two exceptions. In this sense, a positive statement that has to be highlighted is that society compels quality standards. Beside this factor some others set up this group such:

- There is some formal support on quality initiatives;
- Highly centralised management of public services does not decrease operational aspects;
- The value "autonomy" is important to create and develop quality practices;
- ODL is not anymore a marginal means of learning;
- The importance of "humanism training" is increasing in universities.

22.6.2   Barriers for quality development

Before going in detail with the third and fourth categories, there are some factors that were perceived as blocking ones at the beginning of the work but they were finally concluded as "non blocking factors", this do not mean they are favourable but just "non blocking":

- Lack of training as "virtual teachers";
- Lack of high speed networks which do not allow to work with some ICT tools;
- Institutions do not provide clear methodology on how to use the ICT to learning;
- ODL policies not promoting enough a specific use of ICT and methodologies in ODL;
- No budget allocation for quality implementation;
- No known models of quality used in universities;
- Universities using unknown models of quality do not have a clear definition about the theoretical aspects and implementation of such a model (the process is not documented);
- Existing national agencies do not propose special models for ODL courses;
- National agencies do not provide specific certificates which guarantee that a university is applying quality measures[80] (lack of quality certificates);
- Management of quality is highly centralised at a national level;
- No specific policies in quality implementation.

Another set of factors is still under discussion, in other words, the *e-quality* team has not yet decided whether they are or not blocking factors:

- Quality systems in ODL do not have clear indicators, these are not well defined and there are no orientations on how to measure;
- The quality system is not integrated in the management system of the institution.

There is a clear consensus on the third established category that starts treating the non favourable aspects and consequently deals with the common blocking factors. The ones listed below should be taken into a very serious consideration because

---

[80] It is not a perceived blocking factor because basically the issue is more related to certification than to quality.

they are mentioned in the five national reports. Furthermore, these factors are all of them very relevant in quality terms:

- High focus is put on teaching instead of learning;
- To design quality ODL material is time consuming.

In the following table we present some examples of blocking factors in 2 to 4 countries.

Table 22-1: Blocking factors and their distribution within the 5 participating countries

	Fi	Fr	Pl	Sp	Sw
Blocking factors common to 4 countries					
Teachers are reluctant to be evaluated	x	x		x	x
Low value of the pedagogical issues: when recruiting new university teachers, the pedagogical skills are not a prerequisite	x	x	x		x
Copyright issues are not taken into account	x	x	x		x
Traditional low consideration of ODL and consequently no recognition of ODL teaching	x	x	x	x	
Blocking factors common to 3 countries					
Lack of technical assistance for the staff		x	x	x	
Lack of preparation to new methodologies and tools		x	x	x	
'You can teach face-to-face when you know the content, and you can teach at distance when you can teach face-to-face'	x	x			x
Blocking factors common to 2 countries					
Need for good infrastructures, high standards in education, high technologic skills	x		x		
Role of the teacher[81]	x			x	
Lack of training on the use of ICT for the staff	x			x	
Diverse concepts of success in education			x	x	
Diversity and too many educational reforms			x	x	
Lack of transparency in decisions		x		x	
Costs			x	x	
Unclear criteria to reward e-authors and e-trainers		x		x	
Teachers' training in ODL is not favoured within the universities		x			x

(In bold: factors directly linked with quality in ODL)

---

[81] In Spain for instance, there are considerable differences between the values of the teachers, the assumptions of the educational reforms and the requests of parents and society.

22.7   Conclusions: Main challenges for implementation of quality in higher education

Most challenges are related with management in Higher Education institutions and the difficulty of considering students as "clients" more than "users" and definitely different of "products".

In addition, there are not particular quality models fully adapted to the educational reality. In some countries, lack of formal regulations considering ODL in the same level of conventional education is also an important handicap. On the other hand, some norms are too manufacturing process-based integrating too many administrative issues, so a need of inclusion of pedagogical approaches is needed.

Nevertheless, the *e-quality* project is an interesting opportunity to develop and validate a set of pertinent and clear indicators that enable the measurement of results and give confidence enough in order to make growing a good image of ODL quality.

23 Rethinking quality for building a learning society

Maureen Layte, Serge Ravet

EIfEL, France

The article explores how the issue of quality in the knowledge economy and learning society of the 21st century might dramatically differ from that we have known in the industrial age. Until now, most approaches to quality were based on the idea that there is a clear separation between the producer of a good or service and its consumer. How should we define the quality of a learning environment where learners are not simply consumers of knowledge, but co-producers of their own as well as their organisation's and community's knowledge? How de we define quality in a system of *presumption*, where consumers and producers merge?
1.   To suggest a response to this issue, the article will examine how the understanding of the organic link between individual, community, organisational and territorial learning is critical to realise the true power of e-Learning, i.e. the e-transformation and quality of all the processes linked to education, training, human resource and community development.

23.1   Introduction

> "What we want to see is the child in pursuit of knowledge, and not knowledge in pursuit of the child." — George Bernard Shaw

We are now entering into a new world, a world where learning is an integral part of work and the fabric of society, a learning society. As John Dewey wrote: "*Education is not preparing for life; education is life itself*"; or to paraphrase Descartes, one could say: "*I live, therefore I learn.*"

In this article[82], then, we shall be looking at how the need to rethink education, training and learning to meet the needs of a knowledge economy and a learning society[83] inevitably leads to a new approach to building, exploiting and validating the quality of lifelong, and life wide learning. We will explore how the concept of quality must move from a piecemeal to a holistic approach, placing the individual learner as the key component of a quality policy with a set of new competencies at the centre of a network of relationships: learning organisations, learning communities, learning cities and learning regions. Our particular focus is on the critical role to be played by technology.

So, when looking at quality approaches designed for learning, the questions one should ask are:

- How do they take into account the new political, economical, sociological and technological environment? What do they offer that was not, or could not have been, offered 20 years ago? This latter question is an excellent 'acid test' to determine whether something is really new or is a mere revamping of old ideas.

- How can we ensure that our approach to quality meets the real needs of a knowledge economy and a learning society? How might maintaining an old framework create obstacles to progress and innovation?

- Is it possible to adapt quality systems tailored to the industrial age to a knowledge economy and a learning society, or should we invent other quality reference frameworks? These are classical epistemological questions: do we need (are we participating in) a paradigm shift (Kuhn 1970) or a mere adaptation of the old theoretical framework?

- What are the relations between the different learning dimensions (individual, community, organisational, territorial) and how do they impact quality systems? Many quality systems developed in the field of education and probably even more in the field of e-learning are focused on the 'inputs': quality of the learning resources (e.g. CERFAD, Italy), competencies of the tutor (e.g. EIfEL standards of competencies), quality of the training provider (e.g. OPQFC, France), very few, provide a holistic view of learning as a social and community process.

It is clear that we are witnessing the emergence of a new environment requiring citizens with a whole new set of skills (skills for life) that are in contradiction with some of the educational and managerial models inherited from an industrial society (Tapscott, 1998). Learning is now an integral part of work, and not something

---

[82] NB: this article is the result of the work undertaken by EIfEL and our contribution to different European projects on quality and learning (SEEL, SEEQUEL, ReLL), in particular SEEL (supporting Excellence in E-Learning) explored the concept of quality applied to learning regions – looking at the role of technology in the activities of eLearning regions.

[83] Knowledge economy refers to the transformation of the economy, its mode of producing added value, goods and services leading to the emergence of a new class of knowledge workers; learning society refers to the emergence of a new relationship between citizens, organisations, firms, associations, public authorities, cultural heritage, etc. leading to the construction of learning communities, learning cities, learning regions (Florida, Wolfe) and learning countries. Knowledge economy focuses on capital growth, learning society focuses on social capital growth.

that is limited to a dedicated time, space or modality (classroom, physical or virtual) (Schank, 1997).

A quick *PEST* analysis will elicit some of the trends.

- *Political: the move from independent education policies (subsidiary) to cooperation and coordination* – as seen in the need for transparency of qualifications (e.g. Common Qualification Framework and European Diploma Supplement) and mobility of the work force (e.g. Europass Mobility) in an extended Europe.
- *Economic: the move from an industrial economy to a knowledge economy* – e.g. changing the relations of the nature of the goods produced, their production and delivery methods, the qualification of employees, the change in obsolescence patterns of goods and services.
- *Sociological: the move from brawn intensive to brain intensive labour* (Tapscott, 1996) – e.g. change of the relations between organisations, employees and employers, the development of telework, organisation of the space, the need to develop new schemes for accreditation of prior learning.
- *Technological: the move from mass media to knowledge media* – e.g. the ubiquitous access to a "world brain" (Wells, 1937) empowering individuals, not just as consumers, but as co-producers of information, knowledge and culture.

The European 2010 objective, to build "[...] *the most competitive knowledge economy* [...]"is an attempt to give political leadership to a phenomenon that needs to be controlled in order to ensure "sustainable development and social inclusion" – which is part of the same Lisbon declaration, but too often forgotten. Rethinking quality for a learning society needs to take into account all these dimensions.

In the following section we will explore:

- How the emergence of a knowledge economy and learning society are changing our vision of learning and quality of learning?
- What new references we can use for planning learning quality?
- What a typical 21st century e-learner will be like, and what will be his/ her unique contribution to quality?

This discussion will lead us to the conclusion that only an organic vision of learning and quality, including all their dimensions (individual, community, organisational, territorial, societal) will be able to support the quality approach to learning required in a learning society.

Linking individual, community, organisational and territorial learning: Learning is about "...establishing new premises (i.e. paradigms, schemata, mental models, or perspectives) to override the existing ones." (Nonaka, 1995). This applies to individuals, communities, as well as regions. The concepts of learning community (Argyris, Schön, 1978), learning organisation (Senge, 1990) or learning region (Florida, 1995), (Wolfe, 2002) should not refer to independent entities and processes. In order to succeed, the learning regions require a critical mass of skills and knowledge that organisations, companies, associations and citizens can provide. As authorities they have the power to remove (or create) obstacles to individual and community learning and to behave (or not) as learning organisations. They have the ability to place learning at the centre of their communities, challenging people's views about learning and contribute significantly to the development of a learning culture. This will ensure that learning is integrated into all aspects of everyday life, an approach to continuous improvement and citizenship, rather than something isolated or a distraction. In the industrial society, human resource management was principally focused on training and was not really involved in organisational learning, a domain that was left to operations managers. Learning management systems were the technology of choice, a system focused on managing formal training with little or no ability to support organisational or informal learning. In the knowledge economy, it is critical that human resource managers integrate organisational learning as a key component of their learning policies.

23.2   The need for a new quality framework

It is clear today that there are different and often conflicting visions of what learning quality is about (as indeed is reflected in this handbook). There may be conflicts of interest between the same categories of stakeholders as well as across different categories.

To start with, the organisation and activities of learning inevitably reflect the value systems of (the most powerful) stakeholders and society. For example, learners with a middle class background may be perfectly satisfied with the 'quality' of an elitist educational system resulting in a high failure rate for children from a less fortunate background. An elitist system has structural failure built in and is not concerned to exploit all the talents available in a community.

Although a recent study (Berry, 2004), confirming several previous studies, has found that raising the general skill levels in a country 1% leads to 1,5% increase in productivity and 2,5% in GDP growth, such research will only have an impact in a society ready to learn from facts and research and implement corrective policies and actions. An elitist society can thrive perfectly well on exclusion, nurturing a kind of "third world" – France uses the concept of "*quart monde*" – *fourth world* – to describe its inner third world. Another indicator of an exclusive society might be the general level of education of its immigrant populations; it is clear that it is certainly difficult for a country to claim to have a quality education system, when it tolerates the continued existence of a large population of unqualified immigrants.

Beyond the global context of learning policies, there are issues with even more tangible issues, such as the quality of educational resources: some resources might be recognised as 'quality' educational resources for people without disabilities, while being completely inaccessible to learners with disabilities. This time, the structural exclusion may be found in the technology being used, the development process, the competencies of the authors, the values of the publisher or accessibility policies and regulations.

Similarly, a training organisation can be certified ISO 9000, and not meet the needs of today's employment market, producing 'quality' unemployable workers. This is typically what happens in some programmes for unemployed people, where training is being used to reduce the unemployment figures rather than genuinely re-skilling and re-qualifying.

There are also still conflicting visions between those focusing on the *learning path*[84] (in reality, often *the training path*) and those focusing primarily on *learning outcomes*. Most credit systems rely on the number of study hours (centred on classroom time[85]) rarely on the ability to create meaningful outcomes. Also, someone can be perfectly competent yet denied a qualification on the basis that they have not attended the right number of courses and exams.

Moreover, although most learning occurs informally and non-formally, most quality systems are primarily focused on formal education and training – probably because this is where most of the funding goes!

In addition to fundamental issues of values, there is also the ongoing debate about quality in terms of quality control/ assurance/ management systems. Is quality about conforming to standards? Is it about simply satisfying – or delighting – the client or end-user? Is it about fostering innovation or reproducing the same good or service over and over again?

To meet the challenge of building learning quality for the 21st century, two main options are open to us: accommodation and assimilation.

Accommodation vs. Assimilation is used here metaphorically, in reference to the work of Piaget (Hatwell, 1966) on learning as being a combination of assimilation (of new facts and processes) and accommodation (changing one's representations in order to be able to interpret the new facts). In this article, *training* is understood as a process principally *externally driven* and mainly focused on *assimilation* of new rules, procedures and facts; while learning is understood as a process driven internally and mainly focused on *accommodation*.

Accommodation of quality to a learning society requires a complete rethinking of what quality is about and the modalities for implementing, supporting and verifying it. Contrary to *accommodation*, the *assimilation* process does not fundamentally rethink quality values, models or processes, but is an attempt to maintain the old order of things by introducing amendments to a mainly invariant reference framework – e.g. add an 'e-' in front of words and place 'ICT' here and there in the old framework. It is our view that the persistent use of such terms as 'open and

---

[84] Most Learning Management Systems (LMS) focus on the management of predefined "learning paths" programmed by the response to multiple choice questions (or equivalent) to give the right to move to the next section or not, reducing the learning environment to a series of inputs and tests, confusing deep reflective learning with the drill and practice used in boot camps.

[85] Making a distinction between face to face or online is not really relevant in this context.

distance *training,* rather than *learning,* in many European countries is typical of the desire to cling to the old approaches that were organisation and teacher-centred rather than learner-centred. It is as though the Lisbon agenda, the Bologna and Copenhagen process, the movement towards accreditation of prior learning, recognition of informal and non-formal learning, the e-transformation of many processes linked to education and human resource development, the massive invasion of knowledge media (as opposed to mass media) has had no impact.

One particular development in the field of knowledge, information and learning technologies has been the raise of the knowledge media (Eisenstadt, 1995), which has a major impact on the value chain of learning resources and environments. While we have developed the expertise to assess the quality of *mass media based* learning resources, the adaptation of this expertise from traditional *mass media* (e.g. print, television and radio) to digital *mass media* technology (e.g. delivery of contents through CD-ROMs, DVDs or the Internet) has been done through a simple *assimilation* process – by adding a few criteria, such as *being interoperable* or *accessible.*

Knowledge media: "Vast amounts of high quality moving graphics and sound, instantly accessible anywhere on the, er, Infobahn. [...] Now we need to discuss what goes into the multimedia: what fits on those CD-ROMs, what sits on massive file servers, what travels down the Information Superhighway? What do you call it? The conventional wisdom says that you call it 'content', and the hip view says 'bits are bits'. Both of these views are widespread, and in my view dangerous, because if we adopt either of these views we are selling ourselves tragically short. Yes, from the perspective of a Hollywood studio, 'content' is ok. And from the perspective of an editing technician, 'bits' are ok too. But its kind of like saying that Mozart wrote notes (content) and used ink (bits). What's missing in the widely-discussed convergence of telecommunications and computing is a very important third strand: the learning and cognitive sciences. This three-way convergence gives rise to what I call 'Knowledge Media'. I therefore want to raise the stakes and talk about 'knowledge' rather than 'content', and show how that relates to multimedia and the information superhighway" (Eisenstadt, 1995).

In a *knowledge media* model, where the Internet is not just used as a means of delivering pre-packaged contents but as a tool for helping learners to co-produce, co-organise, co-exploit and share knowledge – e.g. wiki-based resources, blogs or e-portfolios – the reference model for quality is certainly very different. What is important in this context is not so much the *intrinsic* quality of pre-packaged educational objects, but the quality of an environment able to foster knowledge co-construction. Reassessing learning resources that were viewed as 'quality' in the old context could lead to some radically different results in this new context. Conversely, keeping the same old quality reference framework could lead to providing objectively poor quality learning resources. The quality of *knowledge media based* resources needs a new reference framework that goes beyond the mere quality of the media and the traditional view on instructional design of *mass media-based* learning resources. A more holistic view must be taken. To those who years ago used the slogan that "content is king", we are happy to respond "context is dynasty."

While we used the difference between *mass* and *knowledge* media to illustrate the need to revise old quality frameworks (moving the focus from *contents* to *context*), the major reason for such a revision remains the move from an industrial society to a knowledge economy and learning society: the learner is now at the centre of a multidimensional learning space through an active participation in learning communities (personal and professional), learning organisations, learning territories (municipalities, regions) and society.

Fig. 23-1: Placing the learner at the centre

Learning is an active process *blended* into everyday life. "*Placing the learner at the centre*", in this context, does not mean that he/ she is the *centre of attention* of well-meaning teachers and trainers, but the *centre of production* of knowledge that occurs in a series of different contexts, involving a series of different stakeholders, from schools, teachers, parents and municipalities to peers, professionals, awarding bodies, training institutions, public authorities, employers, unions and professional bodies.

This new context will have an impact on the *qualities* (competencies) required from learners, as well as on the nature of a quality framework that should be organically linked to the different dimensions of learning: formal and informal, personal, community and organisational. This should require more than mere assimilation into the old quality framework. A new framework is probably required.

23.3   Measuring the quality of learning

While it is true that many different factors contribute to the quality of the learning experience (e.g. resources, processes and contexts), at the end of the learning process there are a series of simple indicators that will provide relevant information about the quality of the learning experience. Meaningful discussion and action to improve the quality of learning must provide evidence about:

- *Who has learned?* This can be provided by statistical information at international, national, organisational or classroom level.
- *What has been learned – and how?* What are the *learning practices*, formal, non-formal and informal? What are the instructional practices? What are the environments? What is the quality of individuals' *learning engagement and activities*? This can be provided through evidence collected by reflective practitioners and communities of practice.
- *What is the impact of the learning activities?* What are the measurable outcomes? How has the performance of individuals, organisations and society as a whole improved? Have we achieved our learning goals? This can be provided through the evidence collected in personal, organisational and community e-portfolios.

We are going to look at each of these and then consider a future-facing model for the 21st century learner.

23.3.1   Who has learned?

If we now refer to the Lisbon and Bologna agenda, and take a look at the reality of learning in Europe, it is clear that the current system is not paying sufficient attention to informal and non-formal learning opportunities. There are for example interesting statistics published by Eurostat about who is engaged in all forms of learning, formal and informal, professional or personal: the statistics shows that there are great discrepancies in the participation of citizens in learning activities across Europe (fig. 23-2).

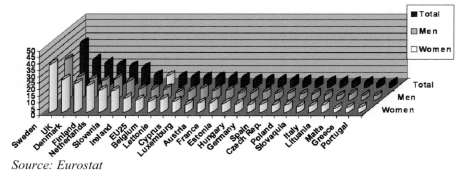

Source: Eurostat

Fig. 23-2: % of adults engaged in a training or educational activity within the 4 weeks preceding the 2002 annual poll

These discrepancies at European level can be amplified at national level. France, for example, which has a mandatory training levy, with the objective of providing professional continuing training to all, in reality has a system that increases the gap between qualified and non-qualified workers as well as between SMEs and large corporations. As the figures compiled by CEREQ (fig. 23-3), an official body studying employment and qualifications, indicate, while SMEs represent nearly 90% of employed people, very little training goes to small enterprises – what the graphic doesn't show is that men get more training than women.

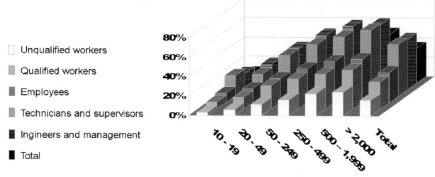

☐ Unqualified workers

▨ Qualified workers

■ Employees

▨ Technicians and supervisors

■ Ingineers and management

■ Total

Source: CEREQ, 2002

Fig. 23-3: Training in relation to qualifications and organisations' staff size in 2002

Although France has a system of continuing education that, despite the initial vision of its founders[86], expands the gap between qualified and unqualified people, it does not mean that people with no or few qualifications, or working in an SME do not learn. If they were not capable of learning, many of the SMEs would be pretty soon out of business! But this learning has not been identified or recognised until recently (2004[87]), with the development of *Validation des Acquis de l'Expérience* (Accreditation of Prior Experience) and a *Droit Individuel à la Formation* (individual training right) providing each employee with 20 hours training per year, managed by themselves.

We need to stress that France is not unique. We have taken one example in order to illustrate the need to change our approach to the organisation and validation of learning. We need to recognise that learning is not synonymous with training – people learn despite the existence of mandatory training or the existence of a training levy – and therefore, quality of *learning* can't be reduced to the quality of *training* and traditional quality systems are of little help to measure the quality of true or deep learning.

So, in order to respond to the first question about the quality of learning (Who?) it is important to take a look at the big picture, and to benchmark policies across countries and organisations in order to understand who really participates in learn-

---

[86] Nobody can doubt the goodwill of those who inspired (Jacques Delors) and voted the 1971 law on continuing education, but the facts demonstrate that creating a training levy and enshrining in law the idea of continuing education would have positive effects. It is interesting to note that, in the 90s, the Australians tried to imitate the French system of training levy, only to abandon it a few years later, recognising that far from closing the gap in education, it created even wider disparities.

[87] It is the Loi de Modernisation Sociale (Social Modernisation Law), after an unsuccessful attempt, since 1894 to offer the opportunity for Validation des Acquis Professionnels (Accreditation of Professional Experience).

ing activities, in the classroom (for formal learning) and outside (for informal and non-formal learning), in the organisation, the community, the region and the nation. It is critical that we develop statistical instruments to be able to measure beyond the obvious number of trainee hours that some countries use to establish official statistics. It is vital to be able to understand, support and value all those *other* learning activities that some say represent more than 80% of all learning.

As we shall see later, what has also changed is the increasing responsibility placed on learners to take their own learning into their own hands, as well as on society to empower individuals. This requires a new set of competencies and rights. Learning technology has a critical role to play in extending and improving learning opportunities as we now see as we consider the second measure of learning quality.

23.3.2   What has been learned – and how? The contribution of technology to quality

We turn our attention now to the issue of learning activities. How can we ensure that learners are carrying out meaningful learning activities that will help them to achieve the desired objectives? It is our view that a new approach is needed and that this is facilitated by technological advances. We have already developed the beginning of an answer for the first point. We should like now to concentrate on the second point, linking new requirements for learning with the new environment, in particular technological.

- *Learning is about transforming representations* – it is a process combining *assimilation* of new facts or procedures (training) and *accommodation* of our brain to new ideas and concepts changing our interpretation and vision of the world as well as our values (Piaget, 1975).
- *Learning is co-constructed* - all new knowledge is constructed on a foundation of prior knowledge, and this new knowledge, once inter-linked and referenced to the prior knowledge, forms a foundation of new prior knowledge. The learning brain is constantly re-organising itself by adding and subtracting information. (Salmon, 2002)
- *Learning is experiential* and explorative – learning takes place by engaging in meaningful practice; experiential learning is at the heart of the acquisition of new competencies and skills (physical and intellectual) (Kolb, 1975). The proof of having acquired such competencies is the ability to replicate them over time with the required level of performance.
- *Learning is proactive* – learners take responsibility for their own learning – the role of learning supports (teachers, trainers, mentors, coaches, etc.) is to set up the circumstances under which learners are likely to teach themselves and to encourage learners to do so. Empowerment is a key element in learners' motivation to learn and a strong determinant of the outcomes and success of learning.

- *Learning is social* – and it changes one's ability to participate into the society. Learning requires feedbacks and interaction with peers, team support, colleagues or customers. This feedback and interaction may vary in quantity and quality, but it provides a critical element for providing meaning and value to learning activities (Vygotsky, 1934).

- *Learning is reflective* – The active work of constructing a base of new knowledge by linking it to prior knowledge can be compared to receiving inventory in a warehouse. Higher order thinking and learning occurs in the lull following the active work of intake as the brain orders and reorders what it has received. The learning brain requires the periodic expanses of mental white space we refer to as reflection (Dewey, 1933).

- *Learning requires regular feedback and diagnostic* – learning requires exploration, trial, error, and sympathetic feedback. Learning is also enhanced by challenge and inhibited by threat.

- *Learning design is about empowering learners* – the function of instructional design is not to apply some predefined formula to shape contents to ease digestion of contents, but to provide an environment where learners will be able to co-construct their knowledge and skills. We have no evidence that a given "instructional chunk" yields a single identifiable "learning chunk" in the learner's brain.

- *Learning is about pleasure* – there are evidence that even the most basic learning mechanisms, such as memorisations are enhanced when associated with pleasure.

Of course, this series of statement is not new and could itself *"have been written 20 years ago"*! – even if the concepts have not been universally applied! What we now need to recognise is the need to interweave (Wenger, 2002) the different dimensions of learning: individual, community, organisational and territorial. This organic link and interweaved dimensions of learning can now be translated into a series of knowledge, information and learning technologies that elicit and support the underlying processes, enabling the emergence of new practices, in rupture with the previous ones. This should have consequences on quality models and processes – which are in fact learning processes, like the EFQM cycle – and should therefore be able to be supported and transformed by knowledge, information and learning technologies (KILT), moving from quality to e-quality, that is the e-transformation of quality assurance mechanisms.

So what would quality look like when dressed in KILT: E-quality? Initially, we need to dissociate two domains where technology will play a role in the quality of learning:

- technology as support to, transformation of the learning process – *e-learning*
- technology as support to, transformation of the quality process – *e-quality*

In order to understand the relation between *e-quality* and *quality*, we need initially to review how *e-learning* is defined in relation to *learning*.

It is our view it is regrettable that a widespread understanding of *e-learning* is that is a kind of distance *training* using digital media (online or offline). This misconception has led to the introduction of the concept of 'blended learning' as a way to correct the so-called 'mistakes' of e-learning, by adding of a portion of face to face to it.

For EIfEL, it is clear that e-learning is not only distance or online training/learning. E-learning, for example, includes e-portfolios, interactive white boards, school intranets, knowledge management systems (for organisational learning) which have nothing to do with *distance* or *blended* learning! Presented as an *enhancement of* e-learning, the concept of *blended learning* is irrelevant as it merely reinforces the initial misconceptions about learning *and* e-learning – this 'mixed' mode of training delivery has been in fact available for decades and is far from new to those who with experience of open and flexible learning.

It is also clear that we should acknowledge the fundamental difference between learning and training and use both words in a meaningful and contextualised manner. For example, we feel that one of the technologies used in education and training is improperly named "Learning Management System" (LMS), rather than "Training Management System" although most LMSs are only efficient at managing training[88] and poor at managing real learning, that is supporting authentic self-management of learning, too often obliging individuals to move in constrained predefined learning paths.

A *learning organisation* is thus certainly not a *training organisation* – although it most likely provides training to its employees – and a *learning region* (or city) (Florida, 1995) is not a region providing more training than others, but a region valuing all its assets (people, organisations, networks, associations, places, culture, history, etc.). And an e-learning region, as an extension of the concept of learning region, is certainly not a region providing "e-learning" in the limited interpretation of the term – nor "blended learning" - but a region using KILT to achieve its goal as learning region.

Richard Florida specifies his concept of the learning region by offering a comparison with "mass production regions". As far as he is concerned, "learning regions provide the crucial inputs required for knowledge-intensive economic organisation to flourish : a manufacturing infrastructure of interconnected vendors and suppliers ; a human infrastructure that can produce knowledge workers, facilitates the development of team orientation, and which is organised around long-life learning; a physical and communication infrastructure which facilitates and supports constant sharing of information, electronic exchange of data and information, just-in-time delivery of goods and services, and integration into the global economy ; and capital allocation and industrial governance systems attuned to the needs of knowledge-intensive organisations" (Maillat, Kebir, 1998).

---

[88] Poor e-training is too often based on rote memorisation (read, watch and respond to multiple choice questions) and mimicking poor educational models.

Starting from a clear understanding of e-learning, which is fundamentally different from *e-training*, we would like to discuss the relation of quality and e-learning. Is it about

- quality of e-learning? Or
- e-quality of learning?

In order to understand the difference between the two concepts, we suggest the following definitions.

E-learning: The e-Transformation of all the processes linked to individual, community, organisational and territorial learning, from education to culture, from training to human resources development and social capital development. E-learning is about using knowledge, information and learning technologies (KILT) to value the assets of an individual, a community an organisation and the society at large.

E-quality: The e-transformation of all the processes linked to quality using knowledge, information and learning technologies (KILT). E-quality is about using KILT to design, document and update standards, implement and document assessment, audit and verification processes. It is about using KILT to facilitate the contribution of all stakeholders in the different processes linked to quality.

E-quality e-learning is about using KILT to support, document and assess the e-transformation process of education, training and human resource development required to sustain learning individuals, communities, organisations and the society at large.

Back to the initial question (the difference between *e-quality learning* and *Quality e-learning*) one could say that one is focusing on the *e-transformation of quality processes* linked to learning, while the other focuses more on the *quality of the e-transformation of learning processes*. If we define quality as a learning process (stating objectives, documenting progresses, getting feedback, reflecting on what has been achieved, modifying plans, tools, standards, etc. according to what has been learned) then we could elicit a much more organic link between e-quality and e-learning. For example, the e-portfolio is at the same time a tool to support e-learning and e-quality (assessment process, individual as well as organisational, i.e. documenting what the organisation has achieved).

Of course, there are different orders of magnitude in the e-transformation of quality, from the mere integration of technologies into existing processes, to the transformation of the processes themselves. We would like to define a first level of granularity in these different levels of change.

The very first level of e-transformation of quality, could be putting the quality documentation online. This can be of course useful to maintain such documentation, making sure that everyone has access to the latest version in real time; among the advantages are reduction of maintenance and distribution costs. This cannot really be considered as innovation - no more than putting the contents of *open and flexible learning* courses online, using the Internet as a mere delivery channel instead of a CD-ROM or text books.

The next level of e-transformation of quality (e-quality) would be in supporting existing quality processes: quality assurance is about collecting evidence that is then submitted to an auditor delivering a certificate. It could be also using the Internet to manage customer service, letting customers having an asynchronous dialogue with maintenance engineers, building FAQs. There again, this not a real innovation, simply changing channels and media to support old processes.

Real innovation with e-quality starts when KILT transforms the quality process from some kind of external process to an organic process *embedded* into everyday activities, into communities and life itself, and where the power shifts from one actor to another, or when the concept of quality itself is being challenged and transformed – e.g. relaying on interactive networks of learners and citizens as an alternative to 'accreditation agencies' to deliver 'quality marks.' This is something that is now emerging where customers and users of products are building communities to share knowledge, make recommendations, etc. These kinds of services that were before provided by consumer advocacy groups through *mass media* can now use *knowledge media* to built interactive, dynamically updated information system. Search engines such as Google, new generations of tools like RSS and aggregators of blogs provide a *transformation* of the relationship between consumers as a group, as well as between consumers and providers of goods and services.

The concept of e-quality is an opportunity to move from "quality *of* learning" to "quality *for* learning" in the same way as we need to move from "assessment *of* learning" to "assessment *for* learning." The e-portfolio is one example of how technology can at the same time support *learning, assessment for learning* and the *quality* of the assessment process. E-portfolios provide an *organic link* between learning and quality, eliciting the *quality process as a learning process*. This is clearly moving one step further than the mere assessment of the quality of a course delivered on a DVD or on the Internet or assessing the competencies of teachers and trainers as was done before. For example, the quality of learning resources can be assessed from the collection of assessment from the different users, providing useful information of the value of the resource in different contexts – a resource can be excellent in a given context and a nuisance in another. Similarly, the competencies of teachers can be assessed by an external assessor, their peers and/ or their students. For example, a learner looking for a specific course, can visit the e-portfolio of the teacher and consult the e-portfolio of his/ her previous cohort of students in order to assess whether his/ her style of teaching his/ her philosophy of teaching is adapted to his/ her style. The power of social networking of e-portfolios, could transform the traditional approach to quality.

23.3.3   The 21st century e-learner

What will the 21st century e-learner look like? What will be his/ her contribution to the quality of his/ her own learning, his/ her community or organisation?

In our view, an e-learner is not someone attending an 'e-learning course', especially in the restricted definition of "online course") but someone with a deep understanding of the link between individual, organisational and community learning and who takes personal responsibility for it.

A 21st century learner is someone who 'extracts learning from everyday activities', at work and in the community, through mainly informal, non-formal, intentional, incidental or accidental learning activities, and shares his/ her learning with peers within relevant communities.

The 21st century e-learner's "responsibilities"

- Plans own learning – identifies and creates his/ her own learning opportunities; sees learning as an integral part of every-day life, e.g. "extracts learning from the workplace"; does not wait for a course to learn.
- Measures learning achieved – looks for authentic assessment, practices self-assessment, asks and provides feedback to peers – in preference to multiple choice questions and all forms of automatic testing.
- Uses all forms of learning: formal, in-formal, non-formal, incidental or accidental, professional, cultural and citizen, individual- team- or community-based, face to face and at a distance, synchronous and asynchronous.
- Looks for authentic learning experiences – meaningful and challenging, providing relevant practice producing meaningful learning outcomes and artefacts.
- Selects relevant sources of learning - books, seminars, Internet, courses, visits, interviews, travel, work, leisure, community activities; makes informed judgement on learning provision.
- Gets support for learning – gets feed-back from peers, colleagues, friends, family, manager and seeks counselling from career professionals.
- Contributes to learning communities – professional body, work colleagues, municipality, shares lessons learned with others, supports the learning of others Contributes to professional, personal and community networks; reflects on and share the lessons learned with communities (of interest, practice, professional, social, etc.).
- Value the learning gained – values his/ her personal assets: knowledge, skills, competencies, networks, etc., using relevant technology. Gets accreditation for prior learning or experience, obtains a promotion, seeks a position or job change.
- Uses relevant knowledge, information and learning technology to plan, organise, assess and reflect on his/ her own learning, e.g. e-portfolios; is information literate: finds, sorts, edits, presents, classifies, shares information; uses relevant technology to solve problems or finds people who can help.

The main competence that should be possessed by e-learners in the 21st century is their ability to develop and value their personal assets, i.e. knowledge, competencies and networks. This goes beyond the requirement for self-guided or self-directed learning. It is about the emergence of the knowledge worker and his/ her power, using knowledge, information and learning technologies to take back the control of his/ her own life and personal capital (competencies, knowledge, networks). This is probably one of the reasons for the emergence of the e-portfolio which is to personal capital what the financial portfolio is to finance.

Of course, a list of responsibilities should be balanced by an equivalent list of rights (table 23-1).

Table 23-1: The e-learner's bill of rights

	Right	Learners have the right to
1.	Access to learning	open and equal access to education, training and other learning opportunities
2.	Information on learning provision	full and accurate information on learning provision
3.	Learning guidance	open information and guidance on all aspects of adult education, opportunities and rights
4.	Learning Administration	fast, efficient and courteous administration
5.	Learning support staff	be supported by qualified and competent staff who are actively engaged in their continuing professional development
6.	Learning environment	a suitable, accessible and state of the art learning environment facilitating peer support
7.	E-portfolio	an e-portfolio to plan, and manage learning, and value one's assets within communities
8.	Learning activities	learning which is relevant to learners' lives
9.	Learning resources	appropriate learning resources to facilitate self-directed learning
10.	Occupational standards	accurate and up-to-date occupational standards
11.	Planning learning	participate or be appropriately represented in planning learning activities
12.	Prior learning	prior learning recognition
13.	Learning induction	appropriate induction
14.	Learning strategies	a personalised and balanced range of learning and teaching strategies
15.	Self-directed learning	personal control over the learning experience
16.	Monitoring and assessment	a fair and transparent assessment process
17.	Feedback & complaints	a fair and effective feedback and complaints procedure

Source: EIfEL, 2005

23.4   Linking learning individuals, communities, organisations and territories for quality

Alongside our earlier question, *Who has learnt?* We should also be asking who has contributed to the definition of the learning policies. Learning is not just the consumption of a service decided by others, but a system where all stakeholders, including the learner and the citizen, directly or indirectly (through representatives, trade unions, associations or lobby groups) influencing the policies at local, regional and national levels.

Without leadership, without strategy, without knowing into which direction to move, no real learning can happen, therefore no *learning quality* is possible. Learning quality at local or regional level starts with leadership, based on partnership with citizens, learning and professional communities, providers of education and learning as well as businesses. Learning communities are at the heart of the idea of a learning territory, whose mission is not to provide more education or training, but to value all its assets: individuals (e.g. competencies, expertise, talents, and networks), organisations, communities, associations, networks, historic, natural and cultural patrimonies, etc.

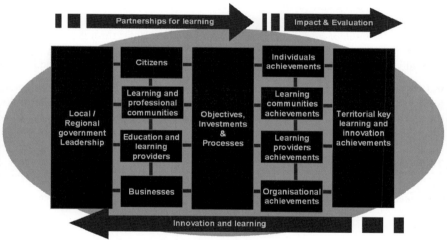

Source: SEEL, adapted from the EFQM model

Fig. 23-4: Quality model for a territory

A learning territory (city, region, community) is the place providing a social context to learning, even to the formal learning happening within a classroom. The 'quality' of the education taking place in an educational institution is intimately linked to the ability of a territory to provide a meaningful context to this learning through interactions which go beyond the annual school field trip or the student work placement. This involves the education of learners as citizens understanding the complexity of the interactions between the different levels of learning and their ability to contribute, at their levels, as pupil, student, active or retired worker, to the policies of the organisations they belong to, in cooperation with the people with whom they interact within various communities.

This leads us to observe again that learning is not primarily about *content*, but about *context*, the ability for an individual (resp. organisation, community or territory) to take control over its learning environment. Learning to learn is not just a *psychological* issue (e.g. what are my learning styles) but a *sociological* one as well, the ability of one individual to contribute actively and consciously to learning organisations, learning communities and a learning society at large (Wenger).

We see this not as an idealistic vision, but an extremely practical approach required for today's education and training (in the sense of 'creating the conditions for learning') that can be translated into operational activities:

- *Linking individual and community learning* (schools): there are many opportunities for children to contribute actively to the resolution of local (or global) problems, sharing their talents with their community making an extended environment (beyond the school walls) be their active learning environment.
- *Linking individual and organisational learning*: through documenting professional practice, linking with professional networks and associations, professionals can bring into their organisation the knowledge developed by a larger community.
- *Linking individual and professional community learning*: through reflection on their practice, professionals can share knowledge in their community, demonstrate informed practice, contribute to the evolution of professional standards.

Put into the context of articulating individual, community, organisational and territorial learning, here is a series of indicators for an approach to learning that links the different dimensions of learning (individual, community, organisation, territory and society).

Table 23-2: Dimensions of learning

	Who	What	How
Individual	% of time spent learning (formal, informal, non-formal)	How what I have learned has changed my life as citizen, worker, spouse, etc.?	What are my preferred learning styles?
Programme	% of individuals who have achieved successfully the programme	What is the impact of the programme on the organisation's performance?	What are the teaching and learning methods used?
Community (professional)	% of professionals engaged in a community and continuing professional development	What are the emerging practices elicited by the community?	How do communities support reflective and informed practice?
Organisation	% of staff engaged in learning activities	Development/ adaptation learning ratio	How is informal and non-formal learning recognised?

	Who	What	How
Community (city, region)	% of citizens actively engaged in associations, clubs, networks	% population registered in adult learning centres culture centres/ popular universities	Mentoring schemes, community centres, public and mobile libraries
Society	% of citizens and workers engaged at any time in learning activities	Cultural/ professional learning ratio	% of qualifications delivered through accreditation of prior learning

The study of the three basic questions about learning (Who?, What? and How?) shows that there are great discrepancies across countries[89], some still demonstrating a provider-driven approach, while others develop a more holistic approach to learning, including the development of local adult community and cultural centres, popular universities, etc. The emergence of a learning society should elicit converging factors.

23.5   Conclusion for an organic approach to quality

The emergence of a learning society and knowledge economy requires the transformation of the old quality reference framework. This transformation cannot be a mere adaptation of the old framework, but a radical transformation based on the new political, economical, sociological and technological context.

This empowerment of individuals through technologies has transformed the nature of the relations between learners and learning support staff, the learning employee and her employer and the learning citizen and his learning communities. The pervasive presence of, and ubiquitous access to, knowledge technologies provide the foundations for a seamless learning environment, linking individual, community, organisational and territorial learning, recognising to a fuller extent that learning occurs in context, learning is active, learning is social, learning is reflective. So is quality – and e-quality!

---

[89] A European project (OSMOSYS) is currently studying those questions through the comparative analysis of adult learning centres in Europe (www.osmosys.se).

24 Myths and realities in learner oriented e-learning-quality

Ulf-Daniel Ehlers

University of Duisburg-Essen, Germany

The article describes the concept of learner oriented quality development for e-learning in various educational sectors. Learner orientation is viewed as a necessity rather than an option for quality development in e-learning. Learners' quality concepts are introduced as the reference point for negotiation processes between the stakeholders in a quality development process. Participative environments are viewed as the future challenge – rather than following concepts which view quality development as an isolated activity of single actors in educational organisations. As a solution for this challenge a new concept of participative quality development which involvers all stakeholders is suggested. Participation is here combined with negotiation to find common objectives for quality development. Four questions are answered in particular: What is learner orientation? Why is it important? What do learners think about quality? How can learner orientation in quality development be achieved in a participative way?

24.1 Learner orientation: Myth or reality in an European quality debate

It has always been the dream of researchers and developers of e-learning systems to build a system which automatically takes into account all factors relevant to a high quality learning experience. At the same time the reality of today's e-learning proves different. Twigg (2001) puts the finger on it by pointing out: „All too frequently, even innovative institutions fall back on a one-fits-all approach [...] forgetting that students are different and have different needs" (Twigg 2001 in Schulmeister 2004). It is this field in which the debate of a learner related quality development is set.

Although learner orientation is a widely accepted principle, the quality debate is often focussing on other aspects. Therefore it seems to be legitimate to ask the question why a learner oriented approach is important at all. Schulmeister (2004) reports findings which show that the diversity and the differences – in motivation and anxiety – amongst students[90] are highly influential on learning processes and outcomes. These differences are most likely rooted in different experiences, attitudes, and approaches towards learning. He concludes that "disregarding the diversity of students may result in failure" (ibid: 2). Regarding *learning styles* and *cognition* he emphasises the importance to treat students as individuals rather than as a homogenous group (ibid: 3) and argues that one of the most severe errors made in e-learning today, is the neglect of the diversity of students and the choice of a learning model that does not allow differentiation and learner oriented learning.

However, learner orientation, on the other hand, is not meant to base e-learning-arrangements purely on *learner satisfaction* and *learners' wishes* and *preferences* – apparently there is no connection between pure satisfaction scores and learning outcomes (Sloan-C, 2003). At the same time the number of variables of student diversity and their interactions is too high, fitting teaching methods to learning methods has no sound basis in research and there is no empirical evidence telling us which instructional methods are most suitable for which individual attitudes. Also, the gap between theoretical assumptions and pragmatic decisions when designing learning environments and when teaching, cannot be bridged by simple deduction, but is subject to norms and value judgments (ibid.) in the learning and also in the teaching situation.

The field of learner oriented quality development is still an open debate. So far, it is unclear in which learner variables/ characteristics have which impact on learning. From a scientific point of view, the concept of learner orientation therefore remains in the dark. Quality certificates claiming organisations compliance to learners' requirements (e.g. the German Certificate LQW II) have to be aware of that, and have to show that this is not rooted only in trendy debates.

Despite the educational reality and the uncertainty of how the concept of learner orientation can be put into practice, a close look at the European educational debate reveals that Europe is completely learner oriented in its educational philosophy. All official policy documents follow a modern constructive rhetoric and take on the leitmotiv of a competent acting individual, developing skills and competencies in a self-organised manner for the active participation in the "knowledge society"[91]. For the sector of higher education this can be seen in the Bologna declaration (European Comission, 1999), for the field of vocational education and training this can be derived from the Copenhagen declaration (Euro-

---

[90] The study was set in the field of motivation and anxiety towards learning statistics in university courses.

[91] The terminology for the transformation of society into a knowledge based, information based, media based society are divers. There are constantly new concepts which show that the industrial age has come to an end: „Global Society" (Rost 1996), „Knowledge Society" (Stehr 1994), „Media Society" (Mettler von Meiborn 1994) or „Information Society" (Bühl 1995). They all focus on one and the same phenomenon which is described as „kowledge Society" in the article, as it is elaborated in the theory of knowledge Society by Peter Drucker (1969), Daniel Bell (1973) and Nico Stehr (1994). This theoretical approach is especially interesting for education because it focuses not only on scientific knowledge but emphasises the rising importance of knowledge as a basis for social interaction and relations.

pean Commission, 2002c) and for schools this is discussed in al European countries after the PISA results hit the ground.

It is the expressed goal also in most of today's mission statements and educational philosophies of professional staff working in the educational field to put the learner in the centre of attention, resp. in the drivers seat. No actor in the field of education, be it on the policy level, the administrative level, in the field of pedagogical practice as well as in educational science is taken seriously in the debate anymore, when failing to mention this point as the basic principal of the presented activity or concept.

However – there are as many opinions as to what learner orientation actually is, as there are stakeholders promoting it. It is neither clear what learner orientation exactly means, how it can be put in practice and thus if it is taken as the basis of educational offers often remains unclear. Learner orientation can be seen a one myth of educational reality today, often quoted and less often achieved[92]. The article aims at bringing light into the debate. Four questions are focussed on:

1. What is learner-oriented quality development and which theoretical implications are suitable to ground the debate newly?
2. What are reasons in literature and educational reality to follow the model of learner-orientation in the quality debate rather than to be provider-centred or technology-centred?
3. What do learners think about quality? What are learners' quality conceptions? And how can a research agenda for learner oriented quality development look like?
4. How can learner orientation in quality development be achieved in a participative way?

24.2   Learner oriented quality development: Impact on the learning process

There is no theory for "educational quality" so far,[93] and thus no theoretical definition of the concept *learner oriented quality*. However, there are theoretical approaches to the question what successful learning is. It is useful to have a look at these concepts in order to be able to define the topic of learner oriented quality in a more concise way. The following account of a *subjective learning theory* allows a concise description of aspects and factors of learner oriented quality development.

---

[92] The survey "E-Learning in Europe – Results and Recommendations, Thematic Monitoring under the Leonardo Da Vinci-Programme" (Nationale Agentur Bildung für Europa 2005) even comes to the conclusion that the majotity of European e-learning projects (56%) are technology driven, as opposed to 44% characterised as learner oriented.

[93] Sometimes the lack of theory for educational quality is substituted by the debate on competencies – on the learner side, or a discussion on professionalism – on the teachers side. However, there are theories which a "quality theory" could be grounded on, like learning theories, evaluation models, socio-educational theories, etc.

24.2.1   What is learner orientation in e-learning? A definition attempt

Klaus Holzkamp's subject-scientific approach to learning (Holzkamp, 1993) is suitable to bring light into how a learner oriented quality concept could be conceptualised. It emphasises that learning from a subjective point of view is not considered enough in previous learning theories. He concludes that the learner is not enough represented as a self-directed individual in learning theoretical approaches so far. According to his opinion, behaviouristic and cognitivistic approaches view learning as an externally controlled process, and that learning in traditional learning theory is not viewed from a *learners subjective perspective* (ibid: 14). It is obvious that this is also the reason for the lack of theories elaborating the idea of quality for learning from a subjective point of view.

According to Holzkamp, learning activities are mostly conceptualised as an *impertinence* for the learning subject – and learning and teaching are seen as directly dependant on each other. Consequently, learning takes place best if a teacher supplies learning activities and materials and/ or the curriculum is institutionally organised. In such approaches it is theoretically not explainable *why* an individual should learn out of ones own motivation and will. The perspective of the learning subject is systematically denied.

Holzkamp suggests a different approach. He views learning from the subjective point of view of the individual learner: Accordingly humans make their world accessible in an intentional way and acquire it from their own perspective. Reality is interpreted from their own point of view against the background of their experiences and intentions (ibid: 21). Subject form a "centre of intention" and experience others as well as "centres of intention" with their own perspective-related viewpoint. From this point of view, the world is interpreted as significantly and meaningful. These meanings are turned into „propositions for actions" on which activities and decisions are based (ibid: 26). "Learning", in his approach, is represented as "action which differentiates itself from other actions by its goal to extend ones own control possibilities" (ibid.).

At this point the parallels between a subjective theory of *learning* and quality development from a learners' perspective becomes obvious: if learning takes place and is judged against individual propositions then also the assessment of the *quality* of a learning process takes place against the background of these propositions. It can be assumed that these propositions determine the individual learners' (quality) requirements because they determine the demands for learning to realise the propositions. If learners have the possibility to assess a learning situation – in our case an e-learning-arrangement – they will do this against the background of their individual propositions, e.g. the intention to extend their competences in a certain field.

Since it can be assumed as safe that the propositions of learners are heterogeneous – individually different – quality development according to the principal „one for all" does not seem to be feasible anymore.

To define a *learner oriented quality concept* means therefore to take the learners motivation, cognitive and personal situation/ context as the basis for the assessment of learning scenarios – and not 'objective'/ external criteria. Objectivity in this sense has no relevance for learning quality, because learning is a process deeply rooted in the subjective situation/ context and the requirements and propositions of the learning individuals[94].

The problem at this point is an economical one: If learner oriented quality is defined in this way, then a variety of learning scenarios for the same course might be needed to fulfil the divers' demands of learners' individual learning propositions. How can this be done in a realistic way? Today there is no answer to this question. It is the challenge of quality research to find methods and ways how to take the learner's requirements as a starting point for the design and provision of learning scenarios. Schulmeister (2004) argues here in the direction of open learning environments (OLEs) which allow learners to explore their own learning path – and thus gain an individualised learning experience according to their individual demands.

Of course it can be argued that learning is not always taking place on basis of free individual chosen propositions but also in "forced", prescribed compulsory environments (e.g. in schools). The assessment of learning arrangements would then also take place on basis of not of individual propositions but rather of externally defined propositions, because the objectives are defined from the outside. Holzkamp (1993) takes this into account and differentiates between two kinds of learning: defensive learning and expansive learning. Defensive learning is a learning mode which takes place under the threat of sanctions. Under the threat of sanctions learning can be pretended or it comes to defensive learning. That means that the learner then tries to overcome the given problem through learning but tries to get it accomplished with as little effort as possible.

For the definition of a subjective quality concept, on the contrary, the concept of expansive learning is more suitable. Expansive learning starts with a perception of a discrepancy between what I would like to do and what I am able to do. Due to individual propositions it appears meaningful to extend the control possibilities in order to master a specific task or action. Thus an interest in learning develops. The learner perceives his/ her current abilities as being not sufficient for the current task. This perception of self inadequacy is called 'experience of discrepancy'. Learning is not initiated by instructors in this case. Learning is initiated because a current learning object evolves from a potential learning object due to an experience of discrepancy. This releases an 'emotional condition of inadequacy' (Holzkamp, 1993, p. 214). Such an experience is the basis for learning motivation. In order to evolve into expansive learning, the learner must anticipate that the 'extension of control' is attainable through learning. If the necessary learning effort is appropriate, it is reasonable to learn expansively in order to solve the problem. According to this thesis, namely that each person acts on reasonable basis, learn-

---

[94] For an account of the debate of the concepts of "objectivity" and "subjectivity" in science see Ehlers 2004.

ing follows as a necessity. The willingness to accept adversities and even setbacks is higher than with defensive learning. Expansive learning is to this extent more effective than defensive learning.

As a basis for learner oriented quality approaches and strategies the subject-scientific approach to learning appears to be more suitable than objective assumptions because it can be assumed as safe that the motivation and personal situation for learning is highly heterogeneous, especially in adult learning. On basis of Holzkamp's theoretical approach, learning is thus a process which is rooted in subjective motives and in each individual context. A learner oriented quality concept has to take this into account for the definition of quality.

A look at most of today's concept of teaching reveals the consequences which a learner oriented quality concept points at: It is widely believed that there is a direct connection between good teaching and good learning. However, Siebert (1985) points out that teaching aims can be abused if they include the idea that learning can be completely planned, that learning processes are determinable by instructors, and that learning results are quantifiable (ibid: 67). Holzkamp (1993) disagrees with this "fiction of administrative planability" of learning processes as well. It is denied in this viewpoint that subjective reasons could motivate learning and learning is thus reduced to 'Teaching equals Learning'. This Fallacy of Teaching=Learning holds that one hour of teaching would have the effect of one hour of learning (ibid: 397). This idea ignores subjective interests of learning. Learning output must be planable. The initiation of expansive, and therefore more effective, learning however, is subject to the coincidence of experiences of discrepancy and school can not want to promote expansive learning.

A learner oriented quality concept thus means to take into account that the assessment of learning environments takes pace on basis of individual propositions. This means from a learner's point of view quality of e-learning would be a judgement of how suitable an e-learning-environment is designed to help them overcome their personal experience of discrepancy through learning.

Here, a paradox can be noted: If a learning scenario is provided only according to the wishes a learner has then – it can be argued – it is not possible for the learner to go beyond the borders of what he knows so far – to develop beyond his limitations. This is one main question of today's pedagogical practice which has remained unanswered so far – empirically and theoretically: How can a learner be guided in his/ her self-development process, resp. self-guided learning process, by external guidance? (Can you educate someone to freedom?) It is the well-known change of the role of a teacher as "sage on the stage" to the "guide by the side" which is needed, to accomplish this challenge, and which is addresses inmost of the modern constructivist rhetoric[95]. Teachers in this understanding take on the

---

[95] Since the 1990s the constructive approach is the „newcomer" of didactical theory (Olberg 2004, 123). Constructivist approaches claim a new approach and at the same time present ideas to integrate it into the practical work. Meanwhile there are a lot publications about constructivist pedagogy and education. For the German speaking community H. Siebert (1994, 1999, 2003), E. von Glasersfeld (1996) as well as K. Müller (1996), E. Kösel (1997) and K. Reich (1996, 2002) can be listed as protagonists of the constructivist debate. The english speaking debate can be followed in works of T.M. Duffy und D.H. Jonassen (1992), T.M. Duffy u.a. (1993), K. Tobin (1993) and L.P. Steffe/ J. Gale (1995).Critical

role of facilitators. It demands for a pedagogical model which allows the learner to first develop his/ her own questions and then develops solutions him-/ herself in an exploratory manner (the connection to Schulmeister (2004) and his concept of Open Learning Environments is as well suitable here).

The relation between instruction and construction remains unclear in today's pedagogical practice and is everyday filed by pragmatic activities of teachers in schools and universities. However it remains unclear how the two – instruction/ teaching and construction/ learning – can form an alliance. Mandl and Reinmann-Rothemeier (1995) point out that construction and instruction can not be realised according to the "all or nothing" principle. Learning requires always motivation, interest and activity on the learner's side. Learning is thus always constructive and is has to be the utmost goal of every teaching to allow and stimulate construction processes for learners. On the other hand learning can be improved through the "guide by the side". Mandl and Reinmann-Rothmeier emphasise therefore that learning is also interactive and that teaching has the central task to support learners and to help them with instruction (Mandl, Reinmann-Rothmeier 1995, p. 52), (Wellenreuther, 2004, p. 69).

Taking into account the subjective theory of learning from Holzkamp and the paradox of instruction and construction, a learner oriented quality concept can be described as follows: Learner oriented quality development means to take the personal, mental situation as well as the learners propositions as the reference point for the decision which have to be made in the design and delivery process for e-learning-environments. It includes enabling learners to have discrepancy experiences and to guide learners (instructional component) in their own construction processes (construction component).

24.2.2   Four plus one reasons for learner orientation

Why is a learner oriented quality concept in today's quality debate important? The discussion going on around education in Europe reveals a discrepancy between a post-modern, constructivist and learner-oriented rhetoric on the one hand, and the reality of e-learning provision on the other hand. However, the debate about the relevance of learner orientation is not only a myth but good reasons can be identified which make learner orientation in the quality debate a necessity rather than an option. There are four good reasons for learner orientation which can be identified from the debate:

1. Economic Developments
2. Pedagogical Concepts
3. Development of Society
4. E-learning-related factors

A fifth reason for learner orientation is the notion of *co-production* of the learning

---

and opposing voices can be found in works of A.M. Kuhl (1993), C. Diesbergen (1998) und E. Terhart (1999).

process between the learner and the learning environment (resources, teachers, materials, other learners, goals/ objectives, curriculum, social learning context, etc.). It can be seen as a general concept which in the sector of education and social services (e.g. the health sector) in general can be observed as more and more important. It goes beyond the pure notion of customer or consumer orientation. In fact the term "customer" and "consumer" do not describe the active participation requirement in a co-produced educational process. Fendt (2000) uses the analogy of persons buying a car. To transfer the concept of co-production from the educational field to the 'market' terminology would mean that before buying it, they would have to help produce it, and then afterwards the quality would be highly varying.

The 'quality' of person-related social services is understood as a social relationship, i.e. it cannot be unilaterally defined and validated, but is seen as a result of negotiation and compromise of those involved in the service process (Ehlers, 2004). Due to their different positions, those involved in the process – users, professionals, management/ organisation and government/ society – have divergent criteria with regard to the 'quality' of services. What is defined as "good" quality is the result of disputes based on differing interests in the course of a negotiation process. From a service-theoretical perspective a new orientation is increasingly discernible, which is also reflected in further education: the 'addressees' of social services – i. e. the learners – are seen as co-producers, who use these services as part of their respective strategies for coping with life (cf. 2004, Pollitt 1998). Therefore the lasting practical value of services for the user is a highly important quality criterion in the service process. Applied to the education sector, this would refer to the practical value of the acquired knowledge, skills and competences.

The concept of co-production strengthens the influence of the learner for the definition of quality in education. In addition to that, Gnahs (1998, 1999) states four more reasons which lead to a higher responsibility in the definition and negotiation process on quality in education.

1. Economic: An increase in the personal financial contribution of learners is anticipated, either directly, by financing private further training measures, or indirectly, e.g. by sacrificing spare-time to take part in company organised advanced training or further education.
2. Pedagogically and didactically, this finds expression in less instructional-based and more experience-based pedagogy. The change is based on a shift from behaviour-oriented learning theories to cognitive learning models and from instructional approaches to constructivist approaches. That means less overall standardisation and more situation and subject orientation.
3. On a social level: One reason for this development is the evolution of a knowledge society. The amount of knowledge available world-wide is currently doubling every 4-5 years. The American sociologist Richard Sennet (1998) anticipates that an American college student will change his job eleven times in the course of his professional life and completely change his knowledge base three times. This process of life-long learning cannot be standardised because it is different for each individual. The challenge for e-

learning is to offer learning arrangements which fit individual requirements as closely as possible.

4. E-learning: A fourth reason for increasing learner responsibility in defining quality in e-learning lies in the special features of e-learning itself (for a detailed account see Baumgartner 1997). The special features of networked learning (with regard to access, needs structure and starting situation) are capable of providing individualised (in the sense of "tailored", not in the sense of "isolated"!) learning scenarios. They enable an orientation of learning offers towards needs – which also demands for a more learner oriented quality. A consistent learner orientation in all processes arising in the production and provision of e-learning-services thus becomes imperative.

24.3   Learners' quality concepts on stake

Quality development always means to negotiate values and to apply them to educational processes. For a learner oriented quality approach this means to find out learners subjective quality concepts, their requirements, personal contexts in order to take these as a starting point for quality development. It has to be emphasised again that this is not meant to plainly "do as learners wish". It is rather important to take into account their motivational situation, their learning biographical experiences, their preferred learning mode for e-learning, to base courses on their pre-knowledge, to name only a few factors. The greatest misunderstanding with learner-orientation is to forget the notion of co-production which emphasises to involve *all* factors relevant for a learning environment, as there are the curriculum, the learning goals or the physical or social learning environment. A learner orientation thus means to take the learners situation, references and knowledge about his or her situation as the reference point for the didactical, technological and other organisational decisions when designing a learning environment – but not the only guideline.

In order to learn what subjective concepts of quality can look like the results of a comprehensive study in this field are given below. The so called "model of learner oriented quality" can be taken and used as orientation for the construction of learning environments.

24.3.1   Quality from a learner's perspective

The presented survey 'Quality from a learners´ perspective'[96] analyses quality from exactly this point of view. In this article, the main results are presented, for a detailed description see Ehlers (2004b). Two goals are being aimed at: First, the research is concerned with the question which dimensions are constituting quality in e-learning from a learner's perspective, i.e. which quality aspects, dimensions or criteria are important for learners? Secondly, quality is no longer viewed as a concept in which the same quality approaches or quality criteria apply to all learners alike, but rather where different learners have different preferences regarding quality in e-learning. The empirical results clearly confirm this hypothesis. For the first time, the research project makes available an empirical based classification of subjective quality concepts in e-learning. Thus now there is an empirical base for learner focussed quality development in e-learning. It shows clearly that a learner focussed quality concept has to be more comprehensive than just focussing on aspects of pedagogical or technological interface design.

Subjective quality concepts

The so-called "subjective model of quality" is organised in a three level structure. 153 subjective quality factors form the basis of the empirical model. They are the result of an in-depth oral interview inquiry with learners. This *inventory* formed the basis of a standardised online survey. The result allowed to structure the factors into 30 dimensions of quality in e-learning, by using a Principal Component Analysis. The dimensions represent bundles of factors that – empirically – belong together (correlate). On the third level the resulting 30 dimensions are then structured into seven fields of subjective quality according to thematic resemblance (fig. 24-1).

The dimensions are the result of a principal component analysis (PCA). This method allows reducing the variety of many factors (153) to few powerful bundles of factors – or: dimensions – that can explain the differences in the quality preferences of the learners. It is important to notice that the 30 preference dimensions are not all equally important to learners. They rather form a grid of dimensions that *can* be of relevance to a specific learner. For each learner the described dimensions therefore are likely to be of a different importance for quality in e-learning. The dimensions thus form the line along which learners (can) differ in their quality preferences.

Each of the 30 dimensions represents a set of criteria of learners preferences

---

[96] The survey used qualitative data as well as quantitative data. The connection between these different approaches – also known as the methodological concept of triangulation (cf. Treumann 1998) – enables researchers to gain a more in-depth insight into the field of subjective quality preferences. The survey was conducted in two phases: First a qualitative inventory was gathered from interview data of 56 interviews with learners who had considerable experience in the field of e-learning. This inventory formed the bases for a quantitative research phase in which 2000 learners answered a questionnaire on their quality preferences for e-learning (n=1994). The data were then analysed using multivariate statistics – principal component analytical and cluster analytical methodology.

that are clustered to a dimension on basis of empirical evidence. The following overview describes the 30 dimensions of subjective quality. They are presented according to the 7 fields of quality they each belong to.

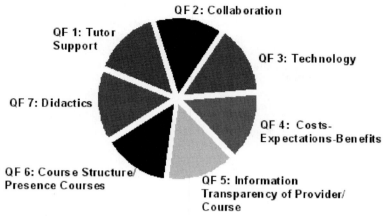

Source: cf. Ehlers, 2004b

Fig. 24-1: Model of subjective quality requirements

Quality field 1: Tutor support

In this field quality preferences are represented that learners have towards the communication and cooperation with a tutor. The survey shows that tutor support is very important for learners in general – regardless their other preferences: Between 74,4% and 97,7% of learners in the different preference groups (fig. 24-2) value tutor support in general as 'important' or 'very important'. However – there are great differences between the learners as to *how* the tutor support should be performed. Their preferences differ along the following dimensions:

Table 24-1: Dimensions 1 - 5

Dimension 1: Interaction	This dimension relates to communication and interaction between tutors and learners. Especially important for this interaction is the aspect of a bi-directional interaction: The learner does not only want to receive a tutorial feedback but wants to give feedback to the tutor as well.
Dimension 2: Moderation of Learning Processes	The dimension expresses the preference for an active moderation of learning processes through the tutor in a communicative manner.
Dimension 3: Learner vs. Content Centredness	Learners vary in their preferences of tutorial behavior along the lines of a rather learner oriented interaction style, referring to their personal learning process on the one hand, and a more content/ subject matter oriented interaction and communication processes between tutors and themselves on the other hand.
Dimension 4: Individualised Learner Support	This dimension relates to a form of tutor support that focuses especially on the learners' situation and supports – apart from the course topic – the learner with additional information according to his/ her interests.
Dimension 5: Goal- vs. Development Centredness	This differentiation describes a tutorial behavior that focuses primarily on the course goals on the one hand and a more learner oriented tutoring style that supports the personal development of learners' learning- and social competences.

Learners do not only vary according to their preference sets in regard to tutorial communication and cooperation performances but also in the kind of media they wish to use for getting in contact with tutors.

Table 24-2: Dimensions 6 - 8

Dimension 6: Traditional Communication Media	Telephone, Fax, Letter (mail)
Dimension 7: Synchronous Communication Media	Video conferencing, Chat
Dimension 8 Asynchronous Communication Media	E-mail, Discussion Forums

Quality field 2: Cooperation and communication

This field contains quality requirements that learners express towards a learning scenario concerning the communication and cooperation environment with other learners, in learning groups, with experts or the tutor.

Table 24-3: Dimensions 9 - 10

Dimension 9: Social Cooperation	The cooperation sequences in the online course should especially focus on the aspect of social interactions, i.e. online discussions, group activities, face-to-face communication in presence phases.
Dimension 10: Discursive Cooperation	The cooperation sequences in the online course should especially focus on the integration of discursive course settings and controversial topics. Not the social aspect is emphasised here but the active knowledge creation in argumentative settings.

Quality field 3: Technology

The field of technical requirements can also be important to learners in regard to the described three dimensions. Technical requirements however seem to have the status of *hygienic factors*. That means that if technical requirements are fulfilled they do not raise the perceived quality very much – as they are taken for granted. Yet, if the expected technical standards are not met the learners quality assessment decreases.

Table 24-4: Dimensions 11 - 13

Dimension 11: Adaptivity and Personalisation	It is important that the learning platform has the capability adapting to the users settings and provides the possibility "starting where the user logged off last time". (This does not relate to learning styles or learning paths.)
Dimension 12: Synchronous Communication possibilities	The Platform should provide the possibility of synchronous communication (Chat, Video Conferencing).
Dimension 13: Availability of contents (technical)	The content should be available in different formats. It should be possible for the user to save course material on his/ her home computer.

Quality field 4: Costs - expectations - benefit

Learner's cost-benefit assessment is one factor that determines their quality judgment. It can be seen in close relation to the expectations they have towards a course setting. The cost and effort that learners have to assign to the learning experience has to be in a subjective adequate relation to the benefits and the outcome.

Table 24-5: Dimensions 14 - 18

Dimension 14: **Expectation of Individualisation and Need Orientation**	This factor expresses the expectation towards online learning that it is flexible (time wise) and individualised in the course structure regarding to content and support.
Dimension 15: **Individual Non-Economic Costs**	The most important cost category is the effort it takes to learn motivated and concentrate on the course although it is an individualised learning scenario.
Dimension 16: **Economic Costs**	The most important costs are the financial costs.
Dimension 17: **Practical Benefits**	Learners expects a practical benefit for their every day working life.
Dimension 18: **Interest in Course and Media Usage**	The user is interested in the course not only because of the course topic but also because of interest in online learning and the usage of the internet.

Quality field 5: Information transparency

Another field of quality preferences covers the information requirements learners have before starting a course, and about the institution/ organisation which is offering the course. It contains the provision of formal and standard information as well as individualised counselling on course contents, learning methodology or technical advise.

Table 24-6: Dimensions 19 - 21

Dimension 19: **Counseling, Advise**	Counseling and advise before learners enter an e-learning-course can be an important dimension of quality.
Dimension 20: **Organisational Information**	It can be of importance to learners that they can not only access information about the course they want to take but also about issues concerning the course certificate, the tutor's qualification and the organisation that offers the course.
Dimension 21: **Information About Course Goals and Contents**	This dimension expresses the importance for learners to access detailed information about the course they are going to take (e.g. a prototype schedule).

Quality field 6: Structure of the learning scenario

This field contains learners' requirements concerning the structure of an e-learning-course. Learners' quality preferences clearly show that presence lessons as part of an e-learning-course are of high importance to certain groups of learners, whereas others do not value them as important. The dimensions of this particular quality field summarise the functions theses presence courses have from a learners' perspective.

Table 24-7: Dimensions 22 - 24

Dimension 22: Personal Support of Learning Processes	This dimension specifies the importance of a personal and individualised course support structure in form of presence courses.
Dimension 23: Introduction to Technical Aspects and to the Content	It can be of importance to learners to have an introduction in form of a presence workshop to important technical and content aspects of the course.
Dimension 24: Tests and Exams	An important function in presence phases can be the possibility to take exams and tests.

Quality field 7: Didactics

The survey shows that a lot of quality preferences that were analysed fall into this category. It covers the content, learning goals, methods and materials. Experienced e-learners are often very precise in their requirements concerning the didactical setting of an e-learning course.

Table 24-8: Dimensions 25 - 30

Dimension 25: Background Material	This dimension expresses the importance of having access to background materials on the course topics.
Dimension 26: Multimedia Enriched Presentation Material	For certain groups of learners it is important to use materials that are enriched by multimedia and use not only one but several media resources (audio, visual, movies, texts, etc.).
Dimension 27: Structured and Goal Oriented Course Material	An important quality dimension can be to structure the course material in a goal oriented way.
Dimension 28: Support of Learning	This dimension contains criteria that express that the course should enable users to gain learning literacy and become more skilled in their life long learning competencies.
Dimension 29: Feedback on Learning Progress	Tests and exams should be integrated into the course material to get feedback on the learning progress.
Dimension 30: Individualised Tasks	The tasks should be especially designed to fit the learner's needs and goals.

Learners quality preferences: Individual – but still manageable

As shown, learners' quality needs can be described in terms of their preferences towards each of the 30 specified dimensions. Using this grid of dimensions, it is easily possible to construct an individual preference profile for each learner. Every learner has a specific position on each of the previously described dimensions.

Der Individualist	**Der Ergebnisorientierte**
(N=328)	(N=235)
▪ **Inhaltsorientiert**	▪ **eigenständig & zielorientiert**
▪ Inhaltsbezogene Qualitätsansprüche ❍	▪ Individualisierung ☺: Standardangebote
▪ Individualisierte Angebote ❍	▪ Arbeitsintegriertes Lernen ❍
▪ Didaktische Strukturierung ❍	▪ Instrumentelle Zweckorientierung ❍
▪ Selbstgesteuertes Lernen ❍	▪ Lern- und Medienkompetenz ❍
▪ Präsenzveranstaltungen, Interaktion- und Kommunikation ☺	▪ Präsenzveranstaltungen, Interaktion- und Kommunikation ☺

Der Pragmatiker	**Der Avantgardist**
(N=293)	(N=392)
▪ **Bedarfsorientiert**	▪ **Interaktionsorientiert**
▪ Individualisierte Angebote ☺	▪ Diskussion/ Kommunikation ❍
▪ Tutorielle Betreuung sachorientiert ❍	▪ Tutorielle Betreuung lernerorientiert ❍
▪ Außerökonomische Kosten ❍	▪ Medien/ Technik avantgardistisch ❍
▪ Information & Beratung ❍	▪ Virtuelle Lerngruppen ❍
▪ Personalisierung der LP ❍	▪ Information & Beratung ❍
▪ Didaktische Anforderungen ❍	▪ Didaktische Reichhaltigkeit ❍

Fig. 24-2: Four quality specific target groups

If the individual profiles of all 1944 learners are now compared with each other, it becomes apparent that there are certain groups of persons with similar profiles. In a next research step, the data was analysed in order to understand if it was possible to find similarities in user's quality preferences, and to describe them in a meaningful way. Therefore an additional analysis of the gathered data was performed with a subset of cases (n=1321) using cluster algorithms. Each users individual preference profile was analysed and compared to those of other learners in order to find resembling profiles that could be combined to groups that are alike concerning their quality needs – but which on the other hand are different to other groups (cluster analysis). The result shows that four target groups can be identified. Figure 24-2 shows the four target groups and gives their main characteristics. The four target groups differ very much in their demands for communication and tutor support as well as group activities and social contacts in an online course.

The findings show that learners´ quality concepts in the field of e-learning can be clearly elaborated (see Ehlers 2004b for a detailed description with theoretical references and conceptual links). However, it has to be emphasised again that this does not mean to plainly follow the learner wish but rather to take it a reference for didactical decisions in the design process for learning scenarios.

The article so far has shown that learner orientation in quality development has to be seen as a necessity rather than an option grounded into the immanent structure of education and based in educational theory. A learning-theoretical approach to *learner orientation* has been worked out and mapped on quality development. Empirically constructed dimensions of a subjective quality concept were identified. However, e-learning-research is still at the beginning of providing educational scenarios in a learner-oriented way and supporting individual learning paths. In this regards the developments in adaptive hypermedia can be seen as a necessary but not sufficient and satisfactory step. It is rather a *suitable* didactical approach which enables learners to use technology to support their learning. "Suitable" in this sense expresses the relation between the provided environment and the learner's demands. If this relation can be realised in a suitable way, the learning process most probably will be successful.

"Suitability", however, does not comply with the concept of customer satisfaction at this point. It is not the ultimate aim to "satisfy" the "wishes" of learners in the learning process. Successful learning and competence development processes could also involve frustration and irritation. Therefore "suitability" rather means to find a learning scenario which – in the sense of Holzkamp (see chapter 2) – leads to a learning experience on the grounds of the learners situations and demands, coming from their propositions. This is first of all a didactical and learning methodological question which then also involves technical, administrative and economical decisions.

24.3.2   Agenda for learner oriented quality development in e-learning

One crucial question for a learner oriented provision of e-learning-scenarios is, how subjective approaches to *learning* and subjective quality concepts can be identified, and which services and demands they involves. The above presented research shows that it is possible to work out subjective quality concepts. However, it is only a first attempt in a certain defined sector of education, and not representative. It reveals that subjective quality conceptions can be described concisely and differentiated but can not be taken as the ultimate complete catalogue for every possible scenario. Therefore the field of research and practice has to be opened further and in a systematic and structured way. Elements, aspects and factors which influence the quality of the learning process, which is determined by the learner and which can contribute to a better understanding of the learners' context and the learning process have to be worked out. They can then form the first bits and pieces of a theoretical model for learner oriented quality development in e-learning.

It is important to better understand the converging processes of working and learning, gaining information, knowledge acquisition and competence development, in private and professional contexts. For these purposes the field of *user centred* research has to be defined clearly. The following four areas state questions which describe the field of *user centred* research which are necessarily to be addressed in order to develop future learner oriented quality development concepts.

1. Evaluation of *individual strategies* in different learning scenarios/ contexts: This covers research topics which assess individual strategies of acquiring knowledge and competences in different contexts, i.e. working environments, educational and private environments. A special attention has to be paid to converging processes in these contexts. Developments of empower-

ment and the responsibility shift from a teaching-oriented to a learning-oriented environment have to be surveyed. How do individuals cope with the new challenges they are faced with in the knowledge society and what implies the concept of a knowledge society for their context of living, working and learning?

2. Research on *individual quality preferences* and subjective quality concepts: What is quality from the point of view of a learner? How can subjective quality concepts be operationalised and generalised. Can a theory of quality from a learners perspective be formulated and state the interdependencies between individual learning contexts and quality concepts. How do learners see their involvement into the co-production process of learning-quality? And which strategies help learners to develop the necessary competences to acquire abilities and knowledge they need for their personal situation?

3. Research on *individual educational/ competence biographies* and their influence on subjective demands and requirements for e-learning-processes: How are demands and requirements, also learning motivation, rooted in the personal situation of learners? What do we need to understand from learners biographical contexts in order to provide learning scenarios which empower learners? How can we bridge the gap between the personal, individual reality of learners, and the post modern constructivist rhetoric of Open Learning Environments?

4. Research on *negotiation methods* to integrate learners' preferences: How can we integrate learners into the design process of e-learning-scenarios? What are suitable negotiation methods for the co-production of learning processes? How do teachers and organisations have to change in order to be able to enter into "goal-open" (Schäffter, 2001) negotiation and learning-processes with learners which are then seen as quality experts for their own learning processes?

24.4   Learner participation in quality development

Quality development hast to involve all stakeholders into a negotiation process (Manelle, 2000) in which the learners needs are taken as a reference concept. This is confirmed by Ravichandran and Rai (2000): „Participation of users, vendors, and developers in the core design and development process promotes mutual understanding of issues and constraints to be addressed to improve quality" (Ravichandran, Rai, 2000). Tietgens (2003) views stakeholders in a learning context as quality experts. They are exposed to a constantly changing environment and can only themselves assure that education meets the requirements which they have in accordance with their contexts. In this sense a participation of learners in the design process of e-learning-environments is of key importance (Tietgens, 2003). Zech (1997) suggests to combine an external perspective of the organisation of learning – the learners perspective – with an internal perspective – the point of view of the educational organisation. He suggests to view the different perspectives as equally important.

To provide learning according to the learners' needs, we suggest to conceptualise quality development should be conceptualised as a negotiation process in which all stakeholders – and thus also the learners – have to participate in. It means to abandon the idea of using "objective", externally prescribed rules and norms for quality development only, and to negotiate the norms and rules amongst the stakeholders. An important part in quality development – the definition of objectives and values – then is negotiated. This has two implications: a) All stakeholders of the e-learning-process are involved and have to be able (or have to be empowered) to voice their needs in the quality development process. b) Quality is a continuously ongoing process which is not ending after a defined time when goals and objectives have been defined and measures are in place. They constantly have to be adapted to the contexts and requirements of learners and other involved stakeholders. In order to enter into a negotiation process to find objectives for quality development four aspects have to be defined: (1) The participating group of persons (stakeholders), (2) the object of negotiation, i.e. what has to be negotiated, (3) values and norms that have to be negotiated, and (4) a method of negotiation has to be specified.

A practical example: In a school, three teachers want to introduce a new e-learning-course in history. They have to prepare materials, define teaching/ learning objectives and have to find a suitable methodology. For quality development we would now need to define the four afore mentioned factors.

---

(1) The first factor answers the question: Who has to be involved in the quality development process? The participating group of persons, the stakeholders, would be obviously the teachers themselves and the students, learning in the course. In a broader definition we would also take into account the participation of the parents and their interests, of the school management and its interest, we would also have to take into account the interest and rules of the school administration to a certain extent – and in the broadest sense all this happens on grounds of the interest of the governmental regulations. It is important to take into account the views and perspectives of relevant actors and weigh their participation in the negotiation process. Not all of them should have veto rights, for example.

(2) The second factor answers the question: What is the object of quality development? The object of quality development in our example is the new program. However, a program is a complex construct of objectives, materials, methodologies, organisation and structure. We can break it down into several components and processes. A concise operationalisation is therefore necessary to isolate certain objects (e.g. the course structure, materials, learning objectives , etc.) in order to enter into a straight negotiation process about how these processes should be carried out properly.

It is important to note that not all of the defined stakeholders need to be present for all negotiation objects. The parents for example would probably not be interested to participate in questions of administration (e.g. room scheduling, staff planning, etc.) and the administrative staff would probably not be interested to participate in curriculum planning.

(3) In a next step we would then have to answer the question: How is quality defined for each process step? This question relates to possible quality models, e.g. pedagogical models, technical- or business models, learner's subjective quality conceptions. At this stage quality development needs norms and values which define 'good' quality. Coming back to the example from the beginning, the teachers in the conception/ design process could for example decide to choose an instructional model of self-organised, collaborative learning. The quality therefore would be high if this goal would be met in the learning situation. For that reason, they would have to choose an analysis instrument which is capable of examining exactly this goal.

(4) The fourth and last step then has to answer the question: How is the negotiation process performed? Methods of negotiation have to be defined and the questions of responsibility have to be clarified. It is important to weigh the votes of stakeholders for the decisions which have to be taken – not everyone is equally responsible for every decision. In our example a serious of workshops would have to be organised for the teachers themselves, for presenting the ideas and discussion them with parents and all other stakeholders.

The example shows how all actors can be involved into the negotiation process. They all participate in the process of defining the quality objectives and the criteria/ indicators which are necessary to decide if an objective has been fulfilled or not. The described factors characterise the negotiation process and can be taken as a basis for structuring further research activities. Rather than closing the debate with this concept there are a lot of questions arising from the concept of learner oriented quality development, starting with the with the issue of the necessary organisational culture for allowing such participative processes, which negotiation methods are suitable and not finishing with the professionalisation of facilitators which guide such a learning oriented environment.

24.5   Conclusions: Towards e-learning quality through learner orientation

The article elaborates learner oriented quality development as a necessity rather than an option if quality development is aimed at having an impact on the learning process. Quality development always has to be a connection of processes and procedures with values and normative decisions. Every facilitator, guiding a group of learners, needs a normative decision concept, like a didactical theory, to have a sound basis for his activities. Quality development which is relevant for educational processes therefore can be described as the sum of all activities and efforts carried in order to improve the learning process. The emphasis of the educational process indicates at this point already that it is not possible to certify such a learning process oriented quality. It can only be perceived when the actual educational process takes place and is always a co-production between the learner and the learning environment. In recent quality debates it is an often made mistake, to assess educational environments isolated from the educational processes and to not take into account the target groups and other stakeholders within the environment. Since quality is not a given, stable characteristic of an educational environment but evolves only from the relation between the learner and the learning environment, quality can only be perceived and assessed in the actual context. Also, there is no possibility to define quality criteria which define quality apart from a concrete educational context.

As a consequence quality development has to be seen as a process of negotiation in which all stakeholders need to participate. The aim of such a participative model for quality development is to define the values and objectives of the learning process together between the stakeholders. Such an active participation of learners will play an important role in future quality development systems. The learners have an active role in these concepts and need to be aware of their personal propositions and demands. In a way of self-management of their own educational biography they have to identify necessary characteristics which learning scenarios have to meet in order to enter into a successful educational process. Such participation processes demand for better information, transparency and counselling on the side of e-learning-providers. At the same time learners have to be aware that their own responsibility for quality development rises, as they themselves are viewed as quality experts in the learning process.

25 The e-learning path model: A specific quality approach to satisfy the needs of customers in e-learning

Anne-Marie Husson

Le Preau/Chamber of Commerce and Industry, Paris, France

Defining a right quality approach for the multiple environments generated by the use of ICT in education, access to information and training, requires a systemic analysis and the choice of a set of references and values in order to define the good criteria to be retained. Focusing on the satisfaction on the various customers all along the offering, the quality approach presented has been elaborated by a team of "quality" and "e-learning" experts under the leadership of Le Préau (the Paris Chamber of Commerce and Industry e-learning Resource Centre). Built from the return of field experiences and a rigorous quality methodology, the quality tool generated is organised according a two fold approach: a process and a quality assurance approach. Since its publication in February 2002, this model has been largely implemented by e-learning designers and providers, used as an evaluation tool for the improvement of existing disposals or as a decision making tool for customers in need of a pertinent offering.

25.1   Introduction

What is success in e-learning? If you ask this question, you will get as many answers as you have categories of actors. By definition, quality which is described as "the set of properties and characteristics of a product or a service which confers to him the ability to satisfy expressed or implicit needs" (AFNOR) cannot be totally objective. Quality is always related to a context and in a given one, quality will be appreciated differently, according to the mindsets and objectives of its key actors. In others words, "the quality of the ones is not the quality of the others" (Mispelblom-Meyer, 1999).

E-learning, because of its inner complexity, its multiplicity of devices and representations, its high level of segmentation mobilising a multiplicity of actors all along its designing and its implementation, its functioning in a rapidly evolving context under the constant pressure both from managers and technological innovations, is particularly in need of quality and, on an other hand, in difficulty to define it: Quality: Why? For who? When? And How?

25.1.1   Our choice: The point of view of the customers

In accordance with many e-learning researchers, like Jane Massy who states that "the two most important criteria for evaluating e-learning are that it should 'function technically without problems across all users' and have 'clearly explicit pedagogical design principles appropriate to learner type, needs and context" (Massy, 2002), the working group directed by Le Préau made *the deliberate choice to approach the issue of quality in e-learning from the point of view of its various customers* (especially *the learner*, the end user in the pedagogical chain).

At the time of the work (years 2000-2002), the majority of the scientific debates going on, on the topic of quality for e-learning, tend to focus on its technological aspects (easiness of use, accessibility, interoperability and traceability of workflow)[97]. Very few publications seemed interested by the instructional and psychological side of these learning experiences. The working group, carried out by Le Préau, chose to retain this angle:

- because the goal of e-learning is to offer a pedagogical service to its major customers: the learners. It seemed important to the working group not to forget that focus and to verify the conditions required to achieve it;
- because e-learning is making a lot of promises to its users: learner's centredness, individualisation, (just in time, just what you need), cost-saving, effectiveness (really helps somebody learns what he wants to learn), efficiency (taking less time, with more memorisation, in an easier a cheaper way). In which conditions, e-learning would be able to satisfy these claims?
- because e-learning answers to a logic of great numbers, performance and cost-savings which has the tendency to treat the learner as the product of a linear, formatted process, who, at the end of the training, either conforms or does not. As Leslie Freeman quotes, "the profession is acting as if designing a learning experience were roughly equivalent to manufacturing cars" (Freeman, 2002). To cope with that risk, how can we conciliate these constraints of industrialisation without putting aside the human factors (confidentiality, motivation, learning preferences...) involved in every educational process and treat the learner as a citizen and a consumer, protected by laws and regulations?

---

[97] IMS, IEEE, ARIADNE, AICC, SCORM, CanCore.

25.1.2   The choice of a particular period: The delivery of the offering

A previous master degree work, produced by Pierre Scheffer (Scheffer, 2001) on the topic: *"Which quality model for e-learning?"* gave the working group the intellectual framework to carry out this study. According to this previous research work, the phase of the delivery appears to be the critical one for a quality approach:

- it is the only one the customers (particularly the learners) are involved in;
- it is the resultant of all the previous processes which went on in the back office: dimensioning of the project, designing of the offering, production of instructional tools, choices of technical solutions, choices of pedagogical approach, options of tutoring. Getting a clear idea of the effects of these initial choices on the final customers is a real option to measure their quality;
- it is a very fruitful to get input and data (qualitative and quantitative ones) on the options previously done. A lot of measures are possible there: those generated by the management system or those we can decide to collect for a specific purpose.

25.1.3   Guiding questions

What are the specific needs, expectancies of the various customers of e-leaning in the diverse fields involved (technical, pedagogical, managerial, financial, organisational, …)? Is it possible to index them and to organise them in an optimised pathway? Is it possible to consider and to conciliate, in the same approach, the human factors that belong to each educational or learning experience and the industrial factors that are part of the use of technology? Which quality approach should better give confidence to the customers and end-users on the validity and quality of all the various aspects of the service they are buying?

25.2   Methodology

To answer this questions, we:

1. defined the contours of our field of investigation,
2. set up a group of experts with specific tasks,
3. entered in a step of work characteristic of a total quality management approach,
4. benchmarked with major initiatives going on at the same time on the topic.

25.2.1   Our field of investigation

E-learning covers a wide range of highly diversified representations and practical organisations (from access to digital resources on your own to informal communities of practise without formal content). As conditions, environments, needs in these various settings are very different, we needed to clarify the architectural framework of e-learning we will consider in order to be able to work coherently in the carrying out of this research.

A set of three criteria, considered as indispensable, helped us define our research framework:

- ICT must be part and parcel of the e-learning set-up (this allows to measure status of on-line provision during the delivery).
- The e-learning offer must be dispensed by a third party/ specific organisation which accompanies the learner on his/ her learning path (no complete autodidactical approach).
- The e-learning supply must provide a form of validation (whatever its level) to the learner and/ or to the prescriber of the course. The instructional effectiveness and efficiency of the service could be evaluated.

25.2.2   Representative and complementary partners

In order to conciliate the diverse perspectives needed in the achievement of our initial questioning, two groups: the *"quality experts"* group and the *"e-learning experts"* group worked both separately and on a collaborative basis to:

- identify the e-learning customers, describe their legal, social, economical, technical environments and their needs;
- describe the e-learning process, from the customers' perspective, in providing a list of relevant indicators able to evaluate the results of the pedagogical approaches envisaged;
- identify the quality tools that may be used in e-learning and evaluate their degree of pertinence and appropriateness versus the characteristics, requirements and specificities of e-learning ;
- elaborate an analysis grid of quality frameworks.

25.2.3   A work methodology belonging to the register of quality

Personal work, research work, surveys and collaborative work were grounded on tools devoted to problem solving frequently used by quality project managers (Ishikawa, 1996) like:

- the diagram of affinities (useful in structuring sessions of brainstorming where the voice of everyone should be equivalent),

- the tree diagram (to split up a global objective in detailed levels of action) and
- the cause-effect diagram (to describe, in an exhaustive way, the resources necessary and essential to the realisation of a procedure).

25.2.4   Benchmarking

All this work was done in connection with various initiatives going one at the same time on the topic of quality in e-learning: the ISO SC36/ JTC1 work (under the umbrella of AFNOR) the GEMME laboratory, the FFFOD workshop, Ariadne initiative, IMS and IEEE publications, etc.

25.3   The e-learning's customers

In a third party legislation, as we have it in our national structures, three categories of customers must be considered: the learner, the organisation/ person prescribing the learning and the funding body. The boundaries between them are not tight as, according to the various situations, the roles of each one of them may be permuted. Nevertheless, each one of these categories has his specific needs, constraints and expectancies.

25.3.1   Identification of the learners' needs

The learners' needs, identified by the 'quality experts' group, have been classified in two major categories: the needs belonging to every situation of learning (i.e.: information on the overall program, clarification of personal objectives, means of evaluation, description of methods used, …) and the needs specific to e-learning (this second list appeared to be much longer than the first one). In the specific needs generated by e-learning, we distinguished three areas: the technical level (i.e.: equipment, assistance, training, debugging, easiness of use, ergonomics, stability, …), the instructional and pedagogical level (individualisation, preferences, self-study, collaboration, flexibility, nature of assessments, …) and the service level (like availability and roles of tutors, confidentiality, networking, communities of practice, sharing areas, deepening, updates, …). A set up of about 70 different needs have been identified.

25.3.2   Other customers' needs

The main characteristic of the relationship established between the learning provider and its institutional customers (prescribers and financers) is a commercial one. According to situations and contexts, the negotiated products may be on-the-shelf or tailored-made. But in every situation, the customer has to get confidence in the provider's ability to satisfy his needs. This particular position gives the provider, a major constraint of being able to prove his knowing-how and his skills (previous realisations, references, prototypes, ...) and to put the two stakeholders in a requirement of contract where expiries, budget, methods, guarantees, tools, endorsements or alike can be clarified.

25.4   Design of an e-learning path model

25.4.1   A description on three levels

The final results have been organised according to a process description with its classical framework made of three levels:

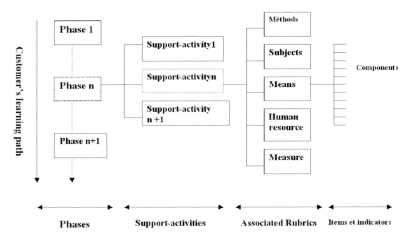

Fig. 25-1: A three levels description

1. *the Phase:* A basic process, clearly distinct from the others, by its goal (clearly identifiable and specific), its duration (each phase has a beginning and an end), its withdrawal option for customers concerned (at the end of it, they have a decision to take to stop or to go on) and its compulsory aspect for the designers (it is recommended to not «skip» a phase). All phases are described via the organisation of
2. *the Support activities:* The 'support activities' (or sub-processes) within each process correspond to its minimum help functions. The identification, the definition and the equipment of these support activities enabled us to elaborate a quality manual for e-learning.
3. *5M 'associated rubrics':* In order to guarantee a level of rigour, coherence and homogeneity in carrying out the description of the support activities, we

used the 5M methodology (which covers the 5 following areas: Methods, Subject areas, Means, Human Resources and Measures) to scan the range of the different fields required.

25.4.2   The learning path model of customers in e-learning

The model, produced as a result of these investigations, organises the needs in a global learning process, expectations and various responsibilities of the different stakeholders involved all along an e-learning delivery aimed at satisfying all of its claims (individualisation, flexibility, confidentiality, etc). In its final form, this global process consists of 8 phases, 24 support activities, 116 associated rubrics composed of a total of 1200 components (5M) to describe them.

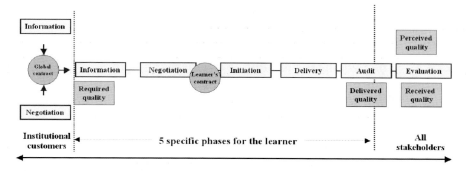

Fig. 25-2: The customers' learning path model in e-learning

Three major sections compose this e-learning path model, each one of them corresponding to a specific target of customers or stakeholders:

• *upstream the arrival of the learner*, two phases of business transactions between the demand and the supply which leads to the signature of a commercial contract between the institutional customers (prescriber and financer) and the provider. Through this contract, the proposed quality of the delivery is specified.

• *the service to the learner* where the learning offering is done. This steps includes 5 phases. The reader will notice that the "Delivery" phase which corresponds to the one where the learner is really in his learning activities comes only on the fourth position (on the five) [or on the sixth position on the whole model].At the end of this section, the delivered quality can be measured.

• *downstream*, two evaluation phases which concern all the stakeholders: the institutional customers, the learners but also the providers. This phase measure the effectiveness and the efficiency of the global provision.

Let us have a short description of these various sections with a particular emphasis on the one which is more critical to us: the learner's phases.

25.4.3   The two phases upstream the arrival of the learner

1.   **Final delivery of these two phases:**
2.   **a commercial contract**

Actors concerned:

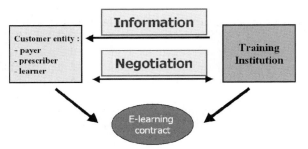

- *The institutional customers:* The prescriber of the learning offer, the financer and possibly the learner (if he/ she is his/ her own prescriber and/ or payer)
- *The providing organisation(s)*

Fig. 25-3: The two phases upstream the arrival of the learner

25.4.4   The five phases relating to the learner's path

In our opinion, these phases are essential, whatever the programme set-up chosen and particularly as regards its length and management process. These phases will obviously be more or less developed to take into account the specificities of each programme but their chronological order should be respected.

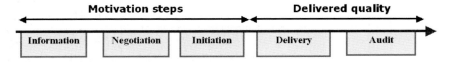

Fig. 25-4: The five phases relating to the learner

- The first three phases will play a vital role in the structuring of e-learning and will contribute to reduce the high drop-out rate associated with this kind of offer.
- The final two phases ("Audit" and "Evaluation") which follow the phase of "Delivery", are key for the implementation of a quality approach.

Actors involved in these central phases:

- the learner,
- the learning provider,
- and with a lower but nonetheless essential level of implication:
- the training facilitator of the learner, in other words the learner's institution whose job is to facilitate the practical organisation and running of the learning processes (technical, organisational, financial facilitations, opportunities of practice, etc).

Let us detail, one by one, these important phases.

Phase 3: Information to the learner

Overall objective of this phase:

At the end of this phase, the learner has accessed to all the necessary elements to choose (or at least to adhere to) his/ her learning supply.

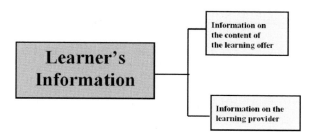

Fig. 25-5: Phase of information to the learner

A key phase to build *the learner's motivation* for the provision chosen by (or given to) him:

Two sub-processes belong to this phase:

Table 25-1: Phase 3

Phase 3	Support-activities	Description	Associated rubrics
Information to the learner	on the content of the training offer	Provide access to all useful information on the e-learning offer concerned.	Description of the process
			Description of contents of training offer
			Communication means
			Personnel involved
			Information records
	on the training organisation	Provide access to all useful information concerning the training organisation, which justify its credibility and its ability to guarantee the provision of a service of quality.	Description of the processes
			Presentation of the training organisation
			Communication means
			Communication team
			Reliability rating

Phase 4: Negotiation with the learner

Overall objective of this phase:

At the end of this phase, the learner has negotiated a pedagogical contract with the different stakeholders involved in his/ her e-learning set-up (at least his training provider and the facilitating institution giving him the means of access to his e-learning).

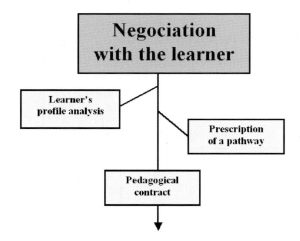

Fig. 25-6: Phase of negotiation with the learner

Three sub-processes belong to this phase, very important for individualisation of the offer, empowerment of the learners in his provision and for the definition of every stakeholders 'rights and duties in the e-learning provision.

Table 25-2: Phase 4

Phase 4	Support-activities	Description	Associated rubrics
Negotiation with the learner	Learner's profile analysis	Take into account the learner's motivation, context, training objectives, prior learning, prerequisites, so as to prescribe a right service.	Identification protocol
			Analysis procedures
			Partners
			Documentation system
	Prescribing a learning program	Proposal of a training path, corresponding to the learner's needs, prior learning, learning profile, level of autonomy and prerequisites identified.	Description of the process
			Terms of condition of training offer
			Procedures
			Authorised persons
			Verification
	Pedagogical contract	Formalisation between all contractors (the learner, the facilitator and the supplier) of all the terms and conditions pertaining to the service.	Description of the process
			Contents of pedagogical contract
			The contractors
			Information records

Phase 5: Initiation

Overall objective:

    At the end of this process, the learner is totally equipped to engage successfully in his/ her learning activities.

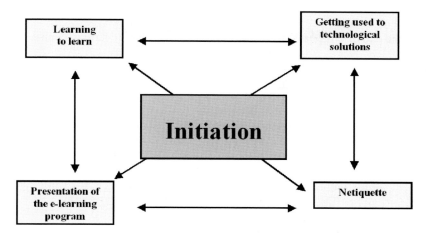

Fig. 25-7: Phase of initiation

This phase, made of 4 sub-processes, is crucial to overcome the feelings of isolation, the loss of motivation, to minimise the risks of drop-outs and to reduce energy used unproductively (technical bugs, lack of personal strategy for learning, insecurity, loss of points of reference, misunderstanding of organisation). It is a phase of empowerment for the learner, giving him the means to become a co-producer in his learning activities.

Table 25-3: Phase 5

Phase 5	Support-activities	Description	Associated rubrics
Initiation	Presentation of the e-learning program	The learner receives exhaustive information on the methods underpinning the learning course proposed.	Description of the process
			Management of the process
			Resources
			Personnel
			Verification/ Traceability/ Information records
	Learning to learn	Provide the learner with effective means of 'know how' on learning within his/ her learning environment.	Description of the learning process
			Learning methodology
			Means
			Learning community
	Technical assistance	All that enables the optimisation of the technical solutions proposed within the learning set-up.	Description of the process
			Management of the process
			Means
			Persons concerned
			Indicators and traceability
	Netiquette	Good practice codes/ Formalisation of standard practice.	Description of process
			Content
			Assistance
			Pedagogical team
			Traceability

Phase 6: E-learning delivery

Overall objective:
At the end of this phase, the learner completes his/ her e-learning course.

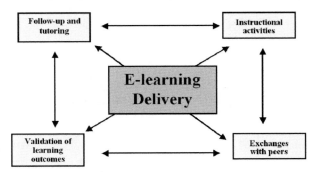

Fig. 25-8: Phase of e-learning delivery

Four sub-processes describe this phase:

Table 25-4: Phase 6

Phase 6	Support-activities	Description	Associated rubrics
Delivery of e-learning	Pedagogical activities	The learner carries out the pedagogical activities (individual and collective) as stipulated in the training path	Description of the process
			Learning contents
			Learning approach
			Means
			Co-producers
			Traceability, information records
	Exchanges with peers	The learner exchanges with peers in any way s/he chooses, via collaborative activities, accompanied or not by a tutor, and/ or in a professional context.	Description of process
			Communautarisation
			Putting at disposal
			Community
			Measures and information records
	Follow-up and tutoring	Follow-up and accompanying on technical, motivational, organisational and pedagogical levels: all that contributes to monitoring and regulating the learner's learning progression	Description of the process
			Adjustment system
			Adjustment tools
			Participants concerned
			Measures and information records
	Validation of prior learning	All that enables carrying out assessments and evaluations of the learner during the training process	Description of the process
			Validation tests
			Means
			Human Resources
			Measures and information records

Phases 7 and 8 devoted to quality measure

In order to be effective, the e-learning path model should demonstrate all levels of quality:

The delivered quality: Identified via a conformity audit, the delivered quality, checks to see whether the initial proposal was respected or not (gap between the expected quality level and the delivered quality level).

The received and perceived qualities: They measure, right at the end of the delivery and on a long term period, the results and the effects (efficiency and effectiveness) of the e-learning offer.

A total quality approach

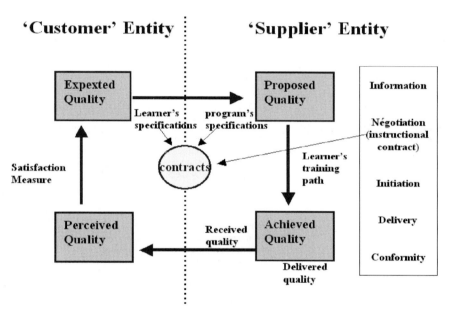

Fig. 25-9: The different levels of quality

Let us check how these different quality levels are equipped in the model:

Phase 7: Audit of the delivered quality

Overall objective:

At the end of this phase, an audit has been carried out to check whether or not the supplying items agreed on, have been respected.

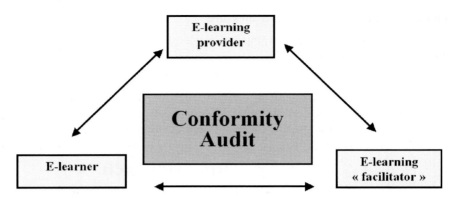

Fig. 25-10: Phase of conformity audit

Three sub-processes belong to this phase, giving each stakeholder the opportunity of a review in order to audit whether or not the specific duties and rights given to every part have been done accordingly to the initial contract.

Table 25-5: Phase 7

Phase 7	Support-activities	Description	Associated rubrics
Audit of the delivered quality	e-learning provider	Conformity audit to identify whether or not the means and actions of the initial proposal have been respected by the training organisation.	Description of the process
			Carrying out of the service
			Management of the overall monitoring system
			Actors concerned
			Measures and information records
	e-learning facilitator	Conformity audit to identify whether or not the means and actions of the initial proposal have been respected by the facilitator.	Description of the process
			Facilitation
			Management of overall monitoring system
			Actors concerned
			Measures and information records
	e-learner	Conformity audit to identify whether or not the means and actions of the initial proposal have been respected by the learner.	Description of the process
			Production
			Management of the overall monitoring system
			Actors concerned
			Traceability of training path/ information records

Phase 8: Evaluation

This phase, often neglected in traditional quality approaches, was considered indispensable by the working group. It gives outputs on the effectiveness (received quality) and efficiency (perceived quality) of the service. In this phase, all stakeholders are concerned:

- The learning provider
- All the customer entities (learners, prescriber and financers)
- Those indirectly concerned (employer, learner's immediate supervisor, e-learning community...)

Overall objective:

At the end of this phase, a value judgement, based on objectified criteria, regarding the quality of the e-learning provision is delivered.

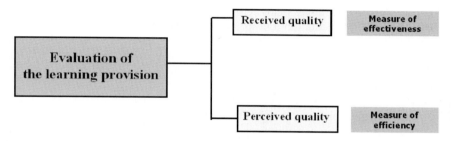

Fig. 25-11: Phase of quality evaluation

Table 25-6: Phase 8

Phase 8	Support-activities	Description	Associated rubrics
Evaluation	Received quality	On-the-spot assessment of the effectiveness of the training offer, using objectified criteria and measurement of the learner's satisfaction.	Description of the process
			Fields of investigation
			Evaluation methods and means
			Persons concerned
			Indicators to evaluate the effectiveness of the e-training offer
	Perceived quality	Post-training evaluation of the efficiency of the training offer, via an evaluation of the indirect effects on all the client entities.	Description of the process
			Fields of investigation
			Evaluations methods and means
			Persons concerned
			Indicators to evaluate the efficiency of the e-training offer

25.5   Practical uses of this model

The quality Model introduced in this chapter has been largely disseminated though articles and conferences in France and on the European level (ICALT, 204, etc.) Two major developments can be noticed as a consequence of its edition: its use as a practical tool for e-learning designers (in their work of conception and evaluation) and a conceptual model for further work on quality for e-learning.

25.5.1   A tool for e-learning designers

Largely implemented by e-learning designers and providers, the E-learning Path Model is having a two folds use:

- As a designing tool to proceed the engineering of e-learning provisions. Many experiences and feedbacks can be given by project managers[98] who testify its easiness of implementation and its major contribution as a reminder and as a structuring tool of the important processes and components to be implemented in their offer. Particularly helpful for users: the two levels of contracts, the Initiation phase, the chronology of the whole process, the guidelines to treat the evaluation.
- as a quality evaluation tool to diagnose already existing set-ups and to enter in an improvement process. A significant feedback given on that topic was presented during the French-European Workshop on quality in Distance Learning held by EQO held in Paris (France) in June 2004. The University of Maine explained how it used this conceptual model to evaluate the delivery of an online master degree and the way this evaluation lead them to re-design the organisation of their offer (Lopez, 2004).

25.5.2   A conceptual model for further work on quality

In 2002, the e-learning Path Model has been used as a grid of analysis to compare the adequacy of 14 different quality tools (usable in the e-learning field) to the needs of customers. The research matched, in a matrix analysis, each phase and its sub-processes with the different areas covered by the diverse quality tools. The

---

[98] Many set-ups have used this model. Amongst them: IFAGE, (2005) www.ifage.ch On the shelf e-learning offer for Open Source training. Contact : jacqueline.uldry@ifage.ch, CNP Assurance (2005) Diagnosis of competencies and individualised follow-up for the field force Contact : laurence.mienniel@cnp.fr, FESTO (2004) www.festo.com Set-up of a learning community for the sales force jean-pierre.bouverans@fr.festo.com, ECOFIC (2004) On-line vocational training for companies' purchasers cdeclercq@eure.cci.fr, NOVARTIS (2003) Set-up of the initial and continuous training of the field force frederic.salignon@novartis.com, PAU University (2003) Reengineering of the degree of history castagnet.veronique@wanadoo.fr, GRETA (2003) www.education.gouv.fr/fp/greta.htm On-line preparation for C2I philippe.boischot@ac-orleans-tours.fr, AFPIC (2002) www.afpic.com Safety instruction on chemical prevention on SEVESO sites g.rouyer@afpic.com, DDJS (2003) On-line degree for sporting coaching Contact : pierre-yves.chassard@jeunesse-sports.gouv.fr.

analysis showed it is difficult to find a quality approach that meets all the specifications listed in our model and when they seem to better fit (ISO, Quality Mark, AFNOR), it is to the price of a lot of work and accommodations with regards to the initial standard[99]. So, as to simplify the task for training bodies to implement a quality approach and make it more comprehensible for end users, we recommended the elaboration of a specific framework for the certification of e-learning services which would provide guarantees on reliability, transparency, security and clarity for all actors involved. Since that period many international works converge on that proposal (Johnstone, 2002).

In 2004, the e-learning Path Model served as a grounding reference for the building of the Code of Best Practises lead by the FFFOD (French Forum of ODL) in cooperation with the French Office of Normalisation (AFNOR). Organised in five processes, this Code embraces all the activities due to the e-learning manager[100].

25.6   Convergent researches

Since its publication, this model has not only been validated by returns of field users in many diverse contexts but also by outside scientific works converging on the same focus: the needs of the diverse customers in e-learning supplies and the means to refocus on the pedagogical and instructional dimensions of e-learning: Collaborative work, constructivism, cognitivism are making their way in new e-learning devices. A high proportion of the 4th IEEE International Conference on Advanced Learning Technologies (ICALT, 2004) treated topics related to pedagogy and customers' needs. The Online Educa Conference in Berlin (2004) had the same kind of focus, giving large place to collaborative technologies and roles and functions in tutoring.

Among the numerous publications and research works done through the recent months, we would like to mention especially three of them for their interesting scope, reinforcing our results:

- A research work held on in 2004 by Ehlers from the University of Duisburg-Essen in Germany (Ehlers, 2004b) questioned in an extensive survey (2000 learners involved) the learners' preferences for e-learning.
- The SEEQUEL "E-learner bill of rights" (SEEQUEL) which under the umbrella of the European Commission published in October 2004 the 17 areas of rights concerning e-learners. One reading this bill will be interested to notice how much of these areas converge with the sub-processes addressed in our quality Model (i.e. information on learning provision, learning guidance, prior learning, learning strategies, learning activities, planning learning, learning

---

[99] In-length study in French (155p) and abstract in English (44p)at http://www.preau.ccip.fr/qualite/publication.htm >téléchargement >pdf "Which quality model for e-learning?"

[100] The Code of Practice for e-learning: AFNOR BP Z76-001-an English version (S2NET) available on the web http://www.fffod.org/fr/doc/RBPZ76001-EN.doc

support staff, monitoring and assessment, feedbacks and complaints) while others open new spaces to investigate (access, e-portfolio or learning induction).

- The Canadian Recommended E-learning Guidelines (CanReg) (EQCHECK) initiated by "FuturEd Inc" (a Vancouver company) who edited a two fold e-learning quality tool: a customer guideline and a guide of best practice for e-learning designers. The customer's guideline helps the future learner to choose his e-learning provision by giving him a three levels questioning: the level 1 corresponds approximately to the learner's contract of our model, the level 2 is about deeper concerns like (actualisation of resources, time organisation, nature of relationships with experts ...) and the level 3 tries to treat the customer relationship between the learner and the e-learning provider.

25.7   Conclusion

Readers interested to get more on this quality model can download the complete version of the study in French and a lengthy abstract in English on Le Préau's website (Preau)[101]. They can also get a thorough description of it on the EQO (European Quality Observatory) Repository[102] and add, on the same data base, their return of experience while using it. It will be very interesting to confront how it fits in the various contexts of implementation and cultures of users. Probably, all together, we can refine it and make it more suited to a real European culture and context. A discussion forum, hosted by EQO, may help us to achieve this goal.

---

[101] "Which Quality Model for e-learning » In-length study in French (155p) and abstract in English (44p)at http://www.preau.ccip.fr/qualite/publication.htm.

[102] Description of the e-learning path Model on the EQO database: www.eqo.info request "The learning path model". Return of experiences go on the same address.

26 Pedagogic quality – supporting the next UK generation of e-learning[103]

John Anderson

Department of Education in Northern Ireland, United Kingdom

Robert McCormick

The Open University, United Kingdom

The editors of this European handbook make the valid point that quality development in the field of e-learning is of growing diversity and is difficult to handle. The argument that there can be 'cross-fire' between the pedagogic, technological, content and economic dimensions is well made. The overall aim of this work is to develop a framework and guidance which can:

Enable educational practitioners (teachers and learners) to make more informed decisions about the value of resources and tools to support effective pedagogical practice in their context;

Improve the quality of available and future resources - in terms of potential to support effective pedagogical practice - by supporting and informing the design decisions of developers and publishers.

We believe the work in progress which is reported here in September 2005, and which was initially developed in response to the "Harnessing Technology" strategy published recently by the Department of Education and Skills in England[104], would benefit from being extended and coordinated on a European-wide basis.

---

[103] Becta (the British Educational Communications and Technology Agency), the UK national agency, asserts its moral and legal rights in respect of the intellectual property of the work reported here.

[104] Harnessing Technology: transforming learning and children's services. 2005 Department for Education and Skills (England) http://www.dfes.gov.uk/publications/e-strategy.

26.1   Introduction

At present there are many approaches and views of what constitutes a 'quality' e-learning resource or course. Differing vocabularies are used to describe similar associated concepts and attributes. The range of e-learning resources available to educational institutions varies significantly, as does the capacity of institutions and teachers to research, review and select those most appropriate to their needs and those of their pupils.

This chapter focuses on the school sector, that is to say, on the phases of compulsory state education for pupils, and, in that context, on two specific aspects of quality:

- The creation of a overarching, common, consensus-based framework to clarify the relationships between and the distinctiveness of the various elements of e-learning quality;
- Work underway to establish and illustrate agreed core principles, quality criteria and indicators for a pedagogic approach to the quality of e-learning.

The intention is to illuminate those principles with exemplary materials tailored (in the first instance) for two primary audiences: designers and developers; and practitioners (mainly, teachers).

More often than not, the issue of e-learning quality is approached in terms of *the quality of the content or the resource product itself.*

Pedagogic quality: In this work we use the term *pedagogic quality* to refer to the quality of *learning and teaching activity* using technology-based resources and tools. The quality of the tools and the resources underpins the quality of the learning experience, but we believe that it will *afford* rather than determine the quality of learning. Quality is ultimately dependent on the decisions and behaviours of learning and teaching practitioners and participants themselves.

The quality of resources must be framed within, and guided by, an understanding of the broader quality of learning activity.

For our purposes, we also extend the term 'pedagogy' to relate to contexts in the school sector where teachers normally direct the learner, to those where learners have a stronger role in directing the learning for themselves (Knowles, 1970). Beyond that, we are also interested in the impact of technology on those contexts where there is no underlying teacher/ learner relationship, and learners largely or wholly determine their own learning (Hase, Kenyon, 2001).

26.2   Methodology of creating a quality reference framework[105]

It can be said of 'e-learning' that if the "e" is removed, then we are really talking about quality teaching and learning. While this is undoubtedly true, it is not the whole story. The scope of the current work is to better understand what additional dimensions – competences, knowledge and understanding - are brought to education when technology is used as the enabler of learning.

Thus far, the work undertaken so far in the UK has been approached in a way which is integral to the wider range of initiatives in the field of quality. We believe that is essential that this work on e-learning is connected and collaborative, is seen as part of the 'family of quality' in education and should not take place in isolation. A similar, integrated, approach ought to be adopted on a European-wide basis.

Pilot projects in e-learning and investigations of classroom practice in the use of learning technologies and ICT resource were analysed to identify common threads. These threads were synthesised into common indicators and were used to establish a framework for e-learning quality which could, in turn, be validated and further developed against yet other sources of evidence and examples of practice. From this framework, reference models and views for particular areas of interest can be extracted; these will consist of subsets of the components and criteria from the broader framework. These specific views will then be used to produce specific outputs, such as tools and guidance, for example a matrix for evaluation of online content for particular scenarios.

The main aim of our work in this field is:

Pedagogic criteria

- drawing on existing work, including the UK BETT Awards (*ibid*), develop criteria and indicators for the *pedagogic* quality elements of the framework, validating these with (i) the research community, (ii) the commercial sector and (iii) with practitioners, hosting further workshops and seminars;
- design a format for the presentation of the criteria that can support the development and evaluation of professional education programmes by teacher education providers.

Overarching common framework for e-learning quality

- continue to develop and refine the common framework, ensuring its alignment with related developments such as the Becta ICT Maturity Model (*ibid*);

---

[105] For more details on Becta's views about work in this field, see: "A quality framework for e-learning resources: Becta's view"
http://www.becta.org.uk/corporate/publications/documents/Becta_view-quality.pdf.

- use the framework as a basis to reconcile and plan an overarching programme of work, involving key stakeholders.

Content quality model

- ensure that work on content quality models and on pedagogic criteria are inter-linked, can support the development of effective tools and guidance and can be tied into vehicles for their dissemination and adoption.

26.3   Context and rationale

In England, the Department for Education and Skill's 'Harnessing Technology' strategy sets out, as one of six priorities, the need to provide a *collaborative approach to personalised learning activities* (Dfes).

It commits us all in Britain to do all we can to accelerate the move to the next generation of e-learning activities and resources. It says that we need better digital resources more widely available and more flexible learning packages that teachers can adapt to their learners' needs. This work programme described in this chapter is in response to the Government's call to

> "support innovation in the market by improving our knowledge of where e-learning works particularly well, and up-date our standards for pedagogic quality, accessibility and safety."

If this goal is to be achieved, then we need to bring a sharper focus to the *pedagogic* quality aspects of e-learning than is currently the case.

Improving the pedagogic quality of e-learning is best approached through an inclusive dialogue in which all of the main educational agencies help to set priorities and build capacity and capability for two prime audiences:

- developers and publishers, (whether practitioner or professional, e.g.: commercial, non-commercial and teachers) who are designing and publishing the new generation of e-learning resources, and need to develop specialist skills
- education users, (teachers and learners) who are selecting e-learning approaches and need to develop their skills to deploy and use ICT effectively to support teaching and learning

Second-order, but no less important audiences are:

- Managers/ leaders, (whether institutional or independent, local, regional or national) who are making decisions about when to deploy e-learning, and are often responsible for access and effective delivery. They need to develop the understanding and skills to manage ICT appropriately to enhance and transform the way in which education is delivered.

- Intermediaries – such as school development/ improvement and support agencies, and virtual learning environment developers
- Evaluators, inspectors, researchers
- Policy-makers.

Quality improvement is not just a question of clarifying vocabulary, and publishing quality criteria and indicators - much as that work is essential. It is largely a matter of levering professional and institutional development within these communities. In effect, it should be conceived as an 'education project'.

Therefore the overall aim of the programme of work is to build the shared understanding of *'what works well and why it works,'* and what makes e-learning compelling and effective. Shared frameworks will enable a coherent approach to this across a range of activities, including the provision of advice and guidance, the promotion of exemplars and the design of professional development projects and programmes.

26.4   The common framework for e-learning quality

The overarching common framework for e-learning quality presented here (Figure 26-1) identifies 5 broad and distinct categories of:

1. infrastructure provision
2. technical standards
3. content development
4. pedagogic affordances and practices
5. institutional development

These divide further into 17 sub-categories as shown. Whilst the framework in Figure 26-1 displays on paper or screen as a list, with a top and a bottom (and therefore seems to imply a hierarchy) it should not be viewed as such. For, most readers, "learning and the learner" will be the pivotal point of the framework.

The boundary running through the centre of the framework is significant. Some researchers believe that it is on this boundary where most tensions can arise:

> "…educational multimedia depends on the combined good practice of both instructional designers and multimedia designers. But seldom does this expertise reside in one individual….the collaborative focus is that the design should work. But this is the very thing that often causes educational multimedia to be dysfunctional since educational functionality and structural functionality are not always compatible and the two may be in a state of tension"[106].

---

[106] Dillon, P.; Prosser, D.; Howe, T. *Design Transactions in educational multimedia*. The Design Journal 7(2), 2004.

Above the line, decisions about quality depend on *conformance* to *specifications* and *standards*. These are largely, but not necessarily, exclusively technical in nature. For computer systems to work there has to be compliance.

Below the line, is where issues of pedagogic quality are to be found. Here, *judgements* about quality are situated in *fitness for purpose*, depending wholly on the education context. The context will include, for instance, the intended objectives and outcomes of teaching and learning, the needs of the target group/ s and the expertise of the teacher. There are of course some specifications and standards either above or on the line that have pedagogic affordances (design principles, quality of assets and fit to the curriculum).

The appropriate quality language is that of *criteria and indicators*.

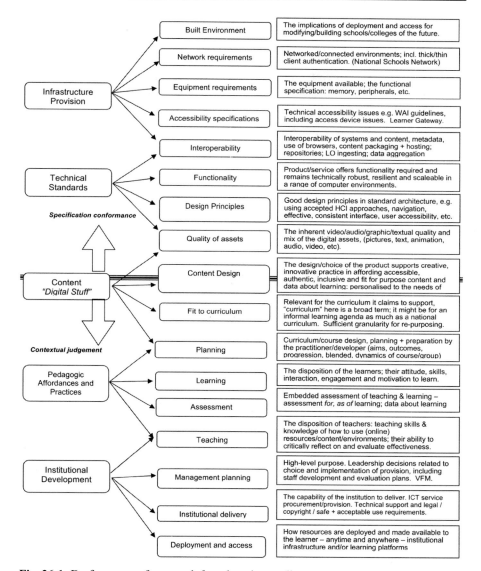

Fig. 26-1: Draft common framework for e-learning quality

The overarching framework (figure 26-1) is not a model. Its role is to provide a high-level overview of all relevant quality components, where they are placed and how they relate to each other. The main purpose of it is to clarify the relationships and boundaries of the range of work on quality (and the related terms used), encompassing the different quality interests and priorities of different stakeholders: industry, academia, professional development, learners and so on. It exposes intentional overlaps and synergies and possible tensions at the interfaces. It is also designed to be generic – that is to say, meaningful at all levels in the system.

The framework has some self-evident limitations however. This is the current version of a *work in progress* and is offered in a spirit of discussion. While it has reached a level of consensus with some significant stakeholders, further validation and testing is required with wider constituencies to ensure that it is as fully inclusive as possible.

Being a static framework (and not a model), it does not model dynamic flow or reveal all the interactions between neighbouring components. The boxes, for instance, do not imply an equivalence of weight or significance. In addition, if the framework were to be applied in a rigid way, rather than in the developmental and educational manner advocated in this paper, there might be some risk of inhibiting innovation. However, we will consider the role that feedback might play in introducing some understanding of the dynamics between the pedagogic components within the framework. 'Feedback' could enable us to capture how, for instance, content impacts on learning. Such an approach could then strengthen the developmental and educational principles of this framework, and begin to turn it from a framework into a dynamic model.

For now, the framework provides a common core of quality elements, which can be flexibly applied to a diverse range of applications of e-learning.

But what does e-learning mean in this context?

E-learning may encompass part, or all of the elements, from a spectrum:

- information/ data for and about learning – including digital assets
- Learning Objects
- authentic online research resources
- models and simulations
- tools for e-learning applications
- ICT learning support, learning resources or ICT packages
- user guidance materials
- courses packages (pathways)
- which may be delivered off-line or, in blended or in full mode, online, at a distance
- and may be supported, support and/ or be exploited by an online community of learners.

At this stage, virtual learning environments are not within the scope of our principles.

Depending upon the educational context, one element, or a specific combination of elements might be selected and used in a variety of different ways which are fit for purpose and reflect different approaches to teaching and learning.

26.5   Core pedagogic principles

This section moves from considering the common framework for the quality of e-learning to focus on the components lying below the central line in the common framework which are most central to teaching and learning and to the development of pedagogic criteria to underpin the next generation of e-learning: curriculum fit; content design; planning; learning; assessment and teaching.

Working through a number of consultative workshops we adopted a 'principled' approach to e-learning quality and have identified, through debate and iteration, ten key principles which are fundamental to our work on pedagogic quality.

The judgement of pedagogic quality has to be principled, in that any particular decision to create and use digital material should be underpinned by some agreed principles of good teaching and learning. These principles may be derived from: particular views of the purposes of education (e.g. that it should be inclusive); sound theoretical and research-based ideas of learning; distilled practice as found in educational institutions.

There is an implicit assumption in this principled approach that the better the quality of material and its uses, the more of the principles will be embodied; and the lower the quality, the less. It is acknowledged that e-learning developments may not embody all of the principles, but that the supporting teaching and learning activities could address 'missing' principles. These missing principles should be addressed in advice to users (whether teachers or learners). This approach recognises the interdependence of 'design' and 'teaching', in that the designer is able to afford the user a wide range of opportunities in the design and where he does not, the user has to compensate for the limited affordance in other ways. There may well be exceptions for certain types of e-learning product such as ICT productivity tools (such as web design and publishing packages for example) which have a specific design focus and are purposed to be used in a wide variety of different ways by the user; in this case it may be that only a limited set of the ten principles are relevant.

The principles should be able to help designers construct e-learning material and associated activities in a way that will enact sound principles of pedagogy; in as much as we have them (we don't know everything). They should also be able to help teachers to choose resources, to design teaching and learning activity that uses it, and to support such activity while it takes place. (The division of designers and teachers does not preclude teachers from being designers, but they are in this case *acting* as a designer.) Both of these actors must address the needs of the learners. However, learners are not passive recipients, indeed one of the pedagogic principles draws on the idea that learners have *agency*. Learning does not take place without the learner exercising some form of agency, thus a passive learner exercises no agency and hence learning will be limited. The passive idea is the opposite of what happens in a genuine learning situation, where learners construct their knowledge. If they don't do this knowledge construction, they don't learn, because knowledge cannot be *given* to them, so the basic argument in constructivism goes. This implies not just *activity* but also ownership and involvement; digital learning material is in danger of encouraging activity (such as clicking around screens), without the necessary 'ownership' and with little involvement in thinking. The consequence of learner agency is that they too have responsibilities and imperatives to develop their own learning. E-learning must support them in this.

We have tried to make the principles which follow:

- simple, comprehensible, compelling and therefore easy to use;
- comprehensive and individually distinctive, one from the other (and therefore 'core'), however, they are inter-related and not independent from each other[107];
- consensus-based - by being developed and applied through debate and partnership;
- promoting of quality consciousness[108] and supportive of quality self-assurance;
- context-sensitive, and founded on the needs of learners, practice in school classrooms, on moves toward whole school improvement and on professional development settings for teachers;
- amenable to approaching quality assurance as a professional development process;
- part of a family of quality for learning in schools;
- complementary and supportive of self-improvement and innovation processes.

The ten principles which follow are not carved in stone, but are offered to open a dialogue and help us reflect on the role of the learning citizen in the 21st century.

26.6   The 10 principles

These principles try to encapsulate all that is important to pedagogic quality, and as such are couched in general terms. The specificity will come through their exemplification in the various approaches to e-learning.

Principle 1: match to the curriculum

The material should be matched with and aligned to the appropriate curriculum through:

- clear objectives (at an appropriate level and form of specification);
- the relevance of content covered;
- the appropriateness of student activities;
- the nature of the assessment (where this is present).

---

[107] Particularly the two principles related to assessment, which are singled out because, in general, e-learning has not been good at implementing these successfully. Designers, teachers and learners are likely to have most difficulty in seeing the issues involved or in knowing how to implement good assessment.

[108] Quality criteria of online learning resources. Liisa Lind. National Education Board of Finland. 10th May 2005.

(It is accepted that there may not be a simple division among some of these elements; for example, the student activities may have assessment elements or be part of the 'content'.)

The more this match is made explicit, the easier it will for those who use the material. Thus a producer of materials could provide a statement that says how the material matches the curriculum in these four dimensions. Material that relies on the user doing a detailed analysis to see if these (even if they are indeed satisfied) may satisfy good quality *specified* material, but unhelpful for *enactment*, and possibly *experience* (by the learners).

Principle 2: inclusion

The material should support inclusive practice seen in terms of:

- different types and range of achievement (including special needs);
- physical disabilities that can be particularly supported by electronic material (e.g. those with visual impairment);
- different social and ethnic groups;
- gender;
- learners who have missed a period of schooling and need to catch up.

The imperative here is not just that a particular group is served by the material (and that this is made explicit), but that it does not exclude a group. Thus material that is aimed at a high achievement group would not be seen as being of as high a quality as that which includes both high and low achievers.

Principle 3: learner engagement

The material should engage and motivate learners. This engagement should be evident in an ethos of being:

- educational i.e. have a 'worthwhile' educational aim, and not just be used to occupy or entertain learners, although it might employ 'game-like' approaches to learning;
- motivating such that it is both enjoyable for learners and makes them want to continue using the material or want to carry on with learning the topic;
- such that it does not produce adverse emotional reactions that are likely to cause reduced motivation to learn in general, or to use digital material in particular;
- motivating such that it improves the class atmosphere for learning and makes it a good experience for teachers and learners alike.

This engagement and motivation may be achieved through one or all of aesthetic, technical and educational design.

Principle 4: innovative approaches

It should be evident why learning technologies are being used, rather than a non-technological approach which achieves the same end as effectively. Digital forms should be used where they bring an innovative approach which cannot be achieved in any other way. E-learning should, in other words, be fit for purpose. The design and implementation of the material may also be innovative, in the sense that it takes an approach that is new and has not been done either by previous non-technological or by digital material for this particular topic or area of the curriculum. This does not imply that it has to be a new basic design of the digital material; it could be, for example, an existing software engine applied to a new area of the curriculum.

Principle 5: effective learning

This principle can be demonstrated in a variety of ways:

- by the use of a range of approaches that will allow the learner to chose one that suits her, or can be personalised to her, or will extend the learner's repertoire of approaches to learning (such as 'learning how to learn');
- by providing empirical evidence of effective outcomes of the material;
- by satisfying a number of the characteristics of good learning (learner agency; learner autonomy; encourages metacognitive (including high order) thinking; enables or encourages collaboration);
- by providing authentic material (authentic to situations outside school and to the learners' perspectives and situations), and that also exhibits multiple perspectives on a topic (this could be seen as another aspect of authenticity).

Principle 6: formative assessment

The material should provide formative assessment, i.e. assessment that is primarily aimed at improving learning. This may be achieved by a number of ways:

- by providing rapid feedback that helps learners to see how they can improve and what they must do to improve;
- by providing opportunities for peer assessment, with appropriate understanding of the criteria or standards of performance required;
- by providing opportunities for self assessment, with appropriate understanding of the criteria or standards of performance required.

While it is possible (although not easy) within e-learning to provide more rapid and personalised feedback to learners that will tell them what areas of their understanding are lacking, and where in the material they must put more effort, these by themselves are unlikely to make any difference to learner improvement. Similarly feedback that is too general for the learners' particular problems is unlikely to be effective. Feedback has to be specific to the learner's problems and specific to their needs for improvement.

Principle 7: summative assessment

Summative assessment here is understood as that which is used to grade students for guidance as to, or selection for, future educational or work opportunities. Although not all digital material will have summative assessment (but it should have formative assessment), where it does, it must be:

- valid and reliable (i.e. assess what is aimed at in the objectives, and do this in a way that can be demonstrated by things like expert views, or ways of testing construct validity; give consistent results for particular learners or other users);
- comprehensible by teachers, learners and parents (as appropriate);
- able to deal with a range of achievement levels;
- free from adverse emotional impact on the learner.

Principle 8: coherence, consistency and transparency

The material must be internally coherent and consistent in the way the objectives, content, student activity and assessment (where present) match to each other. It must be open and accessible in its design. This implies that the components should each match and that the match should be transparent in its intention; for example the activities should be consistent with the objectives and the assessment should assess these objectives (and not un-stated or unknown ones). It should be clear to the user what they are expected to do.

Principle 9: ease of use

The material should be transparent in its ease of use through:

- being open and accessible;
- being intuitive and not requiring guidance on use (for either the teacher or the learner);
- the provision of appropriate guidance for the learner or the teacher and, in the case of the learner, should not require extensive training or instructions that are not themselves part of the educational aims of the material;
- appropriate assumptions about the ICT skills of users (both learners and teachers), or the provision of straightforward guidance on this.

It is accepted that for teachers there may be some training in use, but where possible this should focus on pedagogy and not on software requirements. (However, in some cases, where software tools are to be used, some training is unavoidable, but it should be specified, in context and available.)

Principle 10: cost-effectiveness

E-learning approaches are expensive. There are costs for technology, software, provision, maintenance, training, design, development, deployment. Technology solutions need to be justifiable, affordable and the costs sustainable. Using learning technology is not a cheap option for enhancing educational opportunity, broadening choice and raising standards; nor is it a 'silver bullet'. The investment needs to be justified in terms of cost benefits and savings through efficiencies of scale, or in terms of affordance of pedagogic opportunities and enrichment, or in meeting educational needs and goals which are not achievable in other ways. However, as with many of these principles, there are some formidable definitional problems, about what to include in the costs (or indeed the benefits).

26.7   Conclusion

This chapter presents two significant, generic contributions to the work of better understanding the pedagogic quality of e-learning. The first of these is a common framework for e-learning quality generally, which enables the players to see where and how their work in specific aspects of quality (technical, institutional, content, etc) relates to all of the other components. This framework, while still a draft and open to further refinement, is already demonstrating its worth in bringing coherence to the planning of the responses of national agencies in the UK to government policy to drive forwards investment in learning technologies.

The second of these contributions is a set of ten core principles which express, in an economic and elegant fashion, the underpinning values that can apply to a range of expressions of e-learning (whether in the face to face classroom, or online, or both), and be meaningful in the point of view of a range of audiences – designers, teachers and learners, in the first instance. We believe that while comprehending the pedagogic aspects of quality is a wholly contextual activity, these core principles are sufficiently generic to be relevant across European school systems despite the difference in emphasis, from country to country, on the approach to teaching and learning.

The way in which the various actors in the process (designers, teachers and learners) might address these principles will be different, and so in the UK we are exploring an approach which involves building guidance resources to help educate e-learning designers and users. We will also develop, through these resources, criteria and indicators for making judgements, around the principles best suited to the actors or those supporting them.

There is more work that needs to be done. On its own, the framework and the principles could appear both prescriptive in tone, and rather general in terms of pedagogic advice about e-learning, if they are not clothed in a wide variety of e-learning resources which exemplify the value added by "e" to already good teaching and learning in different contexts.

We are already developing these several 'toolkits' of exemplary materials and highlighting evidence of the benefits and challenges of e-learning. These toolkits may include exemplary materials, illustrative snapshots of practice, guidelines, operational best practice, benchmarks, metrics, methodologies, advice, protocols, proformas, relevant rules and regulations – all of which are aimed at the prime audiences of developer and user. We will ensure that they are also relevant to the secondary audiences.

These principles and resources will help users to design and select effective, and fit for purpose, content and provide information on how to deploy and use it appropriately. The choice of examples will cover the use of technology which is stand-alone as well as online.

We recognise that is a substantial piece of work and involves a wide range of stakeholders. It will require a programme of development over time, coordinated carefully with other major initiatives. We believe that the common quality framework for e-learning will assist partners in navigating through related programmes of work.

We believe that this work needs to be set firmly in a European Union and international context, where appropriate and relevant. The Lisbon agreement sets us some challenges for lifelong learning and the development of independent learners. The achievement of these goals is going to require a much stronger recognition of, and focus on, pedagogy than is currently typical across Europe. There are instances of some excellent thinking, research and practice relating to pedagogical quality. We now have an opportunity to bring all of this work together and, as a consequence, enable some powerful learning.

Becta would be pleased to discuss, with relevant and appropriate agencies and potential partners in other national jurisdictions, and with European and international agencies and partners with an interest in the pedagogic aspects of e-learning, the potential for taking this work forward in the spirit of cooperation and, potentially, of genuine collaboration.

27 Quality in cross national business models for technology based educational services

Martin Gutbrod, Helmut W. Jung

Institute for Applied Learning Technologies, Germany

Stefan Fischer

University of Lübeck, Germany

Technology based educational services (former e-learning) build on a complex partner network with most different service sectors (Jung, Fischer, 2002). In the ideal case, this partner network is build upon a cooperation model integrating processes in form of a detailed business model. The pure definition of necessary processes does not suffice, though, because they do not describe the composition of the rendered services but only the way of the attainment. Economically successful educational concepts build on the implementation of cross national business models which integrate technical, educational and primarily economic quality criteria.

27.1 Introduction

Costs are a major quality factor for the success of e-learning. Well known cost structures of traditional learning scenarios can only be reached by economy of scales effects. The biggest potential for cost savings lies in the content. As an example, it could be purchased from competitive international sources or developed in countries with low income levels. The necessary critical sales volume of services can only be achieved by addressing the global market (Jung, 2005). These conditions require an implementation of cross national e-learning networks.

Europe itself houses a huge market potential and has a good chance due to its historical educational competences to take on a leading role worldwide in the supply of educational services – but its time to start with building consortia.

Cross national e-learning networks: International and interdisciplinary consortia to develop and provide educational services for the world market. They take into account economic and cultural conditions of the target markets.

During the last 5 years, European fundamental e-learning research already focussed intensively on quality criteria for technology and education. Despite all qualitative progress it was not successful to establish e-learning services in the market. One reason was that often economic quality criteria were neglected.

Within the next 5 years, we believe in market-oriented and technology-based educational services which will be driven by global business models. These models must integrate technical, educational and economic quality criteria and ranges of values.

These criteria, built on a predefined process-oriented framework such as EFQM or PAS 1032-1, must be accepted by all partners of a network (Jung, 2005). The compliance with agreed minimum standards supports an efficient and thus more cost-effective production of educational services.

In the concept introduced here, the learners' requirements form a firm reference point which can be described qualitatively (Ehlers, 2001), (Ehlers, 2002). This is valid for technical, for study-specific and for economic aspects.

27.2   Quality as a strategic perspective

An important success factor at the marketing of educational services is the relation of quality to the sales price. Our concept challenges the widespread view of quality just as one factor amongst many others. We see quality as an integrating factor around all development objectives. Thereby a new strategic perspective "quality" arises from a former factor "quality".

One driver to a fundamental change in the design of educational services is based on the management of employees. The approaches to self-financing and high-quality educational services are determined by the need to integrate future educational processes into Human Capital Management (HCM) systems which are integrated in Systems such as SAP/ R3. These systems need quality criteria with defined parameters. These quality parameters work as an important instrument to control all processes inside a HCM-System.

The area of training at the workplace houses the most complex quality requirements of technology, pedagogy and business aspects. These different areas have quality prerequisites, and quality concepts of their own. These are not always coupled, sometimes even contradictory. A successful quality concept for educational scenarios therefore requires a general quality strategy merging different requirements together from a technical, educational and economical point of view. As an additional requirement, the strategy must take international and intercultural aspects into account to enable organisations to act on the global market.

Today process-oriented quality principles exist, e.g. the Total-Quality-Management (TQM)-oriented EFQM approach (www. efqm.org). These approaches focus on process flows. The development of parameters and concrete ranges of values is left to the enterprises themselves. To provide business-independent and enterprise-independent quality principles, this procedure is useful. Educational processes are not different from this principle compared to other production modes. Therefore, generic process-oriented quality principles can also be transferred to the area of educational processes.

The generic frame, however, must then be refined with concrete 'normative' elements. This leads to the positive effect that instruments were developed providing clear descriptions of quality values and guidelines. These normative elements are based on scientific research results as well as ethical, social values and common sense values.

Our favourite future scenario of the development of educational services sees large international transdisciplinary networks. They are designed with strong process-oriented structures similar to the motor industry with a car manufacturer in the centre and lots of international suppliers. From their experiences, an education network must develop a primary normative lining of the process-oriented frame. This arrangement is carried out in negotiations between the partners of the business network involved. An adoption of values and norms must be agreed within the network. This process should lead to a quality strategy which connects a generic process model with normative values and norms.

The major task can therefore be summarised in the following questions:

How can a general quality model be designed for the requirements of technology, education and economy?

How to which integrate the different requirements, and what are the relevant parameters and ranges of values?

27.3   The learner as the central reference point for divergent requirements

27.3.1   Multidimensional divergent prospects

The perspective from which quality is evaluated and viewed on is of decisive importance to the assessment of quality of technology supported educational services. These services include the development, provision and execution of educational courses. From a technical perspective, there are completely other quality requirements than from an educational or economic perspective. As an example, learners can be seen either as customers or as co-producers of the learning process.

27.3.2   Learner orientation

There is a debate going on whether the quality of education scenarios should not be determined from a training provider point of view but from the learners' point of view. There exist some indications to the need of a stronger participant/ learner orientation. (Fend, 2000), (Maleri, 1997).

Gnahs (1999) sees the future learner more and more equipped with the definition power for quality in educational contexts – mainly in four areas: economic, pedagogic, social and technological perspective (see chapter 28).

27.3.3   Quality strategy for learner-oriented educational services

If different organisations such as:

- Content providers with teaching material,
- Infrastructure providers with network technique,
- Private and state educational organisations which operate studying centres,

plan to co-operate in an educational service network they will face several challenges. Usually these organisations have own quality requirements, quality perspectives and processes.

To solve that problem, they have to design a common value-added chain which starts from a further education motivation and ends with a successful billing and accounting. The process control is very complex and needs an adopted quality management system to guarantee the quality demanded by learners.

The following model describes the innovative development and implementation of a new quality concept. It integrates existing technical, educational and economical quality approaches into a learner-oriented quality strategy.

27.4   Learner-oriented quality strategy

27.4.1   Basics

The quality strategy introduced here bases on existing quality developments in the respective disciplines technology, education didactics and economy. It integrates three areas gradually (see figure below).

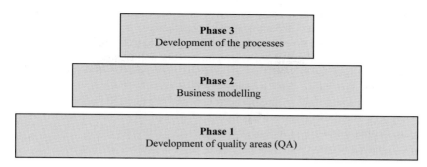

Fig. 27-1: 3 phases to develop a quality strategy

27.4.2   Phase 1

The first phase represents the development of a frame with nine quality areas. This number of quality areas is coincidental. It originates from an executed process of coordination between quality researchers, content providers, service providers, as well as private and state training providers. The quality areas cover the value chain of technology-based educational services. The definition of the areas is not finished at the moment of defining them. They are subject to a permanent optimisation procedure.

The approach organises relevant quality criteria in a grid of existing and new quality standards (see figure 27-2).

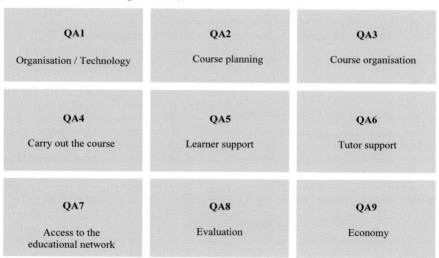

Fig. 27-2: 9 quality areas of the learner-oriented quality strategy

The quality areas base on a comprehensive analysis of known activities to generate educational processes - from a learners´ perspective.

The model uses - where ever it is possible - already existing and accepted standards. These are technological software and quality approaches as „Quality on the line" from Institute for Higher Education Policy, e.g. (N.N., 2004). Own settings must be defined for those quality requirements where no standard are existing.

All organisational units of the educational network have to cooperate according to the agreed standards. Regular processes of accreditation check the compliance with the common quality policy of the network (see figure 27-5).

The 9 quality areas contain the following quality requirements:

QF1: Organisation/ technology

- Development and implementation of guidelines and measures to guarantee the technical quality;
- Description of the technical equipment;
- Compliance with existing international technological standards.

QF2: Course planning

- Standard course design;
- Assessment and evaluation of the courses by the participants;
- Regular check of course content and design;
- Minimum standards for the content development.

QF3: Course organisation

- Individual learner consulting;
- Check of individual learner prerequisites;
- Showing possible studying paths and methods;
- Tutors accompany the learners' individual learning processes.

QF4: Education course

- Integration of regular learning control;
- Constructive and contemporary feedback to the learner;
- Interaction between learners.

QF5: Learner support

- Support in technical and organisational and content-oriented questions;
- Standardised support processes.

QF6: Support of the tutors

- Regular further education and training;
- Self evaluation;
- Technical support.

QF7: Access to the educational network

- Data security and privacy;
- Access control mechanisms;
- Quality of the availability.

QF8: Requirements of the evaluation

- Effectiveness of the courses;
- Best Practice concept;
- Regular data elevation and evaluation;
- Check of learning objectives.

QF9: Economy

- Regular market potential analyses and product adjustments;
- Supervision and control of the value chain with Return On Investment (ROI) methods;
- Inquiry and regular optimisation of processing costs.

27.4.3   Phase 2

The development of the business model is based on the 9 quality areas.

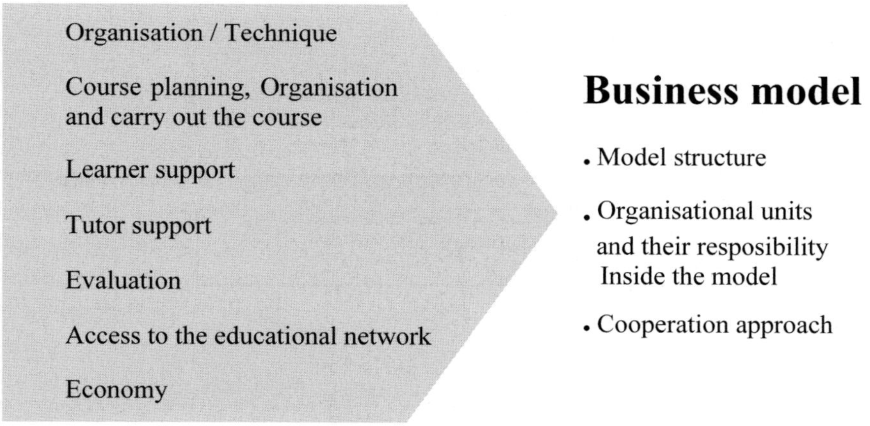

Organisation / Technique

Course planning, Organisation
and carry out the course

Learner support

Tutor support

Evaluation

Access to the educational network

Economy

Business model

- Model structure

- Organisational units
  and their resposibility
  Inside the model

- Cooperation approach

Fig. 27-3: Transfer of the 9 quality areas into a business model

27.4.4   Phase 3

It contains the transfer of the business model with its organisational units into a specified process model.

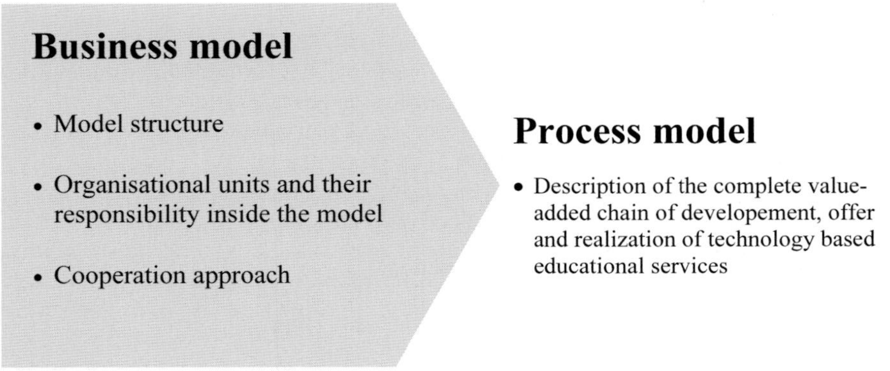

Business model

- Model structure

- Organisational units and their responsibility inside the model

- Cooperation approach

Process model

- Description of the complete value-added chain of developement, offer and realization of technology based educational services

Fig. 27-4: Transfer of the business model into a process model

Extensive processes of coordination are necessary to implement quality requirements into an education network. At first, the organisational units agree on quality principles. In a next step they have to define normative quality requirements.

Processes in and between the organisations are executed according to the defined quality requirements. Particularly important elements are regular reviews. Within these processes the quality and the concept will be checked frequently.

A typical example of a frequent process is the integration of a new organisation into the educational network (see figure 27-5).

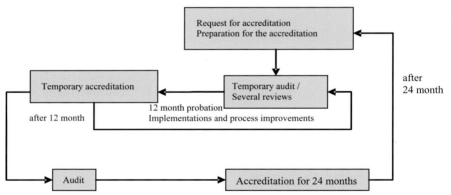

Fig. 27-5: Process of accreditation

In the first process step, the new organisation applies for accreditation into the educational network. In a first temporary audit, the implementation of the agreed quality standards will be checked by a responsible department of the educational network. If the audit has been passed the new organisation is authorised to offer services into the educational network within the next 12 months.

Several reviews improve embedding of the new organisation. The regular audit must be passed every 24 months and takes place for the first time after 12 month.

27.5   Conclusion

Quality becomes a decisive success factor in cross national business models for technology based educational services - besides the cost factor.

Existing quality approaches have a general disadvantage. The focus isolated quality aspects of technology, education or business factors.

The concept introduced here transfers traditional quality approaches to a new strategic approach. With the overall objective to provide successful business models, it integrates the traditional quality approaches into an integral perspective to quality. At this integration level technological, educational and economical quality parameters are related appropriately. The learner perspective serves as the central reference point.

The concept improves the quality significantly by concrete normative quality parameters which are embedded in a generic process-oriented quality framework.

28 E-learning quality and standards from a business perspective

Thomas Reglin

f-bb gGmbH, Germany

This article discusses quality requirements for e-learning from the perspective of vocational education and training (VET). It points out that the complexity of e-learning projects demands a specific *process model,* as realised in PAS 1032-1/ ISO 19796-1, that describes the manifold feedback loops between producers and customers as well as within interdisciplinary teams of experts, didacts, technicians etc. The specific demands of e-learning in enterprises concern all relevant process categories, i.e. requirement analysis, context, concept development, introduction, implementation and evaluation. *Standardisation* is an important economic factor, because the expected economisation of VET by means of e-learning cannot be realised without addressing large user groups. Reliable *quality criteria for products* require a differentiated description of e-learning according to objectives (e.g. information, exercise, discussion). Therefore the article finally submits an e-learning typology.

28.1 Learning and quality

The discussion concerning the quality of e-learning has been taking place on a wide scale since the mid-nineties and has gained tremendous momentum in recent years. In Germany, research institutes, professional associations and large companies had developed catalogues of assessment criteria that acknowledged different interests in its application (see Fricke, 2000), (Meier, 2000). Over here e-learning has been placed on the agenda of (among others) the department for the assessment of learning – launched in 2002 within the Stiftung Warentest – in which it has been subjected to analysis since 2001 (Töpper, 2003). The German Institute for Standardisation (DIN) has created work groups within the framework of the standardisation of ongoing developments that deal with the quality of e-learning on three levels: processes, products and didactics (Lindner, 2003). These efforts are currently being continued on a national and European level and the results of ongoing standardisation processes are now being introduced on an international level.

The *Transferability of quality management approaches into learning* was also sceptically received right from the start (Galiläer, 2005). The position of "customer orientation" − delivering services based on a particular demand of a customer − was criticised in favour of the position of "participant orientation"(Nittel, 1999) since it seemed that an "orientation based on subjective demand" would require being supplemented by a reflection concerning "objective demand" (ibid., p.177). The argument was that if learning focused on the mere provision of demanded "services" then it would gamble away its critical potential as well as its professionalism. Moreover, "vocational training" would finally dissociate itself from its pedagogical ethos, if it offered 'anything that pleases'" (Siebert, 1996, p. 53). Similar fundamental objections, however, are rather unusual in the field of vocational learning:

- Methods in quality management have been well integrated into the economy for many years.
- From a business perspective on human resource development, learning processes are less about "learning for self-enrichment purposes without a clear goal in mind" whose efficacy is hardly predictable (according to Schäffter, 2001) than they are about achieving explicitly defined objectives that are relevant to a firm's success. Processes and products are, then, consistently assessed based on their contribution towards the achievement of objectives. (To what extent this „qualification paradigm" is becoming obsolete in vocational learning, in light of the pressure to innovate which characterises a 'knowledge society,' cannot be discussed here).
- In companies lacking an employee education department, people in charge of vocational training depend upon formalised methods of quality control that allow them to generate action-relevant decisions whose efforts can be justified.

Essentially, there are four approaches to categorising methods of quality control of internal and external learning providers: *input-oriented* methods which focus on the quality of the resources utilised for processes of achievement; *output-oriented* methods that assess ex post facto whether and to what extent targeted goals were actually met; *process-oriented* methods focusing on potentials that are objectified within the organisational structure; finally *participant-protective and demand-oriented* methods that provide results of product tests or criteria for a demand-related evaluation of products being offered on the market (see table 28-1).

Table 28-1: Types of quality concepts

Type	Points of reference	Basis for assessment
input-oriented approaches	e.g. organisation, technology, personnel and methods of the e-learning provider	documents of the provider, references, etc.
output-oriented approaches	learning results and practical success of the participants	program evaluation
process-oriented approaches	the process of creating a learning program	certification
participant-protective and demand-oriented approaches	accredited quality controls, decision support for learning providers	test results, independent counseling, check lists, counseling literature

Source: According to the ideas of Faulstich, Gnahs, Sauter, 2003, p. 9ff.; supplemented

With regard to the *distribution* of elaborated methods of quality assurance, a differentiated perspective seems to be adequate. Besides (e.g. according to DIN ISO 9000) certified companies, which, moreover, set the quality criteria in the field of vocational training, there are also companies in which neither general nor special methods are used (see. table 28-2).

Table 28-2: Typology of business quality strategies in vocational training

quality management (QM)-systematics efforts towards "good" content quality in vocational training	+	–
+	**type 1** QM-systematics and efforts towards content quality in vocational training	**type 2** efforts towards content quality without a QM-systematics
–	**type 3** system related formalism of quality assurance in vocational training	**type 4** neither QM-systematics nor efforts towards "good" content quality in training

Source: Geldermann, Baigger, Geldermann, 2003, p. 85

If in what follows there are quality requirements for e-learning described from the perspective of companies involved in vocational training, then this is because this is based on the process model of the PAS 1032-1 (Publicly Available Specification) that was published at the beginning of 2004 under the supervision of the Department of Standardisation at the research and development stage within the DIN e.V. This is not the appropriate place to indicate a preference for any of the process approaches. (The PAS 1032-1 actually contains in its second part a catalogue of criteria concerning *product*-qualification − see also the article on the PAS in this issue). The process model of the PAS 1032-1, however, seems particularly suitable in its consistent acknowledgement of negotiation and interface problems and the variety of actors involved in e-learning projects. Here e-learning projects are mostly characterised – to various extents and degrees– by time-consuming briefings, counselling phases and instances of collaborative product development. At least several different feedback loops are required in the introductory phase to prevent e-learning in companies from becoming a foreign element within an environment hardly conducive to learning.

28.2   Process quality of e-learning from a business perspective

E-learning-services are developed in cooperative processes that synthesise the work of learning managers, experts, business practitioners, screenwriters, screen-designers, lecturers and other specialists (for a general overview see table 28-3). This results in a highly complex project management and specific feedback loops that become even more complicated through the interplay which occurs between clients in a company and external e-learning producers (but also: *internal* training providers offering e-learning).

Table 28-3: E-learning for business: process-participants

	Strategy/ concept	**Media production**	**Program implementation**
Provider	management pedagogical staff management controlling	experts experts in media didactics screen-writers screen-designers graphic-designers programmers cameramen/ -women speaker/ actors/ actresses	specialists/ administration LMS-administration lecturers evaluators
Business	management HR staff in company communication IT management controlling employee representatives	business-experts people in charge of vocational training representatives of target groups representatives of the IT department	learning employees colleagues immediate managers network-administrators evaluators

The PAS 1032-1 offers a reference model for quality management and quality assurance which, while going beyond the highly abstract and generic approach of the DIN ISO 9000ff., takes into account the particularities of vocational training and especially the processes involved in e-learning. It supports the quality management of e-learning providers and helps contribute towards transparency on the e-learning market. Thus, the prerequisites are established for minimising financial risk for both providers as well as for customers of e-learning. The PAS takes into consideration the particularities of technically supported learning processes by inserting certain process-elements – which are quite relevant to all learning offerings much in the way that layers of food are needed to make up a sandwich ("the sandwich principle")– whose necessity explicitly derives from the nature of media production in e-learning.

Table 28-4 displays process categories and processes involved in e-learning according to PAS 1032-1 and attributes problems to these categories that are (perhaps not only) relevant to vocational training in business.

Table 28-4: Process-categories of the PAS 1032-1 and particular problems of e-learning in business

Process category	Requirements in businesses
requirement analysis	e-learning-strategy
context	learning in contexts that are not optimised for learning processes
concept	adaptability
production	feedback loops
introduction	participation of actors
implementation	flexibility, certification
evaluation	quality assurance and economising

The particular demands of e-learning in business, noted in the second column, will be outlined in more detail below.

28.2.1   Requirement analysis

The need to emphasise on the planning phase in e-learning – compared to classical training in courses – applies to *every* field of asynchronical e-learning. Developing educational media is not only quite impossible without thinking about those who are going to be addressed by it and the context in which the learning offering will take place (this is also relevant to course planning). These presumptions, once they have become objectified in the media that has been designed –in contrast with scenarios involving a teacher and students where communication processes play a central role- *can no longer be amended through the interplay of pedagogical interactions.* Flawed decisions made in the planning phase are rather frustrating for learners and could be economically ruinous. Additionally, the objectified learning media have to be coupled with the pedagogical interactions in an intelligent manner (tele-tutoring, tele-coaching and virtual courses). While structuring these interactions in advance, crucial decisions occur that can only later be corrected with great difficulty.

In the context of organisational situated learning, this argument gains additional weight. The requirements are high when it comes to customising learning offerings. Tailor-made offerings are in demand (Stahl, Stölzl, 1994), (Severing, Stahl, 1995).

So the various actors who have specific needs are to be considered, which requires an increased effort in analysing how much and what demand exists and, consequently, also entails there being a particular relevance of *counselling services* for both internal and external e-learning providers – all the more so since most businesses have not yet elaborated an e-learning strategy. Counselling should not be too narrowly understood (in the sense of: "Get your company ready for e-learning."). The introduction of electronic learning media often leads to the establishment of *culture of autonomous learning* in the enterprise in question – and thus to changes that go well beyond mere technical transformations and include transitions towards organisational development. Counselling has to be able to bolster and facilitate this qualitative jump.

28.2.2   Context

The assumption that learning is "independent of space and time," which is often invoked by e-learning advertising, (for a critique see Reglin, 2005), (for an in-depth treatment see Schulmeister, 2005) means not least that learning takes place in contexts that are not optimised for learning processes (Grotlüschen, 2003). A demand for counselling also results from this. Moreover, media are to be developed with regard to context (e.g. a consideration of firewall regulations and the types of computer models available.).

28.2.3   Concept

Often collaborative product development will be the method of choice: that is, all relevant actors will already be participating in the phase of media development. If module-based learning offerings are developed, then the content availability would have to be ensured through adequate meta-data. The LOM-standard can prove to be rather cumbersome regarding maintenance as well as usability for end-users. For individual developments in HR departments, regulations on corporate design and on other internal standards have to be taken into consideration in most companies. This can also immediately involve questions concerning content, if work-instructions and business documents have to be included due to specific themes. (It will often be appropriate to provide opportunities for customisation for those offerings that will also be available to the public.)

28.2.4   Production

Feedback loops should also be provided for in the phase of media compilation (e.g. prototype tests which allow the relevant groups in companies to experience the learning offering in the first stages of its development – in particular the learners involved in vocational training). They ensure a sophisticated adaptation of learning media as well as learning infrastructure to the company's goals, to the needs of the actors and to the specific context of the company.

28.2.5   Introduction

Issues concerning the learning offering's adaptability to an organisational context and individual habits are at the very least critical to success, if an 'e-learning tradition' does not yet exist within a company. Then again it is also crucial to identify the target groups and to allow for their participation in the processes of change. ("Just confront your learners with the end-results and trust that they will appreciate the undeniable advantages of e-learning", so the seventh tip among "10 Tips for learning providers or how you will definitely fail by introducing e-learning" (Heller, 2003).)

28.2.6   Implementation

E-learning within the contexts of living and working requires a high degree of flexibility from learners. Providers – aware that some participants who participate in the introductory sequence of a course sometimes may decide not to log on any more (this might even be for a period of weeks) and who then might only access the learning service shortly before their account expires in order to 'deal with their e-learning syllabus' – can make concessions by offering the possibility of extending accounts in a way that does not require a lot of bureaucracy. It might be necessary to develop a close relationship between the IT departments of the e-learning provider and of the customer. Finally, a sophisticated and convincing certification program is an integral part of making the learning offering more attractive to learners in business.

28.2.7   Evaluation

Economic motives play a significant role in the transition to forms of web-based learning in vocational training. The issues of quality as well as cost are hardly separable in many arguments that have been brought forth in favour of implementing web-based learning in the context of vocational training programs. The benefits of e-learning are essentially assessed based on its economising effects that can be achieved when compared to vocational training that takes place in courses: e-learning fully substitutes phases of presence or partly does so within the context of hybrid scenarios ("blended learning"). It is to this extent that issues of quality and controlling are closely interwoven. Evaluations have to deal with the issue concerning to what extent it is possible to ensure high quality of the vocational training while decreasing at least its long-term costs. And: evaluation systems themselves have to be run on a small budget as well.

28.3   Significance of standards

The profitability of a web-based learning offering basically depends on whether it can be sold to large groups of people – either it is *originally* produced to meet the needs of a lot learners or it is initially only conceived to address the needs of a small group of learners and yet the circle of its users *expands* by means of marketing cooperation. An argument in favour of the significance of the latter solution is that three out of four identifiable business models in e-learning are based on the principle of marketing cooperation (Keating, 2002).

The possibility of such cooperation necessarily presupposes that standards for complex technical products are available: efforts towards standardisation and methods of quality assurance have to create the conditions for learning with electronic media that are of high quality and are cost effective. The required exchange between producer and distributor can only be realised – regarding technology and content – if standards are available that "increase the interconnection between systems particularly regarding transparency" (Pawlowski, 2004, p. 94). Well-known keywords here are *interoperability, reusability* and *metadata.* Content exchange can only be successful in crossing borders of complex and functionally varied, subdivided systems if internal differentiations can take place in an analogous way regarding structure and communication between the systems can occur on a consistent basis.

Standardisation, in the areas mentioned above, creates the required *prerequisites for market enlargement* that an e-learning product has to face – or, at any rate, it creates this market. In this respect, e-learning standards have immediate economic implications – particularly for the central aspect of the added value of e-learning – the content it offers. If this process of standardisation opens up new markets for e-learning providers, then customers from medium-sized businesses will profit from lower product prices. Large companies that develop e-learning products themselves or order them from external producers make use of the rationalisation effects of already existing product frameworks. Furthermore, the possibility then arises of marketing the product for a second time beyond the borders of one's business.

28.4   Perspectives in the discussion concerning product quality: Objectives for implementing e-learning as a mediating category?

Essentially, the discussion concerning the quality of learning *products* –and especially with regard to e-learning is currently moving between two extremes. On the one hand, "objective" approaches are positioned to attain product quality by means of (often extensive) catalogues of criteria. The following characteristics seem to be mostly plausible: learning software ought to be ergonomically optimised, factually correct, technically adaptable and so on and so forth. Each one of these assessment criteria can be subdivided into a variety of items (see table 28-5). The *unity* of an analysed product, however, runs the risk of being dissolved into a variety of details that need to be examined. Offerings, which are addressed to people in the world of business, reduce the complexity by means of multilevel assessment methods − e.g.: testing whether e-learning makes sense; the selecting of k.o. criteria for e-learning; offering further reaching quality criteria (see Tergan, Schenkel, 2004, p. 168f.). In online-solutions, the evaluation process − done by non-experts − can be facilitated through the provision of context support (see ibid, p. 170ff.).

On the other hand, there are "subjective" approaches that relate the quality of e-learning to user-typologies and individual attitudes (Ehlers, 2004b), (Zimmer, Psaralidis, 2000) and which conclude from a learner-orientated perspective that there is no e-learning quality "as such." This conclusion is supported by the fact that *personal judgements* concerning quality tend to be characterised by a sense of relativity. Depending upon the phase of life he finds himself in and on other existential factors, *any user* may reach different conclusions regarding the quality of a product if asked at different times.

Both perspectives do not exclude each other. Learning media are supportive tools for users in the context of individual developmental processes. They are not able to guarantee learning success − this expectation would lead to a teaching-learning short-circuit according to Holzkamp (Holzkamp, 1995) −, but they can be assessed according to their "usability" in the broad sense of the word (not only technically). "The usability of a product is the extent to which it can be utilised by a particular user to effectively, efficiently and satisfactorily reach certain goals within a particular context" (ISO-Norm 9241). Quality assessment, then, is concerned with the *potentials* of a tool that is used in relation to targeted objectives of its addressees within a particular *context*. Thus, the category of the objective mediates between "subjective" and "objective" aspects. The specification of objectives enables the structuring of extensive catalogues of criteria and the creation of evaluations, from which profiles concerning individual needs can be derived (see Kiedrowski, 2005).

The quality of e-learning "as such" does not exist just as e-learning "as such" does not. Usable criteria simply arise from a differentiated description of respective objectives. If learning objectives in companies are going to be described, then crucial differences will arise from the relation of media-design as well as the (technical and organisational) learning infrastructure to *practical action at work* (Reglin, Hölbling, 2004). Should learning be supported by work-place related production tools or information tools? Should employees be extensively prepared for new activities? Or should there exist processes for practising skills and techniques provided that they remain independent from real contexts through simulation software in order to avoid risks and minimise costs? A systematics of objectives, software types and quality criteria that are to be treated with priority are outlined in table 28-5.

Table 28-5: E-learning-typology according to objectives, my own overview

Objectives	Learning-software-type	Characteristics	Attributable priorities
quick access to required information	information tool	open structure, free access; low level of didactics; practical tools; "reference modus"	convenient search functions (full text, keyword, sitemap…)
enhancing present knowledge in a focused way	module-based learning tool	plurality of learning paths; systematically or ad hoc usable; requires autonomous learning competence (selection, transfer)	meta data, LMS/ shop system with quick access possibilities
appropriation of new fields of business knowledge	electronic course	sequentialisation based on content systematics; reflexivity on actions at work is required	orientation-system, function for notes, e-tutoring, certification
skills/ gain action potency (subjectivity) in a protective environment	exercise tool	sequentialisation based on practical critical incidents up to experienced problems; simulative character; practicing routines and behavioral scripts e.g. in a software application	high quality of multi-media elements with an adequate level of abstraction, realism
support in creative problem solving processes	discussion forum, exchange platform	scaffolding of problem-solving, communication platform	clarity, version management, notification function
structuring of creative processes	production tools	tools for visualisation and structuring	intuitive usability, export possibilities, decision latitude

Source: Reglin, 2003

Differentiated analyses of objectives do not only allow for the creation of catalogues of criteria on behalf of the provider but they also contribute towards the profiling of media undergoing development.

29   A framework for quality of learning resources

Frans van Assche, Riina Vuorikari

European Schoolnet, Belgium

To better understand the complex question of quality of web-based learning resources it is beneficial to look at the different processes during the life of a learning resource; what are the aspects of quality that are related to the creation of material, its discovery and eventually its use and re-use for learning purposes. Obviously this involves different roles which should be distinguished as quality aspects are different for those roles.

This chapter therefore looks at the different processes related to learning resources and the roles involved in these processes with the aim to understand the quality aspects of the processes as well as the roles, which have responsibilities regarding the quality for these processes.

29.1   Introduction

Digital learning resources[109] are increasingly used in education thanks to the variety of ways that they can be created, delivered, used and re-used in different learning contexts. Since the creation and use of digital learning material is getting within the reach of every learner and teacher, more focus is placed on the quality of digital learning resources. As millions of digital learning resources are currently available the question is how does a user (teacher, learner, author etc.) obtain the few quality learning resources she can use? The discussion ranges from usability aspects of digital resources to technical and pedagogical requirements, touching upon issues about standards and interoperability regarding the storage, discovery, retrieval and delivery of content. Furthermore, as repositories are accessible across the globe, the transferability of resources to a different educational culture, lingual or pedagogical setting becomes more important.

---

[109] A digital learning resource is defined as any entity, which can be used or re-used or referenced during technology supported learning. The range is from a simple asset such as a picture to a complete course.

29.2   What processes and roles are involved?

In this section, first the processes related to learning resources are explained and next the roles involved are expounded. In figure 29-1 these processes are depicted as actions of a typical usage scenario during the life of a learning resource. Similar usage scenarios for learning resources exist in the field[110], they are usually based on formal use cases acting as a base for UML models. While many variants to this typical usage scenario may exist and actions can be skipped, all the actions should be taken into account when discussing the topic of quality. Each action will need to be of sufficiently high technical quality AND be accepted by the roles involved.

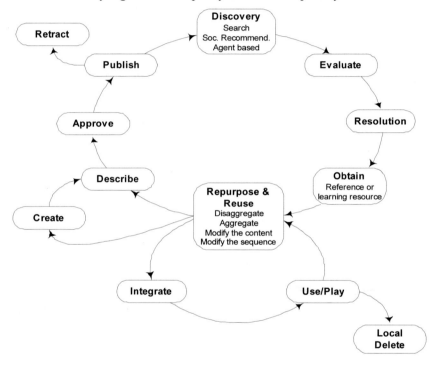

Fig. 29-1: A typical usage scenario for learning resources

The actions on learning resources are:

---

[110] A number of European Schoolnet's consortium members carry out work on learning resources, for example Kennisnet has used similar scenarios to depict the value chain of learning resources (http://contentketen.kennisnet.nl/programma/toelichting/contentketen).

Create

The creation of a digital learning resource might involve base material, tools, a methodology, and skilled persons. The creation process might differ very much on what one is creating; a picture might involve a simple click on a digital camera, a complete course might involve a complete team of subject experts, graphical artists, software engineers, etc.

Describe

Describing a learning resource is providing the metadata of it and follows nowadays usually a standard or a specification, more in particular the IEEE LOM standard (IEEE, 2002) or the DCMI metadata term specification (DCMI).

Approve

Approving a learning resource is the endorsement to make it available to the intended audience. It might be a formal process with a publisher, or a ministry of education which approves a learning resource for use in schools, or a peer review by fellow teachers. The approval process may be more or less formal.

Publish

Once the learning resource is approved, it is made available, under commercial conditions or freely, to the intended audience. This might range from making it available to a single learner up to everyone in the world. Typically for a digital learning resource the internet and the World Wide Web is used as a channel for publishing its metadata.

Discovery

While the publishing of a learning resource makes it available to someone, this person needs to become aware of its existence before she can make use of it.

Evaluate

After having discovered a learning resource a user would evaluate it according to her own criteria.

Resolution

Once a suitable learning resource has been found, a digital learning resource requires a handle (e.g. a token) in order to obtain it. Before getting such a handle it might be that a digital rights agreement needs to be generated and checked.

Obtain

There are various ways in which a digital learning resource can be obtained, but typically in a World Wide Web context it would be through downloading or playing it remotely.

Repurpose & reuse

Before using a learning resource it might require some adaptation in terms of language, cultural, or pedagogic aspects, etc. In addition one might wish to use only parts of the learning resource or aggregate it with more material. In this way learning resources can be re-used in the creation of new ones that in turn can be described, approved, published, etc.

Integrate

The learning resource, whether modified or not, is used in a variety of technical contexts. For example using an interactive whiteboard or incorporated into any one of the hundreds of virtual learning environments available. The institutional context is also an issue:

- New integrated approaches to re-thinking learning.
- Whole school approaches to ICT-based learning.
- The wider institutional context of municipality (e.g. centralised purchase and hosting of learning resources) and national government (e.g. national schemes of assessment of learning with digital learning resources).

A key activity is to identify opportunities and challenges for institutions to integrate learning resources to improve teaching and learning.

Using[111]

Eventually the learning resource is used in a learning setting which may be the classroom, at home, in collaboration with others, etc. The learning context is often constructivist and activities encourage active, learner-centred pedagogies.

Local delete

In a scenario where a teacher or learner has obtained a learning resource, she eventually may dispose it.

---

[111] A number of European Schoolnet's consortium members carry out work on learning resources, for example Kennisnet has used similar scenarios to depict the value chain of learning resources (http://contentketen.kennisnet.nl/programma/toelichting/contentketen).

Retract

The persons/ organisations that published a learning resource might decide to retract it.

In figure 29-1, there are two cycles intersecting at the modifying point (actually running in parallel through finding, evaluating and obtaining):

- The product development and marketing cycle: creating, publishing, discovery, evaluating, resolution, obtaining, modifying.
- The teaching cycle: finding, evaluating, obtaining learning resources, and then modifying, integrating and using learning resources.

While in smaller settings not every action is done, success of a complete system for learning resources depends on the success of all actions. Each action will need to be of sufficiently high technical quality AND be accepted by the user community.

Quality is often succinctly defined as 'fitness for purpose' and hence quality might be appreciated very subjectively. However for practical purposes, in order to come to some shared view on quality in the context of learning resources, it is necessary to relate quality to the shared objectives, requirements and needs of the different roles involved in the processes during the life of a learning resource. The involvement into the different activities will vary according to the roles as shown in table 29-1.

Table 29-1: User roles and involvement at different stages

	Author	Publisher	Teacher	Learner	Librarian
Create	xx		x	x	
Describe	xx	xx	x	x	xx
Approve	xx	xx	x	x	xx
Publish	x	xx	x	x	x
Discover	xx	xx	xx	xx	xx
Evaluate	xx	xx	xx	xx	xx
Resolution	xx	xx	xx	xx	
Obtain	xx	xx	xx	xx	
Adapt & Reuse	xx		xx	x	
Integrate			xx	xx	
Use/ play			xx	xx	

xx-strong involvement, x-occasional involvement

29.3   Quality aspects of the usage scenario

This section looks into the different processes of figure 29-1 and identifies major issues related to the quality at each stage giving examples of good practice or discussing the current research done in the field. As pointed out in section 1, quality is related to the roles involved in the process and is much related to the *effective-*

ness of the process; i.e. did the teacher find what he was looking for, can the learning resource effectively be integrated, to what extent did the learner learn, etc. The major factors influencing quality of the processes outlined in the previous section are the material, the tools and infrastructure, the methodology (e.g. pedagogy, learning resource construction methods), and the people. The following explanation of the usage scenario is in reversal order starting from the usage stage, as the actions are built upon another.

29.3.1   Use

The quality of use of a learning resource is related to what the learner(s) eventually learned. This is determined by the intrinsic quality of the learning resource itself, the pedagogy, the tools and infrastructure, and the people delivering and/ or using the learning resource.

Aspects of the learning resource itself

A learning resource will be used most effectively if it fits the desired learning situation as defined by the person (e.g. teacher) or system (e.g. LMS) that is supporting the learning process. Typical quality characteristics (see for example (Benigno, 2001)) one will find are:

- Accuracy: the resource must be reliable, valid and authoritative.
- Clarity; the resource must provide a clear link between the purpose (goals, objectives) and the content and procedures suggested.
- Appropriateness: the resource must contained information for the intended learners' level. The information must use appropriate vocabulary, language and concepts.
- Completeness: the resource must include wide information related to self-contained activities, material required, prerequisites, information for obtaining related resources, assessment criteria, link to quality indicators.
- Motivation: the information must engage the learner with interest and satisfaction. A great motivator is the capability to attract attention.
- Composition and organisation: the resource must be easy to use both for teacher and pupil. It must flow in an orderly manner, using organising tools (heading, map) and avoiding the use unrelated elements that are potentially ineffective or overpowering.

Pedagogy

Different scenarios such as independent adult learning, group learning, or the learning resource used by a teacher in a classroom should be considered. Obviously, in the latter case the quality of the learning experience will not solely depend on the quality of the learning resource but also on how effectively it is delivered and used by the teacher. In particular where the pedagogy should be has been subject to much debate. For example McCormick (McCormick, 2003) concluded that the pedagogy should be outside the learning resource.

> "I have argued that LOs that try to contain pedagogy, which draws upon contemporary ideas of learning are unlikely to satisfy learning theorists. Where collections of LOs are put together in pedagogically sound ways, this then moves away from the focus on the LOs themselves to the planning tool used by teachers to assemble them or the learning environment within which they are used. At one level it might be better to take a minimalist view of LOs and instead use learning assets, at another level, teachers will want to benefit from the high production values that content and software producers can muster."

However, in a context of distance learning or training, the learning resource itself might benefit of some built-in pedagogical aspects. That could come in four ways:

- Built-in, for instance in an assessment based sequencing following IMS Learning Design (cf. chapter 16).
- Added by the teacher in the integration and delivery processes.
- In the metadata: the metadata may contain clues of how to use the learning resource.
- In another learning resource. This is sometimes referred to as 'teaching resource'. For example one might have a learning resource built around a piece of music like 'The Moldau' or 'Peter and the wolf' and some other resources may then explain how a teacher can use the musical resources in the classroom.

Tools and infrastructure

The tools and infrastructure used will significantly influence the learning. Obviously, there should be a minimum ICT infrastructure in order to enable e-learning. Some specific measures may make a difference. For example the introduction of a beamer in the classroom had a significant effect in one country, as now students were able to show what they had been producing on the web.

Positive effects of personal hand-held and mobile devices were reported already a few years ago. For an example see (Curtis, 2002).

Technical requirements of a learning resource are usually explained in the metadata (see section 3.6), but many times the average user is not aware of the requirements. Platform dependence or required software can cause major headaches to teachers who would like to use digital resources but lack the knowledge and skills. More ways to avoid these situations should be investigated, for example before downloading, the resource system could make a check of relevant software (operating system) availability and prompt before downloading that required software or plug-in is missing. The earlier the warning the better.

People

The learning experience is also heavily influenced by the way the learning resource is delivered. Typically in a school setting, it will very much depend on the quality of delivery by the teacher. In this context, professional training is key. However, it entirely depends on what professional training teachers can get in the field of pedagogical use of learning resources. Only recently more in depth research has started and it will still take a while before good practice becomes more common.

29.3.2   Integration, repurpose & reuse

Integration has two aspects: technical integration and integration into the class room use (pedagogical integration).

Technical integration

A learning resource will have a specific format often expressed as a MIME type or it may be a combination of different specific formats such as in a web page where text, audio, pictures, and even interactive applets may appear. Technical integration will be effective to the extent that the user can integrate the learning resource in the technical environment and/ or with other material. Typically one would be concerned with the hardware infrastructure, the players or viewers required, and the integration might involve some form of conversion to fit the technical environment.

Repurpose, adaptation and pedagogical integration

Pedagogical integration is effective to the extent that the learning resource can be fitted into the overall pedagogical approach. This may involve some adaptation of the learning resource, sometimes called 'repurposing'. The repurposing may be for a different audience - with different language; culture, or age group - or for a different pedagogical approach.

How teachers actually use learning resources in their teaching can be quite independent of the intended pedagogical approach that the learning resource has, as observed in the CELEBRATE case studies (Ilomäki, 2004). This observation relates to the pedagogical consideration of section 3.1 and more in depth research on these aspects is needed.

Reuse

Reuse is effective to the extent that a learning resource or any part of it can be fit into another learning resource or in another context for learning. Reuse in the broad sense includes proper description of how the resource can be reused, providing the necessary discovery and retrieval tools, dealing with the rights for reuse, and the actual reuse itself. The latter might involve disaggregating a learning resource, aggregating it with other components, changing the structure of a learning resource, etc. Creating a reusable learning resource, as a digital artifact, is reasonably similar to creating a reusable component as in the object oriented approach for software engineering. The principles of encapsulation, appropriate granularity, maximum cohesion and minimum coupling can be applied as well.

Allowing re-use of learning resources has economical consequences, but also adds to the quality, because often improvements are suggested and implemented in this way. The possibility to re- and dis-aggregate the resource enhances the learner's ability to construct one's own knowledge and actively reflect upon the learning experience, as well as share it with other learners and users, which are natural parts of any learning experience.

29.3.3   Resolution & obtain

Obtaining

Obtaining a learning resource is effective to the extent that the learning resource has become available to the user. There are three basic models:

- The learning resource is played remotely. For example a piece of music or a video might be provided as streaming media.
- The learning resource is downloaded and played under the control of a shared system such as an MLE, or LMS, LCMS, local server.
- The learning resource is downloaded to the user's personal computer.

From a users' perspective the easier the resource is accessible and faster it is downloaded, the better it is. Here, the variables are many and are located both at the repository's end and at users' local. The issue might even become more complex in the case of (a network of) brokerage systems. To illustrate issues related, for instance, in the CELEBRATE evaluation users and teachers who preferred to download resources to their own (or classroom) computer and play/ view the learning resource from there had major points of frustration doing it.

Resolution

Resolution is effective to the extent that a handle to obtain the learning resource is clearly given or rejected based on the identification of the learning resource and possibly the user. The complexity of this operation might vary; for example, if the identifier (e.g. a URL) obtained during discovery is also the handle to obtain the learning resource. In this case the resolution activity is void. A more complex case is when the learning resource is subject to the enforcement of a digital rights expression. In this case it might involve the identification of the user or user role by an identity management system, the generation of an agreement based on the licenses specified for this user (role), and the enforcement of the agreement.

Currently, a number of Digital Rights Expression Languages (IEEE, 2003) and schemes exist as well as identity management schemes. The application of digital rights ranges from closed and commercial content, as for example applied by publishers, to open and free content. For the latter, the Creative Commons Licence[112] has gained popularity as a simple means to ensure that the copyright is respected, as well as to send a clear message for others about the terms of re-use.

As resolution may involve some other services such as an identity management system and digital rights management system, the quality of resolution will also depend on the quality (reliability, availability, accessibility, response time etc.) of those services. In addition, interoperability between the players/ viewers of the learning resources and the other services must be effective. The requirements will be different dependent on the way the learning resource is obtained; i.e. download versus remote play.

29.3.4   Discover & evaluate

"Water, water everywhere, nor any drop to drink"[113]

Discovery and evaluation is effective to the extent that it results into the identification of all relevant learning resources and only the relevant learning resources. This definition of quality for discovery and evaluation builds on well-known concepts of information retrieval: silence and noise.

- Silence: the ratio of the number of relevant learning resources not found over the number of learning resources found;
- Noise: the ratio of the number of irrelevant learning resources found over the number of learning resources found[114].

---

[112] Creative Commons, http://www.creativecommons.org.

[113] Lines from "The Rime of the Ancient Mariner" by Samuel Taylor Coleridge.

[114] In information retrieval the terms recall and precision are also used. Low silence means high recall and vice versa. Low noise means high precision and vice versa.

Search engines such as Google, for example, have a reasonably low silence (high recall) but a very high noise (low precision). It is often the case that a user (teacher, learner) is looking for a single learning resource that suits her best. This has been the reason for introducing better discovery and evaluation techniques. The more precise the discovery is the less effort needs to be spent on evaluation.

Discovery

Many techniques can be used for discovery, including

- Browsing
- Searching
- Different forms of recommendations and advisory models such as based on previous actions 'users interested in learning resource A are also interested in these learning resources X, Y, and Z', user modelling and social networks
- Agent-based systems
- Selective dissemination of information

Usually it results in a list of candidate learning resources to be evaluated. The list may be ordered by some property such as relevance, price, publication date, etc. More advanced result presentation schemes may use two (or three) dimensional presentations or zoomable tree structures, clusters, with different colours or font size, etc to indicate relevance or another criterion. These information visualisation techniques, see for example (Klerkx, 2004), can also be an effective way to display the availability of resources in a repository.

Evaluation

The user may have many criteria for evaluation and typically they would be related to what he wants to do with it, i.e. the activities following evaluation (see figure 29-1). For example a user might select a learning resource on the basis of one or more of the following criteria:

- Does the learning resource contribute sufficiently to the pedagogical goals? Is it clear what students should already know and what they can learn? How should it be used? Are examples given?
- Does it fit the one of my learning settings? Is it the right level of difficulty?
- Has it adequate usability (Human Computer Interaction and didactics)?
- Is it for my audience: educational direction, age group?
- Is it in the right language? Is it on the right subject? Does it fit the curriculum?
- If I want to adapt it can I easily do it? Do I have sufficient time to do it?
- Can I easily integrate it? Can the assignment for students easily be formulated?
- What use does the copyright allow? Is it affordable?
- How much preparation do I need? How much do I need to learn myself?

- Is it safe for my students to use it? Has it the right accessibility?
- What are the technical requirements?
- How easy is the coaching (including assessment) when using it?

In order to come to a successful evaluation, the teacher or learner should have access to the learning resource itself, a learning resource preview, or metadata. Metadata in the broad sense includes all annotations, comments, evaluation, and feedback from other users. More and more, the feedback, reviews and evaluations, either by board of experts or other users have become a valuable source of information on resource's usability.

One of the major issues in the area of discovery and evaluation is the *semantic interoperability*. Does the user trying to discover and evaluate a learning resource understand the information in the same way as the person who provided this information? Semantic interoperability seeks to ensure that this is indeed the case. It poses challenges of bridging differences in language, culture, vocabularies, etc.

It is only when the evaluation is satisfactory that one can say that a user has found a learning resource. Since discovery and evaluation are usually subjective, more advanced techniques, such as agents, will also use information about the user and her preferences.

29.3.5   Approve and publish

Many models of publishing mechanism and channels exist for digital learning resources, roughly those being institutionalised such as commercial publishers and public institutions or consortia (can have commercial interest too), whereas the others are based on economy of exchange between individuals in an organised or not-so-organised way. Before publishing resources the resources go through either an explicit or implicit approval process with the intention to assure the high standards and quality of the content provided.

Quality, conformance and other labels are used fairly extensively in e-learning products in general and nowadays to a certain extent also within learning resources. Some countries, institutions and consortium have labels approving for example technical compliance, the curriculum compliance or appropriateness of the resources. Many learning platforms and learning resource producers, for example, note their compliance to IMS specifications, in Canada a quality mark is in use for e-learning products and in France the General Inspectorate to the Ministry of Education has a process to review all the learning resources before they receive a label of approval and can be distributed through the official web-based repositories and channels.

The effectiveness of the approval process depends however very much on the context. For example a publisher will have a formal procedure while a teacher might find the opinion of a colleague sufficient. Experience has shown that the approval context should fit the creation and publishing context. Formal quality assurance procedures are very likely to fail in an informal creation and publishing context. In this case voluntary and peer reviews are more effective.

Being explicit about the approval process and the origin of the resource is much appreciated.

29.3.6   Describe

The aim of describing a learning resource is to facilitate the activities of the usage scenario (see figure 29-1). The description is effective to the extent that it indeed helps in the discovery, the evaluation, obtaining, modifying, integrating, and using the resource. The description may be human readable, for instance the pedagogical objective, and/ or machine readable, for instance a digital rights expression in ODRL (Open Digital Rights Language).

Description is more effective if it uses a model that is shared between the information providers, the readers of the information and the tools they are using. It is for this purpose that models such as the LOM and DC have been proposed. A further specification tailored to a user community is elaborated in a so-called application profile. An example is given in (van Assche, 2003).

29.3.7   Create

The production of learning resources, whether it was creation from scratch or aggregating from already existing components, is the crucial stage where aspects of interoperability, accessibility, transferability, repurposing and re-use are determined. The qualities that have the most effect on the overall quality are based on the usefulness of the content for the learning experience (desired learning outcomes), possibilities to reuse the content or its components (cost-effectiveness), and the pedagogical affordance (i.e. the pedagogical clue to the use of an object) of the resources.

At the creation stage the attention is on the design and implementation. Digital learning resources come in almost as many formats and models as there are authors of them, a feature that, on the one hand, makes the richness of the media. On the other hand, as there are very few models that practitioners follow, it also makes the bulk of digital learning content very heterogeneous which consequently makes the quality assurance somewhat harder. At the creation level, re-usability is related to the choices of technical standards. In some of the cases, authors and publishers do not even intend to make their resources reusable, as the decision might be part of a business model.

29.3.8   Retract and delete

Retract and delete are effective to the extent that all obsolete material is retracted/ deleted and useful material is not retracted/ deleted.

29.3.9   Summary and conclusions

This chapter discusses the quality of learning resources from a product and process oriented perspective. It covers all processes involved from creation to use. Whereas on an individual level not every listed process will happen, all processes are important from a systemic point of view and the system will be as good as its weakest link. As quality is related to purpose, this chapter highlights the different roles involved in the processes. For example quality characteristics of a learning resource will be different for an author who must maintain a learning resource than to a learner who will value that it runs in her technical environment.

Improving the quality requires an understanding of and action on all the processes and roles involved. Therefore, also the context in which these processes appear is emphasised. As such this chapter provides a full framework for dealing with quality of learning resources.

30 LearnRank: Towards a *real* quality measure for learning

Erik Duval

Katholieke Universiteit Leuven, Belgium

This paper starts from the notion that quality is context dependent and proposes "LearnRank", a context-dependent ranking algorithm focused on learning applications, as a vision for how to *really* measure quality. This proposal is based on early experiences with the ARIADNE learning object repository and avoids the focus on characteristics that may be easier to measure, but that are less relevant to the usefulness and usability that determines the relevancy of a learning object. This paper does not develop a precise definition of LearnRank. Rather, it analyses in some detail the notion of context and how that influences LearnRank.

30.1 Introduction[115]

This chapter starts from the notion that "quality" is not so much a characteristic of a learning object[116], but rather a characteristic of how such object is used in a particular context. Many facets influence the quality of a learning object in a particular context: target audience, learning objective, time, location etc. This notion of context applies to quite traditional learning resources as well as to more technology based ones, as the following examples illustrate:

---

[115] Acknowledgements: This work is financially supported by the "Onderzoeksfonds K.U.Leuven//Research Fund K.U.Leuven" and the ProLearn Network of Excellence (http://www.prolearn-project.org/, itself supported by the European Commission). The work also benefited greatly from the discussions in the CEN/ISSS Workshop on Learning Technologies (http://www.cenorm.be/isss/Workshop/lt/) and within my research unit (http://ariadne.cs.kuleuven .ac.be/hmdb/jsp/Wiki?Research). Special thanks to Wayne Hodgins for the inspiring conversations!

[116] We will use the term "learning object" in a very loose sense here, referring to any kind of resource that is useful and relevant for learning. In this context, a learning object can be any kind of content, of any kind of granularity. It can also include other kinds of entities that are relevant for learning, like activities or people. See (Verbert et al., 2005) for a more in-depth analysis of a learning object content model with a much more precise definition of "learning object".

- A physics handbook for 16-year-old children will have a different "quality" for PhD. students in physics than for the audience it was originally intended for.
- A handbook that is very well suited for self-directed learning by PhD. students is not necessarily that useful as a teaching support in classroom settings.
- A physics handbook can be well suited as a general introduction in the overall field of physics, but may be less suited for a maintenance repair technician who needs to refresh a particular physics principle.

Not only is quality, by its very nature, context dependent, it is also intrinsically subjective. In that sense, the subject (for our purposes: the learner) is part of the context – or determines the context, that is more of a philosophical difference that is less relevant here.

30.2   Early Ariadne experiences

Our experiences over the last decade in the ARIADNE Foundation (Ariadne) illustrate how seemingly sensible strategies to deal with quality, typically derived from the non-digital world or methodologies developed for academic publishing, are naïve and misguided in the context of a large-scale repository.

We originally intended to impose a quality policy that would restrict the introduction of learning objects into our repository (Forte et al., 1999). After long and difficult discussions, we had to recognise that there was no consensus on precise and usable criteria that would determine the quality. One of the important reasons why such consensus could not be reached was the severe cultural difference in how such quality was viewed in for instance Latin and Nordic European countries.

We then compromised for quality review of the *metadata about* the learning objects, rather than reviewing the objects themselves. The idea was that, if for instance the metadata asserted that a handbook was meant for graduate students, then that was a piece of information that could be reviewed for its relevancy and accurateness. In order to implement this approach, we operated a scheme in which reviewers were assigned a domain of expertise (related to subject, but also, for instance, to language), and reviewed periodically new learning objects, or rather: the accuracy of their metadata. Initially, only the objects whose metadata were reviewed were made available to end users. However, this created a serious bottleneck, as it would sometimes take a long time before the new content would actually be reviewed[117].

In the end, we opted for a scheme wherein the *ranking* of a learning object in a list of search results could be influenced by, among others, the fact that its metadata had been reviewed. Reflecting on this evolution with the benefit of hindsight, it seems to me that there is a deeper trend here: rather than thinking about quality in a binary way, where resources either do or do not qualify to quality criteria, we

---

[117] (Zemsky and Massy, 2004) report a similar finding with the MERLOT repository, where less than 10% of the material is peer reviewed – although this concerns an actual review of the content itself, rather than the metadata only, the findings go in the same direction as our experience.

should reconsider this notion as one that is multi-facetted and that influences the ranking rather than the inclusion of an object in a particular context.

30.3   The problem with quality

The fact that quality is context dependent complicates its automated processing: it suggests that algorithms need to take into account a wide variety of characteristics for a realistic determination of quality. Worse, the subjective nature of quality suggests that such automated processing may be intrinsically impossible: how can an algorithm capture the highly personal preferences and characteristics that determine the experience of an individual?

I believe that the complication described above leads to an overly strong focus in the "learning quality world" on less relevant quality aspects that *can* be measured and processed, like process characteristics or simple learning object properties. Whereas it is clear that these aspects are relevant to some extent, they avoid the real problem of trying to measure quality *in context*.

I believe that a different approach to quality is needed altogether and will refer to it here as a "LearnRank": the basic idea is that we can very well process automatically *real* quality aspects, very much in the same way that for instance Google can serve quality web pages, or Amazon can serve quality books and other products, or Tivo can serve quality television content[118].

30.4   LearnRank

30.4.1   Context revisited

The notion of context, and how it determines quality, is worth considering in more detail. There has been substantial research on the subject of context in the field of ubiquitous computing – see for instance (Coutaz et al., 2005).

However, here we briefly analyse some of the characteristics of quality and how they relate to learning.

- *Learning goal:* What the learner wants to learn (Miller et al., 1996)
  This is quite obvious: a student in medicine will not learn about the functioning of the human heart with material on economical statistics… In a slightly more subtle way, that same material on economical statistics may be relevant to someone studying the evolution of disruptive technologies. However, if the learner is not aware of the relevancy of the material, then it will still fail to support his learning in an efficient and effective way.

---

[118] This theme was also explored in (Rehak, 2004) and (Duval, Hodgins, 2004).

- *Learning motivation:* Why the learner wants to learn (Murphy, Alexander, 2000)
  An inherently motivated student will need less explicit rationale for why she is engaged in a particular activity, whereas a student going through mandatory material in a formal learning session may need to be reminded of why statistics is relevant in the context of learning about for instance business administration. Of course, if the relevancy of the material needs to be made explicit, then that seems to suggest that there is a problem with the instructional design in the first place.
- *Learning setting:* Activities surrounding the learning object (Dalziel, 2003)
  The sort of activities that Learning Design (IMS) or Learning Activity Management System (LAMS) define around learning objects (or within the objects, that distinction is not important here) also influence quality: as an example, a provocative historical document may be very appropriate in a discussion context, and much less so in an unsupported self study mode.
- *Time:* Available time, as well as time of day
  When a mechanic needs to learn how to repair a piece of equipment necessary for an ongoing emergency operation, the time-to-learn should be minimised at all cost. However, when the same mechanic is learning about the same kind of repair procedure during a master class, a more in-depth learning process, which also considers the underlying principles of physics may be more appropriate.
  Time may well have an effect in a different way, as many of us learn differently according to the time of day: there is at least anecdotal evidence that suggests that many learners are better at more abstract learning in the morning, and more background learning in the evenings.
- *Space:* Geographical as well as architecture
  Especially in "mobile learning" applications, the influence of space on quality of learning objects is obvious: connecting the learning experience to the physical environment can reinforce its effect tremendously.
  Physical spaces in general, and architecture in particular, also influence the efficiency and effectiveness of learning. Ambient learning through educational "roomware" could have a deep impact on the quality of learning resources.
- *Culture and language:* Not only geographically (Niles, 1995)
  Especially in a multi-cultural and –lingual context like Europe, the effect of language and culture is obvious: a learning object in a language that the learner doesn't master will not have the same quality as an otherwise similar object in her mother tongue.
  What is often neglected, is that this observation applies not only to geographically determined differences in culture, but also to the difference between other kinds of cultures, such as the academic versus the corporate culture, or a learning context for engineers versus scientists versus medical learners, etc.
- *Educational level:* Age and learning background
  It is rather obvious that toddlers learn differently from elderly learners, and that age has an impact on how for instance colours and sound can either reinforce or detract from the learning experience.

Similarly, academic researchers and "knowledge workers" probably have a different set of expectations and requirements for learning objects from repair mechanics or nurses.

- *Accessibility:* Design for all (Stephanidis, 2001)
  Finally, it is important to note that some objects may require specific auditory, visual, motor or other skills from the learners. Designing resources with that in mind, so that alternative interaction modes are possible, in a "design for all" approach, often benefits everybody, and not just the "disabled" learner.
  As an example, most of us have problems learning from highly visual material while driving a car, as our eyes tend to be engaged with the task of driving. Making the relevant resources also available in a non-visual way (for instance: in an auditory way) not only benefits the learner with a visual disability, but also all the driving learners!

30.4.2   PageRank revisited

As long as the web was relatively small, the main selling point of search engines was how much material they indexed and how efficient they were in processing a query.

However, as the web moved past the "tipping point" and the number of results to a typical query rose from tens to hundreds to many thousands and even millions, ranking the results in a meaningful way became more and more important. Nowadays, the success of search engines like Google and Yahoo depends to a large extent on their ability to rank results in response to a query. Indeed, Google's success is often attributed to its PageRank algorithm, used to rank search results. Contrary to common belief, this algorithm is only to a minimal level based on keywords, the number of times they occur and the location in the document where they occur.

Much more innovative and crucial is the use in PageRank of incoming links to determine the relevancy of a particular document. As explained in (Boldi et al., 2005):

> "One suggestive way to describe the idea behind PageRank is as follows: consider a random surfer that starts from a random page, and at every time chooses the next page by clicking on one of the links in the current page (selected uniformly at random among the links present in the page). As a first approximation, we could define the rank of a page as the fraction of time that the surfer spent on that page on the average. Clearly, important pages (i.e., pages that happen to be linked by many other pages, or by few important ones) will be visited more often, which justifies the definition."

In this way, PageRank exploits the human activities of all web authors who decide to link to pages that they consider relevant. Note that this sort of algorithm does not require any librarian type of effort, but rather is integrated into the very act of authoring material in the first place: this is important, as "librarian metadata don't scale" (Duval, Hodgins, 2004b), (Weibel, 2005)!

30.4.3   Towards the development of LearnRank

If we apply the basic idea behind PageRank to learning, then the "LearnRank" of a resource should indicate how useful people have found this object for their learning. And, as with PageRank, we would need to be able to determine this without asking the learner, author or librarians to provide additional metadata about the object in question.

Objects that have been used in many contexts, or, more importantly, in many contexts that are relevant to a specific learner, should have a higher LearnRank for that learner. The underlying assumption here is that learning objects with a higher quality for a particular context will end up being reused more often in that context than lower quality ones. As LearnRank becomes more and more established, that assumption will become a self fulfilling prophecy, as the higher quality material will be higher ranked, and therefore more used, and therefore this effect will strengthen itself in a quality feedback loop.

In an ideal world, we would actually bootstrap and steer this process through empirical data on the learning effect that specific objects have actually caused (or helped to realise) in specific contexts: if we were able to track that a particular simulation helped graduate students understand with a high degree of efficiency and effectiveness certain effects of the laws of thermodynamics, then, surely, the LearnRank of this object could be quite high when a similar learner is trying to master similar material in a similar context.

However, even though we are optimistic that progress is being made on gathering that kind of empirical data on learning effect (especially in a corporate or military context, where, admittedly, the task of measuring the relevant indicator is often simpler), there are alternatives available already now to help bootstrap the LearnRank algorithm.

- Imagine that 10% of professors in Human-Computer Interaction in the French language for undergraduate students start using a particular tool with their students. Is that not a strong indication that this tool has a high "quality" in that context? What about 20%? Or 80%?
- Suppose that we track (as we can!) the correlation between the objects that learners work with and their performance on a post-test that assesses whether they have actually mastered a specific law of thermodynamics. Would that correlation not give a good indication of "quality"?

Of course, there is much work to be done on elaborating and evaluating the fine details of the LearnRank idea, but the principle should be clear from what has been presented above. Now that the technical standards are finally in place to enable the development of an open infrastructure for learning, we can finally achieve the scale that is necessary to get to the numbers where the idiosyncrasies of one learner or teacher or context will no longer skew everybody's results.

30.4.4   If content is king, then context is queen

Moreover, just like Google and other search engines rely on search terms (and more and more on context, such as location, past search histories, etc.!) to constrain the web graph to the portion that is relevant to the user at that moment, learning applications can constrain the search space to only those resources that are relevant to the learner.

Most interestingly, in a learning context, we can actually go much further than web search engines, because we can exploit much richer metadata about the user, his context and the learning object:

- Learning objects can be described with much richer (learning object) metadata than is typically the case for arbitrary web pages. Moreover, these metadata can automatically be generated, taking into account the learning context (Cardinals et al., 2005). As a consequence, we can restrict the search space of the user to *really* relevant learning objects, with the appropriate technical characteristics, suitable for his budget, accommodating his learning approach, in a language that he can learn in, etc.
- As learning objects are typically deployed in Learning Management Systems that provide explicit context, LearnRank can also rely on this information to take into account the characteristics mentioned in section 3.1.
- Using attention metadata, we can track what a user actually does with a learning object, beyond simple downloading or accessing it (Najjar, 2005). The potential here is huge as it allows us to create a "usage trail" of a learning object, which will eventually enable us to deduce metrics that indicate how good an enabler for learning a learning object is in a particular context.

30.5   Conclusion

Now that we have the open standards in place to build a large scale infrastructure for learning, we can start focusing on quality, much in the same way that web search engines shifted focus from being exhaustive to providing relevant results.

With this paper, I'd like to call for more focus on the development of good LearnRank measures, rather than on only indirectly and partially relevant indicators of quality for learning.

31 Quality of e-learning in tertiary education: Managing a balance between divergence and convergence

Miho Taguma

CERI, OECD, France

The article reports on current initiatives regarding 'quality' in tertiary education e-learning drawing upon the results of the OECD/ CERI international case studies. The case studies examined the tertiary e-learning practices in 19 postsecondary education institutions from 13 countries (Australia, Brazil, Canada, France, Germany, Japan, Mexico, New Zealand, Spain, Switzerland, Thailand, UK, and US). Six institutions are from Europe. Within a global setting, e-learning is in the initial phase of development and diffusion. In this phase, different practices are explored and there are complex streams of divergence and convergence surrounding 'quality' in diverse practices – understanding these complex streams is a major challenge for both governments and institutions. The article presents governmental as well as institutional responses to such challenge. It compares different approaches between European countries in comparison with other regions, and describes potential future challenges.

31.1   Introduction[119]

What is 'quality' in tertiary e-learning? How can we define quality? Are there any indicators that can demonstrate quality in tertiary e-learning: reliable infrastructure, affordable connectivity, existence of government policies, programmes, projects, existence of institutional e-learning strategies, students' satisfaction, learning outcomes, retention rates, faculty satisfaction, wealth of contents, sustainability of course programmes, cost-effectiveness/efficiency? The list can be inexhaustive. Currently, there are no agreed indicators to measure 'quality' in tertiary e-learning. The meaning of 'quality' may differ among different stakeholders, from government policy-makers, institutional managers, researchers, practitioners and learners. It may also differ among different countries which demonstrate varying degrees of "e-learning readiness". There are also likely to be different educational, cultural and social expectations of 'quality' in tertiary education means. To disentangle the complex interpretation of 'quality', there needs to be a strong commitment to 'quality' development, in terms of both definition and practice, among different stakeholders worldwide.

> Tertiary education: Tertiary education is the third-level or third-staged education following secondary education. Tertiary education is provided by institutions such as universities, colleges and higher professional schools. To make international comparison, the International Standard Classification of Education (1997) is often used and tertiary education is classified into ISCED levels 5, 6 and 7. The ISCED is the instrument designed by the United Nations Educational and Scientific Organisation.

31.2   Methodologies

Two sources are used for the article: the OECD/ CERI international case studies (OECD, 2005) and the desk research with a specific focus on governments.

---

[119] Disclaimer: This article partially presents the results of the international case studies carried out by the OECD/CERI (Centre for Educational Research and Innovation). However, the opinions expressed by the author in this article do not reflect the opinion or position of the OECD/CERI.

Acknowledgements: The author wishes to thanks the OECD, the experts of the participating institutions in the OECD/CERI case studies (Yoni Ryan, Bruce Kind, Carlos Alberto Barbosa Dantas, Michelle Lamberson, Tony Bates, Neil Guppy, Christiane Guillard, Ulrich Schmid, Multimedia Kontor Hamburg, Thomas Berkel, Andrea Haferburg, Michihiko Minoh, Fumio Itoh, Munenori Nakasato and Yasushi Shimizu, Jose Escamilla de los Santos, Ken Udas, Andreu Bellot Urbano, Sylvia Gonzalez, Emma Kiselyova, Eva Seiler Schiedt, Jean-Phillippe Thouard, Richard Lewis, Paul Clark, Joel Smith, Robert Lapiner, University, Robert Jerome, Gary Matkin) and her colleagues Patrick Werquin and Fionnuala Canning.

31.2.1   The OECD/CERI international case studies

The OECD/CERI launched an international case study project in order to explore the opportunities and challenges for post-secondary education institutions and governments attempting to provide e-learning. To promote an evidence-based realistic approach to policy-making, the project carried out qualitative research, eliciting case studies with an in-depth questionnaire. The questionnaire covered a wide range of themes, from institutional strategy and e-learning forms; platforms and infrastructure; access to e-learning; teaching and learning; students and markets; staff and materials; funding and government; organisational change as well as scenarios and barriers. The questionnaire is made available online to the public. The topic of 'quality' was not directly addressed in the questionnaire; however, it came out as an important sub-theme across many areas.

The case studies included 19 tertiary education institutions[120] from 13 countries. The regions include Asia and the Pacific (Australia, Japan, New Zealand, and Thailand), Europe (Germany, France, Spain, Switzerland and the UK), North America (Canada and the USA), and Latin America. (Brazil and Mexico). The final synthesis report is being prepared in collaboration with the Observatory Borderless Higher Education (OBHE)[121]. This article benefits from international comparisons as it sheds light on quality in tertiary e-learning within Europe with reference and comparison to other regions. It is possible to cast future scenarios suggesting routes for development of 'quality' within e-learning within Europe.

31.2.2   Desk research

The OECD/CERI case study questionnaire addressed the issue of the governments' involvement in e-learning. However, it was found that there is a gap between what institutions know about government-led initiatives and the actually existing initiatives. To fill this gap, the desk research was conducted to map existing and most relevant government-led or national initiatives. Relevant authorities from the countries were given an opportunity to consult and confirm the compiled details.

---

[120] The case studies institutions are: Aoyama Gakuin University (Japan), Asian Institute of Technology (Thailand), Carnegie Mellon University (US), Kyoto University (Japan), Monash University (Australia), Multimedia Kontor Hamburg (Germany), University of British Columbia (Canada), University of California Irvine (US), University of Paris X-Nanterre (France), University of Sao Paolo (Brazil), University of Zurich (Switzerland), FernUniversität Hagen (Germany), Open Polytechnic of New Zealand (New Zealand), UK Open University (UK), Open University of Catalunya (Spain), Virtual University of Tec de Monterrey (Mexico), University of California Los Angeles Extension (US), University of South Australia (Australia), and University of Maryland University College (US).

[121] Publication. OECD (2005) E-learning in tertiary education: where do we stand?

31.3   Government-led or national initiatives[122]

What can governments do, or are expected to do, to promote quality in e-learning practices in tertiary education? Due to the different jurisdictional practices of governments over tertiary education and the cross-sectoral nature of e-learning, the list of government-led or national initiatives is inexhaustive. Moreover, they may not always be comparable across countries. This section gives an overview of various governments' or national initiatives with a comparative approach. The initiatives are examined in two aspects. First, the section looks into whether or not the governments or relevant bodies have produced e-learning policies, strategies and/ or official documents in order to embed the 'quality' issues in such decodification for accountability and visibility. Second, the section examines what kinds of programmes/ projects the governments have launched with a special focus on quality issues. Third, the section maps out portals/ databases that the governments have developed to manage information concerning e-learning. Finally, the section summarises the initiatives in Europe in comparison with other regions.

31.3.1   E-learning policies, strategies and official documents: Integrated or distinct

Government's policies, strategies, and official documents for e-learning are of increasing importance as tools to demonstrate accountability and visibility. However, due to the cross-sectoral nature of e-learning, e-learning policies on tertiary education do not usually stand alone, and are generally found as part of a larger policy framework: they may be part of generic ICT policies (e.g. Brazil, Canada, France, Germany, Japan, Mexico, New Zealand, Switzerland, and Thailand), generic education policies towards the information society (e.g. Australia, England, Germany, and the US), higher education strategies (e.g. England, Mexico, New Zealand, and Switzerland), distance learning policies (e.g. Brazil, Japan, Mexico and the US), e-learning strategies at all levels of education (e.g. UK), and/ or labour policies (e.g. Germany) (OECD, 2005). The quality-related issues are embedded either explicitly or implicitly in the policy objectives in these integrated documents under infrastructure, access, contents, and the divide issue.

The rare exceptions of having distinct documents on e-learning in tertiary education (in addition to having generic policies) are found within New Zealand and Canada. The E-learning Advisory Group of the Associate Minister of Education, Tertiary Education (New Zealand) has produced *Highways and Pathways: Exploring New Zealand's E-learning Opportunities* (2002). Its goal is to shift the paradigm of 'e-learning' from a state of being recognised as mere part of distance education to recognising its wider potential. It sets out four specific objectives: 1) to improve quality; 2) to increase participation; 3) to change cost structures; and 4) to

---

[122] The section does not limit itself to the government-led initiatives as in some countries, the role of government is minimal and non-governmental organisations or private foundations play a role in the national initiatives (e.g. US).

change distribution/ delivery methods. In Canada, the Advisory Committee for Online Learning was created by the Council of Ministers of Education Canada and Industry Canada. The Committee produced *The E-learning Evolution in Colleges and Universities: a Pan-Canadian Challenge* (2002). The paper lays out five key determinants to accelerate the use of e-learning in post-secondary education: 1) accessibility; 2) flexibility; 3) quality; 4) pan-Canadian synergy; and 5) critical mass.

31.3.2   E-learning programmes and projects: Quality enhancement and quality assurance

In alignment with e-learning policies, e-learning programmes and projects are also implemented simultaneously by different ministries such as the Ministry of Education, the Ministry of Telecommunications and Information, the Ministry of Industries and the Ministry of Labour, etc. The objectives of programmes/ projects cover a wide range of areas, ranging from infrastructure, course materials/ courseware development, development and/ or provision of e-learning products, promoting lifelong learning via e-learning, standardisation and specifications, quality assurance / consumer protection, fostering of transparent e-learning markets, international cooperation and aids projects for developing countries, etc. (OECD, 2005). The shift in focus of the government programmes/ projects are observed across areas from infrastructure to contents development, and process development (such as staff development) as well as quality issue (OECD, 2005; Information Society Technologies, 2004).

The quality issue is becoming a major concern for many countries worldwide. However, it may be assumed that 'access' is more prioritised than 'quality'. In other words, within countries where infrastructure and affordable access has yet to be developed, quality issues may remain on the backburner. However an exception to this assumption can be found within Brazil and Thailand, who are far behind many of the developed countries in terms of e-learning infrastructural development (ranked 34 and 36 out of 60 countries, respectively according to the Economist Intelligence Unit, 2003), and yet have already started to work on the 'quality' issues of online programmes. It is also worth noting the focus and approach to 'quality' may differ from country to country, depending on their jurisdiction, economic, and cultural contexts. The section below now takes a brief overview of some major programmes/ projects concerning specifically 'quality'.

'Quality' is generally addressed from two different perspectives within the national programmes and projects: 1) quality enhancement and/ or 2) quality assurance and consumer protection. Quality enhancement is concerned with how to *enhance the quality* of teaching/ learning in general through the use of e-learning. Quality assurance and consumer protection is concerned, evidently, with how to *assure quality* of e-learning practices. The desk research observed the quality enhancement approach in Australia, Brazil, and France; the quality assurance approach, in Canada, Japan, New Zealand, and Thailand; and both approaches in parallel, in England, Germany, and the US. (See table 31-1). From either perspective, growing attention is placed on learner-/ customer-orientation, faculty development, and evaluation/ assessment. In addition, there are growing tendencies to focus on a certain aspect of e-learning such as e-learning implementation (e.g. the Higher Education Academy's e-learning thematic projects in the UK), quality models of the e-learning market (e.g. The Ministry of Economics and Labour in Germany), and quality assurance in cross-border e-learning (e.g. The Ministry of Education, Culture, Sports, Science and Technology in Japan). The quality assurance and consumer protection approach is characterised by the developments of codes of practice, guidelines, and standards, and accreditation[123].

Table 31-1: Government-led or national/ state programmes/ projects concerning 'quality' in e-learning

Country	Type	Details of Programme/ Project
Australia	Quality Enhancement	The *Australian Flexible Leaning Framework* (2005-2007) aims to increase the sustainable uptake of 'quality' e-learning in vocational and education and training (VET). One of the projects focuses on quality in e-learning resources, aiming at enhancing quality though flexibility and innovation. Another is an international project, which includes an exercise to internationally benchmark Australian VET in terms of global relevance and capacity.
Brazil	Quality Enhancement	The Ministry of Telecommunication supports the *Sistema Brasileiro de Televisão Digital Project* (2003-2006) to develop the Brazilian system for digital interactive TV. The 'quality' is valued on 'a user-centred approach' and e-learning is illustrated to advance developments of learning objects repository for training support, interfacing for tele-education, and applications with the approach.
Canada	Quality Assurance	The Office of Learning Technologies of the Human Resources Development Canada, in collaboration with the Canadian Association of Community Education, prepared a tool for learners to help evaluate programmes before purchasing online courses: the *Consumers Guide to E-learning*. It also prepared a tool for service/ product providers to design and deliver e-learning that meets consumer's expectations: the *Canadian Recommended E-learning Guidelines*.
England	Quality Enhancement	The Higher Education Academy (HEA) acknowledges the need for a holistic approach to embedding e-learning and focuses on implementation. It builds on existing collaboration with the Joint Information Systems Committee (JISC) and has launched the *Distributed e-learning Program*. HEA's *E-learning thematic projects* aim at enhancing quality by providing opportunities to share resources and good practices as well as investigating pedagogic and sustainability issues.

---

[123] The definition and use of 'accreditation' may differ from country to country. See Council For Higher Education Accreditation (CHEA) 2001, Glossary of Key Terms in Quality Assurance and Accreditation, http://www.chea.org/international/inter_glossary01.html (last modified on October 23, 2002).

Country	Type	Details of Programme/ Project
		The *Teaching and Learning Technology Programme (TLTP)* was launched to foster collaboration among the higher education sector to explore how new technologies could help to improve the quality of teaching and learning. Phases one and two focused on developing computer-based teaching and learning course materials. Phase three focuses on how to embed the use of new technologies and how to evaluate its effectiveness.
		The Learning and Skills Development Agency (LSDA) manages projects to evaluate the impact of technology on learning and teaching.
		The *Quality in Information and Learning Technology (QUILT)* was launched as a five-year project (1997-2002) aiming at raising standards in further education by providing staff development in the use of ICT.
	Quality Assurance	The *Quality Assurance Agency's Code of Practice Section 2* (revised in September, 2004) addresses collaborative provision and flexible and distributed learning, including e-learning for higher education. The Agency states, while affirming that some technical specific aspects are unique to 'e-learning', the academic management issues should be the same as the general flexible and distributed learning and, thus, e-learning is included in the section. It addresses the issues for delivery, learner support and assessment of students.
		The Raising Standards Steering Group discussion forum was coordinated by the British Educational Communications and Technology Agency (BECTA) among quality assurance inspectorates and key sector bodies such as college practitioners and inspectorate representatives (e.g. Ofsted, Adult Learning Inspectorate, Quality Assurance Agency for higher education, and the Education and Training Inspectorate, Northern Ireland, University for Industry (Ufi), the Learning and Skills council and the Department for Education and Skills.) The *Demonstrating Transformation* is a programme to offer guidance on inspection and e-learning in post-secondary education by providing information on a free CD-ROM.
France	Quality Enhancement	The Ministry of Education launched the *Campus Numerique (Digital Campus) project* with an aim for higher education institutions to offer 'flexbile' and 'personalised' open distance postsecondary training via new technologies. E-learning is seen as a tool to allow diverse teaching methods and, by adopting formative assessments, to enhance quality teaching/ learning.
Germany	Quality Enhancement	Within the framework of the *Neue Medien in der Bildung (New media in Education) Programme* (2002-2004), the Federal Ministry of Education and Research (BMBF) aims to add value to teaching/ learning. The programme covers schools, vocational training and higher education. Objectives specific to higher education include improving the 'quality of teaching and learning', create new distance-learning programmes, keeping up with the international competition, fostering e-learning markets for lifelong learning on a global scale, etc.

Country	Type	Details of Programme/ Project
	Quality Assurance	The Federal Ministry of Economics and Labour (BMWi) supports the *Quality Initiative e-learning in Germany (Q.E.D.)* to develop a new harmonised quality model for more transparent e-learning market.
Japan	Quality Assurance.	The Ministry of Education, Culture, Sports, Science and Technology (MEXT) set up a research project on quality assurance of higher education with an aim to respond to cross-border education. One of the research themes includes quality assurance of e-learning in higher education.
New Zealand	Quality Assurance	The Ministry of Education launched the *e-Learning Collaborative Development Fund (eCDF)* (2003-7) to improve the capability of e-learning delivery among tertiary education institutions though collaboration. Projects funded by the scheme include developments of guidelines and standards to ensure the quality of e-learning.
Thailand	Quality Assurance	The Ministry of Education has proposed the *Standard Criteria for Establishing Internet-Based Program of Studies by Thai Universities* to regulate setting up online programmes in universities.
The United States	Quality Enhancement.	The US Department of Education's Office of Educational Technology supports the *Regional Technology in Education Consortia* to provide professional development, technical assistance and information about the use of technologies to enhance teaching and learning to educational institutions.
	Quality Assurance	A national accreditation coordinating body, the Council for Higher Education Accreditation (CHEA) voices the importance of quality assurance in the form of 'accreditation' in the era of universalisation, commercialisation and internationalisation of higher education.
		A regional accreditation agency, the Council of Regional Accrediting Commissions, in cooperation with the Western Cooperative for Educational Telecommunications, published the draft document: *Guidelines for the Evaluation of Electronically Offered Degree and Certificate Program.*
		Apart from initiatives taken by accreditation bodies, the Institute for Higher Education Policy (2000) attempted to benchmark e-learning practices: *Quality On the Line: Benchmarks for Success in Internet-Based Distance Education* (2000) . The benchmark looks at seven categories: Institutional support; Course development; Teaching/ learning process; Course structure; Student support; Faculty support; and Evaluation and assessment.
		The American Council on Education has produced the *Distance Learning Evaluation Guide* (2001) as evaluation criteria for distance learning. The Guide includes seven categories: Learning design; Learning objectives and outcomes; Learning materials; Technology; Learner support, Organisational commitment; and Subject matter/ content of course (module or program).

Country	Type	Details of Programme/ Project
		The American Distance Education Consortium attempted to formulate distance education guidelines and prepared the *ADEC Guiding Principles for Distance Learning* (2003). The principles include four categories: Design for active and effective learning; Support the needs of learners; Develop and maintain the technological and human infrastructure; and Sustain administrative and organisational commitment.

31.3.3   Divergence versus convergence

By definition, current national initiatives raise the quality issue in e-learning policies and strategies, and programmes/ projects are concentrated with the 'quality enhancement' of teaching and learning at mainly campus-based institutions with the use of ICT. This may drive diversity of teaching and learning approaches by promoting a range of different practices and innovations. Simultaneously, however, a 'quality assurance' approach may convert practices into standards by generating benchmarks, guidelines, accreditation processes, and indicators. Such attempts are observed in Anglophone countries (e.g. Australia, Canada, New Zealand, UK, and US).

Convergence: Convergence in this context means the coming together and crossover of different traits (i.e. standards, criteria, guiding principles, or references) as each trait adapts to or develops into a de-facto standard. The driver for this type of convergence is the actual and dominant use and practices of certain traits which are selected by the law of the fittest (c.f. harmonisation).

Quality assurance is considered important for accountability purposes and is driven not only by domestic requirements such as institutional codification and evaluation but also by external drivers such as commercialisation and internationalisation of higher education. An example of the quality assurance approach towards convergence in the form of 'accreditation' is observed in an institutional consortium, Universitas 21 Global. It is an international network of research intensive universities mainly composed of Anglophone countries[124] and it aims to offer quality graduate-level e-learning business programmes. Universitas 21 Global established its own 'accreditation' body, U21 Pedagogica, which not only sets standards but also assists member institutions that adopt their specific approach to pedagogies. The U21 Pedagogica also offers consultation services to other higher education institutions. This can be an example of emerging convergence of pedagogic practices in a specific discipline, driven by 'accreditation in consortium'.

Another example of an international collaboration in quality assurance is "standard-setting". To respond to the internationalisation of higher education, governments are working in collaboration to assure quality of cross-border provision, re-

---

[124] The participating institutions to date come from Australia, Canada, China, Germany, Hong Kong, New Zealand, Singapore, Sweden, UK, and US.

specting diverse jurisdiction practices over higher education quality assurance in each country. This does not aim at convergence of quality assurance practices. The UNESCO and OECD are jointly preparing the *Guidelines on Quality Provision in Cross-border Higher Education* as a non-binding instrument and, thus, to assure quality provision via peer pressure. The process discussions suggest that of e-learning also needs to be addressed.

In Europe, a challenge in standard-setting would be how to manage the tension between 'unity' and 'diversity' in e-learning quality. Europe is represented by the motto 'Unity in Diversity' adopted for the European Union by the Constitutional Treaty. To maintain a fine balance between regional standards and local diversity, an extensive and inclusive dialogue is thought to be of critical importance, within which, harmonised indicators, methods and guidelines can be developed. Within the framework of the e-learning Programme, the European Commission supports various initiatives and launched the portal *elearningeuropa.info* to promote the use of ICT in improving learning. The portal encompasses information generic to education/ training at: schools, higher education, work and learning, and lifelong learning. The HELIOS project was recently launched to establish a sustainable observation platform to monitor the progress of e-learning with a specific focus on policy objectives.

Harmonisation: Harmonisation in this context means coordination among different stakeholders (e.g. governments, educational institutions, private e-learning providers, e-learning industries, and learners) with an aim to increase the compatibility of policies, legislation, quality criteria, and guiding principles as well as the interoperability of different technical standards and references within and across countries. Harmonisation aims to ensure cultural diversity and to allow existing different policies, criteria, standards, etc to coexist. It is made possible by an inclusive dialogue between stakeholders.

Building on existing initiatives is a critical element in fostering harmonised collaboration. A good example is the Triangle project: a project specific to the e-learning quality issue. It was built on three existing initiatives, each of which has a specific purpose: European Quality Observatory (EQO) to develop a quality observatory; Supporting Excellence in E-learning (SEEL) to develop guidelines and benchmarks; and Sustainable Evaluation Environment for Quality in E-learning (SEEQUEL) to develop the forum for dialogue and exchange of information. The overall project aim is to provide a sustainable single point for discussions and sharing information and to promote the European diversity of quality approaches. The project launched the European Foundation for Quality in e-learning (EFQEL), which acts as a catalyst for convergence of efforts by identifying and actively encouraging the participation of different actors involved with quality in European e-learning. Given that there are diverse quality e-learning models in Europe, it also aims to establish a Quality Mark for e-learning (EQM) to explore different accreditation and certification models for different educational sectors.

In Asia, the Asia E-learning Network was established among China, Korea, Japan and the ASEAN Economic Ministers. It aims to provide a forum to share information on the latest trends and technologies, promote interoperability of learning (and content) management systems (LMS), and exchange good e-learning practices in the region. The network is engaged in four focused working group themes, one of which is 'e-learning content quality assurance'. The working group looks at five aspects of 'quality': organisational quality, product quality, process quality, quality of use and learning quality. It explores agreed standard criteria for quality assurance such as ISO 9000 for organisational quality, ISO/ IECS36[125] 36 for process quality (see chapter 6, ASTD/ ECC for product quality, ISO 9126 for quality of use, and setting up an original standard for learning quality[126]. As a practical next step, it aims to examine terminologies, reviewing quality items and criteria, producing the quality assurance guideline for e-Learning contents and services and developing an experimental check tool (planned for 2005). While the European Commission values diverse approaches and practices to quality assurance in the region, the Asia E-learning Network at the present focuses on convergence of practices by standardisation. However, it was reported at the 2004 Conference that the dialogue and research has just started on the issue and, thus, the mapping exercise currently implemented on existing quality models in the region might raise the issue of diversity.

In the US, as mentioned earlier, higher education, especially concerning quality issues, is independent from the government. The jurisdiction is highly decentralised and yet the increasing academic autonomy is set within a framework of accountability and 'accreditation'. Thus, it is non-governmental organisations, private foundations and institutional consortium rather than the governments that take initiatives in this regard. The Council of Higher Education for Accreditation (CHEA), a national accreditation coordinating body, voices the importance of quality assurance in the form of 'accreditation' in the era of universalisation, commercialisation and internationalisation of higher education, in which the quality of e-learning is considered as a 'paramount issue'[127]. Regional accreditation agencies as well as non-governmental organisations have attempted to prepare guidelines, benchmarks, evaluation guide, and guiding principles (See Table 31-1). All include 'learner support' as one of the core categories; this is one of the resonant features in the post-modern pedagogy (Fink, 2003), (Taylor, 2004), (Weimer, 2002) as well as the market-oriented approach, manifesting the American approach to quality assurance.

Market oriented quality development: Market-oriented quality development in this context implies the process through which quality is developed not by governmental intervention but by the *expectations of the market* which push for high quality provision through the *competitive process.*

---

[125] SC36 develops International Standards in information technology in the areas of Learning, Education, and Training.

[126] http://www.asia-elearning.net/content/conference/2004/file/S3_WG4.pdf.

[127] Letter from the President, http://www.chea.org/Research/president-letters/01-08.cfm, 2001.

31.4   Institutional strategies: Managing divergence and convergence

The case studies demonstrate, in-line with recent literature, that the current state of tertiary e-learning is complex and can be characterised by the simultaneous occurrence of divergence and convergence just as seen in the previous chapter, and the government-led section (Information Society Technologies, 2004). This section illustrates the complex phenomena of divergence and convergence and to exemplify institutional strategies to manage such complexity in order to assure quality.

31.4.1   Institutional response to divergence: E-learning strategies, faculty development, research and programme evaluation

The case studies observed three major drivers for divergence of practices: 1) blurring of campus-based and distance-based institutions, 2) gaps between enthusiastic and reluctant faculty about innovation, and 3) post-modern pedagogic rhetoric in line with ever-developing new technologies.

First, the use of ICT as well as partnership opportunities have enabled campus-based institutions to embark on distance-based education provision and allowed distance-based institutions to provide face-to-face education provision vice versa. Consequently there is a blurred distinction between campus-based institutions and open and distance education institutions. Given that there are more and more diverse ways for institutions to be engaged in e-learning, there is no one-size-fit-for-all development model. The case study institutions, however, can be grouped into six e-learning development trajectories: 1) campus-based institutions going online, 2) campus-based institutions going online with increasing distance-based characteristics, 3) mixed (having both campus-and distance-based) institution developing a dual mode of fully online and face-to-face, 4) distance-based institutions going online with increasing campus-based characteristics, 5) open/ distance-based institutions going online, and 6) start-up institutions fully online (see figure 31-1).

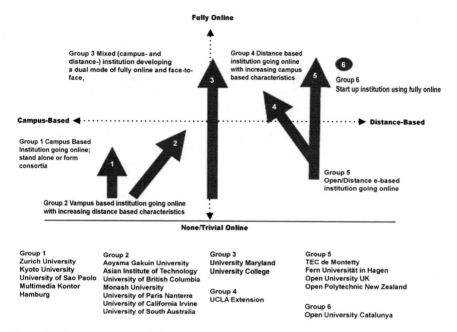

Fully Online

Group 3 Mixed (campus- and distance-) institution developing a dual mode of fully online and face-to-face,

Group 4 Distance based institution going online with increasing campus based characteristics

Group 6
Start up institution using fully online

Campus-Based ◄ · ► Distance-Based

Group 1 Campus Based Institution going online; stand alone or form consortia

Group 5
Open/Distance e-based institution going online

Group 2 Vampus based institution going online with increasing distance based characteristics

None/Trivial Online

Group 1	Group 2	Group 3	Group 5
Zurich University	Aoyama Gakuin University	University Maryland	TEC de Montetty
Kyoto University	Asian Institute of Technology	University College	Fern Universität in Hagen
University of Sao Paolo	University of British Columbia		Open University UK
Multimedia Kontor	Monash University	Group 4	Open Polytechnic New Zealand
Hamburg	University of Paris Nanterre	UCLA Extension	
	University of California Irvine		Group 6
	University of South Australia		Open University Catalunya

Fig. 31-1: The six e-learning development trajectories

One of the institutional responses to such divergent trajectories is to embed the use of e-learning in some form of institutional policy, in-line with organisational missions. Although the existence or absence of an institutional e-learning policy/ strategy does not in itself prove that e-learning is non-existent, the majority of the case studies institutions (eighteen out of nineteen) cited the existence of some form of institutional e-learning policy or strategy. Such policy or strategy may be a distinct institution-wide policy, part of other central policies (e.g. ICT policies, and teaching and learning policies), or a department-level policy/ strategy.

Second, a growing gap between practices occurs due to the intrinsic academic culture on the e-learning diffusion. According to a recent study on e-learning diffusion pattern (Tiffin, 1980), (Romiszowski, 2003), there are three phases of diffusion: 1) the initial exponential growth phrase, driven by the enthusiastic early adopters and supported by various funded programmes and projects; 2) the "trumble back" phrase after the experience of projects' failure; and 3) slow and careful "re-birth" phase for programmes/ projects where, with lessons learnt from the failure, they will be skilfully planned, implemented, and managed if the theoretical benefits are promised. Some of the features of Phrase 2 can be observed such as the post-dot.com stage and the demise of the UK e-University (Bacsich, 2005), (Conole et al, 2004), (Slater, 2005). However, within the global picture, e-learning is still in the infancy stage. During this stage, time-lags occur between early adopters/ enthusiasts and sceptical/ faculty reluctant to change. The time-lag can induce different directions in terms of adoption between the two groups. In fact, the case study found that 'faculty resistance' was one of the most critical barriers to e-learning developments – particularly when formulating institutional e-learning strategies, selecting of learning management systems, actual implementation of e-learning in practices, and course evaluation.

The institutional response is to strengthen faculty development, which is seen to play a pivotal role in advancing e-learning practices. Most case study institutions (fifteen out of nineteen) have worked on either faculty-led or project-level development. While faculty development was mainly on a voluntary basis at campus-based institutions, distance-based institutions or mixed (combination of campus-based and distance-based) institutions make faculty attendance to seminars or workshops mandatory. Although day-to-day practice-based development could be left to each faculty, promoting and enriching diverse practices, a rare example of an institution-wide development was observed at a mixed institution from Australia. At this institution, all faculty are required to be able to integrate online techniques in their teaching and publish teaching materials on their homepage.

Third, e-learning is not static and post-modern pedagogy rhetoric focuses on 'personalisation', 'participation', and 'collaborative and constructivist learning' (Fink, 2003), (Moslehian, 2003), (Taylor, 2004), (Weimer, 2002). E-learning is increasingly seen and explored as a potential tool to make the rhetoric a reality. There are diverse ways to foster personalisation, participation and collaboration, using emerging technologies such as m-learning (via the use of mobile phone), artificial intelligence assessment, e-portfolio, simulation software, etc. Students are more exposed to diverse ways of learning and teaching with the use of tutors, the development of collaborative learning platforms, the development of adoptive feedback systems, the deployment of each student' portals to record his/ her learning assets, and the production of constructivist learning objects, etc. Has e-learning substantively changed the ways of teaching and learning in line with the post-modern rhetoric? If so, how? All case study institutions reported positive pedagogic impact. Few, however, were able to offer detailed research based evidence. Anecdotal evidence shows that the focus is being shifted to students satisfaction, learning outcomes, and students support. Indirect evidence, e.g. student satisfaction surveys and retention/ attainment data, were provided but programme evaluations are not focused on specific aspects of pedagogies, nor may necessarily measure 'quality' in e-learning in general. Further research on the impact on pedagogies and programme evaluation are needed for future.

31.4.2   Institutional response to convergence: Standardisation and system integration

A learning (and content) management system (LMS) is a term used almost synchronously with e-learning in tertiary education. The international interoperability standards are believed to ensure the smooth transfer of data between diverse applications as well as to facilitate consistent configuration of data. There are governmental and non-governmental initiatives to set-up such standards – for example, the Sharable Content Object Reference Model (SCORM)[128] and IMS standards[129]. Convergence is increased because SCORM and IMS are by definition complementary in their specifications. The case studies show that institutional responses to such initiatives are, however, limited to their conscience level, and have not yet reached to the actual adoption level except for a few cases. One case study institution from the UK is already an active contributor to the IMS, and another institution from Germany mentioned that it planned to make international standards mandatory for all e-learning developments - to 'enhance the quality of learning materials'. In the future, with the increased adoption of learning (and content) management systems as well as the growing interests in learning objects, institutions are envisaged to participate in the standardisation process.

As more and more information is generated for institutions to manage digitally (e.g. learning contents, digitalised library resources, students records, etc.), there is a pressing demand for facilitation of information storing, management, and retrieval. The institutional response is to convert the learning and management systems and other systems such as administration, student portals, libraries, etc. into one system. One case study institution from Canada cited the lack of well-developed technical standards as a major reason for delaying the adoption of the integrated systems. In the US, there are emerging standardisation processes such as Advanced Distributed Learning (ADL) Initiatives the Content Object Repository Discovery and Resolution Architecture (CORDRA) aimed at integrating learning and content management and delivery repositories and digital libraries. The challenges are not only technical but also revolve around social and cultural issues. Institutions need to overcome non-technical barriers such as shortcoming in data quality/ consistency, requirements of supporting documents for admission (e.g. proof of English language competence), payment regulations (for overseas students), etc.

31.4.3   Institutional response: Localisation, transverse dissemination, and development

The case studies identified distribution of standardised contents/ curriculum and platforms as an emerging trend. The example of the standardised curriculum may be disseminated in a form of 'Open Educational Resources'. While the precise definition of Open Educational Resources (OER) is being developed, it can be broadly referred to as an educational resources made available for non-commercial purposes. It was initially led by the Massachusetts Institute of Technology's (MIT) Open Courseware since 2002. Implications include international capacity building activity by providing their 'quality' courseware ('reputation' or 'branding'in his sense) for overseas countries including developing countries. A case study institu-

---

[128] It was developed by the US Department of Defence under the "Advanced Distributed Learning" initiative.

[129] It was developed by the IMS Global Learning Consortium, consisted of technical standards bodies, vendors, governments and education institutions/agencies. to collaborate on the development of standards for the interoperability of learning resources.

tion from the US, Carnegie Mellon University, has also launched the Open Learning Initiative (OLI). This type of initiative is US-driven partially due to the financing support system available to experiment such an attempt. In the US, private foundations play a significant role in advancing innovation. Both the MIT and Carnegie Mellon University projects are in fact funded by a private foundation, the William and Flora Hewlett Foundation, partnering with another foundation, the Andrew W. Mellon Foundation. Having one of its missions as securing access to high-quality post-secondary education and educational materials to those who otherwise would be excluded due to geographic, economic or time constraints, the Hewlett Foundation supports other universities for the open courseware initiative: e.g. Rice University's Connexions, Utah State University's Open Courseware, Eastern Oregon University's EduRecources Portal, community colleges' Sharing of Free Intellectual Assets (SOFIA) and Taft's University's Open Courseware to date. Another example of a private foundation's lead is the Sloan Foundation, which supports the sharing of courses with a specific focus. It supports the League for Innovation in the Community Colleges which is confronted with a dilemma between limited funding resources and burgeoning educational needs defined by the industry and, therefore, launched the Specialty Asynchronous Industry Learning (SAIL) project to best capitalise resources.

Apart from private foundations, academics or institutions also take such an initiative from within. A substantive example is the portal, the MERLOT. The portal links to online learning materials for free of charge for faculty and students to share. Another example of the initiative in consortium is the Gateway to Educational Materials (GEM), which includes all levels of education.

Will these OER initiatives be seen as the neo-imperialism of the American academic culture (contents and pedagogies)? The institutional response from other regions to this initiative concerns the localisation of the languages and contents, allowing local cultural (academic) diversity. The former MIT Open Courseware is being translated into Mandarin Chinese by a consortium of Chinese universities approved by the China Ministry of Education, named China Open Resources for Education (CORE). Among Spanish and Portuguese speaking countries, a consortium of more than 720 colleges and universities in Latin America, Spain, and Portugal called Universias have translated about 75 MIT OCW courses into their languages. These courses are being widely used. Apart from languages, an example of localisation of contents can be seen when the UK Open University sells its product (contents and consulting services) to Arab Open University. It was reported that the contents need to be tailored to suit the local needs of the Arab cultural, religious and societal contexts and cannot be used just as they are used at their home institute.

Open Educational Resources: The term 'Open Educational Resources' was first adopted at UNESCO 2002 Forum on the Impact of Open Courseware for Higher Education in Developing Countries. It is defined 'the open provision of educational resources, enabled by information and communication technologies, for consultation, use and adaptation by a community of users for non-commercial purposes.' The recent definition has developed and also includes open software tools, standards, repositories of learning objects, and open materials for capacity building of faculty staff.

In addition to localising the use of the standard contents at the receiving end, institutions in other regions than the US start to aim at 'contributing' their own contents through the network while using the MIT courseware. To this end, Japanese universities have launched the Open Courseware (OCW) consortium with 6 founding member institutions in 2005. It aims to increase the visibility of the Japanese university's excellence worldwide. The case studies report points that cross-border e-learning is still very much in small-scale and generally failed to emerge as a significant market to date (OECD, 2005). With the OER or OCW movements, the cross-border e-learning activities may be vitalised with higher education missions towards knowledge-based society rather than driven by a 'market' rationale.

In Europe, the OER or OCW initiatives are rarely documented to date at the tertiary level partially due to the mixture of academic autonomy, academic resistance or scepticism to a new idea, and lack of development of intellectual property rights in the area. However, a rare example was reported by a case study institution, University of Paris Nanterre. It cited its participation in an international virtual university, the Encylopédie sonore, where nearly 8,000 downloadable courses are available (as of 2004). Despite the fact that the role of private foundations is not as active as in the US, we have an example in Germany. The Bertelsmann Foundation has created an "e-teaching" portal for staff development. As the stakeholders may be a heterogeneous audience, the portal aims to offer access to a wide range of resources, and to act as a forum among faculty, senior managers and policy makers.

In the actual development of contents and dissemination process, institutions need to be aware of emerging issues such as technological and technical issues, copyrights, sustainable models in costing, the management of the courseware, etc.

Apart from the contents, a standardised learning management system can also be disseminated world wide as an open source platform or with the purchase of a proprietary system. The two major vendors which currently dominate the tertiary education market are the Web CT and Blackboard (Observatory on Borderless Higher Education, 2002). In addition to these two systems, the case studies identified the growing development of in-house systems, the adoption of an off-the-shelf open source platform (e.g. Moodle) as well as the development of an open source platform in consortium (e.g. the Learning Activity Management System in Australia, the Sakai in the US, and the Open Source Virtual Learning Environment in New Zealand. These initiatives may be either government-supported, private foundation- or institutions-led. Open source learning management developments are seen mainly in Anglophone countries and it is envisaged that such initiatives will be soon taken up in other parts of the world. In addition to the learning management system, an emerging open source tool is e-portfolio. The former cited foundation, the Andrew W. Mellon Foundation supports the development of the Open Source E-portfolio Initiative. It is designed, having code mobility in mind, to be based on learning management systems development, i.e. the Sakai project's tool portability profile as well as the Open Knowledge Initiative at the MIT.

Difficulties and challenges concern system integration issues, interoperability, collaborative learning environments, and the future development of Open Educational Resources.

The quality concerning Open Educational Resources is becoming a concerned issue, the more its practices prevail within and across the countries. The UNESCO 2002 Forum on the Impact of Open Courseware for Higher Education in Developing Countries already raised the issue of quality assurance and listed concerned topics such as openness and accessibility, costs, user evaluation, indexing systems, pedagogical approaches, the quality of materials, etc. To testify the growing interests in as well as concerns about the OER initiatives, international organisations have started to study the issue. As an awareness-raising as well as information-sharing activity, the UNESCO International Institute for Educational Planning has been acting as a point of sharing information and experiences among experts since 2004. The Commonwealth of Learning is also promoting the OER approach with some cautions on such as accessibility, confidence of users, appropriateness, copyrights, accreditation, and affordability. On the research side, OECD has recently launched a project to study the current scope and nature of OER activity, covering the key issues such as sustainable costs/ benefits models, the intellectual property right issues, access issues for the users, and incentives and barriers for the universities and faculty staff concerning the delivery of the materials.

While OER is still in the very infancy stage of its development and use, many questions remain regarding quality: what indicators can be used to measure the OER? What impact will the OER have in the end on the quality of overall e-learning such as resources developed in-house within educational institutions or resources sold by private enterprises?

31.5   Conclusion and implications

E-learning is still in the initial phase of the educational innovation diffusion pattern. Within the diverse practices currently seen within and across countries, there are complex streams of divergence and convergence surrounding 'quality' in e-learning. The challenge is for governments and institutions to manage both divergence as well as convergence of e-learning practices.

Within this phase, institutions and faculty explore diverse practices in e-learning developments by trial and error. By adopting 'e-learning' in various ways, institutions attempt to seize the opportunities to enhance institutional capacities. In this way, institutions expand its educational provision borders, optimising faculty capacities, and revolutionalising pedagogies. Institutions can, therefore, embed 'quality' by formulating an institutional e-learning policy/ strategy in line with the institutional mission, effectuate the faculty development process, systematise programme evaluation and promote research on pedagogic impacts.

Convergence is occurring especially at the technical level, namely surrounding learning (and content) management systems. This convergence is envisaged to continue. Therefore, institutions are expected to comply with the emerging standards at the meta-data level, whether they be setting up their own platform, or developing an open source system in consortium. Dissemination of standarised contents have emerged as an issue in a form of Open Educational Resources or Open Courseware. Regarding open source developments (contents and platform), the Anglophone countries are more ahead than other regions. Cross-regional collaboration is therefore expected to play a role in setting up converged standards as well as localisation of contents, given that cross-border e-learning is growing albeit slowly.

Governments' roles may differ depending on each country's jurisdiction. Overall, governments can embed quality issues in its policies or strategies. The policies and strategies can be an interministerial document on information society, an integrated educational policy, or a distinct e-learning policy. The governments can also support programmes with focus on both quality enhancement and quality assurance. The challenge in quality assurance is to find a balance between international or regional standards and national and local diverse practices. At the technology side, governments' are expected take a strong lead in standardisation to advance cross-border provision.

To further map the global picture, future studies should include examples from other global regions to accommodate diversifying models of adoption and use of e-learning. For instance examples include high-tech models from Nordic countries, mega-universities from India, emerging models from the Middle-East with fast-growing e-learning markets, new venture models from China with fast-expanding access, virtual universities from developing countries, etc.). By accommodating diverse models future studies will be able to explore international trends and regional differences. They may reveal rationales within different economic, social, cultural, demographic and e-readiness contexts. The end result would be to identify challenges and opportunities in responding to the internationalisation of tertiary education. In addition, a longitudinal study of the e-learning developments at different types of tertiary institutions (e.g. higher education institutions, further education institutions or community colleges, vocational education and training institutions - that may be public, not-for-profit private and for-profit private) may add value to the analysis on comparisons of different missions of different sectors in tertiary education as well as on the blurring public-private dimensions of tertiary education. Government policy makers, funding organisations, and institutional managers could use this knowledge to support their strategic decision-making in enhancing 'quality' e-learning.

32 Best practices for e-learning

Rob Edmonds

SRI Consulting Business Intelligence, England

Best practices are an important concept for improving the quality of e-learning implementations. This article lists more than 40 best practices in e-learning (and provides full details of 17) based on recent research and consulting work conducted by SRI Consulting Business Intelligence's Learning on Demand research program. The practices come from research and consulting projects across multiple industries, including financial services, life sciences, automobiles, and oil and gas. The results are particularly useful for organisations looking to improve their e-learning and learning implementations but are also useful for learning developers and vendors that need to improve the efficiency and effectiveness of their customers' learning operations.

32.1   Introduction

Best practices are an important concept for improving the quality of e-learning implementations. They provide real-world benchmarks as well as practical techniques that organisations can use to increase quality. Best practices apply equally to new e-learning implementations for quality assessment and to existing e-learning initiatives for continuous improvement.

This article provides more than 40 best practices in e-learning based on recent research and consulting work conducted by SRI Consulting Business Intelligence's (SRIC-BI's) Learning on Demand research program. In the interest of brevity, all practices are listed and 17 are selected for a more detailed examination. An SRIC-BI report, *Best Practices in e-learning*, provides full details of all practices (see *References* below).

Best practice: A "best practice" is based upon what an organisation has actually done (it cannot be purely theoretical) and shows an approach to performing a particularly activity or process that improves upon alternative approaches.

The practices come from research and consulting projects across multiple industries, including financial services, life sciences, automobiles, and oil and gas. Most research focussed on the United States, Germany, United Kingdom and the Nordic countries.

The results are particularly useful for organisations looking to improve their e-learning and learning implementations but are also useful for learning developers and vendors that need to improve the efficiency and effectiveness of their customers' learning operations. We expect that organisations using the practices as part of a performance-improvement exercise will want to add their own internal practices as well as new external practices that pertain to their own set of issues and opportunities.

32.2   Design, methodology and summary of results

SRIC-BI conducted the e-learning best practice analysis based upon the body of research and knowledge it had built up through its Learning on Demand research program and consulting practice (see *References* for relevant research reports and projects). Our analysis reviewed this existing knowledge base to identify and capture best practices. Practices were selected based on their actual or potential business impact, on their transfer potential (to other companies) and on their level of innovation. We segmented best practices into the four key areas - strategy, organisation and process, content, and infrastructure - that companies need to have right in order to create successful learning programs.

The following table lists all best practices we identified and indicates which best practices we detail in full in this article.

Table 32-1: Best practices summary

Learning Strategy	Organisation and Process	Learning Content	Learning Infrastructure
Use e-learning to address the learning challenges of a distributed workforce.

Use e-learning and related techniques to create learning programs for customers and resellers.*

Use e-learning to improve synergies between internal and external participants in complex business | Create a centralised learning and development team.*

Source content both centrally and locally.*

Create standards and benchmarks for e-learning content.*

Share internal and external best practices with all teams | Develop a mix of off-the-shelf content and custom content to match the business situation.*

Create integrated learning programs including online and classroom activities.*

Supplement formal courses with informal learning activities.* | Rationalise learning-infrastructure investments by taking a centralised approach.*

Create a learning architecture.

Integrate learning-management systems (LMS) with other enterprise systems.*

Consider LMS from enterprise-application vendors. |

Learning Strategy	Organisation and Process	Learning Content	Learning Infrastructure
processes and projects.* Provide e-learning to the sales department for fast, measurable, business impact. Fulfil compliance-training requirements cheaply and efficiently using e-learning.* Use e-learning to provide on-demand learning for call-centre operatives. Use e-learning to improve time to return on investment during new corporate cost-cutting initiatives. Tie learning to performance. Assess learning outsourcing options.	active in developing, commissioning, or implementing learning.* Negotiate risk-sharing deals for off-the-shelf content libraries. Represent learning early during new strategic initiatives. Gain support from senior management.* Find ways to win over middle and line managers. Foster a good partnership between the training department and information technology. Create meaningful learning objectives. Invest in change management and ongoing user support. Create incentives for informal learning and knowledge sharing.	Combine basic with just-in-time learning.* Take a learning-objects approach.* Design all content with reusability in mind. Use easy-to-use development tools to create low-cost custom content in-house.* Create a "knowledge assembly line" of high-impact presentations by subject-matter experts. Migrate from physical to virtual classrooms to extend reach and reduce cost. Create content-selection practices that meet requirements for deployment speed. Obtain mass-customised content from generic-content vendors.	Develop infrastructure to enable greater multiuse of digital content for formal and informal learning activities.* Incorporate learning into employee portals. Be careful of political and technical issues when scaling up a local LMS for the enterprise. Consider custom LMS systems for low-cost tactical solutions. Treat LMS systems for business partners like consumer Web sites. Evaluate academic alternatives to commercial e-learning tools.

documented in full in this article
Source: SRIC-BI

32.3   Best practices in detail

The remainder of this article provides a detailed, "paper database" of learning and e-learning best practices. Each best practice has a description of what the practice involves, the benefits that organisation can derive, and examples of the practice in action.

32.3.1   Learning strategy

The following best practices concern learning-strategy issues such as learning needs and priorities, revenue generation, cost reduction, and performance improvement.

Use e-learning and related techniques to create learning programs for customers and resellers

- *Description.* As a Web-based medium, e-learning can easily extend to a company's customers and channel partners as well as its internal staff. Such learning initiatives often attract significant interest from senior managers because they address revenue generation and not simply cost reduction.
- *Benefits.* Customer learning can attract new customers and improve customer loyalty. It can also help reduce customer-service costs and educate customers about upcoming products to help drive demand. E-learning for resellers helps to create a sales channel that is better informed and therefore better prepared to win new business.
- Examples:
    - ING MoneyMentor (part of Internationale Nederlanden Group dealing in insurance, banking, and asset management) provides customer education about financial matters using entertainment content from Time Warner.
    - Charles Schwab is one of the pioneers of customer e-learning, having created a variety of financial-training material for its customers. The company realised that by educating customers and making them smarter investors, it could increase customer loyalty: More knowledgeable investors with greater use of online services would be more likely to remain (or become) strong customers of Schwab's services.
    - Cisco has developed a strong learning program for its channel partners. The "Partner e-learning Connection" portal includes courses and information about Cisco professional qualifications and product and technology updates. The site also delivers productivity tools such as learning maps to help registrants plan a curriculum for specific certifications. Content formats include Web-based courses, video on demand, virtual labs, online mentoring, and reference material. Some 90% of the 30 000 Cisco channel partners use the portal.

Use e-learning to improve synergies between internal and external participants in complex business processes and projects

- *Description.* E-learning and synergistic collaboration tools can help create an online community and improve communication between a geographically diverse set of workers. Many companies face certain processes and projects that involve individuals from different departments and external companies, each of whom must play a part in ensuring that a process or project completes successfully.
- *Benefits.* For certain business processes and projects that include a large number of players, e-learning and collaboration tools can help improve efficiency and reduce cost by enabling faster, clearer knowledge sharing.
- Examples:
  - For the drug-development process, various pharmaceutical companies are using e-learning and collaboration tools to integrate players from an internal value chain (such as R&D, business groups, technical operations, and support functions), as well as external players such as universities, health-care providers, biotech companies, and contract marketing and sales organisations.
  - Oil and gas exploration companies often use e-learning and knowledge-management tools to improve knowledge sharing on (and between) new infrastructure projects. Such projects, to extract oil or gas from new wells, involve large capital expenditures and a wide variety of internal and external participants.

Fulfil compliance training requirements cheaply and efficiently using e-learning

- *Description.* Many industries—including financial services, life sciences, and oil and gas—face increasing requirements for regulatory and compliance training. Such training is typically a legal requirement and not a "nice to have" like some other types of training sometimes seem to be. Because of its ability to deliver content to a large number of employees at low cost and to track course completions, e-learning has proved very popular for compliance training.
- *Benefits.* E-learning enables cheap, efficient, and traceable compliance training.
- Examples:
  - Like other energy companies, Statoil (a large Norwegian oil company) faces extensive regulatory training requirements relating to the environment and health and safety. Statoil uses e-learning tools to help track and administer regulatory training.
  - Credit Suisse recently hired WBT Systems to help it comply with new financial regulation. Demonstrating compliance involves tracking employees' progress, documenting courses taken, and demonstrating understanding through test results. This deal, which follows an initial three-year deploy-

ment, calls for an enterprise wide e-learning program that will include compliance training for 50 000 staff members.

32.3.2   Organisation and process

The following best practices concern organisation and process issues such as learning initiatives, learner support, incentive structures, and learning management.

Create a centralised learning and development team

- Description. Historically, many large companies managed learning and development on a very decentralised basis. Although the decentralised approach helps to ensure that learning meets immediate business needs, it does little to leverage the economies of scale possible with e-learning. Large companies have often paid for the same content many times over and even installed multiple learning-management systems. As e-learning matures, large companies are creating central learning and e-learning teams to manage learning infrastructure and coordinate, or advise about, content creation and acquisition. Key tasks of centralised teams are to provide infrastructure, set standards and procedures for content creation and acquisition, and use group purchasing power to drive down cost of infrastructure and generic content libraries that can serve across the group.
- *Benefits.* Centralised learning and development teams can reduce training redundancies (such as multiple LMS systems), increase capability through providing a common infrastructure, and help raise the impact of learning by providing standards and guidelines for content.
- Examples:
  - Deutsche Bank has created a new learning and development division with a newly appointed chief learning officer. One primary objective is to improve learning and e-learning coordination and collaboration across the group. An early task is to streamline and consolidate investments in e-learning infrastructure. Unlike many other central e-learning and learning teams that operate as "influencers," Deutsche Bank has created new reporting lines so that all learning and development staff now report into the central group. This change, although unsuitable for some types of organisations, suited the culture at Deutsche Bank and was necessary to push through some of the rationalisation activities.
  - Reuters has created a new centralised learning and development team to reduce training cost and improve consistency. Key tasks are to implement a shared infrastructure (from Oracle) and to create standards for content creation and purchasing. Reuters plans to integrate content purchasing with the Oracle procurement system and use a preferred supplier list with which it has negotiated preferential terms and has confirmed quality standards.

- A U.S. insurance company found that a variety of skills—including business, technology, and pedagogy—are necessary to create a successful centralised learning and development team.

Source content both centrally and locally

- *Description.* Large organisations often create and source classroom and online learning content locally. Most often, large organisations need to take this approach because centralised learning and development teams would be too far removed from business needs, or they would become a bottleneck for learning. However, we do not suggest that central learning and development teams should play no role in content creation and selection. Central teams should set standards, benchmarks, and guidelines to ensure that content meets quality, technical, and cost requirements. In addition, many leading adopters of e-learning have sourced generic content catalogues (such as desktop IT training and soft skills) at the central level to drive down cost.
- *Benefits.* Taking a decentralised approach to most content creation and acquisition reduces bottlenecks and helps keep content close to business needs. Central groups can set standards and benchmarks to ensure consideration of quality, cost, and interoperability issues and also to obtain preferential deals on generic content catalogues.
- Examples:
  - A global banking group sources content at the global, regional, and divisional levels. Global content at the bank is off-the-shelf IT and finance content. Regional content is driven by language constraints and different requirements for compliance training. Regional content typically includes business-skills training. Divisional content is specific to a line of business and often custom developed.
  - BP relies on training professionals close to the lines of business to decide on content needs, though it does source generic IT and business-skills catalogues—that can serve across business groups—more centrally.

Create standards and benchmarks for e-learning content

- *Description.* Central learning and development teams need to set a variety of technical, quality, and process standards and benchmarks for learning content that may be created and procured by many departments across the organisation. Standards may range from requirements for SCORM (sharable content object reference model) compliance to processes for selecting custom content suppliers and managing a development project.
- *Benefits.* Standards and benchmarks help ensure that a large organisation has quality learning materials that are value for money and that no duplication of effort occurs. Standards and benchmarks also can ensure that e-learning content is interoperable.

- Examples:
  - One key task for the recently appointed chief learning officer (CLO) at Deutsche Bank is to integrate and rationalise the different learning and e-learning activities across the group. As part of this effort, the CLO's team is setting a variety of new standards, processes, and rules to ensure that learning and development activities are consistent and compatible. As part of the process, the team is reducing the number of content suppliers the company uses—from some 1000 to nearer 100.
  - Cisco centralises its e-learning infrastructure but decentralises content creation and acquisition—relying on a set of standards, guidelines, and benchmarks. Reuters takes a similar approach.

Share internal and external best practices with all teams active in developing, commissioning, or implementing learning

- *Description.* Most large corporations have different teams, departments, and even companies that are active in learning implementation. Even if a corporation wishes to retain a decentralised approach to learning and development, it should ensure that mechanisms are in place to enable internal players to share and learn from best practices in implementing e-learning and blended learning. Best practices might be lessons from internal projects as well as from external studies.
- *Benefits.* Use of best practices ensures that the same mistake is less likely to happen twice and that successful approaches are replicable across different parts of an organisation. Mechanisms for sharing best practices are particularly useful for organisations with decentralised training and learning functions.
- Examples:
  - Roche Diagnostic's central team advises the business units and training teams active in learning implementation about best practices in e-learning and enterprise learning. The company also has an internal "e-learning council" in which some 25 people spanning 15 business areas share best practices. As input to the ongoing process, Roche has leveraged an external benchmarking study to learn about the practices of other leading adopters.
  - Although it has a decentralised learning structure, pharmaceutical company Merck runs an internal focus group of some 40 e-learning practitioners for sharing best practices and collaborating on e-learning initiatives.
  - State Farm, a large insurance provider, created an e-learning-focused community of practice to allow in-house training professionals to communicate and collaborate more easily about e-learning issues. The community of practice has helped people avoid duplication of effort and enabled collaboration between smaller groups that focus on specific learning issues. Specific task forces within the community share pain points, document the current e-learning tools and products in use at State Farm, and identify relevant external research.

Gain support from senior management

- *Description.* Many examples exist of e-learning projects' failing because—although innovative—they lacked support from senior management and therefore became difficult to sustain or to roll out beyond a small-scale implementation. How best to gain senior management support depends on a company's situation and culture, though often creating some early wins with measurable cost savings or revenue gains creates a good starting point.
- *Benefits.* Backing from senior management helps ensure that a company can sustain and scale up a learning initiative and can address barriers to success.
- Examples:
  - At the Bank of Montreal, the head of HR is also the head of Strategic Management. Early success in using e-learning to train and ensure completion of a major branch system's implementation in 1994 led to an invitation to the head of the team to participate in new business initiatives and build a role for e-learning from the start.
  - Deutsche Bank has found that workers are more motivated to take courses when senior managers openly support the initiative. Projects that have no proper backing often disappear from the radar screen.

32.3.3   Learning content

The following best practices concern content issues such as curriculum design, content creation, and acquisition, as well as informal learning and reusability.

Develop a mix of off-the-shelf content and custom content to match the business situation

- *Description.* Companies need to decide how much and what types of off-the-shelf, generic content they will use and how much in-house, customised content (some of which may come out of informal learning and work activities) they will develop. Most companies use off-the-shelf content for IT, generic soft skills, and compliance training. Custom content is important for core-business issues to maximise performance and stay competitive. Custom content is also necessary where off-the-shelf content is in short supply, such as in non-English-speaking countries and in industries where e-learning content is less common. Companies need to monitor the supply of generic content carefully because quality is steadily improving, as is the range of covered topics (including an increasing number of industry-specific titles).
- *Benefits.* Off-the-shelf content is usually cheaper than custom content but targets an organisation's specific needs less. Balancing the two approaches according to business requirements and the availability of suppliers enables adopters to derive the best value for money from e-learning.

- Examples:
  - Citibank, ABN AMRO, HSBC, Wachovia, Bank of America, Barclays, and many others use generic content for desktop applications and other IT training. Financial services also use generic content for a variety of soft skills, but especially for sales and customer service.
  - A global banking group uses 75% generic and 25% custom content. It sees this balance as relatively stable and actively tries not to use more custom content to keep costs to a minimum.
  - A major European bank custom develops as much as 90% of its content because it is unable to find quality content in German. It outsources development to local suppliers.
  - Gjensidige NOR develops all content in-house using internal staff. Improving quality of authoring tools and templates that enable quicker and more cost-effective content creation by subject-matter experts encourages internal, customised content development.

Create integrated learning programs including online and classroom activities

- *Description.* Although most companies have claimed to offer "blended learning" for many years, this offering typically meant only that they used classroom training and online learning—not that the two integrated into a coherent learning program. Leading practitioners now have well-defined curricula and learning paths that integrate online learning (and the different types of online learning) with face-to-face activities. Face-to-face activities need not be traditional teaching sessions but could be workshops, discussion groups, and networking events.
- *Benefits.* Developing a truly integrated learning program enables learners to derive the best of both worlds from online and face-to-face learning. An integrated program also ensures that the different media work together to achieve a company's learning objectives. These advantages add up to improved ROI through better learning and cost reduction by eliminating redundancy and duplication in training and development (such as offering the same content both online and offline).
- Examples:
  - Gjensidige NOR has created a "learning garden"—a physical space where a variety of learning activities, using both face-to-face and e-learning tools and technologies, can take place. Among the technologies that find use in the learning garden are MindManager and SmartBoard.
  - Charles Schwab's blended-learning programs include live facilitation at the beginning and at the end of a course.
  - Sun Life Financial is building its new learning program by drawing on online communities-of-practice experiences of Clarica as well as the more traditional training programs of Sun Life.

Supplement formal courses with informal learning activities

- *Description.* Although formal, course-based training still dominates today's corporate learning and development, debate is growing about the effectiveness of formal training alone. A growing number of studies and surveys show that people believe that they learn most effectively during informal learning activities. When putting together learning programs, leading companies include informal learning activities such as communities of practice in their training mix.
- *Benefits.* By harnessing informal learning activities, companies can create a better mix of formal and informal learning initiatives to increase employees' ability to gain new knowledge and skills.
- Examples:
  - Clarica (now Sun Life Financial) made strong efforts to build and support online collaboration and communities of practice for both internal staff and its network of agents and financial advisors. A community of practice to support agents gained public visibility when Deb Wallace, consultant in the Strategic Capabilities Group at Clarica, wrote *Leveraging Communities of Practice for Strategic Advantage* with Hubert Saint-Onge. Building on the company's success with its agent network, Clarica went on to establish communities for agency-management personnel, innovation standards, and group-insurance-account executives.
  - Prudential has used an online collaboration platform from Communispace to create an alumni community for graduates of the company's emerging-business-leaders program. The community will support the delivery of projects that originate in the program, incubate new ideas and projects, and promote networking among alumni across Prudential's businesses.
  - BP, Shell, and other oil companies use communities of practice to share knowledge within the organisation—typically focusing around a business function or process. Both BP and Shell have found that simple systems, where workers can ask questions of a group and receive answers, are the most effective methods of knowledge management. Workers often see stored and codified knowledge as less useful than live answers from other workers because they are unsure if the codified information is up-to-date. BP is using a community of practice to share knowledge among individuals responsible for implementing e-learning solutions. Within e-learning, Shell also emphasises the importance of community and collaboration—for example, most e-learning sessions at Shell begin with meeting one's peers in the virtual class.

Combine basic with just-in-time learning

- *Description.* For the past few years e-learning proponents have encouraged a shift toward short modules (or objects) of learning that are deliverable just in time to learners in the context of their workplace. Although this idea is compelling and of great benefit for many types of learning, leading practitioners recognise that learning programs must teach basic skills in-depth as well as providing just-in-time performance support.

- *Benefits.* Providing deeper training in core topics as well as just-in-time performance support ensures that companies can not only deliver the right piece of knowledge to the right person at the right time but also develop fundamental skills over time.
- Examples:

  - Both Shell and Statoil support more fundamental learning as well as just-in-time, problem-based e-learning. Most learning professionals recognise that a mix of basic learning in fundamental principles and just-in-time learning is necessary. Statoil voiced concern that the pendulum is swinging too far back the other way—e-learning is encouraging learning professionals to overemphasise just-in-time learning and deemphasise basic training.
  - A U.S. consumer-products company expects that "deep-development" training in areas such as leadership will remain face-to-face but plans to move more of its information-intensive learning online.

Take a learning-objects approach

- *Description.* Leading practitioners are taking an object-based approach to creating, managing, and storing content. Instead of large Web-based courses, object approaches advocate breaking e-learning content down into small pieces (learning objects). Open e-learning standards that allow interoperability between learning objects and with standards-based tools are driving adoption of learning objects, though these standards are still in their formative stages. Learning objects often work in conjunction with learning-content–management systems (LCMS) that typically comprise an authoring component, tools for converting legacy content into object form, and a database repository with content-management tools for storing and managing learning objects. Many LMS systems now include an LCMS application.
- *Benefit.* Two of the main benefits of a learning-objects approach are the easy updating of content by swapping in new objects for outdated ones and the ability to reuse content by using learning objects with other object-based content. Adopters of learning objects also find them more amenable than other course designs to blended-learning approaches that combine e-learning and instructor-led training.
- Examples:

  - Autodesk uses a library of 100 000 or more learning objects to mass-customise its product training for different customers.
  - Cisco Systems has developed a reusable-learning-objects (RLO) strategy and amassed a large library of object-based content that it stores alongside other object-based content for use for learning and other content-based areas such as Web-site construction.

- GeneEd, a content developer that focuses on the life-sciences industry, has embraced the use of learning objects and has developed several thousand learning objects, each of which presents a single concept in a two- to seven-minute animation. GeneEd serves numerous pharmaceutical companies, including Pfizer and AstraZeneca.

Use easy-to-use development tools to create low-cost custom content in-house

- *Description.* E-learning-content authoring tools are improving, and some organisations are finding that they can provide a low-cost alternative to outsourcing custom-content creation. In-house e-learning staff can often create templates from which subject-matter experts can create e-learning content in conjunction with training staff.
- *Benefits.* Bringing content creation in-house can reduce cost and may improve creation time. Arguably, quality may also improve if third-party developers did not understand the content very well. Often organisations are giving up a "professional feel" to the content when it comes in-house but they must measure this trade-off against cost and other factors. Content-development tools are particularly beneficial in sectors where little off-the-shelf material is available and so custom content development costs are high.
- Examples:
  - Merck selected the TrainerSoft authoring tool to bring custom-content creation in-house. Developers created templates for consistent look and feel, and a large team of 150 developers creates custom content using the tool. Merck has cut content-creation costs as a result of the move.
  - A U.S. insurance company users TrainerSoft to create its own e-learning content in-house, at low cost. However, the provider is facing staffing challenges as it increases the volume of content.
  - The U.S. military is an early adopter and leading practitioner of e-learning, including advanced simulations and game-based learning. New tools now enable the military to modify off-the-shelf computer games and thus produce more cost-effective products.

32.3.4   Learning infrastructure

The following best practices concern infrastructure issues such as learning architecture, LMS, content management, and enterprise systems.

Rationalise learning-infrastructure investments by taking a centralised approach

- *Description.* When e-learning first arrived, many large companies invested in LMS in an ad hoc fashion, leading to duplicated functionality across different parts of the business. Leading practitioners have now created central task forces or councils to oversee the deployment of centralised learning-management systems and related learning infrastructure. Although a single, centralised LMS will be preferable in many cases, alternatives exist that companies can still manage centrally. For example, as an interim measure, companies can reduce the number of learning-management systems in place. Another approach is to integrate different LMS systems to enable centralised reporting while keeping administration and control separate.

- *Benefit.* Centralised learning infrastructure reduces the cost of software licenses and ongoing support. In addition, the common infrastructure means that many other benefits of e-learning (such as reaching a globally distributed workforce quickly and easily) are possible. At the user level, rationalisation can mean small but significant improvements such as a single log-in and user interface for e-learning.
- Example practitioners:

  - Deutsche Bank is streamlining and consolidating its e-learning systems and components. The bank expects to see significant cost savings and to ease integration of systems. By integrating and consolidating systems, Deutsche Bank is taking a centralised learning infrastructure approach but without making the investment in a single, centralised LMS.
  - Reuters has moved to a single, global LMS from Oracle.
  - One European Bank is planning a hub-and-spoke architecture for a corporate LMS—one central system for reporting and other systems that otherwise run independently.
  - Cisco Systems centralises all learning infrastructure—but decentralises content creation.

Integrate LMS with other enterprise systems

- *Description.* Many companies are integrating LMS systems with other enterprise systems such as human-resources–management systems, customer-relationship–management (CRM) systems, and enterprise-resources–planning suites. "C-level" (CEO, CFO, CLO, CIO, and so on) executives from leading adopters now increasingly see e-learning, content-management, knowledge-management, and related application areas as merely related subsets and elements of the big picture, part of the mosaic of large enterprise systems. Most leading practitioners have integrated or are planning to integrate their LMS with other enterprise systems—even at a basic level to ensure that employee records are correct.
- *Benefits.* To achieve maximum benefit from LMS systems, companies need to integrate LMS systems with other enterprise systems. For example, integration with HR systems ensures a single employee database, and integration with finance systems allows cost allocation using common systems.
- Examples:

  - Genentech's implementation of Pathlore integrates with PeopleSoft.

- Skandia runs a learning portal that integrates with the company's workforce-management system (from PeopleSoft), enabling automated updating of personnel files and tracking for auditing and certification.
- Merck plans to move to an enterprise wide LMS but not until it has completed its implementation of its enterprise human-resource–information system from PeopleSoft.

Develop infrastructure to enable greater multiuse of digital content for formal and informal learning activities

- *Description.* Develop infrastructure to enable use of the same content for a range of formal and informal learning activities. Infrastructure should integrate or combine e-learning, knowledge-management, and enterprise-contentmanagement systems.
- *Benefit.* Common or integrated infrastructure to support all forms of learning in the enterprise means greater capacity for reuse of content and therefore greater efficiency and reduced cost. "Joined-up" learning infrastructure is also likely to improve the overall ability of employees to gain new knowledge effectively.
- Examples:
  - Bristol-Myers Squibb uses a content-management system from Documentum to handle documentation of R&D and clinical trials. The system integrates with the LMS from Plateau and standard-operating-procedure training.
  - Cisco Systems uses a common enterprise-content–management system to manage content for a variety of different purposes, including learning.

32.4   Conclusion

By looking at the list of practices in Table 32-1, and documented in this article, one can quickly see that the complexity and success factors in creating and sustaining quality in e-learning are about far more than dealing with technology and finding the right content. Half of the practices relate to either learning strategy or organisation and process issues. Table 32-1 also reveals several common themes that appear across practices and across practice categories:

- *Growing role of informal learning.* Many organisations are undergoing efforts to create learning programs with a more balanced mix of formal and informal content.
- *Increasing centralisation of learning and e-learning management.* Many leading practitioners are taking a more global view of their e-learning and learning investments.

- *Reduction in the cost of e-learning.* Companies are trying to rationalise e-learning investment beyond the early experimental days and find ongoing practices that provide value for money.

Current gaps in best practices include strategies for generating new revenue from learning, performance measurement, and web services. We expect to see more best practices emerge in these areas over time.

Of course, any list of best practices is academic unless organisations can actually implement them to improve quality. SRIC-BI's consulting practice has developed a generic methodology for applying best practices that is adaptable to different circumstances. The methodology involves five key steps:

- Define mission and focus.
- Conduct diagnostic of current practices and needs.
- Develop or expand a compendium of relevant best practices.
- Rate practice performance against others.
- Create best-practices strategy and implementation plan.

Full details of this methodology appear in the report *Best Practices in e-learning*.

List of projects, organisations and initiatives

Acronym/ Abbreviation:	Project, organisation or initiative description/ Website:	Country/ Region:	Reference in chapter:
AACSB	Association to Advance Collegiate Schools of Business www.aacsb.edu	USA	7
ACE	The American Council on Education www.acenet.edu	USA	31
ADEC	The American Distance Education Consortium www.adec.edu	USA	31
ADL	Advanced Distributed Learning www.adlnet.org	USA	13, 21, 31
AFLF	The Australian Flexible Learning Framework www.flexiblelearning.net.au	Australia	31
AFNOR	Association française de normalisation www.afnor.fr	France	7, 25
AICC	Aviation Industry CBT Committee www.aicc.org	International	21
AIV	Italian Evaluation Association www.valutazioneitaliana.it	Italy	11
ALI	Adult Learning Inspectorate www.ali.gov.uk	UK	31
A-MBA	Association of MBA's/Ambassadors for MBA www.mbaworld.com	International	7
ANECA	Agencia Nacional de Evaluación de la Calidad y Acreditación www.aneca.es	Spain	4, 22
ANSI	American National Standards Institute www.ansi.org	USA	14
AQAS	Agentur für Qualitätssicherung durch Akkreditierung von Studiengängen www.aqas.de	Germany	4
ARIADNE	Ariadne Foundation www.ariadne-eu.org	Europe	21, 25, 30

Acronym/ Abbreviation:	Project, organisation or initiative description/ Website:	Country/ Region:	Reference in chapter:
ArtSet LQW	Lernerorientierte Qualitätstestierung in der Weiterbildung	Germany	8
	www.artset-lqw.de		
ASFOR	Associazione per la formazione alla direzione aziendale	Italy	4
	www.asfor.it		
ASTD	American Society for Training & Development	USA	7, 31
	www.astd.org		
ASTD/ECC	American Society for Training and Development, E-learning Courseware Certification	International	31
	www.astd.org		
Attention.xml	Attention.xml	International	21
	developers.technorati.com/wiki/attentionxml		
BAOL	Reference quality model for e-learning developed by the British Association for Open Learning	UK	25
	www.british-learning.org.uk		
BECTA, Demonstrating Transformation	The Demonstrating Transformation	UK	26
	ferl.becta.org.uk		
BECTA	The British Educational and Communications Technology Agency	UK	31
	www.becta.org.uk		
BLA	British Learning Association, Quality Mark	UK	31
	www.british-learning.org.uk		
BMBF	The Neue Medien in der Bildung Programme	Germany	31
	www.medien-bildung.net		
BME	Bundesverband Materialwirtschaft, Einkauf und Logistik e.V.	Germany	19
	www.bme.de		
BMF	The Federal Ministry of Education and Research	Germany	31
	www.bmbf.de		
BMWA	The Federal Ministry of Economics and Labour	Austria	31
	www.bmwa.gv.at		
BOLOGNA	Bologna declaration	Germany	24
	www.bologna-berlin2003.de		
CACE	The Canadian Association of Community Education	Canada	31
	www.nald.ca/cacenet.htm		
CanCore	Canadian Body for Learning Resource Metadata Initiative	Canada	15, 20
	www.careo.org/cancore		
CanReg	Canadian Recommended E-learning Guidelines	Canada	25, 31
	www.eqcheck.com		

Acronym/ Abbreviation:	Project, organisation or initiative description/ Website:	Country/ Region:	Reference in chapter:
CC	Creative Commons www.creativecommons.org	International	29
CELEBRATE	Celebrate, project of European SchoolNet celebrate.eun.org	International	20, 29
CEN/ISS	European committee for standardisation of information systems, Workshop Learning Technologies www.cenorm.org	Europe/ Belgium	12, 13, 14, 16, 17, 18, 19, 20, 20
CEREQ	Centre d'études et de recherches sur les qualifications www.cereq.fr	France	23
CERFAD	Commissione Regionale per la Certificazione dei Materiali Didattici e dei Servizi per la Formazione a Distanza www.regione.emilia-romagna.it	Italy	3, 23
CHEA	Council for Higher Education Accreditation in the United States www.chea.org	USA	4, 31
CNE	French National Committee for Evaluation www.cne-evaluation.fr	France	22
COL	The Consumers Guide to E-learning www.col.org	Canada	31
CORDRA	The Content Object Repository Discovery and Resolution Architecture cordra.lsal.cmu.edu	International	21, 31
CORE	The China Open Resources for Education www.core.org.cn	China	31
CRAC	The Council of Regional Accrediting Commissions www.neasc.org	USA	31
DC	The Campus Numerique (Digital Campus) project www.cs.ucsb.edu	France	31
DCMI	DCMI Metadata Terms dublincore.org	International	21, 29
DELNI	The Education and Training Inspectorate www.delni.gov.uk	UK	31
DES	Danish Evaluation Society www.danskevalueringsselskab.dk	Denmark	11
DETC	Distance Education and Training Council www.detc.org	International	7, 31
DfES	The Department for Education and Skills www.dfes.gov.uk	UK	26, 31
Digita	Deutsher Bildungssoftware-Pres www.digita.de	Germany	7

Acronym/ Abbreviation:	Project, organisation or initiative description/ Website:	Country/ Region:	Reference in chapter:
DIN	Deutsches Institut für Normung e. V. www.din.de, www.beuth.de	Germany	6, 7, 13, 14
DLS	The Distributed eLearning Program www.dls.army.mil	UK	31
DOD	The US Department of Defence www.defenselink.mil	USA	31
eAccess	Developing web content supporting learning and training of disadvantaged user communities www.ask.iti.gr	Greece	20
ebXML	Electronic business XML www.ebxml.org	International	19
EC	European Commission europa.eu.int	Europe	2, 20
ECA	European Consortium for Accreditation www.ecaconsortium.net	Europe	4
eCDF	The e-Learning Collaborative Development Fund www.govt.nz	New Zealand	31
EDUCATION	Ministère de l'éducation nationale, de l'enseignement supérieur et de la recherché www.education.fr	France	25
EDUCAUSE	EDUCAUSE Learning Initiative (formerly NLII) www.educause.edu	Interantional	17
eduQua	A specific norm developed for Swiss continuing education institutions www.eduqua.ch	Switzerland	22
EE	E-learning europa - the portal elearningeuropa.info	International	31
EELQF	European eLearning Quality forum communities.trainingvillage.gr/elearning_forum	Europe	3
EES	European Evaluation Society www.europeanevaluation.org	Europe	11
EFMD	European Foundation for Management Development www.efmd.org	Europe	7, 8
EFQM	European Foundation for Quality Management www.efqm.org	Europe	6, 7
EFQUEL	European Quality Foundation in e-learning www.qualityfoundation.org	Europe	3
EIfEL	Building a learning Europe www.eife-l.org	Europe	23
ELAN	eLearning Academic Network, Lower Saxony www.elan-niedersachsen.de	Germany	27

Acronym/ Abbreviation:	Project, organisation or initiative description/ Website:	Country/ Region:	Reference in chapter:
ELF	The e-learing Framework elframework.org	International	19
ENQA	European Association for Quality Assurance in Higher Education www.enqa.net	Europe	4, 22
ENV	Enterprise Model Execution and Integration Services (ENV 13550) www.cimosa.de	Germany	19
EOU	Eastern Oregon University - EduRecources Portal sage.eou.edu	USA	31
EPICC	European Portfolio Initiatives Co-ordination Committee www.epiccproject.info	Europe	17
eQCheck	QualitE-Learning Assurance Inc. www.eqcheck.com	Europe	7, 25
EQO	European Quality Observatory www.eqo.info	Europe	3, 7, 12, 25
ETB	European Treasury Browser etb.eun.org	International	31
E-TEACHING	The "e-teaching" project www.e-teaching.org	Germany	31
eudQua	Schweizerisches Qualitätszertifikat für Weiterbildungsinstitutionen www.eduQua.ch	Switzerland	7
EUR-ACE	Accreditation of European Engineering Programmes and Graduates www.feani.org	Europe	4
EureleA	European eLearning Award www.eurelea.org	Europe	7
FES	Finnish Evaluation Society www.finnishevaluationsociety.net	Finland	11
FFFOD	Forum Français pour la Formation Ouverte et à Distance www.fffod.org	France	25
FINHEEC	Finnish Higher Education Evaluation Council www.kka.fi	Finland	22
GAC	German Accreditation Council www.akkreditierungsrat.de	Germany	4
GEM	The Gateway to Educational Materials www.thegateway.org	USA	31
GES	German Evaluation Society www.degeval.de	Germany	11

Acronym/ Abbreviation:	Project, organisation or initiative description/ Website:	Country/ Region:	Reference in chapter:
GPI	Gesellschaft für Pädagogik und Information e. V. www.gpi-online.de	Germany	7
HEA	The Higher Education Academy www.heacademy.ac.uk	UK	31
HELIOS	The HELIOS project diva.library.cmu.edu/HELIOS/about.html	International	31
HOPE	Project, Interactive training for a better future: eLearning for the socially excluded www.hope-project.org	International	20
HRSDC	The Office of Learning Technologies of the Human Resources Development Canada www.hrsdc.gc.ca	Canada	31
HR-XML	Human resources xml www.hr-xml.org	International	19
IEC	International Electrotechnical Committee www.iec.ch	Switzerland	14, 19
IEEE/ICALT	IEEE International Conference on Advanced Learning Technologies (ICALT) lttf.ieee.org/events.htm	International	25
IDEALS	IEEE Learning Technology Standards Committee, WG4: Digital Rights Expression Language ltsc.ieee.org	International	13, 14, 17, 21, 29
IEN	Irish Evaluation Network www.policyinstitute.tcd.ie	Irland	11
IET	The E-learning thematic projects iet.open.ac.uk	UK	31
IETF	The Internet Engineering Task Force www.ietf.org	International	19
IHEP	Institute for Higher Education Policy, The Quality On the Line: Benchmarks for Success in Internet-Based Distance Education www.ihep.com, www.ihep.org	International	7, 31
IITT	Institute of IT Training, University of Warwick www.iitt.org.uk	UK	7
IMS	International Management Standards, Global www.imsglobal.org	International	13, 14, 15, 16, 17, 18, 19, 20, 21, 25, 31
INFLOW	Informal Learning Opportunities in the Workplace www.inflow.eu.com	Europe	17
INQAAHE	International Network of Quality Assurance Agencies in Higher Education www.inqaahe.org	International	7

Acronym/ Abbreviation:	Project, organisation or initiative description/ Website:	Country/ Region:	Reference in chapter:
IPEN	International Program Evaluation Network ipen21.org	International	11
ISO	International Organisation for Standardisation, 9000, 9126 www.iso.org	International	6, 7, 13, 14, 19, 31
ISO/JTC SC36	Joint Technical Committee 1 (JTC1) dedicated to Information Technology for learning, education and training (sub-committee 36) of ISO (International organisation of Standardisation) jtc1sc36.org	UK	5, 13, 17, 21, 25, 31
ITU	International Telecommunication Union www.itu.int	International	14
JISC	Japanese Industrial Standards Committee www.jisc.go.jp	Japan	14
KAON-WS	The Karlsruhe Ontology Web Service Tool Suite www.aifb.uni-karlsruhe.de	Germany	19
Key-PAL	relevance and potential impact of the ePortfolio on the development and assessment of key-skills www.eife-l.org	International	17
KILT	King´s institute of learning and teaching www.kcl.ac.uk	UK	23
L3	L3-Lebenslanges Lernen, BMBF www.l-3.info	Germany	27
LAMS	The Learning Activity Management System www.lamsinternational.com	Australia	30, 31
LDV	Leonardo Da Vinci-Programme europa.eu.int	Europe	24
LQW	Lernerorientierte Qualitätssicherung in der Weiterbildung www.artset-lqw.de	Germany	24
LSAL	The Carnegie Mellon University Learning Systems Architecture Lab www.lsal.cmu.edu	International	21, 29
LSC	The Learning and Skills council www.lsc.gov.uk	UK	31
LSDA	The Learning and Skills Development Agency www.lsda.org.uk	UK	31
Medida-Prix	Mediendidaktischer Hochschulpreis www.medidaprix.de	Germany	7
MELLON	The Andrew W. Mellon Foundation www.mellon.org	USA	21, 31
MERLOT	The MERLOT- Multimedia Educational Rersource for Learning and Online Teaching www.merlot.org	USA	31

Acronym/ Abbreviation:	Project, organisation or initiative description/ Website:	Country/ Region:	Reference in chapter:
MEXT	The Ministry of Education, Culture, Sports, Science and Technology www.mext.go.jp	Japan	31
MINERVA	Minerva Project (Socrates Programme) Project number: 110231-CP-1-2003-1-MINERVA-M – 2003-2006 www.e-quality-eu.org	Europe	22
MoE	The Ministry of Education www.education.gouv.fr	France	31
MPEG	Moving Picture Experts Group www.chiariglione.org	International	14
MPT	The Ministry of Telecommunication ieeexplore.ieee.org	Brazil	31
NCSL	The National College for School Leadership www.ncls.org.uk	UK	26
NEASC	The Guidelines for the Evaluation of Electronically Offered Degree and Certificate Program www.neasc.org	USA	31
NVAO	Nederlands-Vlaamse Akkreditatieorganisatie www.nvao.nl	Netherlands	4
OAGi	Open Applcation Group www.openapplications.org	International	19
OAQ	Centre of Accreditation and Quality Assurance of the Swiss Universities www.oaq.ch	Switzerland	22
OCW	Taft's University - Open Courseware ocw.tufts.edu	USA	31
OCW1	The Japanese universities - Open Courseware consortium www.jocw.jp	Japan	31
OCW2	Utah State University - Open Courseware ocw.usu.edu	USA	31
ODRL	Open Digital Rights Language odrl.net	International	31
OECD	Organisation for Economic Co-operation and Development www.oecd.org	International	2, 25
OET	The US Department of Education's Office of Educational Technology www.ed.gov/Technology	USA	31
OFSTED	The Office for Standards in Education www.ofsted.gov.uk	UK	26, 31

Acronym/ Abbreviation:	Project, organisation or initiative description/ Website:	Country/ Region:	Reference in chapter:
OLI	Carnegie Mellon University - the Open Learning Initiative	USA	31
	www.cmu.edu/oli		
OMA/CORBA	Open Management Architecture/ Common Object Request Broker Architecture	International	19
	www.omg.org		
OMG	Object Management Group	International	19
	www.omg.org		
onlineEduca	yearly worldwide conferences on e-learning (On Line Educa)	International	25
	www.oeb2005.com		
OPQFC	Office Professionnel de Qualification des organismes de Formation et des Conseils	France	23
	www.opqfc.org		
OSE	The Open Source Virtual Learning Environment	New Zealand	31
	www.ose.org.nz		
OSMOSYS	Organising SMO´s employees approaches to life-long learning at system level	International	17, 23
	www.osmosys.se		
PISA	Programme for international student assessment	International	24
	www.pisa.oecd.org		
Portiko	Portiko, BMBF	Germany	27
	www.portiko.de		
PROLEARN	Prolearn Project	Europe	21, 27
	www.prolearn-project.org		
PTE	Polish Evaluation Society	Poland	11
	www.pte.org.pl		
QAA	Quality Assurance Agency for Higher Education	UK	7, 25, 31
	www.qaa.ac.uk		
QED	The Quality Initiative eLearning in Germany	Germany	5, 6, 12, 31
	www.qed-info.de		
QUILT	The Quality in Information and Learning Technology	UK	31
	www.nccic.org/quilt		
ReLL	Regional Network to Develop Lifelong Learning Strategies	International	23
	www.education-observatories.net		
RICE	Rice University	USA	31
	cnx.rice.edu		
RTEC	The Regional Technology in Education Consortia	USA	31
	rtec.org		
SAC	Polish State Accreditation Committee	Poland	22
	www.men.waw.pl		

Acronym/ Abbreviation:	Project, organisation or initiative description/ Website:	Country/ Region:	Reference in chapter:
SAIL	The League for Innovation in the Community Colleges - the Specialty Asynchronous Industry Learning www.league.org	US	31
SCIL	Swiss Centre for Innovations in Learning www.scil.ch	Switzerland	7
SCORM	The Sharable Content Object Reference Model www.adlnet.org	International	15, 16, 22, 25, 31, 32
SEE	Spanish Public Policy Evaluation Society www.sociedadevaluacion.org	Spain	11
SEEL	Supporting Excellence in E-Learning ww.eife-l.org/activities/past/seel	Europe	3, 23
SEEQUEL	Sustainable Environment for the Evaluation of Quality in e-Learning www.education-observatories.net	Internaional	3, 23, 25
SEVAL	Swiss Evaluation Society www.seval.ch	Switzerland	11
SFE	French Evaluation Society www.sfe.asso.fr	France	11
SIG-DLAE	Special Interest Group Distance Learning Accreditation dlae.enpc.fr	France	4
SLOAN	The Sloan Foundation www.sloan.org	USA	31
SMILE	A Sign Language and Multimedia-based Interactive Language Course for the Deaf for the Training of European Written Languages www.arcsmed.at/projects/smile	Austria	20
SMTP	Simple mail transfer protocol www.ietf.org	International	19
SOFIA	Consortium of community colleges - Sharing of Free Intellectual Assets sofia.fhda.edu	USA	31
SRI-BI	The SRIC-BI Learning on Demand Program www.sric-bi.com	International	32
SVUF	Swedish Evaluation Society www.svuf.nu	Sweden	11
SWEP	Walloon Evaluation Society www.prospeval.org	France	11
TBF	The Bertelsmann Foundation www.bertelsmann-stiftung.de	Germany	31
TCP/IP	Transmission control protocol/internet protocol www.ietf.org	International	19

Acronym/ Abbreviation:	Project, organisation or initiative description/ Website:	Country/ Region:	Reference in chapter:
TELCERT	Technology Enhanced Learning Conformance - European Requirements and Testing www.opengroup.org	International	17
TLTP	The Teaching and Learning Technology Programme www.brad.ac.uk	UK	31
TUD	Technical University of Darmstadt, Gütesiegel www.elc.tu-darmstadt.de	Germany	8
U21	Universitas 21 Global www.u21global.com	International	31
UDDI	Universal Description, Discovery and Integration www.uddi.org	International	19
Ufi	University for Industry www.ufi.com	UK	31
UKES	UK Evaluation Society www.evaluation.org.uk	UK	11
UKEU	The UK e-University www.ukeu.com	UK	31
UN/EDIFACT	United Nations Directories for Electronic Data Interchange for Administration, Commerce and Transport www.unece.org	International	19
UNESCO, Criteria for University Programmes	The Standard Criteria for Establishing Internet-Based Program of Studies by Thai Universities asiapacific-odl.oum.edu.my	Thailand	31
UNESCO, Crossboarder Higher Education Guidelines	The UNESCO/OECD Guidelines on Quality Provision in Cross-border Higher Education www.oecd.org	International	2,31
UNESCO, Inernational Institution for Educational Planning	UNESCO International Institution for Educational Planning www.unesco.org/iiep	International	31
ViSiCAST	Virtual Signing: Capture, Animation, Storage and Transmission www.niwi.knaw.nl	Netherlands	30
W3C	World Wide Web Consortium www.w3.org	International	14, 19, 30
WBNRW	WebKollegNRW Zulassungsordnung www.webkolleg.nrw.de	Germany	8
WCET	The Western Cooperative for Educational Telecommunications www.wcet.info	USA	31

Acronym/ Abbreviation:	Project, organisation or initiative description/ Website:	Country/ Region:	Reference in chapter:
WFH	The William and Flora Hewlett Foundation www.hewlett.org	USA	31
WS-1	Web Services Interoperability Organisation www.ws-i.org	International	19
WSDL	Web Services Description Language www.w3.org/TR/wsdl	International	19
XML	Extensible Markup Language www.w3.org/XML	International	19

List of references

Acker, S. *Overcoming Obstacles to ePortfolio Assessment*. Campus Technology Newsletter: Technology-Enabled Teaching/eLearning Dialogue, 2005 [online]. Available from Internet: www.campus-technology.com/print.asp?ID=10788 [cited 20.09.2005].

Adelsberger, H. H.; Bick, M.; Lodzinski, T.; Pawlowski, J. M. *Electronic Performance Support Systems in Production and Operations Management – State of the Art and Future Development*. FACES, 2005, Vol. 20, No 4, in print.

ADL. Advanced Distributed Learning (a). *Introduction to the SCORM for Instructional Designers,* 2004 [online]. Available from Internet: http://www.adlnet.org/scorm/articles/3.cfm [cited 21.06.2005].

ADL. Advanced Distributed Learning (b). *SCORM Run-Time Environment (RTE),* 2004 [online]. Available from Internet: http://www.adlnet.org/downloads/files/67.cfm [cite 21.06.2005].

ADL. Advanced Distributed Learning (c). *SCORM Content Aggregation Model (CAM),* 2004 [online]. Available from Internet: http://www.adlnet.org/downloads/files/67.cfm [cite 21.06.2005].

AFNOR. *Code of practice: Information technologies – e-Learning Guidelines* (French Code of Practice), 2004 [online]. Available from Internet: http://www.fffod.org/fr/doc/RBPZ76001-EN.doc [cited 06.12.2004].

AFNOR. *Definition of Quality*. Standard AFNOR X50-120.

AFNOR. *The Code of Practice for e-learning: AFNOR BP Z76-001-an English version* (S2NET), 2005 [online] Available from Internet: http://www.fffod.org/fr/doc/RBPZ76001-EN.doc [cited 20.09.2005].

Akademie des Deutschen Beamtenbundes (Hrsg.). *Beurteilungskriterien für Lernprogramme*. In: Akademie des Deutschen Beamtenbundes für die berufliche Fortbildung e.V. Info-Paket, Report Nr. 4, 1986.

Allen, C.; Pilot, L. *HR-XML: Enabling Pervasive HR e-Business*. XML Europe, 2001 [online]. Available from Internet: http://www.gca.org/papers/xmleurope2001/papers/html/s18-2b.html [cited 31.05.2005].

Anderson, J. R.; Freeman, W. H. *Cognitive Psychology and its Implications*. 4th edition. New York, 1995.

American Council on Education. *Distance Learning Evaluation Guide.* Washington, DC: American Council on Education, 2001.

American Federation of Teachers. *Distance Education: Guidelines for Good Practice,* 2000 [online]. Available from Internet: http://www.aft.org/higher_ed/downloadable/distance.pdf [cited 18.11.2003].

ANSI. *American National Standards Institute,* 2005 [online] Available from Internet: http://www.ansi.org [cited 04.10.2005].

Argyris, C.; Schön, D. *Organisational learning: A theory of action perspective.* Addison Wesley, 1987.

Arnold, R. *Qualifikation.* In: Arnold, R., Nolda, S., Nuissl, E.: Wörterbuch Er-wachsenenpädagogik. Bad Heilbrunn, S.269, 2000.

Bacsich, P. (ed.). *The UKeU Reports,* 2005 [online]. Available from Internet: http://www.heacademy.ac.uk/e-learning.htm [cited 20.09.2005].

Baker, K.; Johns, K.; Williams, S. *Collaborative Development of a Conceptual Framework.* For Quality in eLearning. Department of Computer Science, University of Reading, UK, 2004.

Balli, C., Krekel, E. M.; Sauter, E. *Qualitätsentwicklung in der Weiterbildung aus der Sicht von Bildungsanbietern – Diskussionsstand, Verfahren, Entwicklungstendenzen.* In C. Balli; E. M. Krekel; E. Sauter (Eds.), Qualitätsentwicklung in der Weiterbildung – Zum Stand der Anwendung von Qualitätssicherungs- und Qualitätsmanagementsystemen bei Weiterbildungsanbietern (p. 5–24). Bonn: Bundesinstitut für Berufsbildung, 2002.

Bangham, A.; Cox, S.; Elliott, R.; Glauert, J.; Marshall, I.; Rankov, S.; Wells, M. *Virtual signing: capture, animation, storage and transmission-an overview of the ViSiCAST project.* In IEE Seminar on Speech and Language Processing for Disabled and Elderly People (Ref. No. 2000/025), London, United Kingdom, 2000.

Baumgartner, P. *Evaluation vernetzten Lernens: 4 Thesen.* In: Simon, H. (Hrsg.): Virtueller Campus. Forschung und Entwicklung für neues Lehren und Lernen. Münster, 1997. P.: 131-146.

BECTA. *Innovation in e-learning: lessons to be learned BJET,* July 2005, Volume 36, Number 4 - ISSN 007-1013.

Bell, D. *The Coming of Post-Industrial Society. A Venture in Social Forecasting.* New York, 1973.

Bellinger, A. *Good Course, Bad Course,* 2004 [online]. Available from Internet: http://www.trainingfoundation.com/articles/default.asp?PageID=1844 [cited 19.11.2004].

Benigno, V.; Dippe, G.; Vuorikari R. *Recommendation on Quality Assurance and Selection of resources for the ETB network,* deliverable D3.2 of the European Treasury Browser project, 2001.

Benmahamed, D.; Ermine, J.-L.; Tchounikine, P. *From Mask KM Methodology to Learning Activities Described with IMS-LD.* In WM2005: Professional Knowledge Management Experiences and Visions, Kaiserslautern: Kerkerdruck, 2005. P. 129-134.

Berendt, B.; Stary, J. (Hrsg.). *Evaluation zur Verbesserung der Qualität der Lehre und weitere Maßnahmen.* Weinheim, 1993.

Berry M. *Paper to The CRITICAL Cities Conference.* RMIT University, Melbourne, 29 September 2004.

Bertzeletou, T. *Accreditation Bodies,* 2003 [online]. Available from Internet: http://cedefop.communityzero.com/content?go=199198&cid=161784 [cited 09.08.2003].

Bertzeletou, T. *Presentation of the Work of the European Forum on Quality in VET: Main Outcomes and List of Possible Quality Dimensions, Driteria and Indicators on Quality Management Approaches (QMA), Self Assessment, Examination and Certification Arrangements, Quality Indicators,* 2002 [online]. Available from Internet: http://www2.trainingvillage.gr/etv/quality/Summary_of_the_main_results.doc [cited 29.10.2004].

Bjornavold, J. *Lernen sichtbar machen. Ermittlung, Bewertung und Anerkennung nicht formal erworbener Kompetenzen in Europa.* Thessaloniki, 2001.

Blease, D. *Evaluating Educational Software.* London, 1986.

Bleicher, K. *Das Konzept Integriertes Management. Visionen, Missionen, Programme;* Frankfurt/ New York: Campus, 1999.

Bliesener, T. *Evaluation betrieblicher Weiterbildung.* In: Schwuchow, K.; Gutmann, J. (Hrsg.): Weiterbildung Jahrbuch 1997. Düsseldorf: 163-167.

Blinco, K.; Rehak, D.; Wilson, S. *Service-Oriented Frameworks: Modelling the infrastructure for the next generation of e-Learning Systems,* 2005 [online]. Available from Internet: http://www.jisc.ac.uk/uploaded_documents/AltilabServiceOrientedFrameworks.pdf [cited 04.10.2005]

BME. *BMEcat,* 2005 [online]. Available from Internet: http://www.bmecat.org [cited 31.05.2005].

Boldi, P.; Santini, M.; Vigna, S. *PageRank as a Function of the Damping Factor. WWW2005,* International World Wide Web Conference, 10-14 May 2005, Chiba, Japan, 2005.

Bötel, C.; Krekel, E. M. *Trends und Strukturen der Qualitätsentwicklung bei Bildungsträgern.* In C. Balli, E. M. Krekel; E. Sauter (Eds.), Qualitätsentwicklung in der Weiterbildung – Wo steht die Praxis? (p. 19–40). Bielefeld: Bertelsmann, 2004.

Bötel, C.; Seusing, B.; Behrensdorf, B. *Qualitätssicherungs- und Qualitäts-managementsysteme bei Weiterbildungsanbietern: Ergebnisse der CATI-Befragung.* In C. Balli, E. M. Krekel; E. Sauter (Eds.), Qualitätsentwicklung in der Weiterbildung – Zum Stand der Anwendung von Qualitätssicherungs- und Qualitätsmanagement-

systemen bei Weiterbildungsanbietern (p. 25–44). Bonn: Bundesinstitut für Berufsbildung, 2002.

Brauer, M. *OpenOffice.org XML File Format*, 2005 [online]. Available from Internet:
http://xml.openoffice.org [cited 21.06.2005].

Brindley, J. E.; Walti, C.; Zawaxki-Richter, O. (Eds.). *Learner Support in Open, Distance
and Online Learning Environments*. Volume 9, 2004, Bibliotheks und Infor-
mationssystem der Carl von Ossietzky Unirsität Oldenburg (BIS), Verlag - ISBN 3-
8142-0923-0.

Brinker, T. *Dialogvideo im Führungskräfte-Training. Eine Studie zur Effektivität und
Akzeptanz*. Frankfurt am Main, 1991.

British Association for Open Learning. *Overview of the BAOL Quality Mark for Learning
Centres*, 2001 [online]. Available form Internet: http://www.baol.co.uk/qmlcover.doc
[20.09.2005].

Brown, J. S.; Collins, A.; Duguid, P. *Cognitive Apprenticeship, Situated Cognition and
Social Interaction, Technical report no. 6886*. Cambridge, 1988.

Bruder, R., Offenbartl, S., Osswald, K., Sauer, S. *Third party certification of computer-
based learning environments*, EISTA, Orlando,2004.

Bruhn, M. *Qualitätsmanagement für Dienstleistungen*. Grundlagen, Konzepte, Methoden;
Berlin, Heidelberg, New York: Springer, 2004.

Bühl, W. L. *Wissenschaft und Technologie. An der Schwelle zur Informationsgesellschaft*.
Göttingen, 1995.

Cardinaels, K.; Duval, E.; Meire, M. *Automating Metadata Generation: the Simple Indexing Interface*. International World Wide Web Conference Committee, WWW 2005,
May 10-14, 2005, Chiba, Japan, see also
http://ariadne.cs.kuleuven.ac.be/amg/publications.php.

Castells, M. *The Internet Galaxy*. Reflections on the Internet, Business and Society. Oxford
UP, 2001.

Castells, M. *The Rise of the Network Society*. Volume 1 of the Information Age. Blackwell
Publishers, 1996.

Cauldwell, P. et al. *Professional XML Web Services*. Birmingham: Wrox Press Ltd., 2001.

CeKom. *Cekom Deutschland*, 2004. [online]. Available from Internet: www.cekom-
deutschland.de [cited 21.09.2005].

CEN/ISS (a). *Initiative for Privacy Standardisation in Europe (IPSE)*, 2002 [online].
Available from Internet: http://www.hi-europe.info/files/2002/9963.htm [20.09.2005].

CEN/ISSS (b). *WS-LT. CWA 14590:2002 Description of language capabilities*. Brussels,
2002.

CEN/ISSS. *Workshop Learning Technologies. CWA14644 Quality Assurance Standards*,
CEN, Brussels, 2003.

CEN/ISSS. *WS-LT. CWA 14926:2004 Guidelines for the production of learner information standards and specifications.* Brussels, 2004.

CEN/ISSS (a). *Workshop on Data Protection and Privacy (WS/DPP)*, 2005.

CEN/ISSS (b). *Learning Technologies Workshop, Project Team "Accessibility properties for Learning Resources", 2005* [online]. Available from Internet: http://www2.ni.din.de/sixcms/detail.php?id=5984 [cited 20.9.2005].

CEN/ISSS (c). *WS-LT. Draft CWA A European Model for Learner Competencies*, 2005.

CEN/ISSS (d). *CWA 15262:2005. CWA on Data Protection and Privacy. Inventory of Data Protection Auditing Practices*; CWA 15263:2005 Technology Impact Assessment; CWA 15292:2005 Standard form contract to assist compliance with obligations imposed by article 17 of the Data Protection Directive 95/46/EC (and implementation guide), 2005 [online]. Available from Internet: http://www.cenorm.be/isss/cwa [cited 20.09.2005].8

CERFAD (a). *Emilia - Romagna Regional Commission for the certification of ODL material.* Guida alla qualità dei sistemi e-Learning. Bologna, 2004. ISBN 88-8186-102-X – ISSN 1722-361X.

CERFAD (b). *Emilia - Romagna Regional Commission for the certification of ODL material.* Analisi di linee guida, sistemi di benchmarking, principi e criteri a supporto della qualità nell'eLearning e nella FAD Research Paper, Bologna, May 2004, www.emilia-romagna.it/cerfad.

CETIS (a). *Learner Information Packaging Group,* 2005 [online]. Available from Internet: http://www.cetis.ac.uk/groups/20010801124300/viewGroup [cited 20.09.2005].

CETIS (b). Centre for educational technology interoperability standards, 2005. *The UK LOM Core home page* [online]. Available from Internet: http://www.cetis.ac.uk/profiles/uklomcore/ [cited 21.06.2005].

Chaiklin, S.; Lave, J. *Understanding Practice: Perspectives on Activity and Context.* New York, 1993.

Champy, J. *Reengineering Management.* The mandate for new leadership; New York: HarperBusiness, 1995.

CHEA. Council For Higher Education Accreditation. *Glossary of Key Terms in Quality Assurance and Accreditation*, 2001 [online]. Available from Internet: http://www.chea.org/international/inter_glossary01.html [cited 06.04.2005].

Chen, D.; Vernadat, F. *Standards on enterprise integration and engineering –state of the art.* International Journal of Computer Integrated Manufacturing, April-May 2004, Vol. 17, No 3, p. 235-253.

Clauss, G., Kulka, H., Rösler, H.-D., Lompscher, J., Timpe, K.-P., Vorwerg, G. (Hrg.) *Wörterbuch der Psychologie.* 5. völlig überarbeitete Auflage. Frankfurt/M. S. 126, 1995.

CMU. *Carnegie Mellon University: Learning and Web Services*, 2004 [online]. Available from Internet:

http://www.lsal.cmu.edu/lsal/expertise/technologies/learningservices/index.html [cited 31.05.2005].

Coad, P.; Yourdon, E. *Object Oriented Analysis*, 2nd edition, Prentice Hall PTR, 1990, ISBN: 0 13629 981 4.

Cobb, J.; Nelson M. *Blurring the Lines: the Convergence of Higher Education and Corporate Universities*. University Access, 1999.

Collins, A.; Brown, J. S.; Newman, S. E. *Cognitive apprenticeship: Teaching the crafts of reading, writing, and mathematics*. In: Resnick, L. B. (Hrsg.). Knowing, learning, and instruction: Essays in honor of Robert Glaser. Hillsdale, 1989. P.: 453-494.

Conole, G.; Garusi, A.; De Laat, M. *Learning from the UKeU experience*, 2004 [online]. Available from Internet: http://www.elrc.ac.uk/download/documents/Learning%20from%20the%20UKeU%20e xperience.doc [cited 3.09.2005].

Council of the European Union. *Report from the Education Council to the European Council: "The concrete future objectives of education and training systems"*. 2001 [online]. Available from Internet: http://europa.eu.int/comm/education/policies/2010/doc/rep_fut_obj_en.pdf [cited 27.05.2005].

Coutaz, J.; Crowley, J. L.; Dobson, S.; Garlan, D. *Context is key*, Communications of the ACM, Volume 48, Number 3, 2005, Pages 49-53.

Cronbach, L.J.; Snow, R.E. *Aptitudes and Instructional Methodes*. New York, 1977.

Crosby, P. B. *Quality is Free*. The art of making quality certain; New York: McGraw-Hill, 1980.

Curtis, G.; Cobham, D. *Business Information Systems: analysis, design and practice*. 5th ed.; Pearson Education, 2005.

Curtis, M.; Luchini, K.; Bobrowsky, W.; Quintana, C.; Soloway, E. *Handheld Use in K-12: A Descriptive Account*, Proceedings of the IEEE International Workshop on Wireless and Mobile Technologies in Education, 2002.

cXML. *commerce eXtensible Markup Language*, 2005 [online]. Available from Internet: http://www.cxml.org [cited 31.05.2005].

Dalziel, J. *Implementing Learning Design: The Learning Activity Management System (LAMS)*. Proceedings of the 20th Annual Conference of the Australian Society for Computers in Tertiary Education (ASCILITE), December 7-10, 2003. Adelaide, 2003.

Danish Evaluation Institute. *Quality procedures in European Higher Education: An ENQA survey. ENQA Occasional Papers 5*, 2003 [online]. Available from Internet: http://www.enqa.net/texts/procedures.pdf [cited 22.12.2003].

Davis, M. W. *Applied Decision Support*. Prentice-Hall: New Jersey, 1988.

DCMI. Dublin Core Metadata Initiative. *Accessibility Working Group*, 2001 [online]. Available from Internet: http://dublincore.org/groups/access/ [cited 20.9.2005].

DCMI. Dublin Core Metadata Initiative. *DCMI Metadata Terms*, 2005 [online]. Available from Internet: http://dublincore.org/documents/dcmi-terms/ [cited 21.06.2005].

Degler, D.; Battle, L. *Knowledge Management in Pursuit of Performance: the Challenge of Context.* Performance Improvement Journal (EPSS Special Edition). ISPI, 39(6), July 2000.

Deitel; H. et al. *Web Services: A Technical Introduction.* London: Pearson Education Ltd., 2003.

DeJoy, J. K.; Mills, H. H. *Criteria for Evaluation Interactive Instruction materials for Adult Self-Directed Learners.* In: Educational technology, 1989, 29, 2, P.: 39-41.

Dembski, M.; Lorenz, T. *Zertifizierung von Qualitätsmanagementsystemen bei Bildungsträgern (volume 428).* Renningen-Malmsheim: Expert Verlag, 1995.

Deming, W. E. *Out of the Crisis*; Cambridge, MA: MIT, 1986.

Deming, W. E. *Quality, productivity and competitive position*; Cambridge, MA: MIT, 1982.

DETC. Distance Education and Training Council. *DETC Accreditation Handbook*, 2005 [online]. Available from Internet: www.detc.org [cited 08.04.2005].

Deutsch, P. *RFC1951 - DEFLATE Compressed Data Format Specification version* 1.3, 1996 [online]. Available from Internet: http://rfc.net/rfc1951.html [cited 21.06.2005].

Dewey, J. *How We Think.* New York: D. C. Heath, 1993.

DfES. *Harnessing Technology: transforming learning and children's services.*

Diekmann, A. *Empirische Sozialforschung.* Grundlagen, Methoden, Anwendungen. Reinbek bei Hamburg, 1995.

Diesbergen, C. *Radikal- konstruktivistische Pädagogik als problematische Konstruktion.* Eine Studie zum Radikalen Konstruktivismus und einer Anwendung in der Pädagogik. Frankfurt am Main, 1998.

Dijkstra, S.; Seel, N. M.; Schott, F.; Tennyson, R. D. (Hrsg.). *Instructional Design: International Perspectives.* Volume II: Solving of Instructional Design Problems. Mahwah, 1997.

DIN Deutsches Institut für Normung e.V. (ed.). *e-Learning. Qualitätssicherung und Qualitätsmanagement im e-Learning*; Berlin: Beuth, 2005 [in print].

DIN (a) Deutsches Institut für Normung e.V. (ed.). *PAS 1032-1: Aus- und Weiterbildung unter besonderer Berücksichtigung von e-Learning - Referenzmodell für Qualitätsmanagement und Qualitätssicherung - Planung, Entwicklung, Durchführung und Evaluation von Bildungsprozessen und Bildungsangeboten* = Learning, Education and Training focussing on e-Learning - Part 1: Reference Model for Quality Management and Quality Assurance - Planning, Development, Realisation and Evaluation of Processes and Offers in Learning, Education and Training; Berlin: Beuth [= PAS 1032-1], 2004.

DIN (b) Deutsches Institut für Normung e.V. *Aus- und Weiterbildung unter besonderer Berücksichtigung von e-Learning – Teil 2: Didaktisches Objektmodell – Modellierung und Beschreibung*, Teil 2, 1032-2:2004. Berlin: Beuth Verlag, 2004.

DIN Deutsches Institut für Normung e.V. (ed.). *Qualitätsmanagement*. Normen. Berlin; Wien; Zürich: Beuth, 2001.

Donabedian, A. (a) *Explorations in Quality Assessment and Monitoring*. Ann Arbor, 1980.

Donabedian, A (b). *The Definition of Quality and Approaches to Its Assessment*; Ann Arbor: Health Administration Press, 1980.

Dondi, C. *Are Open Distance Learning and eLearning relevant to the Bologna Process?* EUCEN BERGEN CONFERENCE, 28-30 April 2005 "Form Bologna to Bergen and Beyond".

Dondi, C. *The introduction of VLE in a conventional university contexts: an institutional perspective*. In: Barajas, M. (Ed., 2003): Learning Innovations with ICT: socio-economic. Perspectives in Europe. Barcelona, Publicacions de la Universitat de Barcelona – ISBN 84-475-2748-4.

Dondi, C.; Moretti, M. *Why quality is a key factor in the speed of adoption of e-Learning*. Economia Global e Gestão, Global Ecionomics and Management Review, Voume IX , N.3/2004 , ISSN 0873-7444.

Dougiamas, M.; Taylor, Peter C. *Moodle: Using Learning Communities to Create an Open Source Course Management System*. EDMEDIA 2003 Conference. Honolulu, Hawaii, 2002.

Draschoff, S. *Lernen am Computer durch Konfliktinduzierung*. Münster, New York, München, Berlin, 2000.

Drucker, P. *The Age of Discontinuity*. Guidelines to our Changing Society. New York, 1969.

Duffy, T. M., Lowyck, J., Jonassen, D. (Hrsg.). *Designing Environments for Constructive Learning*. Berlin, 1993.

Duffy, Thomas M., Jonassen, D. H.,(Hgrs.). *Constructivism and the Technology of Instruction*. A Conversation. Hillsdale, 1992.

Duval, E. *Standards for contents: Beyond Learning Object Metadata*. European Handbook for Quality and Standardisation in E-Learning. CEDEFOP publication 2005.

Duval, E.; Hodgins, W. *A LOM Research Agenda. In Proceedings of WWW2003* - Twelfth International World Wide Web Conference, 20-24 May 2003, Budapest, Hungary. Retrieved July 1, 2005 [online]. Available from inernet: http://www2003.org/cdrom/papers/alternate/P659/p659-duval.html [cited 11.10.2005].

Duval, E.; Hodgins, W. (a). *Metadata Metters. International Conference on Dublin Core and Metadata Applications*, Shanghai, China, 11-14 October 2004. See also http://ariadne.cs.kuleuven.ac.be:8989/mt/blogs/ErikLog/archives/000566.html.

Duval, E.; Hodgins, W. (b). *Making metadata go away: Hiding everything but the benefits*, Keynote address at DC-2004, Shanghai, China, October 2004.

Duval, E.; Hodgins, W.; Sutton; S.; Weibel, S. L. *'Metadata Principles and Practicalities'*, d-Lib Magazine, vol. 8, no. 4, 2002. [online]. Available from Internet: http://www.dlib.org/dlib/april02/weibel/04weibel.html [cited 11.10.2005].

eAccess Project. *Developing web content supporting learning and training of disadvantaged user communities*, 2005 [online]. Available from Internet: http://www.ask.iti.gr/e-Access [cited 20.9.2005].

Eaton, J. S. *Before You Bash Accreditation*, Consider the Alternatives. The Chronicle of Higher Education, 49(25), B15, 2003.

Ebel, B. *Qualitätsmanagement*; Herne; Berlin: Verlag Neue Wirtschafts-Briefe, 2003.

EDUCAUSE Learning Initiative (formerly NLII). 2005 [online]. Available from Internet: http://www.educause.edu/content.asp?SECTION_ID=86&bhcp=1 [cited 20.09.2005].

EFQM European Foundation for Quality Management (ed.) (a). *The Fundamental Concepts of Excellence*; Brussels: European Foundation for Quality Management, 2003.

EFQM European Foundation for Quality Management (ed.) (b). *EFQM Excellence Model*; Brussels: European Foundation for Quality Management, 2003.

EFQM European Foundation for Quality Management (ed.) (c). *EFQM Assessing for Excellence*. A practical guide for successfully developing executing and reviewing a self-assessment strategy for your organisation; Brussels: European Foundation for Quality Management, 2003.

Ehlers, U.-D. (a). *Qualität im E-Learning aus Lernersicht*. Grundlagen, Empirie und Modellkonzeption subjektiver Qualität. Wiesbaden, 2004.

Ehlers, U.-D. (b). *Quality in E-Learning from a learner's perspectives*. Third Eden Research Worksop 2004, Olderburg, Germany, 2004.

Ehlers, U.-D. (c). *Erfolgsfaktoren für E-Learning: Die Sicht der Lernenden und mediendidaktische Konsequenzen*. In: Tergan, S.-O.; Schenkel, P. 2004. P. 29–49.

Ehlers, U.-D. *Qualität beim E-Learning*, 2003 [online]. Available from Internet: http://www.lernqualitaet.de/qualität ehlers.pdf. [cited 01.08.2003].

Ehlers, U.-D. *Qualitätsstrategie der Lernzentren im L3-Projekt*. In: Internes Arbeitspapierr L3-Projekt. Bielefeld, Deutschland, 2001.

Ehlers, U.-D. *Quality in E-Learning – The Learner as a key quality assurance category*. Vocational Training European Journal, N. 29 May – August 2003/II, ISSN 0378 – 5068.

Ehlers, U.-D. *What Do you Need for Quality in e-Learning?* March 2005, elearningeuropa.info.

Ehlers, U.-D.; Gerteis, W.; Holmer, T.; Jung, H. (Hrsg.). *E-Learning-Services im Spannungsfeld von Pädagogik, Ökonomie und Technologie*. L³-Lebenslanges Lernen im Bildungsnetzwerk der Zukunft. Bielefeld, 2003.

Ehlers, U.-D., Hildebrandt, B., Goertz, L., Pawlowski, J. M. *Use and Distribution of Quality Approaches in European E-Learning*. CEDEFOP, 2005.

Ehlers, U.-D.; Pawlowski, J. M.; Goertz, L. *Qualität von E-Learning kontrollieren – Die Bedeutung von Qualität im E-Learning.* In: Hohenstein, Andeas; Wilbers, Karl (Publisher): Handbuch E-Learning, Köln: Deutscher Wirtschaftsdienst, 2003.

Ehlers, U.-D.; Pawlowski, J. M. *E-Learning-Quality: A Decision Support Model for European Quality Approaches.* In: Fietz, Gabriele; Junge, Annette; Mason, Robin et al. (ed.). E-learning for Internationale Markets - Development and Implementation of E-learning in Europe, Bielefeld, 2004.

Eisenstadt M. *The Knowledge Media Generation.* The Times Higher Education Supplement, Multimedia Section, pp. vi-vii, 7th April 1995.

ENIC/NARIC centres. *The European gateway to recognition of academic and professional qualifications*, 2005 [online]. Available from Internet: http://www.enic-naric.net/ [cited 20.09.2005].

ENQA *Standards and Guidelines for Quality Assurance in the European Higher Education Area*, European Association for Quality Assurance in Higher Education, Helsinki, 2005, 41 p.

EPICC. *European Portfolio Initiatives Co-ordination Committee*, 2005 [online]. Available from Internet: http://www.epiccproject.info/ [cited 20.09.2005].

EPortConsortium. *White Paper for North America*, 2003 [online]. Available from Internet: http://www.eportconsortium.org/ [cited 20.09.2005].

EQO French-European workshop.*Comparing Quality models adequacy to the needs of clients in e-learning*, 2004 [online]. Available from Internet: http://www.eqo.info/?fuseaction=news.extraspecial_062004; Contribution to the implementation of relevant Quality approaches in the European Higher Education http://www.enpc.fr/fr/formations/ecole_virt/nte/rencontresGEVP/index.htm [cited 20.09.2005].

Erpenbeck, J. *Was bleibt? Kompetenzmessung als Wirksamkeitsnachweis von E-Learning. Was kommt? Kompetenzentwicklung als Prüfstein von E-Learning.* In: Hohenstein, A., Wilbers, K. (Hrg.): Handbuch E-Learning. 8. Ergänzungslieferung. Beitrag 6.6 Köln; Ders. (2004): Was kommt? Kompetenzentwicklung als Prüfstein von E-Learning. In: Hohenstein, A., Wilbers, K. (Hrg.): Handbuch E-Learning. 9. Ergänzungslieferung. Beitrag 6.7 Köln, 2004.

Erpenbeck, J.; Heyse, V.; Max, H. *KODE®X.* Berlin, Regensburg, Lakeland (FL); System. Vertrieb. Training. ACT GbR, Regensburg, 2001.

Erpenbeck, J.; von Rosenstiel, L. (Hrg.). *Handbuch Kompetenzmessung.* Stuttgart, 2003.

Erpenbeck, J.; Weinberg, J. *Menschenbild und Menschenbildung*, Münster, 1993.

Euler, D.; Seufert, S.; Wirth, M. *Gestaltung des Qualitätsmanagements zur Zertifizierung von E-Learning-Programmen* [Design of Quality Management for the Certification of E-Learning Programs]. In Euler, D.; Seufert, S. (Eds.), E-Learning in Hochschulen und Bildungszentren [E-Learning in Higher Education and Education Centers]. Oldenbourg, München, Wien, 2004.

Europass CV, *Europass Mobility, Europass Diploma Supplement, Europass Certificate Supplement, Europass Language Portfolio.* Europass: a new instrument for better recognition of qualifications and skills in the enlarged Europe, 2004 [online]. Available from Internet: http://www.lex.unict.it/cde/documenti/vari/2004/040107europass_en.pdf; http://europa.eu.int/comm/education/programmes/europass/index_en.html; http://europa.eu.int/agencies/cedefop/index_en.htm [20.09.2005].

European Association for Quality Assurance in Higher Education (ENQA): *Quality procedures in European Higher Education.* An ENQA survey (= ENQA occasional papers 5). Helsinki, 2003.

European Commission. *Bologny declaration,* 1999 [online]. Available from Internet: www.bologna-berlin2003.de/pdf/bologna_declaration.pdf [cited 22.09.2005].

European Commission. *Presidency Conclusions Lisbon European Council 23 and 24 March 2000* [online]. Available from Internet: http://www.bologna-berlin2003.de/pdf/PRESIDENCY_CONCLUSIONS_Lissabon.pdf [cited 20.9.2005].

European Commission. *Communication from the Commission to the Council and the European Parliament,* The eLearning Action Plan, Designing Tomorrow's Education. Brussel. COM(2001)172 final, 2001.

European Commission (a). 2002. [online]. Available from Internet: http://europa.eu.int/rapid/pressReleasesAction.do?reference=DOC/02/9&format=HTML&aged=0&language=EN&guiLanguage=en [cited 21.09.2005].

European Commission (b). *eEurope 2002 Action Plan* [online]. Available from Internet: http://europa.eu.int/information_society/eeurope/2002/action_plan/pdf/actionplan_en.pdf [cited 20.9.2005].

European Commission (c). *Copenhagen Decalaration,* 2002.

European Commission (d). *Call for proposals - Preparatory and Innovative Actions* 2002/b – eLearning Initiative, quality projects [onine]. Available from Internet: http://www.europa.eu.int/comm/education/programmes/elearning/projects_descr_en.html#2002 [cited 20.09.2005].

European Commission (a). *Implementation of "Education & Training 2010": Progress Report November 2003* [online]. Available from Internet: http://europa.eu.int/comm/education/policies/2010/doc/it-technologies_en.pdf [cited 27.11.2003].

European Commission (b). *Council Resolution on eAccessibility improving the access of people with disabilities to the Knowledge. Based Society,* 2003 [online]. Available from Internet: http://europa.eu.int/comm/employment_social/knowledge_society/res_eacc_en.pdf [cited 20.9.2005].

European Commission (c). *Communication from the Commission, "Education & Training 2010", The success of the Lisbon Strategy hinges on urgent reforms* (Draft joint interim report on the implementation of the detailed work programme on the follow-up of the objectives of education and training systems in Europe). Brussels, 11.11.2003. COM

685 final [online]. Available from Internet:
http://www.europa.eu.int/comm/education/policies/2010/et_2010_en.html
[cited 20.09.2005].

European Commission (d). *Decision No 2318/2003/Ec of The European Parliament and of The Council of 5 December 2003 adopting a multiannual programme* (2004 to 2006) for the effective integration of information and communication technologies (ICT) in education and training systems in Europe (eLearning Programme). Official Journal of the European Union, 2003.

European Commission (e). *Implementation of "Education & Training 2010" Work Programme, Working Group "ICT in Education and Training", Progress Report*, 2003 [online]. Available from Internet:
http://www.europa.eu.int/comm/education/policies/2010/objectives_en.html#informatio n [cited 20.09.2005].

European Commission (a). *Call for proposals – eLearning Programme, Transversal actions*, 2004 [online]. Available from Internet:
http://www.europa.eu.int/comm/education/programmes/elearning/projects_descr_en.ht ml#2004 [cited 20.09.2005].

European Commission (b). *Information Society Benchmarks, Survey Results*, Objective 2, Investing in people and skills, 2004.

European Commission (c). *Proposal for a Decision of The European Parliament and of The Council establishing an integrated action programme in the field of lifelong learning. Brussels*, COM 474 final, 2004.

European Commission (d). *Decision No 2241/2004/EC of the European Parliament and of the Council on a single Community framework for the transparency of qualifications and competences* (Europass), December 2004 / Official Journal of the European Union, 2004.

European Commission (a). *Council Conclusions on update of eEurope*, 2005 [oline]. Available from Internet:
http://ue.eu.int/ueDocs/cms_Data/docs/pressData/en/trans/80931.pdf [cited 20.9.2005].

European Commission (b). *Progress towards the Lisbon Objectives in Education and Training*. Staff working paper. Brussels, SEC 419, 2005.

European Commission (c). *The Commission's education and training policy for the next 5 years: diverse systems, shared goals*, Commissioner Jan Figel' speech at the Forum de la mobilité étudiante, Brussels, 2005.

European Commission (d). *Education and Training 2010, diverse systems, shared goals*, 2005 [online]. Available from Internet:
www.europa.eu.int/comm/education/policies/2010/et_2010_en.html [cited 11.10.2005].

European Commission (e). *eLearning*, 2005 [online]. Available from Internet:
www.europa.eu.int/comm/education/programmes/elearning/index_en.html [cited 11.10.2005].

European Consortium for Accreditation (ECA). *Accreditation in the European Higher Education Area.* In preparation for the Conference of European Ministers for Education in Bergen 2005 [online]. Available from Internet: www.ecaconsortium.net [cited 06.04.2005].

European Council. *Report from the Education Council to the European Council* "The concrete future objectives of education and training systems". Brussels, 5980/01, 2001.

European ePortfolio. *White Papers in INSIGHT European project*, 2005 [online]. Available from Internet:
http://www.eun.org/eun.org2/eun/en/Insight_SchoolPractice/content.cfm?ov=33464&lang=en [cited 20.09.2005].

European Foundation for Management Development (a). *EFMD Certification of e-Learning (CEL).* CEL Quality Criteria Overview, 2004 [online]. Available from Internet:
http://www.efmd.org/attachments/tmpl_1_art_041115geyj_att_050725hfzk.pdf [cited 01.08.2005].

European Foundation for Management Development (b). *EFMD Certification of e-Learning (CEL).* CEL Criteria, Indicators, Standards, 2004 [online]. Available from Internet:
http://www.efmd.org/attachments/tmpl_1_art_050606zxrc_att_050712rpku.pdf [01.08.2005].

European ODL *Liaison Committee. Distance Learning and eLearning in European Policy and Practice: The Vision and the Reality.* Policy Paper 17 November 2004, http://www.odl-liaison.org/.

European Quality Observatory. *European Quality Observatory: The EQO Model*, 2004 [online]. Draft version 1.2: University of Duisburg-Essen. Available from Internet: http://www.eqo.info [cited 20.09.2005].

Falk, R. *Betriebliches Bildungsmanagement: Arbeitsbuch für Studium und Praxis.* Köln: Wirtschaftsverlag Bachem, 2000.

Faulstich, P.; Gnahs, D.; Sauter, E. *Qualitätsmanagement in der beruflichen Weiterbildung: ein Gestaltungsvorschlag*, 2003 [online]. Available from Internet: http://www.europanozert.de/epz/dokumente/Studie-Weiterbildung.pdf [cited 15.01.2005].

Federkeil, G. *Benchmarking und Ranking als Instrumente des Leistungsvergleichs.* In W. Fröhlich; W. Jütte (Eds.), Qualitätsentwicklung in der postgradualen Weiterbildung: Internationale Entwicklungen und Perspektiven (p. 62–72). Berlin, München, Münster, New York: Waxmann, 2004.

Feeman, L. *7th annual GATE conference*, Paris, 2002.

Feigenbaum, A. V. *Total Quality Control. Engineering and management*, New York: McGraw-Hill, 1986.

Fend, H. *Qualität und Qualitätssicherung im Bildungswesen: Wohlfahrtsstaatliche Modelle und Marktmodelle.* In: Helmke, A., Hornstein, W., Terhart, E. (Hrsg.) (2000): 41. Beiheft zur Zeitschrift für Pädagogik. Qualität und Qualitätssicherung im Bildungsbereich: Schule, Sozialpädagogik, Hochschule. Weinheim, Basel, 2000, P.: 55-72.

Fink, L. D. *Creating Significant Learning Experiences.* San Francisco: Jossey-Bass, 2003.

Flanders, N. A. *Analyzing Teaching Behaviour.* Reading, 1970.

Florida, R. *Towards the Learning Region.* Futures, 1995. P. 27.

Forte, E., Haenni, T., Warkentyne, K., Duval, E., Cardinaels, K., Vervaet, E., Hendrikx, K., Wentland-Forte, M. and Simillion, F. *Semantic and pedagogic interoperability mechanisms in the ARIADNE educational repository.* ACM SIGMOD Rec. 28, 1 (Mar. 1999), 20–25; see http://www.acm.org/sigmod/record/issues/9903/ index.html.

Francés, V. L., Bonora, A. G., Riddy, P., Fill, K., Wolf, K. D., Rosato, S. et al. *MECA-ODL: Der methodologische Leitfaden für die Qualitätsanalyse von internetbasierten Open-And-Distance-Learning-Anwendungen,* 2003 [online]. Available from Internet: http://www.adeit.uv.es/mecaodl/docs/guide_mecaodl_german.pdf [cited 24.10.2004].

Franz, H.-W. *"Nur systematisch muss es sein?": Ein Plädoyer für mehr Einheit in der Vielfalt der Qualitätsansätze.* In C. Balli, E. M. Krekel; E. Sauter (Eds.), Qualitätsentwicklung in der Weiterbildung – Wo steht die Praxis? (p. 107–121). Bielefeld: Bertelsmann, 2004.

Fraunhofer IPSI. *Gemeinsam Online-Lernen: Technologien & Lernszenarien - Auswertung einer Umfrage des Fraunhofer IPSI bei Weiterbildungsanbietern im August/September 2003* [online]. Available from Internet: http://www.ipsi.fraunhofer.de/concert/projects_new/alba/Gemeinsam_Online_Lernen.p df [cited 07.03.2004].

Frehr, H.-U. *Total Quality Management;* München: Carl Hanser, 1993.

Fricke, R. *Evaluation von Multimedia.* In: Issing, L. J.; Klimsa, P. (Hrsg.) (2002): Information und lernen mit Multimedia. Weinheim, 1995, 2002.

Fricke, R. *Qualitätsbeurteilung durch Kriterienkataloge. Auf der Suche nach validen Vorhersagemodellen.* In: Schenkel, P.; Tergan, S.-O.; Lottmann, A. (eds): Qualitätsbeurteilung multimedialer Lern- und Informationssysteme. Evaluationsmethoden auf dem Prüfstand, Nürnberg, p. 75–88, 2000.

Friend-Pereira, J. C., Lutz, K.; Heerens, N. *European Student Handbook on Quality Assurance in Higher Education* 2002 [online]. Available from Internet: http://www.esib.org/projects/qap/QAhandbook/QAhandbook.doc [cited 09.02.2004].

Fröhlich, W.; Jütte, W. *Qualitätsentwicklung in der wissenschaftlichen Weiterbildung.* In W. Fröhlich; W. Jütte (Eds.), Qualitätsentwicklung in der postgradualen Weiterbildung: Internationale Entwicklungen und Perspektiven (p. 9–17). Berlin, München, Münster, New York: Waxmann, 2004.

Frydenberg, J. *Quality Standards in eLearning: A Matrix of Analysis. International Review of Research in Open and Distance Learning,* 2002 [online]. Available from Internet: http://www.irrodl.org/content/v3.2/frydenberg.html [cited 11.10.2005].

Galiläer, L. *Pädagogische Qualität. Perspektiven der Qualitätsdiskurse über Schule, Soziale Arbeit und Erwachsenenbildung.* Weinheim/München, 2005.

García, J. A. E. *Bailing out on learning,* The Learning Citizen Newsletter, vol. 9(1), April 2002.

Geldermann, R.; Baigger, J. F.; Geldermann, B. *Qualitätssicherung in der betrieblichen Bildung.* Eine Studie mit sechs Fallbeispielen. Bielefeld, 2003.

Gerl, H.; Pehl, K. *Evaluation in der Erwachsenenbildung.* Bad Heilbrunn, 1983.

Glasersfeld, E. von *Radikaler Konstruktivismus. Ideen, Ergebnisse, Probleme.* Frankfurt am Main, 1996.

Global-learning. *On Line Educa.* Berlin, 2004 [online]. Available from Internet: http://www.global-learning.de/g-learn/cgi-bin/gl_userpage.cgi?StructuredContent=m130221 [cited 20.09.2005].

Gnahs, D. *Vergleichende Analyse von Qualitätskonzepten in der beruflichen Weiterbildung, Materialien des Institutes für Entwicklungsplanung und Strukturforschung 164.* Hannover, 1998.

Gnahs, D. *Zwischenbilanz der Qualitätsdebatte. In: Deutsches Institut für Erwachsenenbildung* (DIE), Nuissl, E., Schiersmann, Ch., Siebert, H., Weinberg, J. (Hrsg.): Literatur- und Forschungsreport Weiterbildung Juni 1999, Report 43. Thema: Qualität, Wissenschaftliche Halbjahresschrift des DIE, Juni 1999. Bielefeld, 1999.

Gnahs, D.; Kuwan, H. *Qualitätsentwicklung in der Weiterbildung – Effekte, Erfolgsbedingungen und Barrieren.* In C. Balli; E. M. Krekel; E. Sauter (Eds.), Qualitätsentwicklung in der Weiterbildung – Wo steht die Praxis? (p. 41–59). Bielefeld: Bertelsmann, 2004.

Go Basel. *Glossary of Quality Management,* 2005 [online]. Available from Internet: www.go-cert.de/htm/glossar.htm [cited 17.03.2005].

Goertz, L.; Johanning, A. *Das Kunststück, alle unter einen Hut zu bringen. Zielkonflikte bei der Akzeptanz des E-Learning.* In: Tergan, S.-O.; Schenkel, P., P. 83–92. 2004.

Götz, K. *Zur Evaluierung beruflicher Weiterbildung.* Band 1: Theoretische Grundlagen. Weinheim, 1993.

Gonon, P. *Qualitätssysteme auf dem Prüfstand. Die neue Qualitätsdiskussion in Schule und Bildung* (3., aktualisierte Aufl., Band 5). Aarau: Bildung Sauerländer, 1998.

Gottfried, C., Hager, G.; Scharl, W. *Kriterienkatalog zur qualitativen Bewertung von Lernsoftware,* 2002 [online]. Available from Internet: http://www.esffubb.at/lektion/kriterienkatalog.pdf [cited 26.11.2004].

Gräber, W. *Das Instrument MEDA – Ein Verfahren zur Beschreibung, Analyse und Bewertung didaktischer Software im berufsbildenden Bereich.* In: Dick, A. (1991): AUDIO VISUELL – neue Technologien: gelungene oder misslungene Medialisierung von lernen, Staatliche Landesbildstelle Hessen. Frankfurt am Main, 1991.

Gräber, W. *Kriterien und Verfahren zur Sicherung der Qualität von Lernsoftware in der beruflichen Weiterbildung.* Kiel, 1996.

Gräber, W.; Lauterbach, R. *EPASoft – Instrument zur Bewertung pädagogischer Software.* Kiel, 1992.

Grant, S.; Rees Jones, P.; Ward, R. *Mapping Personal Development Records to IMS LIP to support Lifelong Learning: Consultation Document,* UK: Joint Information Systems Committee, The Centre for Recording Achievement and the Centre for Educational Technology Interoperability Standards, 2003.

Griffiths, D.; Blat, J.; Garcia, R.; Vogten, H.; Kwong, K. L. *Learning Design Tools.* In: Koper, R.; Tattersall, C. (Eds.), Learning Design. A Handbook on Modelling and Delivering Networked Education and Training (S. 109-135). Berlin, Heidelberg, New York: Springer, 2005.

Gröhbiel, U. *Kosten und Nutzen des E-Learning an der Fachhochschule,* 2003 [online]. Available from Internet: http://www.dwi.fhbb.ch/e-learning [cited 02.2003].

Grotlüschen, A. *Widerständiges Lernen im Web – virtuell selbstbestimmt? Eine qualitative Studie über E-Learning in der beruflichen Erwachsenenbildung.* München/New York/Münster/Berlin, 2003.

Haase, K. *Internationales Monitoring zum Forschungs- und Entwicklungsgebiet „Lernkultur Kompetenzentwicklung", Schwerpunkt „Grundlagen der Kompetenz-messung"* Statusberichte. Berlin, 2001 (http://www.abwf.de).

Hammer, M.; Champy, J. *Reengineering the Corporation. A manifesto for business revolution;* New York: HarperBusiness, 1994.

Hansson, H. (Ed.) *Eight Contributions on Quality and Flexible Learning.* Swedish Agency for Distance Education, Report 1:2002 – ISBN 91-973907-5-5.

Harry, M. J.; Schroeder, R. *Six Sigma. The breakthrough management strategy revolutionizing the world's top corporations;* New York: Doubleday, 2000.

Harvey, L.; Green, D. *Qualität definieren. Fünf unterschiedliche Ansätze.* In: Helmke, A., Hornstein, W., Terhart, E. (Hrsg.) (2000): Qualität und Qualitätssicherung im Bildungsbereich: Schule, Sozialpädagogik, Hochschule, Zeitschrift für Pädagogik, 41. Beiheft. Weinheim, Basel, 2000.

Harvey, L. *The Power of Accreditation: views of academics,* 2003 [online]. Available from Internet: http://www.enqa.net/files/workshop_material/UK.pdf [cited 11.10.2005].

Hase, S.; Kenyon, C. *From Andragogy to Heutagogy.* Southern Cross University. 2001 [online]. Available from Internet: http://ultibase.rmit.edu.au//Articles/dec00/hase2.htm [cited 20-10-2005].

Hasher, L.; Zacks, R .T. *Automatic processing of fundamental information: the case of frequency of occurrence.* American Psychologist 39(12), 1984. P. 1372-1388.

Hatwell Y. *Notions d'assimilation et d'accomodation dans les processus cognitifs.* In Psychologie et épistémologie génétiques, Dunod, Sciences du Comportement, 1966.

Heddergott, K.; Pawlowski, J. M. *Qualität mit verlässlichen Standards sichern.* In: Personalwirtschaft. Special Issue 11/2002, p. 20-23.

Heiduk, G. *Integration von E-Learning in übergeordnete betriebswirtschaftliche Prozesse.* In: E-Learning-Services im Spannungsfeld von Pädagogik, Ökonomie und Technologie. WBV-Verlag. Bielefeld, Deutschland, 2003.

Heller, M. *Einführung netzgestützter Angebote bei Bildungsträgern - Von der strategischen Planung bis zur Umsetzung. Präsentation im Ministerium für Wirtschaft und Arbeit NRW,* 2003 [online]. Available from Internet: http://www.mekonet.de/doku/ws_03/03_ws2_heller.pdf [cited 28.09.2005].

Heyse, V.; Erpenbeck, J. *Kompetenztraining. 64 Informations- und Trainingsprogramme.* Stuttgart; Heyse, V., Erpenbeck, J., Max, H. (Hrg.): Kompetenzen erkennen, bilanzieren und entwickeln. Münster, New York, München, Berlin, 1994.

Heyse, V.; Erpenbeck, J.; Michel, L. *Kompetenzprofiling. Weiterbildungsbedarf und Lernformen in Zukunftsbranchen.* Münster, New York, München, Berlin, 2002.

Hildebrandt, B., Pawlowski, Jan M., Stracke, C. *Support Systeme für Qualitätsmanagement im E-Learning.* In: Proc. Of Delfi 2005 – die 3. Fachtagung der Gesellschaft für Informatik e.V. Lecture Notes in Informatics, GI-Edition, 2005.

Hofman, J. *An Expanding Universe. Metadata and Accessibility of Digital Information,* 3d DLM-Forum, Barcelona, 7-8 May 2002.

Hollands, N. *Online Testing: Best Practices from the Field,* 2000 [online]. Available from Internet: http://198.85.71.76/english/blackboard/testingadvice.html [cited 10.04.2004].

Holzkamp, K. *Lernen. Subjektwissenschaftliche Grundlegung.* Frankfurt/New York, 1995.

HOPE Project. *Interactive training for a better future: eLearning for the socially excluded,* 2002 [online]. Available from Internet: http://www.hope-project.org/ [cited 20.9.2005].

HR-XML. *HR-XML Consortium* [online]. Available from Internet: http://www.hr-xml.org [cited 31.05.2005].

ICALT. *4th Conference. Finland* [online]. Available from Internet: http://lttf.ieee.org/icalt2004 [cited 20.09.2005].

IDEALS MTS. *IDEALS Modular Training System, General Project Information, European Commission DGXIII, Telematics applications for education, training and research networks, Project Reference ET1012,* 1996 [online]. Available from Internet: http://www.cordis.lu/data/MSS_PROJ_FP4_BE_EN/QF_EP_SPF_AeqTELEMATICS 2CatBdlndPASSVARclTITLEeqFP4ps20Projectsclps20Telematics.htm [cited 04.10.2005].

IEEE Learning Technology Standards Committee. *IEEE Computer Society. IEEE P1484.1/D9, Draft Standard for Learning Technology—Learning Technology Systems Architecture (LTSA), latest publicly available LTSA draft,* 2001 [online] Available from Internet: http://ltsc.ieee.org/wg1/files/IEEE_1484_01_D09_LTSA.pdf [cited 04.10.2005].

IEEE Learning Technology Standards Committee. *History. IEEE Computer Society. IEEE Learning Technology Systems Architecture (LTSA), History of Drafts,* 2001 [online] Available from Internet: http://ltsc.ieee.org/wg1/materials.html [cited 04.10.2005].

IEEE Learning Technologies Standardisation Committee (a). *IEEE Public and Private Information Draft 8 specification*, 2002 [online]. Available from Internet: http://www.edutool.com/papi [cited 27.05.2005].

IEEE Learning Technology Standards Committee (b). *Learning Object Metadata Standard, IEEE 1484.12.1*-2002 [online]. Available from Internet: http://ltsc.ieee.org/wg12/files/LOM_1484_12_1_v1_Final_Draft.pdf [cited 20.09.2005].

IEEE Learning Technology Standards Committee. *IEEE Computer Society. IEEE Std 1484.1™-2003 Standard for Learning Technology—Learning Technology Systems Architecture (LTSA)*, The Institute of Electrical and Electronics Engineers, Inc., New York 2003.

IEEE. Learning Technology Standards Committee. *WG4: Digital Rights Expression Language*, 2003 [online]. Available from Internet: http://ltsc.ieee.org/wg4/index.html [cited 20.10.2005].

IEEE SA. *IEEE Standards Association*, 2005 [online] Available from Internet: http://standards.ieee.org [cited 04.10.2005].

IETF *IETF/W3C XML-DSig Working Group*, 2003 [online]. Available from Internet: http://www.w3.org/Signature/ [cited 20.09.2005].

Ilomäki et al. *Learning Objects in classroom settings: A report of 13 case studies conducted in Finland*, France, Hungary, Ireland, and UK. CELEBRATE deliverable 7. case 5 and 8, 2004.

Imai, M. *Gemba Kaizen. A commonsense, low-cost approach to management*; New York: McGraw-Hill, 1997.

Imai, M. *Kaizen. The key to Japan's competitive success*; New York: McGraw-Hill, 1986.

IMS (a). *Learner Information Package Accessibility for LIP, Version 1, Final Specification*, 2003 [online]. Available from Internet: http://www.imsglobal.org/accessibility/index.cfm [cited 20.9.2005].

IMS ePortfolios Development Committee. *IMS ePortfolio InformationModel*, 2005 [online]. Available from Internet: http://www.imsglobal.org/ep/epv1p0/imsep_infov1p0.html [cited 20.09.2005].

IMS Global. *IMS Global Learning Consortium: Enterprise Specification*, 2000 [online]. Available from Internet: http://www.imsglobal.org/enterprise [cited 31.08.2005]

IMS Global. *IMS Learner Information Package specification*, 2001 [online]. Available from Internet: http://www.imsglobal.org/profiles/ lipinfo01.html [cited 27.05.2005].

IMS Global (a). *IMS Reusable Definition of Competency or Educational Objective - Information Model. Version 1.0 Final Specification*, 2002 [online]. Available from Internet: http://www.imsglobal.org/competencies/rdceov1p0/imsrdceo_infov1p0.html [cited 20.09.2005].

IMS Global (b). *IMS Global Learning Consortium: Enterprise Specification*, 2002 [online]. Available from Internet: http://www.imsglobal.org/enterprise [cited 31.08.2005].

IMS Global (c). *Accessibility Working Group (IMS AWG)*, 2002 [online]. Availbale from Internet: http://www.imsproject.org/accessibility/accessiblevers/ [cited 20.9.2005].

IMS Global (a). *IMS Digital Repositories Interoperability - Core Functions Best Practice Guide. Version 1.0 Final Specification*, 2003 [online]. Available from Internet: http://www.imsglobal.org/digitalrepositories/driv1p0/imsdri_bestv1p0.html [cited 20.09.2005].

IMS Global (b). *IMS Learning Design Best Practice and Implementation Guide*, 2003 [online]. Available from Internet: http://www.imsglobal.org/learningdesign/ldv1p0/imsld_bestv1p0.html [cited 21.06.2005].

IMS Global (c). *IMS Simple Sequencing Information and Behavior Model*, 2003 [online]. Available from Internet: http://www.imsglobal.org/simplesequencing/ [cited 21.06.2005].

IMS Global (d). *Learner Information Package Accessibility for LIP Conformance Specification. Version 1.0 Final Specification*, 2003 [online]. Available from Internet: http://www.imsglobal.org/accessibility/acclipv1p0/imsacclip_confv1p0.html [cited 20.09.2005].

IMS Global (e). *IMS Global Learning Consortium: Learning Design Specification*, 2003[online]. Available from Internet: http://www.imsglobal.org/learningdesign [cited 31.05.2005].

IMS Global (f). *Abstract Framework*. White Paper, 2003 [online] Available from Internet: http://www.imsglobal.org/af/index.html [cited 04.10.2005].

IMS Global (a). *IMS Content Packaging Information Model*, 2004 [online]. Available from Internet: http://www.imsglobal.org/content/packaging/cpv1p1p4/imscp_infov1p1p4.html [cited 21.06.2005].

IMS Global (b). *IMS Content Packaging Best Practice and Implementation Guide*, 2004[online]. Available from Internet: http://www.imsglobal.org/content/packaging/cpv1p1p4/imscp_bestv1p1p4.html [cited 21.06.2005].

IMS Global (c). *IMS Content Packaging XML Binding*. V 1.1.4 final Specification, 2004 [online]. Available from Internet: http://www.imsglobal.org/content/packaging/cpv1p1p4/imscp_bindv1p1p4.html [cited 21.06.2005].

IMS Global (d). *AccessForAll Metadata, Version 1, Final Specification*, 2004 [online]. Available from Internet: http://www.imsglobal.org/accessibility/index.cfm [cited 20.9.2005].

IMS Global (a). *IMS ePortfolio Information Model*. Version 1.0 Final Specification, 2 June 2005 [online]. Available from Internet: http://www.imsglobal.org/ep/epv1p0/imsep_infov1p0.html [cited 20.09.2005].

IMS Global (b). *IMS ePortfolio Best Practice and Implementation Guide.* Version 1.0 Final Specification, 2 June 2005 [online]. Available from Internet: http://www.imsglobal.org/ep/epv1p0/imsep_bestv1p0.html [cited 20.09.2005].

IMS Global (c). *IMS ePortfolio XML Binding.* Version 1.0 Final Specification, 2 June 2005 [online]. Available from Internet:http://www.imsglobal.org/ep/epv1p0/imsep_bindv1p0.html [cited 20.09.2005].

IMS Global (d). *IMS Rubric Specification.* Version 1.0 Final Specification, 2 June 2005 [online]. Available from Internet: http://www.imsglobal.org/ep/epv1p0/imsrubric_specv1p0.html [20.09.2005].

IMS Global (e). *IMS Learner Information Package Specification,* 2005 [online]. Available from Internet: http://www.imsglobal.org/profiles/index.html [cited 20.09.2005].

IMS Global (f). *IMS Global Learning Consortium: General Web Services,* 2005[online]. Available from Internet: http://www.imsglobal.org/gws [cited 31.05.2005].

IMS Global (g). *IMS Global Learning Consortium: Learner Information Package Specification,* 2005 [online]. Available from Internet: http://www.imsglobal.org/profiles [cited 31.08.2005].

IMS Global (h). *IMS Global Learning Consortium,* 2005 [online]. Available from Internet: http://imsglobal.org [cited 21.06.2005]

INFLOW. *Informal Learning Opportunities in the Workplace,* 2005 [online]. Available from Internet: http://www.inflow.eu.com/ [cited 20.09.2005].

INSIGHT. *European schoolnet knowledge base for new technology and education,* 2005 [online]. Available from Internet: http://insight.eun.org/ww/en/pub/insight/index.htm [cited 20.09.2005].

Institute of Electrical and Electronical Engineers Standards Department. *Draft Standard for Learning Object Metadata,* 2002 [online]. Available from Internet: http://ltsc.ieee.org/wg12/20020612-Final-LOM-Draft.html [cited 21.06.2005].

Ishikawa, K. *La gestion de la qualité,* outils et applications pratiques, Editions Dunod, 1996.

Ishikawa, K. *What is Total Quality Control?* The Japanese Way; Englewood Cliffs, NJ: Prentice-Hall, 1985.

ISO 14915 – Parts 1-3: *Software ergonomics for multimedia user interfaces.*

ISO 19011:2002 = DIN EN ISO 19011:2002-12. *Guidelines for quality and;or environmental management systems auditing*; DIN Deutsches Institut für Normung e. V. (ed.); Berlin: Beuth, 2002.

ISO 8402:1995 = DIN EN ISO 8402. *Qualitätsmanagement und Qualitätssicherung. Begriffe.* DIN Deutsches Institut für Normung e. V. (ed.); Berlin: Beuth, 1995.

ISO 9000:2000 = DIN EN ISO 9000:2000-12. *Quality management systems. Fundamentals and vocabulary.* DIN Deutsches Institut für Normung e. V. (ed.); Berlin: Beuth, 2000.

ISO 9000:2000 = DIN EN ISO 9000:2000-12; Ber 1: 2003-04. *Corrigenda 1 to DIN EN ISO 9000:2000-12*. DIN Deutsches Institut für Normung e. V. (ed.); Berlin: Beuth, 2003.

ISO 9000:2000 = DIN EN ISO 9000:2000-12;DAM 1:2004. *Draft: Quality management systems. Fundamentals and vocabulary*, Amendment 1 – Draft. DIN Deutsches Institut für Normung e. V. (ed.); Berlin: Beuth, 2004.

ISO 9001:2000 = DIN EN ISO 9001:2000-12. *Quality management systems*. Requirements; DIN Deutsches Institut für Normung e. V. (ed.); Berlin: Beuth, 2000.

ISO 9004:2000 = DIN EN ISO 9004:2000-12. *Quality management systems. Guidelines for performance improvements*. DIN Deutsches Institut für Normung e. V. (ed.); Berlin: Beuth, 2000.

ISO 9241 – Parts 1-17: *Ergonomic requirements for office work with visual display terminals*.

ISO- SC36 *Versailles International SymposiumMarch*. Norms and standards for online learning, 2003.

ISO. *How are ISO standards developed?* 2003 [online]. Available from Internet: http://www.iso.org/iso/en/stdsdevelopment/whowhenhow/how.html [cited 09.01.2005].

ISO/IEC (a). ISO/IEC 19796-1:2005. *Information Technology - Learning, Education, and Training — Quality Management, Assurance and Metrics*— Part 1: General Approach. Final Draft International Standard (FDIS), 2005.

ISO/IEC (b). *Technical report presented in JTC1SC36-WG3 about proposed standards concerning Participant Information data models*, 2005 [online]. Available from Internet: http://jtc1sc36.org/doc/36N0965.pdf [cited 20.09.2005].

ISO/IEC. *Expertise and Role Identification for Learning Environments (ERILE)*, Working Paper, 2001 [online]. Available from Internet: http://jtc1sc36.org/doc/36N0077.pdf [cited 04.10.2005].

Johnstone, S. M. *A US approach to Quality assurance of post-secondary on-line programs"*, 2002 [online]. Available from: http://www.mylara.com/elearn/forum/default.asp [cited 20.09.2005].

Joint Information Systems Committee (JISC) and Centre for Educational Technology Interoperability Standards (CETIS). *UK Learner Profile* Version 1.1, 2001.

Jonstone, S. M. *Open educational resources serve the world*. EDUCAUSE Quaterly, 2005 [online]. Available from Internet: http://www.educause.edu/apps/eq/eqm05/eqm0533.asp [cited 3.09.2005].

Jung, H. M. *Multimedia in der Softwareschulung*, Frankfurt am Main, 1994.

Jung, H. W. *Qualitätsorientierte Integration technischer, pädagogisch-didaktischer und ökonomischer Systemkomponenten zur nachhaltigen Implementierung technologie-gestützter Bildungsservices*. Dissertationsschrift, Braunschweig, 2005.

Jung, H. W.; Fischer, S. *A New Partner Concept For Distributed E-Learning*. In: Workshop auf der LEARNTEC 2002. Karlsruhe, Deutschland, 2002.

Juran, J. M. (ed*.). Quality Control Handbook.* New York: McGraw-Hill, 1951.

Juran, J. M. *Juran on quality by design. The new steps for planning quality into goods and services.* New York: Free Press, 1992.

KAON. *KAON Web Services Tool Suite,* 2005 [online]. Available from Internet: http://www.aifb.uni-karlsruhe.de/Projekte/viewProjekt?id_db=51 [cited 31.05.2005]

Kappelhoff, P. *Kompetenzentwicklung in Netzwerken.* In: Die Sicht der Komplexitäts- und allgemeinen Evolutionstheorie. Berlin, 2004.

Karampiperis, P.; Sampson, D. (a). *Learning Object Metadata for Learning Content Accessibility.* In 16th World Conference on Educational Multimedia, Hypermedia and Telecommunications ED-MEDIA 2004, Lugano, Switzerland, 2004.

Karampiperis, P.; Sampson, D. (b). *Supporting Accessible Hypermedia in Web-based Learning Systems: Defining an Accessibility Application Profile for Learning Resources.* The New Review of Hypermedia and Multimedia, Vol. 10, No 2, 2004.

Karampiperis, P.; Sampson, D. (a). *Designing Learning Systems to Provide Accessible Services.* In 2nd International Cross-Disciplinary Workshop on Web Accessibility, 14th International World Wide Web Conference (WWW2005), Chiba, Japan, 10-14 May 2005.

Karampiperis, P.; Sampson, D. (b). *An Architectural Approach for Supporting Accessible Hypermedia in Web-based Learning Systems.* In 5th IEEE International Conference on Advanced Learning Technologies ICALT 2005, Kaohsiung, Taiwan, 2005.

Kaselaar, G. *Computer und Lernen: der Lehrer als Subjekt oder Objekt.* In: Bogner, C.; Burger, H.; Weiß, K. (Hrsg.) (1992): Computer und Kulturtechniken. München, 1992. P.: 132-165.

Keating, M. *Geschäftsmodelle für Bildungsportale – Einsichten in den US-amerikanischen Markt.* In: Bentlage, U.; Glotz, P.; Hamm, I.; Hummel, J. (eds): E-Learning. Märkte, Geschäftsmodelle, Perspektiven, Gütersloh, p. 57–77, 2002.

Kells, H. *Sistemas nacionales de garantía y control de la calidad académica.* In Evaluación Académica, París: UNESCO, 1993.

Key-PAL. *Relevance and potential impact of the ePortfolio on the development and assessment of key-skills,* 2005 [online]. Available from Internet: http://www.eife-l.org/activities/keypal [cited 20.09.2005].

Kiedrowski, J. v. *Lernplattformen für e-Learning-Prozesse beruflicher Weiterbildungs-träger: Bewertung und Auswahl mit Methoden des Total Quality Managements* (volume 36). Köln: Botermann & Botermann, 2001.

Kiedrowski, J. v. *Qualitätsmanagement von E-Learning mit dem House of Quality.* In: Ehlers, U.-D.; Schenkel, P. (eds): Bildungscontrolling im E-Learning. Erfolgreiche Strategien und Erfahrungen jenseits des ROI, Berlin/Heidelberg/New York, p. 165–174, 2005.

Kirkpatrick, D. L. *Evaluation Training Programs.* The Four Levels. San Francisco, 1994.

Klebl, M. *Nachhaltiges Design digitaler Bildungsmedien.* Netzgestützte Bildungsprozesse mit IMS Learning Design. Mössingen-Talheim: Talheimer Verlag, 2005.

Klerkx, J., Duval, E.; Meire, M. *Using Information Visualisation for Accessing Learning Object Repositories, Information Visualisation, Eighth International Conference on (IV 04).* London, England, pp. 465-470. 2004 [online]. Available from Internet: http://csdl.computer.org/comp/proceedings/iv/2004/2177/00/21770465abs.htm   [cited 20.09.2005].

Knight, J. *Monitoring the Quality and Progress of Internationalisation. Journal of Studies in International Education,* 5(3), P. 228–243. 2001 [online]. Available from Internet: http://jsi.sagepub.com/cgi/reprint/5/3/228 [cited 29.09.2004].

Knowles, M. *The Modern Practice of Adult Education: Andragogy versus Pedagogy.* Associated Press, 1970.

Kohrt, L. Probleme *und Perspektiven der Evaluation computerunterstützter Instruktion.* Arbeiten aus dem Seminar für Pädagogik der TU Braunschweig, Bericht Nr. 1/95. Braunschweig, 1995.

Kolb. D. A.; Fry, R. *Toward an applied theory of experiential learning.* In C. Cooper (ed.) Theories of Group Process, London: John Wiley, 1975.

Koper, R. *Modeling units of study from a pedagogical perspective. The pedagogical meta-model behind EML,* 2001 [online]. Available from Internet: http://eml.ou.nl/introduction/docs/ped-metamodel.pdf [cited 15.04.2005].

Koper, R.; Olivier, B.; Anderson, T. (a). *IMS Learning Design Best Practice and Implementation Guide.* IMS Global Learning Consortium, Inc., 2003 [online]. Available from Internet: http://www.imsglobal.org/learningdesign/ldv1p0/imsld_bestv1p0.html [cited 17.02.2003].

Koper, R.; Olivier, B.; Anderson, T. (b). *IMS Learning Design Information Model.* IMS Global Learning Consortium, Inc., 2003 [online]. Available from Internet: http://www.imsglobal.org/learningdesign/ldv1p0/imsld_infov1p0.html [17.02.2003].

Koper, R.; Olivier, B.; Anderson, T. (c). *IMS Learning Design XML Binding.* IMS Global Learning Consortium, Inc., 2003 [online]. Available from Internet: http://www.imsglobal.org/learningdesign/ldv1p0/imsld_bindv1p0.html [cited 17.02.2003].

Kösel, E. *Subjektive Didaktik. Die Modellierung von Lernwelten.* 3. Aufl. Elztal-Dallau, 1997.

Kronreif, G.; Dotter, F.; Bergmeister, E.; Krammer, K.; Hilzensauer, M.; Skant, A.; Barreto, B. *SMILE: Demonstration of Cognitively oriented Solution to the Improvement of Written Language Competence of Deaf People.* In 7th International Conference on Computers Helping People with Special Needs ICCHP 2000, Karlsruhe, Germany, 2000.

Kuhl, A. M. *Soll die Didaktik konstruktivistisch werden?* In: Pädagogische Korrespondenz, Jg. 12, 33-55, 1993.

Kuhn, T. *The Structure of Scientific Revolutions.* The University of Chicago Press, 1970.

Kulik, C.-L.; Kulik, J. *Effectiveness of Computerbased Instruction: An Update Analysis.* In: Computers in Human Behaviour, 1991, 7, P.: 75-94.

Kulik, J. *Meta-analytic studies of findings on computer-based instruction.* In: Baker, E.L.; O'Neil, H.F. (Eds.): Technology Assessment in Education and Training. Hillsdale, 1994.

L-Change. *Change in European education and training systems related to information society technologies: yearly report* 2003/2004 / L-Change, Brussels: Information Society Technologies, 2004.

Lange, E. *Zur Entwicklung und Methodik der Evaluationsforschung in der Bundesrepublik Deutschland.* Zeitschrift für Soziologie, 1983, 12, P.: 253-270.

Lagrosen, S., Seyyed-Hashemi, R.; Leitner, M. *Examination of the dimensions of quality in higher education.* Quality Assurance in Education, 12(2), 61–69, 2004.

Laudon, K. C; Laudon, J. P. *Management information systems: managing the digital firm.* Pearson Education: USA, 2006.

Laux, H. *Entscheidungstheorie.* Fünfte, verbesserte Auflage. Springer: Berlin, 2003.

Lave, J. *Cognition in Practice: Mind, mathematics, and culture in everyday life.* Cambridge, 1988.

Lave, J.; Wenger, E. *Situated Learning: Legitimate Peripheral Participation.* Cambridge, 1990.

Le Préau. *Which quality model for e-learning*, 2005 [online]. Available from Internet: www.preau.ccip.fr [cited 20.09.2005].

Leef, G. C. *Accreditation is no Guarantee of Academic Quality.* The Chronicle of Higher Education, 49(30), B17, 2003.

Leukel, J. *Katalogdatenmanagement im B2B E-Commerce.* Lohmar/Köln: Josef Eul Verlag, 2004.

Leukel, J.; Schmitz, V.; Kelkar, O. *XML-based Data exchange of product model data in E-Procurement and E-Sales: The Case of BMEcat 2.0.* In Proceedings of the International Conference on Economic, Technical and Organisational aspects of Product Configuration Systems (PETO 2004), Copenhagen: 2004, p. 97-107.

Liber, O. *The revolutionary possibilities of eLearning standards.* In: Bachmann, G.; Haefeli, O.; Kindt, M. (Eds.), Campus 2002. Die Virtuelle Hochschule in der Konsolidierungsphase (S. 197-208). Münster, New York, München, Berlin: Waxmann, 2002.

Lindner, R. *Normung zu e-learning und ihre absehbaren wirtschaftlichen Auswirkungen.* In: Reglin, Th.; Severing, E. u. a. (eds): e-learning für die betriebliche Praxis, Bielefeld, p. 119–131, 2003.

Lindquist, K. *Quality*, The European Learning Quality Framework. 2003.

Lockee, B., Moore, M.; Burton, J. *Measuring Success: Evaluation Strategies for Distance Education*. Educause Quarterly, 2002 [online]. Available from Internet: http://www.educause.edu/ir/library/pdf/EQM0213.pdf [cited 26.06.2004].

Lomas, L. *Does the development of mass education necessarily mean the end of quality?* The Sixth QHE seminar, Birmingham, 2001.

Lopez, M. *Radioscopie d'une formation ouverte et à distance »,* French-European workshop on Quality of distance learning, 2005 [online]. Available from Internet: http://www.eqo.info/files/FE-WS/FE-WS%20Radioscopie%20d_une%20Formation%20ouverte%20et%20a%20distance.pdf [cited 20.09.2005].

Lorenzo, G.; Ittelson, J. *An Overview of E-Portfolios*, The EDUCAUSE Learning Initiative, 2005.

Luhmann, N. *Die Gesellschaft der Gesellschaft*; Frankfurt; Main: Suhrkamp, 1998.

Mag, W. *Entscheidung und Information*. Vahlen: München, 1977.

Maillat, D.; Kebir, L. *The Learning Region and Territorial Production Systems*. Neuchatel University IRER, 1998.

Maleri, R. *Grundlagen der Dienstleistungsproduktion*. Springer-Verlag. Berlin/ Heidelberg, 1997.

Mandl, H.; Heinz, G.; Renkl, A. *Lernen mit dem Computer*. Empirisch Pädagogische Forschung in der BRD zwischen 1970 und 1990 Forschungsbericht Nr. 7. München, 1992.

Mandl, H.; Reinmann-Rothmeier, G. *Unterrichten und Lernumgebungen gestalten*. Forschungsbericht Nr. 60. München, 1995.

Manelle, J. *Veränderungen – eine Betrachtungsweise aus psychologischer Sicht*. In: Österle, H.; Winter, R. (Hrsg.): Business Engineering. Auf dem Weg zum Unternehmen des Informationszeitalters. Springer, Berlin u. a., 2000.

Manouselis, N.; Sampson, D. *Recommendation of Quality Approaches for the European Quality Observatory*. In: Proc. of ICALT 2004, Joensuu, Aug. 2004.

Martens, H.; Vogten, H. *A Reference Implementation of a Learning Design Engine*. In: Koper, R.; Tattersall, C. (Eds.), Learning Design. A Handbook on Modelling and Delivering Networked Education and Training (S. 91-108). Berlin, Heidelberg, New York: Springer, 2005.

Martin, B. L. *A Checklist for Designing Instruction in the Affective Domain*. Educational Technology, 1989, (29) 8, P.:7-15.

Massy, J. *Quality and e-learning in Europe*, Bizmedia report, 2002 [online]. Available from Internet: www.elaerningage.co.uk [cited 20.09.2005].

Mayring, P. *Einführung in die qualitative Sozialforschung: Eine Anleitung zu qualitativem Denken*. Weinheim, Basel: Beltz, 2002.

McCormick, R. *Keeping the Pedagogy out of Learning Objects.* Symposium Designing Virtual Learning Material, EARLI 10th Biennial Conference Improving Learning, Fostering the Will to Learn, 2003.

Meier, A.; MEDA; AKAB. *Zwei Kriterienkataloge auf dem Prüfstand.* In: Schenkel, P.; Tergan, S.-O.; Lottmann, A. (eds): Qualitätsbeurteilung multimedialer Lern- und Informationssysteme. Evaluationsmethoden auf dem Prüfstand. Nürnberg, p. 164 – 189, 2000.

Meier, A. *Qualitätsbeurteilung von Lernsoftware durch Kriterienkataloge.* In: Schenkel, P., Holz, H. (Hrsg.) (1995): Evaluation multimedialer Lernprogramme und Lernkonzepte, BIBB-Reihe Multimediales Lernen in der Berufsbildung. Nürnberg, 1995. P.:149-190.

Meier, F.; Baratelli, S. *Wissenspsychologische Evaluation selbstgesteuerten Lernens mit modernen Medien und rechnergestützten Instruktionen, Medienpsychologie,* 3, 1991. P.: 109-123.

Merchel, J. *Qualitätsentwicklung statt Zertifizierung: Zur Problematik der Zertifizierung von Einrichtungen und Diensten der Sozialen Arbeit.* Nachrichtendienst des Deutschen Vereins für öffentliche und private Fürsorge, 81(3), 2001.

Mettler von Meiborn, B. *Kommunikation in der Mediengesellschaft.* Berlin, 1994.

Meyer, K. A. *Quality in Distance Education: Focus on On-Line Learning.* ASHE-ERIC Higher Education Report, 29(4), 1–121, 2002.

Miller, R. B.; Greene, B.A.; Montalvo, G.P.; Ravindran, B.; Nichols J.D. *Engagement in Academic Work: The Role of Learning Goals, Future Consequences, Pleasing Others, and Perceived Ability, Contemporary Educational Psychology,* Volume 21, Number 4, October 1996, pp. 388-422(35).

Mirabella, V.; Kimani, S.; Catarci T. A *No Frills Approach for Accessible Web Based Learning Material.* In International Cross-Disciplinary Workshop on Web Accessibility 2004 (W4A), 13th International World Wide Web Conference, New York, USA, 17-22 May 2004.

Mispelblom-Meyer, F. *Au-delà de la Qualité,* Edition SYROS, 1999.

Moonen, J. *Design Methodology.* In: Adelsberger, H. H.; Collis, B.; Pawlowski, J. M. (Eds.), Handbook on Information Systems for Education and Training. Berlin, Heidelberg, New York, Barcelona, Hong Kong, London, Milan, Paris, Tokyo: Springer, 2001.

Moslehien, S. M. *A glance at postmodern pedagogy of mathematics.* Philosophy of mathematics education, May 2003[online]. Available from Internet: http://www.ex.ac.uk/~PErnest/pome17/contents.htm [cited 3.09.2005].

Müller, Klaus, Hg. *Konstruktivismus. Lehren - Lernen - Ästhetische Prozesse.* Neuwied, 1996.

Murphy, P. K.; Alexander, P.A. *A Motivated Exploration of Motivation Terminology, Contemporary Educational Psychology,* Volume 25, Number 1, January 2000, pp. 3-53(51).

Musa, D. L.; Muñoz, L. S.; Moreira de Oliveira, J. P. *Sharing Learner Profile through an Ontology and Web Services*. In Proceedings of: MIW 2004 - 5th International Workshop on Management of Information on the Web, p. 415-419, 2004.

N.N. *Quality on the line*, 2004 [online]. Available from Internet: http://www.ihep.com/Pubs/PDF/Quality.pdf [cited 21.09.2005].

Najjar, J.; Meire, M.; Duval, E. *Attention Metadata Management: Tracking the Use of Learning Objects through Attention*. XML, ED-MEDIA 2005 World Conference on Educational Multimedia, Hypermedia and Telecommunications, Montréal, Canada, June 27-July 2, 2005; see also http://www.cs.kuleuven.ac.be/~najjar/.

Nationale Agentur Bildung für Europa (Hrsg). *E-Learning in Europe – Results and Recommendations*. Bonn, 2005

Nevile, L. *Why is Accessibility Metadata Proving Difficult? In International Conference on Dublin Core and Metadata for e-Communities: 2002 conference proceedings*; Florence, Italy, 13-17 October 2002.

Nevile, L.; Cooper, M.; Heath, A.; Rothberg, M.; Treviranus, J. *Learner-centered Accessibility for Interoperable Web-based Educational Systems*. In Interoperability of Web-Based Educational Systems Workshop, 14th International World Wide Web Conference (WWW2005), Chiba, Japan, 10-14 May 2005.

Niles, F. S. *Cultural differences in learning motivation and learning strategies: A comparison of overseas and Australian students at an Australian university*, International Journal of Intercultural Relations, Volume 19, Issue 3, Summer 1995, Pages 369-385; see also doi:10.1016/0147-1767(94)00025-S.

Nittel, D. *Von der „Teilnehmerorientierung" zur „Kundenorientierung" – Zur Bedeutung von systematischen Begriffen für pädagogische Feldanalysen*. In: Arnold, R.; Gieseke, W. (eds): Die Weiterbildungsgesellschaft, vol. 1: Bildungstheoretische Grundlagen und Analysen, Neuwied/Kriftel, p. 161–184, 1999.

Nonaka, I.; Takeucki, H. *The Knowledge-Creating Company*. Oxford University Press, 1995.

Nuventive. *iWebFolio*, 2005 [online]. Available from Internet: http://www.nuventive.com/iwebfolio.htm [cited 20.09.2005].

Observatory on Borderless Higher Education. No. 2, March 2002. *Leading Learning Platforms: International Market Presence*. 2002.

OECD. *E-learning in tertiary Education: Where do we stand?* OECD. Paris, OECD, 2005.

OECD. *Learning to Change: ICT in Schools*, 2001 [online]. Available from Internet: www.sourceoecd.org [cited 20.09.2005].

Oess, A. *Total Quality Management. Die ganzheitliche Qualitätsstrategie*. Wiesbaden: Gabler, 1993.

Olberg, H.-J. von. *Didaktik auf dem Wege zur Vermittlungswissenschaft?* In: Zeitschrift für Pädagogik, Jg. 50 (1), 119-131, 2004.

Olivier, B.; Tattersall, C. *The Learning Design Specification.* In: Koper, R.; Tattersall, C. (Eds.), Learning Design. A Handbook on Modelling and Delivering Networked Education and Training (S. 21-40). Berlin, Heidelberg, New York: Springer, 2005.

OMG. *Introduction to OMG's Specifications* 2005 [online]. Available from Internet: http://www.omg.org/gettingstarted/specintro.htm#OMA [cited 31.05.2005]

Open and Distance Learning Quality Council (ODLQC) [2001]. *Standards in open and distance education* [online] Available from Internet: http://www.odlqc.org.uk/st-int.htm [cited 11.02.2004].

OSI. *The ISO Open Systems Interconnection Reference Model*, ISO/IEC 7498-1, 1994 [online] Available from Internet: http://standards.iso.org/ittf/PubliclyAvailableStandards/s020269_ISO_IEC_7498-1_1994(E).zip [cited 04.10.2005].

OSMOSYS. *Organising SMO's employees approaches to lifelong learning at system level*, 2005 [online]. Available from Internet: http://www.osmosys.se; http://www.reu.pub.ro:9080/osmosys/ [cited 20.09.2005].

Österle, H. *Integration: Schlüssel zur.* In Middleware, Braunschweig/Wiesbaden: Vieweg Verlag, 1996.

Parker, N. K. *The Quality Dilemma in Online Education.* In Anderson, T. D.; Elloumi, F. (Eds.), Theory and Practice of Online Learning (p. 385–421). Athabasca: Athabasca University, 2004.

Pawlowski, J M. (b). *The Didactical Object Model: Managing Didactical Expertise.* European Handbook for Quality and Standardisation in E-Learning. CEDEFOP publication, 2005.

Pawlowski, J M. *Das Essener-Lern-Modell (ELM): Ein Vorgehensmodell zur Entwicklung computerunterstützter Lernumgebungen.* Essen: PhD Thesis at the University of Essen, 2001.

Pawlowski, J. M. (a). *Quality Initiative E-Learning in Germany: The Future of Learning Technology Standardisation.* In: Proc. of Second joint workshop on Cognition and Learning through Media-Communication for Advanced e-Learning. Tokio, 2005.

Pawlowski, J. M. *Lerntechnologiestandards: Gegenwart und Zukunft.* In Was macht E-Learning erfolgreich? Berlin: Springer, 2004. P. 93-112.

Pellert, A.; Welan, M. *Die formierte Anarchie – die Herausforderung der Universitäts-organisation.* Wien: WUV-Universitätsverlag, 1995.

Phipps, R. A.; Merisotis, J. *Quality On The Line: Benchmarks For Success.* In Internet-Based Distance Education. Washington, DC: The Institute For Higher Education Policy, 2000.

Piaget J.; Chomsky N. *Théories du langage et théories de l'apprentissage (Le débat entre Jean PIAGET et Noam CHOMSKY).* Le Seuil – Paris, 1975.

PLS Ramboll Management. *Studies in the Context of the E-learning Initiative: Virtual Models of European Universities (Lot 1): Final Report to the EU Commission*, DG

Education & Culture, 2004 [online]. Available from Internet: http://wwwupload.pls.ramboll.dk/eng/Publications/PublicAdministration/VirtualModels .pdf [cited 01.10.2004].

Pollitt, C. *Improving the Quality of Social Services: New Opportunities for Participation?* In: Flösser, G., Otto, H.-U. (Hrsg.): Towards more democrazy in Social Services. Berlin u.a., 1008.

Pollok, J. *The Big Issue: Interoperability vs. Integration.* EAI Journal, October 2001, p. 48-52.

Prell, S. *Evaluation.* In: Schiefele, H., Krapp, A. (Hrsg.) (1981): Handlexikon zur Pädagogischen Psychologie. München, 1981. P.:116-120.

Prell, S. *Evaluation.* In: Sarges, W., Fricke, R. (Hrsg.), (1986): Psychologie für die Erwachsenenbildung-Weiterbildung. Göttingen, 1986. P.: 208-213.

Quality Assurance Association for Higher Education. *Guidelines on the Quality Assurance of Distance Learning,* 1999 [online]. Available from Internet: http://www.qaa.ac.uk/dlg [cited 01-08-2000].

Ravet, S. *Quality in e-learning: are the models inherited from the industrial economy still valid in a knowledge economy?* Vortrag Online Educa, Berlin, 2002.

Ravet, S. *Universités virtuelles: révolution réelle ou révolution virtuelle?* Ed. Hermes, 2003.

Ravichandran, T., Rai, A. *Quality Management in Systems Development: An Organisational System Perspective.* In: MIS Quarterly, 24,3, 381-410, 2000.

Ravitch, D. *National standards in American education: A citizen's guide.* Washington, DC: Brookings Institution Press, 1995.

Rawlings, A.; Rosmalen, P. van; Koper, R.; Rodríguez-Artacho, M.; Lefrere, P. *Survey of Educational Modelling Languages (EMLs). (Version 1) CEN/ISSS WS/LT Learning Technologies Workshop,* 2002 [online]. Available from Internet: http://dspace.learningnetworks.org/retrieve/444/eml-report-cen-isss.pdf [cited 15.04.2005].

Realising the European Higher Education Area: Communiqué of the Conference of Ministers responsible for Higher Education. Bologna Process, Berlin, 2003 [online]. Available from Internet: http://www.bologna-berlin2003.de/pdf/ Communique1.pdf [cited 27.05.2005].

Reay, D. G. *Evaluating Educational Software in the Classroom.* In: Reid, I., Rushton, J. (Hrsg.) (1985): Teachers, Computers and the Classroom. Mancheseter, 1985. P.: 184-195.

Rees, J. P. *Developing a Reference model of ePorfolio, JISC Specifying an e-Portfolio,* 2005 [online]. Available from Internet: http://www.nottingham.ac.uk/e-portfolio/outcomes.htm [20.09.2005].

Reeves, T. C. (1992): Evaluating Interactive Multimedia. Athens, 1992.

Reeves, T. C.; Harmon, S. W. *Systematic Evaluation Procedures for Interactive Multimedia for Education and Training*. Paper presented at the Annual Meeting of the American Educational Research Association. Atlanta, 1994.

Reglin, T. (b). *E-Learning zur Unterstützung arbeitsintegrierten Lernens: Klarheit über die Ziele schaffen*. In: Hohenstein, A.; Wilbers, K. (eds): Handbuch E-Learning. Expertenwissen aus Wissenschaft und Praxis, Köln 2001ff., 6. Erg.-Lfg. Chapter. 4.6.3, 2003.

Reglin, T. *Blended-Learning-Angebote richtig vermarkten – Ergebnisse einer qualitativen Analyse von Leistungsversprechungen*. In: Hohenstein, A.; Wilbers, K. (eds) Handbuch E-Learning. Expertenwissen aus Wissenschaft und Praxis, Köln, 13. Erg.-Lfg. August 2005, chapter 3.9, 2005.

Reglin, T.; Hölbling, G. (a). *Kompetenzentwicklung mit Neuen Medien?* In: QUEM (Hrg.): Lernen im Netz und mit Multimedia. Vier Gutachten. Berlin, S.9-74, 2003.

Reglin, T.; Hölbling, G. *Computerlernen und Kompetenz*, Bielefeld, 2004.

Rehak, D. *Good&plenty, Googlezon, your grandmother and Nike: challenges for ubiquitous learning & learning technology*, 2004; see also http://www.lsal.cmu.edu/lsal/expertise/papers/conference/pgl2004/googlezon20041001.pdf.

Reich, K. *Konstruktivistische Didaktik*. Neuwied, 2002.

Reich, K. *Systemisch-konstruktivistische Pädagogik*. Einführung in Grundlagen einer interaktionistisch-konstruktivistischen Pädagogik. Neuwied, 1996.

Reigeluth, Ch. M. *Instructional design: What is it and why is it?* In: Reigeluth, Ch. M. (Hrsg.): Instructional Theories and Models: An Overview of Their Current Status. Hillsdale, 1983. P.: 3-36.

Reinmann-Rothmeier, G.; Mandl, H. *Lernen auf der Basis des Konstruktivismus: Wie Lernen aktiver und anwendungsorientierter wird*. In: Computer und Unterricht 23/1996. P.: 41-44.

Ridder, H.-G., Bruns, H.-J., Brünn, S. *Online und Multimediainstrumente zur Kompetenzerfassung*. Berlin; vgl. auch Hanft, A., Müskens, W.(2003): Prüfungs- und Dokumentationsmethoden als Instrumente der kompetenzorientierten Erfolgskontrolle internetgestützten Lernens. In: QUEM (Hrg.): Lernen im Netz und mit Multimedia. Vier Gutachten. Berlin, S.177-254, 2004.

Riddy, P., Fill, K., Wolf, K. D., Rosato, S.; Balasca, N. *MECA-ODL: Compendium of Reference Materials on Quality in Open and Distance Learning Delivered via Internet*, 2002 [online]. Available from Internet: http://www.adeit.uv.es/mecaodl/docs/compendium_english.pdf [cited 24.10.2004].

Riehm, R.; Vogler, P. *Middleware: Infrastruktur für die Integration*. In Middleware, Braunschweig/Wiesbaden: Vieweg Verlag, 1996.

Rifkin, J. *The European Dream*. Polity press. ISBN 0-7456-3425-7, 2004.

Rockmann, U. (a). *Produktkriterien für e-learning – Abgrenzung und Verortung bestehender Standards und die PAS 1032-1*. Din. E.V. (Hrsg.) Fachbericht Learning, Education and Training focusing on e-learning Verlag Beuth, 2004.

Rockmann, U. (b). *Qualitätskriterien für IT-basierte Lernmedien – nützlich oder unsinnig?* In: Schenkel, P.; Tergan, O. Was macht E-learning erfolgreich? Grundlagen und Instrumente der Qualitätsbeurteilung. Springer Verlag, 2004.

Rockmann, U. (c). *Qualitätskriterien für IT-basierte Lernmedien – nützlich oder unsinnig?* In: Tergan, S.-O.; Schenkel, P., p. 71–81, 2004.

Rockmann, U. *Software-Ergonomie und Normung von eLearning-Produkten.* dvs-Nachrichten, 2002.

Rockmann, U.; Olivier, N. (a). *Quality of E-learning Products - Illustrated by Examples from the Online Sport Science Academy ILIS* - F. Seifriz, J. Mester, J. Perl, O. Spaniol, J. Wiemeyer (Eds.) 1st International Working Confereence IT and Sport and 5th Conference dvs-Section Computer Science in Sport, Cologne, 2005, ISBN 3-00-014576-1.

Rockmann, U.; Reiter, C.; Olivier, N. (b). *Internet-Lehrbuch-Integration in der Sportwissenschaft (ILIS) – Konzeption und Nutzungserfahrungen*. Wiemeyer, J. (Hrsg.). "Education, Research, and New Media. Chances and Challenges for Science" im Verlag Czwalina, Hamburg, 2005.

Romiszowski, A. *The future of e-learning as an educational innovation: factors influencing project success and failure. Brazilian Review of Open and Distance Learning,* September 2003 [online]. Available from Internet: http://www.abed.org.br/publique/cgi/cgilua.exe/sys/start.htm?UserActiveTemplate=2in g&infoid=834&sid=70 [cited 3.09.2005].

Rosenshine, B.; Furst, N. *Research in Teacher Performance Criteria.* In: Smith, B.O. (Hrsg.): Research in Teacher Education. A Symposium. Englewood Cliffs, 1971.

Rossi, P. H.; Freemann, H. E.; Hoffmann, G. *Programm-Evaluation.* Einführung in die Methoden angewandter Sozialforschung. Stuttgart, 1988

Rost, M. *Die Netzrevolution. Auf dem Weg in die Weltgesellschaft.* Frankfurt/ M., 1996.

Rousseau, B. et al. *In The 19th Annual ACM Symposium on Applied Computing: conference proceedings*; Nicosia, Cyprus, 14-17 March 2004, ACM Press, 2004.

Rychen, S., Salganik, L. (Hrg.). *Defining and selecting key competencies.* Seattle, Toronto, Bern, Göttingen, 2001.

S3. *Industry Report on "Making Sense of Standards & Specifications: A Guide for Decision Makers"* 2nd edition, published by The Masie Center, 2003 [online]. Available from Internet: http://www.masie.com/standards/s3_2nd_edition.pdf [cited 11.10.2005].

Sadoski, D.; Comella-Dorda, S. *Three Tier Software Architectures - Software Technology Roadmap,* 2004 [online] Available from Internet: http://www.sei.cmu.edu/str/descriptions/threetier_body.html [cited 04.10.2005]

Salmon, G. *E-tivities: The Key To Active Online Learning.* London, Kogan Page, 2002.

Sauter, A., Sauter, W. *Blended Learning. Effiziente Integration von E-Learning und Präsenztraining.* Neuwied, 2002.

Scalan, C. L. *Reliability and Validity of a Student Scale for Assessing the Quality of Internet-Based Distance Learning. Distance Learning Administration,* VII(III), 2003.

Schäffter, O. *Perspektiven weiterbildender Schulen. Der Beitrag der Hochschulen zum lebensbegleitenden Lernen.* In: Hessische Blätter für Volksbildung, 1/1997, S.: 37-52.

Schäffter, O. *Weiterbildung in der Transformationsgesellschaft. Zur Grundlegung einer Theorie der Institutionalisierung.* Hohengehren 2001.

Schank R. *Virtual Learning: a Revolutionary Approach to Building a Highly Skilled Workforce.* McGraw Hill, 1997.

Scheffer, P. *DESS Stratégies Qualité,* Université d'Evry, 95000, France, 2001.

Schenkel, P. *Zum Thema „Qualität von Lernsoftware".* In: Arbeitshilfen für die Erwachsenenbildung, Nr. 4, 1998 [online]. Available from Internet: http://www.shuttle.de/pae/ah4-98/schenkel.htm [cited 02.2003].

Schenkel, P. (Hrsg.). *Qualitätsbeurteilung multimedialer Lern- und Informationssysteme.* Evaluationsmethoden auf dem Prüfstand. Nürnberg, 2000.

Schenkel, P.; Holz, H. (Hrsg.). *Evaluation multimedialer Lernprogramme und Lernkonzepte.* Berichte aus der Berufsbildungspraxis. Nürnberg, 1995.

Schmelzer, H. J.; Sesselmann, W. *Geschäftsprozessmanagement in der Praxis.* München; Wien: Carl Hanser, 2003.

Schmetzke, A. *Online distance education: 'Anytime, anywhere' but not for everyone.* Information Technology and Disability Journal, vol. 7(2), 2001.

Schmidt, S.J. *Lernen, Wissen, Kompetenz.* In: Überlegungen zu drei Unbekannten. Donauwörth (i.D.), 2005.

Schott, F.; Krien, F.; Sachse, S.; Schubert, T. *Evaluation von multimedialer Lernsoftware auf der Basis von ELISE (1.0).* Ein Ansatz zu einer theorie-, adressaten- und anwendungsorientierten Methode zur Evaluation von multimedialen Lern- und Informationssystemen. In: Schenkel, P. (Hrsg.) (2000): Qualitätsbeurteilung multimedialer Lern- und Informationssysteme. Evaluationsmethoden auf dem Prüfstand. Nürnberg, 2000.

Schroeter, S., Martina, G., Köppe, D.; Keck, R. *Qualitätsmanagementsysteme.* Erkrath: Toennes, 2003 [online]. Available from Internet: http://www.aachen.ihk.de/de/innovation_umwelt/download/pi_012.pdf [cited 10.01.2005].

Schulmeister, R. *Diversity of students and the consequences for e-learning.* 6. ICNEE, 27-30 September 2004, Neuchâtel / Switzerland, 2004.

Schulmeister, R. *Kriterien didaktischer Qualität im E-Learning zur Sicherung der Akzeptanz und Nachhaltigkeit.* In: Euler, D.; Seufert, S. (eds): E-Learning in Hochschulen und Bildungszentren, München/Wien, p. 473–492, 2005.

Schwarz, I.; Lewis, M. *Basic Concept Microcomputer Courseware: A Critical Evaluation System for Educators*. Educational technology, 1989. 29, 5, P.: 16-21.

SCORM (a). *SCORM Best Practices Guide for Content Developers*, 2004 [online]. Available from Internet: http://www.lsal.cmu.edu/lsal/expertise/projects/developersguide/index.html [cited 11.10.2005].

SCORM (b). *SCORM Reload Editor*, 2004 [online]. Available from Internet: http://www.lsal.cmu.edu/adl/scorm/tools/reload/index.html [cited 11.10.2005].

SEEQUEL. *Sustainable Environment for the Evaluation of Quality in e-Learning, "the e-learner Bill of rights"*, 2005 [online]. Available from Internet: http://www.education-observatories.net/seequel/SEEQUEL%20_elearners_Bill_of_rights.pdf [cited 20.09.2005].

Seghezzi, H. D. *Integriertes Qualitätsmanagement: Das St.Galler Konzept* (2., vollst. überarb. und erw. Aufl.). München, Wien: Carl Hanser, 2003.

Seidel, R.J.; Park, O. *An historical perspective and a model for evaluation of intelligent tutoring systems*. In: Journal of Educational Computing Research, 10, 1994. P.: 103-128.

Senge, P. *The Fifth Discipline*. Random House, 1990.

Sennet, R. *Der flexible Mensch. Die Kultur des neuen Kapitalismus*. Berlin, 1998.

Seufert, S.; Euler, D. Nachhaltigkeit von eLearning-Innovationen. St. Gallen: SCIL, 2003 [online]. Available from Internet: http://www.scil.ch/publications/docs/2003-06-seufert-euler-nachhaltigkeit-elearning.pdf [cited 29.11.2004].

Seufert, S.; Euler, D. *Nachhaltigkeit von eLearning-Innovationen: Ergebnisse einer Delphi-Studie (SCIL-Arbeitsbericht 2)*, 2004 [online]. St. Gallen: SCIL. Available from Internet: http://www.scil.ch/publications/docs/2004-01-seufert-euler-nachhaltigkeit-elearning.pdf [cited 29.11.2004].

Seufert, S.; Euler, D. *Nachhaltigkeit von eLearning-Innovationen: Fallstudien zu Implementierungsstrategien von eLearning als Innovationen an Hochschulen*, 2005 [online] St. Gallen: Swiss Centre for Innovations in Learning. Available from Internet: http://www.scil.ch/publications/docs/2005-01-seufert-euler-nachhaltigkeit-elearning.pdf [cited 05.05.2005].

Severing, E.; Stahl, Th. *Qualitätssicherung in der betrieblichen Weiterbildung – Fallstudien aus Europa*. In: GdWZ 3/1995, p. 161–165, 1995.

Sgouropoulou, C.; Koutoumanos, A. *Applying metadata standards to multilingual learning objects*. Int. J. Learning Technology, Vol. 1, No 4, p. 425-442, 2005.

Siebert, H. *Curriculumplanung und Teilnehmerorientierung*. In: Raapke, Hans-Dietrich; Schulenberg, Walter (Hrsg.): Handbuch der Erwachsenenbildung. Band 7: Didaktik der Erwachsenenbildung. Stuttgart, Berlin, Köln u.a. 1985. S. 62-74., 1985.

Siebert, H. *Didaktisches Handeln in der Erwachsenenbildung*. Neuwied/Kriftel, 1996.

Siebert, H. *Lernen als Konstruktion von Lebenswelten. Entwurf einer konstruktivistischen Didaktik.* Frankfurt am Main., 1994.

Siebert, H. *Pädagogischer Konstruktivismus. Eine Bilanz der Konstruktivismusdiskussion für die Bildungspraxis.* Neuwied, 1999.

Siebert, H. *Vernetztes Lernen.* München, 2003.

SIG DLAE. *Special Interest Group for Distance Learning Accreditation in Europe (SIG DLAE): Proposal for a European e-learning and blended-learning accreditation system.* Paris/Essen, in preparation.

Simon, B. *E-Learning an Hochschulen: Gestaltungsräume und Erfolgsfaktoren von Wissensmedien.* Köln: Eul, 2001.

Slater, J. *Spent Force or Revolution in Progress? eLearning after the eUniversity.* Oxford: Higher Education Policy Institute, 2005 [online]. Available from Internet: http://www.hepi.ac.uk/pubdetail.asp?ID=173&DOC=Reports [cited 03.09.2005].

SLOAN-*C VIEW ISSN 1541*-2806 Volume 2 Issue 2 – April, 2003.

SMILE Project. *A Sign Language and Multimedia-based Interactive Language Course for the Deaf for the Training of European Written Languages,* 2003 [online]. Available from Internet: http://www.arcsmed.at/projects/smile [cited 20.9.2005].

Snock, A. *Quality in e-learning: a critical issue. E-learning Accredit conferences,* 2002 [online]. Available from Internet: http://www.mylara.com/elearn/forum/default.asp [cited 20.09.2005].

SODIS. *Informationen über SODIS,* without date [online]. Available from Internet: http://www.sodis.de/info/kriterien.html [cited 24.10.2004].

Soin, Sarv Singh. *Total Quality Essentials.* New York: McGraw-Hill, 1992.

Squires, D.; McDougall, A. *Choosing and Using Educational Software: A teachers' guide.* London, 1994.

SRIC-BI (2002-2004). *Learning on Demand Reports. Best Practices in e-learning (2004); Learning Outsourcing: Strategic Opportunity (2004); Next-Generation Mentoring for e-learning (2003); e-learning in the Life-Sciences Industry (2003); Enterprise-Application Vendors in the e-learning Marketplace (2003); e-learning in Financial Services: A Case-Based Analysis (2003); Quality and Effectiveness of e-learning: Views of Industry Experts and Practitioners (2003); Mobile Learning: A Perspective on Present and Future (Bulletin: 2003); Integration of e-learning, Knowledge, and Digital Content Management in Next-Generation Learning (2003); Lessons in e-learning from the Oil and Gas Industry (2002)* [online]. Available from Internet: www.sric-bi.com/lod [cited 20.09.2004].

SRIC-BI. *Consulting Studies. Strategic Review and Benchmarking of Financial-Services Company's e-learning Capability (2003); Content Partner Analysis and Strategy for Learning-Services Provider (2003); e-learning Technology Roadmaps for the Automotive Industry (2003)* [online]. Available from Internet www.sric-bi.com/consulting/learningstrategy.shtml [cited 20.09.2005].

Srikanthan, G.; Dalrymple, J. F. *Developing a Holistic Model for Quality in Higher Education.* Quality in Higher Education, 8(3), 215–224, 2002.

Stahl, T.; Stölzl, M. *Bildungsmarketing im Spannungsfeld von Organisationsentwicklung und Personalentwicklung, edited by BIBB* (Modellversuche zur beruflichen Bildung, vol. 33) Berlin/Bonn 1994.

Stallmann, R. M. *Can you trust your computer?* In: Free Software, Free Society: The Selected Essays of Richard M. Stallman, p. 115-118., 2002.

Steffe, L. P.; Gale, J. Hg. *Constructivism in Education.* Hillsdale, 1995.

Stehr, N. *Arbeit, Eigentum und Wissen. Zur Theorie von Wissensgesellschaften.* Frankfurt/ M, 1994.

Stehr, N.; Ericson, R. V. *The Culture and Power of Knowledge.* Inquiries into Contemporary Societies. Berlin/ New York, 1992.

Stephanidis, C. (ed.). *User Interfaces for All,* Concepts, Methods and Tools, 2001.

Stiefel, R. Th. *Grundfragen der Evaluierung in der Management-Schulung.* Lernen und Leistung. Frankfurt am Main, 1974.

Stufflebeam, D. L. *Evaluation as enlightenment for decision-making.* In: Worthen, B.R., Sanders, J.R. (Hrsg.) (1973): Educational evaluation: Theory and practice. Worthington, 1973.

Stufflebeam, D. L. *Professional Standards for Educational Evaluation: United States.* In: Husén, T., Posthlethwaite, T. N. (Hrsg.) (1994): The International Encyclopedia of Education. Oxford, 1994.

Stufflebeam, D. L. *The relevance of the CIPP evaluation model for educational accountability,* SRIS Quarterly, 5(1), 1972.

Stufflebeam, D. L. *The CIPP model for evaluation.* In: Stufflebeam, D.L., Madaus, G.F., Kellaghan, T. (Hrsg.): Evaluation Models. Boston, 2000.

Suchman, L. *Plans and Situated Actions: The Problem of Human/Machine Communication.* Cambridge, 1988.

Tapscott, D. *Growing up Digital.* McGraw Hill, 1998.

Tapscott, D. *The Digital Economy.* McGraw Hill, 1996.

Taylor, M. *Generation NeXt Comes to College, A Collection of Papers on Student and Institutional Improvement,* Volume 2, pp. 19-23, 2004.

TELCERT. *Technology Enhanced Learning Conformance - European Requirements and Testing,* 2005 [online]. Available from Internet: http://www.opengroup.org/telcert/ [cited 20.09.2005].

Tennyson, R. D.; Schott, F.; Seel, N. M.; Dijkstra, S. (Hrsg.). *Instructional Design: International Perspectives.* Volume I: Theories and Models of Instructional Design. Mahwah, 1997.

Tergan, S.-O.; Schenkel, P. (a). *Ein Instrument zur Beurteilung des Lernpotenzials von E-Learning-Anwendungen.* In: Tergan, S.-O.; Schenkel, P., 2004. P. 167–177.

Tergan, S.-O.; Schenkel, P. (b). *Was macht E-Learning erfolgreich? Grundlagen und Instrumente der Qualitätsbeurteilung.* Berlin/Heidelberg/New York, 2004.

Terhart, E. *Konstruktivismus und Unterricht. Gibt es einen neuen Ansatz in der Allgemeinen Didaktik?* In: Zeitschrift für Pädagogik, Jg. 45 (5), 629-647, 1999.

Terhart, E. *Qualität und Qualitätssicherung im Schulsystem.* Hintergründe - Konzepte - Probleme. Zeitschrift für Pädagogik, 2000, 46 (6), 809-829.

The CanCore Metadata Initiative (CanCore) (a). *CanCore homepage*, 2005[online]. Available from Internet: http://www.cancore.ca/ [cited 21.06.2005].

The CanCore Metadata Iniziative (CanCore) (b). *CanCore: Dynamic Guidelines 2.0*, 2005 [online]. Available from Internet: http://www.cancore.ca/en/dynamic/ [cited 21.06.2005].

The Council. Decision of the Council (Education). *Detailed work programme for the follow-up of the objectives of education and training in Europe*, 2002.

The Council. Report from the Education Council to the European Council, *The concrete future objectives of education and training systems.* 5980/01, 2001.

The European Higher Education Area - *Achieving the Goals Communiqué of the Conference of European Ministers Responsible for Higher Education*, Bergen, 19-20 May 2005, 6 p.

The Institute for Higher Education Policy. *Quality on the Line – Benchmarks for Success in Internet-based Distance Education*, Washington, 2001.

The Open Source Portfolio Initiative. *The Open Source Portfolio Initiative*, 2005 [online]. Available from Internet: http://www.osportfolio.org [cited 20.09.2005].

Thomé, D. *Kriterien zur Bewertung von Lernsoftware.* Berlin, 1988.

Tietgens, H. *Theorie und Praxis der Erwachsenenbildung.* Bertelsmann Verlag, Bielefeld, 2003.

Tiffin, J. *Educational television: a phoenix in Latin America?* Programmed learning and educational technology, Vol. 17, No.4, p. 257-61, 1980.

Timmermann, Dieter; Färber, Gisela; Backes-Gellner, Uschi; Bosch, Gerhard; Nagel, Bernhard (Hrsg.). *Finanzierung lebenslangen Lernens - der Weg in die Zukunft.* Schlussbericht der Expertenkommission Finanzierung Lebenslangen Lernens. Bielefeld: Bertelsmann. Schriftenreihe der Expertenkommission FinanzierungLebenslangen Lernens, Bd. 6. Available from Internet: http://www.bmbf.de/pub/schlussbericht_kommission_lll.pdf, 2004.

Tobin, K. (Hrsg.). *The Practise of Constructivism in Science Education.* Hillsdale, 1993.

Töpper, A. *Qualität von e-learning.* In: Reglin, Th.; Severing, E. u. a.: e-learning für die betriebliche Praxis, Bielefeld, p. 97–118, 2003.

Treumann, K. P. *Triangulation als Kombination qualitativer und quantitativer Forschung.* In: Abel, J., Möller, R., Treumann, K. P. (1998): Einführung in die Empirische Pädagogik. Stuttgart u.a., S.: 154-188, 1998.

Tulloch, J. B.; Sneed, J. R. *Quality enhancing practices in distance education: Teaching and learning.* Washington, DC: Instructional Telecommunications Council, 2000.

Twigg, C. A. (a). *Quality Assurance for Whom? Providers and Consumers in Today's Distributed Learning Environment,* 2001 [online]. Available from Internet: http://www.center.rpi.edu/PewSym/Mono3.pdf [cited 20.09.2005].

Twigg, C. A. (b). *Innovations in Online Learning: Moving Beyond No Significant Difference* (Pew Learning and Technology Program). Center für Academic Transformation. Troy, NY, 2001.

U.S. Copyright Office. *The Digital Millennium Copyright Act of 1998,* December 1998 [online]. Available from Internet: http://www.copyright.gov/legislation/dmca.pdf [cited 21.06.2005].

Ulrich, P.; Fluri, Ed. *Management. Eine konzentrierte Einführung.* Bern; Stuttgart: Haupt, 1992.

UNESCO [2002]. *Free access to 2,000 MIT courses online: a huge opportunity for universities in poor countries* [online]. Available from Internet: http://portal.unesco.org/ [cited 20.09.2005].

Unicmind. *Die Nutzung von eLearning-Content in den Top350-Unternehmen der deutschen Wirtschaft. Eine Studie im Auftrag der unicmind.com AG,* 2002 [online]. Available from Internet: http://www.unicmind.com/unicmindstudie2002.pdf [cited 11.02.2004].

UNISYS. *E-learning in Continuing Vocational Training, particularly at the Workplace, with emphasis on Small and Medium Enterprises, contract number 2003-3237 for the European Commission,* Final Report, 2003 [online]. Available from Internet: http://europa.eu.int/comm/education/programmes/elearning/studies_en.html [cited 20.09.2005].

van Assche, F.; Collett, M. *CEN/ISSS WS-LT: The European Standardisation Body for Learning Technologies.* UPGRADE: The European Journal for the Informatics Professional, Vol. IV, No 5, p. 16-20, 2003.

van Assche, F.; Massart, D. *Federation and brokerage of learning objects and their metadata.* In Kinshuk, C.K. Looi, E. Sultinen, D. Sampson, I. Aedo, L. Uden, and E. Kähkönen, editors, Proc. of The Fourth IEEE International Conference on Advanced Learning Technologies, ICALT'04, pages 316--320, Joensuu, Finland. IEEE Computer Society, Los Alamitos, California, 2004.

van Assche, F.; Nirhamo, L. *Celebrate LOM Application Profile,* version 1.1, 2003 [online]. Available from Internet: http://celebrate.eun.org/docs/ [cited 20.09.2005].

van Damme, D. *Accreditation in global higher education. The need for international information and cooperation. Outline of a IAUP approach. Memo for the Commission on Global Accreditation of the International Association of University Presidents,* 2000 [online]. Available from Internet:

http://www.ia-up.org/grp5/dvandamme%20-%20memo%20-%20may%202000.doc [cited 08.03.2004].

Verbert, K.; Jovanovic, J.;Gasevic, D.; Duval, E.; Meire, M. *Towards a global component architecture for learning objects: a slide presentation framework*, World Conference on Educational Multimedia, Hypermedia & Telecommunications, ED-MEDIA 2005, June 27 - July 2, 2005, Montreal, Canada.

Vernadat, F. *Enterprise Modelling and Integration: Principles and Applications*. London: Chapman & Hall, 1996.

Verordnung zur Schaffung barrierefreier Informationstechnik nach dem Behinderten-gleichstellungsgesetz (Barrierefreie Informationstechnik-Verordnung – BITV) vom 17.7.2002, Bundesgesetzblatt Jahrgang 2002 Teil 1 Nr. 49.

ViSiCAST Project. *Virtual Signing Capture, Animation, Storage and Transmission*, 2000 [online]. Available from Internet: http://www.niwi.knaw.nl/en/oi/nod/onderzoek/OND1277077/toon [cited 20.9.2005].

Vygotski, L. S. *Pensée et langage Col. Terrains - Éditions Sociales/Messidor* - Paris - 1985 - Édition russe originale : 1934.

W3C. *Extensible Markup Language (XML)*, 2003 [online]. Available from Internet: http://www.w3.org/XML [cited 31.05.2005]

W3C. *Techniques For Accessibility Evaluation And Repair Tools*. W3C Working Draft, 2000 [online]. Available from Internet: http://www.w3.org/TR/AERT [cited 24.09.2005].

W3C. *Web Content Accessibility Guidelines (WCAG). W3C Recommendation*, 1999 [online]. Available from Internet: http://www.w3.org/WAI/intro/wcag.php [cited 20.9.2005].

WebKolleg (a). *Zulassungsordnung*, 2003 [online]. Available from Internet: www.webkolleg-nrw.de [cited 01.04.2005].

WebKolleg (b). *WebKolleg NRW - ein zeitgemäßes medienbasiertes Bildungsangebot in NRW, Zulassungsordnung WebKollgNRW – contemporary media-based education & training, admission regualtions*, 2003 [online]. Available from Internet: http://www.webkolleg.de/anbieterInfo/Zulassungsordnung/WebKolleg-Zulassungsordnung-Gesamt-0309021.pdf [cited 11.02.2005].

Weibel, S. L. *Border Crossings - Reflections on a Decade of Metadata Consensus Building*, D-Lib Magazine, July/August 2005, Volume 11 Number 7/8, see also http://mirrored.ukoln.ac.uk/lis-journals/dlib/dlib/dlib/july05/weibel/07weibel.html.

Weidenmann, B. *„Multimedia": Mehrere Medien, mehrere Codes, mehrere Sinneskanäle?* In: Unterrichtswissenschaft 2/1997. P.: 197-206.

Weimer, M. *Learner-Centered Teaching*. San Francisco: Jossey-Bass, 2002.

Weitz, W. *BasisarchitekturenWeb-basierter Informationssysteme*. Wirtschaftsinformatik, June 2002, Vol. 44, No 3, p. 207–216.

Wellenreuther, M. *Lehren und Lernen - aber wie?* Baltmannsweiler, 2004.

Wells, H. G. Lecture. *"The Brain Organisation of the Modern World"* October and November. Quoted in Ithiel de Sola Pool, Technologies Without Boundaries: On Telecommunications in a Global Age (Cambridge: Harvard University Press, 1990), 1937, 88-89.

Wenger, E; McDermott; Snyder. *Cultivating Communities of Practice.* HBS press, 2002.

Westerbusch, R. *Qualitätsmanagementsysteme. Die Zertifizierung nach DIN EN ISO 9000ff.* Wiesbaden: Vieweg, 1998.

White paper from the Economist Intelligence Unit – the 2003 e-learning readiness rankings / the Economist Intelligence Unit: New York, the Economist Intelligence Unit, 2003.

Wiki (a). *Enterprise Application Integration,* 2005 [online]. Available from Internet: http://en.wikipedia.org/wiki/EAI [cited 31.05.2005]

Wiki (b). *Enterprise Data Interchange,* 2005[online]. Available from Internet: http://en.wikipedia.org/wiki/EDI [cited 31.05.2005]

Wiki (c). *Middleware,* 2005 [online]. Available from Internet: http://en.wikipedia.org/wiki/Middleware [cited 31.05.2005]

Wiki (d). *SOAP,* 2005 [online]. Available from Internet: http://en.wikipedia.org/wiki/SOAP [cited 31.05.2005]

Wiki (e). *Universal Description, Discovery, and Integration,* 2005 [online]. Available from Internet: http://en.wikipedia.org/wiki/UDDI [cited 31.05.2005]

Wiki (f). *Web Service Description Language,* 2005 [online]. Available from Internet: http://en.wikipedia.org/wiki/WSDL [cited 31.05.2005]

Will, H.; Winteler, A.; Krapp, A. *Von der Erfolgskontrolle zur Evaluation.* In: Will, H., Winteler, A., Krapp, A. (Hrsg.) (1987): Evaluation in der beruflichen Aus- und Weiterbildung. Konzepte und Strategien. Heidelberg, 1987. P.:11-42.

Wilson, S. *Architectures to Support Authoring and Content Management with Learning Design.* In: Koper, R.; Tattersall, C. (Eds.), Learning Design. A Handbook on Modelling and Delivering Networked Education and Training (S. 41-62). Berlin, Heidelberg, New York: Springer, 2005.

Winship, J. *Software Review or Evaluation: Are They Both Roses Or Is One a Lemon?* Paper presented at the Proceedings of the Australian Computer Education Conference. Perth, 1988.

Wirth, M. *Qualität in eLearning: Konzepte und Methoden zur Beurteilung der Qualität eLearning-gestützter Aus- und Weiterbildungsprogramme* (At the same time Dissertation Nr. 3119 at the University of St. Gallen). Paderborn: Eusl, in print.

Wittmann, W. W. *Evaluationsforschung - Aufgaben, Probleme, Anwendungen.* Berlin, 1987.

Wolfe, D. *Innovation Policy for the Knowledge-Based Economy: From the Red Book to the White Paper.* In How Ottawa Spends, 2001-2002. G. Bruce Doern ed., Toronto: Oxford University Press, 2002.

Womack, J.P.; Jones, D.T.; Roos, D. *The machine that changed the world*. New York: Rawson Associates, 1990.

Woodhouse, D. *The Quality of Quality Assurance Agencies*, 2003 [online]. Available from Internet: http://www.inqaahe.nl/public/docs/ThequalityofEQAs.doc [cited 30.07.2003].

World Wide Web Consortium (W3C). *Extensible Markup Language (XML)*, June 2005 [online]. Available from Internet: http://www.w3.org/XML/ [cited 21.06.2005].

Wottawa, H.; Thierau, H. *Lehrbuch Evaluation*. Stuttgart, 1990.

Wright, C. R. *Criteria for Evaluating the Quality of Online Courses*, wihtout date [online]. Available from Internet: http://www.imd.macewan.ca/imd/content.php?contentid=36 [cited 25.03.2005].

Wulf, Ch. (Hrsg.). *Evaluation. Beschreibung und Bewertung von Unterricht, Curricula und Schulversuchen*, München, 1972.

xCBL. *XML Common Business Library (xCBL)*, 2000 [online]. Available from Internet: http://www.xcbl.org/ [cited 31.05.2005]

Zech, R. (Hrsg.) *Pädagogische Antworten auf gesellschaftliche Modernisierungsanforderungen*. Klinkhardt, Bad Heilbronn, 1997.

Zech, R. *Lernerorientierte Qualitätstestierung in der Weiterbildung. LQW2: Das Handbuch* [Learner-oriented quality assessment in further education – LQW2: Handbook]. Hannover, Expressum, 2003.

Zemsky, R.; Massy, W. F. *Thwarted Innovation: What Happened to e-learning and Why. A Final Report for The Weatherstation Project of The Learning Alliance at the University of Pennsylvania in cooperation with the Thomson Corporation; see* http://www.thelearningalliance.info/WeatherStation.html, 2004.

Zimmer, G.; Psaralidis, E. *„Der Lernerfolg bestimmt die Qualität einer Lernsoftware!" – Evaluation von Lernerfolg als logische Rekonstruktion von Handlungen*. In: Schenkel, P. et al. (eds): Qualitätsbeurteilung multimedialer Lern und Informationssysteme, Nürnberg, 2000.

Zink, K. J. *TQM als integratives Managementkonzept. Das EFQM Excellence Modell und seine Umsetzung*. München; Wien: Carl Hanser, 2004.

Zink, K. J.; Schick, G. *Quality Circles, Vol. 1 and 2*; München: Carl Hanser, 1998.

Zollondz, H.-D. *Grundlagen Qualitätsmanagement. Einführung in Geschichte, Begriffe, Systeme und Konzepte*. München; Wien: Oldenbourg, 2002.

Editors of the handbook

Dr. Ulf-Daniel Ehlers

Ulf-Daniel Ehlers studied English, Social Sciences and Educational Sciences at the University of Bielefeld where he finished his Ph.D. on "Quality in E-Learning" in 2003. He is now coordinating European projects for the Department for Informa-tion Systems for Production and Operations Management at the University Duisburg-Essen. He served as lecturer in several German universities and had responsibility in German lighthouse projects in e-learning.

Dr. Ehlers is an internationally recognised researcher and innovator in the area of e-learning. His main research interest cover quality management for and competence development with e-learning. He has extensive experience in helping individuals and organisations achieving superior learning performances and has run several projects and evaluations in the field of e-learning and knowledge management as well as e-business including new-technology-consulting for small and medium sized enterprises. Dr. Ehlers developed the *Learners' Quality Model* for e-learning, which is recognise nationally and internationally and serves as a basis for learner centred quality development in e-learning. He is the author/ publisher of several books and more than 50 articles and book chapters, has been a featured speaker at numerous European and international conferences, and is member of several professional associations for e-learning and education in Germany, and director of the European Foundation for Quality in E-Learning.

E-mail: ulf.ehlers@icb.uni-essen.de

Dr. Jan M. Pawlowski

Dr. Jan M. Pawlowski is the Director of the workgroup on E-Learning & Quality Management within the Institute for Computer Science and Business Information Systems. This includes the research coordination of several German and European projects (e.g., Essen Learning Model, Virtual Education in Business Information Systems, European Quality Observatory, European Foundation for Quality Management for E-Learning, Quality Initiative E-Learning in Germany). He is the editor of the "International Handbook on Information Systems for Education and Training" and has published numerous articles in books, journals, and conference proceedings. His main research interests and activities are in the field of E-Learning, Modelling Learning-related Processes, Procedural Models, Learning Technology Standardisation, Quality Management and Quality Assurance for Education, and Mobile / Ambient Learning. He is in the Board of the German E-Learning Association D-ELAN, responsible for International Cooperation. He is Chair for Education in the IEEE Technical Committee for Learning Technology. He actively involved in research organisations (AACE, GI, etc) and coordinates the quality workgroups within standardisation organisations (DIN, CEN, ISO/ IEC JTC1 SC36).

E-mail: jan.pawlowski@icb.uni-essen.de

List of contributors

John Anderson

John Anderson is from the Department of Education in Northern Ireland and is responsible for the policy and strategy for information and communications technology for Northern Ireland schools. He oversees the implementation of e-learning strategy undertaken by all the education partners in Northern Ireland. He is currently directing a project for the British Educational Communications and Technology Agency (Becta) on the pedagogic quality of e-learning in schools. He is also a member of the Department's Education and Training Inspectorate.

He is a member the Becta's UK government strategy group and of the Curriculum Online Content Advisory Board. He lectures widely in the UK, Europe and in the USA, and also undertakes projects and provides consultancy for a range of agencies, including the EUN European Schoolnet. Most recently he has been involved in a P2P (Peer to Peer) ICT policy review with Finland and France.

E-mail: john.anderson.deni@nics.gov.uk

Prof. Michel Arnaud

Researcher at the laboratory on electronic knowledge industries (CRIS/SERIES) with a focus on ICT tools for online learning. Specific domains of interest cover public access to Internet and standards for e-learning.

In charge of an online Master to train professionals for designing and managing digital territorial development projects.

Since 2001, AFNOR, CEN ISSS LT and ISO/JTC1/SC36 expert, in charge of an AFNOR working group on collaborative technologies and LMS open architectures.

E-mail: michel.arnaud@u-paris10.fr

Thomas Berger

Thomas Berger has been managing director of the Institute of interdisciplinary Research inter.research e.V. since 1999 (www.inter-research.de). The non-profit institute supports research and education in the areas of Computer Supported Learning, Information Society Technologies and International Student Exchange Programmes. Mr. Berger holds a diploma degree in Applied Computer Science of the University of Applied Sciences Fulda, Germany. He is involved in various European projects in the area of E-learning such as "Teaching Culture!"

(www.teaching-culture.de) and "media-net-works" (www.media-net-works.de). His field of research are virtual communities of learning. Mr. Berger participates in working groups at the German Instiute of Standardisation (DIN e.V.) and ISO SC 36 and contributed to the Public Available Specification PAS 1032-1.
E-mail: berger@inter-research.de

Prof. Dr. Markus Bick

Professor of Business Information Systems at the ESCP-EAP European School of Management, Germany. His main research interests and activities are related to knowledge management, e-learning, convergent systems, ambient intelligence, and simulation. He teaches business and management information systems in the Masters, Ph.D., and MBA programs of the ESCP-EAP Berlin, as well as knowledge management and simulation in the Master program (M.Sc.) *Virtual Education in Business Information Systems (VAWi)* at the Universities of Bamberg and Duisburg-Essen. He earned a Ph.D. in economics from the University of Duisburg-Essen, and a Diploma (M.Sc. equivalent) in business information systems from the University of Essen.
E-mail: markus.bick@escp-eap.de

Dr. Claudio Dondi

Claudio Dondi, born in Modena in 1958 and an industrial economist as a university background, is the President of SCIENTER – Ricerca e Innovazione per la formazione (IT), – a non-profit research organisation and active Europe-wide in the field of innovation of education and training systems. In this position his main activities are the co-ordination of large national and European projects, as well as policy advice and evaluation at regional, national and international level. His other positions include: Professor of Human Resource Development at the College of Europe in Bruges (1998 – 2003), Member of the Board of the MENON EEIG (enabling e-learning) in Brussels, Member of the Editorial Boards of the British Journal of Educational Technology and of the European Journal of ODL, Vice-President of Eifel – the European Institute for e-learning, Vice-President of EDEN – European Distance Education Network, President of EFQUEL (European Foundation for Quality in e-learning).
E-mail: cdondi@scienter.org

Dr. Bernard Dumont

Bernard Dumont is a senior consultant on ODL and the use of ICT for Education. His background is in Mathematics with a State Doctorate in Sciences. He is a former full Professor of Educational Sciences at the University of Paris 7 and invited Professor at the TéléUniversité of Quebec. He is an evaluator for the European Commission (Information Society and Media Directorate General) and an expert by the Council of Europe.
E-mail: bdumont.consultant@free.fr

Prof. Erik Duval

Erik Duval is a professor of computer science at the K.U.Leuven in Belgium. His research interests include metadata in a wide sense and learning object metadata in particular, technical standards for an open, global learning infrastructure, human-computer interaction in general, and in a learning or digital repository context in particular, an the application of information and communication technology in education and training.

Erik teaches courses on Human-Computer Interaction, Multimedia, and Problem Solving and Design. Prof. Duval is president of the ARIADNE Foundation and technical editor for the standard on Learning Object Metadata. He coordinates the work on learning objects, metadata and interoperability within the ProLearn Network of Excellence. Erik is a fellow of the AACE and serves on the Scientific and Technical Council of the SURF Foundation.

E-mail: Erik.Duval@cs.kuleuven.be

Rob Edmonds

Rob Edmonds is a senior consultant in SRI Consulting Business Intelligence's (SRIC-BI's) Learning-on-Demand program, and he coordinates the program in Europe. He has also led and participated in a wide variety of consulting projects on learning technology. For the Learning-on-Demand, program Edmonds has written numerous learning-technology research reports on topics including best practices, enterprise vendors, mentoring, learning objects, cultural issues, government initiatives, the oil and gas sector, and e-learning for strategy. In addition, Edmonds is frequently invited to present and lead workshops at international learning technology conferences and events. Before joining SRIC-BI, Edmonds worked for CMG plc and IBM Global Services. Edmonds holds a M.Sc. in cognitive science from Birmingham University (England) and a B.A. in philosophy from Middlesex University (England).

E-mail: redmonds@sric-bi.com

Prof. Dr. John Erpenbeck

Born in 1942 in Ufa/Bashkiria, he graduated in 1968 with the experimental bio-physical study "Contercurrent Diffusion in the Fluid Phase with Subsequent Multiplication by Circulation". He worked as an experimental physicist at the Institute for Biophysics at the Berlin Academy of Sciences. From 1973 to 1990, he was a scientific employee at the Central Institute for Philosophy at the Berlin Academy of Sciences working on the problems of philosophy, history, and the theory of science involved in the psychology of cognitive, emotional-motivational, and volitional processes. In 1978, he earned his habilitation as a Doctor of Philosophical Science (Dr.sc.phil.) with the paper "Epistemology and the Psychophysics of Cognitive Processes". In 1984, he was made a professor. Since 1991, his research emphasis (at the Max-Planck-Society) has been on the history of science and the theory of science with analogous questions.

E-mail: john.erpenbeck@gmx.de

Prof. Dr. Stefan Fischer

Institut für Angewandte LernTechnologien. Professor for Information Technology 1998-2001, International University in Germany, Bruchsal. September 2001 until October 2004: Professor for Computer Science at the Institute for Operating Systems and Computer Network of the TU Brunswick. Since November 2004: Professor for Practical Computer Science at University of Lübeck.
E-mail: fischer@ifalt.de

Julia Flasdick

Julia Flasdick is project manager at MMB Institute for Applied Media and Competence Research. She studied communication science, psychology and politics in Münster/Germany. After her degree as Magistra Artium (M.A.) she worked for the media research department of a public broadcaster and other research institutes. Afterwards, she was involved in a project for computer-based learning as a scientific assistant at the University of Erfurt. Since then, the scientific preoccupation with e-learning is one of her main fields of activity. In July 2003 she started working at MMB as a junior project manager, since October 2004 as a project manager. She is responsible for studies and accompanying research in the field of e-learning.
E-mail: flasdick@mmb-institut.de

Dr. Lutz Goertz

Dr. Lutz Goertz is head of department for educational research at MMB Institute for Applied Media and Competence Research since 2002. Before he was head of department for research and education at the German Multimedia Association (bvdw), he has studied communication sciences at the WWU Münster. His main fields of activity are education in the German Digital Economy, the German multimedia market, E-Learning in firms; monitoring of projects.
E-mail: goertz@mmb-institut.de

Martin Gutbrod

Institut für Angewandte LernTechnologien. After studies in Reutlingen and Shanghai/ China 1997 Master of Business Administration into International marketing at the European School of business (ESB Reutlingen). Development of the company Cobis GmbH and various Internet projects. Since February 2002 scientific employee in the area of distributed systems, TU-Braunschweig.
E-mail: gutbrod@ifalt.de

Kai Heddergott

Kai Heddergott studied communication sciences, sociology and newer history at Westphalian Wilhelms-University Muenster, Germany. Subject of his thesis: "e-learning in the academic journalism education". From 1995 to 1998 he was collegiate assistant at the Institute for communication research, department of journalism, at the University of Muenster and responsible for the buildup of the electronic news room and led courses on magazine production. From 1996 to 1999 as a free-lancer he was author and trainer on the use of multimedia. Since 1999 he is project manager "e-learning" at MMB Institute for Applied Media and Competence Research in Essen, Germany, and is responsible for several studies and projects dealing with the diffusion of e-learning in the vocational training. Moreover, he supported the foundation of the German Network of E-Learning Actors (D-ELAN) and is responsible for the press relations of this network.

E-mail: heddergott@mmb-institut.de

Barbara U. Hildebrandt

Barbara U. Hildebrandt finished an apprenticeship as industrial sales representative at the Deutsche Shell AG in Düsseldorf, Hamburg and Cologne. She worked as clerical assistant for the accounting department of a medium-sized business in Düsseldorf before she started studying business informatics at the University of Essen. Throughout the years of study she worked at the custom's support at Hewlett-Packard GmbH as well as for a small start-up business as a programmer. Also she became a MCSE and published several professional articles. Since her diploma she has been working as a research assistant for several European and German projects at the department of Information Systems for Production and Operations Management at the University of Duisburg-Essen. Her main research is learning technologies, standardisation and classification schemes, quality in e-learning and accessibility.

E-mail: barbara.hildebrandt@icb.uni-essen.de

Wayne Hodgins

Wayne Hodgins is recognised around the world as a strategic futurist and leading expert on human performance improvement, knowledge management, learning and training technology. With over 30-years of experience in business and education, Wayne has developed thought-provoking and visionary perspectives on how learning, technology, and standards can revolutionise human performance improvement and workforce productivity.

He is at the forefront of learning technology standards, serving as Chair of the IEEE Learning Technology Standards Committee, Learning Object Metadata Working Group, and serves as a strategic advisor to groups such as the US Department of Defence, the European Commission and many research and development groups worldwide.

Wayne is commonly referred to as the "father" of Learning Objects and IEEE recognised Wayne in 2004 with its prestigious *Hans Karlsson Award for Leadership and Achievement through Collaboration* for his work in defining the Learning Object Metadata Standard, the world's first accredited standard for learning and technology.

E-mail: wayne@learnativity.org

Brian Holmes

Brian Holmes is Principal Administrator in the unit dealing with European policy for innovation in education and training, in DG Education and Culture at the European Commission. He is primarily responsible for ICT policy development (*e-l*earning), for links with industry, professional skills development, standards and quality for e-learning.

E-mail: Brian.Holmes@cec.eu.int

Anne-Marie Husson

Quality Project Manager of Le Préau/CCIP (the e-learning dedicated service of the Paris Chamber of Commerce and Industry) acts as a quality consultant in e-learning departments of companies and educational bodies, helping providers to enter into a continuous improving process. In charge from 2000 to 2002 of the study "Which Quality model for e-learning" lead by Le Préau/CCIP and its 10 partners, she participated in the Editorial Board of the "Code of Practice for e-learning" (BPZ76-001) held by the French community of e-learning professionals under the auspices of the FFFOD (French Forum for ODL) and AFNOR (French Body of Standardisation). She is also in charge, in partnership with the University of Nanterre (Paris X) of several e-learning programs, including a Bachelor degree (CAFEL), meant to train the e-learning managers with the new skills they need.

E-mail: amhusson@ccip.fr

Dr. Helmut W. Jung

Institut für Angewandte LernTechnologien, Debuty Director. Deutsche Telekom´s international corporate strategy. Design of business models and QoS-parameters for web based training from a technological, didactical and economical point of view, Institute of Operating Systems and Computer Networks, Technical University of Braunschweig; Institut für Angewandte LernTechnologien, since 2004.

E-mail: jung@ifalt.de

Pythagoras Karampiperis

Holds a Diploma (2000) and MSc in Electronics and Computer Engineering (2002) and an MSc on Operational Research (2002), all from the Technical University of Crete, Greece. Currently, he is a PhD candidate at the Department of Technology Education and Digital Systems, of University of Piraeus, Greece and a Member of the Advanced Electronic Services for the Knowledge Society Research Unit (ASK) at the Informatics and Telematics Institute (ITI) of the Centre of Research and Technology Hellas (CERTH). He received the Best Paper Award in IEEE International Conference on Advanced Learning Technologies ICALT04, Joensuu, Finland (August 2004). He is a Student Member of IEEE and a Member of the Technical Chamber of Greece.

E-mail: pythk@iti.gr

Dr. Michael Klebl

After his exam in educational science Michael Klebl has been working five years as consultant and information architect. He specialised in knowledge management, content management systems and cross media publishing, mainly for corporate communication and training. At present he is assistant lecturer and scientific assistant at Catholic University Eichstätt-Ingolstadt, Germany at the Chair of Ergonomics and Industrial Pedagogy. Starting from 2003 and finished in 2004, his PhD-thesis was dedicated to the conceptual examination and empirical review of IMS Learning Design Level A. He developed a prototypical runtime environment called 'lab005', based on 'Moodle'. His research interests lie on the conceptual foundations of educational media and information systems from an educational perspective. His main areas of research are mixed mode learning scenarios in higher education, vocational training and further education, IMS Learning Design in the instructional design process as well as issues of internationalisation and localisation of learning scenarios.

E-mail: michael.klebl@ku-eichstaett.de

Maureen Layte

Maureen Layte is Development Director of EIfEL, responsible for the development and promotion of the Institute's activities, including the management of, and participation in, a wide range of European projects, the development and implementation of competency-based programmes, membership services and the organisation of international conference and seminars.

Maureen has had many years of experience in the design and delivery of programmes of training, development and certification in further and adult education. She has extensive experience of the production of learning resources and is the co-author of Technology Based Training (Kogan Page 1997) and Valider les compétences avec les NVQs (Demos, 1998). Principal activities in EIfEL include pioneering work on e-portfolios in Europe, standards of competence for learning practitioners and quality in e-learning. The SEEL project, which she co-ordinated produced a range of outcomes that are having a significant impact on the way regions ensure the quality of their e-learning initiatives, and will continue to be developed under the aegis of the European Foundation for Quality in e-learning, of which EIfEL is a founding member.

E-mail: maureen.layte@eife-l.org

Dr. Amaury Legait

Amaury Legait is an independent consultant, developing distance learning and management of European Projects. For seven years, he served as manager in higher education institutions in Paris, developing life long learning. He also worked eleven years for the Thales group from project manager to strategy manager. He was educated in France (Ecole Normale Supérieure de la rue d'Ulm) and England (University of Cambridge) and has two PhDs in Astrophysics.

E-mail: amaury.legait@mail.enpc.fr

Dr. Rolf Lindner

Dr. Rolf Lindner has a background starting with Electrical Engineering in 1964 (Diploma in 1971), migrating towards Computer Science in 1971, working on Computer Graphics since 1975 (PhD in 1979), and specializing on Computer-based Training since 1990. At the TUD Interactive Graphics Systems Group, he is responsible for the preservation of scientific expertise. He has done extensive lecturing and leads a research group on Computer-based Training. In the nineties, he was a key person in the European projects DEDICATED (D2014) and IDEALS (ET1012) and further related research activities. He has chaired the SIG Design in the European PROMETEUS Initiative and is active in the CEN/ISSS "Workshop on Learning Technologies", being its liaison officer towards ISO/IEC JTC1 SC36. He is actively involved in the activities of the IEEE LTSC, until 2002 in its WG1 "Architecture and Reference Model" and presently in its WG11 "Computer Managed Instruction". Since the foundation of the ISO/IEC JTC1 SC36 "Information Technology for Learning, Education, and Training", he is the German HoD, chairing the German mirror committee DIN NI-36 "Lerntechnologien". He is the convener of the ISO/IEC JTC1 SC36/WG5 "Quality Assurance and Descriptive Frameworks". He is in the Board of the German E-Learning Association D-ELAN, responsible for Academia.
E-mail: Rolf.Lindner@gris.informatik.tu-darmstadt.de

Thomas Lodzinski

Thomas Lodzinski is Officer in the IT-Operations department of the German Federal Office of Administration. This includes strategical and procedural support for the department of IT-Operation, as well as knowledge and information management efforts for administrative use. In 2002-2005 he was a member the E-Learning & Quality Management workgroup within the Institute for Computer Science and Business Information Systems at the University of Duisburg-Essen. He has worked on several market studies in the field of Quality Management and Quality Assurance for Education and was co-author of several workgroup's publications. His main research interests are in the field of Quality Marks and Quality Assurance for Education as well as in the Field of Knowledge Management and Electronic Performance Support.
E-mail: Thomas@Lodzinski.de

Prof. Robert McCormick

Professor Robert McCormick is in the Centre for Curriculum and Teaching Studies, Faculty of Education and Language Studies, The Open University (OU) UK. He has directed several research projects in technology education: a UK Economic and Social Research Council (ESRC) funded study of problem solving and co-directed an evaluation of a project to encourage electronics in the curriculum. He has recently finished a study of the use of ICT research evidence to inform policy (ERNIST) and an evaluation of the use of digital material in European classrooms (CELEBRATE), and is working on peer-to-peer review of the use of ICT in

schools (P2P); all co-ordinated by European Schoolnet. Currently he is co-director of the ESRC Teaching and Learning Programme research project *Learning how to learn - in classrooms, schools and networks*, and directing an evaluation of the National College for School Leadership online environment.
E-mail: R.Mccormick@open.ac.uk

Dr. Lutz P. Michel

Lutz P. Michel is owner and managing director of MMB Institute for Applied Media and Competence Research, a private, independent research institute, founded in 1996 and located in Essen and Berlin. MMB carries out studies in the fields of education & training and labour market development; the institute is specialised on e-learning as well as quality assessment of professional training and education. Lutz P. Michel has a Master Degree and a Ph.D. in Slavic Studies, Communications and Sociology. Before founding the MMB Institute, he lectured at the University of Münster/Germany and worked as senior research fellow at the Infas Institute in Bonn/Bad Godesberg. He is chairman of D-ELAN (German Network of E-Learning Actors) and member of different organisations, e.g. the German Society for Communication Science (DGPuK) and the Society for Research in Professional Education and Training (ABWF, Berlin).
E-mail: michel@mmb-michel.de

Michela Moretti

Michela Moretti took a degree in Educational Science (Pedagogy) at University of Bologna in 1988 and attended a two years post-graduated course in Management and Development of Human Resources.
She is the Head of the Evaluation and Training Design unit of Scienter (IT). She is involved at national and European levels in projects focused on: assessment of ODL and e-learning materials/resources, quality of ODL/e-learning services and systems, pedagogy of ODL and e-learning, game based learning, quality assessment of innovative projects which employ ICT in the process of teaching and learning.
E-mail: mmoretti@scienter.org

Fabio Nascimbeni

MENON Network Officer, has a Degree in Economics, with an international business management specialisation, and is finalising a Ph. D. on ICT for Development in the Knowledge Society. Since 2001 he has been collaborating with the MENON Network as Network Officer in charge of business development, coordination of international working groups, policy advisory and strategic consultancy. He conducts research and management activities in the frame of a number of trans-national projects in the field of e-learning (namely ACTIVe, eWATCH, L-Change, DELOS, POLE, SEEQUEL, Valnet). He was involved in the set up of a number of international entities (MENON EEIG, Multipalio EEIG, European Foundation for e-learning Quality) and he is managing the International Stake-

holders Component of the @LIS Programme in collaboration with the European Commission, for the cooperation of Europe and Latin America in the fields of e-learning, health, e-government, e-inclusion.
E-mail: fabio.nascimbeni@menon.org

Christian Prpitsch

Christian Prpitsch got his diploma in business information systems in 2004. Since then he has been working as a research assistant in the fields of E-Learning and system convergence at the department of Information Systems for Production and Operation Management at the University of Duisburg-Essen.

His research topics are standardisation in E-learning and the convergence of systems. He currently works in a project supported by the Deutsche Forschungsgemeinschaft, DFG (www.systemkonvergenz.org). Apart from that he assists in a virtual course of study called VAWi (www.vawi.de).
E-mail: christian.prpitsch@icb.uni-essen.de

Serge Ravet

Serge Ravet is Chief Executive of the European Institute for e-Learning (EIfEL). Combining both technological (computer science graduate) and pedagogical expertise (20 years experience in training and human resources development) with working experience in Europe and the US, he is retained as an expert in the assessment of research projects for a French government agency and the European Commission. Publications include 'Technology-based Training' (Kogan Page, 1997); 'Valider les Compétences avec les NVQs' (DEMOS, 1999); a Guide to e-learning Solutions (2001) and numerous articles.

Created in 2001, EIfEL is the leading cross-sectoral professional body whose mission is to support the development of a knowledge and learning society, in particular by recognising the organic link between individual, organisational a community learning and the role played by knowledge, information and learning technologies (KILT) to achieve this goal. EIfEL is leading Europortfolio, a consortium that has set as its objective that in 2010, every citizen will have an e-portfolio, believing that this will be a key policy element in achieving the goal set in 2000 at the Lisbon European Commission Conference: to make Europe the most competitive, sustainable and inclusive knowledge based economy in the world.
E-mail: serge.ravet@eife-l.org

Thomas Reglin

Holder of a M.A. in arts, Thomas Reglin has worked in vocational learning and media development since 1995 at the bfz Bildungsforschung as a project management and as a coordinator in the field of new learning media. Since 2003 he has also been the vice-president of f-bb (www.f-bb.de). His main areas of interest are learning among elderly people, learning management in businesses, e-learning knowledge management and European strategies in vocational training.
E-mail: reglin.thomas@f-bb.de

Prof. Dr. Ulrike Rockmann

Since 1991 Prof. Dr. Rockmann is working in the area computer-based learning. She developed CBTs and online courses for commercial usage and several software applications for research purposes (http://www.sportwissenschaft-akademie.de/www/quitl/index.html). Her research especially focused on the behaviour of learners when using e-learning products, the consequences of product design on learning, the influence of previous knowledge and experiences on the usage of learning strategies. She developed usability concepts and evaluated conformity of software with ISO 9241.
E-mail: bww@uni-oldenburg.de

Prof. Albert Sangra

Albert Sangra is full Professor at the Education and Psychology Department, *Universitat Oberta de Catalunya (UOC)*. Academic Director of the International Master's Degree in e-learning. His background is in Educational Sciences with a Postgraduate in *Applications of IT in ODE* (UKOU) and a Diploma on *Strategic Use of IT in Education* (Harvard University). Former professor at Universitat Ramon Llull, Barcelona. He has led educational consulting projects in Europe, America and Asia. His research focus is on organisational models and Quality in e-learning. Evaluator for the Spanish Higher Education Quality Agency (ANECA).
E-mail: asangra@uoc.edu

Prof. Dr. Demetrios G. Sampson

Holds a Diploma in Electrical Engineering (1989) from Demokritus University of Thrace and Ph.D. in Multimedia Communications (1995) from University of Essex, UK. He is the Head of the Advanced eServices for the Knowledge Society Research Unit (ASK) at the Informatics and Telematics Institute (ITI) of the Centre of Research and Technology Hellas (CERTH) and an Assistant Professor on e-learning at the Department of Technology Education and Digital Systems of the University of Piraeus. He is a Senior Member of IEEE and serves as the Vice Chairman of the IEEE Computer Society Technical Committee on Learning Technology. His main scientific interests are in the areas of Technology-enhanced Learning. He is the co-author of more than 160 publications in scientific books, journals and conferences with at least 135 known citations. He received the Best Paper Award in IEEE International Conference on Advanced Learning Technologies ICALT01, Madisson, USA (August 2001) and in IEEE International Conference on Advanced Learning Technologies ICALT04, Joensuu, Finland (August 2004). He is the Co-Editor-in-Chief of the Educational Technology and Society Journal, and a Member of the Editorial Board of eight International Journals.
E-mail: sampson@iti.gr

Dr. Cleo Sgouropoulou

Dr. Cleo Sgouropoulou is an associate lecturer at the National Technical University of Athens (NTUA) and an associate professor at the Technological Educational Institute of Athens. Her research interests lie in the field of Learning Technologies and specifically, in the development of data models for interoperable systems. She is an active member of the CEN/ISSS Workshop on Learning Technologies and has participated in several of its project teams on learning objects, learner information and learner competences modelling. She is also involved in the activities of the ISO/IEC JTC1 Sub-Committee 36 "Standards for: Information Technology for Learning, Education and Training", acting as a representative of the Learning Technologies teams of the NTUA and the Hellenic Organisation for Standardisation (ELOT).

E-mail: csgouro@cs.ntua.gr

Christian Stracke

Christian Stracke manages the Quality Initiative E-Learning in Germany (Q.E.D.), supported and funded by the German Federal Ministry of Economics and Technology (BMWi). He studied Educational Sciences (M.A.) at the University of Bonn yet dedicating his Master Thesis on e-Learning software. Christian Stracke has been a project manager, consultant, designer and researcher in the fields of e-Learning and Human Resources for over 10 years. He gained experiences as e-Learning project manager and business consultant working at e-Learning providers and consultancies. Now he is doing his doctorate at the University Duisburg-Essen, Department of Information Systems for Production and Operations Management focusing on quality management and quality standards in e-Learning and international methods and metrics for quality assurance and evaluation. His main research interests and activities are quality and standards in e-Learning, quality management in education and HR, Learning Regions and Intercultural e-Learning, ICT in development cooperation, change management and controlling in learning processes. He is engaged in several workgroups of standardisation organisations (EBN, DIN, CEN/ISSS, ISO/IEC JTC1 SC36, IEEE) and co-author of both e-Learning specifications PAS 1032-1 including the DIN reference model of quality management in education and PAS 1032-2 with the DIN-DOM (Didactical Object Model). He is co-initiator and member of the Board of the German e-Learning Association D-ELAN and elected speaker of the SIG "International e-Learning". He has established the eLC Institute for e-Learning, information and Cooperation, founding member of D-ELAN.

E-mail: christian.stracke@icb.uni-essen.de

Miho Taguma

Miho Taguma has always worked in the higher education field, first as a practitioner and researcher for academic community and then a researcher for policy makers. She joined OECD as an Associate Expert within the framework of the Japanese Government's Ministry of Foreign Affairs' scheme. She has been working on

OECD projects concerning post-secondary e-learning, recognition of non-formal and informal learning and credit transfer to promote lifelong learning, and internationalisation of higher education. Before joining OECD, she worked at UNESCO. She was involved in a project to promote peace education, human rights education, dialogue among civilisation, intercultural understanding and communication. As a practitioner, she worked at some Japanese universities and a Japanese university affiliate campus located in the US as one of the earliest adopters using the ICT into teaching. She has also worked in developing countries and bases her research agenda for education how the UN Millennium Goals can be met through education. She experiences internationalisation of higher education with her own experiences: she has a bachelor's degree from Sophia University (Japan), a master's degree from Boston University (US) and another master's degree from Institute Nationale des Langues et Civilisations Orientales (France).
E-mail: Miho.taguma@oecd.org

Sinje J. Teschler

Sinje J. Teschler finished the study of economics at the University of Duisburg-Essen at the end of 2002. In January 2003 she started working as a research assistant in the same University at the department "Information Systems for Production and Operations Management". She worked in the European project "European Quality Observatory (EQO)" dealing with Quality Approaches for European e-Learning. Currently she is working in two projects: the first one is the "Quality initiative for e-learning in Germany (Q.E.D.)" and the second one is dealing with quality assurance in further education. Her main research is quality management, quality assurance and standardisation in the field of e-learning and education.
E-mail: sinje.teschler@icb.uni-essen.de

Prof. Frans van Assche

Frans van Assche works as Strategy manager in European Schoolnet. He is in charge of the Standards and Interoperability Strand, is the chief architect of the CELEBRATE brokerage system, the Knowledge Management System, and semantic interoperability tools. Mr. van Assche is vice-chair of the CEN/ISSS workshop on Learning Technologies, and leads the CEN/ISSS project team on 'Harmonisation of vocabularies'. He is Director of European IMS Network and holds an associate professor at the School of Economics EHSAL, Brussels.

Mr. van Assche was the technical manager of the recently finalised project CELEBRATE. Previously, he was project manager for EU funded projects such as RUBRIC, Web for Schools (WfS), WfS-ESIS, and the EUN multimedia project. he has been reviewer, evaluator, and rapporteur for EU projects and various working groups of the European Commission.

He has written numerous articles and books and has served on various scientific

programme committees. He is silver core member of the International Federation of Information Processing (IFIP) and former secretary of WG 8.1.
E-mail: Frans.van.Assche@eun.org

Patrick Veith

After successfully finishing his apprenticeship as IT clerk at the Alfred Friedrich Flender AG in Bocholt/ Germany, he started studying business informatics at the University of Essen. 2001 he got his diploma in business informatics and since then he has been working as a research assistant in the field of E-Learning at the department of Information Systems for Production and Operation Management at the University of Duisburg-Essen.

His main research topic is analysing the standardisation potential of M-Learning and to improve actively the quality of M-Learning solutions. His work includes assisting in the lectures within a virtual course of study called VAWi (www.vawi.de), developing new standards and revealing new markets and business models within the Quality Initiative E-Learning in Germany (Q.E.D., www.qed-info.de).
E-mail: patrick.veith@icb.uni-essen.de

Riina Vuorikari

Riina Vuorikari has worked in European Schoolnet since March 2000 as a research analyst. She deals with a wide variety of issues ranging from e-learning interoperability in the context of learning resources to the collaborative use of ICTs in schools. She is a member of CEN/ISSS workshop on Learning Technologies, where she has participated in the work on quality as well as harmonisation of vocabularies. She is the editor for the Interoperability-section of the Insight portal. She has degrees in education and hypermedia, and currently pursues her PhD in learning technologies.
E-mail: riina.vuorikari@eun.org

Dr. Markus A. Wirth

Markus A. Wirth studied business administration with a specialisation on business education and educational management at the University of St.Gallen, Switzerland. He has been working with the Institute for Business Education and Educational Management at the University of St.Gallen as a research fellow, as a lecturer, as a quality auditor for EFMD's Certification of e-learning (CEL), and as a project manager for the campus wide e-learning implementation since beginning of 2001. At the same time, he was working with IBM Business Consulting Services as a certified consultant in the strategy and change profession with focus on e-learning and knowledge management. Combining both, experiences from academia and the corporate sector, he successfully concluded his doctoral thesis on quality in e-learning supported and management oriented higher and further education programmes which builds the scientific framework for EFMD's new

e-learning certification initiative CEL (www.efmd.org/CEL).
E-mail: markus.wirth@unisg.ch

Index

Printing: Krips bv, Meppel
Binding: Stürtz, Würzburg